LEGITIMACY AND LEGALITY IN INTERNATIONAL LAW

It has never been more important to understand how international law enables and constrains international politics. By drawing together the legal theory of Lon Fuller and the insights of constructivist international relations scholars, this book articulates a pragmatic view of how international obligation is created and maintained. First, legal norms can only arise in the context of social norms based on shared understandings. Second, internal features of law, or 'criteria of legality', are crucial to law's ability to promote adherence, to inspire 'fidelity'. Third, legal norms are built, maintained or destroyed through a continuing practice of legality. Through case studies of the climate-change regime, the anti-torture norm, and the prohibition on the use of force, it is shown that these three elements produce a distinctive legal legitimacy and a sense of commitment among those to whom law is addressed.

JUTTA BRUNNÉE is Professor of Law and Metcalf Chair in Environmental Law at the University of Toronto.

STEPHEN J. TOOPE is President and Vice-Chancellor of the University of British Columbia.

CAMBRIDGE STUDIES IN INTERNATIONAL AND COMPARATIVE LAW

Established in 1946, this series produces high-quality scholarship in the fields of public and private international law and comparative law. Although these are distinct legal sub-disciplines, developments since 1946 confirm their interrelation.

Comparative law is increasingly used as a tool in the making of law at national, regional and international levels. Private international law is now often affected by international conventions, and the issues faced by classical conflicts rules are frequently dealt with by substantive harmonization of law under international auspices. Mixed international arbitrations, especially those involving state economic activity, raise mixed questions of public and private international law, while in many fields (such as the protection of human rights and democratic standards, investment guarantees and international criminal law) international and national systems interact. National constitutional arrangements relating to 'foreign affairs', and to the implementation of international norms, are a focus of attention.

The Board welcomes works of a theoretical or interdisciplinary character, and those focusing on the new approaches to international or comparative law or conflicts of law. Studies of particular institutions or problems are equally welcome, as are translations of the best work published in other languages.

A list of books in the series can be found at the end of this volume.

LEGITIMACY AND LEGALITY IN INTERNATIONAL LAW

An Interactional Account

JUTTA BRUNNÉE

AND

STEPHEN J. TOOPE

CAMBRIDGE
UNIVERSITY PRESS

CAMBRIDGE UNIVERSITY PRESS
Cambridge, New York, Melbourne, Madrid, Cape Town,
Singapore, São Paulo, Delhi, Mexico City

Cambridge University Press
The Edinburgh Building, Cambridge CB2 8RU, UK

Published in the United States of America by Cambridge University Press, New York

www.cambridge.org
Information on this title: www.cambridge.org/9780521706834

First published 2010

A catalogue record for this publication is available from the British Library

Library of Congress Cataloguing in Publication Data

Brunné e, Jutta.
Legitimacy and legality in international law : an interactional account / Jutta Brunnée,
Stephen J. Toope.
p. cm. – (Cambridge studies in international and comparative law ; 67)
Includes bibliographical references and index.
ISBN 978-0-521-88065-7 – ISBN 978-0-521-70683-4 (pbk.)
1. International law–Social aspects. 2. International law–
Psychological aspects. 3. Obedience (Law) 4. Rule of law. 5. Effectiveness and
validity of law. I. Toope, Stephen J. (Stephen John) II. Title. III. Series.
KZ1251.B78 2010
341–dc22
2010021906

ISBN 978-0-521-88065-7 Hardback
ISBN 978-0-521-70683-4 Paperback

For Laura, for whom nothing is impossible
And for Paula, who makes all things possible

CONTENTS

TABLE OF CASES

International Court of Justice

Case Concerning Armed Activities on the Territory of the Congo (*Democratic Republic of Congo* v. *Uganda*), Judgment, I.C.J. Reports 2005, p. 116.

Case Concerning The Temple of Preah Vihear (*Cambodia* v. *Thailand*), Judgment, I.C.J. Reports 1962, p. 6.

Concerning the Application of the Convention on the Prevention and Punishment of the Crime of Genocide (*Bosnia and Herzegovina v. Serbia and Montenegro*), Judgment, I.C.J. Reports 2007, p. 140.

Gabčíkovo-Nagymaros Project (*Hungary/Slovakia*), Judgment, I.C.J. Reports 1997, p. 7.

Legal Consequences of the Construction of a Wall in the Occupied Palestinian Territory, Advisory Opinion, I.C.J. Reports 2004, p. 136.

Legality of Use of Force Case (*Yugoslavia* v. *Belgium*), Provisional Measures, I.C.J. 1999, pleadings of Belgium, 10 May 1999, CR 99/14.

Military and Paramilitary Activities in and against Nicaragua (*Nicaragua* v. *United States of America*), Judgment, I.C.J Reports 1986, p. 14.

North Sea Continental Shelf (*Federal Republic of Germany/Denmark*), Judgment, I.C.J. Reports 1969, p. 3.

Oil Platforms (*Islamic Republic of Iran* v. *United States of America*) Judgment, I.C.J. Reports 2003, p. 161.

Reservations to the Convention on the Prevention and Punishment of the Crime of Genocide, Advisory Opinion, I.C.J. Reports 1951, p.15.

Arbitral Awards

Eritrea Ethiopia Claims Commission, Partial Award – Jus Ad Bellum, Ethiopia's Claims 1–8, 19 December 2005, repr. in (2006) I. L. M. 45 430–5.

International Criminal Tribunals

Prosecutor v. *Dusko Tadic* (*Appeal Judgment*), IT-94–1-A, International Criminal Tribunal for the former Yugoslavia, 15 July 1999.

Prosecutor v. *Furundzija* (*Trial Judgment*) IT-95–17/1-T, International Criminal Tribunal for the former Yugoslavia, Trial Chamber, 10 December 1998.

European Court of Human Rights

Askoy v. *Turkey* (1996), 23 Eur HR 553.
Ireland v. *United Kingdom*, 1976 YB Eur Conv on HR 512.

Canada

Canada (Justice) v. *Khadr*, 2008 SCC 28 [2008] SCR 125.
Suresh v. Canada (Citizenship and Immigration), 2002 SCC 1, [2002] 1 SCR 3.

Israel

HC *428/86, Barzilai* v. *Government of Israel, 40(3) PD 505 (1986).*
Public Committee against Torture v. *Israel*, (1999) HCJ 5100/94.

United Kingdom

A(FC) and others v. *Secretary of State for the Home Department* [2005] UKHL 71, 3 All ER 169.
R. v. *Bow Street Metropolitan Stipendiary Magistrate, ex parte Pinochet Ugarte (Amnesty International and others intervening) (No. 3)* [1999] 2 All ER 897 (HL).

United States

Boumediene et al v. *Bush*, 553 US 723 (2008).
Hamdi v. *Rumsfeld*, 542 US 507 (2004).
Rasul v. *Bush*, 542 US 466 (2004).
Jacobellis v. *Ohio*, 378 US 184 (1964).

TABLE OF TREATIES

Rome Statute of the International Criminal Court, 2187 U.N.T.S. 90, (1998) 37 I.L.M. 999.

Cartagena Protocol on Biosafety to the Convention on Biological Diversity (2000) 39 I.L.M. 1027.

Kyoto Protocol to the United Nations Framework Convention on Climate Change, (1998) 37 I.L.M. 22.

United Nations Framework Convention on Climate Change, (1992) 31 I.L.M. 849.

African Charter on Human and People's Rights, 1520 U.N.T.S. 217.

Convention against Torture and Other Cruel, Inhuman or Degrading Treatment or Punishment, 1465 U.N.T.S. 85, (1984) 23 I.L.M. 1027.

American Convention on Human Rights, (1969) 9 I.L.M. 99.

International Covenant on Civil and Political Rights, 999 U.N.T.S. 171, (1967) 6 I.L.M. 368.

Vienna Convention on the Law of Treaties, Vienna, 1155 U.N.T.S. 331 (1980) 8 I.L.M. 679.

Convention for the Protection of Human Rights and Fundamental Freedoms, 213 U.N.T.S. 221 at 223, Eur. T.S. 5.

Geneva Convention relative to the Treatment of Prisoners of War, 75 U.N.T.S. 135, 6 U.S.T. 3316.

Geneva Convention relative to the Protection of Civilian Persons, 75 U.N.T.S. 287.

Statute of the International Court of Justice, as annexed to the Charter of the United Nations, 1 U.N.T.S. 3.

PREFACE

We have been working together for more than fifteen years. Our engagement with the subject matter of this book began when we were first invited to participate in interdisciplinary seminars bringing together international lawyers and international relations theorists. As lawyers we were in the minority, and were sometimes called upon to explain what practical difference international law made in international society, and often to describe how international legal norms differed from other social norms. International lawyers tend to take for granted the importance of the discipline, but our engagement with related disciplines prompted us to reflect more carefully on what it is that accounts for the effectiveness and distinctiveness of legal norms. Our consequent work has often required that we move outside familiar debates and established conceptual frameworks, and we are grateful for the hard questions that launched our interest in the research agenda that underlies this book.

Our work together would not have been possible without the consistent and generous support of the Social Sciences and Humanities Research Council of Canada. We have benefited from the collegial environments of the Faculties of Law of the University of British Columbia, McGill University and the University of Toronto, as well as sabbatical leaves and further financial support from these institutions. The Connaught Fund of the University of Toronto provided a generous Research Fellowship. We also appreciate the workshop funding provided by the former Canadian Centre for Foreign Policy Development of the Department of Foreign Affairs and International Trade.

As this book has evolved over almost five years, we have benefited from discussions with many colleagues, including Emanuel Adler, Asher Alkoby, José Alvarez, Michael Barnett, Steven Bernstein, Alan Boyle, Michael Byers, Christine Chinkin, Matthew Craven, Dan Drezner, Jeffrey Dunoff, David Dyzenhaus, Jaye Ellis, Marty Finnemore, the late Thomas Franck, Christopher Greenwood, Paul Heinbecker, Ellen Hey, Duncan Hollis, Andrew Hurrell, the late Douglas Johnston, Ian Johnstone,

Nicholas Katzenstein, Robert Keohane, Benedict Kingsbury, Jan Klabbers, Karen Knop, Harold Koh, Friedrich Kratochwil, David Lazer, Vaughan Lowe, Rod Macdonald, Margaret MacMillan, Georg Nolte, Mary Ellen O'Connell, Yasuaki Onuma, Andreas Paulus, Mark Pollack, Richard Price, Mario Prost, René Provost, Steven Ratner, Sean Rehaag, Beth Simmonds, Anne-Marie Slaughter, Peter Spiro, Janice Stein, Joel Trachtman, Jim Tully, Wilbren van der Burg, Jeremy Webber, Nicholas Wheeler, Antje Wiener, and Elizabeth Wilmshurst. We also thank the anonymous reviewers for Cambridge University Press, who helped us sharpen our approach to this book.

We have presented parts of this book in seminars and workshops at Duke University, The Fletcher School of Law and Diplomacy, Harvard University, the Max Planck Institute for Comparative Public Law and International Law, Oxford University, Queen Mary College of the University of London, The Royal Institute of International Affairs and the British Institute of International and Comparative Law (jointly), Temple University, The University of British Columbia, The University of Maryland, The University of Ottawa, The University of Toronto, The University of Wisconsin, and Yale University. We are grateful to the participants for their helpful comments.

In undertaking the research for this book, and in finalizing the manuscript, we have been fortunate indeed to benefit from the work of many outstanding students. We thank Ioana Bala, Kate Brookson-Morris, Andrew Bryan, Rebekah Church, Michael Fakhri, Amos Friedland, Hadley Friedland, James Hunter, Adrian di Giovanni, Henry Lovat, Eric Mendelsohn, Ali Mian, Elena Middelkamp, Shane Moffatt, Sasha Nowicki, Umut Őszu, Sarah Perkins, Jarrett Plonka, Vincent-Joel Proulx, Robert Rastorp, Vinay Sarin, Kate Skipton, Dierk Ullrich, Mike Varey, Jared Will, Cora Zeeman, and Laura Zizzo.

We thank Richard Woodham and Lynn Aitchison, as well as Jodie Barnes, Christina Sarigiannidou and the entire team at Cambridge University Press. We owe a particular debt of gratitude to CUP's Finola O'Sullivan for her faith and patience.

This book offers new research and thinking about our interactional law framework and its application. In presenting this new material, we drew upon the following previously published works:

Jutta Brunnée, 'COPing with Consent: Lawmaking under Multilateral Environmental Agreements' (2002) 15 *Leiden Journal of International Law* 16 (Ch. 4); 'The Kyoto Protocol: A Testing Ground for Compliance Theories?' (2003) 63 *Zeitschrift für ausländisches öffentliches Recht und*

Völkerrecht (Heidelberg Journal of International Law) 255 (Ch. 4); 'Europe, the United States, and the Global Climate Regime: All Together Now?' (2008) 24 *Journal of Land Use and Environmental Law* 1 (Ch. 4); 'Climate Change, Global Environmental Justice and International Environmental Law', in Jonas Ebbesson and Phoebe Okowa (eds.), *Environmental Law and Justice in Context* (Cambridge University Press, 2009), p. 316 (Ch. 4); 'From Bali to Copenhagen: Towards a Shared Vision for a Post-2012 Climate Regime?' forthcoming in (2010) 25 Maryland Journal of International Law (Ch. 4).

Jutta Brunnée and Kelly Levin, 'Climate Policy beyond Kyoto: The Perspective of the European Union', in Steven Bernstein, Jutta Brunnée, David Duff and Andrew Green (eds.), *A Globally Integrated Climate Policy for Canada* (University of Toronto Press, 2007), p. 57 (Ch. 4).

Jutta Brunnée and Stephen J. Toope, 'International Law and Constructivism: Elements of an Interactional Theory of International Law' (2000) 39 *Columbia Journal of Transnational Law* 19 (Chs. 1, 2, 3, 6); 'Persuasion and Enforcement: Explaining Compliance with International Law' (2002) 13 *Finnish Yearbook of International Law* 273 (Chs. 1, 2, 6); 'Slouching Towards New "Just Wars": International Law and the Use of Force after September 11th' (2004) 51 *Netherlands International Law Review* 363 (Chs. 2, 6); 'The Use of Force: International Law After Iraq' (2004) 53 *International and Comparative Law Quarterly* 785 (Chs. 2, 6).; 'Norms, Institutions and UN Reform: The Responsibility to Protect' (2006) 2 *Journal of International Law and International Relations* 121 (Ch. 2): 'The Responsibility to Protect and the Use of Force: Building Legality?' forthcoming in (2010) 2 *Global Responsibility to Protect* (Ch. 6).

Stephen J. Toope, 'Formality and Informality' in Daniel Bodansky, Jutta Brunnée and Ellen Hey (eds.), *Oxford Handbook of International Environmental Law* (Oxford University Press, 2007) p. 107; 'Public Commitment To International Law: Canadian and British Media Perspectives on the Use of Force' in Christopher P.M. Waters (ed.), *British and Canadian Perspectives on International Law* (Dordrecht: Martinus Nijhoff, 2006) p. 13; 'The Roles of International Law and of International Lawyers' in H. Kindred (gen. ed.), *International Law Chiefly as Interpreted and Applied in Canada*, 7th edn. (Toronto: Emond Montgomery, 2006), p. 1 (Ch.1); 'Disparitions, prisons secrètes et restitutions extraordinaires: comment perdre la "guerre contre la terrorisme"' (2007) *Esprit* (octobre) 41 (trans. Julien Cantegreil).

Aside from our professional debts, we both owe more than we can possibly say to the people who make our personal lives so rich. Stephen's parents-in-law, Harry and Delores Rosen, contradict in life and practice every possible in-law joke. Paula Rosen, his wife, is a fountain of humour, good judgment and incredible support. His children Hannah, Alexander and Rachel are a constant source of joy; they also helpfully puncture any incipient inflation of the ego. Jutta's partner, Laura, and two amazing girls, Leah and Noa, make life a ride in technicolor – or is that in HD-3D? And, yes, the chapter is finished. The book, even!

Introduction

On 15 February 2003, millions of people around the world marched in the streets of their towns and cities to protest the impending invasion of Iraq by a 'coalition of the willing' led by the government of the United States of America. Media reports conservatively estimated crowds of 750,000 in London, 600,000 in Madrid, 500,000 in Berlin, 150,000 in Melbourne, 100,000 in New York, and possibly over a million in Rome, where estimates varied wildly. Smaller, but vocal demonstrations were held in scores of cities around the world.[1] When all the numbers are pulled together, this was probably one of the largest mass protests in human history.

The motivations behind individual decisions to protest were undoubtedly various, but underlying many decisions was a sense that the planned invasion broke the rules of international law. In a contemporaneous address, Pope John Paul II invoked the Charter of the United Nations Organization 'and international law itself' to conclude that 'war cannot be decided upon, even when it is a matter of ensuring the common good, except as the very last option and in accordance with very strict conditions, without ignoring the consequences for the civilian population both during and after the military operations'.[2] A protester in Boston described the Iraq war as 'unjust' and 'a war of aggression'.[3] An 11-year-old Muslim boy protesting in Los Angeles declared: 'We are here to show our support because we think [President George W.] Bush is doing something

[1] BBC News Service, *Worldwide Protests Mark Iraq War*, 21 March 2004, at http://news.bbc.co.uk/2/hi/middle_east/3552147.stm; and CNN News Service, *Cities Jammed in Worldwide Protest of War in Iraq*, 16 February 2003, at www.cnn.com/2003/US/02/15/sprj.irq.protests.main/index.html?iref=newssearch; see also, Chapter 6 on the use of force, text accompanying note 21.

[2] John Paul II, 'Address of His Holiness to the Diplomatic Corps', 13 January 2003, at www.vatican.va/holy_father/john_paul_ii/speeches/2003/january/documents/hf_jp-ii_spe_20030113_diplomatic-corps_en.html.

[3] Quoted in Brian MacQuarrie, 'From All Walks, Antiwar Protesters on Same Path', *The Boston Globe*, 15 February 2003, p. B1.

wrong ... The U.N. inspectors, they didn't get much time, and Bush is just bringing, like, flimsy evidence.'[4]

An 11-year-old invoking UN-mandated weapons inspections and the 'evidence' for war, joining with other 'ordinary' people and world leaders to call for respect for international law. Does this tell us anything about how international law might shape global society? Does it signal anything important about the changing face of international law? We believe so, and it is our purpose in this book to explain that changing face, to understand how international law influences the behaviour of actors in contemporary international society.

'Just a minute,' sceptics will interject, 'doesn't the Iraq War show the total failure of international law? Despite the protests all around the globe, the war went ahead. Power trumps law every time.' In this book, we will challenge the conception that law only 'works' when it is an explicit constraint matched with a sanction. It is too early to trace out the entire argument, but the short answer to the sceptics' objection is that the effects of international law were felt throughout the Iraq crisis, and those effects proved to be stronger than the massed military power of coalition armies. The street protests did not prevent the war, but they helped to bolster norms of international law on the use of force and the protection of human rights.

International law really only emerged as a 'discipline' in the nineteenth century. The founders of international law were philosophers and theologians with wide-ranging interests in law and international relations. Indeed, the disciplines were not separate, as they became in the nineteenth century. Aquinas, Grotius, Pufendorf, Suarez – they cannot have imagined themselves as building an edifice of 'pure' law to 'govern' all inter-state relations, much less the relationships amongst states, corporations, international organizations, non-governmental organizations, and individuals. Given the politics of the era, the space for international law was highly restricted. This early international law was at most a law of coexistence, not co-operation, to borrow Wolfgang Friedmann's later Cold War classification of international law.[5] There was certainly no 'common law of mankind' as Wilfred C. Jenks was to imagine.[6]

The aspirations of early international lawyers were ambitious for the time, but modest in retrospect: to provide guidance to monarchs in their

[4] Quoted in CNN News Service, above note 1.

[5] Wolfgang Friedmann, *The Changing Structure of International Law* (New York: Columbia University Press, 1964).

[6] Wilfred C. Jenks, *The Common Law of Mankind* (London: Stevens, 1958).

international intercourse and to provide a framework for trade and some constraints on war. It was only with the nineteenth-century colonial project, when international lawyers began what Martti Koskenniemi calls their 'civilizing mission', that international law took on a transformative calling.[7] These origins are cause for concern for contemporary internationalists. International law as it developed in the nineteenth and twentieth centuries was inextricably linked to social and political processes of domination and control. It was accorded all too easily with raw power, and often seemed to be the mere handmaiden of the national interests of the 'great powers'. This legacy should not be ignored, but neither should it preclude the re-imagining of the international law project today.[8]

The human imagination has never been dictated to by history; history is both limit and promise, as the source of warnings, lessons and hints of possibility. In recent years the history of international law has emerged as a fresh field of scholarly study,[9] but too often the result has been a paralysis in thinking. The burden of the past, the undoubted hypocrisy and constant abuse of law, are served up to suggest that international law is fundamentally flawed, that it can never be more than a mask for power relationships.

In popular parlance, the world is a jungle, and the law of the jungle is simple: the strongest win. In the early twentieth century, liberal internationalists argued that the jungle could be turned into a zoo, with legal institutions acting as the zookeeper. The appetites of states for land, power and glory could be tamed. By contrast, self-styled 'realists' argued that the strongest animals would never allow themselves to be captured and caged.[10] The realists saw their view confirmed in the demise of the League of Nations. After 11 September 2001, the pattern seemed to be repeating. Hope placed in the deliberative forum of the United Nations was said to be naïve idealism.[11] A realist could rely only on material power, not

7 Martti Koskenniemi, *The Gentle Civilizer of Nations: The Rise and Fall of International Law 1870–1960* (Cambridge University Press, 2001), p. 71.

8 Philip Allott, *Eunomia: New Order for a New World* (Oxford University Press, 1990).

9 See e.g. Koskenniemi, above note 7; Antony Anghie, *Imperialism, Sovereignty and the Making of International Law* (Cambridge University Press, 2005); and generally the *Journal of the History of International Law*.

10 Robert Jackson and Georg Sørensen, *Introduction to International Relations* (Oxford University Press, 1999).

11 John Bolton, 'Address before the Federalist Society at the 2003 National Lawyers Convention', 13 November 2003, at www.fed-soc.org/doclib/20070324_bolton.pdf; see also, John Bolton, 'Is There Really "Law" in International Affairs?' (2000) 10 *Transnational Law and Contemporary Problems* 1; Thomas Shanker, 'Rumsfeld Rebukes the U.N. and NATO on Iraq Approach', *The New York Times*, 9 February 2003, p. A14; and David E.

on international law, which was seen to have no real purchase, or even explanatory power, in international relations.[12]

Realism has been powerful in shaping the popular image of international law. In moments of crisis, international law is often invoked in the western popular media. Yet, more often than not it is portrayed as notionally relevant, but practically without impact. Nevertheless, at these same moments of crisis, cynicism is tempered by expressions of hope and expectation. This point returns us to the Iraq War protests of 2003. Aside from the resistance to the war itself, when the first pictures emerged recording sessions of abuse at Abu Ghraib, much of the world's population reacted with horror. Outrage was provoked not just by the scenes of physical brutality and humiliation, but also by the evident violations of fundamental legal norms against torture and the treatment of prisoners of war.[13] One would be hard-pressed to find more media references to humanitarian law in any previous international conflict.

Similar public engagement occurred around the issue of climate change. Public concern was galvanized by the findings of the Intergovernmental Panel on Climate Change and the parallel communication efforts of former US Vice-President, Al Gore.[14] The world's environmental nongovernmental organization (NGO) community banded together in support of the Kyoto Protocol, despite its weaknesses, because it was the only legal framework available to test the commitment of states. The refusal of some key states to take on legally binding emission reduction commitments became a touchstone for those who saw a failure to come to grips with the reality of climate change.

The scholarly literature needs to catch up with the perception of international law's role amongst people on the street. In debates over intervention in Iraq, over ratification of the Kyoto Protocol, over the use of torture to fight terrorism, and over 'humanitarian intervention' in Darfur, Sudan, the public discourse has been about values and interests, of course; but it has also been explicitly about law, and the effects of law upon human and state behaviour. This should not be surprising. Intuitively, people sense

Sanger, 'Iraq Makes U.N. Seem "Foolish", Bush Asserts', *The New York Times*, 29 October 2002, p. A15.

12 Bolton, 'Is There Really Law', above note 11; and Michael J. Glennon, 'The UN Security Council in a Unipolar World' (2004) 44 *Virginia Journal of International Law* 91.

13 Neil MacFarquhar, 'Revulsion at Prison Abuse Provokes Scorn for the U.S.', *The New York Times*, 5 May 2004, p. A18; and Dana Priest and R. Jeffrey Smith, 'Memo Offered Justification for Use of Torture', *The Washington Post*, 8 June 2004, p. A1.

14 CNN News Service, *Gore: Nobel Win a Chance 'to Change the Way People Think'*, 12 October 2007, at www.cnn.com/2007/POLITICS/10/12/nobel.gore/index.html.

that law is more than a reflection of state interests or a measure of who has the biggest stick. If law were nothing more than enforcement by self-interested states, the very concept would not be needed. Power would do its own work.

The central argument of this book is that there is law in the jungle. It is made through the interactions of a variety of actors, including elites, the media, NGOs and 'ordinary' citizens. States – though still dominant – are not the only animals in the jungle, and the law of the jungle is not made only by the strongest: nor is it broken with impunity. The law of the jungle is often unrecognized by the very people who help to make it. We want to confront that dynamic and suggest new ways of imagining the role of law in constructing and shaping global society.

For scholars, policymakers and citizens, it has never been more important to understand how international law enables and constrains international politics. Without a rich understanding of how international law influences the behaviour of key actors, one cannot design effective political and legal strategies to accomplish shared, or even individual, goals. Promoting specific norms matters. Building them in legitimate ways matters. Cultivating their application in particular contexts matters. Understanding the diverse ways in which legal norms can be effective matters. We therefore outline a framework to assist international lawyers and policymakers in identifying the most promising avenues for normative and institutional development. This framework is built primarily upon a theory of international law, but it is supplemented by insights from international relations (IR) theory. We believe that international lawyers have much to gain from IR perspectives on the role of law in international society. In turn, IR scholars stand to gain from exploration of the concept of international legal obligation.

1. An interactional account: the hard work of international law

In thinking and writing about international law over the years, we found ourselves increasingly dissatisfied with the prevailing theoretical accounts of the field. None of these accounts, it seemed to us, provided a theoretical framework that fully resonated with the contemporary practice of international law-making and application, satisfactorily explained the strengths and weaknesses of international law, or illuminated the idea of legal obligation in international society. Our goal in this book is to sketch out a theory that does meet these challenges – an interactional theory of international law. More specifically, we articulate a theory of international legal obligation. We believe that the key to understanding the role that law plays in international society lies in understanding the nature and operation in practice of legal obligation.

In developing our thesis, we draw on the work of one of the foremost legal theorists of the twentieth century, Lon Fuller, although we extend his insights in directions that he might not have imagined. Fuller himself hinted that international society was not ready for the rule of law, and perhaps in the early 1960s, at the height of the Cold War, it wasn't. Today, however, we think that Fuller's insights are actually borne out powerfully in the international area. Yet, there is some irony in our turn to Fuller's theory of domestic law to think about international law. After all, dutiful incantations of caution notwithstanding, international lawyers and commentators on international law (both friendly and unfriendly) frequently draw on domestic law in their assessments of or prescriptions for its international relative. The resulting picture of international law is rarely good, often ugly, and always distorted. That is precisely why Fuller's theory is so important for understanding international law.[15] It reveals that the problem with the domestic law analogy is not necessarily the analogy as such, but the assumptions that commonly shape it. When we assume that the defining features of domestic law – and by extension of all law – are formal enactment by a superior authority, application by courts, and centralized enforcement, we are bound to see international law as a poor cousin. Most importantly, we risk misjudging how law operates in international society, obscuring its potential power, and misdirecting even the best-intentioned efforts to improve it.

What distinguishes law from other types of social ordering is not form, but adherence to specific criteria of legality: generality, promulgation, non-retroactivity, clarity, non-contradiction, not asking the impossible, constancy, and congruence between rules and official action.[16] When norm creation meets these criteria and is matched with norm application

[15] Although Fuller himself did not engage with international law in any detail, he did highlight the implications of legal positivism, and a domestic law optic, for international law. See Lon L. Fuller, *The Morality of Law*, rev. edn (New Haven: Yale University Press, 1969), pp. 232–7. In Fuller's most direct engagement with international law, he grappled with the limits of adjudication in international society, observing that if international law existed at all, 'it exists imperfectly – it is still in process of being born'. See Lon L. Fuller, 'Adjudication and the Rule of Law' (1960) 54 *American Society of International Law Proceedings* 1 at 1. See also Karen Knop, 'The Hart–Fuller Debate's Silence on Human Rights', in Peter Cane (ed.), *The Hart–Fuller Debate: 50 Years On* (Oxford: Hart Publishing, 2010), p. 61.

[16] See Fuller, *The Morality of Law*, above note 15, pp. 39 and 46–90.

that also satisfies the legality requirements – when there exists what we call a 'practice of legality' – actors will be able to pursue their purposes and organize their interactions through law. These features of legality are crucial to generating a distinctive legal legitimacy and a sense of commitment – what Fuller called 'fidelity', – among those to whom law is addressed. They create legal obligation. By focusing our attention on markers of legality that are internal to law, Fuller's theory provides a helpful lens through which to reflect on international law. It shows that the formal and hierarchical manifestations typically associated with domestic law, such as tests of 'validity', are not sufficient to characterize 'law', domestic or international, and indeed may not always be required.[17]

Fuller's legal theory explains law as a purposive enterprise that is both shaped by human interaction and aimed at guiding that interaction in distinctive ways. Law does not depend on hierarchy between law-givers and subjects, but on reciprocity between all participants in the enterprise. By 'reciprocity' we mean that law is not a 'one-way street'. It can exist only when actors collaborate to build shared understandings and uphold a practice of legality. This conception of reciprocity is at the very heart of the interactional account of international law that this book sets forth. Understanding this dynamic is the key to appreciating the nature of legal obligation. In short, we argue that the distinctiveness of law lies not in form or in enforcement but in the creation and effects of legal obligation.

The interactional framework enables international lawyers to take a fresh look at their discipline. Taking that fresh look does not mean that we must dismiss as unimportant state consent, or 'sources' of international law, the creation of courts and tribunals, or better enforcement mechanisms. Rather, it places these elements in the broader context of the international legal enterprise, so as to better appreciate the roles they

[17] For an extended critique of the 'positivist canon', see Fuller, *ibid.*, esp. Chapter V. In summary, Fuller objected to positivism's preoccupation with the pedigree of rules (sources) and to its attendant hierarchical conception of law creation, which Fuller believed to facilitate authoritarianism. He similarly rejected the idea that law is principally an exercise in 'social control', and the linked tendency, evident even in Hart's sophisticated positivism, to view law as co-extensive with the power of the state. Much of his criticism retains great force. We would only caution that Fuller's attempt to paint H.L.A. Hart into the corner of those who would support 'immoral law' is unfair. One of the explicit desires of the analytical positivists was to provide for an external critique of law rooted in morality. Even if something was law, it could still be wrong. See H.L.A. Hart, 'Positivism and the Separation of Law and Morals' (1958) 71 *Harvard Law Review* 593 at 618. Fuller simply thought that the critique would be more effective, and loyal to the purposes of legality, if internal rather than external.

play, their potential, and their limitations. It also reveals that building and maintaining the reciprocity that grounds legal obligation requires sustained effort. As we will illustrate throughout this book, the hard work of international law is never done: not when a treaty is adopted or brought into force, not when a case is decided by an international court, not when the Security Council enforces a resolution through military force. Each of these examples represents but a step in the continuing interactions that make, remake or unmake international law.

For example, sources discourse in law provides a useful shorthand to distinguish law from other types of norms, facilitating the daily calculations of participants in a legal system. Although a duly concluded treaty is formally binding on the parties, when it fails to meet the legality requirements we noted above, the treaty may not generate a sense of obligation. Interactional law helps us to understand that the formal indicator of a rule, in this case a treaty, is not necessarily co-extensive with the legality and practice that generates obligation. A particular treaty rule might satisfy the requirement of promulgation, and yet fail to meet other criteria of legality such as clarity. Failure to meet these requirements at the outset does not mean that legality can never be built through the application and development of the treaty. Indeed, gradual build-up will often be the only way to establish genuine and resilient international legality. By the same token, legality can be squandered through careless practice under a treaty. Either way, states' consent to a treaty, its formal existence, and the presence or absence of judicial or enforcement practice are but reference points for efforts to understand, build or maintain the treaty's potential to bind. Each presents opportunities for international law; but opportunities must be seized. The concept of a truly 'interactional' international law, then, is at once sobering and empowering.

Unlike the prevailing accounts of international law, an interactional understanding of law does not limit effective participation to state actors. The framework explains how diverse actors can interact through law and accommodates both the continuing pre-eminence of states in the international legal system and the rise of non-state actors. In addition, because the requirements of legality are largely procedural in orientation, interactional law is not contingent upon particular political commitments. The fundamental commitment is to enabling participants to pursue their own ends while being guided by law. In other words, while interactional law may well facilitate the legal articulation and pursuit of shared goals, it embraces the diversity of priorities in international society.

Interactional law shares this commitment to diversity with some accounts of international legal positivism,[18] particularly the return to a 'culture of formalism'.[19] But we will argue that interactional international law's internal legality requirements provide stronger safeguards against political domination and power than a purely formal account of international law, precisely because the commitment to autonomous actor choices and diversity is internal to the framework itself (rather than merely an external justification for the framework).

2. IR theory and legal obligation

Political scientists share with international lawyers a concern to understand how norms function in a horizontal normative order such as international society.[20] It is, of course, trite to describe the international order, including international law, as 'horizontal' in structure. The essence of the characterization is that there is no legislative or executive hierarchy within the system. Yet, as Michael Barkun argued in the 1960s, social scientists tend to look at international society through the prism of domestic legal systems and to find international law under-developed or wanting. This approach is not surprising. Indeed, it is characteristic of much of the scholarship that, in recent decades, has sought out new insights in cognate disciplines. In looking for such interdisciplinary insights, scholars have often adopted reductionist definitions of the 'other' discipline because they have not been actively involved in the constitutive internal disciplinary debates and processes that lead to healthy uncertainty and nuance. In the case of social scientists viewing law, the distorting optic of the domestic law analogy was not exclusively a result of these pitfalls of interdisciplinarity but, as Barkun rightly observed, was actually fed by professional deformation within the discipline of law itself. As we have already suggested, many legal theorists and practising lawyers have had trouble understanding – much less articulating – how international law can be law, when viewed from the perspective of seemingly hierarchical domestic legal systems.

[18] See Benedict Kingsbury, 'Legal Positivism as Normative Politics: International Society, Balance of Power and Lassa Oppenheim's Positive International Law' (2002) 13 *European Journal of International Law* 401 (discussing 'political positivism').

[19] See Martti Koskenniemi, *From Apology to Utopia: The Structure of International Legal Argument*, reissue with a new Epilogue (Cambridge University Press, 2005), p. 616.

[20] See Martha Finnemore and Kathryn Sikkink, 'International Norm Dynamics and Political Change' (1998) 52 *International Organization* 887 at 887–8.

The reason for what Barkun called the 'uncritical appropriation' of the domestic law paradigm is not hard to discover:[21] it is the strongly positivistic stance of legal theory throughout much of the late nineteenth and twentieth centuries.[22] For outsiders, even more than for lawyers, positivism promises easy intelligibility: law can be found, defined and labelled.[23] Yet, if law is viewed (as it is in various strands of positivist thinking), as a hierarchically ordered imposition of social control emanating from a *de facto* sovereign,[24] a purely theoretical '*Grundnorm*',[25] or even a 'rule of recognition',[26] then the persistently horizontal structure of international law will prove troublesome. International law will either be declared non-existent, or its operation will have to be distorted to fit the theoretical framework. It was therefore natural for IR scholars in the realist tradition, who were trying to cleanse their discipline of all normative ideas, to ignore international law (or perhaps in their self-conception to grow beyond it).[27]

Historically, realists are the dominant school in IR theory. For realists of all stripes, law is virtually irrelevant, as is the concept of legal

[21] See Michael Barkun, *Law without Sanctions: Order in Primitive Societies and the World Community* (New Haven: Yale University Press, 1968), p. 11; cited in Fuller, *The Morality of Law*, above note 15, p. 237.

[22] A thoughtful description of the appropriation of positivist legal theory by public international lawyers is found in Roberto Ago, 'Positivism', in Rudolph Bernhardt (ed.), *Encyclopedia of Public International Law*, vol. VII (Amsterdam: North-Holland, 1984), p. 385.

[23] For this formulation of the attraction of positivism in law, we are indebted to Rod Macdonald. A clear example of this tendency is found in the 'legalization' project. See Kenneth W. Abbott, Robert O. Keohane, Andrew Moravcsik, Anne-Marie Slaughter and Duncan Snidal, 'The Concept of Legalization' (2000) 54 *International Organization* 401.

[24] John Austin, *Lectures on Jurisprudence*, 5th edn (London: John Murray, 1885), pp. 86–103. For Austin, the command, to be law, must also be 'general' and matched with a potential sanction in the event of non-compliance.

[25] Hans Kelsen, *General Theory of Law and State*, Anders Wedberg (trans.) (New York: Russell & Russell, 1961); and *Principles of International Law* (New York: Rinehart & Company, 1952).

[26] H.L.A. Hart, *The Concept of Law* (Oxford: Clarendon Press, 1961), pp. 89–96 and Chapter 6; and H.L.A. Hart, *Essays in Jurisprudence and Philosophy* (Oxford: Clarendon Press, 1983). Hart's analysis of law was explicitly hierarchical, with primary rules (imposing obligations) rooted in secondary rules (of recognition, change and adjudication), and the entire system of law nesting in a fundamental 'rule of recognition' generated through the practice of state officials.

[27] Hans J. Morgenthau, *Politics Among Nations: The Struggle for Power and Peace*, 2nd edn (New York: Knopf, 1954), p. 8. See also Martti Koskenniemi, 'Carl Schmitt, Hans Morgenthau, and the Image of Law in International Relations', in Michael Byers (ed.), *The Role of Law in International Politics* (Cambridge University Press, 2000), p. 17.

obligation. Relative power and interests determine state conduct. States are seen as homogeneous actors that proceed on the basis of a rationally assessed and pursued self-interest.[28] In the absence of hard enforcement, international law is without effect. For classical realists, the innate human desire for power shapes interaction amongst states, leaving no room for socially generated norms. For neo-realists, the anarchical structure of international society forces states strategically to pursue power in support of their material interests; participation in a regime or adherence to a norm occurs if the net benefits outweigh those of unilateral action. Regimes and norms are seen as reflections of underlying power and interest balances rather than independent factors influencing behaviour. Social norms are entirely subservient to this pursuit. The realist frame of reference has been influential amongst positivist international lawyers, as well as with adherents to the 'New Haven School' and, of course, 'critical' scholars. More recently, realism has been reasserted as the proper way to understand the 'limits of international law' by a strongly nationalist stream of US constitutional law scholarship.[29]

It was equally possible for IR theorists who were actually interested in international law, and its normative force, to misconceive the potential persuasive power of international law by assuming that its relevance lay in the qualities ascribed to all law by positivist lawyers. 'Neo-liberal institutionalists' trace out theoretical terrain that is somewhat more hospitable to international law than are the assumptions of the realists. Law, like other social norms, can provide predictable rules and stable institutional structures. Like realism, neo-liberal IR theory is rooted in rationalist assumptions, but states are not assumed to be homogeneous actors. Rather, states must be understood, at least partly, in relation to the institutions in which they are engaged.[30] Their interactions and deliberations through institutions are important in shaping their self-perceived interests. Actors and their interests are seen as separate from processes of interaction, as largely 'given'. Engagement in institutions may affect behaviour but not the 'givens' as such. For neo-liberal institutionalists,

[28] See Peter J. Katzenstein, Robert O. Keohane and Stephen D. Krasner, 'International Organization and the Study of World Politics' (1998) 52 *International Organization* 645 at 658.

[29] Jack L. Goldsmith and Eric A. Posner, *The Limits of International Law* (Oxford University Press, 2005).

[30] Robert Keohane and Joseph S. Nye, 'Power and Interdependence Revisited' (1987) 41 *International Organization* 725.

legal obligation is simply assumed,[31] but is never the subject of explicit theorizing. Indeed, obligation seems to become relevant only in combination with other independent explanatory variables, in particular 'precision' of rules and 'delegation' of legal decision-making. [32]

In short, rationalist IR theory devotes little attention to the foundations of legal obligation, either because law is viewed as a meaningless concept in international relations or because the obligatory quality of law is subsumed within other variables. If material interests drive human behaviour, then 'obligation' holds no analytical interest; the only important question is what incentives and disincentives can be created to cause people and institutions such as states to calculate and pursue their interests in particular ways. International law will not be able to prevail over contrary state interests, since only rarely can it affect interest calculations through adjudication or enforcement. In other words, IR rationalism neatly maps onto the domestic law analogy, treating most international law as weak, or even 'epiphenomenal'.[33] The vicious circle closes when lawyers mistake the dominant theory of international relations for a true account of the way the world actually works. When melded with rationalist assumptions about human motivation, international lawyers' worst fears about the weakness of international law must be equally true.

In much the same way that the domestic law optic can limit how we think about international law, rationalism can constrain our understanding of international relations. That has been the important message of a more recent strand of IR theory – constructivism – which emerged in part as a reaction to the dominant rationalist explanatory models.[34] Although constructivist scholars have not focused specifically on the issue of legal obligation, we argue that constructivism can help us to think more creatively and fruitfully about obligation in law. It shows how international law can be an important force in socializing actors and shaping their interests and choices. It lends support to our argument that law's obligatory

[31] The most comprehensive effort to date by neo-liberals to understand the role of law in international relations specifically brackets obligation even though it is said to be one of only three indicators of 'legalization'. See Abbott *et al.*, above note 23.

[32] John G. Ruggie, 'What Makes the World Hang Together? Neo-utilitarianism and the Social Constructivist Challenge' (1998) 52 *International Organization* 855 at 862–3; and Alexander Wendt, 'Collective Identity Formation and the International State' (1994) 88 *American Political Science Review* 384 at 384.

[33] See David Bederman, 'Constructivism, Positivism, and Empiricism in International Law' (2001) 89 *Georgetown Law Journal* 469 at 473.

[34] See Antje Wiener, 'Constructivism: The Limits of Bridging the Gaps' (2003) 6 *Journal of International Relations and Development* 252 at 252.

effect results from a commitment or fidelity to law that is generated by adherence to specific traits of legality and maintained by a practice of legality. In turn, as we hope to show, our interactional legal theory can assist constructivism in discerning the distinctive influence exerted by legal obligation.

Constructivists challenge rationalist IR theory to explain the origin of the interests that are said to be determinative of behaviour. Constructivism sees interaction as central to shaping human conduct. The key claim is that interests are not simply 'given' and then rationally pursued, but that social construction of actors' identities is a major factor in interest formation. Importantly, the ends of social interaction are not predetermined, but can be discovered and learned. Constructivists show how, through interaction and communication, actors generate shared knowledge and shared understandings that become the background for subsequent interactions. In the process, social norms may emerge that help shape how actors see themselves, their world and, most importantly for us, their interests.[35]

None of these commitments reveal any intrinsically idealist bias; they do not assume or even aspire to the creation of a shared global identity or deep value coalescence. For example, John Ruggie and Alexander Wendt are both careful to distance their approaches from any postulated world community or collective conscience.[36] Emanuel Adler speaks of several, often overlapping, 'transnational or international communities', which must be understood as 'communities in, and of, *practice*' and, above all, as 'learning communities'.[37] These communities 'cut across state boundaries and mediate between states, individuals, and human agency, on one hand, and social structures and systems, on the other'.[38] Their enterprise does not necessarily imply 'a common goal or vision', only that members 'must share collective understandings' of 'what they are doing and why'.[39]

[35] For an overview see, e.g. Emanuel Adler, 'Constructivism in International Relations', in Walter Carlsnaes, Thomas Risse and Beth Simmons (eds.), *Handbook of International Relations* (London: Sage, 2002), p. 95; and Christian Reus-Smit, 'Constructivism', in Scott Burchill, Andrew Linklater, Richard Devetak, Jack Donnelly, Terry Nardin, Matthew Paterson, Christian Reus-Smit and Jacqui True, *Theories of International Relations*, 3rd edn (Houndsmills, Basingstoke: Palgrave Macmillan, 2005), pp. 198–9.

[36] Ruggie, above note 32 at 869–70; Wendt, above note 32 at 386 (arguing that 'the intersubjective basis of social identities can be cooperative or conflictual').

[37] Emanuel Adler, *Communitarian International Relations: The Epistemic Foundations of International Relations* (London and New York: Routledge, 2005), p. 11 (emphasis in original).

[38] *Ibid.*, p. 15. [39] *Ibid.*, p. 22.

Returning to the central idea that actors' identities are shaped by social interaction, constructivists also stress that identities are not monolithic. Actors may maintain and foster multiple, though typically overlapping, identities depending upon the pattern of interactions into which they enter.[40] Consider the multiple identities of France, for example, as a nation, as European, as a 'great power', residually as a colonial power, or as a member of the Security Council.[41] None of these examples make sense in the absence of social interaction. Even as a 'nation', France's identity is constructed through internal (regional) interaction, but also through interactions with other nations. This is not to deny that material elements are also relevant to identities and interests. France's identity is also shaped by its location and geography, its population size and density, its natural resources or need for resources, and a myriad of other material factors. Of course, constructivists would maintain that 'ideas' still play a significant role in giving meaning to these material factors. Either way, brute facts and social facts both shape identity and interest.[42]

The key for understanding international relations in constructivist terms is that the interaction of states and other actors ('agents') builds and modifies social 'structures'. Echoing the structuration theory of Anthony Giddens and Roy Bhaskar,[43] constructivists emphasize the 'duality of structure': structures constrain social action, but they also enable action, and in turn are affected and potentially altered by the friction of social action against the parameters of the structure.[44] In other words, agents and structures are mutually constituting, and both are inherently social. Emanuel Adler explains:

> As webs of meaning sustained by social communication, intersubjective structures constitute the content and boundaries of identities, practices, and institutions. Without individuals' minds, of course, there would be

[40] Alexander Wendt, 'Anarchy is What States Make of It: The Social Construction of Power Politics' (1992) 46 *International Organization* 391 at 398.

[41] Identities are not constantly shifting, however, so interests may also retain a consistent flavour, allowing for predictability. See *ibid.*, at 411 and 418.

[42] See John Searle, *The Construction of Social Reality* (London: Penguin, 1995), p. 2.

[43] Anthony Giddens, *The Constitution of Society: Outline of the Theory of Structuration* (Cambridge: Polity Press, 1984); and Roy Bhaskar, *The Possibility of Naturalism: A Philosophical Critique of the Contemporary Human Sciences* (Brighton: Harvester Press, 1979).

[44] See Giddens, above note 43, pp. 25–9. See also Anthony Giddens, 'Agency, Structure', in Anthony Giddens (ed.), *Central Problems in Social Theory* (Berkeley, Calif: University of California Press, 1979), p. 69; and Alexander Wendt, 'The Agent–Structure Problem in International Relations' (1987) 41 *International Organization* 335.

> no intersubjective webs of significance; but without these webs, minds would be nearly empty and there would be no institutions.[45]

For present purposes, the main point is that the 'intersubjective structures' to which Adler refers 'have different components that help in specifying the interests that motivate action: norms, identity, knowledge, and culture'.[46] In highlighting both the social creation of norms and their social impact, constructivism thus opens the way for a fresh examination of the role of law in international society.

3. Interactional theory and its application

Our interactional framework adds significantly to the sources on which it draws. It explicitly links the theories of Lon Fuller to the insights of constructivist IR scholars. It also extends Fuller's thinking into the area of international law, which he barely touched. What is more, we take ideas that are hinted at in Fuller, and provide much more detailed analysis. In our engagement with the constructivists we offer an analysis that demonstrates the distinctiveness of legal, as opposed to social, normativity.

In Chapter 1 we provide a thorough account of international legal obligation. By drawing together constructivist insights and Fuller's work, we articulate a pragmatic view of how international law is created and maintained: first, legal norms can only arise in the context of social norms based on shared understandings. Second, internal features of law, which we call criteria of legality, are crucial to law's ability to promote adherence, or to inspire 'fidelity'. Third, legal norms are built, maintained, and sometimes destroyed through a continuing practice of legality. Although these elements were inspired by Fuller and the constuctivists, we extend their ideas and offer an entirely fresh explanation of legal obligation.

In Chapter 2, we show in more detail that the constructivist stream in contemporary IR theory is helpful in explaining how 'communities of practice' are created and maintained. It is through such interaction that actor identities are shaped and shared expectations arise that may ultimately allow for the existence of interactional international law.

[45] Emanuel Adler, 'Barry Buzan's Use of Constructivism to Reconstruct the English School: "Not All the Way Down"' (2005) 34 *Millennium: Journal of International Studies* 171 at 176.

[46] Katzenstein *et al.*, above note 28 at 679. See also Finnemore and Sikkink, above note 20 at 891. Note that it is common for constructivists to talk of 'norms' when they mean 'institutions', the latter being properly viewed as aggregations of interrelated norms. Institutions, both formal and informal, are simply particular cases of 'social structure'.

Constructivist insights reveal how collaborative norm-making is possible, and how norms produce their practical influence. We add that creating a shared understanding itself is not enough to produce a legal norm, and we examine carefully the transition from social norms to legality. In linking Fuller's communicative understanding of law to the constructivists, we enrich both. Although Fuller emphasized the need for continuous, and reciprocal, communication, we suggest that it is in communities of practice that relevant legal communication arises. In describing the importance of the criteria of legality, we show IR theory that it is possible to distinguish amongst different types of norms.

Our interactional theory of international law carries additional insights for IR scholars as well as for lawyers. It provides specific criteria of legality that are essential in creating obligation. Our theory also offers IR scholars, whether rationalist or constructivist, concrete factors to consider as they examine whether and how law 'matters' in international affairs.[47] We will explore the impact of international law on state conduct, and compliance, in detail in Chapter 3. In so doing, we provide a new perspective on Fuller's criterion of congruence. We show that in international society at least, congruence requires the substantial compliance of all participants in a legal system with not only the criteria, but also a continuing practice of legality. Because our interactional approach focuses clearly on the concept of obligation in law, our compliance theory is significantly different not only from those advanced in IR but, perhaps surprisingly, also from the prominent theories in the international law literature.

To be clear, in engaging with IR theory, our ambition is not to create hybrid concepts of international 'governance'.[48] Rather, ours is a *legal* theory and its central element is a theory of *legal* obligation, which we hope can contribute to 'the important enterprise of distinguishing law from the morass of approaches to governance in which it threatens to disappear'.[49] In an era when it appeared – to borrow Yeats's evocative turn of phrase – that the 'centre cannot hold',[50] when concerns over clashing civilizations

[47] See Martha Finnemore, 'Are Legal Norms Distinctive?' (2000) 32 *New York University Journal of International Law and Politics* 699.

[48] Jan Klabbers, 'The Relative Autonomy of International Law or the Forgotten Politics of Interdisciplinarity' (2005) 1 *Journal of International Law and International Relations* 35.

[49] Benedict Kingsbury, 'International Law as Inter-Public Law', in Henry R. Richardson and Melissa S. Williams (eds.), *NOMOS XLIX: Moral Universalism and Pluralism* (New York University Press, 2009), p. 197.

[50] William Butler Yeats, 'The Second Coming', in *Michael Robartes and the Dancer* (Churchtown, Dundrum: Cuala Press, 1920), p. 19.

drowned out the articulation of shared norms at the international level,[51] an interactional approach to law provides concrete guidance in seizing opportunities for effective law-making and also shows when law-making attempts are likely to fail. Chapters 4 to 6, which deal respectively with climate change, torture, and the use of force, will serve to provide detailed illustrations of the operation of the interactional framework. Any choice of specific case studies is necessarily selective and somewhat arbitrary. We tried to identify a range of issue areas that help us to tease out distinctive elements in our framework.

The climate change regime (Chapter 4) provides an example that is particularly congenial to an interactional analysis. It allows us to explore the construction of new norms within a treaty-based regime that provides for repeated negotiation and shared learning. Further, it permits the examination of norm building among actors of diverse perspectives and priorities. This issue area also encompasses serious threats to human well-being, environmental and economic, and does so in a highly charged political and security context that highlights north–south divisions. To address these threats, we require a complex regulatory regime, so the analysis pays attention to the continuing interactions of regime participants, including influential non-governmental actors, over multiple issues that pose what Fuller called 'polycentric problems'.[52] The chapter also shows how the building of shared understandings may be a long-term project, but that this process is required before one can effectively create a detailed regulatory framework. To facilitate that long-term work, the regime participants have focused on procedural issues. We show that in the climate change regime, the procedural elements largely meet the tests of legality, whereas the substantive elements remain works in progress.

Torture (Chapter 5) presents a different set of conceptual challenges. The norm precluding torture exists in treaty and custom, and is said to be absolute. It may even be *jus cogens*, and is certainly widely supported by actors in civil society. Yet we see that the anti-torture norm is also undermined by contrary practice. This fact affects every stage of the interactional analysis, casting doubt on the shared understandings supporting the norm, calling into question some of the criteria of legality, and undermining any continuing practice of legality. The case study illustrates that an analysis that focuses on shared understandings as the

[51] Samuel P. Huntington, *The Clash of Civilisations and the Remaking of World Order* (New York: Simon & Schuster, 1996).

[52] Fuller, 'Adjudication', above note 15 at 395.

foundation of legal obligation does not necessarily paint a positive picture of international law. Whereas the conventional approach would say that the existence of formal law banning torture is definitive, we show that the normative understandings are fragile. This makes sense of the common claim that human rights norms are subject to 'hypocrisy'. The chapter also reveals the increasingly important role of non-state actors in normative development.

Whereas environmental protection and human rights might be seen as areas of relatively low political charge, the use of force in international relations (Chapter 6) goes to the core of state security and is therefore 'high politics'. This area should be a decidedly hard case for any theory that does not rely on realist assumptions. However, our interactional analysis reveals that even in this setting, shared understandings and legality do shape state conduct. Here we explore the well-established prohibition on the use of force, and its exceptions, self-defence and collective security. These norms are at the foundation of the contemporary international legal order. We trace out the ebb and flow of shared understandings that at various points have undermined and reinforced the norm, and show that the criteria and practice of legality have actually influenced this process. Even though the use of force would seem to be an issue area where states would simply assert their vital interests without much room for learning, strong evidence reveals that states do reassess their interests in the light of legal interaction. The norm entrepreneurship around the responsibility to protect also allows us to evaluate the process of norm building in a highly conflictive issue area.

This book was conceived long before the US presidential election of 2008, but the powerful winning theme of that campaign – the mixture of pragmatism and hopeful social engagement – is very much the theme of our work as well. Many observers of international society have worried for the last few years that the world was at a fork in the road – central actors seemed to be entirely dismissive of law and unilateralist in instinct. Our analysis, as any analysis of international law and society in our era must be, is marked profoundly by the events of 11 September 2001, and reactions to those events. The prohibition on torture and the rules on the use of force were subjected to enormous strains. Even in the climate change context, the withdrawal of the United States from robust multilateral engagement seemed to undercut the prospects for global regime building. Our analysis of these three important issue areas confirms that what looked like fundamental shifts in the international order were actually temporary phenomena. This book illustrates that international legal norms are shaped by the shifting currents of shared understandings and efforts to maintain or undermine legality. Although our analysis is sober, and can drive us to hard conclusions, the processes we describe also provide genuine opportunities to strengthen international law. Our interactional framework helps us to understand how the public protests of an 11-year-old boy in Los Angeles can be legally relevant, and how lawyers and political leaders can build on that meaning in undertaking the hard work of creating and upholding international law.

1

An interactional theory of international legal obligation

> If we could come to accept what may be called broadly an interactional view of law, many things would become clear that are now obscured by the prevailing conception of law as a one-way projection of authority.[1]

1. Introduction

Our goal in this chapter is to set out the conceptual framework of interactional international law. To set the stage, we provide an account of Lon Fuller's legal theory. We then turn to international law, and articulate a novel approach to legal obligation that helps to distinguish between social and legal norms, a task that Fuller himself did not wish to undertake. In international society we believe that this distinction is relevant and important because of the weak rule of law tradition that Fuller bemoaned. It also helps to address the common question of international relations (IR) thinkers, what value does 'law' add? Although our approach challenges conventional wisdom about the operation of international law, it addresses some of international law's fundamental problems, such as social and political diversity, sources of law and legitimacy.

2. Fuller's legal theory

Lon Fuller inspires us because he cared deeply about two key ideas: the generation of social norms through interaction and the sense of responsibility that arises only from the human ability to reason with norms. On the first idea, one could adopt constructivist terms from IR theory to explain that Fuller believed in the mutuality of agency and social structure. To understand how law works, we need to pay attention both to autonomous actors and to the institutions through which they interact.

[1] Lon L. Fuller, *The Morality of Law*, rev. edn (New Haven: Yale University Press, 1969), p. 221.

This dual focus highlights that Fuller's commitment to 'autonomy' is best understood in relational terms – as human interaction in social institutions – a constructivist recasting that allows for social and political diversity.[2] Analysing law in this way cuts to the heart of the greatest challenge facing international law: to construct normative institutions while admitting and upholding the diversity of peoples in international society. Fuller explained law, and the rule of law, in a manner that did not require fundamental shared commitments to a single political morality, nor the existence of centralized political authority.[3]

Fuller's conception of the rule of law connects us to his second core idea – reasoning with norms helps to create a sense of responsibility. Fuller's approach to theory was utterly practical. He wanted to show that law enables human beings to organize their lives and their relationships with each other while limiting the potential abuse of authority by insisting on 'criteria of legality' that constrain arbitrary exercises of power. When citizens are enabled to reason with norms, they can begin to develop what Fuller called 'fidelity' not just to particular norms, but to the system of law itself.[4] We will explain shortly how that fidelity is fostered, and demonstrate that it is central to the legal concept of obligation.

Fuller's description of law is forthright, but does not constitute a definition: law is 'the enterprise of subjecting human conduct to the governance of rules'.[5] The description of law as an 'enterprise', a term borrowed from

[2] Similar reinterpretations of autonomy are found in political theory and legal philosophy. See e.g. the work of Jennifer Nedelsky, including 'Communities of Judgment and Human Rights' (2000) 1 *Theoretical Inquiries in Law* 245; or 'Judgment, Diversity, and Relational Autonomy', in Ronald Beiner and Jennifer Nedelsky (eds.), *Judgment, Imagination, and Politics: Themes from Kant and Arendt* (Lanham: Rowman & Littlefield, 2001), p. 103.

[3] For a similar argument, see Terry Nardin, 'Legal Positivism as a Theory of International Society', in David R. Mapel and Terry Nardin (eds.), *International Society: Diverse Ethical Perspectives* (Princeton University Press, 1998), pp. 24 and 31. But see Frederick G. Whelan, 'Legal Positivism and International Society' in *ibid.*, p. 50 (suggesting that the idea that this conception of the rule of law 'can accommodate states with different cultures' ultimately 'combines conceptions of legality with a substantive liberal philosophical principle').

[4] Fuller, above note 1, pp. 39–41; and especially Lon L. Fuller, 'Positivism and Fidelity to Law – A Reply to Professor Hart' (1958) 71 *Harvard Law Review* 630.

[5] Fuller, above note 1, p. 106. On Fuller's lack of interest in definitional exercises, see Kenneth I. Winston, 'Three Models for the Study of Law', in Willem J. Witteveen and Wibren van der Burg (eds.), *Rediscovering Fuller: Essays on Implicit Law and Institutional Design* (Amsterdam University Press, 1999), p. 69 (quoting Fuller criticizing the definitional fixations of lawyers: 'I know of no other field in which we consume so much energy and adrenaline in proposing and attacking definitions').

the sphere of economic life,[6] is meant to signify law's 'purposive' aspect, its incomplete and aspirational (or even entrepreneurial) quality. For Fuller, law is best viewed as a continuing challenge rather than as a finished project.[7] Law is formed and maintained through continuing struggles of social practice.[8] It 'is the work of its everyday participants, a continuous effort to construct and sustain a common institutional framework to meet the exigencies of social life in accordance with certain ideals'.[9] Note the strong parallel to Emanuel Adler's constructivist description of 'communities of practice' as a source for all social norms.[10] It follows that law can exist by degrees, so it is possible to talk about law

[6] Although Fuller's work was rooted in the liberal market economics of mid-twentieth-century America, he was by no means an apologist for unbridled capitalism. Most importantly, Fuller did not believe that cooperation could only be produced through rational maximization of self-interest. See Jeremy Waldron, 'Why Law – Efficacy, Freedom, or Fidelity?' (1994) 13 *Law and Philosophy* 259 at 271; Winston, above note 5, p. 65; Joseph Vining, 'Fuller and Language', in Witteveen and van der Burg, above note 5, p. 471 (distinguishing law from games); David Luban, 'Rediscovering Fuller's Legal Ethics', in Witteveen and van der Burg, above note 5, p. 208 (arguing that Fuller's economics is completely distinct from the 'law and economics' school); and Karol Sołtan, 'A Social Science That Does Not Exist', in Witteveen and van der Burg, above note 5, p. 394 (noting that Fuller is part of a tradition resistant to rational choice theory and its assumptions about human motivation). He was not even a utilitarian, being far too preoccupied with moral theory, and eschewing instrumentalism. See Pauline Westerman, 'Means and Ends', in Witteveen and van der Burg, above note 5, p. 145.

[7] Fuller, above note 1, pp. 106 and 145. See also Lon L. Fuller, 'American Legal Philosophy at Mid-Century' (1954) 6 *Journal of Legal Education* 457 at 467 ('law is not a datum, but an achievement that needs ever to be renewed').

[8] Fuller, above note 1, p. 129. Fuller is indebted to Aristotle for the strong practical orientation of his approach to norms and morality. See Aristotle, *The Nicomachean Ethics*, J.A.K. Thomson (trans.) (Harmondsworth: Penguin 1976), pp. 335 (s. X:ix) *et seq.*, esp. pp. 340–1. See also Peter R. Teachout, '"Uncreated Conscience": The Civilizing Force of Fuller's Jurisprudence', in Witteveen and van der Burg, above note 5, p. 240; Gerald J. Postema, 'Implicit Law' (1994) 13 *Law and Philosophy* 361, repr. in Witteveen and van der Burg, above note 5, p. 256; and Roderick A. Macdonald, 'Legislation and Governance', in Witteveen and van der Burg, above note 5, pp. 286–7. Oddly enough, Fuller's understanding of law as social struggle serves as a link between his work and that of the consummate realist, Hans Morgenthau, who also rejected positivism because of its lack of connection to actual social forces shaping humanity's structures and fate. However, this connection is superficial, for Morgenthau would never have accepted Fuller's conclusions, most pointedly, that legal norms are tested in part through adherence to an internal morality. For Morgenthau, 'realism' dictated that law could be defined only by the psychology and sociology of force or sanction. See Martti Koskenniemi, 'Carl Schmitt, Hans Morgenthau, and the Image of Law in International Relations', in Michael Byers (ed.), *The Role of Law in International Politics* (Cambridge University Press, 2000) pp. 22–4.

[9] Winston, above note 5, p. 63.

[10] See above Introduction, text accompanying notes 37–9.

that is being constructed; law is not an all-or-nothing proposition.[11] Fuller admits that this continuum of legality[12] can make it difficult to know exactly when a system, or a particular rule, has made the transition from social to legal normativity, but he proposes a specific approach to assessing the strength of legality, which we will shortly discuss.[13]

Despite the use of the word 'subjecting' in Fuller's description of law, Fuller rejected a command model of legal effectiveness. Law is not grounded in the will of the sovereign or of Parliament; it is not simply the fiat of state power, nor is it rooted in a hierarchy of rules.[14] *Humans* are not subjected to law; human *conduct* is subjected to the governance of rules. No law, even law in seemingly hierarchical state systems, is merely the imposition of authority (read as 'power') from above.[15] That is because, when understood as a purposive activity, law depends for its existence 'on effective interaction and cooperation between citizens and lawmaking and law-applying officials'.[16] For Fuller, this reciprocity was necessary because

11 Fuller, above note 1, pp. 117 and 123 (rejecting a bright line distinction between law and non-law) and 122 ('[B]oth rules of law and legal systems can and do half exist. This condition results when the purposive effort necessary to bring them into full being has been, as it were, only half successful').

12 In earlier work we described the idea of such a continuum in a discussion of what we called 'contextual regimes'. See Jutta Brunnée and Stephen J. Toope, 'Environmental Security and Freshwater Resources: Ecosystem Regime Building' (1997) 91 *American Journal of International Law* 26.

13 Fuller, above note 1, p. 131. See also the discussion of the 'internal morality' of law, below notes 24–5 and accompanying text.

14 Fuller, above note 1, pp. 63 (warning against a confusion between fidelity to law and 'deference for established authority'), 107 (distinguishing the rule of law from public order), 115, 148 (emphasizing that lawful authority is the 'product of law', not its precursor), 168 (explaining why not all governmental action is 'legal' in nature), 110 (rejecting the 'pyramidal structure of state power' as the essence of law), and 133–45 (discussing and discarding Hart's normative hierarchy).

15 *Ibid.*, pp. 221 and 233. Neither official texts nor officials' acts can be treated as exclusive sources of normativity. See Macdonald, above note 8, pp. 305 and 309. For a characteristic positivist focus upon explicit texts as the primary source of legal obligation, see Thomas M. Franck, *The Power of Legitimacy Among Nations* (Oxford University Press, 1990), pp. 42 and 52.

16 Postema, above note 8, p. 260. See also Fuller, above note 1, pp. 194–5 ('The quality and terms of the parties' emergent relationship – its "laws" if you will – constitute an important social reality, but it is a reality brought into being and kept alive by purposive effort and by the way each of the parties interprets the purposes of the other'), and 209 (arguing that in a legal system 'the existence of a relatively stable reciprocity of expectations between lawgiver and subject is part of the very idea of a functioning legal order'). See also Lon L. Fuller, 'Human Interaction and the Law' (1969) 14 *American Journal of Jurisprudence* 1, repr. in Kenneth I. Winston (ed.), *The Principles of Social Order: Selected Essays of Lon L. Fuller*, rev. edn (Oxford: Hart Publishing, 2001), pp. 231–3; and Lon L. Fuller, 'A Reply to Professors Cohen and Dworkin' (1965) 10 *Villanova Law Review* 655 at 661.

of the fundamental autonomy of human beings. Indeed, one might say that Fuller's entire theory was directed at ensuring that autonomy.[17] However, Fuller always balanced 'autonomy' against a fundamental need for human communication, so as noted above, autonomy is conceived in social terms. Citizens are not merely subjects, but are interacting agents creating law through specific processes of communication.

Fuller's 'interactionism'[18] is central to the upholding of autonomy. Law guides human action by addressing *reasons for action* to agents, but these reasons are of a general nature, and agents must reason further with the norms to apply them in specific contexts, characteristically relying upon analogy to argue a point.[19] It is therefore essential that relatively stable patterns of expectation emerge both amongst the governed and between the governed and the governing. But relatively stable expectations or, to adopt constructivist language, shared understandings, are only likely to arise from repeated social practice. Postema refers to this idea as the 'congruence thesis', emphasizing that 'legal norms and authoritative directives can guide self-directed social interaction only if they are broadly congruent with the practices and patterns of interaction extant in the society generally.'[20]

It follows that law is not dependent upon force for its existence,[21] nor is it best imagined as an exercise of authority, if by 'authority' one means 'power over' others.[22] Law is 'authoritative', but only when it is

[17] Colleen Murphy, 'Lon Fuller and the Moral Value of the Rule of Law' (2005) 24 *Law and Philosophy* 239. See also Kristen Rundle, 'The Impossibility of an Exterminatory Legality: Law and the Holocaust' (2009) 59 *University of Toronto Law Journal* 65.

[18] See Fuller, above note 1, pp. 221, 237 and 241. See also the discussion in Postema, above note 8, pp. 256–65 and 270.

[19] See Vaughan Lowe, 'The Politics of Law-Making: Are the Method and Character of Norm Creation Changing?', in Byers, above note 8, pp. 210, n. 5 and 214. Lowe's approach to the 'character' of norm creation is analogous to Fuller's, for Lowe emphasizes the power of 'interstitial norms' in driving change within the international legal system, *ibid.*, pp. 212 *et seq.* Of course, the idea that norms must inevitably be interpreted, and that rules must be conditioned by context to be equitable is deeply rooted in Aristotelian thought. See Jonathan Barnes, 'Introduction' in Aristotle, above note 8, p. 21 and *ibid.*, pp. 177 (s. V:iii) and 198 (s. V:x).

[20] Postema, above note 8, p. 265.

[21] Fuller, above note 1, pp. 108 and 139 (though force may usefully be exercised in some circumstances). The lack of emphasis upon coercion is one of the key elements distinguishing Fuller from American Legal Realists. Their interest in 'practice' was largely limited to predicting the exercises of power by official actors (especially judges), matched with the enforcement capacity of the state. See Oliver Wendell Holmes, Jr., 'The Path of the Law' (1897) 10 *Harvard Law Review* 457.

[22] Postema, above note 8, p. 272. See also Andrew Hurrell, 'International Law and the Changing Constitution of International Society', in Byers, above note 8, p. 328. This

mutually constructed. Finally, in a system that is reciprocally generated, issues of interpretation occupy 'a sensitive, central position' in the legal imagination.[23]

Within a conception of law that is non-hierarchical, not defined by the use of force, and mutually constructed by actors who may be both governors and governed (creators and subjects of law), what gives rise to a legal norm, distinguishing it from other social norms? Here Fuller posits his most controversial thesis: one knows law by requiring strong adherence to its 'internal morality'.[24] Fuller's concept of 'internal morality' was rooted in his belief that certain conditions must be in place to allow human beings to pursue their purposes through law and for law to guide their actions and interactions.[25] If the internal morality of the law is not fulfilled, if the conditions are not met, then the process of law creation, be it through legislation, adjudication or negotiation, is fundamentally flawed and, we will argue, lacks distinctive legal legitimacy. The formation of a simple contract provides a useful example. If the imbalance of power between the parties is great, if there is no real opportunity for negotiations, and if no true reciprocity is evident, then one really has not created a contract at all, but has merely acted in the form of 'contract'.

claim is more radical than the denial of 'force' as a central element of the definition of law, for even positivists such as Hart wanted to jettison the reliance upon force inherent in Austinian command theories of law: see Winston, above note 5, p. 60. But to move 'authority over subjects' from the centre of our preoccupations profoundly challenges any hierarchical understandings of law. Postema correctly emphasizes that both force (or coercion), and authority are 'salient' for Fuller, but he moves them away from 'the center of our conceptions of law'.

23 Fuller, above note 1, p. 91.

24 Fuller also posited the existence of a weak 'external morality' that was the repository of a limited substantive conception of justice and fairness. See *ibid.*, Chapters 2 and 4. The ambiguity introduced by Fuller's references to external morality has been highlighted by both friendly and critical commentators. See Westerman, above note 6, p. 155 (observing, while otherwise sympathetic to Fuller's account, that 'his distinction between internal and external morality seems to reintroduce the distinction between technicity and morality' and, along with his endorsement of a 'procedural natural law', 'seems to strengthen the interpretation that Fuller conceives of law primarily as … a means to … external "substantive aims"'). That appears to be precisely the interpretation arrived at in critiques such as that by Frederick Schauer, 'Fuller's Internal Point of View' (1994) 13 *Law and Philosophy* 285 at 296 (noting that 'if the argument for calling Fuller's internal procedural requirements moral ones is the belief in their probabilistic instrumental relationship to substantive or external morality, then there is not that much distance between Fuller's position … and a more traditional natural law position').

25 See David Dyzenhaus, 'Fuller's Novelty', in Witteveen and van der Burg, above note 5, p. 97.

Fuller's linkage of law and morality raised storms of protest. It is a first principle of positivism that 'the law that is' should be viewed separately from 'the law that ought to be', that law and morality are distinct spheres of human endeavour with different structures of argument.[26] But Fuller never argued that law and morality are co-extensive.[27] Indeed, he recognized that legal norms are distinguishable by the explicit responsibilities they impose and, we add, by the specific sense of obligation that they generate. However, the idea that law is constructed, that it can partly exist, makes it hard to distinguish the exact point when broad moral concerns in society become legal concerns. For Fuller, the key to the distinction lies in eight internal criteria of legality – his 'internal morality of law' – that apply to both individual rules and systems of rule-making. Legal norms must be general, prohibiting, requiring or permitting certain conduct. They must also be promulgated, and therefore accessible to the public, enabling citizens to know what the law requires. Law should not be retroactive, but prospective, enabling citizens to take the law into account in their decision-making. Citizens must also be able to understand what is permitted, prohibited or required by law – the law must be clear: law should avoid contradiction, not requiring or permitting and prohibiting at the same time; law must be realistic and not demand the impossible; its requirements of citizens must remain relatively constant; finally, there should be congruence between legal norms and the actions of officials operating under the law.[28]

It is fair to say that for Fuller, identifying the distinctive obligatory effect of law was not a major concern. Given his strong pluralism, his interest in the wide variety of mechanisms of normative social ordering outside law, Fuller was never much concerned to trace out a fixed boundary between law and other forms of social normativity.[29] Our view is somewhat different. For international society, some distinction between legal obligations and broader social norms is crucial in upholding an admittedly weak

[26] See e.g. H.L.A. Hart, 'Positivism and the Separation of Law and Morals' (1958) 71 *Harvard Law Review* 593 at 606; and Ronald Dworkin, 'Philosophy, Morality, and Law – Observations Prompted by Professor Fuller's Novel Claim' (1965) 113 *University of Pennsylvania Law Review* 668. Hart also thought that positivism's separation of law and morals properly emphasized the nature of law as authority rooted in criteria of validity found ultimately in the rule of recognition. See the posthumously published postscript to the second edition of *The Concept of Law* (Oxford University Press, 1994), pp. 238 *et seq.*

[27] See below note 40 and accompanying text.

[28] See Murphy, above note 17 at 240–1.

[29] Fuller, above note 1, p. 131 and 'Human Interaction', above note 16.

rule-of-law tradition.[30] What is more, despite his refusal to highlight the issue, we think that one can nonetheless extrapolate an approach toward the relative specificity of law – what we call its obligatory quality – from Fuller's arguments.[31] When the eight criteria of legality are met, law will tend to attract its own adherence. As mentioned previously, Fuller called this effect 'fidelity' to law;[32] others have termed it law's 'loyalty-advantages'[33] or the 'self-bindingness of law'.[34] Legal 'obligation' is therefore best viewed as an internalized commitment and not as an externally imposed duty matched with a sanction for non-performance.

Fidelity is generated, and in our terminology obligation is felt, because adherence to the eight criteria of legality (a 'practice of legality') produces law that is legitimate in the eyes of the persons to whom it is addressed. To take two simple examples: no one really enjoys paying taxes; nor do riparian states readily concede their 'right' to the use of water. However, when tax law is seen to be fair, the rules relatively understandable, and when the rules are seen to be applied by officials in an equitable manner, most people will voluntarily pay their taxes. The contrary is equally true, and in many states with a weak set of 'rule-of-law' principles, the rate of effective tax collection is low.[35] Similarly, our work on shared water

30 We believe that the distinction between being legally obliged to follow a rule and being encouraged to do so through social pressure alone is important to the political calculations of international actors. In addition, a theory of legal obligation helps social actors to take strategic decisions about how to act so as to shape, uphold or change norms. See further in Chapter 3.

31 The closest Fuller comes to discussing the distinction between law and other forms of social normativity is in the concluding chapter of Lon L. Fuller, *The Law in Quest of Itself* (Chicago: The Foundation Press, 1940). See also, but more opaquely, Lon L. Fuller, 'Freedom as a Problem of Allocating Choice' (1968) 112 *Proceedings of the American Philosophical Society* 101; and Fuller, above note 1, pp. 33–8 (on mythical King Rex coming to understand an interactional legal order as relying on internalized conceptions of bindingness). See also Jan Klabbers, 'Constitutionalism and the Making of International Law: Fuller's Procedural Natural Law' (April 2008) 5 *No Foundations: Journal of Extreme Legal Positivism* 84 at 106–8 (arguing that Fuller's eight requirements might be seen as approaching a fully fledged sources theory of international law, 'combining formal and substantive criteria for the identification of legal rules').

32 See above note 4 and accompanying text. Even Fuller's principal intellectual opponent, Professor Hart, emphasized that norms required a sense of internally felt obligation on the part of officials who must follow a rule, but in Hart's theory this was more a measure of effectiveness, for rules derived their *force* from their existence in a normative hierarchy. See H.L.A. Hart, *The Concept of Law* (Oxford: Clarendon Press, 1961), *passim*.

33 Waldron, above note 6 at 282.

34 Roderick A. Macdonald, personal communication with authors.

35 See e.g. Marcelo Bergman, *Tax Evasion and the Rule of Law in Latin America: The Political Culture of Cheating and Compliance in Argentina and Chile* (Philadelphia: Penn State

resources has demonstrated that when states participate in norm creation through open interactional processes, communities of practice are created that allow for the evolution of stronger normative regimes, as has recently been the case in the Nile Basin.[36] To reiterate, a distinctive form of legitimacy is internal to interactional law; it is not an external measure of political value or preference.

The criteria of legality suggested by Fuller are largely uncontroversial. Few lawyers or legal theorists would argue against promulgation, clarity or predictability in rules. In fact, even Fuller's primary opponent, H.L.A. Hart, agreed that the criteria were important.[37] However, in well-known objections to Fuller's characterization of his eight tests of legality as 'moral', both Hart and Joseph Raz argued that the criteria were purely about efficacy. Raz offered up the metaphor of a knife.[38] As a knife becomes more and more blunt, it ceases to serve its function, and at some point can no longer be called a knife. So Hart and Raz agreed with Fuller that, when certain criteria are not met, law ceases to be law, but they considered this question to be a purely instrumental, and not a moral, issue. Hart and Raz are positivists who argued strongly that moral concerns were necessarily external to law. But Raz's very metaphor reveals the difficulty in treating law as essentially functional and instrumental, without internal 'moral' content. Just as law remains law even when it is not directly enforced, there are circumstances when a 'knife' can still be a knife even when it is entirely blunt, or when it cannot be used for a functional purpose. First of all, a knife can have tremendous symbolic value. When a small boy asks his father for a knife, the father might be reluctant to give the requested Swiss Army knife, but a beautiful 'jewel-encrusted'

University Press, 2009) (arguing that the willingness of citizens to pay taxes is closely related to the social norms that underpin the rule of law; while the threat of enforcement plays a role, its impact is greatest when citizens have other reasons to comply, rooted in a sense that the system is fair and that fellow citizens generally comply; thus, different rule-of-law traditions explain why tax evasion is relatively common in Argentina whereas compliance rates are relatively high in Chile). See also Dan M. Kahan, 'The Logic of Reciprocity: Trust, Collective Action, and Law' (2003) 102 *Michigan Law Review* 71 at 82 (commenting on the role of different tax compliance cultures).

[36] See Brunnée and Toope, above note 12.

[37] Hart considered the criteria to be important for efficient law, acknowledging also that they were descriptive of the rule of law. However, he did not consider them to be central to the concept of law as such and, crucially, he did not consider them to be moral in nature. See Hart, above note 32, pp. 202 and 207; and H.L.A. Hart, *Essays in Jurisprudence and Philosophy* (Oxford: Clarendon Press, 1983), p. 350.

[38] Joseph Raz, *The Authority of Law: Essays on Law and Morality* (Oxford: Clarendon Press, 1979), pp. 223–6.

dagger bought on vacation for a few dollars at a Tunisian market might be very much appreciated by the boy as a symbol of 'knife' even with its dull, functionless blade. Similarly, the Kirpan worn by orthodox Sikh males may be wrapped in a ceremonial casing that makes it impossible to draw the knife. That has not stopped some worried parents from trying to have Kirpans banned from schools in Western countries.[39] 'Knife' has value aside from function, and law has internal value aside from its instrumentality: that was one of Fuller's central insights.

We nevertheless acknowledge that describing the criteria of legality as 'moral' can cause confusion, because of the link to natural law theory, and a resulting sense that Fuller may be requiring too much social agreement as to the ends of law. Given the long history of scholarly debate, people tend to assume that natural law necessarily implies a deep commitment to a range of substantive values. For Fuller, it did not. Fuller himself described his theory as a 'procedural version of natural law'.[40] By that he meant that the 'morality' to which he refers is contained primarily within the procedures of law itself – in the eight criteria of legality. One could describe this procedural natural law as a 'weak' variety of natural law, in the sense that it contains only a very limited range of substantive commitments. Indeed, for Fuller, there were only two essential commitments in law: human autonomy *and* communication or interaction. It is crucial that these values themselves interact, so that, as we suggested above, Fuller's 'autonomy' was an autonomy created and supported through communication. For Fuller, it is only to the extent that law supports autonomy while facilitating social interaction that law pursues 'moral' ends.[41]

Fuller's particular conception of the 'moral' content of law requires further exposition. He insisted that his internal criteria were moral in part because they upheld and promoted agency; they enabled citizens to reason

39 For details regarding a recent Canadian attempt to ban the wearing of kirpans in schools, see Richard Blackwell and Terry Weber, 'Supreme Court Rules Kirpans Okay in School', *The Globe and Mail*, 2 March 2006, at www.theglobeandmail.com/servlet/story/RTGAM.20060302.wkirpan0302/BNStory/National/. For details regarding similar attempts in a number of US states, see The Sikh Coalition, *United States Judicial Opinions Regarding the Sikh Religious Identity*, 2009, at www.sikhcoalition.org/LegalUS0.asp.

40 Fuller, above note 1, pp. 96–7 ('What I have called the internal morality of law is … a procedural version of natural law … [it is] concerned, not with the substantive aims of legal rules, but with the ways in which a system of rules for governing human conduct must be constructed and administered if it is to be efficacious and at the same time remain what it purports to be').

41 Dyzenhaus, above note 25, p. 97 (noting that, for Fuller, '[t]he moral foundation of law has to be manifest in the institutions of law so that law can fulfil its moral task – the promotion of interaction between individuals subject to the law …').

with law, to make choices about their own lives and appropriate conduct. Therefore 'the rule of law provides some normative grounds for thinking that citizens have a moral obligation to obey the law'.[42] The obligation to obey is self-generated – 'fidelity' – and is rooted in a sense of legitimacy gained primarily from upholding the 'internal morality of law' (the eight criteria of legality). We concur that promoting agency, and therefore responsibility, is an important social goal. But, as we have already hinted, in respect of international law the commitment to agency and autonomy, when linked to the second 'moral' commitment to communication or interaction, implies that another good is embedded in the conditions of legality: respect for the diversity of peoples. If fidelity to law is generated by the adherence to the criteria of legality, then agents are willing to have their behaviour guided by the promulgated rules even if they disagree with them on substantive moral grounds.[43] Or, as Jeremy Waldron put it, the crucial point is that fidelity to law 'is predicated on what law is, not just on what it is used for'.[44] Remember the knife analogy: a knife can have meaning aside from function, and so can law. Perhaps despite his own preference to support the autonomy of individuals as an overarching moral value, Fuller actually helps us to see how law is possible in societies where diverse moral ends are being pursued by citizens or peoples, including even challenges to individual autonomy.

The second internal 'moral' element of law is rooted in an assumption about human nature, which is that the main goal of human life is not mere survival, but 'maintaining communication with our fellows'.[45] Indeed, humanity's survival has been predicated upon the acquisition and transmission of knowledge, and upon a conscious and deliberate coordination of effort among human beings.[46] Following Ludwig Wittgenstein, Fuller

[42] Murphy, above note 17 at 242.

[43] But see also Dyzenhaus, above note 25, p. 98 (suggesting that 'in particular legal orders, that is, in liberal democratic societies, one will find that allegiance is possible only if the legal order respects the liberty-loving character of the citizenry').

[44] Waldron, above note 6 at 275.

[45] Fuller, above note 1, p. 185. See also *ibid.*, p. 210 ('[L]aw … is basically a matter of providing the citizenry with a sound and stable framework for their interactions with one another …'). On the role of communication in human life see also the following, evocative passage in Tim Blanning, *The Pursuit of Glory: Europe 1648–1815* (London: Allen Lane, 2007), p. 3 ('Communication is central to human existence. Apart from basic physical functions such as eating and defecating, waking and sleeping, nothing is more central. Whether the form it takes is symbolic, as in speech, or physical, as in travel, it is communication between people and people, or between people and places, that weaves the social fabric.').

[46] Fuller, above note 1, pp. 185–6. Winston argues that Fuller's essentially benign view of human nature is what led him to 'conceive of law not as coercive and controlling but as

argues that '[h]ow and when we accomplish communication with one another can expand or contract the boundaries of life itself'.[47] Constructivists would add that it is through communication and social practice that actors' identities are shaped and their world acquires meaning.[48]

Fuller's belief that law facilitates communication was grounded in his allegiance to the long and rich Aristotelian tradition of rhetoric. He shared Aristotle's purposive understanding of human action: 'Every art and every investigation, and similarly every action and pursuit, is considered to aim at some good ...'[49] From this basis flowed a commitment to 'rhetorical activity' as 'a means of discerning and evaluating the ends available to a given community'.[50] Chaim Perelman articulated this commitment in philosophical terms by distinguishing between 'rational truths' and 'reasonable arguments'; the former were meant to be self-evident and compelling, while the latter were convincing reasons for action, but could not *cause* action.[51] Rhetorical claims can be persuasive because they are

facilitative and enabling'. Winston, above note 5, p. 58. See also Aristotle, above note 8, pp. 74 (s. I:vii) and 258 (s. VIII:1) (on humans as 'social beings' who live to communicate, and to develop friendships).

[47] Fuller, above note 1, p. 186. Or in Macdonald's words, '[o]ur acts and our sayings are both the reflection of, and the aspiration towards, normativity'. Macdonald, above note 8, p. 305. We noted above that this communicative focus in Fuller connects as well to Anthony Giddens's and Ray Bhakshar's structuration theory, which is why Fuller speaks so helpfully to constructivist approaches to international relations. Anthony Giddens, *The Constitution of Society: Outline of the Theory of Structuration* (Cambridge: Polity Press, 1984) and Roy Bhaskar, *The Possibility of Naturalism: A Philosophical Critique of the Contemporary Human Sciences* (Brighton: Harvester Press, 1979).

[48] Emanuel Adler, *Communitarian International Relations: The Epistemic Foundations of International Relations* (London and New York: Routledge, 2005), p. 11.

[49] Aristotle, above note 8, p. 63 (s. I:i). See also the discussion of 'purposive jurisprudence' in Teachout, above note 8, pp. 238–45.

[50] Francis J. Mootz III, 'Natural Law and the Cultivation of Legal Rhetoric' in Witteveen and van der Burg, above note 5, p. 444. See also Lowe, above note 19, p. 221 (describing international law as a system 'where the plausibility of analogical reasoning and the persuasiveness of topical, rhetorical argument lie at the root of the perception of legitimacy').

[51] Here we are relying on the thoughtful and compelling reading of Perelman by Mootz, above note 50, pp. 440–4. For Perelman's philosophy in detail, see Chaim Perelman, *The New Rhetoric and the Humanities: Essays on Rhetoric and Its Applications*, W. Kluback (trans.) (Dordrecht: D. Reidel Publishing Company, 1979); and Chaim Perelman, *Logique Juridique* (Paris: Dalloz, 1976). Postema and Macdonald also read Fuller as positing that legal rules are reasons, not causes, for human action. See Postema, above note 8, p. 262; and Macdonald, above note 8, p. 304. Given Fuller's grounding in Aristotle, this conclusion is completely coherent, for Aristotle emphasized that rhetorical argument could not be as precise as other forms of more 'exact' science. Questions of cause and effect had to be evaluated differently in rhetoric (as part of politics) and physical science: Aristotle, above note 8, p. 65 (s. I:iii).

rooted in 'prior agreements' or contexts of shared understanding.[52] On one reading, Fuller's internal morality of the law is an attempt to structure legal processes so that they are most likely to produce rhetorical knowledge, to facilitate interactive communication without presupposing specified ends.[53] When law fulfils the eight criteria of legality it shapes the practical reasoning of citizens and their deliberations about how they should act.[54] 'Rhetoric' captures Fuller's commitment to self-rule through the interaction of government and governed, and to the construction of law through everyday practice by all participants in the system, respecting diverse views as to the definition of the good life.[55]

At this point in the argument, now that questions of Fuller's moral characterization of law have been addressed, we return to the congruence of legal norms with social practice.[56] We reiterate that 'social practice', or in constructivist terms 'shared understandings', need not represent (in fact, they rarely do) deep moral commitments. It is possible to imagine law rooted in thin, shared moral commitments, such as autonomy and communication. For example, basic rules of contract law may be grounded in notions of free consent (autonomy) and transaction (a blending of material and psychic forms of communication). However, as societies attempt to articulate more ambitious rules related to human interaction, such as anti-discrimination statutes or surrogate mother contracts, we find that substantive moral commitments are expressed in law. To be effective, ambitious substantive norms require deeper shared understandings of the right ordering of society. There is no possibility of simply imposing significant social change by fiat in the absence of some degree of social consensus, expressed in practice.

[52] See Adler, above note 48, p. 15. Aristotle called these understandings 'topics' or 'commonplaces', that is, accepted frames or starting points for argument. See Aristotle, *Rhetoric*, E.S. Forster (trans.) (Cambridge, Mass: Harvard University Press, 1966).

[53] Rhetoric, as a daily practice, 'is a continual denial of literalness in meaning and of the reducibility of language to rules'. Vining, above note 6, p. 457.

[54] Murphy, above note 17 at 241.

[55] Willem J. Witteveen, 'Rediscovering Fuller: An Introduction' in Witteveen and van der Burg, above note 5, p. 37. As we will illustrate in Chapter 2, this practice-driven account of the generation of law is, of course, closely allied to Adler's 'community of practice' description of the generation of all social norms.

[56] See Postema, above note 8, p. 265 and accompanying text on Postema's 'congruence thesis'. It is important to distinguish Postema's concept of congruence between law and wider social practice from Fuller's emphasis on the need for congruence between official action and the law. The two ideas are of course interrelated, but, whereas Fuller's notion of congruence is one of the requirements of legality he posited, Postema's congruence thesis is concerned with the preconditions that must exist for legality to evolve.

We are not suggesting that there is no 'educative value' in law, only that any such value is but a starting point for the hard work of norm entrepreneurs. As we have already argued, the form of law alone is not enough to generate behavioural change. Nor does our argument imply that we must simply defer to existing practice; it is possible – our point is that it is necessary – to work to construct shared understandings.[57] In summary, law is rooted in social practice that generates shared understandings, and we can work to make these shared understandings deeper through more and more interaction. This can, but will not necessarily, lead to law that is more ambitious, that regulates more intrusively. Merely declaring the form of 'law' alone will not accomplish this end, a point to which we return towards the end of this chapter.

Fuller's legal theory, as should be obvious from this brief *tour d'horizon*, is not instrumental, in the sense that he never seemed to be setting up arguments simply to further a particular moral or political agenda,[58] with the exception of his weak liberal commitment to human autonomy matched with the human need to communicate. As we have suggested, what enables interactional law to promote autonomy is that it is independent of stronger moral or political commitments. That, in turn, enables it to facilitate communication and to protect diversity, one of its strengths in conceptualizing the role of law in international society.[59]

3. Fuller and international law

Fuller wrote primarily with domestic law in mind,[60] and his principal area of interest was property and contract theory, but his fundamental preoccupation was with law as a set of non-hierarchical practices

[57] See also Adler, above note 48, p. 12 (stressing that 'constructivism takes a dynamic view of social life in which new practices, identities, and interests emerge with new constitutive rules and newly evolving social structures').

[58] But see Murphy, above note 17 at 242 (concerns raised by e.g. Westerman and Schauer).

[59] See below note 94 and accompanying text.

[60] Fuller did not apply his insights to the realm of international law in any sustained way. Indeed, in one of his brief references, he seemed to deny that international society could aspire to a rule of law. See Lon L. Fuller, 'The Forms and Limits of Adjudication', in Winston, above note 16, p. 102. We think that he was wrong, and that he missed opportunities in international society both to apply and to find support for his own insights. It may be that Fuller's thinking was so much shaped by the Cold War that he could not imagine the purposes of international law beyond 'preventing a holocaust'. For a brief, but more engaged, discussion of international law and its relationship to his own theoretical approaches, see Fuller, above note 1, pp. 232–3 and 236–7.

ordering human interaction. To that extent, he speaks directly to the parallel preoccupations of international legal theorists, all of whom inevitably struggle to understand how norms function in the horizontal normative order that is international society. Fuller helps us to understand five key points. First, that domestic law is also 'horizontal' in important ways; indeed horizontality is an asset for, not a defect of, law. Second, that appreciating law's grounding in social interaction reveals the real locus of its power to shape human behaviour, through the generation of fidelity (a sense of obligation), rather than through reciprocal advantage as rationalists would maintain. Third, that a thin, largely procedural, conception of the rule of law upholds and supports diversity in moral and political ends while at the same time helping to build a stronger global society, perhaps with pockets of deeper normative communities. Fourth, international lawyers rely too heavily upon formalistic accounts of legality, missing important opportunities for a richer understanding of customary, treaty and soft law. Fifth, 'legitimacy' can have a specific, legal meaning. Additionally, we suggest that Fuller's theories, when linked to constructivist insights from IR, help to better explain the contemporary practice of international law.

3.1 The horizontal nature of law

First, in addressing the horizontal nature of law, it bears repeating that within *all* systems of legal normativity, even state systems of law, social norms are constructed through rhetorical activity and social practice, producing increasingly influential mutual expectations or shared understandings of actors. In turn, if these shared understandings are reinforced through action based upon Fuller's criteria of legality, it becomes possible to generate obligation, or fidelity to law.

This point applies not just to law-making, but also to implementation and even to formal enforcement of law. Fuller's central argument is that law does not depend upon enforcement for its existence, much less on the use of physical force, though power and force are relevant in understanding human interaction in law, as elsewhere. This insight is fundamental for international lawyers who are constantly challenged to show how a rule that is not backed by a sanction can be law. Like Fuller, we accept that power and force are salient to law, but they do not explain the sense of obligation that must exist in international society for legal enforcement to be possible and effective. We distinguish between raw power and legal authority.

It is nonetheless important to recognize that a failure to enforce does tend to undermine fidelity to law, not because of the need for external validation through 'force', but because laws that are 'kept on the books as a kind of symbolic act, with the knowledge that they will not and cannot be enforced' lead to a sense of hypocrisy that damages any commitment to the rule of law.[61] Fuller's understanding of the failure to enforce norms helps us appreciate why it is that so many people are frustrated by international law: it is not because law requires enforcement to be law, but because law requires fidelity. That fidelity is damaged when law is seen to have no possibility of effect. This is the lesson of Fuller's eighth criterion of legality: congruence between law and official action or, in the case of international law, congruence amongst the actions of a majority of international actors. When explicit rules are unrelated to how states and other international actors actually behave, fidelity is destroyed.[62]

The interactional view, in which agents participate actively in the construction of law, helps make sense of central features of the international legal system, for example Georges Scelle's '*dédoublement fonctionnel*',[63] the idea that states are both subject to and sovereign in international law, that cannot comfortably be accommodated within theories of law predicated upon hierarchical projections of authority. The parallel to Fuller's commitment to autonomy in the domestic sphere is the traditional commitment in international society to sovereignty: but this observation requires some nuance.

There is an important difference between human agency in Fuller's interactional law and state sovereignty in interactional international law. Human agency is central to Fuller's account, in that autonomy is at once the basis of interactional law and in part, along with the possibility of communication, what it is meant to protect. Thus, while individuals' decisions may be guided by law and their social identities are shaped by interaction through law, their socially constructed autonomy is the prerequisite for interactional law. By contrast, sovereign states are but an imperfect proxy for human agency. It is nonetheless plausible to think of states' interaction through law as comparable to that of individual human

[61] See Fuller, above note 1, p. 153.

[62] See also above note 55 and below notes 89–90 and accompanying text.

[63] See Georges Scelle, 'Le Phénomène Juridique de Dédoublement Fonctionnel', in Walter Schätzel and Hans-Jürgen Schlochauer (eds.), *Rechtsfragen der internationalen Organisation: Festschrift für Hans Wehberg zu seinem 70 Geburtstag* (Frankfurt: Klostermann, 1956), p. 324 (Scelle highlighted the dual role of states as both subjects of international law and law-makers).

beings within a system of law that has not traditionally recognized the agency of any other entities.[64] What is more, states are collective entities constituted and represented by individual human beings. For that reason, it does make analytical sense to speak of states as individual agents, and to treat sovereignty as a proxy for autonomy. Similarly, constructivists are right to base their analysis of international relations on the proposition that states have 'identities' and that their identities and actions are shaped in part by social interaction, including interaction through law.[65]

Yet, none of this means that state sovereignty is indispensable for interactional international law in the same way that human agency is for Fuller's theory. Rather, in the case of states, it is international law that constitutes their autonomy in the first place, by defining what sovereignty means at any given point, or what attributes make a collective entity a 'state'. An individual human being exists outside law, though his or her ability to act in society may be strongly affected by law. A 'state' exists only within a normative framework – in our era the framework of international law. In other words, unlike individual human beings, states are entirely creatures of interaction. States are but one manner in which people can organize themselves to pursue their goals. Obviously, in contemporary international society, states remain the dominant players, often even at the expense of individuals' autonomy. But the increasing participation of individuals and non-state collectivities, such as governmental or non-governmental organizations or corporations, is indicative of the potential for major shifts in the breadth of international legal interaction. At the same time, the interactional perspective helps us to make sense of existing patterns of participation in international law-making where norms, although formally sanctioned by states alone, in fact are influenced strongly by a diversity of actors.[66]

[64] Gerald J. Postema, 'Custom in International Law: A Normative Practice Account', in Amanda Perreau-Saussine and James Bernard Murphy (eds.), *The Nature of Customary Law: Legal, Historical and Philosophical Perspectives* (Cambridge University Press, 2007), p. 306 (arguing that, '[d]espite obvious disanalogies, international actors, like individual human agents, can and do engage in discursive, practically concrete normative practices'. Of course, our interactional approach also tries to show how contemporary international law is more open to the actions of participants other than states).

[65] For a detailed discussion, see Trine Flockhart, ' "Complex Socialization": A Framework for the Study of State Socialization' (2006) 12 *European Journal of International Relations* 89.

[66] See also Benedict Kingsbury, 'International Law as Inter-Public Law', in Henry R. Richardson and Melissa S. Williams (eds.), *NOMOS XLIX: Moral Universalism and Pluralism* (New York University Press, 2009), pp. 175–9 (also suggesting that diverse actors can participate in international law-making, but arguing more narrowly that these actors must either be public entities, or exercise governing power).

3.2 *Reciprocity and obligation*

Turning, second, to the creation of obligation, we note that rationalists in IR and positivists in international law also describe interactional processes, and they typically rely on 'reciprocity' as the explanation for law. For them, however, reciprocity is simply a series of transactions in which interests are traded for advantages. Law enables the efficient functioning of society by sending coherent signals that make interaction predictable. Participation in such a system is rational because an individual agent is benefited by both the possibility of exchange in material interests and predictability in relationships. The paradigmatic example is trade agreements.[67] To the extent that rationalist-positivists would acknowledge any binding effect of law, it is rooted in a form of reciprocity that ensures that the constraint imposed on one is imposed on all. The system is stable because of the implied threat that if one agent 'defects', others will as well.[68] The rationalist version of reciprocity is helpful in understanding how interests affect norms and behaviour, but it does not go far enough. As we have argued above, 'interests' come from somewhere, and are not created solely by rational assessments of material conditions. Interests are rooted in identity and identity is formed in large measure through social interaction.[69]

Still, reciprocity in the rationalist sense just described is the most common explanation given by international lawyers for the existence of legal norms. Following on from the New Haven School, Rosalyn Higgins argued that there is no point in searching for an explanation of obligation.

[67] See e.g. Beth Simmons, 'The Legalization of International Monetary Affairs' (2000) 54 *International Organization* 573; and Beth Simmons and Daniel Hopkins, 'The Constraining Power of International Treaties' (2005) 99 *American Political Science Review* 623.

[68] See e.g. Robert Axelrod, *The Evolution of Cooperation* (New York: Basic Books, 1984); Robert O. Keohane, 'Reciprocity in International Relations' (1986) 40 *International Organization* 1; George W. Downs, David M. Rocke and Peter N. Barsoom, 'Is the Good News About Compliance Good News About Cooperation?' (1996) 50 *International Organization* 379. And see Andrew T. Guzman, *How International Law Works: A Rational Choice Theory* (Oxford University Press, 2008), pp. 42–5 and 211–12 (arguing that this dynamic increases the costs of violations and so can promote compliance).

[69] See also Kahan, above note 35 at 72–80 (arguing that individuals in collective action settings are best understood as 'moral and emotional reciprocators' whose decisions to contribute or withhold contribution to collective goods is dependent on their perceptions of others' willingness to contribute – that is, on trust; social interaction impacts individuals' decisions insofar as it changes their perceptions of others, for better or worse).

In her view, international law functions purely on the basis of reciprocal obligations rooted in interests.[70] Other legal theorists have looked to a type of systemic reciprocity explained by the long-term interests of states in the predictability provided by law.[71] As part of a recent surge of purely rationalist explanations of international law by American scholars, Eric Posner and Jack Goldsmith have suggested that states may cooperate to uphold a rule of international law if they anticipate long-term interaction on the issue and if the pay-offs from defection do not significantly outweigh those from cooperation.[72]

For Fuller, and for us, reciprocity is deeper than the exchange flowing from the calculation of material interests, or the direction inherent in what he called 'managerial control'.[73] Fidelity to law depends upon the reciprocal fulfilment of duties.[74] Law-makers must adhere to the criteria of legality because, as we suggested above, in so doing they give

[70] Rosalyn Higgins, *Problems and Process: International Law and How We Use It* (Oxford: Clarendon Press, 1994), p. 16. See also Michael Byers, *Custom, Power and the Power of Rules* (Cambridge University Press, 1999), pp. 89–105. See also below Chapter 3.

[71] See Louis Henkin, *How Nations Behave: Law and Foreign Policy*, 2nd edn (New York: Columbia University Press, 1979), pp. 51–2; Abram Chayes and Antonia Handler Chayes, *The New Sovereignty: Compliance with International Regulatory Agreements* (Cambridge, Mass: Harvard University Press, 1995), pp. 26–7; J.L. Brierly, *The Law of Nations: An Introduction to the International Law of Peace*, Humphrey Waldock (ed.) (Oxford: Clarendon Press, 1963), pp. 55–6; and George Norman and Joel P. Trachtman, 'The Customary International Law Game' (2005) 99 *American Journal of International Law* 541 at 542. See also René Provost, *International Human Rights and Humanitarian Law* (Oxford University Press, 2002), pp. 121–6 (on reciprocal obligations that are bilateral and those that are generalized).

[72] See Jack L. Goldsmith and Eric A. Posner, *The Limits of International Law* (Oxford University Press, 2005), pp. 26 and 29–32 (arguing that reciprocity – 'cooperation' in their terminology – is one of four models that captures the 'behavioural regularities' – or international law – that emerge when states pursue their own self-interest). See also Guzman, above note 68, pp. 25–69 (offering an alternative rational choice model).

[73] See Fuller, above note 1, pp. 203–4 and 214 (suggesting that positivists' claims re 'efficacy' rather than morality stem from assumptions grounded in 'managerial control' rather than law). It is ironic that in criticism of our earlier work, we have been associated with 'managerialist' compliance theorists such as Chayes and Chayes, above note 71. Although we do agree with the Chayes when they highlight the importance of interactional, justificatory processes, we do not share their rationalist explanation of why actors adjust their behaviour in interaction. For a full discussion, see below Chapter 3 and Jutta Brunnée and Stephen J. Toope, 'Persuasion and Enforcement: Explaining Compliance with International Law' (2002) 13 *Finnish Yearbook of International Law* 273.

[74] Thus, for Fuller, 'reciprocity' was the connection between citizens and government with respect to the observance of rules. This version of reciprocity is captured especially in Fuller's eighth criterion of legality. See Waldron, above note 6 at 277.

citizens the opportunity to reason with rules. If the criteria of legality are neglected, these norms will have failed to become law and citizens will feel resentment; they will have no desire to abide by the promulgated norms. Reciprocity will fail. In addition, 'the existence of duties depends partly on the behavior of others'. Why should a person feel obliged to act in certain ways if no similar expectations apply with respect to those judging that person's behaviour?[75]

This analysis resonates strongly with the 'logic of appropriateness' articulated by two sociologists of organization, James March and Johan Olsen.[76] Their influential work has demonstrated that decisions are grounded in two different 'logics'.[77] The first, the logic of consequences, is related to rationalist-positivist reciprocity. On this logic, decisions are purely instrumental: 'How do I get what I want, and what will happen if I behave in a certain way?' The second, the logic of appropriateness, focuses upon social norms, and paves the way towards a theory of legal obligation. This logic engenders self-reflection, prompting the central question, 'What should I do in this situation?'[78]

March and Olsen help us appreciate that the decisions of actors can be motivated both by consequentialist concerns *and* moral considerations.[79] Thus reciprocity is not limited to material exchange, but can also be grounded in the desire to interact, to create sustained relationships.[80]

75 Murphy, above note 17 at 242.

76 See James G. March and Johan P. Olsen, *Rediscovering Institutions* (New York: Free Press, 1989).

77 March and Olsen's initial work was focused upon democratic politics at the national level. See March and Olsen, *ibid.*; and James G. March and Johan P. Olsen, *Democratic Governance* (New York: Free Press, 1995). They subsequently applied it to international political relations. See James G. March and Johan P. Olsen, 'The Institutional Dynamics of International Political Orders' (1998) 52 *International Organization* 943.

78 March and Olsen, above note 76. See also Martha Finnemore and Kathryn Sikkink, 'International Norm Dynamics and Political Change' (1998) 52 *International Organization* 887 at 914.

79 See March and Olsen, 'The Institutional Dynamics', above note 77 at 952; and James Fearon and Alexander Wendt, 'Rationalism v. Constructivism: A Skeptical View', in Walter Carlsnaes, Thomas Risse and Beth Simmons (eds.), *Handbook of International Relations* (London: Sage, 2002), p. 60. See also Harald Müller, 'Arguing, Bargaining and All That: Communicative Action, Rationalist Theory and the Logic of Appropriateness in International Relations' (2004) 10 *European Journal of International Relations* 395 at 400–1.

80 Note that, in any event, the very 'capacity for rational thought and behavior is not only an individual, but also and above all a [social] capacity ... Rationality lies less in the act of instrumental choice between alternatives on the basis of true theories than in behaving in ways that stand to reason, given people's background expectations and dispositions.'

Our reading of Fuller shows how, in *law*, the logic of appropriateness can develop into a sense of *legal* obligation.[81]

In international society, the deeper sense of reciprocity is even more salient because states are both subjects and law-makers. To the extent that international law is created without adhering to congruence with shared understandings and Fuller's criteria of legality, fidelity to law – the sense of obligation – amongst states will not be generated.[82] The central insight is that the kind of reciprocity that we are speaking of is not about 'tit-for-tat' interactions between individual actors. Rather, reciprocity is created and maintained collectively. To be sure, not all members of international society must be engaged in this enterprise. Interactional law can withstand individual defiance so long as a majority of actors works to uphold legality. Yet, the fact that reciprocity requires collective effort also serves to underscore why claims to legal 'exceptionalism' by powerful states can be so corrosive. Some states will be actively resentful when confronted with such claims, or with other failures to meet the requirements of legality.

This way of addressing reciprocity also explains why it is that the governments of so many developing states express frustration, even anger, over the evolution of international law. Our point is that this resentment cannot be ascribed purely to moral differences as to the proper ends of law, to 'politics'. They arise because of failures in the very creation of law, failures that in too many cases render international law illegitimate. The formation of a simple treaty provides a useful illustration. If the imbalance of power between the parties is great, if there is no real opportunity for negotiations, and if no mutual sense of duty is evident, then states have not really created a treaty at all, but have merely acted in the

See Emanuel Adler, 'Constructivism in International Relations', in Carlsnaes *et al.* above note 79, p. 103. In short, constructivists 'consider rationality and reason to be of critical importance', but they do not accept 'the notion that rationality means only instrumental rationality'. Adler, *ibid.*, p. 102.

81 For March and Olsen, the logic of appropriateness entails 'duties' and 'obligations' to act. See March and Olsen, above note 76, pp. 23 and 59. Our work suggests why a particular type of 'logic of appropriateness' is engaged by *legal* obligation.

82 For a discussion of how ideas conceived in the context of individual persons may nonetheless apply to entities like states, see above notes 64–66 and accompanying text, and below Chapter 3. Briefly put, state governments are made up of individual decision-makers who are capable of belief and who can experience a sense of obligation, but see Goldsmith and Posner, above note 72, pp. 15 (suggesting that there is no evidence that 'states are pulled to comply with international law because it reflects morally valid procedures, or consent, or internal value sets ...') and 185–202.

form of treaty.[83] For example, the sense of hypocrisy which can generate illegitimacy is apparent in the entire nuclear non-proliferation regime, where the main nuclear powers have failed to discharge their obligation seriously to pursue nuclear disarmament.[84]

Fuller's fidelity argument may seem to relate closely to conceptions of signalling in rationalist IR theory, or to the indicators of 'obligation, precision and delegation' posited by rationalist IR and international law scholars for the purposes of interdisciplinary study of 'legalization'.[85] It could be suggested that all that the criteria of legality do is to get the signalling right so that agents know how they should behave.[86] That would be like saying that law is the same as a set of signs in an airport: if they are coherent, clear, non-contradictory, etc., the passengers will find their planes. But this is too limited an understanding of Fuller's criteria of legality: they are not merely signals, but are conditions for the existence of law. Only when the conditions of legality are met, and embraced by a community of practice, can we imagine agents feeling obliged to shape their behaviour in the light of the promulgated rules.[87] The criteria of legality are directed

83 Gerry Simpson offers the Ottoman capitulations and the Treaty of Nanking of 1842 as two, particularly influential, examples of such treaties. See Gerry Simpson, *Great Powers and Outlaw States: Unequal Sovereigns in the International Legal Order* (Cambridge University Press, 2004), p. 243 and n. 61. Note that in this description, the 'form' of treaty is parallel to the form of 'contract' described in the text following note 25. We are offering an illustration parallel to our earlier discussion of invalid contracts. However, we are not suggesting that treaties should be seen in purely contractual terms.

84 For an analysis of the way in which US administrations have sought to avoid the Nuclear Non-Proliferation Treaty's original goal of disarmament while pressing for increasingly stringent counter-proliferation measures, see Richard Price, 'Nuclear Weapons Don't Kill People, Rogues Do' (2007) 44 *International Politics* 232.

85 On 'signalling' in rationalist IR theory, see Simmons, above note 67. The rationalist idea that actors choose legal form to 'signal' 'credible commitment' also underpins the 'legalization' project, and is reflected in the indicator of 'obligation'. Kenneth W. Abbott and Duncan Snidal, 'Hard and Soft Law in International Governance' (2000) 54 *International Organization* 421 at 426–30. See also See Kenneth W. Abbott, Robert O. Keohane, Andrew Moravcsik, Anne-Marie Slaughter and Duncan Snidal, 'The Concept of Legalization' (2000) 54 *International Organization* 401 at 408–12.

86 See Raz, above note 38, pp. 218 and 223–6 (using the metaphor of a knife to argue that the criteria are about efficacy and not morality); Hart, above note 37, pp. 347–53 (arguing that the criteria are merely principles of 'good craftsmanship', that is, they are principles of efficiency); and Goldsmith and Posner, above note 72, pp. 84–91 (arguing that international law, though it does not pull states towards compliance, is valuable insofar as it clarifies what counts as cooperation or coordination in inter-state relations).

87 This does not mean 'that each law must be regarded as having moral force on its own'. Actors 'may well follow a particular law out of calculated self-interest or to avoid

to the creation of obligation, and obligation is the 'value added' of law, distinguishing it from social desiderata, airport signs, or the rationalist proposition that 'obligation' is a mode of action chosen by actors to signal credible commitment.[88]

3.3 *Interactional law and diversity*

Fuller's thin conception of the rule of law is particularly useful in global society.[89] It is congenial to diversity, but permits and encourages the gradual building up of global interaction. An interactional view of law would suggest that law is only possible within specific times and places where actors have developed certain basic understandings about what they hope to achieve together. They need not agree on a definition of the good life, only on basic objectives. Actors bring their cultural specificity to the table, as it were, but accept that they will not convince other actors of the desirability of a particular world-view. However, if there is no agreement on even the parameters of coordinated social action, legal normativity cannot emerge. Basic understandings can, however, be fostered through pre-legal mutual interaction in informal and formal institutions, through

governmental coercion'. Winston, above note 5, p. 62. Ours is a broader point about fidelity to the legal order.

88 Notably, the 'legalization' project brackets the question of how obligation is explained and employs it as an indicator of commitment. See Abbott *et al.*, above note 85 at 401 (observing that '[*o*]*bligation* means that states or other actors are … *legally* bound by a rule or commitment in the sense that their behavior thereunder is subject to scrutiny under the general rules, procedures, and discourse of international law, and often of domestic law as well'). Our point is that it is precisely obligation that must be generated in the first place, so that the legalization project is weakened by a significant blind spot. See also discussion in Jutta Brunnée, 'Review: Legalization and World Politics. Edited by Judith L. Goldstein, Miles Kahler, Robert O. Keohane, and Anne-Marie Slaughter (2001)' (2003) 1 *Perspectives in Politics* 231; and Martha Finnemore and Stephen J. Toope, 'Alternatives to "Legalization": Richer Views of Law and Politics' (2001) 55 *International Organization* 743.

89 See also Nardin, above note 3, pp. 24–5 (arguing that 'where the rule of law is the mode of association, they are rules of a certain kind. They are *noninstrumental* rules. A noninstrumental rule is concerned solely with the propriety of actions, not their usefulness in achieving or avoiding certain outcomes') and 28 (suggesting that this conception is essential for law in international society, since it avoids 'the extremes of Hobbesian positivism, which makes legality itself the criterion of justice, and natural law, which makes justice into a criterion of legality'). Fuller's understanding of the rule of law is also close to that articulated by Tamanaha. See Brian Z. Tamanaha, *On the Rule of Law* (Cambridge University Press, 2004), p. 94 ('The fact that this version of the rule of law has no content requirements renders it open to a range of ends. … This substantively empty quality has been identified by theorists, and by the World Bank and other development agencies, as what renders it amenable to universal application.').

the work of norm entrepreneurs, through the engagement of epistemic communities and issue networks, and through other processes of socialization affecting the self-perception and identity of actors.[90]

The criteria of legality within Fuller's conception of the rule of law enable states to 'reason' from law to achieve their own objectives, thereby preserving diversity. But Fuller's essentially communicative understanding of law, rooted in the Aristotelian rhetorical tradition, means that it is in the very process of interaction – of reasoning through law – that one can achieve a modest and gradual building up of society.[91] Fuller did, however, aspire to more: as humans (and, we would add, states and other international actors), communicate through law, opportunities arise to deepen shared understandings. Around certain concrete issues, for example an environmental problem or a human rights concern, it may even be possible to cultivate normative convergence. Fuller was not naïve; he never posited an existing global moral community.[92] Though not a moral relativist,[93] Fuller insisted that cultural specificity is relevant to any definition of 'community'.[94] He nonetheless concluded that 'we should

[90] See our discussion of the importance of pre-legal normativity and the evolution of 'contextual regimes' in Brunnée and Toope, above note 12.

[91] This idea also is central to constructivist work, which emphasizes the *intersubjective* nature of societies and communities. See Emanuel Adler, 'Barry Buzan's Use of Constructivism to Reconstruct the English School: "Not All the Way Down"' (2005) 34 *Millennium: Journal of International Studies* 171 at 176, and Peter J. Katzenstein, Robert O. Keohane and Stephen D. Krasner, 'International Organization and the Study of World Politics' (1998) 52 *International Organization* 645 at 679. See also Finnemore and Sikkink, above note 78 at 891. Note that it is common for constructivists to talk of 'norms' when they mean 'institutions', the latter being properly viewed as aggregations of interrelated norms. Institutions, both formal and informal, are simply particular cases of 'social structure'.

[92] Fuller did not insist on the necessity of 'broad agreement on general values' even within specific legal cultures, only shared standards by which disagreements could be identified and discussed meaningfully toward some rational resolution. See Postema, above note 8 at 269. The rejection of a universal definition of the Good (apart from a broadly defined individual happiness) is derived from Aristotle: see above note 8, pp. 69 (s. I:vi) and 73 (s. I:vii).

[93] Mootz, above note 50, p. 450.

[94] Because of Fuller's sensitivity to local culture, he never succumbed to the liberal triumphalism often displayed in western (and particularly U.S.) legal theory. See Lon L. Fuller, 'The Law's Precarious Hold on Life' (1969) 3 *Georgia Law Review* 530 (discussing law in the processes of African decolonization). See also Dyzenhaus, above note 25, pp. 90 and 96–7. Indeed, even a relatively unsympathetic reader is able to enlist Fuller 'into the enterprise of deflating the celebratory posture toward law, legal institutions, and legal actors that pervades so much of American legal thought'. Frederick Schauer, 'Fuller on the Ontological Status of Law' in Witteveen and van der Burg, above note 5, p. 142. See also Klabbers, above note 31 at 100–3 (arguing that Fuller's criteria of legality suggest the possibility of international law that is universally shared and morally acceptable without having to rely on 'substantive values').

aspire to enlarge that community at every opportunity and to include within it ultimately, if we can' all people of good will.[95]

Our point is that although building shared understandings is a goal, with Fuller one must always remember that the enterprise of law-making he described is aspirational. He wanted to challenge societies to work towards the goal of fidelity to law, but he never assumed that the goal would be fully achieved.[96] It is not necessary to have a morally cohesive 'community' before law-making is possible, though some foundation of shared understandings is required. In this sense, Fuller's theory differs from Habermas's concept of communicative action, where it would seem that a 'common lifeworld' is a precondition to effective norm building.[97] Nor is our interactional view of international law predicated upon a vision of a growing liberal world community. Our theory of legal obligation is not aligned with cosmopolitan liberalism,[98] or with theories of the 'democratic peace',[99] or with visions of global

[95] Fuller, above note 1, p. 183. Almost exactly the same formulation of human aspiration is offered within secular, pragmatist philosophy by Richard Rorty, *Contingency, Irony, and Solidarity* (Cambridge University Press, 1989), p. 196 (while treating the notion of common humanity as nothing more than a useful *focus imaginarius*, it 'is a means of reminding ourselves to keep trying to expand our sense of "us" as far as we can').

[96] So much so that he would argue that 'the inner morality of law is condemned to remain largely a morality of aspiration and not of duty. Its primary appeal must be to a sense of trusteeship and to the pride of the craftsman.' See Fuller, above note 1, p. 43.

[97] Habermas's lifeworld appears to consist in common cultural and historical traditions, shared norms and socialized participants. See e.g. Jürgen Habermas, *Between Facts and Norms: Contributions to a Discourse Theory of Law and Democracy* (Cambridge, Mass: MIT Press, 1996), p. 80. But Habermas also appears to contemplate that communicative action can build sufficient commonality: 'The lifeworld forms both the horizon for speech situations and the source of interpretations, while in turn it produces itself only through ongoing communication,' *ibid.*, p. 22. According to Thomas Risse-Kappen, '"Let's Argue!": Communicative Action in World Politics' (2000) 54:1 *International Organization* 1 at 14, 'Habermas's theory is rather silent on the question of how much of a common lifeworld people need to share in order to communicate in a reasonable manner.'

[98] See e.g. Bruce Russett, *Grasping the Democratic Peace: Principles for a Post-Cold War World* (Princeton University Press, 1993); Thomas Risse-Kappen, *Cooperation Among Democracies: The European Influence on US Foreign Policy* (Princeton University Press, 1995); John Rawls, *The Law of Peoples; with 'The Idea of Public Reason Revisited'* (Cambridge, Mass: Harvard University Press, 1999); and Allen Buchanan and Robert O. Keohane, 'The Legitimacy of Global Governance Institutions' (2006) 20 *Ethics and International Affairs* 405.

[99] For various accounts, some more sympathetic than others, see Thomas M. Franck, 'The Emerging Right to Democratic Governance' (1992) 86 *American Journal of International Law* 46; Anne-Marie Slaughter, 'Building Global Democracy' (2000) 1 *Chicago Journal of International Law* 223; and Gregory H. Fox and Brad R. Roth (eds.), *Democratic Governance and International Law* (Cambridge University Press, 2000).

constitutionalism.[100] Rather, we envisage interactional law as a particular kind of 'community of practice', a concept that we will explore in more detail in Chapter 2. We reiterate Adler's important observations that the 'joint enterprise of members of a community of practice does not necessarily mean a common goal or vision', but that members 'must share collective understandings that tell [them] what they are doing and why', which have obvious resonance with the concept of law that we have developed in this chapter.[101]

We have already noted that an interactional theory of law opens up law-making to a diversity of participants, indeed requires it, because of the need for reciprocity in the construction of law. It follows that any description of society at the international level must extend beyond the sphere of states.[102] International organizations, NGOs, corporations, informal intergovernmental expert networks, and a variety of other groups are actively engaged in the creation of shared understandings and the promotion of learning amongst states and other international actors. As we have already emphasized, although states remain dominant within the system, they are influenced (admittedly in different ways and to different extents) by the persuasive activities of less obviously powerful actors. The differential impact of such persuasive efforts is partly dependent upon politics within states, which remains an important focus of attention for norm-interested IR scholars and international lawyers alike.[103]

[100] There are many versions of global constitutionalism. See e.g. discussions in Matthias Kumm, 'The Legitimacy of International Law: A Constitutionalist Framework of Analysis' (2004) 15 *European Journal of International Law* 907; Erika de Wet, 'The International Constitutional Order' (2006) 55 *International and Comparative Law Quarterly* 51; and, for a critical perspective, Jeffrey L. Dunoff, 'Constitutional Conceits: The WTO's "Constitution" and the Discipline of International Law' (2006) 17 *European Journal of International Law* 647.

[101] Adler, above note 48, p. 22. And, for an overview of how constructivism sees interaction as central to shaping human conduct, see Adler, above note 80.

[102] See also Michael Walzer, *Spheres of Justice: A Defense of Pluralism and Equality* (New York: Basic Books, 1983) (on overlapping norm systems).

[103] See e.g. Harold H. Koh's discussion of transnational legal process in 'Transnational Legal Process – The 1994 Roscoe Pound Lecture' (1996) 75 *Nebraska Law Review* 181 at 199–205; Eyal Benevenisti, 'Domestic Politics and International Resources: What Role for International Law?' in Byers, above note 8, p. 109; and Katzenstein *et al.*, above note 91 at 663–70. The widely debated 'democratic peace' literature is founded upon the belief that the primary causal explanation for respect for international norms is internal democratic processes of liberal societies. See e.g. Russett, above note 98; Risse-Kappen, above note 98; and the recent recasting of John Rawls's theory of justice in an international context: see Rawls, above note 98 at 44–54.

3.4 *Formality: custom, treaty and soft law*

A further lesson for international law derived from Fuller's theories is that international lawyers rely too heavily on formalistic accounts of legality.[104] Such accounts do not provide an accurate explanation of legal obligation. Nor do they permit a convincing distinction between law and other forms of normativity.

We have previously noted that Fuller was not particularly interested in the distinction between legal and other social norms. On this point we disagree and share one of positivism's goals: to distinguish between what is legally required and what is desirable or acceptable. We suggest that this distinction is not based in any particular form of rule, but in a sense of obligation generated by fidelity to law. Our concern is that legal formalism pervades the practice of international law today – hence the exclusive reliance on sources of law as a means to define the existence of binding rules, the assumption that decisions of the International Court of Justice apply only 'positive' law derived from the consent of states, and the desire to define a bright line boundary between law and non-law. We argue that great caution is required in trying to trace out the law and non-law distinction. Legal formalism is inadequate for the task.

The key is to distinguish between 'formality' and 'formalism'. By formalism, we mean a view that treats form as the only indicator of law, and which is close to legalism as described by Judith Shklar.[105] Formality is actually an aspect of Fuller's internal criteria of legality: it includes ideas such as promulgation and publicity, and not asking the impossible.[106] Nonetheless, thinking about the creation of law in purely formal terms provides only limited guidance in analysing how obligation is created in international society. Although formal indicators provide useful indicia of the existence of binding rules and, of course, 'validity' on the terms of the system, they are not enough to identify

[104] See also discussion in Dyzenhaus, above note 25, p. 78.

[105] Judith Shklar, *Legalism: Law, Morals, and Political Trials* (Cambridge, Mass.: Harvard University Press, 1986).

[106] See Waldron, above note 6 at 276: 'One way of looking at Fuller's jurisprudence is that he is asking whether there is anything in the formal character of law that can possibly sustain this fidelity, any source of respect inherent in legality as such which may survive a loss of faith in substantive ends which the government is pursuing.' See also Stephen J. Toope, 'Formality and Informality', in Daniel Bodansky, Jutta Brunnée and Ellen Hey (eds.), *Oxford Handbook of International Environmental Law* (Oxford University Press, 2007), p. 107.

'law' because formality alone is not strong enough to generate fidelity. What is more, the move from formality to formalism can actually mask the absence of any real sense of obligation. The interactional account instructs that it is crucial not to mistake the formal representation of law for successful law-making.

Our explanation of the interplay amongst posited norm, shared understandings, the criteria of legality, and the practice of legality makes sense of the most important ways in which international law is made in contemporary practice, through custom, treaty and soft law.

Interactionalism helps to explain the traditional formulation of customary law as arising from state practice plus *opinio juris*. The latter requirement has always proved to be troublesome for international lawyers, who have difficulty in explaining what is meant by a 'belief that [a] practice is rendered obligatory by the existence of a rule of law requiring it'.[107] How is one to understand the idea that an abstract entity like a state 'believes' something? How is the belief to be proved? Typically, one must resort to extrapolation: when practice is consistent and widespread *enough* then the *opinio juris* can be presumed. But this has never been a fully satisfying explanation.

The interactional theory shows that a social norm, reflecting a shared understanding that meets the criteria of legality is upheld through practice that is congruent with the norm. This constitutes a 'practice of legality'. This enriched form of practice is what would traditionally have been called *opinio juris*. Interactional law is not dependent upon practice alone, for that would undermine any distinction between social and legal norms. But neither does it require reference to an artifice – *opinio juris* – that refers to 'belief' on the part of a social construct, thereby upholding the fiction of consent. Instead, we are frank that it is practice itself that grounds continuing obligation, but practice rooted in the criteria of legality. Thus, we provide a more objective, less mystical, account of how customary legal norms become binding.

Our account also addresses the temporal problem often noted in the traditional formulation of customary law. How is it that practice 'counts' as relevant to the creation of a custom if it is not rooted in the belief that the practice is required? In other words, the 'first adopters' of any practice cannot believe that they are bound, because the practice is new. How does the tipping point arise at which the practice becomes 'required'? One can

[107] *North Sea Continental Shelf (Germany/Denmark)*, Judgment, I.C.J. Reports 1969, para. 77.

explain under the traditional theory how custom can be maintained, but not how it can be created. Interactional law can explain both.[108]

Why have treaties become so important to the evolution of international law? We suggest, very much in keeping with the standard account, that it is in large measure because of the desire of states in international society for clarity and relative certainty. Treaties fulfil important roles. First, they can allow for the crystallization and specification of pre-existing shared understandings. Given the very real practical challenge of capturing and communicating shared understandings in the international setting, the treaty will often be an important step in interactional law-making. After all, the number of actors in the international arena is so large and their opportunities for direct interaction are so limited that 'snapshots' of the common ground will often be needed to advance the law-making process.

Second, in the process of treaty negotiation, existing understandings may be pushed or advanced modestly to allow for normative change, as long as the criteria of legality are met. Third, in some cases treaty rules will be posited that are not grounded in shared understandings with the hope that the new 'rule' may become a reference point around which new law may coalesce. We argue that such 'rules' are not interactional law, but may become so over time if they meet the criteria of legality and become the object of a practice of legality. For example, when diplomats return to their capitals after 'successfully' concluding a treaty, we argue that the hard work of international law has often just begun. We must ask if the conditions for the creation of obligation – the existence of shared understandings, and the eight criteria of legality – have been met. Is the treaty rooted in shared understandings reflecting some social consensus that the goals of the treaty are desirable? Alternatively, is it possible to use the treaty as an educative device to work towards shared understandings that can support the transformation of treaty language into real legal obligations? One must then ask whether or not the treaty meets the criteria of legality. Was it concluded through processes that allowed for the genuine participation of relevant actors? Is the language clear enough to be understood in commensurable ways by members of the treaty regime? Does the treaty contradict other international law obligations, or ask the impossible of states? Eventually, one must also confirm the existence of a practice of legality that actually comes to shape the actions of parties. If

[108] We are indebted to Professor Beth Simmons for observations that helped us to clarify this point.

such a practice has not taken hold, then an individual state party is likely to conclude that there is no congruence between the requirements of the treaty and the application of the treaty. It will be ignored because it will have inspired no 'fidelity.'

Interestingly, the Vienna Convention on the Law of Treaties itself is a good example of the interactional processes that we have described. The basic treaty-making rules of the convention were and continue to be grounded in shared understandings. These understandings grew into customary law, and were then 'codified' in treaty form. Other rules pushed the boundaries of the pre-existing law, but were quickly supported by a practice of legality. For example, the rules in Article 20(4)(b) and Article 21(3) changed the customary law by requiring that a state can only avoid the effect of a reservation by another state by explicitly declaring that it would treat that state as a non-party.[109] This change has been widely accepted. By contrast, it remains disputed whether or not it is up to treaty parties to determine if another state's reservation is consonant with the object and purpose of the treaty.[110]

What is more, the Vienna Convention rules themselves, to a very large extent, instantiate Fuller's criteria of legality and insist upon their application to treaties between states, as the following examples illustrate. The treaty applies to all states wishing to conclude treaties and applies to all treaties between or amongst states (Article 1). The treaty also provides for detailed regulation of reservations and of modification of obligations amongst some of the parties so as to promote generality of obligation when possible (Articles 19–23 and 41). Promulgation is specifically required through the rules concerning entry into force of treaties (Article 24) and registration (Article 80). A fundamental rule of interpretation provided for in the Vienna Convention is the presumption of non-retroactivity (Article 28). Clarity is encouraged through the requirement that treaties be set down in writing if they are to fall within the terms of the convention (Article 2(1)(a)) and through the fundamental rule of interpretation that words be given their 'ordinary meaning ... in their context and in the light of [the treaty's] object and purpose'. In addition, the

[109] *Cf. Reservations to the Convention on the Prevention and Punishment of the Crime of Genocide*, Advisory Opinion, I.C.J. Reports 1951.

[110] See Vienna Convention on the Law of Treaties, Vienna, 23 May 1969, in force 27 January 1980, 1155 UNTS 331. Article 19 is cast in objective terms whereas Article 20 is cast in subjective terms. This difference arises in the human rights context especially (US and UK), see Anthony Aust, *Modern Treaty Law and Practice*, 2nd edn (Cambridge University Press, 2007).

rules concerning consent, amendment and entry into force also promote clarity (Articles 9–17, 24 and 39–40).

Fuller's principle of non-contradiction is upheld through the rule of the application of successive treaties (Article 30), the regime of contextual interpretation (Article 31), the requirement that a treaty in more than one language must be interpreted authoritatively in each language, meaning that they must be read together (Article 33), and the provision concerning *jus cogens* which requires that a treaty be void when it conflicts with a peremptory norm of international law (Articles 53 and 64). Not demanding the impossible is expressly ensured through the provisions on supervening impossibility and fundamental change of circumstances (Articles 61 and 62). The Vienna Convention rules on termination or suspension are all designed to ensure constancy and predictability (Articles 54–72), as are rules concerning the non-applicability of treaties to third parties (Articles 34–38). The interpretation, and amendment and modification rules also seek to promote constancy (Articles 31–32 and 39–41). Finally, congruence between treaty norms and the subsequent practice of treaty parties is promoted through the fundamental rule of *pacta sunt servanda* (Article 26) and the rule on material breach (Article 60). In addition, the acceptance of subsequent practice as evidence of changing interpretation is evidence of two tendencies; first, the willingness to allow evolution of obligation (purportedly in the light of original intention), but second, the desire to limit that evolution by requiring formal amendments when the interpretation of original intent cannot be stretched to cover new circumstances (Articles 31–32 and 39–40).

Treaty-making is a device for reaching concrete, substantive agreements, but it is also sometimes a means by which parties simply enable particular forms of the practice of legality to play out within a regime. For example, in some environmental regimes, initial 'framework agreements' are deliberately focused upon the creation of decision-making rules and procedures; they are constitutive, rather than regulatory. In the light of this subsequent evolution, one can now view the Vienna Convention itself in similar terms. Its rules are designed to create a treaty 'framework' that enables more particular normative structures to be created.

International lawyers also regularly grapple with a phenomenon called 'soft law'. Some commentators insist that the term is nonsensical, or even dangerous.[111] Others would accept that soft law is a relevant

[111] See e.g. Jan Klabbers, 'The Redundancy of Soft Law' (1996) 65 *Nordic Journal of International Law* 167; and Prosper Weil, 'Towards Relative Normativity in International Law?' (1983) 77 *American Journal of International Law* 413.

category, and matters in some way, but they cannot fit soft law's effects within formal sources doctrine.[112] We argue that 'soft' norms may sometimes possess more obligatory force than norms derived from formal sources of law. Interactional international law explains why. When norms are rooted in shared understandings and adhere to the conditions of legality, they generate fidelity. Christine Chinkin makes a similar point in reverse:

> While soft law may not be directly used to found a cause of action it has both a legitimising and a delegitimising direct effect: it is extremely difficult for a State that rejected some instrument of soft law to argue that behaviour in conformity with it by those who accepted it is illegitimate.[113]

In other words, it is hard to attack the fidelity produced through interactional law-making. Although at first blush soft norms do not figure in the 'causes of action' allowed in adjudicative international decision-making, for they do not fit within Article 38 of the International Court of Justice statute, such norms can figure in practical legal reasoning of courts, states and other international actors. For example, the precautionary principle is not universally accepted as a norm of customary law, but it has influenced the decisions of international tribunals,[114] framed international treaties[115] and been embraced at the domestic level.[116] In Chapter 4, we detail how the concept of common but differentiated responsibilities, notwithstanding its ambiguous legal status, has been influential in shaping the evolution of the global climate regime.

To summarize, it is crucial to distinguish Fuller's largely procedural, and hence relatively 'thin', conception of the rule of law from 'formalism'. While we are sympathetic to his underlying preoccupations, we are not convinced by Martti Koskenniemi's advocacy of a 'culture of formalism' – the idea that only rigorous insistence upon the 'validity' of rules – measured by the consent of sovereign states – can serve as a bulwark against the domination of world society by great powers, especially by the

112 See e.g. Pierre-Marie Dupuy, 'Soft Law and the International Law of the Environment' (1991) 12 *Michigan Journal of International Law* 420.

113 Christine Chinkin, 'The Challenge of Soft Law: Development and Change in International Law' (1989) 38 *International and Comparative Law Quarterly* 850 at 850–1.

114 *Gabčíkovo-Nagymaros Project (Hungary/Slovakia)*, Judgment, I.C.J. Reports 1997. For information on the activities of the Commission for the Conservation of Southern Bluefin Tuna see www.ccsbt.org/.

115 *Cartagena Protocol on Biosafety to the Convention on Biological Diversity* (2000) 39 I.L.M. 1027.

116 See the Preamble to the Canadian Environmental Protection Act, S.C. 1999, c. 33.

single superpower.[117] The notion of a 'culture' of formalism is intended to highlight the only way for international law to protect global diversity and resist political hegemony: by providing a 'shared surface ... on which political adversaries recognize each other as such and pursue their adversity in terms of something shared'.[118] Still, it is not clear how this 'culture' can be distinguished from state-centric positivism.[119] In our view, formalism provides far less protection against the undermining of law by power and politics than an interactional approach to law; in the absence of legal legitimacy, formal law cannot generate fidelity.[120] What is more, Fuller's version of the rule of law requires rulers to be public and open in their law-making efforts, but formalism makes no such demands.[121]

3.5 *International law and legitimacy*

The last insight we derive from Fuller is that it is useful to specify a particular legal understanding of legitimacy, at which we have already hinted at various points. Most international lawyers seem to assume that international law is legitimate, probably because formal sources of law are employed to create the law. Underlying this assumption is the belief that international law is created by state consent.

Thomas Franck was one of the few international legal theorists to tackle legitimacy head-on, but he shares the dominant assumptions. His starting presumption is that state consent is the necessary but not sufficient condition for international legal legitimacy.

Legitimacy is a key factor in explaining the influence of international law because legitimacy 'accommodates a deeply held popular belief that for a system of rules to be fair, it must be firmly rooted in a framework of formal requirements about how rules are made, interpreted and applied'.[122] Franck sets out four 'objective factors' that, he claims, can assist in the

117 Martii Koskenniemi, *From Apology to Utopia: The Structure of International Legal Argument*, reissue with a new Epilogue (Cambridge University Press, 2005), p. 616.

118 Martti Koskenniemi, 'What is International Law for?', in Malcolm D. Evans (ed.), *International Law*, 2nd edn (Oxford University Press, 2006), p. 77.

119 Toope, above note 106, p. 111.

120 Of course, our differences with Koskenniemi share much common ground with the main points of the debate between Hart and Fuller. See above note 37.

121 Fuller, above note 1, p. 159. See also Klabbers, above note 31 at 102–3 (noting that Fuller's eight requirements propose a minimum baseline for law-making that would make the chances of 'law's substance being odious fairly negligible').

122 Thomas M. Franck, *Fairness in International Law and Institutions* (Oxford: Clarendon Press, 1995), pp. 7–8.

identification of legitimate rules: determinacy (ability of a rule to convey a clear message), symbolic validation (ability of a rule to communicate authority through ritual or regularized practice), coherence (consistency of the rule and its application with other rules), and adherence (vertical nexus of a rule to a pyramid of secondary rules).[123]

We share some common ground with Franck, notably the focus on internal features of law as central to its power to promote commitment. The internal indicators of legitimacy we posit overlap in part with Franck's. However, the internal features of law play a strikingly different role in Franck's legitimacy theory than in our interactional conception. Franck's account remains explicitly positivist, both in its emphasis on state consent and in its reliance upon a rule of recognition to explain the source of international legal obligation. What is more, Franck's legitimacy goes only to the issue of compliance with law; law is created essentially through positivist hierarchies. We will explore the concept of legitimacy and its relationship to compliance in Chapter 3.

For now, it is enough to emphasize that legitimacy is related to compliance,[124] but not through primarily rationalist explanations. When we say that law is 'legitimate' we mean that it has the capacity to generate fidelity to the rule of law itself and not merely to specific rules. Let us be clear, because this claim is strong: only when law is produced through the interactional framework we describe can it be said that the law is 'legitimate'. Our interactional framework reveals how legitimacy is built through broad participation in the construction and maintenance of legal regimes. Specifically, broad participation is encompassed in the requirements that legal norms be grounded in underlying social norms and, in turn, that social practice be congruent with extant legal norms (reciprocity). As we will explain in Chapter 2, if there are absolutely no shared understandings of the role of law, and of particular candidate norms, it will be difficult if not impossible to see the norms emerge as 'law'. So the first step in building interactional law is the creation of social legitimacy through the emergence of widely shared understandings.

For legal rules to emerge it is not enough, however, for there to exist underlying shared understandings with their attendant social legitimacy. To create 'legal legitimacy', the criteria of legality must also substantially

[123] For an overview, see *ibid.*, pp. 30–46. Detailed discussions can be found in Thomas M. Franck, 'Legitimacy in the International System' (1998) 82 *American Journal of International Law* 705 at 713 and, of course, in Franck, *The Power of Legitimacy Among Nations*, above note 15, pp. 25, 32, 35–6 and Chapter 11.

[124] See below Chapter 3.

be met. Those criteria are fundamental in producing norms that have the capacity to be called 'law'. However, even that is not sufficient to instantiate the rule of law, or even particular legal rules. Shared understandings and rules that meet the criteria of legality must be continuously reinforced through a robust practice of legality. In other words, law is created and maintained through interaction. It is interaction that makes this relationship 'horizontal' and 'reciprocal', and is the core of 'legal' legitimacy.

This account highlights that influential norms will not emerge in the absence of processes that allow for the active participation of relevant social actors. To reiterate, the requirement of participation is inherent in the idea of communities of practice that we employ and that explains both the creation of shared social understandings and the importance of a shared practice of legality. 'Active participation' must be understood in specific contexts. Although he does not use the term 'legitimacy', Andrew Hurrell captures the variety of ways in which participation in international society can be conceived:

> some acceptance of equality of status, of respect, and of consideration; some commitment to reciprocity and to the public justification of one's actions; some capacity for autonomous decision making on the basis of reasonable information; a degree of uncoerced willingness to participate; a situation in which the most disadvantaged perceive themselves as having some stake in the system; and some institutional processes by which the weak and disadvantaged are able to make their voice heard and to express claims about unjust treatment.[125]

The idea of continuous practice will hardly be novel to international lawyers. It is central to the concept of customary law and also plays a significant role in the evolution of treaties. What is added through our account of legal legitimacy is the idea that a very particular kind of practice is required to make and sustain international legal norms: inclusive practice that adheres to the criteria of legality. As we will illustrate in subsequent chapters, this perspective reveals the real weakness of many customary or treaty rules. This weakness lies not in the absence of enforcement or other attributes of 'hard' law, but in a legitimacy deficit resulting from limited participation in norm building and insufficient attention to the requirements of legality. At the same time, our framework provides concrete guidance for practice that would strengthen international law.

[125] See Andrew Hurrell, 'Global Inequality and International Institutions', in Thomas W. Pogge (ed.), *Global Justice* (Oxford: Blackwell, 2001), p. 42.

A final point is worth making: even powerful states cannot simply impose 'rules'. If the legal rule is not grounded in shared understandings and if the criteria of legality are only weakly or imperfectly met, the rule will not generate fidelity, and it will not be employed in the reasoning of states as to appropriate behaviour. Conversely, even powerful states cannot escape existing rules that have generated widespread fidelity. Arguing for the ability of interactional law to constrain power is not to deny that powerful states (and other actors) have a privileged place in international law-making. By virtue of their greater resources, they have a stronger capacity to influence communication than poor states.[126]

4. Conclusion

Is there any added value to law and to legal obligation? If so, how is this added value created? The interactional theory of law explains that it is obligation that constitutes law's added value, not form, and that a sense of obligation will only arise when states and other actors perceive law-making to be legitimate. The creation of legal legitimacy is best explained as comprising three elements. First, states and other international actors must build up shared understandings of what they want to accomplish through law, and of specific candidate norms. Second, international actors must work to ensure that the specific criteria of legality are met. Third, shared understandings and rules that adhere to the criteria of legality must be reinforced through a continuing practice of legality. Our description of the hard work of international law underscores that law is not a product that is manufactured in centralized, hierarchical systems and merely distributed to social actors for consumption. Citizens in domestic systems, and states and other actors at the international level are not consumers; they are active agents in the continuing enterprise of law-making, through the elaboration of custom, treaty and soft law.

[126] Joseph S. Nye, Jr., *Soft Power: The Means to Success in World Politics* (New York: Public Affairs, 2004). See also the discussion of power below in Chapter 2.

2

Shared understandings: the underpinnings of law

1. Introduction

We suggested in Chapter 1 that for law to guide human interaction it must be broadly congruent with the practices and patterns in society. Law must rest on a foundation of shared understandings. At the same time, law is also more than simply those understandings; not because it takes a particular form or can be enforced in particular ways, but because it arises only when shared understandings come to be intertwined with distinctive internal qualities of law and practices of legality. In this chapter, we examine these twin propositions in detail.

We begin by exploring how shared understandings emerge in international society. To illuminate the underlying processes, we rely on constructivist IR and social learning theories. Next we examine the relationship between shared understandings and international legal norms. We ask what kinds of shared understandings must exist for law-making to be possible, and take a closer look at the transition from social norms to legality. Finally, we address what kinds of shared understandings can exist in a deeply diverse world and one in which power imbalances are so marked. We argue that while our approach may initially seem unduly optimistic in the light of diversity and power imbalances, the interactional approach actually reveals with clarity the limits to international law-making, while also illuminating opportunities. Interactional international law can exist in weak or strong forms; the deeper the shared understandings, the greater the possibility of ambitious law. Limited shared understandings do not mean no law, but they limit the possibilities of law-making.

2. Shared understandings in international society: the contribution of IR

Not all constructivist accounts of how shared understandings evolve – through collective knowledge, norms, or practices – place equal emphasis on the interplay between agents and structures. Indeed, surprisingly little constructivist work engages in detail with the processes of norm building.[1] We examine three accounts that are particularly relevant for our purposes. The first two, the norm cycle and epistemic community accounts, are primarily agent-focused. The third account, which explores the role of 'communities of practice', pays more attention to the mutuality of agents and structures and, therefore, illuminates both the norm cycle and epistemic community concepts. It also serves to reinforce the concept of interactional law that we developed in Chapter 1.

Martha Finnemore and Kathryn Sikkink have advanced the notion of a norm cycle, triggered by 'norm entrepreneurs' who promote particular standards of appropriate behaviour.[2] The point of this account is that norms 'do not appear out of thin air', but are built by various actors, including states, non-governmental organizations (NGOs) and individuals.[3] Finnemore and Sikkink describe how norm entrepreneurs bring relevant actors to embrace new norms, work that often involves displacing existing standards and establishing a new logic of appropriateness.[4] At the international level, norm entrepreneurs must convince a sufficient number of states to endorse the new norm and, in turn, to promote it in their interactions with other states or through relevant international organizations. Finnemore and Sikkink suggest that a 'tipping point' is reached when a critical number of key states embrace the norm.[5] An international socialization dynamic unfolds, in which states invoke the norm in their diplomatic practice, and governmental organizations or NGOs seek to hold more and more states to the new standard.[6] The dynamic is driven

1 See Martha Finnemore and Kathryn Sikkink, 'International Norm Dynamics and Political Change' (1998) 52 *International Organization* 887 at 896.

2 See *ibid.* 3 *Ibid.* at 896.

4 *Ibid.* at 897–8. On the logic of appropriateness, see Chapter 1, text accompanying notes 76–81. See also related work outside the realm of IR theory, such as: Lawrence Lessig, 'Social Meaning and Social Norms' (1996) 144 *University of Pennsylvania Law Review* 2181 (speaking of 'meaning managers'); and Robert D. Benford and David A. Snow, 'Framing Processes and Social Movements: An Overview and Assessment' (2000) 26 *Annual Review of Sociology* 611 (discussing the norm-initiation process in terms of 'framing').

5 Finnemore and Sikkink, above note 1 at 901 (employing the terminology of 'New Chicago' legal theorists such as Lawrence Lessig and Cass Sunstein).

6 *Ibid.* at 902 (speaking of a 'norm cascade'). See also Thomas Risse-Kappen, 'Transnational Actors and World Politics', in Walter Carlsnaes, Thomas Risse and Beth Simmons (eds.), *Handbook of International Relations* (London: Sage, 2002), p. 265; and Ryan Goodman and Derek Jinks, 'Toward an Institutional Theory of Sovereignty' (2003) 55 *Stanford Law Review* 1749 at 1784.

by processes of persuasion and argumentation, as well as various forms of social influence or pressure.[7] Specifically, while some states might initially pay mere lip-service to the new norm, or embrace it for purely strategic reasons,[8] Finnemore and Sikkink posit that states' desire for 'legitimation, conformity and esteem' is likely eventually to socialize them into accepting it as a new standard for appropriate state conduct.[9] The norm cycle is complete when the new standard is internalized by a wide range of actors, such that it acquires a 'taken-for-granted quality'.[10] It now constitutes a background understanding against which conduct is evaluated and justified, and that any new norms would have to re-shape or displace. Still, it is important to stress that completion of the cycle is not a foregone conclusion; some new norms may never reach the tipping point.[11]

Whether the emergence of an internationally shared understanding is a slow process or progresses relatively quickly will depend on a range of factors. These include the issue area involved, resonance with existing background norms, the strength of norms that would have to be re-shaped or displaced, the particularities of the actors promoting or potentially affected by the norm, and the institutional context within which interactions take place.[12]

[7] See Alastair Iain Johnston, 'Treating International Institutions as Social Environments' (2001) 45 *International Studies Quarterly* 487 at 494–506; Thomas Risse-Kappen, '"Let's Argue!": Communicative Action in World Politics' (2000) 54 *International Organization* 1 at 28–33; Jeffrey T. Checkel, 'Why Comply? Social Learning and European Identity Change' (2001) 55 *International Organization* 553; Ryan Goodman and Derek Jinks, 'How to Influence States: Socialization and International Human Rights Law' (2004) 54 *Duke Law Journal* 621; and Trine Flockhart, '"Complex Socialization": A Framework for the Study of State Socialization' (2006) 12 *European Journal of International Relations* 89 at 97.

[8] Ellen L. Lutz and Kathryn Sikkink, 'International Human Rights Law and Practice in Latin America', in Judith L. Goldstein, Miles Kahler, Robert O. Keohane and Anne-Marie Slaughter (eds.), *Legalization and World Politics* (Cambridge, Mass: MIT Press, 2001), pp. 274–5; and see Oona A. Hathaway, 'Do Human Rights Treaties Make a Difference?' (2002) 111 *Yale Law Journal* 1935 at 1941.

[9] Finnemore and Sikkink, above note 1 at 903; and Lutz and Sikkink, above note 8, p. 275. And see Goodman and Jinks, above note 7 at 642–3 and 700 (speaking of 'acculturation').

[10] Finnemore and Sikkink, above note 1 at 895.

[11] *Ibid.*

[12] See e.g. Johnston, above note 7; Checkel, above note 7; Roger A. Payne, 'Persuasion, Frames and Norm Construction' (2001) 7 *European Journal of International Relations* 37; Amitav Acharya, 'How Ideas Spread: Whose Norms Matter? Norm Localization and Institutional Change in Asian Regionalism' (2004) 58 *International Organization* 239; and Andrew P. Cortell and James W. Davis, 'When Norms Clash: International Norms, Domestic Practices, and Japan's Internalisation of the GATT/WTO' (2005) 31 *Review of International Studies* 3.

There are certainly examples of remarkably speedy international norm cycles, as illustrated by the campaign against landmines. It was launched by a coalition of six NGOs in 1992,[13] was relatively quickly embraced by a significant number of state sponsors, saw the award of the Nobel Peace Prize to the International Campaign to Ban Landmines and its coordinator, Jodi Williams, in 1997, and the adoption of the Landmines Convention in the same year.[14] Today, the Landmines Convention has 155 state parties, and only forty states have neither signed nor ratified the treaty.[15] We will return to the significance of the turn to law in the next section of this chapter, in which we examine the relationship between shared understandings and international law. For the moment, suffice it to say that there exists a good deal of evidence that both parties and non-parties to the convention feel compelled to justify their military practices in light of the norm banning landmines.[16]

Another account of the construction of shared understandings focuses on the work of epistemic communities and their members.[17] Epistemic communities are knowledge-based networks, most often focused on scientific, economic or technical matters. Their members enjoy authority not merely due to their expertise, but also because of the perceived impartiality of their activities.[18] Although membership is often inter-disciplinary, members come to share causal beliefs and arrive at common notions of validity and a common policy enterprise.[19] In other words, as their work evolves, members participate in collective learning processes.[20]

[13] These are: Handicap International, Human Rights Watch, Medico International, Mines Advisory Group, Physicians for Human Rights and Vietnam Veterans of America Foundation. See International Campaign to Ban Landmines (ICBL), at www.icbl.org.

[14] See generally Richard Price, 'Emerging Customary Norms and Anti-Personnel Landmines', in Christian Reus-Smit (ed.), *The Politics of International Law* (Cambridge University Press, 2004), p. 106 (describing how key states were socialized into the emerging anti-mine norm).

[15] See ICBL above note 13, at www.icbl.org/treaty/members.

[16] See Price, above note 14, pp. 125–9.

[17] See Peter Haas, 'Epistemic Communities', in Daniel Bodansky, Jutta Brunnée and Ellen Hey (eds.), *Oxford Handbook of International Environmental Law* (Oxford University Press, 2007), p. 791.

[18] *Ibid.*, p. 793. [19] *Ibid.*

[20] Note that some of the work on epistemic communities sees learning as affecting actors' assessments of their interests and options for pursuing these interests, as opposed to their social identities. See e.g. Joseph S. Nye Jr., 'Nuclear Learning and U.S.–Soviet Security Regimes' (1987) 41 *International Organization* 371 at 380 (distinguishing 'simple' and 'complex' learning); and Ernst Haas, *When Knowledge is Power* (Berkeley: University of California Press, 1990), pp. 23 *et seq.* and 33 *et seq.* By contrast, resolutely constructivist conceptualizations hold that social learning is central to the mutual constitution of agents

From a policy perspective, the critical question is how the shared knowledge generated within an epistemic community comes to be embraced by decision-makers or a wider public. The community's authority usually plays a significant role. For example, the views held by epistemic communities comprised of respected scientists are likely to have considerable persuasive force.[21] The specific pathways of that knowledge diffusion and persuasion will differ from case to case. To the extent that epistemic communities are tied into international, transnational or domestic policy-making, their understandings may become more widely shared.[22] For example, consensus within epistemic communities that operate in the context of international environmental regimes can significantly shift policy debates about the need for, or costs of, collective action.[23] Collective background understandings regarding the environmental problem at hand can also facilitate the emergence of internationally shared norms or reinforce the work of norm entrepreneurs.[24] Similar processes may unfold when participants in international or transnational epistemic communities interact with other experts in national circles, be they governmental or non-governmental.[25] The shared knowledge produced within epistemic communities may also come to be the subject of wider public debates, facilitated by mass media or NGOs. For example, the widely reported and discussed findings of the 2007 report by the Intergovernmental Panel on Climate Change appear to have been a tipping point of sorts, recognized in the awarding of the Nobel Peace Prize, galvanizing the now widely shared view that human-induced global climate is occurring and requires urgent collective action.[26]

and structures, and consider that epistemic communities 'bargain about meanings' and 'socially construct knowledge, including scientific knowledge'. See Emanuel Adler, *Communitarian International Relations: The Epistemic Foundations of International Relations* (London and New York: Routledge, 2005), p. 17.

21 See Johnston, above note 7 at 497.

22 See Emanuel Adler, 'Seizing the Middle Ground: Constructivism in World Politics' (1997) 3 *European Journal of International Relations* 319 at 344 (arguing that 'knowledge is constructed twice – first by members of epistemic communities and later by individuals and institutions interacting in domestic and international political systems').

23 See Peter Haas, 'Introduction: Epistemic Communities and International Policy Coordination', in Peter Haas (ed.), 'Special Issue: Knowledge, Power, and International Policy Coordination' (1992) 46 *International Organization* 1 at 29.

24 See Haas, above note 17, pp. 798–9 (discussing the role of 'ecological epistemic communities' in promoting the adoption of the 'critical loads' approach in the long-range transboundary air pollution regime).

25 See also Adler, above note 20, pp. 26 and 80–3.

26 See Intergovernmental Panel on Climate Change (IPCC), *Climate Change 2007, Working Group I Report: The Physical Science Basis* (February 2007), at www.ipcc.ch/ipccreports/

The examples provided for the unfolding of norm cycles and the impact of epistemic communities illustrate that internationally shared understandings can be successfully promoted by non-state actors, be they groups or influential individuals. In fact, although constructivists often focus on 'states' or other governmental or non-governmental entities endorsing or embracing particular understandings,[27] the salient interactions ultimately occur amongst individuals or groups of people. It is the individuals acting on behalf of these entities, be they diplomats, policy experts or international bureaucrats, who are socialized and who may then influence the entities' uptake of the norm.[28] This is not to say, of course, that a state or an international organization as such cannot come to 'share' in the relevant understandings. For example, once a given norm is woven into a state's public debates, bureaucratic practices or laws, it is likely to shape the government's understanding of appropriate conduct in tangible ways, as Harold Koh's work illuminates.[29] Indeed, constructivists would argue that the norm can shape the state's very identity, and thereby its interests and conduct.[30] The same applies to international organizations, which may best be understood as international bureaucracies and, as such, are subject to similar influences as their domestic counterparts.[31]

Yet, neither the norm cycle nor the epistemic community account alone fully exploits the central constructivist ideas of the mutual influence of actors and cognitive or normative structures, and thus of the interactional roots of shared understandings. While the idea of the norm cycle illustrates the origin and progression of particular understandings, its focus is on the, often strategic, actions of norm entrepreneurs and on how

ar4-wg1.htm; IPCC, *Climate Change 2007, Working Group II Report: Impacts, Adaptation and Vulnerability* (April 2007), at www.ipcc.ch/ipccreports/ar4-wg2.htm; and IPCC, *Climate Change 2007, Working Group II Report: Mitigation* (May 2007), at www.ipcc.ch/ipccreports/ar4-wg3.htm.

27 See Alexander Wendt, 'Collective Identity Formation and the International State' (1994) 88 *American Political Science Review* 384.

28 Johnston, above note 7 at 506–7; Checkel, above note 7; Goodman and Jinks, above note 6 at 654; and Flockhart, above note 7 *passim*.

29 For a discussion of the internalization of legal norms, see Harold H. Koh, 'The 1998 Frankel Lecture: Bringing International Law Home' (1998) 35 *Houston International Law Journal* 623; and 'Transnational Legal Process – The 1994 Roscoe Pound Lecture' (1996) 75 *Nebraska Law Review* 181; and see below Chapter 3. See also Martha Finnemore, *National Interests in International Society* (Ithaca: Cornell University Press, 1996), pp. 2–3; and Flockhart, above note 7 *passim*.

30 See Wendt, above note 27.

31 See Michael Barnett and Martha Finnemore, *Rules for the World: International Organizations and Global Politics* (Ithaca: Cornell University Press, 2004).

norms then come to be embraced by others, be it as a result of calculation or reasoning. This agency-centred account pays relatively less attention to the social communication through which collective understandings are built. Similarly, in much of the writing on the influence of epistemic communities, the emphasis is on 'teaching' by these communities or their members and the reception of their teachings by others.[32] Learning, then, is often conceptualized as the unidirectional diffusion of norms, rather than as an interactional, mutual process.[33]

We therefore turn to a third account of how shared understandings are generated, one that does rest on a genuinely collective concept of learning. The setting for this interactional learning is furnished by 'communities of practice', a notion pioneered by social learning theorists Jean Lave and Etienne Wenger and adapted by Emanuel Adler for the purposes of a constructivist understanding of international relations.[34] Wenger has explored social learning through communities of practice in great detail. He shows that learning is not simply a discrete activity through which individuals acquire knowledge, but is part and parcel of everyday life and occurs through continuing social engagement.[35] People's understandings of the world, and of themselves, are produced and reproduced through continuous interactions and negotiation of meanings.[36]

Inherent in this account is the proposition that it is through their participation in social practice that actors generate and maintain collective understandings.[37] Over time, aspects of people's social experience tend to be given fixed form. Wenger's examples range from the production of tools, to the creation of bureaucratic procedures, to laws, all of which shape subsequent experience.[38] 'Having a tool to perform an activity', he notes, 'changes the nature of that activity.' In turn, the 'fixing' of experience into particular norms or procedures provides reference points in the ongoing negotiation of meanings and facilitates further interactions by providing 'shortcuts' to existing shared understandings.[39] Yet, these

[32] See Jeffrey T. Checkel, 'The Constructivist Turn in International Relations Theory' (1998) 50 *World Politics* 324 at 329.

[33] See also Jeffrey W. Knopf, 'The Importance of International Learning' (2003) 29 *Review of International Studies* 185 at 194–5.

[34] See Adler, above note 20, pp. 15–27. Adler traces the concept to Jean Lave and Etienne Wenger, *Situated Learning: Legitimate Peripheral Participation* (Cambridge University Press, 1991), but draws most extensively on Etienne Wenger, *Communities of Practice: Learning, Meaning, and Identity* (Cambridge University Press, 1998).

[35] Wenger, *ibid.*, pp. 7–9. [36] *Ibid.*, pp. 52–3. [37] *Ibid.*, pp. 55–6.

[38] *Ibid.*, pp. 58–9. [39] *Ibid.*, p. 61.

reference points will retain their salience only to the extent that actors continue to participate in their production and use. Wenger provides the example of a constitution, which is 'empty without the participation of the citizens involved', but which at the same time 'is crucial to the kind of negotiation that is necessary for them to act as citizens, and to bring together the multiple perspectives, interests and interpretations that participation entails'.[40]

Wenger's description of the continuous negotiation of collective meanings leads him to posit the centrality of communities of practice: 'Practice resides in a community of people and the relations of mutual engagement by which they can do whatever they do.'[41] This concept of 'community' has no inherently positive connotations; it can equally 'reproduce counter-productive patterns, injustices, prejudices, racism, sexism and abuses of all kinds'.[42] Also, while the premise of mutual engagement implies social relationships among members of the community, these relationships can just as easily be conflictual or competitive as they can be harmonious or cooperative – members can learn to be enemies or friends.[43] Either way, through mutual engagement and sustained practice, members' identities become 'interlocked' and are shaped by the practice.[44] For example, actors' identities as enemies are just as intertwined with one another and shaped by common practice as those of friends;[45] and the identities of employer and employee are just as mutually dependent as those of equal partners in a business.[46]

Wenger's account of social learning in communities of practice resonates with the central constructivist thesis of the mutuality of agents and structure.[47] Indeed, communities of practice may be at the very heart of this mutuality. They provide the settings in which the knowledge or norms that shape actors' understandings of the world are generated and practices evolve. In turn, it is through actors' participation that these

40 *Ibid.*, p. 62. And see Antje Wiener, *Invisible Constitution of Politics: Contested Norms and International Encounters* (Cambridge University Press, 2008), pp. 26, 30 and 32.

41 Wenger, above note 34, p. 73. 42 *Ibid.*, p. 132.

43 *Ibid.*, pp. 77 and 85. 44 *Ibid.*, pp. 75–6 and 129.

45 See also Alexander Wendt, 'Anarchy is What States Make of It: The Social Construction of Power Politics' (1992) 46 *International Organization* 391 (offering a parallel argument about state identities and international practice).

46 See James Fearon and Alexander Wendt, 'Rationalism v. Constructivism: A Skeptical View', in Carlsnaes *et al.*, above note 6, pp. 52 *et seq.* at 58 (noting that even in the extreme case of slavery, actors 'cannot *be* "masters" and "slaves" except in relation to the other').

47 Wenger specifically cites Giddens's structuration theory and notes that he works with similar assumptions. See Wenger, above note 34, p. 281.

understandings are maintained or shifted. As Emanuel Adler puts it, for individual actors, learning consists in 'redefining reality' in light of 'contextual "community" knowledge'. In turn, for a given community of practice, learning entails the 'evolution of background knowledge'.[48]

The central point is that shared understandings are inherently interactional, being always at once individual and social.[49] Since communities of practice 'cut across state boundaries and mediate between states, individuals, and human agency, on one hand, and social structures and systems, on the other',[50] we can also appreciate knowledge or norm diffusion as something more than a unidirectional process. It involves nothing less than the expansion of the community of practice to include a broader range of actors. In other words, norm entrepreneurs or epistemic communities do not simply 'teach' or exert social influence to bring others on board, nor do ideas just 'jump from mind to mind'.[51] On the one hand, both norm entrepreneurs or experts draw on the background knowledge already existing within the various communities of practice to which they belong:[52] on the other hand, it is only when new actors, be they states, international organizations or non-state actors, become actively engaged in a community of practice that its understandings come to be more widely shared (and, possibly, again re-shaped).[53] The same applies to the diffusion of international norms within states' domestic spheres.

To summarize, shared understandings are collectively held background knowledge, norms or practices; but these understandings do not simply exist, or miraculously emerge as agreed among actors. They are *shared* understandings precisely because they are generated and maintained through social interaction. The constructivist emphasis on the mutuality of agents and structures entails certain assumptions about how such understandings arise, and how they come to influence actors. On the one hand, agents generate and promote particular understandings, whether through norm entrepreneurship or through the work of epistemic communities. Shared understandings then emerge, evolve or

48 Adler, above note 20, p. 20.

49 See Martha Finnemore and Kathryn Sikkink, 'Taking Stock: The Constructivist Research Program in International Relations and Comparative Politics' (2001) 4 *American Review of Political Science* 391 at 392.

50 Adler, above note 20, p. 15.

51 *Ibid.*, p. 20.

52 See *ibid.*, pp. 16–19 (explaining how epistemic communities can be understood as particular types of communities of practice).

53 *Ibid.*, p. 16.

fade through processes of social learning.[54] On the other hand, once in existence, shared understandings become 'structures' that shape how actors perceive themselves and the world, how they form interests and set priorities, and how they make arguments or evaluate others' arguments.[55] The central insight is that social interaction is the engine that drives these processes. Actors work to promote meanings, but what they care about and how they act to pursue it is shaped in part by their interaction with others and the existing patterns of collective knowledge or meanings.[56] The underlying proposition – that norms are constituted by practice and practices are shaped by norms – does not imply that there can never be relatively stable norms. It merely highlights the fact that such stability too is the product of, and contingent upon, practice.

3. Shared understandings and interactional law

There are important linkages between shared understandings, communities of practice, and our interactional framework of international law, but also important differences.

3.1 Fuller's interactional theory

To explore these linkages and differences, we must return to the proposition that law can guide self-directed human interaction only if relatively stable patterns of expectation (or shared understandings) emerge, and if law is anchored in them. Fuller's work demonstrated the importance of this dimension to the effective interaction between the participants in the legal system. In emphasizing the need for reciprocity between officials and citizens in the creation and sustenance of law,[57] he illustrated that what is often assumed to be a vertical relationship (of authority and

[54] See e.g. Alexander Wendt, *Social Theory of International Politics* (Cambridge University Press, 1999), pp. 326–35; and Knopf, above note 33 at 194–5.

[55] See Emanuel Adler and Steven Bernstein, 'Knowledge in Power: The Epistemic Construction of Global Governance', in Michael Barnett and Raymond Duvall (eds.), *Power in Global Governance* (Cambridge University Press, 2005), pp. 295–6.

[56] Karin M. Fierke, 'Constructivism', in Timothy Dunne, Milja Kurki and Stephen Smith (eds.), *International Relations Theory: Discipline and Diversity* (Oxford University Press, 2007), pp. 169–70.

[57] Lon L. Fuller, *The Morality of Law*, rev. edn (New Haven: Yale University Press, 1969), p. 209.

subordination) actually has strong horizontal features.[58] Reciprocity means that law-givers must be able to expect that citizens will 'accept as law and generally observe' the promulgated body of rules.[59] Conversely, citizens must be able to expect that the government will abide by and apply these rules.[60]

This reciprocity is closely connected to Fuller's internal legality requirements. Citizens' ability to rely on the law in their decision-making, and their commitment to the law, is fostered by adherence to the requirements of legality, especially congruence between official action and the law. In turn, legality is tethered to broader social practices, in part because, to understand law's guidance, citizens and law-applying officials must first of all share a basic repertoire of common reference points – 'implicit rules' that are embedded in social practice.[61]

The reciprocity upon which interactional law relies requires constant nurturing. It can break down at several, interrelated points. If the law deviates from the practices and understandings that prevail within society, it risks being unintelligible to citizens – unclear or unreasonable, and impaired in its legality.[62] When the conflict between a society's shared understandings and legal rules is too stark, legality can come under significant strain.

For example, if the vast preponderance of a country's citizens rejects the death penalty as fundamentally incompatible with core values such as the human rights to life and dignity, it is doubtful that its government

58 *Ibid.*, p. 219 (observing that 'the functioning of a legal system depends upon a cooperative effort – and effective and responsible interaction – between law-giver and subject'). See also Paul Schiff Berman, 'From International Law to Law and Globalization' (2005) 43 *Columbia Journal of Transnational Law* 485 at 492 and 497.

59 Lon L. Fuller, 'Human Interaction and the Law' (1969) 14 *American Journal of Jurisprudence* 1, repr. in Kenneth I. Winston (ed.), *The Principles of Social Order: Selected Essays of Lon L. Fuller*, rev. edn (Oxford: Hart Publishing, 2001), p. 235. See also above Chapter 1, note 16 and accompanying text.

60 Fuller, above note 57, pp. 217 and 219. For a detailed discussion of Fuller's conception of reciprocity, in contrast to the rationalist–positivist view, see above Chapter 1, text accompanying notes 67–88.

61 See Gerald J. Postema, 'Implicit Law' (1994) 13 *Law and Philosophy* 361, repr. in Willem J. Witteveen and Wilbren van der Burg (eds.), *Rediscovering Fuller: Essays on Implicit Law and Institutional Design* (Amsterdam University Press, 1999), pp. 259 and 264. See also Friedrich V. Kratochwil, 'How do Norms Matter?', in Michael Byers (ed.), *The Role of Law in International Politics: Essays in International Relations and International Law* (Oxford University Press, 2000), pp. 40–1 (providing the example of the injunction 'Dogs must be carried on the escalator' and of the social understandings needed to correctly understand that rule).

62 Postema, above note 61 at 265.

could reinstate the death penalty through legislation, even if the relevant laws paid scrupulous attention to legality requirements like promulgation, clarity, generality, predictability, consistent implementation and so forth. These requirements force law-makers to be explicit about, and stand by, their purposes. If society deeply abhors the purpose, adherence to legality may not foster citizens' commitment to the new law, but rather debate, protest, and even active resistance. It is in part because it enables these responses, that adherence to legality means treating citizens as equal participants in the legal system, permitting them to rupture the reciprocity on which individual norms or even the legal system rest.

In any event, when laws diverge widely from social understandings, it will likely become increasingly difficult for a government to uphold all legality requirements. For example, faced with mounting protest, the government may cease to carry out executions, so the actions of officials will no longer conform to the written law. Ultimately, the contested norm itself will decay, and either fall into desuetude or the textual expression will be amended to conform to the reality of official practice. We have deliberately chosen a stark example. It illustrates that Fuller's legality requirements, while largely autonomous from substantive values, are not completely divorced from the dominant understandings in society.[63] Fuller insisted that, notwithstanding their procedural nature, the legality requirements would make it harder for substantive injustices to be inflicted by legal means:

> It has been said that most of the world's injustices are inflicted, not with the fists, but with the elbows. When we use our fists we use them for a definite purpose, and we are answerable to others and to ourselves for that purpose. Our elbows, we may comfortably suppose, trace a random pattern for which we are not responsible, although our neighbor may be painfully aware that he is being systematically pushed from his seat. A strong commitment to the principles of legality compels a ruler to answer to himself, not only for his fists, but for his elbows as well.[64]

Our death penalty example is not intended to suggest that there must be complete congruence between law and social understandings. It is meant to show only that it is unlikely to be possible to bridge a yawning gap between law and social understandings by adherence to the legality

[63] Indeed, Fuller argued that his 'internal morality' requirements were still connected to standards of 'external morality'. Fuller, above note 57, pp. 131–2 and 145–67.

[64] *Ibid.*, p. 159. See also more generally, *ibid.*, pp.157–70 (discussing various examples, such as the Nazi and apartheid regimes).

requirements alone. Still, as we have noted at various points, interactional law is possible even without deep substantive agreement among participants. Further, the interactional account suggests how, by adhering to requirements of legality, law-makers can create conditions in which reasoned communication and decision-making can take place, nurturing either deeper agreement or fidelity to law, even in the face of disagreement with the values or policies that it enshrines. The death penalty may exist, at least for a time, in societies where the majority of the population is opposed to its imposition. It has certainly been eliminated in societies where the majority actually supports its imposition. In such cases, one could conclude that the disagreements over the death penalty, although strongly emotive, are actually not central enough to the society's core of required shared understandings to generate outright rebellion. This example demonstrates that as long as the requirements of legality are met, citizens may well accept controversial rules, even when there is deep disagreement over the content of the rule. As we have emphasized, interactional law can accommodate significant diversity.

Of course, it is equally true that congruence between shared social understandings and law alone is not a sufficient condition for successful interactional lawmaking. To continue with the death penalty example, suppose another country's laws provide for capital punishment and its society strongly supports this penalty. Suppose further, however, that the relevant legislation applies only to tall people, that it is unclear what crimes may incur the death penalty, or that the country's authorities do not apply the law consistently and never prosecute people with blond hair, or pardon friends of leading government figures. In this admittedly overdrawn example, notwithstanding the underlying social understandings regarding the death penalty as such, the failure to live up to the requirements of legality is likely to erode whatever commitment to the law that citizens might have.[65]

The death penalty example shows that it is important to distinguish several layers of shared understandings, which play different but interrelated roles in interactional law. First, the shared understandings held in a society and its social practices are relevant to law's intelligibility and to perceptions of reasonableness. As a result, they feed into the requirements of legality that we described, and they help determine when and how

[65] See also Postema, above note 61 at 261 (arguing that when the 'reciprocity [between law-giver and citizens] breaks down, or is greatly compromised, legal order will break down').

much law is possible at any given time. This basic layer of shared understandings is the minimum required for a thin version of interactional law to exist. Second, an interactional legal system also depends upon shared understandings of legality. The participants in a legal system must build and maintain a practice guided by the requirements of legality. Shared understandings of legality can deepen to allow for more complex and intrusive norms to be created – but they can still be largely procedural in nature.[66] Finally, shared legal understandings can be rich and substantive. For example, legislation protecting human rights or banning the death penalty may enshrine deeply held convictions in substantive legal understandings. Like all shared understandings, they are dependent upon social practice. But they are shared *legal* understandings only when general social practice around substantive values becomes intertwined with a practice of legality. This conclusion reaffirms our argument in Chapter 1 that it is adherence to the requirements of legality that distinguishes law from other social practice.

The idea of communities of practice rounds out the picture of the relationship between law and shared understandings. One might think of interactional law as a particular type of community of practice, nourished by broader social practices, but distinct from them. Interactional law does not arise simply because a community of practice has grown around a given issue. Only when there is a practice of legality, built around Fuller's eight criteria of legality, can shared legal understandings, be they procedural or substantive, modest or ambitious, be produced, maintained or altered.

A further important point follows from understanding interactional law as a community of practice: it is not enough to cast socially shared understandings in legal form; they cannot simply be 'posited'. Positive law may be an element of interactional law, often even an important element, but it is not necessarily coextensive with it. The communities of practice concept instructs that positive law is a method of 'fixing' legal understandings, or creating 'short-cuts' to legal substance or procedure – a function that is particularly important in large, diffuse societies. In other words, positive law may help frame a particular community of practice and its legal understandings. It may also assist in meeting requirements of legality, such as clarity, transparency, or predictability; but without sufficiently

[66] Notwithstanding their substantive purposes: enabling human autonomy and self-directed interaction. For a discussion, see above Chapter 1, notes 40–59 and accompanying text.

dense interactions and participation of its members, positive law will remain, or become, dead letter. The interactional account, enriched by the concept of communities of practice, thus enables us to appreciate why, as Postema put it, 'enacted, pedigree-validated, authoritative norms ("made law") represent only the surface phenomena of law'.[67] However, it is important to be clear that our point is not merely that interaction is required to give social recognition to a formally valid legal norm.[68] This process is important, of course, to produce and maintain a shared understanding concerning the norm, but, as we are about to discuss in more detail, only a distinctive type of interaction – a practice of legality – will produce law.

3.2 *Interactional international law*

Communities of practice exist not just in domestic settings, but can also operate in transnational or international relations. For example, the world of diplomacy, or the trade, environment or human rights arenas could all be thought of as particular types of communities of practice in which state and non-state actors participate in international law and policy processes.[69]

Practice, of course, plays a central role in any account of international law. It is indispensable for the very existence of customary international law, and it shapes treaties through doctrines of application and interpretation. Still, international law cannot simply be equated, writ large, with a community of practice. For such a community to exist, participants must be engaged in interactions of a certain density and specificity.[70] In this sense, an international legal community can exist only through a practice that sustains basic shared understandings and, most importantly, a practice that sustains shared understandings of legality. We return to the

[67] Postema, above note 61 at 268. See also David Dyzenhaus, *The Constitution of Law: Legality in a Time of Emergency* (Cambridge University Press, 2006), p. 231 (arguing that a positivist legal order is but 'a step along a continuum of legality').

[68] See Antje Wiener, 'Enacting Meaning-In-Use: Qualitative Research on Norms and International Relations' (2009) 35 *Review of International Studies* 175 at 179.

[69] Adler, above note 20, p. 15.

[70] See Wenger, above note 34, pp. 131–3 (stressing, however, that communities of practice can exist only in settings that allow for sustained mutual engagement). For example, they must have sustained mutual relationships (harmonious or not), shared approaches to interaction, shared indicators of membership, knowledge of others and their roles in the joint enterprise, shared discourses and shortcuts to communication, and common criteria for the appropriateness of actions and outcomes. See *ibid.*, pp. 125–6.

concepts of international community and international legal community in the next section of this chapter. We will suggest that the communities of practice concept resists the facile invocations of 'community' that are found in much international legal rhetoric as well as the universalizing assumptions that often underpin such invocations. For present purposes, however, the important point is that the communities of practice perspective illuminates the interactional framework that we have advanced and enables a more critical look at the practice that international lawyers often take for granted.

Although the stock of shared understandings may be relatively limited in international society, law-making is possible.[71] But law-makers may have to be modest in their aspirations if a sustainable community of legal practice is to emerge. To be meaningful, international law may need to track what little common ground there is, even if that ground is confined to a shared sense that future interactions should be *legal*, rather than purely social or political, interactions. As Fuller's account instructs, the hallmark of legal interactions is reciprocity among participants, sustained by adherence to the requirements of legality.

For example, notwithstanding political differences and vast power differentials among states – indeed, because of them – legal interactions have been built upon a shared understanding of state sovereignty and around the customary law principles of sovereign equality and non-intervention. As much as some states have sought to subject the principle of sovereign equality to human rights standards, a responsibility to protect, or requirements of democratic governance, sovereign equality and non-intervention remain the frame of reference for global legal relations.

Similarly, if states agree that they want their relations on a given issue to be framed by a treaty but do not agree on political values or particular outcomes, there is no reason why they should not be able to engage in interactional law-making and build a practice of legality on that relatively limited basis. For example, climate change law-making began without common understandings of the problem, the urgency of collective action, or the responsibilities of each state. States did, however, agree on the need for a legal regime, on certain basic principles to guide further debates, and on procedures for decision-making and treaty development. Although

[71] See also Gerald J. Postema, 'Custom in International Law: A Normative Practice Account', in Amanda Perreau-Saussine and James Bernard Murphy (eds.), *The Nature of Customary Law: Legal, Historical and Philosophical Perspectives* (Cambridge University Press, 2007), pp. 300–6 (discussing customary international law).

some governments have worked assiduously to undermine the global regime, it has proven resilient.[72] The shared understanding of the dangers of climate change has ensured that the issue continues to resurface, with pressure mounting both domestically and internationally for recalcitrant states to act.[73] This pressure will not necessarily result in the implementation of the Kyoto commitments themselves, but it seems to generate a need for some concrete governmental response, and has focused efforts to create a more robust and lasting climate regime.[74]

Fuller's theory highlights that legal interactions are valuable in and of themselves, precisely because one of law's central purposes is to '[o]pen up, maintain, and preserve the integrity of the channels' through which people can communicate 'across the boundaries and through the barriers that … separate' them.[75] At the same time, adherence to the requirements of legality, in establishing the conditions for reasoned dialogue and reciprocity, assists in the development of a broader base of shared legal understandings. We would argue that building up a practice of legality is ultimately more important to this end than enshrining norms in positive law. We repeat that the creation of formal legal rules as such is a valuable step on the way to legality. The adoption of a treaty, for example, ensures at least some promulgation of the relevant norms, but that alone is not enough. As we have already noted, shared legal understanding cannot simply be enacted. This point is particularly important when international law extends its normative ambition beyond providing basic parameters for legal interaction. The form of law will prove a hollow shell unless law-making is understood as an effort to build and sustain legality – unless law-makers embrace the hard work of international law. For example, simply enshrining the principle of responsibility to protect in a General Assembly resolution does not turn it into interactional law, nor would inclusion in a treaty.[76] Whether or not a genuinely shared legal understanding emerges, and whether or not it can be widened by resolving ambiguities in and disagreements about the principle, will ultimately depend on whether a community of practice grows around the principle and whether that community practices legality.

[72] See detailed discussion below in Chapter 4.

[73] See Jutta Brunnée, 'Shifting the Global Climate Debate: When Bad News is Good News' (Summer 2007) *Nexus* 30.

[74] On the evolving regime and the continuing climate negotiations, see below Chapter 4.

[75] Fuller, above note 57, p. 186.

[76] See generally Jutta Brunnée and Stephen J. Toope, 'Norms, Institutions and UN Reform: The Responsibility to Protect' (2006) 2 *Journal of International Law and International Relations* 121. And see below Chapter 6.

More generally speaking, there will often be a gap between the text of a treaty and interactional law. States might adopt a treaty to provide reference points for their future legal interactions, but they also employ diplomats and lawyers to participate in its ongoing application, clarification or adjustment in practice.[77] As we have just noted, such treaty practice can convert positive law into interactional law, or expand the body of treaty-based interactional law. However, it is equally possible that a treaty gives rise to no interactional law at all (the proverbial paper tiger), or that only part of a treaty is animated by shared legal understandings and practice.

By the same token, one can easily imagine circumstances in which only some of the parties to a treaty are participants in the interactional legal regime that it spawns. For example, while some treaties may enshrine shared understandings regarding human rights and engage parties in a sustained practice of legality, not all states that are formally bound by the treaty may be parties in this interactional sense. A troubling example is found in the practice surrounding the Convention on the Elimination of Discrimination Against Women. A number of states parties have effectively undermined the norms of the convention, sometimes through an abusive use of the legal vehicle of reservations, but just as often through a complete failure to implement their formal commitments.[78] We have argued in the previous chapter that this behaviour by laggards works to destroy law by creating a sense of hypocrisy that diminishes the fidelity to law of other actors.

Inversely, examples abound where important parts of the negotiations leading to the adoption or further development of a treaty are conducted by a relatively small group of influential states. The 'participation' of many other states in law-making is often merely formal; there is no real inclusion, no engagement. Such practices undercut the potential development of both widely shared understandings and the reciprocity that animates interactional legality and invites and encourages fidelity to law. This analysis explains, for example, the strong resistance shown by many developing states to the trade regime negotiated under the World

77 Wenger, above note 34, pp. 63–4.

78 Typical examples are Algeria, which ratified the convention in 1996 with a host of reservations, and Nepal, which has come under fire for its inconsistent implementation record. See Jessica Neuwirth, 'Inequality Before the Law: Holding States Accountable for Sex Discriminatory Laws under the Convention on the Elimination of all Forms of Discrimination Against Women and Through the Beijing Platform for Action' (2005) 18 *Harvard Human Rights Journal* 19 at 27–35.

Trade Organization (WTO). All too often, smaller, less influential states believe that they are not true participants in the negotiations, but rather are bystanders in disputes between increasingly salient regional trading blocs and the single superpower.[79]

It is important to note that even customary international law, which is quintessentially based upon practice, does not necessarily constitute interactional law, at least not for all the states that it purports to bind as a matter of positive law. After all, the standard account of customary international law often presumes engagement with the norm where such engagement may not actually exist.[80] Not all states will actually have participated in the creation of a given norm or be actively involved in maintaining its validity.[81] This applies especially in relation to developing countries, which may not always be aware of the emergence of a customary rule, or be in a position effectively to resist its emergence. Material considerations are important here: small states often lack the legal and diplomatic resources to engage fully in the process of customary law formation and degradation. In such circumstances, states simply do not partake in a given shared understanding. Similarly, inconsistent or selective application or interpretation of existing customary rules, notably by more powerful states, undercuts the very practice of legality that is needed to sustain interactional law. Again, the concept of responsibility to protect lends itself to an illustration. While the concept may have come to be embraced by a growing number of states, some developing countries remain sceptical, in part because the practice around the concept does not fare well when measured against the requirements of legality, particularly the requirement that the actions of officials should conform to the norm. The past and potential selectivity of application of the emerging

[79] Thus, one commentator has argued that '[g]iving all small countries a real voice in all WTO decisions is impossible', and that we should therefore aim to ensure 'that they understand those decisions, that they were engaged in the preliminary discussions and that new rules do not impose conditions they cannot meet'. See Robert Wolfe, 'Decision-Making and Transparency in the "Medieval" WTO: Does the Sutherland Report Have the Right Prescription?' (2005) 8 *Journal of International Economic Law* 631 at 639.

[80] For a very critical discussion of customary international law and its 'fictitious' generality, see Yasuaki Onuma, 'A Transcivilizational Perspective on Global Legal Order in the Twenty-first Century', in Ronald St. J. Macdonald and Douglas M. Johnston (eds.), *Towards World Constitutionalism: Issues in the Legal Ordering of the World Community* (Leiden: Martinus Nijhoff, 2005), pp. 172–85.

[81] See also Oscar Schachter, 'New Custom: Power, *Opinio Juris* and Contrary Practice', in Jerzy Makarczyk (ed.), *Theory of International Law at the Threshold of the 21st Century* (The Hague: Kluwer Law International, 1996), p. 536 (observing that, '[a]s a historical fact, the great body of customary international law was made by remarkably few States').

norm of the responsibility to protect generates a sense of hypocrisy that undermines fidelity to the law.

This discussion points to several practical lessons for international lawyers. First, it should serve as a caution against undue faith in formal law-making. To reiterate, positive law does factor into the legality criteria that we have highlighted, such as promulgation. But formal validity is only a starting point for what is the truly hard work of international law – the building up and maintaining of the legality elements that sustain interactional law.

Second, international law-making must be sensitive to the role of shared understandings. International law depends upon a background of shared understandings that make it intelligible, and upon broad congruence with the patterns and practices in international society. The congruence between such understandings and legal rules is an important but not sufficient foundation for interactional law. In the diffuse social relationships through which international law operates, treaties or custom can provide important snapshots of shared understandings.[82] But shared *legal* understandings are generated by and must be maintained through a practice of legality. When read with constructivist international relations theory discussed in the Introduction, this point implies another important insight: if there are to be shared legal understandings, that is, norms that have the potential to shape identities and interests, law must by definition be interactional. This fact poses a constant and fundamental challenge to international law. Suffice it to point to the example of the prohibition on the use of force. Undoubtedly, the prohibition enshrines one of the most deeply and widely held international understandings, and yet the scope for argument around the fuzzy edges of the norm, its inconsistent invocation and application in international practice, and exceptionalism by powerful states all threaten to undermine its legality. These threats to the norm underscore that all international actors – states, citizens, intergovernmental organizations, NGOs, and the media – must work constantly to uphold its legality. The death of the norm generally prohibiting the use of force has been declared repeatedly in recent generations.[83]

[82] See also above Chapter 1, text following note 106.

[83] See e.g. Thomas M. Franck, 'Who Killed Article 2(4)? Or: Changing Norms Governing the Use of Force by States' (1970) 64 *American Journal of International Law* 809; Thomas M. Franck, *Recourse to Force: State Action Against Threats and Armed Attacks* (Cambridge University Press, 2002); and Michael J. Glennon, 'The Emerging Use-of-Force Paradigm' (2006) 11 *Journal of Conflict and Security Law* 309.

That the norm retains vigour is an example of the triumph of constant effort to support it; its mere formal declaration, even in the UN Charter, would not have been enough to save it.[84]

On the other hand, when a law-making project is markedly at odds with – or ahead of – social background understandings, even the best efforts of the most committed international lawyers may not suffice.[85] A clear example is the Migrant Workers Convention, where ambitious norms for the protection of migrant workers have failed to generate adherence; only 37 states have ratified the convention.[86] In such circumstances, it may be preferable to settle for a less ambitious project, and to patiently build up the legality elements that may enable a community of practice gradually to expand its stock of shared understandings. In other words, the interactional account helps identify circumstances where 'less' law may be 'more' and provides concrete guidance for law-making under such conditions. Our hypothesis is that adherence to the criteria of legality facilitates interaction on the basis of mutual respect and reciprocity and, therefore, fosters the commitment of states and other actors to their joint enterprise. Interactional lawmaking, then, engages actors in a particular type of community of practice, one that is aimed at building and maintaining shared legal understandings.

In summary, the communities of practice account reinforces the central argument of this book: that an interactional concept of law is best able to capture how law influences international actors and guides international relations. Yet, interactional international law is more than the stock of shared understandings existing in international society at any given time, and it exerts its influence in distinctive ways. As we explained in Chapter 1, the key to appreciating the distinctiveness of legal norms and processes lies in Lon Fuller's criteria of legality. Adherence to these requirements promotes a felt sense of obligation among actors. By enabling and guiding interactions among states and other international actors, legal processes or norms that meet the legality requirements also have the

[84] See Jutta Brunnée and Stephen J. Toope, 'Slouching Towards New "Just Wars": International Law and the Use of Force after September 11th' (2004) 51 *Netherlands International Law Review* 363; and Jutta Brunnée and Stephen J. Toope, 'The Use of Force: International Law After Iraq' (2004) 53 *International and Comparative Law Quarterly* 785.

[85] See also Postema, above note 61 at 265.

[86] International Convention on the Protection of the Rights of All Migrant Workers and Members of their Families, New York, 18 December 1990, in force 1 July 2003, 2220 United Nations Treaty Series (UNTS) 93. For current information regarding the convention's ratification status, see United Nations Treaty Collection, at http://treaties.un.org/Pages/ViewDetails.aspx?src=TREATY&mtdsg_no=IV-13&chapter=4&lang=en.

potential to facilitate the widening or deepening of internationally shared legal understandings.

'So what?' may be the reaction of some international lawyers to these arguments. 'Our job is to assess whether customary international law exists, or to ensure that a treaty is legally sound.' Our response to this perhaps not so hypothetical objection is that we share these very concerns. That is why we urge practitioners and scholars of international law to look beyond the formal manifestations of law. Form is not the essential feature of law; adherence to specific criteria of legality is. International lawyers should care about obligation because obligation is the value-added of law. Neither form nor hierarchy of norms can produce obligation in and of themselves. Close attention to the interactional processes that generate legitimacy and concomitant fidelity is a far more promising strategy to create international law.

4. Diversity and power in international society

In recent years, a cacophony of voices has raised challenges to the very possibility of 'international' law, challenges based on the assumption that the diversity of actors in international society makes any form of shared law impossible. The earliest modern arguments from the perspective of diversity go back to the rise of the Soviet Union; it is well known that Lenin initially thought that the USSR could reject the constraints of any bourgeois internationalism.[87] Rejectionist impulses surfaced again in the post-colonial era, with some 'third-world' statespersons and academics challenging the Eurocentric foundations of international law. Today the same critique is extended in a variety of ways by scholars encompassed within the Third World Approaches to International Law (TWAIL) network. Essentially the argument is that international law, once Eurocentric, is now irredeemably 'Western' and ill-attuned to the needs and aspirations of the developing world.[88]

We agree. What is more, these problems are fundamental: they relate both to the mission and the deep structure of the law. The Statute of the Permanent Court of International Justice (1921) encouraged the court

[87] See e.g. Malcolm N. Shaw, *International Law*, 5th edn (Cambridge University Press, 2003), pp. 31–8.

[88] See Makau W. Mutua, 'What Is TWAIL?' (2000) 94 *American Society of International Law Proceedings* 31 at 33; James Thuo Gathii, 'International Law and Eurocentricity' (1998) 9 *European Journal of International Law* 184. IR scholars have pursued related inquiries. See e.g. Siba N. Grovogui, 'Postcolonialism', in Dunne *et al.*, above note 56, p. 235.

to apply 'general principles of law recognized by civilized nations', the assumption being that such nations were limited to Europe (and a handful of 'white' colonies or dominions), the United States of America, a few great Asian civilizations, and a scattering of independent South American states.[89] This phrasing of the Court's jurisdiction was extended to the Statute of the International Court of Justice in 1949. In addition, during the League of Nations era, mandates were created for the 'benefit' of peoples and territories that were seen to require the tutelage of 'civilized' states. Even after the creation of the United Nations, this system was continued as trusteeships, whereby potential states were apportioned out to ex-colonial powers for education into the ranks of civilized nations.[90] Today, the discourse of 'governance' may play a similar role: 'failed' and 'failing' states must be coached into democracy, the rule of law and free market economics;[91] civilized nations may feel compelled to intervene in other states to protect vulnerable populations from tyranny and grave human rights abuse.[92] The totality of this history and current practice is well-described by Martti Koskenniemi as the 'civilizing mission' of international law.[93]

Structurally, the civilizing mission is rooted in the central concept of sovereignty.[94] To be a sovereign is to count as an empowered actor in the system of law. Historically, this concept facilitated colonialism by treating some societies as outside the framework of law, and amenable to acquisition and domination. Today, in a post-colonial era, sovereignty is still invoked to play an exclusionary role, privileging 200-or-so states at the expense of other international actors.[95] One of the central challenges to

[89] Edward Keene, *Beyond the Anarchical Society: Grotius, Colonialism and Order in World Politics* (Cambridge University Press, 2002), pp. 97–119.

[90] See e.g. Antony Anghie, '"The Heart of My Home": Colonialism, Environmental Damage, and the Nauru Case' (1993) 34 *Harvard International Law Journal* 445.

[91] See e.g. Antony Anghie, *Imperialism, Sovereignty and the Making of International Law* (Cambridge University Press, 2004), Chapter 5.

[92] See e.g. Mohammed Ayoob, 'Humanitarian Intervention and State Sovereignty' (2002) 6 *International Journal of Human Rights* 81.

[93] Martti Koskenniemi, *The Gentle Civilizer of Nations: The Rise and Fall of International Law 1870–1960* (Cambridge University Press, 2002).

[94] See e.g. Anghie, above note 91; and Makau W. Mutua, 'Why Redraw the Map of Africa: A Moral and Legal Inquiry' (1995) 16 *Michigan Journal of International Law* 1113.

[95] See e.g. Balakrishnan Rajagopal, 'International Law and Third World Resistance: A Theoretical Inquiry', in Antony Anghie, Bhupinder Chimni, Karin Mickelson and Obiora Chinedu Okafor (eds.), *The Third World and International Order: Law, Politics and Globalization* (New York: Kluwer Law International, 2003), p. 145 (discussing the role of social movements).

contemporary international law is how to incorporate the potential and real contributions of a variety of non-state actors, from inter-governmental organizations to sub-state groups, from NGOs to transnational networks, from corporations to individuals.

Sovereignty is a limiting concept, but the claim is made that the law produced by a limited number of sovereign actors is nonetheless universal.[96] Contemporary expressions included international human rights discourse, joined by neo-liberal market discourse, and more recently by the language of 'democratic governance'.[97] Connected to these universalizing discourses is the idea that the world, or at least the world of states, forms an 'international community'. International bureaucrats, some politicians and many scholars take for granted that international law defends and upholds not just state interests, but community interests.[98] We find these assumptions of an 'international community' to be both misleading and unhelpful. Empirically, it is difficult to point to a community in anything but the most superficial sense. Moreover, universalist claims of a 'community' of states obfuscate the reality of deep cultural and social diversity across our globe; the values said to be represented by the community of states are actually culturally specific, western, values. Indeed, there continues to be much debate over whether or not there exists an international society,[99] let alone an international community. For present purposes, we need not enter into these well-worn debates.[100]

96 See e.g. Antony Anghie, 'Universality and the Concept of Governance in International Law', in Edward Kofi Quashigah and Obiora Chinedu Okafor (eds.), *Legitimate Governance in Africa: International and Domestic Legal Perspectives* (The Hague: Kluwer Law International, 1999), p. 21.

97 See Eve Darian-Smith and Peter Fitzpatrick (eds.), *Laws of the Postcolonial (Law, Meaning, Violence)* (Ann Arbor: University of Michigan Press, 1999) *passim*; James Thuo Gathii, 'The Limits of the *New* International Rule of Law on Good Governance', in Quashigah and Okafor, above note 96, p. 207; David Slater, 'Contesting Occidental Visions of the Global: The Geopolitics of Theory and North–South Relations' (1994) 4 *Beyond Law* 97; and Dianne Otto, 'Subalternity and International Law: The Problem of Global Community and the Incommensurability of Difference' (1996) 5 *Social and Legal Studies* 337.

98 See Edward Kwakwa, 'The International Community, International Law, and the United States: Three in One, Two Against One, or One and the Same?', in Michael Byers and Georg Nolte (eds.), *United States Hegemony and the Foundations of International Law* (Cambridge University Press, 2003), p. 25.

99 See Christian Reus-Smit, 'Society, Power and Ethics', in Christian Reus-Smit (ed.), *The Politics of International Law* (Cambridge University Press, 2004), pp. 274–9.

100 For a comprehensive analysis, see Andreas L. Paulus, *Die Internationale Gemeinschaft im Völkerrecht* (Munich: Verlag C.H. Beck, 2001). See also Dino Kritsiosis, 'Imagining the International Community' (2002) 13 *European Journal of International Law* 268.

Although we place emphasis upon 'communities of practice' in explaining the evolution of shared understandings and of interactional law, it is important to stress that this concept of 'community' is fundamentally different from the notion of community underlying the historical and contemporary universalist claims of international law. Given that a community of practice is constituted by mutual engagement rather than by shared values or goals, membership neither presupposes nor necessarily leads to homogeneity of purposes.[101] The concept embraces diversity and, as Adler stresses, the 'joint enterprise of members of a community of practice' requires only that they share an understanding of 'what they are doing and why'.[102] There exists a 'thin' community of international legal practice based in very limited shared understandings that there is a need for law in shaping international communication and interaction.[103] Thus, a community of diplomats may share a commitment to certain diplomatic practices notwithstanding fundamental political disagreements amongst states.[104] For example, although the members of the Security Council do not share a single belief system, they are 'in an enduring relationship and share certain expectations about the enterprise in which they are engaged'.[105] Or environmentalists may interact on the basis of a shared understanding that climate change is a serious global threat that requires collective action, without any further commitment to specific goals or approaches. Whether, over time, a deeper sense of community coalesces around the emergence of common histories, values or norms, is a separate question. Such coalescence is certainly not inevitable; nor is it required to produce interactional law. On the other hand, we must stress that without a deep engagement in diversity, without robust interaction, law cannot be

[101] Wenger, above note 34, pp. 75–8.

[102] Adler, above note 20, p. 22. See also Ian Johnstone, 'The Plea of Necessity in International Legal Discourse: Humanitarian Intervention and Counter-Terrorism' (2005) 43 *Columbia Journal of International Law* 338 at 382 (advancing the concept of 'interpretive community', and suggesting that 'members of a legal interpretive community may hail from different political and cultural communities' and still share a 'perspective and style of reasoning').

[103] See also Martti Koskenniemi, *From Apology to Utopia: The Structure of International Legal Argument*, reissue with a new Epilogue (Cambridge University Press, 2005), p. 110 (arguing that 'international law provides the shared surface … on which political adversaries recognize each other as such and pursue their adversity in terms of something shared'). And see Postema, above note 71, pp. 301–2.

[104] See Adler, above note 20, p. 15.

[105] See Ian Johnstone, 'Legislation and Adjudication in the UN Security Council: Bringing Down the Deliberative Deficit' (2008) 102 *American Journal of International Law* 275 at 300–1.

created in international society. This is why, on our account, not all formally valid international law reflects genuine legality.

Three further points are worth highlighting with respect to the interplay between communities of practice and diversity. First, aside from diverse values or priorities, communities of practice can also accommodate a plurality of actors. As we have seen, they can bring together state and non-state actors of various kinds.[106] Second, at any given time there also exists a plurality of communities of practice, often with overlapping priorities and memberships.[107] Third, communities of practice are shaped and affected by interactions within institutions such as states. As shared understandings are built through international interaction, they can be reinforced or challenged by the politics within states.[108]

To reiterate, our concept of interactional law presupposes only thin shared understandings, although it allows for deepening of these understandings through interaction. It does not posit a liberal world community,[109] yet it does not deny the possibility that adversaries can learn from each other and expand their common ground beyond the surface of shared formal legality.[110]

We acknowledge that Fuller, and our version of interactional law, are grounded in a western liberal tradition that upholds legal rationality. However, because the only substantive commitment that is required in our version of that tradition is to a symbiotic understanding of autonomy and communication, we believe that a wide range of diversity is facilitated by an interactional understanding of law. For us, 'autonomy' is a cognate for diverse needs and aspirations but is inextricably bound to the human need to communicate. We do not argue for a transposition of liberal individualism to international society, but rather for a clear acknowledgement of the construction of international actors, including the state, through social

106 See *ibid.* at 281 (discussing the permeability of interpretive communities to diverse perspectives).

107 Michael Walzer, *Spheres of Justice: A Defense of Pluralism and Equality* (New York: Basic Books, 1983).

108 See Koh, 'The Frankel Lecture: Bringing International Law Home', above note 29; and Wiener, above note 40, p. 212.

109 See e.g. Anne-Marie Slaughter, 'International Law in a World of Liberal States' (1995) 6 *European Journal of International Law* 503; and Andrew Moravcsik, 'Taking Preferences Seriously: a Liberal Theory of International Politics' (1997) 51 *International Organization* 513.

110 But see Koskenniemi, above note 103, p. 539 (maintaining that international law is bound to express either 'utopian justice' or 'an apology of actual power', rather than genuinely shared norms).

interaction.[111] Nor does interactional law demand the promulgation of a specific set of liberal values. Although some actors would, of course, bring these values to any interaction, they must remain committed to genuine dialogue and sincere attempts at reciprocity of understanding. This is the very point of our argument, that international law must be grounded in shared understandings elaborated through communities of practice, and more specifically a practice of legality. The criteria of legality set out above and the related concept of legal legitimacy are the very means by which diversity is protected; they mediate between the creation and maintenance of a community of practice and autonomy of social actors.

At the same time, interactional law helps us understand the limits to law-making under conditions of deep diversity. Our interactional understanding of law explains why the creation and sustenance of international law requires a commitment to communication, a willingness to listen, and openness to reciprocal modification of outlook. These requirements reveal how hard it is to create law when actors pursue values that they view as 'right' and therefore immutable. One can see the difficulties play out in all interactions premised upon a 'clash of civilizations', whether the 'civilizations' of staunch liberal individualism, neo-conservatism or political Islam. So, at first glance, the existence of any international law may seem very unlikely in our world. Yet, the interactional understanding of law also demonstrates that despite diversity, thin initial commitments to legality are possible and shared legal understandings may deepen through communities of practice. That is the hard work of international law.

If the achievement of international law is made difficult by the diversity of actors, it is further complicated by power differentials. Many commentators, both lawyers and IR theorists, have argued that international law can never be anything more than the expression of the interests of powerful states. At the very least, powerful actors will be disproportionately influential in shaping the content of legal regimes, both to protect and advance their interests, and to instantiate and perpetuate their power. What is more, it is argued that any 'rules' that exist in international law are really paper tigers in confronting powerful states; such states can ignore

[111] See also, for the sake of analogy, the work of Jennifer Nedelsky, particularly 'Communities of Judgment and Human Rights' (2000) 1 *Theoretical Inquiries in Law* 245; and 'Judgment, Diversity, and Relational Autonomy', in Ronald Beiner and Jennifer Nedelsky (eds.), *Judgment, Imagination, and Politics: Themes from Kant and Arendt* (Lanham, Md: Rowman & Littlefield, 2001), p. 103.

rules at will.[112] Seen in this light, the notionally fundamental concept of the sovereign equality of states is mere pretence.[113] The idea that sovereign states must consent to international rules is similarly fictitious. Material imbalances, including vast differences in the availability of human resources to monitor, negotiate or protest, make a mockery of the notions of equality and consent. Power differentials are exacerbated for developing countries. They operate in an international legal system that is steeped in the history of colonialism, generating continuing bitterness and a sense of disenfranchisement. Some scholars suggest that the existing rules and practices serve only to reinforce the colonial legacy, keeping developing states on the periphery, perpetuating weakness and assisting in their continuing exploitation by the developed world.[114]

Power differentials also exist among non-state actors. NGOs from important western countries have resources and influence that are denied to all but a few NGOs from the developing world.[115] Of course, in their interactions with states, even well-resourced NGOs will find their material power goes only so far. States can effectively dictate which non-state actors can participate in international law formation and what capacities and entitlements they may have.[116]

112 See e.g. George F. Kennan, *American Diplomacy 1900–1950* (University of Chicago Press, 1984), p. 95; and Hans J. Morgenthau, *Politics Among Nations: The Struggle for Power and Peace*, 1st edn (New York: Alfred A. Knopf, 1948). See also Michael Byers, *Custom, Power and the Power of Rules* (Cambridge University Press, 1999); and Michael Glennon, 'Why the Security Council Failed' (2003) 82 *Foreign Affairs* 16.

113 See the discussion in Benedict Kingsbury, 'Sovereignty and Inequality' (1998) 9 *European Journal of International Law* 599 (arguing, however, that the concept of sovereignty nonetheless affords weaker states important protections). See also Nico Krisch, 'More equal than the rest? Hierarchy, Equality and US Predominance in International Law', in Michael Byers and Georg Nolte (eds.), *United States Hegemony and the Foundations of International Law* (Cambridge University Press, 2003), p. 135.

114 See e.g. Mohammed Bedjaoui, *Towards a New International Economic Order* (New York: Holmes & Meier Publishers, 1979); Yoke Ling Chee, *How Big Powers Dominate the Third World: The Use and Abuse of International Law* (Penang: Third World Network, 1987); James Thuo Gathii, 'Alternative and Critical: The Contribution of Research and Scholarship on Developing Countries to International Legal Theory' (2000) 41 *Harvard International Law Journal* 263; Balakrishnan Rajagopal, 'Locating the Third World in Cultural Geography' (1998–9) *Third World Legal Studies* 1; and Bhupinder S. Chimni, 'Third World Approaches to International Law: A Manifesto', in Anghie *et al.*, above note 95, pp. 60–1.

115 See e.g. Andrew Hurrell, 'Power, Institutions, and the Production of Inequality', in Michael Barnett and Robert Duvall (eds.), *Power in Global Governance* (Cambridge University Press, 2005), pp. 44–5 (examples illustrating the dominance of western NGOs).

116 See e.g. Anna Holzscheiter, 'Discourse as Capability: Non-State Actors' Capital in Global Governance' (2005) 33 *Millennium: Journal of International Studies* 723 at 725.

It has been suggested that constructivist approaches to IR gloss over power differentials and actually serve to propagate western, especially US, interests.[117] We believe that this critique is too sweeping. Although it may be fair to suggest that some versions of 'norm entrepreneurship' are directed to the dissemination of liberal values, this goal is not inherent in constructivist logic. On the contrary, constructivism reveals that all power, even material power, is 'irreducibly social'.[118] As Barnett and Duvall have shown, power takes multiple forms: *compulsory power* is closest to the common usage of the word 'power', that is, the ability of one actor to exercise direct control over another; *institutional power* is the power that actors exercise through diffuse relationships within institutions[119] (e.g. rules of decision); *structural power* is the direct relationship between actors which allocates differential capacities and advantages (e.g. master–servant); and *productive power* 'is the socially diffuse production of subjectivity in systems of meaning and signification'.[120] This taxonomy reveals that purely materialist conceptions of power are incomplete; 'raw' power matters, but so do the relationships that define and shape power. It is worth reiterating that just because power relationships are socially constructed does not mean that they are benign: interaction can produce oppression, not only cooperation. We previously emphasized this point in relation to communities of practice, which can generate positive or negative norms. The claim that constructivist approaches are unduly optimistic is simply false. An analysis of power relationships is not inherently positive; no more so than an analysis of material resources.

Interactional international law takes us a step further. Recognizing the multifaceted reality of power differentials, the interactional analysis helps to identify the ways in which the ability of powerful actors to dominate

[117] Umut Özsu, 'Towards a Critical Constructivist Theory of Legal "Norm-Internalization": Two Cases from Early Republican Turkey', unpublished LL.M. thesis, University of Toronto, Faculty of Law (2007), Chapter 1; and Milja Kurki and Adriana Sinclair, 'Hidden in Plain Sight: Reflections on the Limitations of the Constructivist Treatment of Social Context' (manuscript on file with authors), (2007).

[118] Michael Barnett and Raymond Duvall, 'Power in International Politics' (2005) 59 *International Organization* 39.

[119] We follow Alexander Wendt in defining an 'institution' as a 'relatively stable set or "structure" of identities and interests'. See Jutta Brunnée and Stephen J. Toope, 'International Law and Constructivism: Elements of an Interactional Theory of International Law' (2000) 39 *Columbia Journal of Transnational Law* 19 at 29–30; and Wendt, above note 45 at 399.

[120] Barnett and Duvall, above note 118 at 43. See also Ian Johnstone, 'The Power of Interpretive Communities', in Barnett and Duvall, above note 115, p. 185 (distinguishing institutional, compulsory and productive power).

legal relationships can be constrained. Interactional law will reveal when compulsory power is exercised arbitrarily and without legitimacy. Simply asserting control in the absence of shared understandings and a practice of legality is abusive. That is why unilateral invasions of states are uniformly viewed as unlawful unless the invasion is justified under the rubric of self-defence.

By requiring a practice of legality, interactional law will also provide a basis for resistance in relationships of structural power. A weaker state within a bilateral treaty regime, for example, will be able to insist upon practices of legality that resist the direct application of greater power; hence, the impetus for schemes of third-party dispute resolution in trade treaties. But the strongest insights to be derived from interactional law apply to relations of institutional and productive power. Institutions can 'represent frozen configurations of privilege and bias'.[121] But in all negotiations around institutional design and evolution, if the insights of interactional law are taken seriously, it will be possible to build a setting that will facilitate a practice of legality and the emergence of communities of practice that could lead to the deepening of social interactions. Developing world challenges to the practices of law-making within the WTO regime are supported by interactional law if it can be demonstrated that key substantive goals are simply being imposed by powerful states, that effective participation by relevant actors is not possible, or that the established rules are simply being ignored by the strongest states.

Similarly, when one considers productive power, the possibility of all actors to influence systems of knowledge and discursive practices is revealed. However, not all social actors have the same capacity to influence, given differentials in material power including human resources. Interactional law undercuts the ability of powerful actors to put forward utterly self-serving or perverse normative claims, because the claims will have to be measured against the eight criteria of legality, and will have to fit within shared understandings generated through inclusive participation of all social actors.[122] In addition, interactional law supports the participation of a range of non-state actors in productive power, thereby recognizing a reality of contemporary legal discourse. Consider the self-serving claim of the George W. Bush administration

[121] Barnett and Duvall, above note 118 at 52.

[122] See also Johnstone, above note 102 at 383 (commenting on the ability of interpretive communities to constrain dominant actors, notwithstanding the latter's greater ability to shape the 'rules of the game').

that the well-established rules of self-defence had been overturned by the events of 11 September 2001 and the subsequent US-declared 'war on terror'. These claims have been undermined by the consistent practice, including rhetoric, of states, large and small, supported by the actions of civil society around the globe.

5. Conclusion

Social norms can only emerge when societies generate shared understandings of the need for norms, and deeper shared understandings of the need for specific norms to guide behaviour. Norm entrepreneurs and epistemic communities are often influential in promoting norms, but the effective creation of norms is not a unidirectional projection of ideas or values. Shared understandings are inherently interactional, created through communities of practice that shape the mutual engagement of various actors in international society. That engagement is framed by existing norms and social structures, and the active participation of actors in turn maintains and re-shapes both norms and structures.

Legal norms are rooted in these shared understandings. Shared understandings may include merely a basic acceptance of the need for law in a society, or they may be more substantive and value-laden. Interactional law only emerges when shared understandings become fused with a 'practice of legality', rooted in Fuller's eight criteria of legality and embraced by a community of practice that adheres to those criteria in day-to-day decision-making. Fuller's criteria of legality are not a mere checklist to tell us whether or not a particular legal form, e.g. a treaty or a court decision, is properly designed as 'law'. Instead, the criteria come alive when actors reason with the rules in continuing processes of mutual engagement, creating a community of legal practice.

Because interactional international law can exist in weak or strong forms, depending upon the intensity of the underlying shared understandings in international society, the interactional description of international law is attuned to cultural diversity and power differentials in our world. It is both hopeful and sobering. Some forms of interactional law may exist without overarching shared substantive values. This law may be 'thin', and primarily procedural, but it is real.

It is not necessary or helpful to imagine the existence of a homogeneous 'international community' for law to emerge. The interactional account reveals that the mere declaration of supposed common values articulated in formal law can be deceptive. Without a community of practice, supposed shared values will remain lofty rhetoric. Yet, communities of practice can actually have impact without deeply-shared substantive values. Fuller shows us that a community of legal practice can exist with only a thin set of substantive commitments; indeed, this is the reality of international law today. That is precisely why it is so important to focus effort on the building up of a more resilient community of legal practice in international society. As mutual engagement increases, it may be possible for even adversaries to learn from each other. Over time, with increasing interaction, communities of practice can become more interconnected and value-based, allowing for richer substantive rules.

3

Interactional law and compliance: law's hidden power

> [T]he concept of 'compliance' with law does not have, and cannot have, any meaning except as a function of prior theories of the nature and operation of the law to which it pertains.[1]

1. Introduction

Compliance questions have now preoccupied international lawyers for almost two decades, and they have animated much of the re-engagement between international law and international relations (IR) theory.[2] We deliberately speak of engagement between 'international law' and 'international relations theory', rather than between 'international law theory' and 'international relations theory'. We believe that a limitation of much recent compliance scholarship is its failure to articulate a theory of international law or, more specifically, a theory of international legal obligation. In much of this writing, theories of international law and obligation operate only in the background, if at all. All too often, international law is treated simply as a fact of international life, or is assumed to emanate from formal sources and the consent of states. The result is that the distinctive 'compliance pull' of international law, to use Thomas Franck's evocative phrase,[3] is disregarded or undervalued, and important opportunities for understanding and promoting compliance are missed.

One might forgive international relations theorists for spending little time distinguishing between 'norms' and legal norms, or for building

[1] Benedict Kingsbury, 'The Concept of Compliance as a Function of Competing Conceptions of International Law' (1998) 19 *Michigan Journal of International Law* 345 at 346.

[2] See Martti Koskenniemi, *The Gentle Civilizer of Nations: The Rise and Fall of International Law 1870–1960* (Cambridge University Press, 2002), Chapter 6 (for an account of how the two disciplines parted company in the early 20th century, largely as a result of the growing dominance of realism in United States international relations circles).

[3] Thomas M. Franck, *The Power of Legitimacy Among Nations* (Oxford University Press, 1990), p. 26.

their frameworks on the positivist accounts of law that remain dominant among international lawyers. As we discussed in the Introduction, the positivist view of law has reinforced the realist and rationalist theories of compliance that have long been dominant within the discipline of international relations. In that dominant view, law, like other social norms, can provide predictable rules and stable institutional structures. But if international law is only a formal phenomenon contingent upon state will, it is at least initially plausible that states' interests and relative powers will determine their compliance. The general absence of compulsory dispute settlement and enforcement mechanisms rounds out the perception of international law as weak or even 'epiphenomenal'.[4] Constructivist international relations scholars, by and large, have not challenged the thin account of law that underpins the majority of compliance theories. Although compliance scholars working in a constructivist vein are by definition 'norm interested', they too have been remarkably uninterested in examining whether legal norms are 'distinctive' in more than merely a formal sense,[5] and what the implications for their capacity to shape identities and induce compliance might be.

Most intriguing, however, is the fact that international lawyers themselves have developed increasingly elaborate compliance theories without spending much time explicating their underlying theories of legal obligation.[6] The reason may again lie in the predominant positivism of the discipline, leading many international lawyers to see obligation as nothing more than the legal consequence of formal validity, or of state consent.[7] Alternatively, in international law's 'post-ontological

[4] See David Bederman, 'Constructivism, Positivism, and Empiricism in International Law' (2001) 89 *Georgetown Law Journal* 469 at 473.

[5] But see Martha Finnemore, 'Are Legal Norms Distinctive?' (2000) 32 *New York University Journal of International Law and Politics* 699.

[6] See William Bradford, 'International Legal Compliance: Surveying the Field' (2005) 36 *Georgetown Journal of International Law* 495 at 496 (providing the following list of general theoretical frameworks: '(a) realism, (b) enforcement theory, (c) rational choice theory, (d) liberal theory, (e) managerial theory, (f) reputational theory, (g) transnational legal process, (h) legitimacy theory, (i) constructivism, (j) organizational-cultural theory, and (k) personality theory').

[7] For a classic statement, see P. Corbett, 'The Consent of States and the Sources of International Law' (1925) 6 *British Yearbook of International Law* 20. It is interesting to note that in many of the principal textbooks on public international law, there is no general discussion of the nature of obligation; validity and consent are assumed within the discourse on 'sources' of law. See e.g. Ian Brownlie, *Principles of Public International Law*, 6th edn (Oxford University Press, 2003); and Malcolm N. Shaw, *International Law*, 5th edn (Cambridge University Press, 2003).

age',[8] the once thorny matter of international legal obligation can be effectively bracketed,[9] or dispatched by simply taking its existence in international practice for granted, the latter approach being dominant amongst international lawyers.[10]

In short, while theoretical inquiry into compliance with international law is all the rage, theoretical inquiry into legal obligation is treated by many international lawyers as 'old hat'. Jack Goldsmith and Eric Posner recently went so far as to assert that the concept of international legal obligation is theoretically unconvincing and practically irrelevant. In moral terms, states do not have an obligation to comply with international law and, empirically speaking, they do not act out of a sense of obligation but *exclusively* in rational pursuit of their interests.[11] As many commentators have observed, Goldsmith and Posner's arguments are driven by a vision of US constitutionalism that seeks to limit the threat that international law is seen to pose to American popular sovereignty and democracy.[12] Whatever the authors' motivations, we need not add here to the already large number of detailed rebuttals of their sweeping claims, including by scholars who are sympathetic to rationalist explanations of state conduct.[13] But we do want to suggest that Goldsmith and Posner's account, whether

[8] Thomas M. Franck, *Fairness in International Law and Institutions* (Oxford: Clarendon Press, 1995), p. 6.

[9] See Kenneth W. Abbott, Robert Keohane, Andrew Moravcsik, Anne-Marie Slaughter and Duncan Snidal, 'The Concept of Legalization' (2000) 54 *International Organization* 401 at 403.

[10] See the description of this 'practical' view in J. L. Brierly, *The Law of Nations: An Introduction to the International Law of Peace*, 6th edn, Humphrey Waldock (ed.) (Oxford: Clarendon Press, 1968), p. 69 (describing how practitioners and diplomats deem debates about the nature of obligation to be 'pedantry of the theorist and not of the practical man').

[11] Jack L. Goldsmith and Eric A. Posner, *The Limits of International Law* (Oxford University Press, 2005), pp. 15 and 185–203.

[12] See Oona A. Hathaway and Ariel N. Lavinbuk, 'Rationalism and Revisionism in International Law' (2006) 119 *Harvard Law Review* 1404 (discussing in detail the 'conservative, revisionist' underpinnings of Goldsmith and Posner's theory). Concerns about the threats posed by international law to US constitutionalism are made both from the left and from the right. See e.g. Jed Rubenfeld, 'Unilateralism and Constitutionalism' (2004) 79 *New York University Law Review* 1971; and Paul W. Kahn, 'Speaking Law to Power: Popular Sovereignty, Human Rights and the New International Order' (2000) 1 *Chicago Journal of International Law* 1.

[13] See e.g. Hathaway and Lavinbuk, above note 12 at 1406; Anke van Aaken, (2006) 'To Do Away with International Law? Some Limits to "The Limits of International Law"' (2006) 17 *European Journal of International Law* 289; Andrew T. Guzman, 'The Promise of International Law' (2006) 92 *Virginia Law Review* 533; and Daniel Bodansky, 'International Law in Black and White' (2006) 34 *Georgia Journal of International and Comparative Law* 285 at 292–5.

convincing or not, serves to illustrate that compliance scholarship must re-engage with the concept of obligation if international law is not to be caricatured as meaningless or weak. While this assessment applies both to international law and to international relations scholarship, our focus in this chapter is exclusively on the former. Only after international law scholars have advanced a compelling theory of legal obligation can IR scholars examine whether and how obligation itself 'matters' in international affairs. And, in any case, it is up to international lawyers to articulate a concept of international obligation that can withstand attacks from within the discipline itself.

In this chapter, we argue that the strength of our interactional approach to compliance lies precisely in the fact that it is primarily a theory of obligation. We begin by distinguishing our account of obligation from explanations of compliance. Second, we explain why interactional obligation, through the distinctive influence it exerts, is relevant to compliance. Third, we show that interactionalism provides concrete guidance to lawyers and policymakers as they seek to understand and promote compliance with international law. Specifically, we argue that the foundations for compliance can be built through law-making processes; that spaces and opportunities must be created for interactions on the basis of legality; that dispute settlement and enforcement too are best understood as elements of a practice of legality; and that the requirements of interactional law-making must also be heeded in the internalization of international law into states' domestic spheres. We also suggest that interactionalism reveals the very concept of 'compliance' to be far more complex than conventional definitions would allow.

The focus on obligation distinguishes our framework from the various rationalist compliance theories advanced by international lawyers.[14] It also marks a crucial difference between our approach and the most prominent norm-oriented compliance theories: Thomas Franck's legitimacy theory, Abram and Antonia Handler Chayes' 'managerial' theory,

[14] It is possible, of course, to offer rationalist explanations of compliance without a theory of obligation, or to do so with only a thin, positivist theory. The very point of such theories is that factors external to law, such as interests, costs and benefits, or power account for compliance. Therefore, while we do not deny that these factors are relevant to compliance, we will not engage in any detail with rationalist theories in this chapter. Suffice it to say that, even if theoretically coherent on their own terms, purely rationalist accounts miss an important part of the compliance picture precisely because they discount obligation. See e.g. Andrew T. Guzman, *How International Law Works: A Rational Choice Theory* (Oxford University Press, 2008), pp. 25–69 and 211–18 (whose explanation of compliance rests on the ways in which international law generates costs for a state).

Ryan Goodman and Derek Jinks's state socialization theory, and Harold Koh's transnational legal process and norm internalization theory. These frameworks share our assumption that law has the potential to shape the conduct of states or other international actors. Franck's account is concerned with the properties of rules that enable them to pull towards compliance; the other frameworks are focused upon the processes through which law is given effect. We draw on these four frameworks to highlight the distinctive features of our own, and to illustrate why compliance theory must pay greater attention to obligation. We argue that a key strength of the interactional account is that it speaks to both norm properties and legal process. The interactional concept of obligation integrates the two, with important implications for compliance.

2. Interactional obligation and compliance distinguished

Our interactional theory of law provides an account of how international legal obligation is created and how it operates. As a theory of obligation, it illuminates why states and other actors commit to international law, and why they do or do not remain committed. And it implies that obligation is relevant to compliance because it is not something that is imposed on actors, but is an attitude towards the law that is part of actors' identities. Obligation rests in the commitment of actors – their 'fidelity' – to a legal system and its rules.

This sketch might suggest that the interactional framework entails an overly optimistic account of compliance. It does not. Explaining commitment is not the same as explaining compliance. We argue that commitment does indeed pull towards compliance. However, 'compliance pull' does not predict whether actors will in fact comply, or explain exhaustively why they do or do not comply. We do not claim that (interactional) obligation inevitably produces compliance; nor do we suggest that all instances of compliance are necessarily the result of obligation. We do, however, take issue with the claim that interests and power are the *only* explanations of state conduct. We have already explained in Chapters 1 and 2, drawing on constructivism, that norms shape the identities and actions of states and other international actors. We argue that legal norms do so in distinctive ways, a point that we pursue further in our discussion of compliance questions in this chapter. Still, we do not deny that rationalist accounts of compliance have explanatory power. Interests and power do matter in international affairs and incentives or disincentives can help promote compliance.

For example, there will be situations where states or other actors violate international law because it is in their perceived interest, or because compliance is deemed to be too costly. Exactly why this occurs is a separate question, and a number of answers are conceivable.[15] The rule in question might have been formally valid, but might not have been interactional law such as to invite a sense of obligation that could have influenced or pulled against interest assessments. In this case, the proper 'compliance strategy' would not necessarily be to resort to incentives or disincentives, but would be to work to turn a formal rule into interactional law. Alternatively, the rule in question might have met the requirements of interactional law and a state or other actor violates it, notwithstanding the sense of obligation that it engenders. Depending on the circumstances, the proper compliance strategy might be strengthening the opportunities for interaction and legal discourse, or to complement interactional strategies through incentives or disincentives. If, in a given situation, the interests in question are too powerful – for example, in cases of perceived threats to the fundamental security of the state or where intervention abroad is seen to be urgently required to protect human beings from grave abuses – neither strategy might avert non-compliance.

Similarly, our claim is not that obligation will always trump power, but rather that it is an over-simplification to say that obligation has no impact at all on powerful actors. Power differentials do affect international relations and they may well grant powerful actors greater elbow room when it comes to compliance with international law. But while power matters, so do the relationships that define and shape it. As we argued in Chapter 2, an interactional analysis, by revealing when power is exercised arbitrarily and without legitimacy, helps to reveal how the ability of powerful actors to dominate legal relationships can be constrained. Interactionalism suggests that powerful actors have less freedom to disregard international law than is commonly assumed, a proposition to which we will return in subsequent chapters. It also suggests that pressure exerted by powerful actors to enforce compliance is unlikely to be effective in the long-run unless it is embedded in a practice of legality.

The previous discussion illustrates that it is impossible to assert the validity of one or the other compliance theory in absolute terms, or even in the context of specific instances of state conduct. Only careful empirical work would enable more conclusive assessments of actors' motivations,

15 See also Thomas M. Franck, 'Legitimacy in the International System' (1988) 82 *American Journal of International Law* 705 at 712.

and of the role that law played in a given situation.[16] Our point is not to make an empirical claim about the accuracy of our interactional theory: it is only to illustrate that both rationalist and norm-driven explanations are plausible, and in some cases may even have parallel relevance. We will discuss a variety of empirical cases in Chapters 4 to 6.

3. The role of obligation

One of the great puzzles in international affairs, the seeming paradox of why states comply with 'powerless rules',[17] prompted Thomas Franck to articulate a legitimacy-based theory of compliance with international law. He demonstrated that states frequently comply with international law even when it seems to run counter to their immediate interests.[18] In the absence of systematic enforcement, he argues, there must be certain features of international law itself that enable it to exert 'compliance pull'.[19] He argues that the salient factor is the 'perception of a rule as legitimate by those to whom it is addressed'.[20]

Franck's account has been a touchstone for much subsequent work on compliance. He was the first contemporary international law scholar to articulate a legal theory of compliance. His framework has also been one of few such theories to be picked up in the IR literature on compliance.[21] We share Franck's conviction that legal legitimacy matters to compliance, and the indicators of legality that we see as relevant to legal legitimacy overlap in part with Franck's legitimacy factors,[22] but there are also two significant differences between our framework and Franck's. First, as we explained in Chapter 1, our concept of legal legitimacy is broader than the

[16] See e.g. Abram Chayes, *The Cuban Missile Crisis* (Oxford University Press, 1974). See also Kal Raustiala, 'Compliance and Effectiveness in International Regulatory Cooperation' (2000) 32 *Case Western Reserve International Law Journal* 387 at 391–9; Ronald B. Mitchell, 'Compliance Theory', in Daniel Bodansky, Jutta Brunnée and Ellen Hey (eds.), *The Oxford Handbook of International Environmental Law* (Oxford University Press, 2007), p. 903.

[17] See Franck, above note 3, p. 3.

[18] See the various examples provided by Franck, above note 15 *passim*.

[19] Franck, above note 3, p. 26. [20] Franck, above note 15 at 706.

[21] See e.g. Kal Raustiala and Anne-Marie Slaughter, 'International Law, International Relations and Compliance', in Walter Carlsnaes, Thomas Risse and Beth Simmons (eds.), *Handbook of International Relations* (London: Sage, 2002), p. 541.

[22] We have already highlighted the legitimacy factors posited by Franck in Chapter 1: determinacy, symbolic validation, coherence, and adherence. See above Chapter 1, text accompanying note 123.

four factors posited by Franck, encompassing a rule's congruence with underlying social norms, continuous participation of relevant actors in norm-building, and a practice based upon substantial fulfilment of the criteria of legality.[23]

Second, and most importantly for present purposes, while Franck sees legitimacy as a trait that can be added to rules that are already obligatory,[24] we see the internal legitimacy of international law, its obligatory force, and its compliance pull as inextricably linked. Franck ties his legitimacy factors into Hart's analytical positivism, emphasizing the importance of adherence of a rule to the secondary rules of the legal system and, in turn, to an ultimate rule of recognition.[25] The differences between Franck's account and ours are encapsulated in his legitimacy factor of 'adherence' and our legality criterion of 'congruence', respectively.

In Franck's theory, 'adherence' is a marker of a rule's formal pedigree, attesting that legal obligation is primarily a formal concept for Franck. Pedigree, in turn, adds to the legitimacy of the rule and so is said to enhance its compliance pull. The question remains how 'adherence' to an assumed rule of recognition creates obligation, and why such adherence would increase legitimacy. Franck's answer is that a rule's legitimacy derives in part from the perception that it originated from 'right process', including from 'valid sources'.[26] We agree, of course, that right process is crucial to legal legitimacy: that is why our account places emphasis on the criteria and practice of legality. We also agree that adherence to formal criteria (including recourse to generally recognized 'sources' of international law) can enhance legal legitimacy. As we explained in Chapter 1, reliance on formal tools, such as treaties or custom, to publicize and

[23] See above Chapter 1, text accompanying notes 122–5.

[24] See Franck, above note 15 at 705.

[25] Building on Hart's conception, Franck argues that the legitimacy of the rule of recognition 'cannot be demonstrated by reference to any other validating rules or procedures, but only by the conduct of nations manifesting their belief in the ultimate rule's validity *as the irreducible prerequisites for an international concept of right process.*' Franck, above note 3, p. 194 (emphasis in original). Franck looks to 'membership' in the international community as the ultimate explanation for law's obligatory force. See *ibid.*, pp. 8, 38 and 190 *et seq.*; Franck, above note 8, p. 29; and Michael Byers, *Custom, Power and the Power of Rules* (Cambridge University Press, 1999), p. 8 (suggesting that the 'social character of inter-State relations' is the basis of obligation). See also Friedrich V. Kratochwil, 'How Do Norms Matter?', in Michael Byers (ed.), *The Role of Law in International Politics: Essays in International Relations and International Law* (Cambridge University Press, 2000), pp. 40–1 (offering a powerful critique of arguments that 'membership' can serve as the basis of legal obligation).

[26] Franck, above note 15 at 706.

clarify law is perfectly consonant with the criteria of legality that we set out. At the same time, on its own, such formality does not illuminate the concept of obligation, nor is it helpful simply to rely on a rule of recognition and, therefore, assume precisely what must be shown to exist – obligation.

That is why 'congruence' plays a central role in our account of legality. The legitimacy of legal rules is enhanced when they substantially meet criteria such as generality, promulgation, reasonableness, clarity or predictability – criteria that overlap with Franck's legitimacy factors. As we have explained, fulfilment of these requirements builds legal legitimacy because these features enable actors to reason with law.[27] But interactional obligation must also be practised to maintain its influence, a crucial point to which we return in the next section. Because obligation depends in large part upon the reciprocity or mutuality of expectations among participants in a legal system – a reciprocity that we have described as collectively built and maintained[28] – it exists only when a society's actual legal practices are 'congruent' with existing norms.

As we have explained in the preceding chapters, this proposition has several interlocking facets. Official action must be within the bounds of the law and there must be a substantial degree of compliance with that law. But for a congruent legal practice to evolve in the first place – for actors to be able to understand the guidance provided by the law and to reason with it – legal norms themselves must be broadly congruent with wider social practices.[29] If not, the law will seem hypocritical or irrelevant, and therefore without real influence. When these conditions are met, a sense of commitment to the legal system – legal obligation – is created. The key point is that interactional law exerts distinctive 'compliance pull' by inspiring a sense of obligation – *fidelity* – in actors. That sense of obligation is contingent upon 'congruence'.[30] To reiterate, it cannot be produced

[27] See above Chapter 1, text accompanying notes 79–82.

[28] As we explained in Chapter 1, Fuller's version of 'reciprocity', which we adopt, is about the mutual engagement that builds up expectations of legality. It is not the rationalist account of reciprocal advantage or material exchange. See above Chapter 1, text accompanying notes 67–88.

[29] See above Chapter 1, text accompanying note 20. See also above Chapter 2, text accompanying notes 63–7.

[30] But, to be clear, our argument is not that compliance equals, or provides evidence of, obligation. The point is that compliance (or 'congruence') is part of what builds obligation.

simply through 'adherence' to a rule of recognition or reliably identified by purely formal indicators.[31]

The plausibility of our interactional account finds confirmation in people's everyday experience with law. Most people respect the law, and tend to feel obligated to comply with it (again, note that whether and why they do or do not comply in any given case is a separate issue). Why? When people say they have to do something because 'it's the law', or refrain from doing something because it is 'against the law', the reason is not that the relevant requirement is enunciated in a statute or court decision. It is that the idea of 'law' encompasses the very things that we have highlighted – congruence with shared understandings, fulfilment of the requirements of legality, and a sustained practice of legality. Thus, people typically respect statutes, for example, because they are shorthand for legality; but, over time, they do so only if formal manifestations of law in fact represent law in the richer, interactional, sense. Similarly, people do not feel respect for the law, or a statute, simply because it emanates from a superior authority, or because it could be or is being centrally enforced. These factors matter, but like formality they are not decisive on their own, as Fuller's well-known allegory of King Rex's failed efforts at law-making illustrates so well.[32] These considerations also apply to international law. If formality, hierarchy and enforcement are not the reasons why the average citizen feels obligated, why would they be markers of international law and its obligatory effect on international actors?

In summary, we argue that interactionalism, in looking behind the formal, hierarchical manifestations of law, reveals that the power of international law rests in a conscious sense of obligation rooted in a specific form of legal legitimacy. This sense of obligation is not coextensive with compliance, but it does provide a rich explanation of the distinctive influence that law exerts, an influence that tends to promote compliance. Understanding obligation also provides guidance in building and enhancing that influence.

Obligation, in turn, is a sense of commitment and pulls towards compliance. Still, a range of factors will determine whether and why actors in fact comply.

[31] But see Bodansky, above note 13 at 293–4 (arguing that a rule's 'status as law' constitutes a reason for action so creates obligation).

[32] See Lon L. Fuller, *The Morality of Law*, rev. edn (New Haven: Yale University Press, 1969), pp. 33–8. See also our examples of failures to uphold legality in above Chapter 2, text accompanying notes 62–6.

4. Promoting compliance: lessons from interactional law

Compliance theories commonly assume that law-making and compliance questions are discrete concerns. Only once customary or treaty law has been created does it make sense to raise compliance questions, or to turn attention to suitable compliance strategies or mechanisms. The compliance literature typically debates questions such as: how is compliance to be monitored?; what procedures are best suited to assessing compliance and addressing non-compliance?; should incentives be provided to promote compliance?; or should there be penalties or other consequences that deter or punish non-compliance?; and should the outcomes of compliance procedures be legally binding?

These are obviously important questions. But we argue that to answer them more fully, compliance theory must take not just one, but two further analytical steps. It must look beyond positivist assumptions and grapple with the concept of obligation, and it must acknowledge that law-making and compliance are not radically distinct. Rather, they are points on a continuum of legal interaction. A purely formal concept of international law glosses over this fact and obscures opportunities for promoting compliance. Because our interactional theory of legal obligation integrates law-making and compliance questions, it sheds new light on the entire compliance continuum, and on the concept of compliance itself.

4.1 Building the foundations for compliance through law-making

The overarching lesson to be derived from interactionalism is one that we have stressed at various points already: law's obligatory power – its 'self-binding' effect – must be cultivated and maintained. The hard work of building obligation begins at the law-making stage, as do the foundations for compliance. The creation of formal legal rules may play an important role in this context, but formal law-making alone is not enough. Interactional law instructs that the creation of obligations presupposes transparent and inclusive processes. Law-makers must also pay attention to the congruence of prospective legal norms with shared understandings, construct norms and regimes in keeping with criteria of legality, and instantiate a practice of legality.

We will examine the practical implications of these insights more closely in subsequent chapters, when we consider specific issue areas through the lens of interactional law. By way of a brief illustration, for present purposes suffice it to point to the experience with the framework-protocol approach to environmental regime building. The foundations for this approach to treaty-making are established in the initial framework agreement. Typically, these agreements do not include demanding commitments, but enshrine basic principles or treaty objectives and provide for institutions and processes through which views can be exchanged and subsequent law-making can occur. At a later stage, specific commitments are added through amendments or protocols to the framework. Interactional law suggests that the prospects of compliance with such a regime will depend in part on the degree to which its principles and goals either represent genuinely shared understandings, or come to be shared by parties as they interact in the context of the treaty. Interactional processes framed by the regime play a crucial role in this regard. In turn, attention to legality criteria helps cultivate the sense of obligation that pulls towards compliance. For example, law-makers should seek to ensure that specific commitments are compatible with the regime's basic principles and goals, that treaty requirements are reasonable and predictable in their implications for parties, and that subsequent interpretations or applications of the treaty are congruent with its terms or with the meanings given to treaty terms by such practice.

We are not the first, of course, to stress the need to identify the features that pull towards compliance with law and to take concrete steps to strengthen them. Thomas Franck made a similar point regarding the practical value of his legitimacy criteria.[33] He has also gone furthest among the norm-oriented compliance theorists in connecting compliance and legal obligation. Indeed, he once observed that 'the degree to which a rule is obeyed affects the *degree* to which a rule is cognizable as a valid obligation. Conversely, the extent to which a rule is cognizable as a legitimate obligation affects the extent to which it is obeyed.'[34] We agree with the second part of this observation; it is central to understanding law's ability to attract compliance. We also agree that compliance (or 'congruence') is part of what nourishes obligation.[35] However, as we have just explained,

[33] See Franck, above note 15 at 711–12.

[34] Franck, above note 3, p. 44 (emphasis in original).

[35] It is in this sense that we have previously argued that law's existence is related to the influence that it exerts. See Jutta Brunnée and Stephen J. Toope, 'International Law and Constructivism: Elements of an Interactional Theory of International Law' (2000) 39 *Columbia Journal of Transnational Law* 19 at 65. This proposition is, of course, inherent in the concept of a community of practice that we employ. However, as our distinction

for us this also means that obligation cannot be explained solely in terms of formal 'validity'. Nor can the formal characteristics of rules by themselves, i.e. how they are created in specific institutions, explain why they exert influence.

Franck's legitimacy theory was quite consciously focused only on the 'rule' component of the compliance picture. While we agree that this focus is important, we also believe that it is incomplete. Franck acknowledged as much through his reference to the importance of the degree to which a legal rule is obeyed in practice. Indeed, he cautioned that the 'focus on the properties of rules ... is not a self-sufficient account of the socialization process'. Attention must also be paid to '[h]ow rules are made, interpreted and applied'.[36] Another central lesson from *interactional* law goes to precisely this point: law's distinctive features are not reducible to the norms it provides; law exists when norms that meet the requirements of legality are embedded in actual *practice*.

4.2 *Building spaces and opportunities for interaction*

If the creation and maintenance of shared understandings requires interactions within a community of practice,[37] and the creation and maintenance of interactional law requires a distinctive practice of legality,[38] then it is crucial to cultivate spaces and opportunities for engagement with and around legal norms.

International institutions, be they international organizations or treaty bodies, can furnish such spaces, and the deliberations that occur under their auspices offer opportunities for legal interaction. Particularly important is the fact that such settings enable ongoing interactions and so allow for the emergence of relatively dense communities of practice.[39] The plenary bodies of many international treaties, for example, meet at regular intervals to review and develop the terms of the treaty, to assess the adequacy of commitments, or to review the performance of treaty parties.

between commitment and compliance makes clear, we do not conflate 'effects with causes', as has been suggested. See Kal Raustiala, 'Form and Substance in International Agreements' (2005) 99 *American Journal of International Law* 581 at 582.

36 Franck, above note 15 at 712–13.

37 See above Chapter 2, text accompanying notes 34–53.

38 See above Chapter 2, text accompanying notes 75–6.

39 See also Antje Wiener, 'Enacting Meaning-in-Use: Qualitative Research on Norms and International Relations' (2009) 35 *Review of International Studies* 175 at 181 (discussing the importance of opportunities for deliberation and norm contestation to build the meaning of norms).

Usually, the activities of various sub-bodies dealing with technical or legal issues feed into and interact with these plenary activities.

To the extent that a regime provides for implementation review processes, or even specific compliance procedures, interactional opportunities are significantly enhanced. Such processes require parties to justify their performance in light of the treaty's requirements. We argue that the compliance pull of the treaty norms will be stronger if the relevant norms meet the requirements of interactional law – congruence with shared understandings, adherence to criteria of legality, and enmeshment of the norms in a practice of legality. Conversely, these factors help ensure that the justificatory burden that rests upon individual parties will be heavier; other parties are less likely to be persuaded by arguments that deviate from interactional law. Sometimes the ensuing interactions will also lead parties to clarify or refine the terms of a treaty. Either way, compliance processes feed back into law-making activities, by reasserting the original norm, by shifting, or even abandoning it. As we suggested earlier, in an interactional understanding of law there is no bright line boundary between law-making and compliance processes. What matters is that attention is paid throughout to the requirements of interactional law.

We have just provided examples of relatively strongly institutionalized international settings. Such settings, in providing ample space and opportunity for ongoing interactions, are particularly well suited to building interactional law and promoting compliance with common norms. Two clarifications are in order. First, institutionalization alone is not enough to generate obligation; institutionalized law-making should not be confused with interactional law-making.[40] Second, highlighting the benefits of institutionalized contexts does not mean that interactional law can

[40] That is why we have insisted that our approach must be distinguished from a cluster of institutionalist theories that have been grouped by some under the label of 'transformationalism'. See George W. Downs, Kyle W. Danish and Peter N. Barsoom, 'The Transformational Model of International Regime Design: Triumph of Hope or Experience?' (2000) 38 *Columbia Journal of Transnational Law* 465 at 467. We have cautioned elsewhere that the transformationalist label has the potential to confuse rather than assist the compliance debate. The ostensible transformationalists, as cited by Downs *et al.* in support of the approach's various design principles, do not share a theoretical outlook but subscribe to a variety of approaches to law and international relations, ranging from critical, to positivist, to game theoretical, to constructivist. See *ibid.* at 467, note 2 (citing Chayes and Chayes, Brunnée and Toope, Levy, Széll, Koskenniemi, and Koh). Elsewhere they cite, for example, Brown Weiss (note 9), Haas (note 11), Bodansky (note 18), Benvenisti (note 33), Lang (note 34), Handl (note 46), and Setear (note 76). For a detailed discussion, see Jutta Brunnée and Stephen J. Toope, 'Persuasion and Enforcement: Explaining Compliance with International Law' (2002) 13 *Finnish Yearbook of International Law* 273 at 280–6.

exist, and exert compliance pull, only in such settings. The communities of practice that make, maintain and re-make international law also operate in the more diffuse setting of the larger international system. As we explained in Chapter 2, communities of practice can encompass states and other international actors. In the face of non-compliance, the efforts of such actors to reassert shared norms play a crucial role in upholding norms, and in drawing delinquent actors back towards compliance. A broad spectrum of spaces and opportunities exists for a widening range of actors to participate in interactional law-making.[41] For example, since 11 September 2001 vigorous efforts to uphold the rule on the prohibition of torture have been undertaken by international organizations, individual diplomats and politicians, government lawyers, high-ranking military officers, non-governmental organizations, academics, journalists, and the proverbial person in the street protesting against attempts to weaken the prohibition. The spaces in which these interactions occurred were equally diverse, ranging from UN meetings to domestic legislatures, and courts to national media, to the internet, and more.[42]

Clearly, in such diffuse settings actors must work all the harder to uphold international legality and maintain law's compliance pull. We are not suggesting that such efforts will always be successful. The challenges are significant and, it bears repeating, they are ongoing – the hard work of international law is never done. If norms are to prevail and maintain compliance pull, they must be reasserted again and again. Upholding interactional law and its attendant practice of legality, then, becomes increasingly difficult in the face of non-compliant behaviour.

The same is true in more institutionalized settings provided by international regimes. Through the continuing law-making and compliance processes that such regimes provide, greater opportunities exist for

[41] See also Kal Raustiala, 'The Architecture of International Cooperation: Transgovernmental Networks and the Future of International Law' (2002) 43 *Virginia Journal of International Law* 1 at 10–16.

[42] Josh White and Carol D. Leonnig, 'U.S. Cites Exception to Torture Ban', *The Washington Post*, 3 March 2006, p. A04. See also Kofi Annan, *Prohibition of Torture 'Absolute', Binding on all States, in all Circumstances, Says Secretary-General in Message on International Day*, 17 April 2004, at www.un.org/News/Press/docs/2004/sgsm9373.doc.htm; Center for Human Rights and Global Justice, *Beyond Guantanámo: Transfers to Torture One Year After* Rasul v. Bush (New York University School of Law, 2005); United Kingdom All Party Parliamentary Group on Extraordinary Rendition, *Briefing: Torture by Proxy: International Law Applicable to 'Extraordinary Renditions'*, prepared by The Center for Human Rights and Global Justice, December 2005; and Jane Mayer, 'Outsourcing Torture', *The New Yorker*, 14 February 2005.

normative interaction and for focused efforts to maintain the regime's compliance pull: but, as we already suggested, the normative horizons can shift in any community of practice, however tightly knit. The interactional framework, then, holds a twofold message for international law and policymakers.

On the one hand, the chances for the emergence of a community of practice and opportunities for interactional law-making with its attendant compliance pull are enhanced by greater density and continuity of interaction. International organizations and treaty-based regimes, although not the only settings in which interactional law can operate, are especially well placed to foster that density. In highlighting the value of institutionalization and repeated interactions, therefore, we share common ground with some of the most prominent norm-oriented compliance theories,[43] notably the managerialism advanced by Abram Chayes and Antonia Handler Chayes,[44] and Ryan Goodman and Derek Jinks's account of state socialization.[45]

On the other hand, however, it is important to understand that not just any kind of institutionalization or interaction will do. This point goes to the core distinction between our account and the managerialist and state socialization theories. As we have argued extensively, law entails a particular form of interaction. Legal obligation, and with it law's compliance pull, is created and maintained through a distinctive practice of legality. We are therefore not convinced by the reliance of the managerialist and state socialization theories on a positivist conception of international law. The attendant lack of interest in the nature and effects of legal obligation undercuts the explanatory potential of both theories.

[43] Note that rationalist compliance theories, too, emphasize the role of institutions. Most prominently, the neo-liberal institutionalism that we described in the Introduction focuses on the role of institutions and repeated interactions in shaping states' self-interest, and in 'lengthening the shadow of the future' so as to counter-balance states' short-term interests. We do not deny that institutionalization can have these effects. Rather, we argue that this perspective, due to its focus on interests and reliance on a positivist account of law, misses important dimensions of the compliance picture. See Introduction, text accompanying notes 30–2. On the idea of the shadow of the future, see Robert Axelrod, *The Evolution of Cooperation*, rev. edn (New York: Basic Books, 2006), pp. 126–32. See also John Setear, 'An Iterative Perspective on Treaties: A Synthesis of International Relations Theory and International Law' (1996) 37 *Harvard International Law Journal* 139.

[44] Abram Chayes and Antonia Handler Chayes, *The New Sovereignty: Compliance with International Regulatory Agreements* (Cambridge, Mass: Harvard University Press, 1995).

[45] Ryan Goodman and Derek Jinks, 'International Law and State Socialization: Conceptual, Empirical, and Normative Challenges' (2005) 54 *Duke Law Journal* 983.

In keeping with its roots in the American legal process school,[46] the central elements of the managerial approach are continuous processes of argument and persuasion, 'justificatory discourse' that ultimately 'jawbones' states into compliance.[47] Building in part on Franck's account of legitimacy,[48] the Chayes highlight the role of international law in framing such discourse. The argument is that states' explanations for their conduct tend to be more compelling when in conformity with a legal rule and that 'good legal argument can generally be distinguished from bad'.[49] We share the Chayes's interest in 'justificatory discourse' and in the ways in which international law influences state behaviour by framing the boundaries of persuasion and argument. We could also not agree more with the Chayes's challenge to the focus 'on a narrow set of externally defined "interests",' which diverts 'analytic attention … from a wide range of institutional and political mechanisms that in practice bear the burden of efforts to enhance treaty compliance'.[50]

However, the Chayesean framework also leaves many of the most important questions unanswered. It does not explore in any detail *how* good legal argument is distinguished from bad, and what accounts for the legitimacy of international law. While Chayes and Chayes build their compliance strategy upon treaty parties' 'general sense of obligation to comply with a legally binding prescription',[51] they do not explain how that sense of obligation is generated. It is simply assumed to exist in response to (formally) binding law.[52] Deeper questions about the binding effect of law are side-stepped, and its role in influencing actors remains obscure.

In fact, when the reference to a 'general sense of obligation' is unpacked, managerialism is dependent upon a rationalist, interest-based account of state behaviour, and not on obligation. According to Chayes and Chayes, it is the condition of the 'new sovereignty', that is states' growing interdependence and enmeshment in a 'complex web of

[46] See e.g. Henry Hart Jr. and Albert Sacks, *The Legal Process: Basic Problems in the Making and Application of Law* (Westbury, N.Y.: Foundation Press, 1994).

[47] Chayes and Chayes, above note 44, pp. 25–6.

[48] *Ibid.*, pp. 127–34. [49] *Ibid.*, p. 119.

[50] See Abram Chayes and Antonia Handler Chayes, 'On Compliance' (1993) 47 *International Organization* 175 at 178.

[51] Chayes and Chayes, above note 44, p. 110.

[52] The Chayes's account too is based upon Hartian positivism. *Ibid.* See also above Chapter 1, text accompanying notes 70–1.

international arrangements',[53] that underpins managerial strategies.[54] Most states today can only realize their sovereignty through participation in various international regimes. The need to remain a member 'in reasonably good standing in the regimes that make up the substance of international life',[55] therefore, is more likely to explain compliance with commitments than costs or benefits in the context of an individual regime.[56]

The premise of the 'new sovereignty' harkens back to long-standing, pragmatic explanations of 'how nations behave': because it is in their interest to maintain orderly international relations and to remain respected and influential players.[57] The Chayes's particular contribution is to augment Henkin by demonstrating the growing enmeshment of states in international regulatory regimes, and the importance of justificatory processes in deepening this enmeshment in individual cases. We do not disagree with the proposition that involvement in regimes can affect actors' interest assessments, but we suggest that the 'enmeshment' described by Chayes and Chayes has the potential to do considerably more. To the extent that actors become engaged in a community of practice that generates shared understandings and ties them into a practice of legality, they will develop a sense of obligation that pulls

[53] Chayes and Chayes, above note 44, p. 27. [54] *Ibid.*, pp. 26 and 28.

[55] *Ibid.*, p. 28. In their emphasis on membership, the Chayes share ground with Franck. However, membership plays an even stronger explanatory role for Franck, who sees membership in the club of states as the very locus of obligation. See Franck, above note 15. By contrast, the Chayes appear to locate the source of obligation in the principle of *pacta sunt servanda*. See Chayes and Chayes, above note 44, pp. 8 and 116.

[56] Chayes and Chayes, *ibid.*, p. 27.

[57] More than thirty years ago, Louis Henkin observed that:

> Nations have a common interest in keeping the society running and keeping international relations orderly. They observe laws they do not care about to maintain others that they value, and to keep 'the system' intact; they observe law when it 'hurts' so that others will observe laws to their benefit ... Considerations of 'honor', 'prestige', 'leadership', 'influence', 'reputation', which figure prominently in governmental decisions, often weigh in favour of observing law.

Louis Henkin, *How Nations Behave: Law and Foreign Policy*, 2nd edn (New York: Columbia University Press, 1979), p. 48. The Chayes's observations regarding the impact of the 'new sovereignty' on state behaviour are strikingly similar:

> The [compliance] process works because modern states are bound in a tightly woven fabric of international agreements, organizations, and institutions ... The integrity and reliability of this system are of overriding importance for most states, most of the time ... Connection to the rest of the world and the political ability to be an actor within it are more important than any tangible benefits in explaining compliance with international regulatory agreements.

Chayes and Chayes, above note 44, pp. 26 and 27.

towards compliance and imbues justificatory discourse with distinctive qualities.

Ryan Goodman and Derek Jinks have developed an account of 'state socialization' that is complementary to managerialism, while also pushing its implications further towards constructivist analysis than Chayes and Chayes were prepared to go. The Chayes were satisfied with the idea that treaty-making and application are processes during which states can learn and discover their interests.[58] By contrast, based on a sociological understanding of state sovereignty, Goodman and Jinks argue that states' identities, interests or organizational structures are all shaped in significant part by global regimes.[59] Although Goodman and Jinks observe that debates about regime design 'inadequately attend to the ways in which law influences state behavior',[60] they too take legal obligation (specifically, formal treaty obligation) for granted and do not inquire into its nature and effects. Instead, their focus is on 'the social mechanisms of law's influence'.[61]

Their contribution is to argue that the influence of international norms and regimes is not fully explained through dynamics of persuasion or coercion. 'Acculturation', they argue, is a crucial third mechanism to bring about state conformity with international norms, even in the absence of persuasive or coercive means.[62] Whereas coercion involves social sanctions that will entail material costs, acculturation entails only social costs.[63] This type of social pressure also distinguishes acculturation from persuasion, which involves social learning.[64] Unlike persuasion, then, acculturation produces 'outward conformity ... without private acceptance'.[65] It leads actors to 'adopt the beliefs and behavioral patterns of the surrounding culture'.[66]

[58] See Chayes and Chayes, above note 50 at 179–85; and Chayes and Chayes, above note 44, pp. 4–8.

[59] Ryan Goodman and Derek Jinks, 'Toward an Institutional Theory of Sovereignty' (2003) 55 *Stanford Law Review* 1749 at 1752.

[60] Goodman and Jinks, above note 45 at 983. [61] *Ibid.*

[62] Ryan Goodman and Derek Jinks, 'How to Influence States: Socialization and International Human Rights Law' (2004) 54 *Duke Law Journal* 621.

[63] *Ibid.* at 645.

[64] *Ibid.* at 635 and 643. As Goodman and Jinks point out, constructivist writing does not always clearly distinguish persuasion from social pressure. See *ibid.* at 631.

[65] *Ibid.* at 643. See also Alastair Iain Johnston, 'Treating International Institutions as Social Environments' (2001) 45 *International Studies Quarterly* 487 at 499.

[66] Goodman and Jinks, above note 45 at 992.

Whether or not it matters that the 'culture' in question is a legal culture, and whether or not the 'social mechanisms of law's influence' are distinctive precisely because they revolve around law, remains unclear. Goodman and Jinks appear to consider these questions to be of secondary interest. Indeed, they specifically state that '[a]cculturation depends less on the properties of the rule than on the properties of the relationship of the actor to the community'.[67] We agree that 'relationships' are crucial, both to norm development and actor compliance with these norms, but we question Goodman and Jinks's neglect of the 'properties' of principles and rules. In their framework, presumably because 'acculturation' involves not persuasion but social pressure,[68] it does not seem to matter whether or not the norms or 'culture' into which actors are socialized are *legal*.

We are not convinced by this approach, which appears to rely on an extremely thin, formal concept of law and depicts actors as motivated by (social) costs and benefits rather than any sense of obligation. Goodman and Jinks's model may have merit when international norms exist only in a formal sense. However, José Alvarez is correct in his observation that persuasion is unlikely to be completely absent, even in circumstances involving social pressure to conform with international law.[69] This assessment applies with even greater force when interactional law comes into play. The 'logic of appropriateness' is driven in distinctive ways by international law. Why else would actors feel a pressure to conform to given community standards and ask 'what should I do in these circumstances'? As Alvarez points out, Goodman and Jinks's account may explain why states join international agreements, but not why they would 'go beyond such symbolic acts' and actively ensure that their commitments are met.[70]

To summarize, like managerialism and state socialization theory, our framework stresses the importance of ongoing interactions for the promotion of compliance. It explains why it is important to create and *use* settings in which such interactions can take place. However, unlike managerialism and state socialization, our theory emphasizes the distinctive

[67] Goodman and Jinks, above note 62 at 643.

[68] *Ibid.* at 626, 643, and 645. See also José E. Alvarez, 'Do States Socialize?' (2004) 54 *Duke Law Journal* 961 at 970 (observing that Goodman and Jinks's approach 'presume[s] that states sometimes act like trendy teenagers unthinkingly following the latest fad').

[69] See Alvarez, *ibid.*

[70] *Ibid.* at 971. For an initial response, see Goodman and Jinks, above note 45 at 991–8.

features of legal interaction and explains why these features, and the manner in which law exerts influence, are inextricably tied to legal obligation.

4.3 *Extending the practice of legality: non-compliance procedures, dispute settlement and enforcement*

The literature on compliance with international law has devoted much attention to the role of compliance mechanisms, dispute settlement, and enforcement measures.[71] Binding dispute settlement and enforcement are often treated as the 'gold standard' that cannot be achieved in most areas of international law. Many in the international environmental movement, for example, express regret that the area lacks mechanisms comparable to those available under the auspices of the World Trade Organization (WTO) to settle trade disputes.[72] Instead of such compulsory and binding processes, compliance processes with legally non-binding outcomes and strong emphasis on facilitation of compliance now dominate fields such as environmental law or human rights law.[73] Some commentators treat these types of 'soft' mechanisms as a compromise, or even a sell-out that threatens to undermine international law.[74] Others argue that managerial

[71] See e.g. U. Beyerlin, P. T. Stoll and R. Wolfrum (eds.), *Ensuring Compliance with Multilateral Environmental Agreements: A Dialogue between Practitioners and Academia* (Leiden: Brill Academic Publishers, 2006); and Geir Ulfstein, Thilo Marauhn and Andreas Zimmermann (eds.), *Making Treaties Work: Dispute Settlement, Compliance Control and Enforcement in Human Rights, Environmental and Arms Control Agreements* (Cambridge University Press, 2006).

[72] See e.g. arguments for a 'Global Environment Organization' (WEO) that would place international environmental governance under a single WTO-like umbrella and include a dispute settlement mechanism. See Frank Biermann, 'The Case for a World Environment Organization' (2000) 42 *Environment* 22; and Daniel C. Esty and Maria H. Ivanova, 'Revitalizing Global Environmental Governance: A Function-Driver Approach', in Daniel C. Esty and Maria H. Ivanova (eds.), *Global Environmental Governance, Options and Opportunities* (New Haven: Yale School of Forestry and Environmental Studies, 2002). But see Steve Charnovitz, 'WTO Dispute Settlement as a Model for International Governance', in Alexandre Kiss, Dinah Shelton and Kanami Ishibashi (eds.), *Economic Globalization and Compliance with International Environmental Law* (The Hague: Kluwer Law International, 2003), pp. 252–3 (arguing that while environmentalists can learn from the WTO's dispute settlement system, the 'stick' of trade sanctions is not the best means to compliance in the international environmental arena).

[73] See Ulfstein *et al.*, above note 71.

[74] See e.g. Jan Klabbers, 'Compliance Procedures', in Bodansky *et al.*, above note 16, p. 995; and Martti Koskenniemi, 'Breach of Treaty or Non-Compliance? Reflections on the Enforcement of the Montreal Protocol' (1992) 3 *Yearbook of International Environmental Law* 123.

mechanisms are actually better suited to promoting compliance with international agreements than enforcement-oriented approaches.[75]

Managerialism was in part a response to realist claims that international law was fatally weakened by the absence of enforcement.[76] It builds on the assumption that states generally enter into commitments with an intention to comply and that non-compliance more often results from norm ambiguities or capacity limitations than from deliberate disregard.[77] For this reason, as Chayes and Chayes have rightly argued, it is important to identify the causes of non-compliance in a given case, and to take them into account in developing response measures. For example, when there are genuine ambiguities in the underlying norms, clarification or further development of the relevant standards would seem to be the most appropriate response, as the interactional account would also suggest. Compliance procedures play an important role in this regard. Similarly, if non-compliance results from capacity limitations rather than deliberate disregard of norms, facilitation and capacity-building are generally the most effective, and also most appropriate, response. In such circumstances, enforcement would seem neither a promising avenue, nor one that is likely to strengthen the legal regime in the longer run.

We agree, therefore, with the basic thrust of the Chayesian argument for a 'cooperative, problem-solving approach' to promoting compliance,[78] and with their prescription of a blend of transparency (with respect to both the norms and procedures of the regime and the performance of its members), dispute settlement, and capacity-building.[79] But we also believe that Chayes and Chayes were too categorical in their assertion that 'sanctioning authority is rarely granted by treaty, rarely used when granted, and likely to be ineffective when used'.[80] We suggest that it is their failure

[75] For an overview on the debate between managerial and enforcement-oriented approaches, see Kyle Danish, 'Management v. Enforcement: The New Debate on Promoting Treaty Compliance' (1997) 37 *Virginia Journal of International Law* 789. See also Anastasia A. Angelova, 'Compelling Compliance with International Regimes: China and the Missile Technology Control Regime' (1999) 38 *Columbia Journal of Transnational Law* 419 at 422–34. Both Danish and Angelova conclude, correctly, that the pointed disagreements between the two schools have obscured the fact that many of their respective claims are actually compatible.

[76] See e.g. Hans Morgenthau, 'Théorie des sanctions internationales' (1935) 16 *Revue de Droit International et de Legislation Comparée* 474 and 809.

[77] Chayes and Chayes, above note 44, pp. 10–15. [78] *Ibid.*, p. 3. [79] *Ibid.*, pp. 22–5.

[80] *Ibid.*, pp. 32–3. This proposition has been challenged by a variety of authors. For example, some compliance scholars emphasize that the relative need for incentives and disincentives, and their feasibility, depend upon the type of 'game' or incentive structures that underlie a given regime. The argument is that sanctions or threats of punishment are

to pay due regard to legal obligation that leads them to this narrow view of the role that enforcement can play in international law. Chayes and Chayes are obviously right to caution that blind faith in enforcement is uncalled for, but they do not sufficiently consider the circumstances in which enforcement measures could be legitimate and therefore acceptable and effective.

In our view, the theoretical debate about the relative merits of 'soft', facilitative compliance mechanisms and 'hard', enforcement-oriented approaches has been unnecessarily polarized.[81] We have already illustrated in above section 2 that a range of different factors (such as a sense of obligation, interests, or power) may determine whether or not actors comply with international law in given circumstances. Similarly, different 'social mechanisms' can come into play in influencing actors. For example, Goodman and Jinks argue that persuasion, coercion and acculturation are each important, although they play different roles and are likely to be most successful in different circumstances.[82] We do not necessarily disagree with these claims. However, unlike Goodman and Jinks, we believe that one of the salient 'differences' is whether or not the underlying norm is a legal norm, and whether that norm is merely valid in the formal sense or also obligatory in the interactional sense.

A further point follows: as presented by Goodman and Jinks, socialization is a uni-directional 'mechanism'.[83] Target actors are persuaded or coerced into compliance, or pressured into conformity with the extant 'culture' or norms. Such 'mechanisms' may well account for some of the dynamics that bring about compliance, but they capture only part of the picture. Inherent in constructivism is the proposition that norms and actors are interdependent. To capture this mutuality, some constructivist accounts of compliance examine processes of 'arguing' or 'contestation'.[84]

necessary where strong incentives to defect exist. This will usually not be the case in a 'coordination game', but will be when agreements resemble 'mixed-motive games'. See especially George W. Downs, David M. Rocke and Peter N. Barsoom, 'Is the Good News about Compliance Good News about Cooperation?' (1996) 50 *International Organization* 379.

[81] See also Jutta Brunnée, 'Enforcement Mechanisms in International Law and International Environmental Law', in Beyerlin *et al.*, above note 71, p. 1.

[82] See Goodman and Jinks, above note 62 at 700–1; and Goodman and Jinks, above note 45 at 992.

[83] On this point, see further below section 4.5.

[84] See e.g. Thomas Risse, '"Let's Argue!": Communicative Action in World Politics' (2000) 54 *International Organization* 1; and Antje Wiener, 'Contested Compliance: Interventions on the Normative Structure in World Politics' (2004) 10 *European Journal of International Relations* 189.

In our view, persuasion, arguing or contestation, acculturation, and coercion are all modes of interaction that are shaped by, and in turn shape, norms that exist within communities of practice. As we explained in Chapter 2, formal legal rules may or may not be norms in this social sense, and they may or may not give expression to interactional law. But when legality *is* interactional, each of these modes of interaction entails collective engagement with, and around, legal norms, and is distinctive because it forms part of a broader practice of legality.

These considerations lead us to suggest that the 'hard' vs. 'soft' dichotomy both over-emphasizes the importance of the formal legal status of compliance mechanisms, and misconstrues the role of attendant enforcement measures. It is misguided to assume that a cure for international law's perceived ills can be found simply in the creation of formal procedures and the pursuit of 'hard' enforcement.[85] To be feasible and productive, enforcement measures, just like compliance mechanisms or dispute settlement, must be embedded in the shared understandings and the practice of legality that generate interactional law and, through it, obligation. To reiterate, the binding nature of an international norm is separate from the question of its enforceability,[86] and, once the idea of obligation is separated from sanction, enforcement can play a role distinct from the

[85] And yet, this view is as pervasive as it is persistent, in both theory and practice. Perhaps unconsciously, many international lawyers still look to enforcement as an answer to the perceived ineffectiveness of international law, hence the recent focus upon binding dispute settlement and the tracing of a trajectory of institutional, even bureaucratic, 'legalization'. See Abbott *et al.*, above note 9. In the political arena, national leaders have sought to reassure constituents by asserting that seemingly intrusive international norms are not genuinely enforceable. For example, in the context of the debate about Canada's ratification of the Kyoto Protocol, then Deputy Prime Minister, John Manley, was quoted in the press as saying that although 'Canada should take its Kyoto obligations seriously if the pact is ratified ... the accord is not a legally enforceable contract.' Patrick Brethour, Steven Chase and Jill Mahoney, 'Kyoto not binding, Manley says', *The Globe and Mail*, 14 November 2002, p. A7. Similarly, Justice Louis LeBel of the Canadian Supreme Court observed that '[a]s international law is generally non-binding or without effective control mechanisms, it does not suffice to simply state that international law requires a certain outcome.' See L. LeBel and G. Chao, 'The Rise of International Law in Canadian Constitutional Litigation: Fugue or Fusion? Recent Developments and Challenges in Internalizing International Law' (2002) 16 *Supreme Court Law Review* 23 at 62.

[86] This point, of course, is also made by strongly positivist international lawyers. See e.g. Prosper Weil, 'Le droit international en quête de son identité' (1992) 237 *Récueil des Cours de l'Academie de Droit International* 13 at 53 (calling for a breaking up of the 'couple diabolique obligation-sanction'). And see Sir Gerald Fitzmaurice, 'The Foundations of the Authority of International Law and the Problem of Enforcement' (1956) 19 *Modern Law Review* 1 at 2 (noting that '[t]he law is not binding because it is enforced: it is enforced because it is already binding').

effective validation of a norm. Thus, enforcement is best viewed as only one element of a practice of legality. It is not a surrogate for the existence of binding law. In an interactional theory of international law, enforcement's role is also symbolic. It is ideally an expression of the intention of international society in advance of any actual breach of a norm to punish the breach through the use of some form of force, be it economic, social or military. Enforcement is the collective disapproval of international society. It is the promise and the reality of collectively imposed punishment. The enforcement is not purely symbolic once it is actually applied, of course: willingness to resort to force remains important to ensure the integrity of the collective disapprobation. The actual application of force should remain exceptional.

Because of the horizontal nature of international society, and the lack of strong hierarchical mechanisms with a monopoly on the legitimate use of force, genuine collective enforcement is rare.[87] The enforcement of norms in the common interest is often pursued through forms of reprisal that are unilateral, yet the unilateral action is justified only on the basis of collective disapprobation.[88] Debates over the 'enforcement' of Security Council resolutions are a vivid illustration of this problem. Once a normative framework has been established through resolutions of the Security Council,[89] but the Council then finds itself unable or unwilling to apply force to implement the norms, is there any residual right for individual states to 'enforce' the Security Council's norms? One reading of the debates over the international response to Iraq would emphasize the US's and UK's justification for potential war as an implementation of Security Council resolutions. The situation is clouded by the parallel justification on the grounds of pre-emptive self-defence, which would not then amount to 'enforcement' but to self-help.

[87] International law remains primarily horizontal in its functioning despite the emergence in the specific treaty contexts of hierarchical mechanisms of interpretation and implementation. The empirical fact of increasing 'delegation' of decision-making authority, to use the terminology of the 'legalization' project (see Abott *et al.* above note 9), does not tell us very much about how meaningful these mechanisms are. As we have argued, formal 'enforcement' alone does not guarantee compliance.

[88] Of course, states are also able unilaterally to enforce norms that go to specific state interests. In other words, reprisals for direct violations of a state's rights remain possible. Even here, however, there is a form of collective constraint in that the rights of individual states are constructed within a normative framework that sometimes legitimates unilateral vindication.

[89] We are not arguing that Security Council resolutions are necessarily legitimate simply because of their provenance. That issue is beyond the scope of this chapter. We are simply trying to illustrate the link between collective norms and unilateral action.

Of course, even without 'hard' enforcement, international law need not be as ineffective as many observers claim. This point is illustrated by the broad conception of 'enforcement' that Paul De Visscher offered in his 1972 *Cours général de droit international public*. Apart from what he referred to as *techniques institutionelles* (involving international institutions), and *techniques d'autoprotection* (including self-defence, reprisals, retorsion, or embargos), De Visscher drew attention to the significance of *techniques spontanées* (voluntary compliance with international norms).[90] Indeed, as he suggested:

> Dans la très large mesure où le droit international reflète fidèlement un état de conscience sociale, à ce point fermement établi que les gouvernements eux-mêmes ne sauraient plus l'ignorer ou le défier, le droit international ne requiert, pour sa réalisation, ni juge ni gendarme.[91]

This passage spotlights a crucial question: if collective enforcement through penalties and binding judicial processes still plays only a limited role, what is it that brings about states' compliance with international law – what accounts for its compliance pull? De Visscher points to 'social conscience', but how is it that international law comes to reflect social conscience? Our answer is that this social conscience (for us, shared understandings of legality) and law's distinctive compliance pull are generated through interactional law-making. Interactional international law helps us to identify the reasons for law's binding quality and its influence. As we showed in the preceding section, the requisite legal interactions can occur, and a practice of legality can be maintained, through a variety of processes, ranging from ongoing law-making to soft or hard compliance procedures, and encompassing the full spectrum of De Visscher's 'enforcement techniques'.

But interactionalism also illustrates why the absence of sanctions can nonetheless amount to a weakness of international law: not because enforcement is needed to compel actors, but because failure to enforce can be indicative of a lack of 'congruence' between existing norms and international practice. So long as legal interactions maintain that congruence, there will be little need for sanctions, be they social or material in nature. But when significant instances of non-compliance by one or more actors meet with no, or only selective, responses – when the community

[90] P. De Visscher, 'Cours général de droit international public' (1972) 136 (II) *Récueil des Cours de l'Academie de Droit International* 9 at 137–53.

[91] *Ibid.* at 139.

of practice does not insist that its rules are obeyed – interactional law will come under increasing strain.[92]

In short, when seen through the lens of our interactional framework, treaty-based non-compliance procedures, binding dispute settlement, and enforcement measures all play potentially important roles both in building legality and in promoting compliance. At the same time, if employed arbitrarily, selectively, or not at all, they can each damage the congruence upon which interactional law depends. The most important question to ask about compliance mechanisms and measures, then, is not whether or not they are 'hard' or legally binding in a formal sense, but whether or not they meet the requirements of interactional legality. Both 'hard' and 'soft' approaches can run afoul of these requirements. An important further message for lawyers and policy-makers is that compliance mechanisms or enforcement measures cannot simply be added to a regime or set of norms and expected to function. They must be embraced by the salient community of practice and must become intertwined with its legal interactions.

4.4 *Understanding the interplay between international and domestic law*

To understand compliance, it is not enough to consider only the interactions between states and other actors in the international arena. As Chayes and Chayes have pointed out, many international standards today are not about matters, or conduct, that states control directly.[93] For example, states can decide how to handle diplomatic relations, whether to mount a military strike, or whether to meet disarmament commitments, but most commitments today require extensive domestic regulatory or policy action, and the alteration of conduct within states' societies. For instance, states will not be able to meet their international commitments to reduce greenhouse gas emissions, or commitments to protect intellectual property laws, unless domestic actors adjust their behaviour. Moreover, many international commitments are owed not only to other states, but also to individuals or business entities (e.g. human rights commitments, foreign investment commitments), or are of concern to them (e.g. environmental commitments). In the absence of suitable international spaces for

[92] See also our discussion of the death penalty example in above Chapter 2, text following text accompanying note 62.

[93] Chayes and Chayes, above note 50 at 193–4.

legal interaction between state and non-state actors, domestic forums often assume particular importance. For these reasons alone, compliance theory cannot limit itself to an inquiry into the horizontal interactions among states.

More fundamentally, however, it is an abstraction to speak of compliance by 'states' (or other entities, such as international organizations). Some theories of state behaviour and compliance, both rationalist and constructivist, deliberately rely on this abstraction to enhance the parsimony of claims, or to reflect their assumption that states remain the dominant actors in the international system.[94] Ultimately, however, the salient actors are individuals, acting on behalf of states and other entities at the international and national levels, or making up the relevant segments of domestic society. The latter insight, of course, is at the heart of self-styled 'liberal' compliance theories. Following terminology originating in IR scholarship,[95] the label denotes theories that see state conduct as primarily determined by domestic political processes through which individuals and groups seek to realize their interests and values.[96] Similarly, Oona Hathaway has posited an 'integrated' theory of international law, which aims to integrate analysis of international and domestic dynamics, as well as 'interest-based' and 'norm-based' accounts of

[94] See e.g. Kenneth W. Waltz, *Theory of International Politics* (Reading: Addison-Wesley, 1979), repr. in Robert E. Keohane (ed.), *Neorealism and Its Critics* (New York: Columbia University Press, 1986), pp. 33–41 and 57–62 (discussing the central place of parsimony in social-science theory) and pp. 87–92 (discussing states as the key units of the system); Guzman, above note 14, pp. 19–22 (noting that his rationalist theory of international law assumes a unitary 'black box' in the interests of parsimony); and Alexander Wendt, 'Anarchy is What States Make of It' (1992) 46 *International Organization* 391 at 424–5 (discussing the state-centrism of his constructivist approach while noting that other international actors merit more research attention).

[95] See Andrew Moravcsik, 'Taking Preferences Seriously: A Liberal Theory of International Politics' (1997) 51 *International Organization* 513.

[96] A prominent perspective on the relevance of domestic factors in promoting compliance is Anne-Marie Slaughter's liberal theory of international law. In earlier work she argued that the features of a state played a central role and, indeed, that 'liberal states' were more likely to comply with international law. See e.g. Anne-Marie Burley, 'Law Among Liberal States: Liberal Internationalism and the Act of State Doctrine' (1992) 92 *Columbia Law Review* 1907. Slaughter's more recent liberal theory work is not explicitly focused upon compliance, so will not be discussed in detail here. Her basic premise is that the extent to which international norms reach individuals is crucial to their ability to shape state conduct. The more directly individuals have recourse to international norms, through international or domestic processes, the more likely are these norms to be engaged. See Anne-Marie Slaughter, 'A Liberal Theory of International Law' (2000) *Proceedings of the 94th Annual Meeting of the American Society of International Law* 240 at 248.

state conduct.[97] Nonetheless, Hathaway's framework is firmly rooted in rationalism, its analytical focus being on 'legal enforcement' and 'collateral consequences' (anticipated reactions of state and non-state actors) as transnational or domestic forces that create 'incentives that affect states' decisions' shows.[98] Thus, although these theories rightly stress the importance of domestic engagement with international norms and offer valuable insights, we leave them aside here because they are too limited for our present purposes.

Focusing on the people who represent, or make up, states and other international actors is particularly important for our framework, which posits that international norms shape not just actors' conduct but their identities, and stresses the importance of interactions in communities of practice.[99] As we explained in Chapter 2, these communities 'cut across state boundaries and mediate between states, individuals, and human agency, on one hand, and social structures and systems, on the other'.[100] Thus, interactionalism instructs that, to understand precisely how legal obligation exerts its compliance pull upon international actors, we must look beyond the 'billiard ball' image of encounters between monolithic entities on the international plane.[101]

In the compliance literature, this point has been made most forcefully by Harold Koh. He shares with Franck and the Chayes the intuition that 'voluntary obedience, not coerced compliance, must be the preferred enforcement mechanism'.[102] But, in Koh's view, both accounts ultimately fall short in explaining obedience (conduct pursuant to a norm that has been internalized into an actor's own value system), as opposed to what

[97] Oona Hathaway, 'Between Power and Principle: A Political Theory of International Law' (2005) 71 *University of Chicago Law Review* 469. See also Oona Hathaway, 'Why Do Countries Commit to Human Rights Treaties?' (2007) 51 *Journal of Conflict Resolution* 588.

[98] Hathaway, *ibid.* at 613.

[99] See above Chapter 2, *passim* and especially text accompanying notes 27–31.

[100] Emanuel Adler, *Communitarian International Relations: The Epistemic Foundations of International Relations* (London and New York: Routledge, 2005), p. 15.

[101] See Alvarez, above note 68 at 968–9 (commenting on Goodman and Jinks's state socialization model).

[102] Harold H. Koh, 'Why Do Nations Obey International Law?, Review of *The New Sovereignty: Compliance with International Regulatory Agreements* by A. Chayes and A. Handler Chayes, and of *Fairness in International Law and Institutions* by T.M. Franck', (1997) 106 *Yale Law Journal* 2599 at 2645. See also Harold H. Koh, 'The 1998 Frankel Lecture: Bringing International Law Home' (1998) 35 *Houston International Law Journal* 623: and '"Transnational Legal Process" – The 1994 Roscoe Pound Lecture' (1996) 75 *Nebraska Law Review* 181.

Koh calls simple conformity of behaviour with standards (for reasons of convenience), or compliance (acceptance of norms due to specific rewards or punishments).[103] The missing link between international norms and state conduct, argues Koh, is the internalization of international norms into the domestic sphere through what he calls transnational legal process.[104]

According to Koh, the internalization of international norms occurs in three stages: first, a transnational actor provokes interactions with another, 'which forces an interpretation or enunciation of the global norm applicable to the situation'.[105] The salient interactions at least initially may occur in an international arena, and may involve states as well as international organizations, NGOs, business entities, and other norm entrepreneurs.[106] These transactions generate a legal rule that guides future interactions between the parties. Finally, 'repeated participation in the process will help to reconstitute the interests and even the identities of the participants in the process'.[107] Internalization into the domestic sphere can occur through a variety of processes – social (the public legitimacy of a norm results in widespread obedience), political (elites accept an international norm and adopt it as government policy), and legal (incorporation of the norm into the domestic legal system).[108]

With its emphasis on repeated interactions and sensitivity to 'identity', Koh's account has strong constructivist features,[109] and considerable

[103] See Koh, 'Why Do Nations Obey International Law?', above note 102 at 2603. Koh also distinguished coincidental conformity between a norm and conduct. Elsewhere Koh draws a distinction between 'grudging compliance' brought about by the threat of sanctions and true 'obedience'. *Ibid.* at 2603 and 2645–6. See also the detailed discussion in Koh, 'The 1998 Frankel Lecture: Bringing International Law Home', above note 102 at 627–33.

[104] See Koh, *ibid.* at 626–7. In its focus on the domestic sphere, Koh's transnational legal process shares common ground with liberal compliance theory. However, while the latter emphasizes the importance of liberal politics within states, Koh's framework stresses interaction, which he assumes can take place in a variety of settings.

[105] Koh, 'Why Do Nations Obey International Law?', above note 102 at 2646.

[106] See Koh, 'Transnational Legal Process', above note 102 at 184. [107] *Ibid.*

[108] Koh, 'Why Do Nations Obey International Law?', above note 102 at 2656–7; and Koh, 'The 1998 Frankel Lecture: Bringing International Law Home', above note 102 at 642–3.

[109] See e.g. Koh, 'Why Do Nations Obey International Law?', above note 102 at 2646 (arguing that transnational legal process helps 'to reconstitute the interests and even the identities of the participants'); and Koh, 'The 1998 Frankel Lecture: Bringing International Law Home', above note 102 at 641 (observing that 'a nation's repeated participation in transnational legal process is internalizing, normative, and constitutive-of-identity').

overlap with the work on norm entrepreneurship and norm cycles that we discussed in the previous chapter.[110] But Koh also faults constructivist approaches, including Goodman and Jinks's state socialization model, for failing to explain through what specific pathways international norms come to be 'internalized' to shape the identities of state actors.[111] We agree that a closer look at the social interactions through which international norms migrate into states' domestic spheres and instantiate themselves in their social, bureaucratic and legal practices is important to understanding whether and to what extent they actually embrace the norms.

Koh's central contribution to the compliance debate, then, is to break the path to obedience down into a series of interactional processes that, as he put it, bring international law 'home'.[112] In so doing, his transnational legal process model complements our interactional account of international law. Moreover, although Koh's account traces the mechanisms for norm internalization, it also allows for the possibility that 'law transforms, mutates, and percolates up and down, from the public to the private, from the domestic to the international level and back down again.'[113] This proposition resonates with our argument that communities of practice shape and re-shape international law. More specifically, norms can shape practice, but practice and interactions among actors also shape norms. Thus, for norm internalization to occur, relevant communities of practice must expand to engage domestic actors in their shared legal understandings. In turn, domestic engagement with norms is likely to have feedback effects back into the international arena.

Notwithstanding the overlap between Koh's transnational legal process account and our interactional framework, there is also a significant difference. Although Koh is interested in the notion of 'obedience', he does not explore the role that the binding quality of international law plays in generating it. We agree with his assessment that it is time to get past the 'does international law matter?' question, but we do not think that it is enough to examine, as do legal process scholars, only 'the social mechanisms that help *make* international law matter'.[114] It remains as important

110 See above Chapter 2, text accompanying notes 2–16.

111 Koh, 'Why Do Nations Obey International Law?', above note 102 at 2651. On Goodman and Jinks, see Harold H. Koh, 'Internalization through Socialization' (2005) 54 *Duke Law Journal* 975 at 981.

112 See Koh, 'The 1998 Frankel Lecture: Bringing International Law Home', above note 102.

113 See Koh, 'Transnational Legal Process', above note 102 at 184.

114 See Koh, 'Internalization through Socialization', above note 111 at 977.

as ever to ask *how* international law matters. As we noted at the outset of this chapter, to answer this broader question, attention must be paid to both norm properties and legal process: after all, they are inextricably linked. Interactionalism, therefore, highlights the role of legal obligation, focusing on the features that give legal norms a distinctive ability to gain internalization and to shape actor identities through transnational *legal* processes. This proposition has important practical implications.

To be sure, we would endorse much of the practical advice that Koh offers on the basis of his transnational legal process account – it complements what we have already outlined in this chapter. For example, Koh highlights the need to enhance actors' opportunities to participate in salient interactions. He also suggests that, in instances where 'horizontal' mechanisms at the international level may be weakly developed, compliance at least with well-established international norms might be best promoted through 'vertical strategies of interaction, interpretation, and internalization'.[115] We would add, however, that paying attention to the requirements of interactional law enhances the potential for norm internalization through expanding communities of practice. Thus, the prerequisites for interactional obligation – the grounding of legal rules in social understandings, adherence to the requirements of legality, and the existence of a practice of legality – must be cultivated at the international level and connected into states' domestic spheres.

For interactional law-making to succeed, each state or its representatives must bring a sound assessment of domestic understandings to the international table. Such assessments are important because, as we argued in the preceding chapter, international law-makers must be careful not to push treaty or customary norms too far beyond internationally shared understandings. This point is especially relevant when it comes to demanding substantive norms (for example, a death penalty prohibition), which are otherwise bound to clash with domestic understandings.[116] Therefore, when the stock of internationally shared substantive understandings is relatively thin, law-making may be more productively focused upon elastic, open-textured substantive norms, or upon norms that are aimed primarily at building legality.[117] Such norms leave scope

[115] See Koh, 'Why Do Nations Obey International Law?', above note 102 at 2656.

[116] See also Andrew P. Cortell and James W. Davis, 'When Norms Clash: International Norms, Domestic Practices, and Japan's Internalization of the GATT/WTO' (2005) 31 *Review of International Studies* 3.

[117] See above Chapter 2, text accompanying and following note 72.

for a domestic margin of appreciation – and thus for diversity – and allow for the gradual building up of shared understandings and an attendant practice of legality.

Our hypothesis is that these factors are indicative of when international norms are most likely to become woven into domestic law, and when a sense of obligation (or, in Koh's terms, 'obedience') is most likely to evolve on the part of the state actor. Arguably, resonance with internationally shared understandings and a strong international practice of legality also assist this process by enhancing the legitimacy and persuasiveness of the relevant norms to domestic audiences. Granted, questions of international legality alone will usually not be of direct concern to citizens at the domestic level (but will be the domain primarily of state governments). Citizens might become engaged, however, when substantive international law is being applied nationally and questions of legality manifest themselves as concerns about democratic deficit, transparency, or popular sovereignty. Similarly, weak (or absent) international practice of legality can undercut the domestic reach even of international norms that are established in customary or treaty law. Thus, while we agree with Koh that domestic legal processes can strengthen and promote compliance with such norms, we also reiterate that formal existence of norms is an insufficient indicator of legality. To be clear, formally valid rules do play an important role in internalization processes, be they international customary or treaty law, or domestic implementing legislation. They can contribute to a practice of legality, and they 'fix' international understandings so as to provide a focal point for domestic engagement. However, once again, congruence with shared understandings, adherence to the requirements of legality and engagement are the crucial factors. Formality alone does not guarantee internalization.[118]

To summarize, we suggest that paying attention to the interlocking requirements of legality helps ensure that interactional law is accommodating of diversity and, as a result, is more likely to allow for internalization into domestic spheres. In interactional law, more demanding norms are built and maintained only when there is congruence with shared understandings, attention to the requirements of legality, and enmeshment in a practice of legality. Legal interactions in the domestic sphere feed into these international processes. When diverse domestic

[118] See also Wiener, above note 39 at 181 (arguing that social recognition of norms, and their meaning, is contingent upon interaction and, therefore, is context-specific and may well 'differ according to the respective experience with norm-use').

practices and interpretations remain within the margin of appreciation left by international norms, the norm is maintained or even strengthened. When they consistently stretch beyond the margin, or even reject the international norm altogether, the latter will eventually be weakened, altered or even destroyed. That, in our view, is how compliance should be understood. It is not merely an outcome produced by the norm, but part of the continuing process of interactional law-making.

4.5 *Rethinking the concept of compliance*

The primary insight to be derived from the interactional perspective is that the promotion of compliance does not begin with mechanisms for the interpretation or application of pre-established rules. The potential for compliance is already present to be encouraged or undermined by the processes through which obligation is generated. Conversely, interactional law is created and upheld through processes of rhetorical claim, action and response. Rules are not simply posited and projected out to willing or unwilling recipients. Like obligation itself, compliance is built in large measure through interactive practices of legality.

Another important point follows from this insight, and from the constructivist theory that informs it: compliance dynamics are not unidirectional. This proposition poses a direct challenge to the assumptions and methodology of most compliance scholarship. International lawyers especially, focused as they are upon questions of compliance with the formal rules found in treaties or custom, tend to define rules in static terms and 'compliance' as 'a state of conformity or identity between an actor's behavior and a specified rule'.[119] While this stance is consistent with rationalist perspectives on international conduct, it is surprising that it also grounds much constructivist compliance scholarship.

Goodman and Jinks's state socialization framework is a recent, and illustrative, example. Recall that this framework is focused upon 'acculturation', which is said to be an important compliance dynamic, notably when persuasion and enforcement are unavailable to give effect to international norms.[120] Goodman and Jinks posit that acculturation entails 'incomplete internalization' of norms, and stress that its importance lies precisely in the fact that it can bring about compliance in the absence

[119] Raustiala and Slaughter, above note 21, p. 539.
[120] See above notes 62–8 and accompanying text.

of full internalization.[121] In other words, although the account posits a mechanism for the expansion of 'global culture', it does not appear to be premised upon the expansion of shared understandings to new actors. It remains unclear how a 'culture', legal or otherwise, can be sustained and extended in this way. Goodman and Jinks are content to argue that the best means of promoting acculturation is that 'embedding target actors in social settings organized around highly institutionalized, broadly shared principles could foster the basic elements necessary for acculturation.'[122] But, again, this claim leaves some crucial questions unanswered: how do 'shared principles' arise and how are they sustained?[123] Our point is that compliance, and efforts to promote compliance, are important parts of the answer. It is an oversimplification to posit the existence of international rules with which actors are then made to comply, be it through socialization or other means.

Such an account is also vulnerable to the concern that what is at issue is 'delivery' of western 'culture' to the rest of the world.[124] We believe that our assumption that norms, collective understandings, and, arguably, also 'cultures' are produced through communities of practice is better suited to dealing with the challenge of diversity. It is important to appreciate international 'relationships' as interactions, rather than unidirectional transmission belts. This point connects back to the interplay between international and domestic law. As we explained in the preceding section, an interactional approach to law-making is sensitive to diverse domestic practices, factoring them into the interplay between shared understandings and practices of legality. Compliance by a state or actors within a state is not merely an outcome produced by the norm or by its enforcement, but part of the ongoing process of interactional law-making. The importance of this point cannot be overstated. As Antje Wiener has argued, even some of the constructivist accounts that do take seriously the interactional and fluid nature of norm development, such as Risse's 'logic of arguing',[125] ultimately limit this approach to interactions at the international level. According to Wiener, '[o]nce a norm is agreed within this context the stability assumption kicks in'

[121] Goodman and Jinks, above note 62 at 644. [122] *Ibid.* at 654.

[123] See also Asher Alkoby, 'Theories of Compliance with International Law and the Challenge of Cultural Difference' (2008) 4 *Journal of International Law and International Relations* 151 at 168.

[124] See e.g. Alvarez, above note 68 at 974. [125] See Risse, above note 84.

for these theorists.[126] As far as the domestic arena is concerned, '[t]he expected result is that norm followers will be persuaded, not the *re*validation or change of norms'.[127] What is neglected is the possibility of subsequent 'contestation of meaning', especially to the extent that it may occur in domestic settings.[128] By contrast, our communities of practice account considers all processes of contestation, whether international or national, to be salient.

Although we have criticized the prevalent conception of compliance as too static, we are not suggesting that it is pointless to promote, or assess, compliance with international law, including customary or treaty rules. On the contrary, our argument throughout this chapter has been that there are many more opportunities to promote compliance than is commonly assumed. So, by all means, we can and indeed should ask whether state A or B is complying with customary rule X or treaty rule Y; but, to get more than a snapshot of a particular moment in the continuing enterprise of international law-making we must look beyond the superficial.[129] We must ask not only whether there is compliance with a given rule, but also whether that rule remains reflective of shared understandings and embedded in a practice of legality: the standard framework of legal analysis certainly allows for the possibility that subsequent practice, interpretation or judicial processes lead to an evolution of the original rule. Our account pushes this point further, revealing that law-making and compliance questions are not radically distinct: they are best seen as located on a continuum. Just as processes or measures designed to promote compliance, even enforcement, help maintain or rebuild interactional law (and are thus essential to the stability of norms),[130] so paying attention in law-making to the prerequisites for interactional obligation builds the foundations for law's compliance pull.

[126] See Antje Wiener, 'The Dual Quality of Norms and Governance Beyond the State: Sociologocal and Normative Approaches to "Interaction"' (2007) 10 *Critical Review of International Social and Political Philosophy* 47 at 53 (showing that even constructivists committed to a 'logic of arguing' assume that norms become stable social facts once arrived at internationally; and advocating an account that allows for norm contestation and norm change at the domestic levels as well).

[127] *Ibid.* [128] See *ibid.* at 50.

[129] See also Benjamin Gregg, *Coping in Politics with Indeterminate Norms: A Theory of Enlightened Localism* (Albany: State University of New York Press, 2003), p. 22 (arguing that a norm's '[m]eaning is created time and again').

[130] See above Chapter 2, text accompanying notes 60–1.

5. Conclusion

Our interactional theory of international law is first and foremost a theory of obligation. It explains why states and other international actors commit to international law, and why they remain committed. Like all social norms, law shapes actors' identities and their interests and so, ultimately, their conduct. Our interactional theory augments this constructivist insight by explaining why legal obligation exerts distinctive influence. In looking behind the formal, hierarchical manifestations of law, interactionalism reveals that the power of international law rests in a felt sense of obligation, rooted in a specific form of legal legitimacy.

Through this concept of obligation, interactionalism provides concrete guidance to lawyers and policy-makers as they seek to understand and promote compliance with international law. It instructs that the foundations for compliance can be built in the law-making process. Interactional obligation – the self-binding effect of law – cannot be posited or enacted; it must be built and maintained. Attention must be paid to the congruence of prospective or existing legal norms with underlying social norms. In addition, law-making requires that the criteria of legality are substantially met and that they become enmeshed in a sustained practice of legality.

By emphasizing the importance of a sustained practice of legality, our theory also highlights the need to build spaces and opportunities for ongoing interaction. Law-making processes and compliance processes must be transparent and inclusive. Importantly, compliance processes are not radically distinct from law-making. They are essential parts of the practice of legality that sustains and re-shapes interactional law. Similarly, 'enforcement' is not merely a method for imposing compliance. Interactionalism reveals both that enforcement can be an important element of the practice of legality, and that it is unlikely to be acceptable or effective unless it is in fact embedded in such a practice.

An interactional understanding of obligation also sheds new light on the interface between international and domestic law. If obligation is built and maintained through a community of practice, then international law cannot simply be implemented domestically. It will unfold its obligatory effect only if shared understandings and a practice of legality are extended into the domestic sphere. If international norms remain contested at the domestic level, the result from the standpoint of international law may be non-compliance or, if the contestation is widespread and sustained, a shift in the norm itself.

Interactionalism, then, also instructs that the very concept of 'compliance' must be handled with care. Interactional law, by definition, is not a one-way street. Compliance and non-compliance are better understood as elements of the broader practice of legality that sustains international law. This does not mean that compliance could never be assessed, or that it is unimportant. It means only that the common image of law as fixed standards against which behaviour is then measured does not do justice to the complexity and import of compliance questions.

Finally, interactional theory reveals that compliance theories must take a closer look at obligation than they have tended to so far. This assessment applies not only to rationalist compliance theories, which tend to discount obligation and focus on external factors, such as interests, costs and benefits, or power, to explain behaviour. Perhaps more surprisingly, it applies also to norm-oriented compliance theories, which share our assumption that international law has the potential to shape the conduct of international actors. The limitation of these theories is that they too rely upon a thin, positivist concept of international law. The attendant formal concept of obligation, in our view, can neither fully explain the 'compliance pull' of international law,[131] nor illuminate why various processes through which actors are persuaded or pressured into compliance can 'help *make* international law matter'.[132] Our interactional framework offers a richer account of law's distinctive influence and reveals that legal process is more than a strategy or technique for promoting compliance. As we have sought to illustrate, the key to understanding compliance – the power of international law – rests in an approach that integrates norm properties and legal process through an interactional concept of obligation

[131] Franck, above note 3, p. 26.

[132] See Koh, 'Internalization through Socialization', above note 111 at 977.

4

Climate change: building a global legal regime

> One very simple truth about Global Warming is this, that it will spare nobody, however rich, mighty and powerful we think we are. ... Mr Tony Blair, the Prime Minister of the UK once said that without proper action now, the average global temperatures would rise by 2 degrees Celsius. Scientists estimate that the subsequent rise in the sea level would be enough to swamp a large proportion of Bangladesh in 30/40 years time. It would be a serious catastrophe for my country and for the whole region if much of the land in Bangladesh disappears under the sea. I become frightened to think that my grandchildren (when I touch them) will have no place to live on this planet earth. I really want to be sure that my grandchildren, and their children after them, will be able to enjoy the beauty of my country that I have enjoyed, and be able to have enough land to live, and enough land for food.
>
> Michael S. Baroi, Anglican Bishop of Bangladesh[1]

1. Introduction

For some observers, climate change is the single most important public policy challenge of our time.[2] But describing the 'problem' is not actually an easy matter. It is dizzying in its complexity, daunting in its implications, and multifaceted in a way that eludes easy categorization. Beginning with the environmental dimension, global warming is a problem of unprecedented scale. It is planetary in scope and inter-generational in its implications. Even more importantly, because climate change implicates virtually all production and consumption processes, addressing it is about nothing less than changing the way we do everything that we do, everywhere in the world. Climate change, then, is also a classic collective

[1] CiNews, *Fight global warming for the sake of my country, pleads Bangladesh bishop*, 4 November 2006, at www.cinews.ie/article.php?artid=2850.

[2] See e.g. David A. King, 'Climate Change Science: Adapt, Mitigate or Ignore?' (2004) 303 *Science* 176.

action problem. It can only be solved if all states, or at least the major greenhouse gas emitters, cooperate.

These difficulties are compounded by the fact that far-reaching decisions must be made under conditions of scientific uncertainty.[3] While both the phenomenon of human-induced climate change and its dangerous potential are now beyond doubt,[4] that was not always the case. On other issues, such as the speed and severity of climatic change, some debate continues. Not surprisingly, therefore, global warming is also an intractable political problem. How does one get states and political leaders to prioritize the issue, nationally and internationally?

In addition, climate change raises a series of difficult questions of equity, some say of global environmental justice.[5] Historically, emissions of greenhouse gases have been far greater in the industrialized world. The emissions of industrialized countries still significantly exceed those of developing countries,[6] although the emissions of some large developing countries are projected to rise sharply over the next two decades.[7] In 2006, China had surpassed the United States as the largest national emitter of greenhouse gases.[8] However, Chinese per capita emissions remain far lower than those of the United States or the

[3] See Daniel Bodansky, Jutta Brunnée and Ellen Hey, 'International Environmental Law: Mapping the Field', in Daniel Bodansky, Jutta Brunnée and Ellen Hey (eds.), *Oxford Handbook of International Environmental Law* (Oxford University Press, 2007), pp. 7–8 (discussing the role of uncertainty in international environmental lawmaking).

[4] It is now well established that anthropogenic changes to the global climate are occurring and will occur in the future, with potentially dangerous consequences. See Intergovernmental Panel on Climate Change (IPCC) Report, Vol. 1 (*Climate Change 2007: The Physical Science Basis*), February 2007; Vol. II (*Climate Change 2007: Impacts, Adaptation and Vulnerability*), April 2007; and Vol. III (*Climate Change 2007: Mitigation*), May 2007. All at www.ipcc.ch. See also text accompanying notes 61–3.

[5] For an extensive, interdisciplinary literature review, see Stephen M. Gardiner, 'Ethics and Global Climate Change' (2004) 114 *Ethics* 555.

[6] This is true for total, per capita and, especially, historic global emissions. See e.g. Kevin Baumert and Jonathan Pershing, *Climate Data: Insights and Observations* (Washington, DC: Pew Center on Global Climate Change, 2004), p. 4 (share of global emissions), p. 11 (per capita emissions) and p. 13 (cumulative CO2 emissions 1850–2000), at www.pewclimate.org/global-warming-in-depth/all_reports/.

[7] *Ibid.*, pp. 15–16.

[8] See Union of Concerned Scientists, *Each Country's Share of CO2 Emissions* (August 2006), at www.ucsusa.org/global_warming/science_and_impacts/science/each-countrys-share-of-co2.html. See also John Vidal and David Adam, 'China overtakes US as World's biggest CO2 Emitter', *The Guardian*, 19 June 2007, at www.guardian.co.uk/environment/2007/jun/19/china.usnews.

European Union.[9] The effects of climate change are likely disproportionately to affect developing countries, many of which are especially vulnerable to such effects.[10] Industrialized countries have vastly larger economic and technological capacity not only to mitigate greenhouse gas emissions, but also to adapt to its consequences.[11] These issues must be addressed if an international climate regime is to succeed. However, the gulf between radically different perceptions of the problem is not easily bridged. Many developing countries see climate politics as part of a larger pattern of historical and economic injustices and so demand that industrialized countries bear the primary burden of combating climate change. In turn, many industrialized countries insist on developing country participation as a matter of pragmatic problem solving, or even 'fairness'.[12]

Climate change can also be framed as a security issue. In 2004, then UK Chief Scientific Adviser, David King, famously referred to it as 'the most severe problem that we are facing today – more serious even than the threat of terrorism'.[13] For some countries, like small island states, climate change poses an existential threat.[14] For others, its physical effects might endanger human settlements, supplies of food, water or energy, or economic stability. All of these effects can exacerbate humanitarian crises, and promote state failures and border disputes, producing more conventional threats to national and international security.[15] Indeed, in April 2007 the United Kingdom took the unprecedented step of bringing climate change before the UN Security Council. The British Foreign Secretary stressed that global warming was not merely a matter of national security for individual states, but a question of 'collective security in a fragile and increasingly interdependent world'.[16]

[9] The Climate Group, *China's Clean Revolution* (July 2008), at www.theclimategroup.org/assets/resources/Chinas_Clean_Revolution.pdf (noting that '[i]n 2007, China reached a per capita level of 5.1 metric tons compared to the European Union's 8.6 metric tons and the USA's 19.4 metric tons').

[10] Baumert and Pershing, above note 6, pp. 17–18.

[11] *Ibid.*, pp. 17–20.

[12] See e.g. J. Timmons Roberts and Bradley C. Parks, *A Climate of Injustice: Global Inequality, North–South Politics, and Climate Policy* (Cambridge, Mass: MIT Press, 2007).

[13] King, above note 2 at 176.

[14] See UN News Centre, *UN sounds alarm on Pacific nations' security posed by climate change*, 6 August 2009, at www.un.org/apps/news/story.asp?NewsID=31694&Cr=Climate+Change&Cr1.

[15] See John M. Broder, 'Climate Change Seen as Threat to U.S. Security', *The New York Times*, 9 August 2009.

[16] See UN Security Council, Sixty-second Session, 5663rd meeting, 17 April 2007, U.N. Doc. S/PV.5663, p. 19 at www.un.org/Docs/journal/asp/ws.asp?m=S/PV.5663. See also statement of the representative of Papua New Guinea, pp. 26–9.

Finally, there is the legal dimension of climate change, which will be the focus of our discussion in this chapter. All states' actions affect the global climate and all states are affected by the consequences. Since the Earth's climate is beyond the jurisdiction of individual states, those states must develop an international climate regime. But bringing all states – and, in particular, the major greenhouse gas emitters – into a meaningful, long-term climate regime is exceedingly difficult. Building and sustaining an international legal regime is hard work in the best of circumstances. In the case of climate change, this effort has now been underway for almost two decades. The United Nations Framework Convention on Climate Change (UNFCCC) was adopted in 1992,[17] and supplemented by the Kyoto Protocol in 1997.[18] However, the Kyoto Protocol imposes emission reduction commitments only on some of the major emitters, and does so only for the period from 2008 to 2012. Negotiations for a more comprehensive set of mid- and long-term commitments were meant to lead to an agreement by the end of 2009. However, the Copenhagen meetings of the parties to the convention and protocol could not resolve the remaining differences. They yielded only a slim instrument, the 'Copenhagen Accord', which was negotiated by a small group of parties in the final hours of the meeting, and then merely taken note of the by the parties to the Climate Convention.[19] The negotiations are now set to continue through 2010.

Notwithstanding many ups and downs, the climate regime has proven to be resilient. It survived the withdrawal of the United States in 2001, saw Europe assume a leadership role in regime development, and is now, in the context of the negotiations for a new commitment regime, witnessing the re-engagement of the United States. Indeed, it appears that a global climate consensus is slowly emerging and, for the first time, major developing countries seem willing to contemplate emissions-related commitments.

The climate regime provides fertile ground for an application of our interactional law framework and, in turn, our framework can illuminate the evolution of the regime. As we explained in the preceding chapters, our framework has three main elements. First, it posits that legal norms

[17] *United Nations Framework Convention on Climate Change*, U.N. Doc. A/AC.237/18 (Part II)/Add.1, reprinted in (1992) 31 I.L.M. 849 (UNFCCC).

[18] *Kyoto Protocol to the United Nations Framework Convention on Climate Change*, 10 December 1997, U.N. Doc. FCCC/CP/1997/L.7/add. 1, reprinted in (1998) 37 I.L.M. 22 (Kyoto Protocol).

[19] See UNFCCC, Decision -/CP 15 at: http://unfccc.int/2860.php (Copenhagen Accord) and below section 6.

can only emerge in the context of social norms based on shared understandings. Second, to count as interactional law, norms must meet a set of criteria of legality. Third, interactional norms are built, maintained, and sometimes destroyed through a continuing practice of legality. It is the combination of these three elements that produces legitimate legal norms and a sense of legal obligation among participants in the system.

This chapter will illustrate that the process of building shared understandings is crucial and, in the case of the climate regime, has been time-consuming. Our discussion will show that the objective of the climate regime – to avert dangerous climate change – and one of its key principles – common but differentiated responsibilities (CBDR) – have been the lynchpins for regime development, notwithstanding the fact that neither establishes binding obligations. Both the objective and CBDR were enshrined in the climate convention, but the treaty text left the underlying scientific and normative controversies unresolved. The efforts to develop a 'Shared Vision for Long-term Cooperative Action', launched at a meeting of the parties in 2007,[20] provide a fascinating opportunity to explore how the objective and CBDR have shaped parties' positions and, in turn, how regime participants have sought to clarify and shift the meaning of these norms. In fact, it turns out that the title of the negotiating mandate is anything but empty rhetoric. Intentionally or not, it captures exactly the challenge that parties face, which is first and foremost to develop a genuinely shared vision. Only now do regime participants appear to be arriving at shared understandings that could guide and sustain an ambitious global commitment regime. Whether they will in fact agree upon such a regime, however, remains uncertain as we write.

As for the emergence of interactional law, the climate regime illustrates our argument in Chapter 2 that communities of practice can emerge, and legality can be cultivated and gradually expanded, even under conditions of deep diversity and on the basis initially of only thin substantive understandings. In such a setting one might expect the legality of the procedural aspects of the regime to be more strongly developed than that of its substantive dimensions. And indeed, we will see that the parties to the climate regime first developed a foundation of shared understandings, and a sustained practice of legality, regarding decision-making bodies

[20] UNFCCC, *Report of the Conference of the Parties on its thirteenth session, held in Bali from 3 to 15 December 2007*, Decision 10/CP.13 (*Action Plan*), U.N. Doc. FCCC/CP/2007/6/Add.1 (14 March 2008) (Bali Action Plan), para. 1(a), online at http://unfccc.int/resource/docs/2007/cop13/eng/06a01.pdf#page=3.

and procedures. We show that the procedural interactional law of the climate regime is a central factor in explaining why the climate regime has endured notwithstanding the participants' strongly divergent interests, the deep divisions between North and South, and the rejection of the Kyoto Protocol by a singularly powerful state. However, we will also see that certain aspects of the regime's procedural practices, notably the practice of consensus decision-making, have come to pose fundamental changes.

In view of the complexity of the climate change regime, we begin with a brief sketch of its salient aspects and its evolution. We then examine some of these elements and developments more closely, through the lens of interactional law. We explore the shared understandings that underpin the regime, concentrating on some of its key features. Specifically, our focus is on shared understandings concerning the need for a global legal regime, its objective, the CBDR principle, and the emission reduction commitments enshrined in the Kyoto Protocol as well as the emerging new commitment regime. Our discussion of shared understandings focuses primarily on the interactions between actors in the context of the climate regime, but we also highlight salient domestic factors. In particular, we explore the reasons for the divergent policy paths followed by the two main industrialized regime participants, the European Union (EU) and the United States. Next we assess the extent to which the UNFCCC, the Kyoto Protocol, and CBDR meet the criteria of legality. Finally, we consider the practice of legality that we believe has evolved under the climate regime, paying particular attention to the role of the Kyoto Protocol's compliance procedure. The bulk of this chapter was written in the summer of 2009, and so examines the evolution of the climate regime up to that point. We consider the adoption and content of the December 2009 Copenhagen Accord, how it measures up to the requirements of interactional law, and its implications for the future of the climate regime, in a separate section at the end of the chapter.

2. The global climate regime: key features and evolution

It is probably fair to say that the Climate Convention owes its existence in part to the green internationalism (reinforced by post-Cold War optimism) that peaked at the 1992 Earth Summit.[21] Still, given the

[21] See Stacy D. VanDeveer, 'Green Fatigue' (2003) 27 *Wilson Quarterly* 55.

complexities of the climate challenge, it is remarkable that the UNFCCC became a truly universal agreement, boasting 192 parties.[22] Perhaps more remarkable is the fact that the regime actually speaks to all of the facets of the climate change problem that we have just sketched.

The convention acknowledges climate change as a global environmental and sustainable development problem with intergenerational implications,[23] requiring 'the widest possible cooperation by all countries and their participation in an effective and appropriate international response'.[24] Indeed, the preamble acknowledges that climate change and its adverse effects constitute a 'common concern of humankind'.[25] It expresses concern that 'human activities have been substantially increasing the atmospheric concentrations of greenhouse gases', and 'that these increases enhance the natural greenhouse effect'.[26] To deal with scientific uncertainty, the regime stipulates that parties should take 'precautionary measures to anticipate, prevent or minimize the causes of climate change and mitigate its adverse effects',[27] and provides an array of information gathering and exchange mechanisms.[28] On the security side, the convention's objective is to achieve a 'stabilization of greenhouse gas concentrations in the atmosphere at a level that would prevent dangerous anthropogenic interference with the climate system'.[29] Particular attention is paid to the concerns of countries vulnerable to sea-level rise, flooding or desertification.[30]

The most important aspect of the climate regime, however, is the fact that it attempts to tackle the global equity dimension. The language of the convention is striking. It states plainly that the largest share of historical and current global emissions of greenhouse gases stems from industrialized countries, and that per capita emissions in developing countries remain relatively low.[31] It recognizes that eradication of poverty and economic growth are legitimate priorities for developing countries.[32] An unusual feature of the convention is that it devotes an article in the operative part of the treaty to certain guiding principles. In particular,

[22] For the list of ratifications, as at 22 August 2007, see *UNFCCC Status of Ratifications*, online at http://unfccc.int/files/essential_background/convention/status_of_ratification/application/pdf/unfccc_conv_rat.pdf.

[23] See UNFCCC, above note 17, Art. 2 (stating that the treaty's objective is to stabilize greenhouse gas emissions in a time-frame that allows 'ecosystems to adapt naturally' and 'economic development to proceed in a sustainable manner').

[24] *Ibid.*, preamble. [25] *Ibid.* [26] *Ibid.* [27] *Ibid.*, Art. 3.3.

[28] *Ibid.*, Arts. 4.1(g) and (h), 5 and 9. [29] *Ibid.*, Art. 2. [30] *Ibid.*, preamble and Art. 4.8.

[31] *Ibid.*, preamble. [32] *Ibid.*

Article 3.1 calls upon parties to protect the climate system 'on the basis of equity and in accordance with their common but differentiated responsibilities and respective capabilities'.[33] The convention also stipulates that 'developed country Parties should take the lead in combating climate change'.[34] Article 4, which refers back to parties' common but differentiated responsibilities, fleshes out the idea of developed country leadership and distinguishes between the respective commitments of developing and developed countries. It provides that, initially, emission reductions be pursued only by the developed countries and countries with economies in transition that are listed in an Annex I to the convention.[35]

To secure global support for the ambitious undertaking of dealing with climate change in all its complexity, the climate regime was built incrementally. In keeping with the framework convention model that has become prevalent in international environmental law and that is specifically designed to promote long-term interaction among treaty parties,[36] the UNFCCC does not impose ambitious substantive commitments on parties. Rather, it contains principles and objectives to guide global climate policy, facilitates gathering and exchange of scientific information, and establishes institutions and processes for further treaty development, including through the adoption of protocols. Much as in the case of an international organization, the convention's plenary body, the Conference of the Parties (COP), and its subsidiary bodies, provide the forum for regular meetings and continuing deliberation.[37]

The Kyoto Protocol was adopted in 1997 to build on the general commitments set out in the convention. It envisaged binding greenhouse gas emission reduction commitments for the parties listed in Annex I to the UNFCCC, but not for developing countries. Although this feature of the protocol has become increasingly controversial, it is consonant with the above-mentioned principles of the convention, especially the principle of common but differentiated responsibilities.[38] Indeed, the

[33] *Ibid.*, Art. 3.1. [34] *Ibid.*

[35] *Ibid.*, Arts. 3.1 and 4.2(a) and (b). Arts. 4.2(a) and (b) contained a non-binding commitment, applicable only to Annex I parties, to stabilize their greenhouse gas emissions at 1990 levels by the year 2000.

[36] See Bodansky *et al.*, above note 3 at 21–3.

[37] See Jutta Brunnée, 'COPing with Consent: Lawmaking under Multilateral Environmental Agreements' (2002) 15 *Leiden Journal of international Law* 16 at 4–5; and Robin Churchill and Geir Ulfstein, 'Autonomous Institutional Arrangements in Multilateral Environmental Agreements: A Little-Noticed Phenomenon in International Law' (2000) 94 *American Journal of International Law* 623.

[38] See Lavanya Rajamani, 'China and India on Climate Change and Development: A Stance that is Legitimate but not Sagacious?', in Steven Bernstein, Jutta Brunnée, David Duff

negotiating mandate ('Berlin Mandate') for the protocol had specified that the process was to be guided by '[t]he provisions of the Convention, including Article 3, in particular the principles in Article 3.1', and would '[n]ot introduce any new commitments for Parties not included in Annex I'.[39] The preamble to the Kyoto Protocol itself states that the parties were '*guided* by Article 3 of the Convention'. Article 10 of the protocol reaffirms and builds on all parties' existing commitments under Article 4.1 of the convention, 'taking into account their common but differentiated responsibilities'. Be that as it may, some of the major emitters of greenhouse gases do not have reduction obligations under the Kyoto Protocol, either because they are developing countries, like China and India, or because they have refused to join the protocol, as did the single largest industrialized country emitter, the United States.[40]

The protocol requires Annex I parties, during a 2008–2012 'commitment period', to achieve specified reductions in comparison to their 1990 emission levels. Compliance with these targets is assessed at the end of that period. Parties' individual commitments vary. For example, while Canada is required to reduce its emissions by 6 per cent below 1990 levels, the European Community, which is party to the protocol in addition to its member states,[41] committed itself to an 8 per cent cut.[42] Russia is committed only to a stabilization of its emissions at 1990 levels, whereas Norway, Australia and Iceland may even increase their emissions. The United States, had it joined the protocol, would have had to cut its emissions by 7 per cent below 1990 levels.[43] To give all Annex I parties greater flexibility in meeting their emission reduction commitments, the Kyoto Protocol establishes several emissions trading mechanisms. Two of these

and Andrew Green (eds.), *A Globally Integrated Climate Policy for Canada* (University of Toronto Press, 2007), pp. 110–12.

[39] Decision 1/CP.1, U.N. Doc. FCCC/CP/1995/7/Add.1, para. 1(a) and para. 2(b) (Berlin Mandate).

[40] See above notes 8–9 and accompanying text.

[41] The EU, which currently has 27 member states, was established through the 1992 Treaty on European Union. The EU and the European Community (EC) are legally distinct, but have the same member states and largely the same institutions. The EC rather than the EU is legally competent to enter into international agreements. On the salient distinctions, see Ludwig Krämer, 'Regional Economic Integration Organizations: The European Union as an Example', in Daniel Bodansky, Jutta Brunnée and Ellen Hey (eds.), *Oxford Handbook of International Environmental Law* (Oxford University Press, 2007), pp. 854–7.

[42] See Kyoto Protocol, above note 18, Art. 3.1, and Annex B. In addition to the Community, its member states have their own commitments.

[43] *Ibid.*

mechanisms envisage trades of emission rights (Article 17) or reduction credits (Article 6) amongst Annex I parties (or legal entities under their jurisdictions). The third, the Clean Development Mechanism, was designed to give further expression to the CBDR principle, enabling Annex I parties to acquire reduction credits from projects undertaken in developing countries (Article 12) while helping to promote sustainable development in these countries.[44] Finally, the parties agreed to adopt 'procedures and mechanisms to determine and address cases of non-compliance' with the protocol.[45]

The Kyoto Protocol too is in some respects a framework agreement. Due to the complexities and scope of the issues under negotiation, it was not possible to settle all the elements of the protocol in time for adoption at the Kyoto meeting.[46] As a result, the protocol contains a series of provisions that anchor the outlines of key elements such as inventory and reporting requirements, the emissions trading mechanisms, and the compliance regime in the treaty.[47] But it was left to the plenary bodies of the convention and the protocol, respectively, to approve the rules, guidelines, and procedures required to transform broad concepts into regimes that are sufficiently detailed to allow implementation and that enable states to decide whether or not to ratify the protocol.

The UNFCCC parties agreed to develop the relevant decisions in time for adoption at their sixth meeting in November 2000.[48] However, rather than produce a final package that could enable entry into force of the protocol, COP-6 saw a breakdown of negotiations.[49] In March 2001, the United States rejected the Kyoto Protocol as fatally flawed, stating that it would not ratify the agreement.[50] One might have expected the

44 See Jacob Werksman, 'The Clean Development Mechanism: Unwrapping the Kyoto Surprise' (1998) 7 *Review of European Community and International Law* 147 (for an account of the negotiating history). See also Emily Boyd *et al.*, 'The Clean Development Mechanism: An assessment of current practice and future approaches for policy' Tyndall Centre Working Paper 114, October 2007, at www.tyndall.ac.uk/publications/working_papers/twp114_summary.shtml (for an assessment).

45 See Kyoto Protocol, above note 18, Art. 18.

46 See Herrmann Ott, 'The Kyoto Protocol: Unfinished Business' (1998) 40 *Environment* 3.

47 See the Kyoto Protocol, above note 18, Arts. 3.4, 5.1, 6.2, 7.4, 8.4, 12.7, 16, 17, and 18.

48 See UNFCCC *Report of the Conference of the Parties to the United Nations Framework Convention on Climate Change on its Fourth Session*, U.N. Doc. FCCC/CP/1998/16/Add.1 (1998), Decision 8/CP.4.

49 See e.g. Michael Grubb and Farhana Yamin, 'Climatic collapse at The Hague: what happened, why, and where do we go from here?' (2001) 77 *International Affairs* 261.

50 See 'Text of a Letter from the President to Senators Hagel, Helms, Craig, and Roberts', 13 March 2001, at http://c-span.org/executive/bush_letter.asp?Cat=Current_Event&

US position to have a sobering effect on the negotiations; some observers even predicted the collapse of the Kyoto Protocol.[51] However, it appears that the US stance actually spurred on other parties' efforts to salvage it.[52] The parties were able to bridge many of the gaps that had separated their positions and to pave the way for the adoption, at COP-7 in November 2001, of a compromise package. The so-called Marrakech Accords consist in a series of draft decisions that the UNFCCC COP recommends to the Kyoto Protocol parties for adoption at their first meeting upon entry into force of the protocol.[53]

The Kyoto Protocol entered into force in February 2005,[54] and it is largely due to determined European lobbying of other states that it did so despite the refusal of the United States to join the regime.[55] The US decision not to join the protocol was seen by many European policy-makers as an affront, and as further evidence of rising American 'unilateralism'.[56] Today, notwithstanding the abstention of the United States, the protocol has been ratified by 184 states and the EU.[57]

Code=Bush_Admin (indicating that the protocol 'exempts 80 percent of the world, including major population centers such as China and India, from compliance, and would cause serious harm to the U.S. economy').

51 See David G. Victor, *The Collapse of the Kyoto Protocol and the Struggle to Slow Global Warming* (Princeton University Press, 2001), at xi (considering the core of the 'Kyoto architecture' to be 'flawed').

52 See Daniel Bodansky, 'Bonn Voyage: Kyoto's Uncertain Revival' (2001) *The National Interest* 45 at 48.

53 See UNFCCC *Report of the Conference of the Parties to the United Nations Framework Convention on Climate Change on its Seventh Session*, U.N. Doc. FCCC/CP/2001/13/Add.1–3 (21 January 2002) (Marrakech Accords). The results of COP-7 are summarized in David A. Wirth, 'The Sixth Session (Part Two) and Seventh Session of the Conference of the Parties to the Framework Convention on Climate Change' (2002) 96 *American Journal of International Law* 648.

54 See UNFCCC, *Kyoto – Entered into Force on 16 February 2005*, at http://unfccc.int/meetings/kyoto_eif/items/3363.php.

55 See e.g., Hermann Ott, 'The Bonn Agreement to the Kyoto Protocol – Paving the Way for Ratification' (2001) 1 *International Environmental Agreements: Politics, Law and Economics* 469.

56 See, e.g., Tony Karon, 'When it Comes to Kyoto, the U.S. is the "Rogue Nation"', *TIME Magazine*, 24 July 2001, at www.time.com/time/world/article/0,8599,168701,00.html. See also David D. Caron, 'Between Empire and Community – The United States and Multilateralism 2001–2003: A Mid-Term Assessment' (2003) 21 *Berkeley Journal of international Law* 395 at 398.

57 As of 8 July 2009, the Kyoto Protocol had 188 parties. See *Kyoto Protocol Status of Ratification*, at http://unfccc.int/files/kyoto_protocol/status_of_ratification/application/pdf/kp_ratification_20090708.pdf.

However, the Kyoto Protocol is clearly not the solution to the world's climate change problem. The protocol's 2008–2012 commitments, even if fully implemented, will fall far short of achieving the convention's objective, something that parties were aware of when the protocol was negotiated. The Kyoto commitments were always seen as only a first step in the right direction. In the protocol, therefore, parties also agreed to begin consideration of new commitments well before expiry of the first commitment period.[58]

Discussions about such additional commitments have been underway for some time now, but have been sluggish and contentious, to say the least. The complexity and scope of the issues to be tackled are reflected in the Byzantine process that the parties agreed upon in 2005, and involving multiple tracks for considering further actions under the UNFCCC umbrella. An Ad-hoc Working Group was tasked, under Article 3.9 of the Kyoto Protocol, with considering new commitments for Annex I parties.[59] Given that the protocol's commitments are limited to Annex I parties, this track precludes consideration of developing country commitments. Article 9 of the protocol would have allowed for a broader review of the adequacy of the protocol and its approach, but the G77 and China resisted the discussion of emissions-related commitments by developing countries. In view of this resistance, industrialized states were unwilling to discuss a concrete negotiating mandate under Article 3.9. However, an open-ended 'dialogue' on 'long-term cooperative action' was launched under the auspices of the framework convention. It was intended in part to keep the United States and Australia, which had also refused to join the Kyoto Protocol, engaged in global deliberations, but also to provide a forum for engagement with developing countries.[60]

58 See Kyoto Protocol to the United Nations Framework Convention on Climate Change, Art. 3.9, at http://unfccc.int/resource/docs/convkp/kpeng.pdf.

59 See UNFCCC/Kyoto Protocol, *Report of the Conference of the Parties serving as the meeting of the Parties to the Kyoto Protocol on its first session, held at Montreal from 28 November to 10 December 2005*, Decision 1/CMP.1 (*Consideration of commitments for subsequent periods for Parties included in Annex I to the Convention under Art. 3, paragraph 9, of the Kyoto Protocol*), U.N. Doc. FCCC/KP/CMP/2005/8/Add.1, at http://unfccc.int/resource/docs/2005/cmp1/eng/08a01.pdf#page=3.

60 UNFCCC, *Report of the Conference of the Parties on its eleventh session, held at Montreal from 28 November to 10 December 2005*, Decision 1/CP.11 (*Dialogue on Long-Term Cooperative Action to Address Climate Change by Enhancing the Implementation of the Convention*), U.N. Doc. FCCC/CP/2005/5/Add.1, (Dialogue), online at http://unfccc.int/resource/docs/2005/cop11/eng/05a01.pdf.

The release of the Intergovernmental Panel on Climate Change's (IPCC) Fourth Assessment Report in 2007 injected a new sense of urgency into the discussions. The IPCC concluded that '[w]arming of the climate system is unequivocal, as is now evident from observations of increases in global average air and ocean temperatures, widespread melting of snow and ice, and rising global average sea level.'[61] It also found that the unprecedented increases of greenhouse gas concentrations in the atmosphere during the industrial era are the result of human activities.[62] Perhaps most importantly, the IPCC drove home the point that global greenhouse gas emissions would have to peak around 2020 and would have to be dramatically reduced by 2050 if there was to be a reasonable chance of averting dangerous warming.[63]

This message finally got through. At their June 2007 summit, G8 leaders agreed to aim for global emission reductions of at least 50 per cent by 2050, and to work within a UN process.[64] The latter pledge was important in that it was supported by the United States, which had been perceived by many observers as engaged in efforts to undercut the UN climate regime by promoting alternative, non-binding initiatives.[65]

At their December 2007 meeting in Bali, the parties to the UNFCCC adopted a decision on 'long-term cooperative action' on climate change.[66]

[61] Richard B. Alley *et al.*, 'IPCC 2007: Summary for Policymakers', in Susan Solomon *et al.* (eds.), *Climate Change 2007: The Physical Science Basis. Contribution of Working Group I to the Fourth Assessment Report of the Intergovernmental Panel on Climate Change* (Cambridge and New York: Cambridge University Press, 2007), p. 5, online at www.ipcc.ch/pdf/assessment-report/ar4/wg1/ar4-wg1-spm.pdf. A growing chorus of voices warns that even the IPCC's worst-case scenarios are in fact too conservative and that global climate change is occurring at a much faster rate than expected, in part due to various feedback effects. See Pew Center on Global Climate Change, *Key Scientific Developments since the IPCC Fourth Assessment Report – Science Brief 2*, June 2009, at www.pewclimate.org/brief/science-developments/June2009.

[62] See Alley *et al.*, note 61 above, pp. 2–3 (considering it to be 'very likely', i.e. more than 90% certain, that human impact accounts for these increases).

[63] See Terry Barker *et al.*, 'Technical Summary', in B. Metz *et al.* (eds.), *Climate Change 2007: Mitigation. Contribution of Working Group III to the Fourth Assessment Report of the Intergovernmental Panel on Climate Change* (Cambridge and New York: Cambridge University Press, 2007), pp. 39 and 90, online at www.ipcc.ch/pdf/assessment-report/ar4/wg3/ar4-wg3-ts.pdf.

[64] See *Chair's Summary*, G8 Summit – Heiligendamm, 8 June 2007, at www.g-8.de/Content/EN/Artikel/__g8-summit/anlagen/chairs-summary,templateId=raw,property=publicationFile.pdf/chairs-summary.pdf.

[65] See e.g. David Hunter, 'The Future of U.S. Climate Change Policy', in Bernstein *et al.*, above note 38, p. 79. And see below notes 100–2 and accompanying text.

[66] For helpful assessments of the Bali outcomes, see Lavanya Rajamani, 'From Berlin to Bali and Beyond: Killing Kyoto Softly' (2008) 57 *International and Comparative Law*

In the decision, dubbed the 'Bali Action Plan', the parties launched 'a comprehensive process' aimed at arriving, by 2009, at an 'agreed outcome' – a 'shared vision' for global climate action, 'including a long-term goal for emission reductions'.[67] To this end, it established an 'Ad hoc Working Group on Long-term Cooperative Action under the Convention',[68] thereby creating a complement to the working group that was already tasked with considering future Kyoto commitments.[69] The plan required that any 'shared vision' be 'in accordance with the provisions and principles of the convention, in particular the principle of common but differentiated responsibilities and respective capabilities'.[70] Part of the significance of the Bali Action Plan lies in the fact that it envisages climate action by all convention parties, rather than only those states currently committed under the Kyoto Protocol. Indeed, the language of the Action Plan moved away from the 'Annex I' and 'non-Annex I' party dichotomy that has constrained the current convention–protocol regime, and refers to future actions by 'developed' and 'developing' countries.[71]

After much wrangling, the United States and the major developing country emitters joined the consensus on this approach.[72] To keep these accomplishments in perspective, while the compromise struck in the Action Plan did not preclude future binding targets, it did not entail a commitment to them either.[73] Similarly, the plan was silent on interim targets for 2020. Instead, the Bali compromise consisted in recognizing that 'deep cuts in global emissions will be required' and, in emphasizing the 'urgency' of climate action, including by means of a footnote that references the IPCC findings.[74] The Ad-Hoc Working Group operating under the Kyoto Protocol went somewhat further and recognized that the IPCC's findings 'would require Annex I Parties as a group to reduce

Quarterly 909; and Chris Spence *et al.*, 'Great Expectations: Understanding Bali and the Climate Change Negotiation Process' (2008) 17 *Review of European Community and International Law* 142.

67 See Bali Action Plan, above note 20. 68 *Ibid.*, para. 2.

69 See above note 59 and accompanying text.

70 See Bali Action Plan, above note 20, para. 1(a).

71 See *ibid.*, para. 1(b). See Spence *et al.*, above note 66 at 150.

72 See Markus Becker, 'Climate Change Deal Reached after US U-Turn', *Der Spiegel Online*, 15 December 2007, at www.spiegel.de/international/world/0,1518,523570,00.html.

73 The Plan contemplates '[m]easurable, reportable and verifiable nationally appropriate mitigation commitments and actions, including quantified emission limitation and reduction objectives'. See Bali Action Plan, above note 20, para. 1(b)(i).

74 *Ibid.*, preamble.

emissions in a range of 25–40 per cent below 1990 levels by 2020'.[75] The group adopted a work programme pursuant to which it too was to report back to the protocol parties by 2009.[76]

Throughout 2009, attention was focused on the preparations for the December meetings of the parties to the UNFCCC and the Kyoto Protocol in Copenhagen, at which a new climate agreement was to be adopted. The deliberations of the convention and protocol working groups proceeded at an accelerated pace, and speculation was rife as to whether the parties would indeed arrive at an 'agreed outcome'.[77] While there was guarded optimism, it also became increasingly clear that, the negotiating states remained divided on a range of key issues, including the scope and stringency of new emission reduction commitments, and what legal form the outcome of the Copenhagen meetings should take.[78] Expectations for the outcome were gradually scaled back from a fully fledged legal agreement to a political agreement sketching the contours of a climate deal, to be fleshed out during 2010.[79]

Meanwhile, in the lead-up to the Copenhagen meetings, movement towards a new climate consensus was discernible. The G8 group of states confirmed their 'strong commitment to the UNFCCC negotiations' and to arriving at an 'ambitious post-2012 agreement in Copenhagen, involving all countries, consistent with the principle of common but differentiated responsibilities and respective capabilities'.[80] Whereas, at their 2007 meeting, the G8 leaders had committed to a 50 per cent cut in global greenhouse gas emissions, the 2009 declaration commits industrialized countries to an 80 per cent cut, albeit 'compared to 1990 or more recent years'.[81]

[75] UNFCCC, *Report of the Ad Hoc Working Group on Further Commitments for Annex I parties under the Kyoto Protocol on its resumed fourth session held in Bali, 3–15 December 2007* (Part III: *Review of work programme, methods of work and schedule of future sessions*), U.N. Doc. FCCC/KP/AWG/2007/5 (5 February 2008), para. 16, online at http://unfccc.int/resource/docs/2007/awg4/eng/05.pdf.

[76] *Ibid.*, para. 22(c).

[77] See e.g. Lavanya Rajamani, 'Addressing the "Post-Kyoto" Stress Disorder: Reflections on the Emerging Legal Architecture of the Climate Regime' (2009) 58 *International and Comparative Law Quarterly* 803.

[78] See Lavanya Rajamani, 'The Copenhagen Agreed Outcome: Form, Shape and Influence' Centre for Policy Research (CPR) *Climate Brief*, October 2009, at 2–3, at www.cprindia.org/policyupload/1259569856-CPR%20Polic%20Brief2.pdf.

[79] *Ibid.*, at 3.

[80] G8 Leaders' Declaration: *Responsible Leadership for a Sustainable Future*, 9 July 2009, para. 64, at www.g8italia2009.it/static/G8_Allegato/G8_Declaration_08_07_09_final,0.pdf.

[81] *Ibid.* See also Brian Laghi and Shawn McCarthy, 'Target found in G8's climate change fight', *The Globe and Mail*, 9 July 2009 (reporting that European countries are advocating

A parallel meeting of the 'Major Economies Forum' (MEF), established by President Obama in March 2009 to engage the seventeen states that account for roughly 80 per cent of global carbon emissions, could not agree on specific goals for emission cuts. Since industrialized countries were unwilling to commit to an interim target for 2020 and to promise financial and technological assistance, China and India refused to agree to a long-term target.[82] However, the MEF too 'reaffirmed the objective, provisions and principles of the UN Framework Convention on Climate Change', referring specifically to the principles of equity and common but differentiated responsibilities. Importantly, in the MEF declaration, the major developed and developing countries also agreed that increases in global temperature should not exceed 2° Celsius.[83] Furthermore, MEF States agreed that 'additional investment in developing countries should be mobilized' to address climate change.[84] During talks, British Prime Minister Gordon Brown went so far as to propose a US$100 billion fund to assist developing countries reduce emissions and adapt to climate change.[85]

3. Shared understandings

Having briefly retraced the lumbering evolution of the global climate regime and the reluctance of many key states to assume emission reduction commitments, one may wonder what shared understandings there

a 1990 reference year, whereas the United States and Canada, respectively, are calling for 2005 and 2006).

[82] See Peter Baker, 'Poorer Nations Reject Target on Emission Cut', *The New York Times*, 9 July 2009 (reporting that Europe and the United States had sought an agreement on a global cut of 50% by 2050, with industrialized countries cutting their emissions by 80%). See also Indrani Bagchi, 'Climbdown on 2° C clause done as a last resort', *The Times of India*, 17 July 2009.

[83] See MEF, *Declaration of the Leaders – The Major Economies Forum on Energy and Climate*, 9 July 2009, at www.whitehouse.gov/the_press_office/Declaration-of-the-Leaders-the-Major-Economies-Forum-on-Energy-and-Climate/. See also G8 Leaders' Declaration, above note 80, para. 65.

[84] MEF Declaration, above note 83.

[85] See Environment News Service, *17 Major Economies Pledge to Set Greenhouse Gas Limit by December*, 9 July 2009, at www.ens-newswire.com/ens/jul2009/2009–07-09–01.asp; and UK Department of Energy and Climate Change, *Make or break time for our climate*, Press Release 26 June 2009 (Prime Minister Gordon Brown 'urged countries to work together on a global figure of around $100 billion per year by 2020 to help developing countries reduce their emissions, tackle deforestation and adapt to the climate change already being experienced'), at www.decc.gov.uk/en/content/cms/news/pn065_1/pn065_1.aspx.

are in the climate change context. A closer look reveals that, while many points of divergence remain, the regime does rest upon a surprisingly solid, and apparently growing, foundation of shared ground. As we will show, there is broad agreement on the need for a global climate regime and a strong set of procedural understandings. As far as specific substantive commitments are concerned, shared understandings do not currently extend much beyond the proposition that the existing regime be developed to include deeper commitments for more parties, with industrialized countries taking the lead. The G8 and MEF meetings of July 2009 suggested that a consensus on 2050 emission targets was slowly emerging, but robust agreement on interim targets for industrialized countries and long-term targets for major developing countries remains elusive. We argue that to arrive at, and then sustain, an appropriate post-2012 commitment regime, parties must first develop strongly shared understandings of the meaning of the regime objective and of the core principle of CBDR. We therefore explore the shared understandings concerning these two central elements of the climate regime in some detail.

3.1 The need for a global legal regime

The universal membership in the convention that anchors the climate regime is *prima facie* evidence of the broad support that the global legal regime to address climate change enjoys. But membership by virtue of ratification is not enough in an interactional framework. Crucial for our purposes are the many indications that an active and enduring community of practice has evolved under the auspices of the convention. This practice community encompasses the states that are parties to the convention as well as a burgeoning network of non-governmental actors.

More than a thousand not-for-profit entities from all around the world, including NGOs (both civil society and business organizations), universities, think tanks and religious organizations, are accredited with the UNFCCC.[86] The sessions of the regime's plenary bodies are typically attended by hundreds of non-governmental observers. Many hold side-events during the official meetings, attended by a governmental and non-governmental audience, or use other venues and methods, including

[86] See UNFCCC, above note 17, Art. 10.6 (providing that 'any body or agency, whether national or international, governmental or non-governmental, which is qualified in matters covered by the Convention' can be admitted as an observer). For a list of accredited organizations, see http://unfccc.int/parties_and_observers/ngo/items/3667.php.

the internet, to present legal or policy proposals to the broader policy community as well as to the government negotiators.[87] An NGO is also central to disseminating factual information about developments within the climate regime. Aside from the official documents and meeting reports available at the UNFCCC website, the most detailed, most up-to-date and most widely relied upon 'reporting service' for the climate meetings is provided by the Earth Negotiations Bulletin (ENB), prepared under the auspices of the International Institute of Sustainable Development.[88] The official UNFCCC website provides a link to the ENB,[89] and negotiators consult the daily reports to bring themselves up to date on developments on various negotiating issues and on what positions were presented.[90]

It is fair to say that there exists a global network of actors closely connected to the climate regime. Some are state actors that participate formally in the negotiations, others observe the negotiations directly and provide 'on-site' input, yet others follow the developments through internet-based means, including the ENB and the UNFCCC website, and provide input from a distance. Epistemic communities, such as the scientists engaged in the work of the IPCC,[91] and norm entrepreneurs, including a broad range of NGOs working for or against further climate commitments,[92] are clearly active in the climate regime. However, we suggest epistemic communities, norm entrepreneurs, and other participants are in turn part of a community of practice, or of several overlapping such communities. The various protagonists pursue diverse and often competing objectives, including official government positions, environmental causes, business or commercial priorities, scientific or educational goals, and development or global justice concerns. Still, all these participants share a repertoire of 'climate expertise', encompassing the technical and legal language of

[87] See generally, Kal Raustiala, 'Non-State Actors in the Global Climate Regime', in Urs Lauterbacher and Detlev F. Sprinz, *International Relations and Global Climate Change* (Cambridge, Mass: MIT Press, 2001), pp. 104–9.

[88] The ENB issues covering various international environmental negotiating processes can be accessed via the IISD website at www.iisd.ca/.

[89] See UNFCCC webpage, *Civil Society and the Climate Change Process*, at http://unfccc.int/parties_and_observers/ngo/items/3667.php.

[90] Personal observation (Brunnée).

[91] See discussion in Chapter 2, text accompanying notes 17–31. On the IPCC, see www.ipcc.ch/; and see below notes 114–16 and accompanying text.

[92] See discussion in Chapter 2, text accompanying notes 2–16. NGOs working to support new climate commitments range from the Pew Center on Global Climate Change, a think tank, all the way to the more activist Climate Action Network. A prominent example of an NGO working against the climate regime is that of the Global Climate Coalition, a once influential association of industry groups that was disbanded in 2002.

the climate regime, working knowledge at least of scientific background information, and an understanding of the main negotiating and policy issues. In other words, they share a collective understanding of the enterprise they are engaged in, and of why the enterprise is important (see our discussion below of the treaty objective), but they do not necessarily have a common outlook regarding all aspects of the problem or common priorities in addressing it.[93] As we have shown in Chapter 2,[94] the presence of such a community of practice is significant. Epistemic communities or norm entrepreneurs initiate and shape debates, but only a community of practice can instantiate and sustain the background knowledge, norms and practices that nourish a regime.

The convention and protocol parties themselves meet twice each year to deliberate on scientific, policy and legal issues pertaining to climate change, doing so on the basis of, and continuously reinforcing, the substantive and procedural requirements of the regime. As we will illustrate below, the convention's objective and its core principles have proven to be influential in framing the deliberations among parties and the evolution of the regime over time. In turn, the decision-making rules of the regime, such as the rules of procedure of the COP, or the rules concerning the adoption of amendments, are a steady staple in the practice within the regime. Parties pay careful attention to these rules, ensuring that decisions of the treaty bodies meet the relevant procedural requirements.

For example, when parties sought to adopt the decisions necessary to flesh out the Kyoto Protocol, they faced a conundrum. The protocol empowers its plenary body, the Meeting of the Parties, to adopt the relevant decisions. In order to decide whether or not to ratify – and bring into force – the protocol, states need to assess the reporting, emissions trading, or compliance rules that emerge from these decisions. However, the Meeting of the Parties comes into existence and meets only after entry into force of the protocol.[95] The Parties solved the dilemma by tasking the convention COP with the elaboration of the decisions, for subsequent adoption by the protocol parties.[96] Similarly, in the negotiations for post-2012 commitments, parties ran up against the rule establishing that amendments to the Kyoto Protocol must be communicated to all Parties

[93] See Chapter 1, text accompanying note 99, and Chapter 2.

[94] See discussion in Chapter 2, text accompanying notes 34–56.

[95] See Art. 13.6 of the Kyoto Protocol, above note 18.

[96] See above note 17 and accompanying text. But see Art. 17 of the Kyoto Protocol, above note 18 (authorizing the COP of the convention directly to adopt the decision on emissions trading).

six months before the meeting at which they are proposed for adoption.[97] Since parties could not agree on a proposal during the June 2009 meetings in Bonn, several parties made individual submissions to keep the door open for amendment discussions in Copenhagen in December 2009.[98] While these examples suggest that parties sometimes apply the procedural rules flexibly, they also illustrate that they do not simply ignore the requirements when inconvenient, but take pains to adhere to their letter and spirit. However, as we hinted in the introduction to this chapter, and will explore in more detail below in section 6, one aspect of the regime's procedural practice, the practice of decision-making by consensus, posed serious challenges during the Copenhagen meetings.

Nonetheless, to date the convention's community of practice has proven resilient enough for the regime to withstand a range of efforts to sideline it and to undercut the widely shared understanding that the global climate regime should be universal, and legal in nature. We have already seen that the Kyoto Protocol survived – and perhaps was even strengthened by – the US decision in 2001 not to ratify the agreement.[99] A few years later, in 2005, the United States helped launch the Asia-Pacific Partnership on Clean Development and Climate.[100] The arrangement was meant to promote direct engagement between the world's fastest growing emitters of greenhouse gases in the South, China and India, along with South Korea, and the United States, Japan, Australia and Canada. However, it received mixed reviews from other states, due to the concern that it could undermine UNFCCC processes including the effort to extend the legally binding emission reduction commitments under the Kyoto Protocol.[101] Similar concerns were raised about the Bush administration's September 2007 effort to launch a 'major emitters' process that would bring the largest industrialized and developing country emitters together to consider voluntary actions to promote research and technology development.[102] By

[97] *Ibid.*, Art. 20.2.

[98] Several Parties made proposals for a new protocol or implementing agreement under the Convention; others proposed amendments to the Kyoto Protocol. See http://unfccc.int/2860.php.

[99] See above note 52 and accompanying text.

[100] See Asia-Pacific Partnership on Clean Development and Climate, at www.asiapacificpartnership.org/.

[101] See Associated Press, *U.S., partners sign own climate pact: Technology focus contrasts with mandatory emission cuts in Kyoto treaty*, 28 July 2005, at www.msnbc.msn.com/id/8730232/.

[102] See U.S. Department of State, *Bureau of Oceans and international Environmental and Scientific Affairs, Major Economies Forum on Energy and Climate Change*, at www.state.

contrast, President Obama's MEF was explicitly cast as intended to 'help generate the political leadership necessary to achieve a successful outcome at the December UN climate change conference in Copenhagen', thereby confirming the centrality of the UN regime.[103] And, as we have seen, in their July 2009 meetings, the MEF states expressed their unequivocal support for the UN regime. By 2009, then, the MEF and the G8 had become venues within which the leaders of major carbon emitting states could attempt to work towards the consensus required for adoption of post-2012 commitments at Copenhagen.

3.2 *The objective of the regime*

The 'ultimate objective' of the climate convention 'and any related legal instrument' is to achieve a 'stabilization of greenhouse gas concentrations in the atmosphere at a level that prevents dangerous climate change' (Art. 2 UNFCCC). Among the state parties to the regime, as well as among the non-state actors engaged in its further development, this objective has achieved a taken-for-granted quality and is routinely invoked in the current discussions about further commitments.[104] It underpins the Kyoto Protocol,[105] and frames the Bali Action Plan pursuant to which post-2012 commitments are being negotiated,[106] and was recognized in the Copenhagen Accord adopted in December 2009.[107]

However, only relatively recently has a stronger shared understanding emerged around the meaning of the regime's objective. Since the adoption of the UNFCCC in 1992, states and other international and domestic actors have debated what constitutes 'dangerous climate

gov/g/oes/climate/mem/; and see Andrew C. Revkin, 'Bush Climate Plan: Amid Nays, Some Maybes', *The New York Times*, 4 June 2007.

103 US Department of State, *Bureau of Public Affairs, Major Economies Forum on Energy and Climate*, Press Release Number 2009/369 (23 April 2009), at www.state.gov/r/pa/prs/ps/2009/04/122097.htm. See also Andrew C. Revkin, 'White House Announces International Meetings to Address Energy and Climate Issues', *The New York Times*, 28 March 2009.

104 See e.g. the routine invocation of the objective in the submissions to the Ad Hoc Working Group on Long-Term Cooperative Action (AWG-LCA) by states, intergovernmental organizations, and non-governmental observers. The submissions made since the AWG-LCA's first session in March 2008 can be accessed at http://unfccc.int/meetings/ad_hoc_working_groups/lca/items/4918.php.

105 See preamble, Kyoto Protocol, above note 18.

106 See Bali Action Plan, above note 20, preamble, para. 1(a).

107 Copenhagen Accord, above note 19, paras. 1 and 2.

change',[108] and at what level the concentration of greenhouse gases in the atmosphere would have to be stabilized to prevent it.

As we noted earlier, the tipping point in the broader debate about climate change was reached when the IPCC published its report in 2007. In the report, hundreds of leading, government-nominated scientists from around the world confirmed that human-induced climate change is occurring, and that it will have dangerous environmental effects if unabated.[109] In terms of capturing public imagination, the ground for the IPCC's message was prepared by Al Gore's efforts to articulate the 'inconvenient truth' in a manner that resonated with the proverbial person on the street.[110] The Nobel Peace Prize that was awarded jointly to the IPCC and Gore speaks to the combined impact that the two initiatives had on generating awareness and shifting the public debate.[111] The shift is also reflected in the marked change in media coverage on climate change. Most notably, media reports abandoned the practice of citing climate sceptics in every news item that invoked the mounting scientific evidence of human-induced warming.[112] Indeed, by September 2007, large majorities of people in both industrialized and developing countries believed that human activity causes climate change, and that all countries must take strong action sooner rather than later.[113]

[108] See Katherine Richardson *et al.*, *Climate Change: Global Risks, Challenges & Decisions Copenhagen 2009, 10–12 March* (Synthesis Report), p. 12, at http://climatecongress.ku.dk/pdf/synthesisreport/ (noting that 'defining "dangerous climate change" is ultimately a value judgment to be made by societies as a whole').

[109] See above notes 61–3 and accompanying text.

[110] See www.climatecrisis.net/.

[111] See *The Nobel Peace Prize 2007*, at http://nobelprize.org/nobel_prizes/peace/laureates/2007/index.html.

[112] See Andrew Revkin, 'Skeptics Dispute Climate Worries and Each Other', *The New York Times*, 8 March 2009; and Sharon Begley, 'The Truth About Denial', *Newsweek*, 13 August 2007 (detailing the extent to which climate sceptics or 'deniers' had been funded by industry, and reporting that 'contrarian scientists' typically did not base their critiques of mainstream studies on original research). See also BBC News Service, *'Maverick' risk to science debate*, 30 November 2006, at http://news.bbc.co.uk/2/hi/science/nature/6159371.stm (citing Lord Martin Reed, President of the UK Royal Society: 'It used to be controversial whether smoking caused lung cancer, it used to be controversial whether HIV caused Aids. Now, there are a few mavericks who deny those things. In the case of climate change, I think the debate is going the same way in that there is a strong consensus that it is a serious matter').

[113] See BBC World Service, *All Countries Need to Take Major Steps on Climate Change: Global Poll*, 25 September 2007, at http://news.bbc.co.uk/2/shared/bsp/hi/pdfs/25_09_07climatepoll.pdf (in the BBC's poll of 22,000 people in 21 countries, an average of eight in ten (79%) say that 'human activity, including industry and

From the perspective of the global climate regime, the shift in the public debate was important in rallying states around the regime's objective. The IPCC report was particularly influential in this regard. It was specifically cast in terms of the UNFCCC objective. Furthermore, it identified the greenhouse gas concentrations that could avert dangerous climate change, and suggested the emission reduction levels and the time-frames that would be required to achieve the objective.[114] While there continues to be debate about the medium- and long-term emission reductions required to achieve the stabilization goal, there is general agreement that delayed reductions significantly constrain the stabilization opportunities and increase the risks of more severe climate impacts.[115]

In any case, the discussions about emission reductions are now clearly structured by the convention's objective and, notwithstanding the reluctance of some delegations,[116] states cannot avoid engaging with the IPCC's findings, which translate the objective into concrete terms. Indeed, one of the major actors in the climate negotiations, the EU, has explicitly tied its negotiating position to the convention objective. Since 2005, EU policy development has been anchored in the goal of limiting global temperature increases to 2° C above pre-industrial levels.[117] While there is not yet global consensus on this temperature target, it is now widely seen as providing a reasonable chance of avoiding 'dangerous' climate change.[118] The

transportation, is a significant cause of climate change', nine out of ten say that action is necessary to address global warming, and a substantial majority (65%) chose the strongest position, saying that 'it is necessary to take major steps starting very soon').

114 See Barker *et al.*, 'Technical Summary' in Metz *et al.* (eds.), above note 63, pp. 32, 39 and 90, at www.ipcc.ch/pdf/assessment-report/ar4/wg3/ar4-wg3-ts.pdf.

115 See R.K. Pachauri and A. Reisinger (eds.), *Climate Change 2007: Synthesis Report. Contribution of Working Groups I, II and III to the Fourth Assessment Report of the Intergovernmental Panel on Climate Change* (Geneva: IPCC, 2008), p. 19, at www.ipcc.ch/pdf/assessment-report/ar4/syr/ar4_syr.pdf.

116 In the Bali Action Plan, above note 20, parties were unable to agree on an explicit acknowledgement of the IPCC findings. Instead, they recognized 'that deep cuts in global emissions will be required to achieve the ultimate objective of the Convention and emphasiz[ed] the urgency', while citing the IPCC report in a footnote.

117 See e.g., Council of the European Union, *Information Note 7242/05 of 11 March 2005 on Climate Change: Medium and longer term emission reduction strategies, including targets: Council conclusions*, at http://register.consilium.europa.eu/pdf/en/05/st07/st07242.en05.pdf.

118 See Malte Meinshausen *et al.*, 'Greenhouse-gas emission targets for limiting global warming to 2 C' (2009) 458 *Nature* 1158 (noting that '[m]ore than 100 countries have adopted a global warming limit of 2° C or below (relative to pre-industrial levels' as a guiding principle for mitigation efforts to reduce climate change risks, impacts and damages'). And see Richardson *et al.*, above note 108.

importance of this emerging shared understanding, and the endorsement of the 2° C target by the G8 and MEF, is difficult to overstate. The latter marks the first time that the major industrialized and developing country emitters agreed on a threshold that quantifies the objective set out in Article 1 of the UNFCCC.[119]

The example of the objective provision illustrates that the formal articulation of a given proposition, even in a universally endorsed treaty, is not necessarily matched by a genuine shared understanding among treaty parties. In the case of Article 1 of the UNFCCC, states arguably agreed on the goal of averting dangerous climate change – a goal that is difficult to argue with. However, it took more than fifteen years for an agreed definition of 'dangerous climate change' to emerge. At the same time, the example illustrates the importance of setting out conceptual reference points to guide the evolution of a regime. Now that its central concept has been defined, the Article 1 objective not only provides general direction to states' efforts, but sets a bar against which the credibility of emission reduction commitments can be measured. From the temperature target maximum concentrations of greenhouse gases in the atmosphere can be extrapolated, which in turn permits conclusions about the timing and extent of the emission reductions required to achieve those concentrations.[120]

It is arguable, therefore, that a shared understanding on the specific meaning of the regime objective will facilitate the emergence of shared understandings surrounding emission reduction commitments. It certainly narrows the elbow room that states have in their deliberations on emission reductions. At first glance, the negotiations leading up to

[119] But note that Indian leaders subsequently suggested that the agreement on the 2° target was merely a political compromise. See Bagchi, above note 82 (quoting the Indian Prime Minister's special envoy on climate change as saying: 'We do not regard this as an arithmetical target; we regard this as a political decision because there is a great deal of uncertainty with respect to what would be the actual rise in temperature, what would be the consequences of that rise of temperature'). Note also that, during the Copenhagen meetings, AOSIS and some African states sought to enshrine a 1.5° C target. See below, section 6.

[120] See here the negotiating position of the EU, which is constructed precisely in this fashion. See Commission of the European Communities, *Communication from the Commission to the Council, the European Parliament, the European Economic and Social Committee and the Committee of the Regions – Limiting global climate change to 2 degrees Celsius – The way ahead for 2020 and beyond*, COM (2007) 2 final, 1 October 2007, pp. 2 and 9, at http://eur-lex.europa.eu/LexUriServ/LexUriServ.do?uri=COM:2007:0002:FIN:EN:PDF.

the Copenhagen meeting seemed to suggest otherwise. After all, in the very same declaration in which they accepted the 2° C target, developed countries also refused to commit to mid-term emissions reductions. Yet, the presence of 2° C target in the documents enabled the UN Secretary-General, Ban Ki-Moon, to admonish developed countries, stating that they:

> ... must lead by example in making firm commitments to reduce their emissions by 2020 on the order of the 25 to 40 per cent below 1990 levels that the Intergovernmental Panel on Climate Change (IPCC) tells us is required. It is disappointing to note that thus far, the mid-term emissions targets announced by developed countries in the MEF are not in this range.[121]

In the same vein, the Chair of the IPCC, Rajendra Pachauri, noted bluntly that the G8 leaders had 'clearly ignored' the IPCC findings, adding:

> If the G8 leaders agreed on this 2-degree increase as being the limit that could be accepted, then I think they should have also accepted the attendant requirement of global emissions peaking by 2015.[122]

These observations illustrate how the 2° C target serves to strengthen arguments in favour of a strong post-2012 commitment regime. In turn, such strong statements by high-profile individuals within the climate community of practice lend support to developing countries as they demand that developed states take on interim targets. The same applies to the position of the EU. Arguably, EU advocacy played an important role in bringing the 2° C target into the G8 and MEF declaration. Conversely, this target, and statements such as those quoted above, bolstered the EU's official position. That position committed the EU to a unilateral emissions cut of 20 per cent by 2020, combined with an offer to reduce emissions by 30 per cent if other developed countries do the same.[123] The hold-outs on

[121] See UN News Centre, *Challenges remain in run-up to Copenhagen climate change conference – UN official*, 15 July 2009, at www.un.org/apps/news/story.asp?NewsID=31479&Cr=climate+change&Cr1.

[122] See UN News Centre, G8 leaders 'ignored' UN's scientific findings on climate change, says official, 20 July 2009; at www.un.org/apps/news/story.asp?NewsID=31524&Cr=climate+change&Cr1.

[123] See Commission of the European Communities, *Communication from the Commission to the Council, the European Parliament, the European Economic and Social Committee and the Committee of the Regions – Towards a comprehensive climate change agreement in Copenhagen*, COM(2009) 39 final (28 January 2009), p. 2, at http://eur-lex.europa.eu/LexUriServ/LexUriServ.do?uri=COM:2009:0039:FIN:EN:PDF.

interim targets were Australia, Canada, and Japan, all of which announced national interim goals that were pegged to a reference year other than 1990.[124] The United States and Russia also remained on the fence. It stands to reason, however, that the increasingly prominent role of the 2° C target amplified the international pressure on these states to accept 2020 reduction commitments. Indeed, in August 2009, New Zealand announced its willingness to cut emissions by between 10 and 20 per cent below 1990 levels by 2020.[125] In November 2009, in the lead-up to the Copenhagen meetings, President Barack Obama announced his administration's willingness to cut US emissions by 17 per cent below 2005 levels by 2020.[126] China and India followed suit shortly after with the announcement of emissions intensity targets.[127]

3.3 The Principle of Common but Differentiated Responsibilities (CBDR)

3.3.1 CBDR and the climate regime

The repeated references to CBDR in the UNFCCC, combined with its prominent position in the Berlin Mandate, the Kyoto Protocol, and the Bali Action Plan, and its endorsement by the July 2009 G8 and MEF meetings, indicate that CBDR is the most important among the principles that frame the climate regime. Aside from the climate regime, the most prominent articulation of the CBDR principle is found in Principle 7 of the 1992 Rio Declaration on Environment and Development, which provides that:

> States shall cooperate in a spirit of global partnership to conserve, protect and restore the health and integrity of the Earth's ecosystem. In view of

[124] See Joint Submission by Australia, Belarus, Canada, the European Community and its Member States, Iceland, Japan, Kazakhstan, Liechtenstein, Monaco, New Zealand, Norway, Russian Federation, Switzerland and Ukraine, *Information relating to possible quantified emissions limitation and reduction objectives as submitted by Parties*, 10 August 2009, at http://unfccc.int/files/kyoto_protocol/application/pdf/australia100809.pdf.

[125] See Alister Doyle, Reuters, *Time running out for December climate pact: U.N.*, 10 August 2009, at www.reuters.com/article/newsOne/idUSTRE57926O20090810.

[126] John M. Broder, 'Obama to go to Copenhagen with Emissions Target', *The New York Times*, 25 November 2009; at www.nytimes.com/2009/11/26/us/politics/26climate.html.

[127] See Edward Wong and Keith Bradsher, 'China Joins U.S. in Pledge of Hard Targets on Emissions', *The New York Times*, 26 November 2009; at www.nytimes.com /2009/11/27/science/earth/27climate.html. And see Rama Lakshmi, 'Moves by U.S., China induce India to do its bit on climate', *The Washington Post*, 2 December 2009; at www.washingtonpost.com/wp-dyn/content/article/2009/12/01/AR2009120102591.html.

> the different contributions to global environmental degradation, States have common but differentiated responsibilities. The developed countries acknowledge the responsibility that they bear in the international pursuit to sustainable development in view of the pressures their societies place on the global environment and of the technologies and financial resources they command.[128]

Elements of the CBDR principle are also expressed or reflected in a range of other agreements on environmental protection, including the Law of the Sea Convention, the Montreal Protocol on Substances that Deplete the Ozone Layer, and the Convention on Biological Diversity.[129] Similarly, in its 2001 report in the *Shrimp-Turtle* case, the WTO panel urged Malaysia and the United States to cooperate on concluding an agreement on sea turtles, 'taking into account the principle that States have common but differentiated responsibilities to conserve and protect the environment'.[130]

As these examples illustrate, the CBDR principle has come to play a pivotal role in international environmental law as it relates to global concerns.[131] We therefore focus our discussion of convention principles in this chapter on CBDR. The principle interests us for a variety of reasons aside from its prominent position in the treaty.

First, it furnishes us with an opportunity to examine the impact and further evolution of a norm that is not easily slotted into the formal legal categories of custom or treaty. Notwithstanding its apparently universal acceptance in international environmental law,[132] the clear weight of opinion is that CBDR has not acquired the status of customary international law.[133]

[128] *Rio Declaration on Environment and Development*, U.N. Doc. A/CONF.151/26 (vol. I); 31 ILM 874 (1992), principle 7.

[129] Patricia Birnie, Alan Boyle and Catherine Redgwell, *International Law and the Environment*, 3rd edn (New York: Oxford University Press, 2009), pp. 132–5.

[130] WTO (2002) United States – Import Prohibition of Certain Shrimp and Shrimp Products: Recourse to Art. 21.5 by Malaysia, WT/DS58/AB/RW, Panel Report 15 June 2001, para. 7.2., at http://docsonline.wto.org/DDFDocuments/t/WT/DS/58RW.doc.

[131] See International Law Association, *Report of the Seventieth Conference, New Delhi, 2002* (London: ILA, 2002) at 394 (Committee on Legal Aspects of Sustainable Development): 'the principle of *common but differentiated responsibilities* has a firm status in … international environmental law' and Philippe Cullet, *Differential Treatment in International Environmental Law* (Brookfield, Vt: Ashgate Publishing Co., 2003).

[132] Birnie *et al.*, above note 129 at p. 132.

[133] See e.g. Lavanya Rajamani, 'The Principle of Common but Differentiated Responsibility and the Balance of Commitments under the Climate Regime' (2000) 9 *Review of European Community and International Environmental Law* 120 at 124; Tuula Honkonen, 'The Principle of Common but Differentiated Responsibility in Post-2012 Climate Negotiations' (2009) 18 *Review of European Community and International Environmental Law* 257, at 258 and Birnie *et al.*, above note 129 at p. 135.

This conclusion follows from the diverse, context-specific articulations of the principle and from the lasting disagreement on some of its elements.[134] Similarly, the principle does not have the same formal status that a substantive or procedural provision contained in the operative part of a treaty would ordinarily have. Great care was taken by some parties to ensure that the principle was contained in the preamble to the UNFCCC, and to circumscribe its inclusion in the operative Article 3 by specifying that parties are to be 'guided' by the principles articulated in that provision.[135] Nonetheless CBDR and the other principles expressed in the convention provide parameters for the interpretation and application of the treaty and for further negotiations by the parties on new commitments.[136] Treaty practice, including in the repeated references to the convention principles in the decisions and instruments adopted to develop the climate regime, confirms this point.

A second feature of CBDR that interests us is the very fact that it is a principle and, as such does not require particular outcomes, but rather provides reasons or considerations that decision-makers must take into account.[137] The climate regime allows us to observe how CBDR has exerted precisely this kind of influence during the course of the efforts to further develop of the climate regime.

Finally, we are intrigued by the fact that CBDR is both firmly established in the climate regime, and the subject of fierce debates about its precise parameters. The negotiations for post-2012 climate commitments provide us with an opportunity to observe the extent to which, and how, CBDR has figured in the interventions of states and other regime participants. Thus, just as we can observe how the principle shapes deliberations within the regime and has proven impossible to dislodge, we can also trace efforts by various regime participants to shape its meaning. Put slightly differently, close attention to the continuing normative debate surrounding CBDR permits us to identify the extent to which actors in

134 On the many differences among states in reading the principle, see also Susan Biniaz, 'Common But Differentiated Responsibility – Remarks' (2002) 96 *American Society of International Law Proceedings* 358 at 359 and 362–3.

135 See Daniel Bodansky, 'The United Nations Framework Convention on Climate Change: A Commentary' (1993) 18 *Yale Journal of International Law* 451 at 502; and Farhana Yamin and Joanna Depledge, *The International Climate Change Regime: A Guide to Rules, Institutions and Procedures* (New York: Cambridge University Press, 2004), p. 66.

136 Lluís Paradell-Trius, 'Principles of International Environmental Law: an Overview' (2000) 9 *Review of European Community and International Environmental Law* 93 at 96.

137 A. E. Boyle, 'Some Reflections on the Relationship of Treaties and Soft Law' (1999) 48 *International and Comparative Law Quarterly* 901 at 907–8.

the climate regime share an understanding of a core meaning of CBDR, and to what extent the norm remains contested.

3.3.2 Shared ground and contested meanings

A closer look at the UNFCCC, related sources, and relevant practice reveals that some elements of CBDR are generally agreed upon, while others are subject to debate. The CBDR principle figures prominently in the submissions by states, intergovernmental organizations, and non-governmental observers in the continuing discussions under the auspices of the Bali Action Plan.[138] It seems fair to say that there is wide agreement on the basic idea that animates the CBDR concept in the present context: that addressing climate change and its consequences is a common responsibility of all states,[139] but that states' attendant individual responsibilities are differentiated.[140] There also appears to be a shared sense that capacity differences among states are relevant to that differentiation of responsibilities. Finally, states seem to agree that industrialized countries should take the lead in combating climate change. Beyond these very basic parameters, however, the common ground between states is not as easily charted.

3.3.2.1 Differentiation While there is broad consensus that differentiation of commitments can take a variety of forms,[141] it is less clear what states' or groups of states' responsibilities are to be differentiated, and what the criteria or reasons are for such differentiation. There is consensus that the respective responsibilities of developed and developing countries under the climate regime are to be differentiated from one another.

138 Submissions to the AWG-LCA can be accessed at http://unfccc.int/meetings/ad_hoc_working_groups/lca/items/4918.php.

139 See UNFCCC, *Views regarding the work programme of the Ad Hoc Working Group on Long-term Cooperative Action under the Convention*, AWGLCA, 1st Sess., UNFCCC Doc. FCCC/AWGLCA/2008/MISC.1 (3 March 2008), at http://unfccc.int/resource/docs/2008/awglca1/eng/misc01.pdf. See e.g. submission of Singapore therein at p. 66, 'Paper No. 19: Singapore – Work Programme for the Ad Hoc Working Group on Long-Term Cooperative Action under the Convention' (stating that 'All countries, both developed and developing, have a part to play to address climate change …').

140 See Lavanya Rajamani, 'From Stockholm to Johannesburg: The Anatomy of Dissonance in the International Environmental Regime' (2003) 12 *Review of European Community and International Environmental Law* 23 at 31.

141 The convention is not specific on the types of differentiation that the CBDR principle can give rise to. Art. 4 suggests that differentiation can relate to the *type of commitment* (e.g. emission reduction commitment in Art. 4.2 *vs* other commitments in Art. 4.1; and emission reduction commitments in Art. 4.2 *vs* financial commitments in Art. 4.3).

This approach is consonant with Principle 7 of the Rio Declaration and with the practice under other MEAs. It is also reflected in the distinction between developed and developing country commitments set out in Article 4 of the UNFCCC, as well as in the Berlin Mandate, Kyoto Protocol, and Bali Action Plan.

What remained controversial is the question whether the CBDR principle can accommodate differentiation within the 'developed' and 'developing' country groupings.[142] In the past, developing countries have tended to take the position that the principle is applicable only to differentiation between industrialized and developing countries, and not among the former or among the latter.[143] However, the requirement in the Bali Action Plan that a shared vision for long-term cooperative action also take into account 'social and economic conditions and other relevant factors' (para. 1(a)), as well the differences in the 'national circumstances' of developed country parties (para. 1(b)(i)), and the focus on 'nationally appropriate' mitigation actions by developing country parties (para. 1(b)(ii)) all suggest that CBDR can accommodate differentiation amongst developed and developing countries, respectively.[144]

Article 4.2(a) of the UNFCCC, as well as para. 2(a) of the Berlin Mandate, require that emission reduction commitments of Annex I parties be set:

> taking into account the differences in ... starting points and approaches, economic structures and resources bases, the need to maintain strong and sustainable economic growth, available technologies and other individual circumstances ...

This idea was then implemented through Article 3.1 and Annex B of the Kyoto Protocol, which establishes differing emission reduction commitments for Annex I parties. Even if this differentiation were not to flow from the CBDR principle as such, the structure of commitments under the climate regime at the very least confirms that the principle does not preclude it. The same argument applies to differentiation amongst developing countries. Indeed, within that group, the preamble to the UNFCCC and its Article 4 explicitly recognize the particular circumstances of, for

[142] See e.g. 'Paper No. 2C: France on behalf of the EC – Enhanced national/international action on mitigation of climate change', in UNFCCC, *Ideas and proposals on the elements contained in Paragraph 1 of the Bali Action Plan. Submissions from Parties. Addendum.*, AWGLCA, 4th Sess., UNFCCC Doc., FCCC/AWGLCA/2008/MISC.5/Add.1 (21 November 2008), p. 14, at http://unfccc.int/resource/docs/2008/awglca4/eng/misc05a01.pdf.

[143] Bodansky, above note 135 at 506.

[144] See Bali Action Plan, above note 20.

example, small island countries, countries prone to desertification, and fossil fuel-producing countries. Furthermore, developing countries that are 'particularly vulnerable to the adverse effects of climate change', are singled out by Article 12.8 of the Kyoto Protocol to receive a share of the proceeds from CDM projects to assist with adaptation measures.

To be sure, some states remained staunchly opposed to such differentiation. For example, according to China:

> The principle of 'common but differentiated responsibilities' between developed and developing countries is the keystone of the Convention and the Bali Action Plan. Any further sub-categorization of developing countries runs against the Convention itself and is not in conformity with the consensus reached in the Bali Action Plan.[145]

For Qatar:

> Efforts to differentiate between developing countries are totally not acceptable and in particular, [*sic*] on basis of GDP or GHG per capita are which are detrimental to Qatar.[146]

However, the conclusion that the CBDR principle, as reflected in the climate regime, does not preclude and may even require differentiation within groups, appears to be shared by a growing number of parties, both developed and developing. For example, Australia argued:

> There has to be yet further differentiation of responsibilities and capabilities other than highlighting the vulnerability and lack of capacity of some Parties to respond to the impacts of climate change. There is considerable variation in the circumstances of the 191 countries in the UNFCCC. Accordingly, there can be many different approaches to differentiating and grouping countries according to such circumstances.[147]

[145] See *Paper No. 5: China – China's Views on Enabling the Full, Effective and Sustained Implementation of the Convention through Long-Term Cooperative Action Now, Up To and Beyond 2012*, in UNFCCC, *Ideas and proposals on the elements contained in paragraph 1 of the Bali Action Plan. Submissions from Parties*, AWGLCA, 4th Sess., UNFCCC Doc. FCCC/AWGLCA/2008/MISC.5 (27 October 2008), p. 34, at http://unfccc.int/resource/docs/2008/awglca4/eng/misc05.pdf.

[146] See Qatar in UNFCCC, *Ideas and proposals on the elements contained in paragraph 1 of the Bali Action Plan. Submissions from Parties. Part II*, AWGLCA, 6th Sess., UNFCCC Doc. FCCC/AWGLCA/2009/MISC.4 (Part II) (19 May 2009), p. 75, at http://unfccc.int/resource/docs/2009/awglca6/eng/misc04p02.pdf. See also *Paper No. 19: Saudi Arabia – Fulfillment of the Bali Action Plan AWG-LCA*, in UNFCCC, *Ideas and proposals on the elements contained in paragraph 1 of the Bali Action Plan. Submissions from Parties*, AWGLCA, 5th Sess., UNFCCC Doc FCCC/AWGLCA/2009/MISC.1 (13 March 2009), p. 73, at http://unfccc.int/resource/docs/2009/awglca5/eng/misc01.pdf.

[147] Australia – 'Initial Views on A long-Term Global Goal for Emission Reductions', in UNFCCC, *Views Regarding the Work Programme of the Ad Hoc Working Group*

Similarly, France submitted on behalf of the European Community that:

> ... a key issue to explore under the BAP [Bali Action Plan] is what the principle of CBDR and respective capabilities means for nationally appropriate mitigation action between and within groupings ...[148]

Canada submitted that:

> Each country has different national circumstances and respective capabilities and the Convention AWG should determine criteria relevant to the definition of these circumstances ...[149]

Developing countries, in turn, have focused their remarks primarily on differentiation within their group. For example, for Bangladesh, the task of the shared vision was to:

> [d]etermine global mitigation targets for post Kyoto climate regime based on common but differentiated responsibility (regarding but not limited to

on Long-term Cooperative Action under the Convention. Submissions from Parties. Addendum, AWGLCA, 1st Sess., UNFCCC Doc. FCCC/AWGLCA/2008/MISC.1/Add.2 (20 March 2008), pp. 7–8, online at http://unfcccbali.org/unfccc/images/document/Action_Under_Convention.pdf.

148 'Paper No. 1A: France on behalf of the EC – Mitigation, including technology and finance', in UNFCCC, *Ideas and proposals on the elements contained in paragraph 1 of the Bali Action Plan. Submissions from Parties*, AWGLCA, 3rd Sess., UNFCCC Doc. FCCC/AWGLCA/2008/MISC.2 (14 August 2008), p.5, online at http://unfccc.int/resource/docs/2008/awglca3/eng/misc02.pdf.

149 'Paper No. 2: Canada – The Bali Action Plan – Views Regarding the Work Programme for the Ad Hoc Working Group on Long-term Cooperative Action Under the Convention', in FCCC/AWGLCA/2008/MISC.1/Add.2, above note 147, p. 10. See also 'Paper No. 24: United States – Submission of the United States under the Bali Action Plan Decision 1/CP.13', in FCCC/AWGLCA/2008/MISC.1, above note 139, p. 87 (noting that the agreed outcome 'will need to accommodate a wide range of national circumstances and approaches'); 'Paper No. 8F: New Zealand – A submission to the Ad hoc Working Group on Long-term Cooperative Action under the Convention Overview Comments on the Bali Action Plan', in FCCC/AWGLCA/2008/MISC.5, above note 145, p. 60 ('Static categories of "developed" and "developing" country, or "Annex I/II" and "non-Annex I" Parties are no longer helpful. Instead, there should be a dynamic continuum with different commitments, actions and support for different countries based on common, objective criteria.'); 'Paper No. 32: Turkey – Information, Views and Proposals by Turkey Regarding Paragraph 1 of the Bali Action Plan of the Ad Hoc Working Group on Long-term Cooperative Action Under the Convention', in UNFCCC, *Ideas and proposals on the elements contained in paragraph 1 of the Bali Action Plan. Submissions from Parties. Addendum. Part II*, AWGLCA, 4th Sess., UNFCCC Doc. FCCC/AWGLCA/2008/MISC.5/Add.2 (Part II) (20 December 2008), pp. 67–8, at http://unfccc.int/resource/docs/2008/awglca4/eng/misc05a02p01.pdf; and 'Paper No. 7: Japan – Japan's Proposal for AWGLCA: For preparation of Chair's document for COP 14', in FCCC/AWGLCA/2008/MISC.5, above note 145, pp. 41–2.

> the time paths, peaking years and allowable limits of emission) between the developed and developing countries and within developing countries, between the LDCs and the rest of them.[150]

Egypt maintained that:

> responsibilities should be seen against the fact that there are different levels of development within developing countries. We therefore call for the inclusion of criterion of income level and growth in the issue of climate change ...[151]

Maldives observed that:

> while the differing national circumstances between developed and developing countries have been acknowledged in Article 1(b)(v) [of the Bali Action Plan], vast differences also exist between many of the developing countries, especially the large ones and the LDCs.[152]

Some NGOs also submitted that the most advanced developing countries should be treated differently, notably that such states should take on emissions targets.[153] The same idea is central to the European Community's proposals for a post-2012 regime, which argue that 'to meet the 2°C objective ... developing countries, as a group, will need to limit the rise in their GHG emissions' and that '[d]iffering national circumstances and stages of development require differentiated actions and levels of ambition'.[154]

[150] 'Paper No. 2: Bangladesh – Bangladesh Submission on Bali Action Plan Regarding Work Programme of the Ad-Hoc Working Group on Long-term Cooperative Action Under the Convention', in FCCC/AWGLCA/2008/MISC.1, above note 139, p. 10.

[151] 'Paper No. 6: Egypt – Egyptian Submission for Ad-Hoc Working Group on Long-term Cooperative Action', in FCCC/AWGLCA/2008/MISC.1, *ibid.*, p. 23.

[152] 'Paper No. 10: Maldives on behalf of the Least Developed Countries – Bali Action Plan Regarding Work Programme of the Ad-Hoc Working Group', in FCCC/AWGLCA/2008/MISC.1, *ibid.*, p. 32.

[153] See e.g. International Trade Union Confederation, 'International Trade Union Confederation (ITUC) submission on the Ad-Hoc Working Group on Long-term Cooperative Action under the Convention (AWGLCA)' (22 February 2008), UNFCCC Doc. SMSN/NGO/2008/004, p. 2, at http://unfccc.int/resource/docs/2008/smsn/ngo/004.pdf. See also the AWG-LCA submission of 6 June 2009 by Greenpeace, WWF, Germanwatch e.V., David Suzuki Foundation, IndyACT and National Ecological Centre of Ukraine, 'A Copenhagen Climate Treaty Version 1.0 – A Proposal for a Copenhagen Agreement by Members of the NGO Community' (6 June 2009), p. 19 (referring to 'newly industrialized countries' like Singapore, South Korea and Saudi Arabia), online at http://unfccc.int/resource/docs/2009/smsn/ngo/157.pdf.

[154] See Commission of the European Communities, *Towards a comprehensive climate change agreement in Copenhagen* (2009), above note 123, p. 5.

Prior to the Rio Earth Summit, differential treatment for developing countries was based primarily on capacity limitations.[155] Within the climate regime too, parties agree that financial and technical capacity is a ground for differentiation of commitments.[156] This notion is reflected, for example, in the formulation of the principle as one of 'common but differentiated responsibilities and respective capabilities'.

By contrast, the question whether 'historical contributions' of states to greenhouse gas concentrations in the atmosphere are a ground for accordingly differentiated commitments remains highly contentious. In the literature, it is often noted that, along with capacity issues, historical (and current) contributions to the environmental concern at hand give rise to differentiated responsibilities.[157] This is also the position taken by some NGOs,[158] and by many developing countries, in particular, China and India.[159] Since the negotiations for the UNFCCC, these countries have consistently pushed for the recognition by developed countries of their 'main responsibility for climate change', and of developed countries' accordingly diminishing share of global emissions.[160] Developed countries, by contrast, have tended to resist these arguments, and the implicit proposition that CBDR represents a principle of 'global environmental justice'.[161]

The legal texts of the climate regime certainly make factual references to developed countries' emission patterns, but carefully avoid a direct linkage to the CBDR principle.[162] Historical and current emissions are mentioned in a preambular paragraph, but not in conjunction with

155 Rajamani, above note 133 at 122 (pointing to the examples of the Law of the Sea Convention, the ozone regime, and the Basel Convention).

156 See e.g. Maldives, above note 152.

157 See e.g. Philippe Sands, *Principles of International Environmental Law*, 2nd edn (New York: Cambridge University Press, 2003), p. 287; Rajamani, above note 133 at 122; and Yoshiro Matsui, 'Some Aspects of the Principle of "Common but Differentiated Responsibilities"' (2002) 2 *International Environmental Agreements* 151 at 154.

158 See AWG-LCA submission of 6 June 2009 by Greenpeace, WWF, Germanwatch, David Suzuki Foundation, INDYACT and NECU, above note 153, p. 6.

159 See Rajamani, above note 38. On China's and India's parallel arguments re per capita emissions, see notes 182 and 185 (below) and accompanying text.

160 Bodansky, above note 135 at 498.

161 See Jutta Brunnée, 'Climate Change, Global Environmental Justice and International Environmental Law', in Jonas Ebbesson and Phoebe Okowa (eds.), *Environmental Law and Justice in Context* (Cambridge University Press, 2009), pp. 326–7.

162 See also the Berlin Mandate, above note 39, para. 1(d), which specifically adverts to the '*fact* that the largest share of historical and current global emissions has originated in developed countries' (emphasis added).

references to CBDR.[163] Indeed, the Kyoto Protocol suggests that, at least amongst industrialized countries, historical contribution is not a central factor. In relating industrialized countries' emission reduction commitments to their 1990 emission levels, the protocol effectively 'grandfathered' earlier emissions. Principle 7 of the Rio Declaration does not shed much further light on the implications of CBDR. It merely adverts to the pressures that industrialized societies currently place on the global environment. The attendant 'responsibility' is also forward-looking, relating to the international pursuit of sustainable development and not correction of past actions. In a 2009 proposal for an amendment to the Kyoto Protocol, developing countries may have implicitly acknowledged that CBDR and historical contributions are separate principles. The submission proposed that Annex I parties' emission reduction commitments under Article 3 be determined 'by applying the principle of historical responsibility, from 1850 to 2005'.[164] Not surprisingly, developed countries have rejected the latter principle as not rooted in the convention.[165]

3.3.2.2 Responsibilities The notion of common but differentiated 'responsibilities' raises the question of what, if any, legal consequences follow from the CBDR principle. Aside from the basic proposition that parties' responsibilities under the climate change regime are to be differentiated, there is little common ground.

Whereas developing countries tend to argue that CBDR imposes legal responsibilities on industrialized countries, the latter tend to insist that the principle simply provides a framework for pragmatic problem-solving and attendant burden-sharing. The United States, for example, has consistently resisted any implication of legal responsibility for past actions,

[163] The same is true for per capita emissions. The preamble states that 'per capita emissions in developing countries are still relatively low' and that their share of global emissions will grow 'to meet their social and development needs'. But this statement is made separately from references to CBDR. See UNFCCC, above note 17, preamble.

[164] See UNFCCC, *Proposal from Algeria, Benin, Brazil, Burkina Faso, Cameroon, Cape Verde, China, Congo (Republic of), Democratic Republic of Congo, El Salvador, Gambia, Ghana, India, Indonesia, Kenya, Liberia, Malawi, Malaysia, Mali, Mauritius, Mongolia, Morocco, Mozambique, Nigeria, Pakistan, Rwanda, Senegal, Seychelles, Sierra Leone, South Africa, Sri Lanka, Swaziland, Togo, Uganda, United Republic of Tanzania, Zambia, and Zimbabwe for an amendment to the Kyoto Protocol*, U.N. Doc. FCCC/KP/CMP/2009/7 (15 June 2009), at http://unfccc.int/resource/docs/2009/cmp5/eng/07.pdf.

[165] See International Institute for Sustainable Development (IISD), 'Summary of the Bonn Climate Change Talks: 1–12 June 2009', *Earth Negotiations Bulletin*, Vol. 12, No. 241 (15 June 2009), pp. 6 and 12, at www.iisd.ca/download/pdf/enb12421e.pdf.

and has repeatedly lodged interpretative statements to that effect.[166] Similarly, the United States has resisted the proposition that, as a result of CBDR, developing countries' legal responsibilities are reduced.[167]

As noted, there is general agreement that, pursuant to the UNFCCC and related instruments, developed countries should 'take the lead' in combating climate change and its adverse effects.[168] After all, this proposition is stated in Article 3.1 of the Convention, and reflected in the structure of commitments under Article 4, as well as under the Kyoto Protocol. It was also endorsed by the G8 members and the 17 MEF countries at their respective meetings in July 2009.[169] However, developing countries maintain that developed countries bear the 'main responsibility' for climate change, whereas developed countries tend to argue that they were willing to take the lead because of their greater financial and technical capacities.[170]

Similar disagreement prevails with respect to the commitments of developed countries to provide financial and technical assistance to developing countries. Developing countries, to be sure, assert that industrialized countries bear this responsibility, and some Northern countries may well agree.[171] But many industrialized countries prefer to see assistance as a matter of pragmatism or benevolence, rather than an outgrowth of CBDR.[172]

The preamble to the Climate Convention, for example, speaks broadly of cooperation by all states and 'participation in an effective and

[166] See e.g. Marc Pallemaerts, 'International Law and Sustainable Development: Any Progress in Johannesburg?' (2003) 12 *Review of European Community and International Environmental Law* 1 at 8–9. See also Karin Mickelson, 'South, North, International Environmental Law, and International Environmental Lawyers' (2000) 11 *Yearbook of International Environmental Law* 52 at 70–2 (showing that developing countries very much conceived of the question as one of legal responsibility when Principle 7 of the Rio Declaration was negotiated).

[167] See e.g. the US interpretative statement to Rio Principle 7, cited in Matsui, above note 157 at 155 ('The United States does not accept any interpretation of principle 7 that would imply a recognition or acceptance by the United States of any international obligations or liabilities, or any diminution in the responsibilities of developing countries').

[168] See UNFCCC, *Fulfilment of the Bali Action Plan and components of the agreed outcome – Note by the Chair,* AWGLCA, 5th Sess., U.N. Doc. FCCC/AWGLCA/2009/4 (Part II) (18 March 2009), para. 30, at http://unfccc.int/resource/docs/2009/awglca5/eng/04p02.pdf.

[169] See G8 Leaders' Declaration, above note 80, para. 5; and MEF, above note 83, section 1.

[170] Bodansky, above note 135 at 503. [171] See Rajamani, above note 140 at 31.

[172] See Jekwu Ikeme, 'Equity, environmental justice and sustainability: incomplete approaches in climate change policies' (2003) 13 *Global Environmental Politics* 195 at 202–3.

appropriate response'. To be sure, Article 4.7 does tie the extent of effective implementation by developing countries of their commitments to the effective implementation by developed countries of their financial and technical assistance commitments. The provision also notes that developing countries' implementation efforts 'will take fully into account' their development priorities. Still, while this phrasing may resonate with the CBDR concept, it must also be noted that Article 4.7 is set apart from the convention's statements on CBDR. Article 4.7 also states that developed country implementation 'will depend' on developed country implementation of their financial commitments. This language certainly suggests a causal relationship between developed and developing country implementation, but it does not establish assistance obligations on the part of developed countries, nor does the factual statement about implementation make the underlying developing country obligations conditional on assistance.[173]

3.3.3 CBDR: Taking stock

In sum, CBDR is firmly anchored in the regime and, in turn, it anchors deliberations about the interpretation and further development of the regime. States do not contest the basic proposition that their commitments under the climate regime will be differentiated, and that a relatively greater onus will be on developed countries. The importance of this fact is difficult to overstate, since the concept of CBDR encapsulates some of the hardest questions that confront the climate negotiations.

To be sure, the gulf between radically different perceptions of the global climate problem is not easily bridged. Many developing countries see climate politics as part of a larger pattern of historical and economic injustices and so demand that industrialized countries bear the primary burden of combating climate change. In turn, many industrialized countries insist on developing country participation as a matter of pragmatic problem solving, or even fairness.[174] In this fraught terrain, CBDR has the potential to provide the very kind of principled foundation in which any onerous global commitment regime must be grounded to be legitimate and resilient.

Notwithstanding lingering debates about its meaning, CBDR has been a crucial factor in stabilizing and directing the regime. The power of the

[173] But see Birnie *et al.*, above note 129 at 134–5.

[174] See e.g. Roberts and Parks, above note 12.

CBDR principle is well illustrated by the inability of the Bush administration to extricate itself from the UN regime. It is arguable that the US attitude towards the Kyoto Protocol antagonized others at least in part because it appeared to challenge head-on the basic ideas that animate CBDR. As we have seen, the notion that addressing climate change is a *common* responsibility is a strongly shared understanding. Against this normative backdrop, the United States' refusal to join the Kyoto Protocol was widely read as unilateralism and thus struck a particularly negative chord.[175] Similarly, it may well be sensible to suggest that all major emitters, including developing countries, must participate for a climate regime to be effective. But the flat refusal by one of the wealthiest states of the world – and its major carbon emitter – to take on emission reduction commitments, clashed with generally shared sense that developed countries should take the lead in combating climate change. Indeed, rarely have states as openly expressed their resentment of US climate policy as did Papua New Guinea's ambassador for climate change when, reacting to the outgoing Bush administration's initial refusal to support the Bali Action Plan on long-term cooperative action, he stated: '[I]f for some reason you're not willing to lead, leave it to the rest of us. Please get out of the way.'[176]

Although the Bush administration remained reluctant to make specific commitments to climate action, especially without developing country commitments, it had softened its overall stance on the global climate regime. It began to show some willingness to consider long-term action under the auspices of the UNFCCC as early as 2007, when it endorsed a G8 statement in which leaders agreed to work within a UN process to consider long-term emission reductions.[177] Arguably, this initial shift was prompted in large part by the diplomatic pressure that the United States faced in the wake of the 2007 findings of the IPCC. However, one year later, roughly halfway through the Bali process, a re-articulation of the US position was discernible, suggesting that the normative framework of the climate regime too has influenced its policy. While the United States still insisted on developing country participation in an emissions regime, its proposals were now expressed in terms that were compatible with

[175] BBC News Service, *Anger at US climate retreat*, 28 March 2001, at http://news.bbc.co.uk/2/hi/science/nature/1248278.stm.

[176] Andrew C. Revkin, 'Issuing a Bold Challenge to the U.S. Over Climate', *The New York Times*, 22 January 2008 (quoting Kevin Conrad). See also Becker, above note 72.

[177] See Becker, *ibid.*

CBDR. Thus, the argument is no longer a bald statement that the United States will not take on commitments unless major developing countries do the same. Instead, the argument is that CBDR actually demands, or at least accommodates, differentiation among developing countries,[178] suggesting that major developing economies with large emissions must accept some emissions commitments. In other words, the United States has stopped arguing against the basic understandings that underpin the regime and has begun to work with the CBDR concept.

Interestingly, the EU has long taken this approach to formulating its international climate policy. As already noted, its negotiating position is explicitly grounded in the UNFCCC objective of averting dangerous climate change.[179] It is also framed in terms of the principles enshrined in the convention. In arguing for a global regime with commitments by all key players, European policy is not merely pragmatic, but treats climate change as a common concern of humankind. Furthermore, EU policy statements acknowledge the greater economic and technological capacity of industrialized countries, and their relatively greater contributions to climate change. In effect, EU policy proposals are guided by the CBDR principle and the idea that developed countries must take the lead in combating climate change. These propositions underpin the differentiated 2020 and 2050 emission goals advocated by Europe.[180] It is arguable that the EU position therefore read as 'principled', rather than purely self-interested.

Finally, major developing countries, like China and India, have always sought to draw rhetorical power from the convention principles. They worked hard during the negotiations for the UNFCCC to enshrine principles such as equity and CBDR in the convention, and consistently raised these concepts in the negotiations for a post-2012 regime.[181]

178 See e.g. the compilation of party submissions in UNFCCC, *Ideas and Proposals on paragraph 1 of the Bali Action Plan, Revised note by the Chair*, AWGLCA, 4th Sess. U.N. Doc. FCCC/AWGLCA/2008/16/Rev.1 (15 January 2009), para. 22(h), at http://unfccc.int/resource/docs/2008/awglca4/eng/16r01.pdf (citing Australia, New Zealand, the Russian Federation, and the United States for the notion that '[n]ew sight on the differentiation among Parties is required [...], based on recent advances in scientific knowledge and changing social and economic situation in the world ...').

179 See above note 117 and accompanying text.

180 See Commission of the European Communities, *Limiting global climate change to 2 degrees Celsius – The way ahead for 2020 and beyond* (2007), above note 120, pp. 2 and 9–10; and Commission of the European Communities, *Towards a comprehensive climate change agreement in Copenhagen* (2009), above note 123, pp. 2–6.

181 See Bodansky, above note 135 at 501–5. And see e.g. 'Paper No. 4: China – China's Comments on the Implementation of the Bali Action Plan', in FCCC/AWGLCA/2008/

As noted, in the past, large developing countries, especially China and India, refused to contemplate any emission reduction commitments whatsoever.[182] The argument was that pursuant to CBDR only industrialized countries should take on such commitments and that, at any rate, they should take the lead in cutting emissions. While the latter point resonates with the shared understandings around CBDR, the former fell increasingly out of step with the basic thrust of the principle. Once China and India emerged as major carbon emitters – in China's case even displacing the United States as the single largest emitter – the CBDR principle began to work against insistence on complete exemption from emission reductions.[183] Instead, the notion of common responsibility actually calls for some action by all major emitters. The most widely shared rationale for CBDR, capacity differentials, suggests that salient differences within the developing and developed country groupings of states should be taken into account. Indeed, even if 'historical' contributions to climate change were generally seen to be a criterion for differentiation, CBDR does not completely insulate major developing country emitters from emissions-related commitments.[184] The 1990 reference year of the UNFCCC and the emissions trajectory in major developed and developing emitters since then militate in favour of the latters' inclusion in a commitment regime, while reducing the exposure of developed countries with respect to their cumulative emissions.[185]

As a result, it has become increasingly difficult for major developing economies with significant carbon emissions to refuse reduction commitments outright. Hence the redoubled efforts of China and India to

MISC.1, above note 139, p. 18: 'In developing … [a shared] vision [for long-term cooperative action], it is important to take into account the principles of equity and common but differentiated responsibilities …' See also 'Paper No. 3C: India – Government of India Submission to UNFCCC on Long Term Co-operative Action', in FCCC/AWGLCA/2008/MISC.5/Add.1, above note 142, p. 32.

182 See above note 82 and accompanying text.

183 This point has not escaped the attention of the new US administration. See Glenn Kessler, 'Clinton, Indian Minister Clash Over Emissions Reduction Pact', *The Washington Post*, 20 July 2009 (citing Secretary of State, Hillary Rodham Clinton as stating that she 'completely' understood Indian arguments about per capita emissions, but noting that the argument 'loses force' as developing countries become the major emitters).

184 See Rajamani, above note 133 at 130.

185 See also Commission of the European Communities, Commission of the European Communities, *Towards a comprehensive climate change agreement in Copenhagen* (2009), above note 123, p. 5 (submitting that the 'accepted Kyoto base year, 1990, should be used as the historical reference point' for further emission reductions by developed countries after 2012).

promote the concepts of per capita entitlement to global 'carbon space' and convergence of per capita emissions in all countries,[186] combined with a softening of their stance on emission reductions. Amidst the growing calls for differentiation amongst developing countries,[187] a shared understanding appears to be emerging, and major developing countries have begun to signal willingness to curb emissions. This shift found expression in the Bali Action Plan, which contemplates mitigation 'actions' by developing countries, while also maintaining some North–South differentiation by envisaging mitigation 'commitments' only for developed countries.[188] As we will see, it is also reflected in the December 2009 Copenhagen Accord, in which developing countries, led by China and India, for the first time pledged emissions-related 'actions'.[189]

As these developments illustrate, CBDR represents only the nucleus of an emerging framework for global burden sharing in the climate regime. A comprehensive shared understanding of how and on what grounds mitigation and adaptation burdens should be allocated has yet to solidify. The negotiations pursuant to the Bali Action Plan reveal concerted efforts by industrialized and developing countries as well as various non-governmental actors, to reinforce, challenge, or shift the meaning of CBDR in various respects. They provide a fascinating window on the evolution and role of shared normative understandings. They illustrate that the articulation of a principle in a treaty is only the beginning of the norm-building process – an important focal point for the activities of a community of normative practice. As with the objective provision, far from being mere rhetorical flourish, the CBDR principle has guided the evolution of the climate regime and has provided the foundation for the gradual emergence of shared understandings concerning emission reduction commitments.

[186] See e.g. 'Paper No. 3B: India – Government of India Submission on Financing Architecture for Meeting Financial Commitments Under The UNFCCC', in UNFCCC, FCCC/AWGLCA/2008/MISC.5/Add.1 (21 November 2008), above note 142, p. 31 (stating that 'A paradigm of convergence of per-capita emissions of developed and developing countries, also accounting for the historical responsibility of developed countries, provides an equitable approach to fair burden sharing'); and see Kessler, above note 183.

[187] See above notes 145–54 and accompanying text.

[188] See Bali Action Plan, above note 20. And see Rajamani, above note 66 at 938 (commenting on the distinction between mitigation 'actions' and 'commitments').

[189] See below note 339 and accompanying text.

3.4 *Emission reduction obligations: Kyoto and beyond*

In moving beyond the basic objective and principles underpinning the climate regime, and the procedural dimensions of the regime, it becomes considerably harder to identify shared understandings among parties. The Kyoto Protocol is a good example of an agreement that is widely ratified, but the substantive elements of which rest on fragile shared ground. The particular commitments taken on by individual industrialized countries were clearly the result of a bargain rather than reflective of a principled agreement on the criteria for the differentiation of individual states' emissions targets. Nonetheless, it would seem that the member states of the EU and a range of other industrialized countries accepted the premise of the protocol – that it was an effort to implement the central CBDR ideas that developed countries should take the lead in combating climate change and that their commitments should differ from those of developing countries. In this broad sense of a necessary first step, then, the Kyoto commitment regime arguably was rooted in the shared understandings of a significant number of states.

Not all key states were on board, however. As we have noted at various points in the chapter, although it fully participated in the negotiation of the Kyoto Protocol, the United States wound up rejecting not only its own commitment but also the protocol's overall approach of imposing emission reductions only on industrialized states.[190] Claiming that it would be harmful to its economy without commitments by the United States and major developing countries, Australia too refused to ratify the protocol, notwithstanding the relatively generous target that it had negotiated for itself.[191] In turn, Canada, which did ratify the Kyoto Protocol in 2002, began pulling away from its commitment to the treaty in 2006, stating that its emission targets were impossible to meet.[192] During the Bali negotiations for post-2012 commitments, Canada insisted that all major emitters, including developing countries, should take on binding

[190] Had the United States ratified the protocol, it would have been required to cut its emissions by 7% compared to 1990 levels. See above note 43 and accompanying text.

[191] See Fred Pearce, 'Coal-rich Australia rejects Kyoto Protocol', *New Scientist*, 5 June 2002, at www.newscientist.com/article/dn2369-coalrich-australia-rejects-kyoto-protocol.html; and BBC News Service, *Australia Rejects Kyoto Pact*, 5 June 2002, at http://news.bbc.co.uk/2/hi/asia-pacific/2026446.stm.

[192] See CBC News Service, *'Impossible' for Canada to reach Kyoto targets: Ambrose*, 7 April 2006, at www.cbc.ca/canada/story/2006/04/07/kyoto060407.html.

targets, prompting some observers to charge that Canada was looking to undermine the principles of the climate regime.[193]

As for post-2012 commitments, we have just illustrated the important role that efforts to settle the meaning of principles such as CBDR have played in the negotiations. The submissions to the Bali process suggest that states, intergovernmental organizations, and non-governmental observers share the view that a successful continuation of the global climate regime must be anchored in its core principles and, in turn, that at least some of the contested meaning of the CBDR principle must be settled as the negotiations proceed.

Our discussion of the emerging shared understandings surrounding the 2° C target and the CBDR principle, respectively, suggests that some basic parameters for the post-2012 regime already exist. Based on the developments that we have traced out, it is arguable that an emission reduction regime must be capable of achieving the 2° C objective to be credible, and must be consonant with the CBDR principle to be broadly acceptable and legitimate.

As for the 2° C target, IPCC findings, confirmed by later analyses, suggest that robust action is urgently required.[194] To have a reasonable chance of meeting the objective, greenhouse gas emissions must peak within the next six years, followed by significant medium- and long-term emission reductions.[195] By 2020, developed country emissions would have to be cut by 25–40 per cent; by 2050, they would have to be reduced by 80–95 per cent.[196] In turn, to respect the CBDR principle, a post-2012 regime must see developed countries take the lead on emission reductions through credible mid-term targets, as well as take on commitments that reflect their greater capacity and share of emissions. Major developing countries, by contrast, may initially commit to mitigation-related actions but not take on specific reduction targets. However, given their rapidly rising share of global emissions, CBDR is compatible with, and even demands, credible reductions by the main developing country emitters, at least in the longer term. Finally, differentiation according to capacity and emissions share suggests that poorer countries or countries

[193] See Tobin Darymple, 'Canada could "derail" Bali climate talks: activists', *The National Post*, 8 December 2007.

[194] See Meinshausen *et al.*, above note 118 at 1160.

[195] See Richardson *et al.*, above note 108, pp. 18–20. And see Barker *et al.*, above note 63.

[196] This is the range of required reductions that was established in the IPCC's 2007 Report. See Pachauri and Reisinger, above note 115 at 66–7.

with negligible emissions should be subject to considerably less onerous requirements.

The discernible trends in the climate discussions are remarkably consonant with these parameters. As we already noted in our earlier discussion of the climate regime, the Bali Action Plan makes only general reference to the urgency of the situation and to the need for 'deep cuts'.[197] Only the Ad Hoc Working Group operating under the Kyoto Protocol has acknowledged that developed countries must achieve an emissions cut of 25–40 per cent below 1990 levels by 2020.[198] Developing countries have since been insisting on this reduction range for emission cuts by developed countries. In 2007, only the EU had undertaken to achieve a 20 per cent reduction by 2020, offering a 30 per cent cut provided other states follow suit.[199] As indicated earlier, in the lead-up to the Copenhagen Summit, a range of other states, including the United States, China and India, came forward with their pledges for 2020.[200] In terms of a long-term target, the G8 Declaration indicates that major developed countries were prepared to accept an 80 per cent emissions cut by 2050, so long as all countries commit to achieving a 50 per cent reduction in global emissions. A similar approach was to find expression in the MEF declaration, but was ultimately rejected by the developing country members of the forum, led by China and India.[201] They were not satisfied with the draft text on mid-term targets for developed countries, which merely declared that the latter would 'undertake robust aggregate and individual mid-term reductions in the 2020-timeframe'.[202] This disagreement carried over into the Copenhagen Accord. Indeed, an earlier draft of the Copenhagen Accord contained a global goal to reduce emissions by 50 per cent by 2050, with an industrialized country pledge of 80 per cent.

197 See Bali Action Plan, above note 20, preamble.

198 See UNFCCC, above note 75.

199 See above notes 122–5 and accompanying text. And see 'The European Union thinks it can be a model for the world on climate change: Can it?' *The Economist*, 15 March 2007); and Doyle, above note 126 (reporting that cuts proposed by developed countries average at 10–14%).

200 See above notes 126–7 and accompanying text.

201 See Alister Doyle, Reuters, *Major economies consider halving world CO2*, 25 June 2009) (reporting a draft text according to which the MEF supported 'an aspirational goal of reducing global emissions by 50 percent by 2050, with developed countries reducing emissions by at least 80 percent by 2050' and declared that developed states would 'undertake robust aggregate and individual mid-term reductions in the 2020 timeframe').

202 *Ibid*. See also Baker, above note 82; and Bagchi, above note 82.

The relevant passages were apparently dropped because of developing country concerns about an implicit commitment to long-term emissions cuts on their parts.[203]

Although the pledges that the Copenhagen Accord is likely to anchor will fall short of the demands of the regime objective,[204] it is arguable that the 2° C target already has exerted pressure on reluctant parties. It also stands to reason that CBDR added normative power to the refusal of the major developing countries to accept long-term commitments in the absence of mid-term commitments by developed countries. In combination, these factors helped to shape the Copenhagen Accord. Arguably, any such agreement had to consist in a package of commitments that are differentiated both between developed and developing countries and within these groups, with credible 2020 and 2050 targets for the major emitters.

3.5 *Shared understandings: final observations*

3.5.1 Domestic factors

In this section, we have explored the extent to which existing and emerging shared understandings support the global climate regime. We have focused primarily on the key actors in the international climate regime. In so doing, we are mindful that it is often an over-simplification to assert that a state, say the United States or Australia, Canada, India, or China, rejects a particular treaty or commitment. Notwithstanding the hard-line positions of their governments, for example, roughly two-thirds of the Indian and Chinese publics considered that their countries should take on emission reduction commitments and a majority rejected the proposition that developing countries should not be required to limit their emissions at all.[205] Similarly, in the case of each of the former three countries'

[203] See David Biello, 'Draft text of new "Copenhagen Accord"', *Scientific American – Observations*, 18 December 2009; at www.scientificamerican.com/blog/post.cfm?id=draft-text-of-new-copenhagen-accord-2009-12-18. And see Chris Holly, 'Disappointed Climate Delegates "Take Note" Of Vague Greenhouse Accord', *The Energy Daily*, 19 December 2009; at www.theenergydaily.com/events/climateconf2009-12-19.html; John Drexhage, 'Copenhagen: A memorable time for all the wrong reasons?' International Institute for Sustainable Development, December 2009, p. 2, at www.iisd.org/pdf/2009/cop_memorable_time_wrong_reasons.pdf.

[204] See below section 6, notes 375–6 and accompanying text.

[205] See WorldPublicOpinion.org, *Most Indians Say India Should Limit its Greenhouse Gases*, 1 March 2006, at www.worldpublicopinion.org/pipa/pdf/feb06/India_Feb06_quaire.pdf (citing a poll conducted in 2005). And see *BBC Global Poll*, above note 113.

attitudes towards the Kyoto Protocol, it would be more accurate to speak of the US, Australian or Canadian governments' rejection of the treaty. Australia, for example, changed its policy and decided to ratify the protocol once a new Labour government came into office in December 2007.[206] Conversely, the Canadian pull-back from Kyoto followed the election of a conservative government.[207] In the United States, finally, concerns about costs and efficacy prompted a unanimous Senate resolution ('Byrd-Hagel Resolution') against joining a Kyoto-style agreement.[208] Yet, notwithstanding the resistance to Kyoto in Washington, at the sub-national level, a wide range of local, state and regional initiatives flourished, many of which referenced themselves to the protocol.[209] Furthermore, even at the height of the Bush administration's rhetoric against the Kyoto Protocol, a sizeable portion of the American public disapproved of the decision to reject the treaty and supported participation.[210] Finally, by 2007, a growing number of legislative proposals specifically aimed at climate change had been placed before the US Congress.[211] While there were significant differences between the major bills, common themes were proposals for cap-and-trade systems, and for emission goals that are focused upon long-term reductions with a 2050 horizon.[212] It is not accurate to say, therefore, that the principles and targets of the climate regime had no resonance in the United States. Indeed, by the time that President Obama took office, the ground had been prepared for the adoption of a federal climate bill and re-engagement in the global regime.[213]

[206] BBC News Service, *Rudd Takes Australia Inside Kyoto*, 3 December 2007, at http://news.bbc.co.uk/2/hi/asia-pacific/7124236.stm.

[207] CBC News Service, *French minister slams Canada's Kyoto retreat*, 16 November 2006, at www.cbc.ca/world/story/2006/11/16/kyoto-ambrose.html.

[208] See Byrd-Hagel Resolution, 143 CONG. REC. S8113–05 (25 July 1997).

[209] For an overview, see Robert B. McKinstry, Jr., 'Laboratories for Local Solutions for Global Problems: State, Local and Private Leadership in Developing Strategies to Mitigate the Causes and Effects of Climate Change' (2004) 12 *Penn State Environmental Law Review* 15.

[210] Matthew C. Nisbet and Teresa Myers, 'The Polls – Trends: Twenty Years of Public Opinion about Global Warming' (2007) 71 *Public Opinion Quarterly* 1 at 23–4 (citing two 2001 polls showing disapproval of the Kyoto withdrawal at 47% and 51%, respectively; and citing 2002, 2004 and 2005 surveys showing support for US participation at 64%, 65% and 73%, respectively).

[211] Pew Center on Global Climate Change, *Legislation in the 110th Congress Related to Global Climate Change*, www.pewclimate.org/what_s_being_done/in_the_congress/110thcongress.cfm (citing 165 bills, resolutions or amendments).

[212] See Hunter, above note 65 at 93–4.

[213] On the status of the federal bill, see below notes 224–6 and accompanying text. But see also Suzanne Goldenberg, 'Global poll finds 73% want higher priority for climate change',

In other words, while international interaction and practice are the primary mechanisms through which shared understandings emerge within a regime, a wide range of domestic factors help explain why a given state is more or less receptive to the regime and its norms.[214] It may seem tempting to put differences in states' attitudes towards the climate regime down to interests. For example, consider the policy differences between the two leading industrialized members of the climate regime. Regarding US climate policy, it seems plausible to conclude that binding emission reductions were quite simply not in the US domestic interest. In light of the upward trajectory of US emissions, the required measures were seen as costly,[215] and their benefit uncertain, especially without the participation of major developing countries:[216] hence the unanimous Byrd-Hagel Resolution. As for the EU, it seems plausible that ratification and implementation of the Kyoto Protocol was a relatively easy step, given the emission trajectories of eastern European countries and the fact that emission reductions in Germany and the United Kingdom could offset increases in other member states.[217] The EU may also have been driven by the desire to embarrass the United States after its rejection of the Kyoto Protocol,[218] and to assume a global leadership role.[219] And yet, such interest-based

The Guardian, 30 July 2009. And see WorldPublicOpinion.org, *Publics Want More Government Action on Climate Change: Global Poll*, 29 July 2009, at www.worldpublicopinion.org/pipa/articles/btenvironmentra/631.php?lb=bte&pnt=631&nid=&id= (suggesting that by August 2009, only 44% of Americans felt that climate change should be a top priority for the new administration).

214 See also the discussion of the interplay between international and domestic law in above Chapter 3, section 4.4.

215 See Cass Sunstein, 'Of Montreal and Kyoto: A Tale of Two Protocols' (2007) 31 *Harvard Environmental Law Review* 1 at 33–6. See also Kathryn Harrison and Lisa McIntosh Sundstrom, 'The Comparative Politics of Climate Change' (2007) 7 *Global Environmental Politics* 1 at 3–5 (attributing variations in Kyoto ratification and compliance in large part to variations in compliance costs).

216 See e.g. Michael P. Vandenbergh, 'Climate Change: The China Problem' (2008) 81 *Southern California Law Review* 905 at 923–5.

217 See Sunstein, above note 215 at 36–7. And see Jonathan B. Wiener 'On the Political Economy of Global Environmental Regulation' (1999) 87 *Georgetown Law Journal* 749 at 773–81.

218 See Sunstein, above note 215.

219 Jon Hovi, Tora Skodvin and Steinar Andresen, 'The Persistence of the Kyoto Protocol: Why Other Annex I Countries Move on Without the United States' (2003) 3 *Global Environmental Politics* 1 at 16. But see also Michael Grubb and Joyeeta Gupta, 'Implementing European Leadership', in Joyeeta Gupta and Michael Grubb (eds.), *Climate Change and European Leadership: A Sustainable Role for Europe* (Berlin: Springer, 2000), pp. 306–9 (arguing that EU leadership was not so much about prestige or political benefits as about the desire to forge a collective EU identity).

considerations do not fully explain why the United States rejected the Kyoto Protocol and why the EU nonetheless stuck with the regime.[220]

The examples of the United States and the EU also illustrate that the structure of a domestic political system is as relevant as the substance of domestic politics. Consider the fact that ratification of a treaty by the United States requires the 'advice and consent' of a two-thirds majority of the Senate.[221] Environmental agreements often become entangled in the deliberations of the Senate's Foreign Relations Committee. They are also exposed to political lobbying by an array of domestic constituencies, especially when MEAs require re-opening the carefully negotiated compromises that are contained in many US domestic environmental laws. These particular dynamics appear to be structural, rather than contingent on the government of the day. While the administration of George W. Bush is generally said to have neglected environmental protection,[222] it is important to recall that even the more sympathetic Clinton administration was unable to navigate its international environmental priorities through the competing domestic agendas in the Senate.[223] The Byrd-Hagel Resolution illustrates that these difficulties cannot simply be attributed to party politics.

That said, since the inauguration of the Obama administration, federal climate change legislation has made progress. On 26 June 2009, the House of Representatives passed the American Clean Energy and Security Act.[224] One element of the bill is the creation of a national cap-and-trade scheme that would reduce green house gas emissions from major sources by 17 per cent by 2020 and 83 per cent by 2050 relative to 2005 levels.[225] The bill is an important step towards the reduction of US

220 For a more comprehensive analysis see Jutta Brunnée, 'Europe, the United States, and the Global Climate Regime: All Together Now?' (2008) 24 *Journal of Land Use and Environmental Law* 1.

221 See Harold K. Jacobson, 'Climate Change: Unilateralism, Realism, and Two-Level Games', in Stewart Patrick and Shep Forman (eds.), *Multilateralism and U.S. Foreign Policy: Ambivalent Engagement* (Boulder, Colo: Lynne Rienner Publishers, 2001) 415 at 427.

222 See, e.g., Editorial, 'An Environmental Deficit', *The New York Times*, 11 February 2004; and Julian Borger, 'Bush disarms the pollution police', *The Guardian Weekly*, 13–19 November 2003.

223 See John Dernbach, 'U.S. Adherence to Its Agenda 21 Commitments: A Five Year Review' (1997) 27 *Environmental Law Reporter* 10504.

224 American Clean Energy and Security Act, ACES, H.R. 2454, at http://thomas.loc.gov/cgi-bin/bdquery/z?d111:H.R.2454.

225 See Suzanne Goldenberg, 'Barack Obama's US climate change bill passes key Congress vote', *The Guardian*, 27 June 2009.

greenhouse gas emissions. However, it does not adopt the 1990 baseline upon which the global climate regime has rested to date. It has also been weakened by a number of concessions, including the exemption of existing coal-fired power plants from its ambit and from the US Clean Air Act.[226]

In any case, the EU's political and legal structure has promoted far greater inclination toward multilateralism than the US constitutional framework and political processes. The EU as an actor is constituted by international law. Its member states have pooled significant aspects of their sovereignty and they have long been comfortable with a supra-national approach to law and policy-making.[227] EU environmental multilateralism can be traced back to the late 1970s. The experience with the negotiation of an international ozone layer regime demonstrated to EU member states the benefits of collective policy-making, and that national interests need not fall victim to a European environmental policy approach. Thus, when climate talks picked up speed in the early 1990s, EU member states had already become comfortable with more flexible interpretations of sovereignty and were generally open to global solutions, even when inconsistent with short-term economic interest.[228] Furthermore, the involvement of a large number of different actors in climate policy (the member states, the European Parliament, the Commission and the Presidency) facilitates mutual reinforcement, with multiple spaces for policy discourse, and multiple actors that can 'pass the leadership baton off to the next player' (or perhaps distribute the blame for onerous policies) when so required.[229]

In other words, the distinctive features of the EU as a supra-national entity seem conducive to the emergence of strong climate policy. The UN climate regime binds both the EU and its member states, and its requirements have come to be enshrined in EU and national laws. The legal framework of the EU promotes continuous interactions between international, European, and national laws, as well as between various international,

[226] Editorial, 'Climate Loopholes', *The New York Times*, 22 July 2009.

[227] See e.g. Pierre-Marie Dupuy, 'The Place and Role of Unilateralism in Contemporary International Law' (2000) 11 *European Journal of International Law* 19 at 21 (arguing that Europe 'knows that it owes its very existence to international law').

[228] See Ludwig Krämer, 'The Roots of Divergence: A European Perspective', in Norman J. Vig and Michael Faure (eds.), *Green Giants? Environmental Policy of the United States and the European Union* (Cambridge, Mass: MIT Press, 2007), p. 67.

[229] Miranda Schreurs and Yves Tiberghien, 'Multi-Level Reinforcement: Explaining European Union Leadership in Climate Change Mitigation' (2007) 7 *Global Environmental Politics* 19 at 40.

European and domestic actors. As we have illustrated, the EU has been actively engaged in the UN climate regime throughout its long evolution. Its climate policy is focused not only on keeping the UNFCCC at the core of the global climate regime, but also framed around the regime's objective and its core principles. Some of the convention principles, notably CBDR, also resonate with the EU's internal practices of blending environmental regionalism and collective priority setting, and of burden sharing between wealthier and poorer member states.[230] In light of these policy patterns it seems fair to say that the EU, its member states and, arguably, even its public,[231] have actually internalized the goals and principles of the global climate regime to a significant degree. These norms have become woven into the legal and policy discourse within Europe, and perhaps even into the identity of the EU as a member of a global climate community.

The approach of the United States to the global climate regime has been very different. As shown earlier in this chapter, until recently the United States attitude towards the UN regime has been one of reluctance and even resistance. While the US remained active in the treaty process, its policy has consistently sought to avoid having its policy options tied down by the regime. This stance was in part due to the rejection of the regime's core commitments by the government of the day, and in part due to domestic political dynamics. There is no comparable range of internal political arenas in which the engagement with the climate regime could take place. The closest parallel to the EU's multi-level processes may be the experimentation and regulatory competition that has been taking place among the

[230] See e.g. Christopher C. Joyner *et al.*, 'Common But Differentiated Responsibility' (2002) 96 *American Society of International Law Proceedings* 358 at 362–3. Regina Axelrod, Norman J. Vig and Miranda Schreurs, 'European Union as an Environmental Governance System', in Regina Axelrod, David Leonard Downie and Norman J. Vig, *The Global Environment: Institutions, Law and Policy*, 2nd edn (Washington, DC: CQ Press, 2005), p. 206.

[231] See e.g. European Commission, *Special Eurobarometer 300 – Europeans' attitudes towards climate change* (Fieldwork March – May 2008; Publication September 2008), p. 5, at http://ec.europa.eu/public_opinion/archives/ebs/ebs_300_full_en.pdf (indicating that 62% of Europeans feel that 'global warming/climate change' is among the most serious problems in the world). See also *BBC Global Poll*, above note 113 (indicating that large majorities of Europeans support 'limiting greenhouse gas emissions in the context of a deal that requires the wealthy countries to provide aid and technology'); and see European Commission, *Standard Eurobarometer 67 – Public Opinion in the European Union* (Fieldwork April–May 2007; Publication November 2007), p. 162, at http://ec.europa.eu/public_opinion/archives/eb/eb67/eb67_en.pdf (indicating that 89% of those polled in 30 European countries felt the 'European Union should urgently put new policies in place to reduce greenhouse gas emissions by at least 20% by 2020').

local, state and federal governments. However, unlike in the EU context, these processes are not specifically focused on the engagement with, or translation of international norms into the domestic realm. Furthermore, the main arena in which such engagement should take place, the US Senate, has long shown itself to be hostile to international regulation since the adoption of the UN climate regime. Indeed, the domestic resistance to the UNFCCC and the Kyoto Protocol is tied into much broader discomfort with the threats that international law is seen (at least by some) to pose to American constitutionalism and sovereignty.[232] Whether shifting domestic attitudes, re-engagement in the international regime, and a sympathetic new administration can in fact overcome these obstacles, and whether the Senate will adopt climate legislation that will allow the United States to live up to its post-2012 pledges is as yet uncertain.

3.5.2 Summary of conclusions on shared understandings

Our review of key aspects of the global climate regime has illustrated that the global climate regime rests on a strong foundation of shared understandings concerning the need for a global legal regime. However, while the regime participants have arrived at a solid set of procedural understandings, the stock of substantive understandings remains relatively lean.

A widely shared understanding appears to be emerging that the objective of the regime to avert dangerous climate change entails a requirement to keep global temperature increases at or below 2° C. There is also broad consensus that states have a common responsibility to address climate change, that their resulting individual responsibilities should be differentiated, and that industrialized countries should lead in climate action. It is generally accepted that capacity differentials, especially between developing and industrialized states are relevant, and there is growing support for differentiation amongst industrialized and developing countries, respectively. However, disagreements remain on whether or not historical and per capita emissions are appropriate criteria for differentiation, and

[232] See e.g. Terry L. Anderson and J. Bishop Grewell, 'It Isn't Easy Being Green: Environmental Policy Implications for Foreign Policy, International Law and Sovereignty' (2001) 2 *Chicago Journal of International Law* 427 at 436 (describing MEAs as 'genuine threats' to American sovereignty); and Jed Rubenfeld, 'Unilateralism and Constitutionalism' (2004) 79 *New York University Law Review* 1971 at 1975 (arguing that international law in general is incompatible with the American constitutional commitment to democratic self-government); Jeremy Rabkin, *Law Without Nations? Why Constitutional Government Requires Sovereign States* (Princeton University Press, 2005).

whether or not CBDR requires industrialized states to provide financial and technical assistance to developing countries.

It is easy to dismiss the Bali Action Plan's notion of a 'shared vision' for long-term climate action as lofty but empty rhetoric. But the participants in the climate negotiations, after years of effort, do appear to understand the importance of arriving at just that – a *shared* vision. Our analysis shows that the success of the global climate regime is not guaranteed by a mere 'deal' among key participants. Of course, it is highly probable that the negotiating states, through the Copenhagen Accord or a subsequent more formal arrangement, will ultimately make some kind of 'deal', including trade-offs, compromises, and various types of side-payments. But, as we have shown, not only is any such deal contingent on a foundation of genuinely shared understandings, it must also be consonant with the overall objective and core principles of the climate regime. Only then will the foundations exist for specific commitments that are legitimate and capable of generating a sense of obligation – provided, of course, that they also meet the requirements of legality, to which we now turn.

4. Criteria of legality

In the previous section, we demonstrated that many of the key elements of the global climate regime – specifically, its overall objective and the central principle of CBDR – are supported by resilient shared understandings. Against the backdrop of this assessment, we now examine the extent to which the regime meets the criteria of legality against which interactional law must be measured. Here we focus on the UNFCCC, the Kyoto Protocol, and the principle of CBDR. An assessment of the Copenhagen Accord will be provided below, in section 6.

4.1 The UNFCCC

The framework convention that anchors the global climate regime, we have seen, rests on a core of widely shared understandings. However, this fact alone does not account for the resilience of the regime. We suggest that the UNFCCC has endured not because it places few demands on states, as some have argued,[233] but at least in part because it meets many

[233] See George W. Downs, Kyle W. Danish and Peter N. Barsoom, 'The Transformational Model of International Regime Design: Triumph of Hope or Experience?' (2000) 38 *Columbia Journal of Transnational Law* 465.

of the criteria of legality that we have posited in earlier chapters. As will become apparent, this assessment applies in particular to the procedural aspects of the convention.

Since the UNFCCC tackles a global problem, it is significant that participation in the agreement is universal. This fact goes to the requirement of generality, as it ensures that all states are subject to the requirements of the convention, and participate in the effort to develop 'an effective and appropriate response'.[234] Even if states' commitments under the convention are differentiated, that differentiation is based upon generally applicable criteria, encapsulated in the CBDR principle, as well as in the distinctions that the convention draws, for example, between Annex I and non-Annex I countries. The convention's global membership also ensures that all states are entitled to participate in decision-making concerning climate change. Since global climate change affects all states, whether they are major greenhouse gas emitters or not, this aspect of the convention's generality is particularly important. Arguably it is a key factor in explaining its enduring legitimacy, notwithstanding the slow progress towards an 'effective and appropriate' emissions reduction regime. As in the context of decision-making on the use of force, examined more closely in Chapter 6,[235] attempts to solve global problems through 'coalitions of the willing' are likely to suffer from a legitimacy deficit.

This does not mean that it is misguided or inappropriate to focus on reducing the emissions of major contributors to global warming, or to engage these states through initiatives like the MEF. It does mean, however, that such efforts must be tied into the global regime rather than bypass it. The strong resistance to the Asia-Pacific partnership and the major emitters process promoted by the Bush administration illustrate the point. The British initiative to make climate change the subject of a debate in the UN Security Council raised the participation issue even more pointedly.[236] Many of the more than 50 states participating in the debate welcomed the effort to re-frame the issue so as to highlight its importance and urgency.[237] Others questioned that the Security Council, with its limited membership, was an appropriate forum. According to

[234] See UNFCCC, above note 17, preamble. [235] See below Chapter 6, section 2.3.

[236] UN Security Council, above note 16.

[237] *Ibid.* (statements of Germany, Papua New Guinea, Congo). See also UN Security Council, *Security Council Holds First-Ever Debate on Impact of Climate Change on Peace, Security, Hearing over 50 Speakers*, Press Release SC/9000, 17 April 2007, at www.un.org/News/Press/docs/2007/sc9000.doc.htm (statements of Bolivia, Denmark, Iceland, New Zealand, Tuvalu, and many others).

the representative of Peru, for example, climate change was 'a problem of a global scale, one that can be tackled only by means of multilateral and concerted action on the part of the entire international community, within the agreed legal framework and the principles underlying it.'[238] Other developing countries saw the move as following a familiar pattern, threatening their full participation in policy-making and raising the spectre of decisions being imposed on them.[239]

The requirement of promulgation is clearly met by the UNFCCC. Further, although the 1992 agreement used 1990 emissions as a baseline for the non-binding requirement that Annex I parties stabilize their greenhouse gas emissions by 2000,[240] it does not have retroactive effect. The year 1990 merely serves as a reference point for future action by the parties. We return to this issue below, in our discussions of the Kyoto Protocol and the CBDR principle, respectively.

On the whole, the UNFCCC also lives up to the clarity requirement. This assessment applies notably to the procedural provisions of the regime, which establish information exchange and reporting requirements, treaty bodies, and decision-making and amendment rules. For some of these procedural rules, clarity was achieved through the subsequent elaboration of subsidiary rules, or through reference to complementary rules. For example, the Conference of the Parties (COP) adopted decisions containing rules that detail the content, timing, and format of the convention's information exchange or reporting requirements.[241] Similarly, while the convention spells out the rules that apply to the adoption of amendments,[242] other decisions by the COP are subject to the rules of procedure that the COP adopts for itself.[243] In turn, the rules of procedure provide detailed decision-making rules, but leave unresolved the voting requirements. Pending agreement on this point, UNFCCC parties chose to adopt the general UN approach of consensus decision-making.[244] Thus,

[238] *Ibid.*, p. 18.

[239] *Ibid.*, p. 13 (citing the Chinese representative as stating that 'The developing countries believe that the Security Council lacks expertise in handling climate change and is not the right place to take decisions with extensive participation leading to widely acceptable proposals'). See also statements by, e.g. Pakistan, Russia, South Africa, and Qatar.

[240] See above note 35; and UNFCCC, above note 17, Art. 4.2(a) and (b).

[241] See e.g. *ibid.*, Arts 4.1(a) and 7.2(d).

[242] See UNFCCC, *ibid.*, Art. 15.2.

[243] See *ibid.*, Art. 7.3.

[244] In elaborating the Rules of Procedure for the COP, the parties were unable to agree on the voting rules. At COP-1, it was decided that the draft Rules of Procedure would be applied provisionally, with the exception of Rule 42 on voting. See *Report of the Conference of the Parties to the United Nations Framework Convention on Climate Change on its First*

through the practice of parties under the convention, clarity was achieved notwithstanding that the treaty rule itself was, on the face of it, unclear, or at least under-developed. But, as noted above, the consensus practice can be in tension with other legality requirements.

As our discussion of shared understandings suggests, clarity has been more of a work in progress with respect to the convention's substantive provisions. Arguably, the initial lack of clarity was necessary to enmesh states in the agreement, although it also made it possible for states to evade obligations. For example, recall that the stated objective of the convention is to achieve a 'stabilization of greenhouse gas concentrations in the atmosphere at a level that would prevent dangerous anthropogenic interference with the climate system'.[245] However, the apparent clarity of this formulation masked several points of scientific contention, including the extent to which climate change is human-induced, the point at which climate change is 'dangerous', and the levels at which greenhouse gas concentrations in the atmosphere would have to be stabilized to prevent reaching that point. As we have shown, only now that agreement on the concept of 'dangerous climate change' is being reached, can the greenhouse gas concentrations that follow from it be determined with some clarity. Thus, although the objectives provision itself does not impose obligations on parties, it is directly relevant to the emission cuts they must make if the objective is to be achieved. As such, it enhances the clarity of the agreement as a whole, as well as sets clear parameters for the negotiation of specific emission reduction commitments.

A similar assessment applies to the CBDR principle, the legality indicators of which we examine in more detail in section 4.3 below. For present purposes suffice it to say that the lack of clarity in the articulation of the principle in the convention may initially have served the parties' desire to paper over widely divergent perceptions of the climate problem and the burden-sharing that it entails. But recent efforts to refine the meaning of the principle indicate that a commitment regime cannot be constructed without clarification of the framing principle. Several other instances of ambiguity in the convention's substantive provisions could be cited.

Session, U.N. Doc. FCCC/CP/1995/7, at http://unfccc.int/resource/docs/cop1/07.pdf. The draft Rules of Procedure are reproduced in *Organizational Matters: Adoption of the Rules of Procedure – Note by the Secretariat*, U.N. Doc. FCCC/CP/1996/2, available at http://unfccc.int/resource/docs/cop2/02.htm. See also Patrick Széll, 'Decision Making under Multilateral Environmental Agreements' (1991) 26 *Environmental Policy and Law* 210.

[245] UNFCCC, above note 17, Art. 2.

The above-mentioned stabilization commitment, for example, was articulated in two lengthy and convoluted paragraphs, models of obscurity rather than clarity.[246] The provisions reflect the arduous negotiations that produced the UNFCCC, and the political sensitivity of emissions-related commitments.

We underscore again that the ambiguity of the UNFCCC's substantive provisions must be put into perspective. It is important here to recall the reason why framework–protocol regimes are employed in international environmental law in the first place.[247] It is precisely to put procedures and institutions in place that can facilitate the gradual development of shared understandings on substantive matters. Absent a sufficient foundation of shared understandings, it would quite simply be impossible to arrive at any substantive commitments, especially in an issue area that is as contentious and complex as climate change. Broadly textured substantive principles or commitment provisions serve as guideposts for this continuous, albeit often slow-moving, law-making enterprise. We have already illustrated that this approach to law-making has borne fruit in the case of the climate regime, which now seems to be moving towards a genuinely global agreement on long-term emissions reductions. Thus, while clarity will be required once emissions reductions are at issue, it is less crucial, perhaps even harmful, in the early stages of regime building, when substantive understandings must first be forged. We conclude that, in the case of the climate regime, the progressive clarification of treaty terms has been an important part of the hard work of international law and has been necessary for the development of interactional law. Clarity could be promoted over time – to such a degree that this criterion of legality is met.

Turning to the criterion of non-contradiction, some parallels can be discerned to the situation concerning clarity. The UNFCCC's procedural provisions pose no major problems when assessed against this criterion. By contrast, some of its substantive provisions, while not strictly speaking contradictory, have been in significant tension. For example, if the objective of the agreement is to prevent dangerous climate change, then a vaguely phrased, modest stabilization target that is applicable only to some of the main emitters may be seen to contradict the very purpose of the agreement. Certainly, in the face of mounting evidence of human-induced climate change and the urgent need for action, the convention's

[246] See Bodansky, above note 135 at 515–17.

[247] See above notes 36–7 and accompanying text.

loose commitments, and the slow movement towards more demanding commitments, prompted considerable frustration with the regime along the way.[248] However, we have already adverted to the deliberately evolutionary nature of the UNFCCC regime, and to the reasons for this approach. We have also suggested that agreement on the relatively precise concept of dangerous climate change was required before the objective provision could unfold its full effect. After all, partisan or ill-supported assessments of danger would not further the cause of the regime. As for the absence of emissions-related commitments for some of the major emitters, including some large developing countries, it does not inevitably contradict the UNFCCC objective. Indeed, according to Article 2, the objective is to be achieved 'in accordance with the relevant provisions of the Convention', which include those setting out the CBDR principle. While there may be some tension between the objective and CDBR, the convention ties them together in a manner that requires each to be read in light of the other.

Finally, insisting on developing country commitments, even if more likely to promote the convention objective, might be in tension with another criterion of legality – the requirement that the law not ask the impossible. This requirement shows that the climate regime's decision against emission reductions on developing countries is not merely pragmatic politics, but also goes to the legal legitimacy of the regime. The principle of CBDR, putting capacity issues in the spotlight, is also a crucial regulator. In any case, the impossibility criterion illustrates that the legality requirements do not necessarily pull in the same direction, and that maintaining legality often involves striking an appropriate balance.

The same applies to the constancy or predictability criterion. For example, while meeting the stabilization commitment was not impossible for the developed country parties to the convention, it arguably proved to be considerably more difficult and costly for them than they

[248] See e.g Hermann Ott, 'Climate Policy post 2012 – A Roadmap: The Global Governance of Climate Change', Discussion paper for the 2007 Tällberg Forum (Stockholm: Tällberg Foundation, 2007), p. 4, at www.wupperinst.org/uploads/tx_wibeitrag/Ott_Taellberg_Post-2012.pdf. And see Greenpeace, *Climate talks brought back from the brink, but lacking substance*, Press Release 15 December 2007, at www.greenpeace.org/international/press/releases/bali ('The climate agreement finalised in Bali today has been stripped of the emission reduction targets that science and humanity demands'); World Wildlife Fund, *Rich countries need to redefine their CO2 targets, Media Statement 10 August 2009*, at www.panda.org/wwf_news/press_releases/press_packs/bonn_press_pack.cfm.

envisaged when the convention was negotiated.[249] Therefore, although the commitment itself was predictable, its ramifications may not have been completely so. The evolutionary nature of the regime, while crucial for its effectiveness in dealing with a problem the contours and urgency of which are not fully understood, can also make it difficult or even impossible to predict what commitments the regime will eventually occasion.[250] The procedural aspects of the UNFCCC play an important role in this context, ensuring that at least the decision-making rules and law-making processes are transparent and predictable.

Finally, the pattern that we have begun to highlight – that the convention's procedural provisions fare well on the legality scale whereas its substantive aspects do less so – extends to the eighth requirement, that of congruence between international practice and the requirements of the UNFCCC. Annex I parties have by and large not adhered even to the relatively weak substantive commitments in the convention, notably their emission stabilization commitments.[251] These failures arguably also undercut the Annex I parties' commitment to take the lead in combating climate change, although the adoption of the Kyoto Protocol may, at least initially, have mitigated this fact. However, so far the weak congruence with the UNFCCC's substantive requirements has not undermined the legality of the convention as a whole, given its procedural focus. We

249 See Warwick J. McKibbin and Peter J. Wilcoxen, 'Estimates of the costs of Kyoto: Marrakesh versus the McKibbin-Wilcoxen blueprint' (2004) 32 *Energy Policy* 467 at 471 ('If anything, cost-benefit calculations based on studies to date tend to suggest that the costs exceed the benefits, at least in developed countries'); and Victor, above note 51, at 11 ('Regulating emission quantities is problematic because emissions are determined by factors such as technological change and economic growth that policy makers are unable to control or anticipate perfectly').

250 Indeed, this is one of the concerns of some US conservative law-makers about MEAs. See Robert F. Blomquist, 'Ratification Resisted: Understanding America's Response to the Convention on Biological Diversity, 1989–2002' (2002) 32 *Golden Gate University Law Review* 493 at 546 (citing Senator Jesse Helms as warning that '[t]his so-called treaty is scarcely more than a mere preamble, not a treaty. The real treaty – the essential nuts and bolts – is yet to be created at the conference of the parties').

251 For example, see *Net Position Report 2009 – New Zealand's projected balance of Kyoto Protocol units during the first commitment period*, p. 1, at www.mfe.govt.nz/publications/climate/net-position-report-2009/net-position-report.pdf (as of 2007 New Zealand's gross greenhouse gas emissions have risen by 22% since 1990); see *Annual European Community greenhouse gas inventory 1990–2007 and inventory report 2009*, Executive Summary, p. 9, at www.eea.europa.eu/publications/european-community-greenhouse-gas-inventory-2009/at_download/file (Ireland has increased its emissions by 25% since 1990, Greece by 24.9% and Spain by 53.5%); and 'Japanese greenhouse gas emissions reach record level, data show', *The New York Times*, 12 October 2008 (claiming that for the year ending March 2008, Japan's emissions had risen by 8.7% since 1990).

observed earlier in the chapter that parties agree on the need for a global legal regime on climate change, and that their practice upholds the treaty's procedural rules. Our conclusion is that the procedures of the climate regime have become interactional law, and have fostered, at least up until the Copenhagen meeting, continuing efforts to build substantive commitments. By contrast, the convention's framework of substantive commitments falls short of the requirements of interactional law.

4.2 *Emission reductions: the Kyoto Protocol*

The Kyoto Protocol entails emission reduction commitments only for parties listed in Annex I to the UNFCCC. One of the most common charges against the protocol is that it 'exempts' some of the largest emitters from its commitment regime.[252] But the protocol is part of the convention regime, and was intended to implement the convention's CBDR principle by imposing only inventory and reporting-related commitments on developing countries – in keeping with the notion that developed countries take the lead in combating climate change. Initially, then, the protocol's emission reduction approach would have met the generality requirement, notwithstanding its selectivity. The protocol's compliance mechanism, intended to 'facilitate, promote and enforce' compliance with the protocol,[253] confirms the generality point. Its aspiration is to apply to all protocol commitments, while accounting for the differences between these commitments. To this end it encompasses an 'Enforcement Branch', designed to determine and address Annex I parties' non-compliance with their emission reduction commitments and related commitments, and

[252] See Gary Becker 'What Price Pollution? Leave That to a Global Market', *BusinessWeek*, 18 October 1999, at www.businessweek.com/archives/1999/b3651059.arc.htm, lamenting that 'thanks to politics, the protocol exempts more than 130 countries, including Brazil, China, India, and Mexico, from any restrictions on their industrial pollution.' More recently, see Todd Stern and William Antholis, 'A Changing Climate: The Road Ahead for the United States' (2007) 31 *The Washington Quarterly* 175 at 179 (asserting that such exemptions from binding commitments are 'no longer sustainable for the more advanced developing countries, such as China and India, in light of current emissions trends').

[253] See UNFCCC, Decision 27/CMP.1 'Procedures and mechanisms relating to compliance under the Kyoto Protocol', in *Report of the Conference of the Parties serving as the meeting of the Parties to the Kyoto Protocol on its first session, held at Montreal from 28 November to 10 December 2005. Addendum. Part Two: Action taken by the Conference of the Parties serving as the meeting of the Parties to the Kyoto Protocol at its first session*, U.N. Doc. FCCC/KP/CMP/2005/8/Add.3 (30 March 2006), p. 93, Section I, at http://unfccc.int/resource/docs/2005/cmp1/eng/08a03.pdf.

a 'Facilitative Branch', intended to facilitate the implementation of all parties' other commitments through advice and assistance.[254] However, the generality of the protocol as originally conceived has come under increasing strain. Recall that the emissions of some large developing countries have grown exponentially, in some cases surpassing those of states with Kyoto commitments. At the same time, the shared understandings concerning the meaning of CBDR have evolved towards an acceptance of differentiation amongst developing countries and hence emission reduction commitments for some of them. In short, while an argument for the protocol as an important first step can still be made, it is increasingly difficult to assert the generality of the emissions regime, and might become impossible if large developing country emitters refused to accept (long-term) emission reduction responsibilities of their own.

The requirement of promulgation is met not only by the protocol itself, but also through the adoption of the so-called 'Marrakech Accords' that fleshed out key parts of the protocol.[255] As we noted earlier in this chapter,[256] the parties were able to agree in the Kyoto Protocol that, for example, an emissions trading mechanism would be available to assist them in meeting emission reduction commitments. However, since there was not enough time to elaborate the specifics of that mechanism in the treaty itself, they charged the COP with defining 'the relevant principles, modalities, rules and guidelines'.[257] The same applies to the protocol's compliance mechanism, which was provided for in the protocol but left to be elaborated and adopted through subsequent plenary decisions.[258] The fact that these 'accords' are contained in a series of decisions of the convention and protocol parties, and so are not formally legally binding, does not detract from their promulgation function. In the practice of the climate regime, supplementary rules are routinely adopted through party decisions, rather than by way of formal amendments.[259] These rules are then published in the meeting reports of the COP or MOP and applied in conjunction with the provisions of the treaty itself.

The emission reduction commitments contained in the Kyoto Protocol, like the UNFCCC's stabilization commitments, are pegged to a 1990 reference year. We have already suggested that the fact that the reference year pre-dates the adoption and entry into force of the climate regime does not

[254] *Ibid.*, Sections II, IV and V. [255] See above note 53 and accompanying text.

[256] See above notes 47–8 and accompanying text.

[257] Kyoto Protocol, above note 18, Art. 17. [258] *Ibid.*, Art. 18.

[259] See Brunnée, above note 37 (discussing the reliance on party decisions in the climate regime and other MEAs).

mean that the regime runs afoul of the non-retroactivity requirement. Granted, the reference year does factor some past emissions trends into the determination of the Kyoto commitments, however this is done not because a state's legal responsibility is triggered by its emissions in 1990, but for practical reasons, to make emission reductions measurable and comparable. If anything, as we explained earlier in the chapter, the 1990 reference year grandfathers prior emissions.

Like most treaties, the Kyoto Protocol contains some terms that are deliberately vague, typically on issues that parties could not resolve in the negotiations. For example, the Kyoto Protocol left undefined the proposition that Annex I parties, by 2005, were to have made 'demonstrable progress' in meeting their reduction commitments.[260] Only in the Marrakech Accords did parties agree on how that progress is to be reviewed and assessed.[261] Similarly, several provisions of the protocol note that parties' recourse to the emissions trading mechanisms, acquiring emissions rights and credits to assist them in meeting their emissions targets, should be 'supplemental' to their own emissions reductions.[262] In the negotiations, the EU had sought a specific percentage to ensure that the majority of a party's commitment is met through its own actions rather than through reliance on reductions made by other countries. Other parties, led by the United States, had sought to keep maximum flexibility for recourse to the trading mechanisms.[263] The term 'supplemental' papered over these differences, which have since resolved themselves through the practice under the Kyoto Protocol.[264] Ironically, the EU became the primary proponent and user of emissions trading, even establishing a European emissions trading system.[265]

Another type of ambiguity involves protocol text that is clear on its face, for example, in stipulating that parties must estimate, and prepare annual inventories of, relevant emissions, or that they 'may participate

[260] Kyoto Protocol, above note 18, Art. 3.2.

[261] Yamin and Depledge, above note 135 at 129.

[262] See Kyoto Protocol, above note 18, Arts. 5, 6, 7, 12 and 17.

[263] Jean-Charles Hourcade and Thierry Le Pesant, 'Negotiating Targets, Negotiating Flex-Mex: The Economic Background to the US-EU Controversy', in Carlo Carraro (ed.), *Efficiency and Equity of Climate Change Policy* (Dordrecht: Kluwer Academic Publishers, 2000), p. 63.

[264] The Marrakech Accords stipulate merely that domestic action should be a 'significant' element of a party's efforts to meet its commitments. See Yamin and Depledge, above note 135 at 145.

[265] See Jutta Brunnée and Kelly Levin, 'Climate Policy beyond Kyoto: The Perspective of the European Union', in Bernstein *et al.*, above note 38, p. 63.

in emissions trading for the purposes of fulfilling their commitments under Article 3'.[266] But, as we just noted, the protocol left it to subsequent meetings of the parties to approve the rules and procedures required to transform treaty terms into regimes that are sufficiently detailed to allow implementation and that enable states to decide whether or not to ratify the protocol. The ambiguity below the surface of the treaty text, then, was remedied only subsequently, through adoption of the relevant decisions in the Marrakech Accords. The resultant clarifications were important also for the protocol's main emission reduction commitment. Although Article 3.1 and Annex B, in enshrining numerical targets, appear to meet the clarity requirement, the actual scope and impact of these commitments too was ascertainable only once the supplementary decisions had been adopted.

At first glance, the Kyoto Protocol may seem to raise one more clarity issue. An average reader would likely find the language of the protocol obscure and, in some instances, almost incomprehensively technical. The latter observation applies in particular to the Marrakech Accords and the highly technical details that they provide, for example, on inventory and reporting requirements, accounting rules for forest sinks, or transaction logs for emissions trading. However, in this respect, the protocol and its supplementary rules do not differ from many other specialized regulatory regimes. Clarity, in this context, is to be assessed from the vantage point of a regime participant – of a member in the regime's community of practice. In the case of the Kyoto Protocol, there exists an overarching community of practice, engaged in the major aspects of the regime and familiar with the main structural concepts. In addition, there exist a series of highly specialized sub-communities, consisting of experts on the various elements of the regime.

The protocol also passes the non-contradiction test. It is certainly internally consistent, and was at least initially consistent with the UNFCCC and its guiding principles, although it may be in increasing tension with the evolving understanding of CBDR. The protocol might also be seen as contradicting the regime objective of preventing dangerous climate change. After all, it is widely agreed that the protocol, even if fully implemented, makes only an insignificant contribution to the required emission reductions. But, once again, this fact must be seen in the context of the need for developed countries to take a first step towards emission reductions while also establishing the basic architecture for a regime that

[266] Kyoto Protocol, above note 18, Art. 17. See also Arts. 3.4, 5.1, 6.2, 7.4, 8.4, 12.7, 16, and 18.

could carry further reductions. The protocol's first 2008–2012 commitment period, was intended to be followed by subsequent commitment periods.[267] Furthermore, the apparent weakness of the protocol's reduction requirements must be considered against the backdrop of a rapid rise of emissions since 1990, making the apparently small percentage reductions accepted by each party considerably more onerous than they might appear at first glance. Canada has even suggested that it has become 'impossible' for it to meet its Kyoto commitment.[268] The argument is that emissions trajectories are such that the Kyoto target can no longer be achieved, and that it is too costly to make up the difference by acquiring emission rights abroad. Other parties too are finding their Kyoto commitments difficult to meet.[269] Whether these difficulties are the result of actual or political impossibility, of course, is another matter. In Canada's case, for example, the problem flows in good part from its failure to adopt an appropriate implementation plan, and from the political decision of a new government not to make efforts to comply with the Kyoto target to which its predecessor agreed.[270]

The predictability requirement raises similar issues. It could be argued that the actual costs of meeting the Kyoto targets were not predictable at the time that the agreement was concluded. However, the targets were set up to give parties maximum flexibility in meeting their commitments,

[267] See above note 58 and accompanying text.

[268] In 2006 Environment Minister Rose Ambrose stated, 'My departmental officials and the department officials from natural resources have indicated that it is impossible, impossible for Canada to reach its Kyoto targets' (see Ambrose, above note 192).

[269] According to NZ Minister for Climate Change Issues, Dr. Nick Smith, 'the only thing that is currently saving New Zealand's bacon on the carbon balance is the large tree planting that occurred in the 1990s'; see Parliament of New Zealand, *Questions for oral answer*, Volume 653, Page 2625, 28 April 2009, at www.parliament.nz/en-NZ/PB/Business/QOA/3/9/8/49HansQ_20090428_00000007-7-Kyoto-Protocol-Compliance.htm. Japan's 8.7% increase in emissions from 1990 to 2008 has cast serious doubts on its ability to meet Kyoto commitments – see France 24, *Japan beats its CO2 emissions record*, 12 November 2008, at www.france24.com/en/20081112-japan-carbon-dioxide-carbon-record-global-warming-kyoto. Even the recent slump in Japan's economy is unlikely to herald a reduction of emissions – see Reuters, *Japan's CO2 emissions may rise despite economic slump*, 3 April 2009, at www.reuters.com/article/environmentNews/idUSTRE53245V20090403 ('outages at [Japan's] biggest nuclear station have likely further pushed up CO2 emissions in the year ended March 2009').

[270] For the shortcomings of the original (Liberal) implementation plan, see the C.D. Howe Institute, *Burning Our Money to Warm the Planet – Canada's Ineffective Efforts to Reduce Greenhouse Gas Emissions*, No. 234, May 2006, at www.cdhowe.org/pdf/commentary_234.pdf. On the subsequent failures of the Conservative government, see CBC News Service, *Kyoto and beyond*, 14 February 2007, at www.cbc.ca/news/background/kyoto/.

including through recourse to emissions trading. By establishing a 2008–2012 commitment period, the 1997 agreement also sought to establish a sufficiently long horizon for policy planning. Similarly, by requiring that the negotiation of subsequent commitments was to be initiated 'at least seven years before the end of the first commitment period',[271] the goal was to create as much predictability as possible for state parties and economic actors.

Has the practice of the parties been congruent with the Kyoto Protocol? At the moment, only compliance with procedural commitments, such as inventory and reporting requirements, can be examined. While it is possible to evaluate the parties' emissions trends, their actual compliance with the emission reduction targets can only be assessed after the end of the first commitment period in 2012. Even if some parties are found at that time not to have met their targets, this would not necessarily detract from an overall congruent practice. To assess congruence, it must also be asked whether parties are meeting their procedural commitments, whether they make reasonable efforts to comply with their emissions targets, and whether they accept the findings of the regime's compliance body, as well as the consequences that attach to non-compliance. We will consider the practice of the compliance regime more closely in the next section, in our discussion of the practice of legality. For the moment, suffice it to say that Canada is the only party that has distanced itself from its emissions target. To date, the compliance body has had to deal with only a relatively small number of implementation issues. Only in two cases, concerning compliance with reporting and inventory commitments by Greece and Canada, respectively, has the Enforcement Branch process been triggered. Both states adjusted their performance in response to the findings of the compliance body.[272]

Overall, then, an assessment of the protocol through the lens of the legality criteria presents a mixed picture. By and large, the protocol's emission reduction requirements meet the criteria. The supplementary decision-making practice inherent in the evolutionary nature of the regime has remedied some of the potential legality concerns, notably those relating clarity. But the emissions trends as well as the evolving understandings among parties during the long time-span between its negotiation and implementation are also presenting some problems. In particular, the protocol's emission reduction regime appears increasingly

[271] Kyoto Protocol, above note 18, Art. 3.9.

[272] See also below notes 313–21 and accompanying text.

to strain against the generality and non-contradiction, and perhaps also the impossibility criteria.

4.3 *The Principle of Common but Differentiated Responsibilities*

Aside from assessing how the CBDR principle affects the legality of the climate regime as a whole, it is also worth exploring to what extent the principle itself meets the requirements of legality. Considering CBDR through this lens is helpful in reflecting on why certain meanings of the principle have come to be widely accepted, while others have met with resistance.

At first glance, CBDR appears to clash with the requirement of generality, given that its premise is that states' responsibilities under the climate regime should be differentiated. However, this conclusion misunderstands the principle in at least two respects. First, CBDR envisages precisely that all states within the climate regime share a common responsibility, thereby actually promoting generality. Second, generality is not the same as treating all actors in identical fashion. We have already suggested that the very point of the principle is to provide generally applicable criteria to determine whether to differentiate, to what extent to do so, and on what basis. In this sense too, and even as it evolves to demand further differentiation within the industrialized and developing country groupings, CBDR very much meets the criterion of generality.

Given that the CBDR principle has found expression in the UNFCCC, the Kyoto Protocol, and a series of decisions by the treaty parties, the criterion of promulgation seems unproblematic. Granted, the meaning of the CBDR principle has been fleshed out over time, so that its precise content can be ascertained only through a careful analysis of the evolving practice within the regime. However, this point does not go to promulgation so much as to clarity. Thus, while the climate regime stipulates CBDR as a core principle, the articulations of the principle in the treaty texts do not meet the requirement of clarity. Take, for example, Article 3.1 of the convention, which states that parties should act 'on the basis of equity and in accordance with their common but differentiated responsibilities and respective capabilities'. This wording suggests, but does not clarify, whether equity and CBDR are separate concepts, and whether capabilities are to be considered as part of or in addition to CBDR. What the criteria for differentiation are, and whether they apply only between developed and developing countries or also within these groupings, remains equally unclear.

As we noted at the beginning of the chapter,[273] it was significant that the principle, and related concepts, found expression in the convention text, including in an article dedicated to 'principles'. We have here an illustration of the interplay between the requirements of legality and the process of building shared understandings. Given the wide divergence of views on one of the central, and most sensitive, issues of the climate change regime, it is not surprising that the treaty text only sketches the contours of CBDR – there were no shared understandings about the meaning of CBDR. However, the promulgation of the principle in the convention, even if in broad strokes, did provide a conceptual platform for the all-important debate about burden-sharing. And, as our earlier discussion of shared understandings has illustrated, a normative debate has indeed been taking place and the CBDR principle is progressively clarified.

The requirement of non-retroactivity, in turn, sheds light on why some readings of CBDR have encountered particular resistance. The argument that the scope of states' responsibilities should be determined not just by their relative capacity to address climate change, but also by their historical contribution to the problem, is a case in point. Whereas the former criterion is forward-looking, the latter attaches responsibility to past activity.[274] The argument that rich countries should be responsible for the 'carbon space' they have taken up through their cumulative emissions certainly has some resonance. But it also entails moral as well as legal problems, as it imposes responsibility for actions taken by previous generations, without awareness of their climatic consequences.[275] In the context of legal responsibility, the historical contribution argument is fundamentally different from a claim that responsibility should be allocated in light of current emissions, or should place reliance on 1990 as a reference year for future emission cuts.[276]

The criterion of non-contradiction is met by CBDR. We already suggested that the concept, to the extent that it reduces or delays emission reductions by major developing countries, may be in tension with, but

[273] See above notes 31–5 and accompanying text.

[274] See e.g. UNFCCC, above note 164, p. 5 (reporting a developing country proposal that Annex I states' commitments be based on 'the principle of historical responsibility, from 1850 to 2005').

[275] See Simon Caney, 'Cosmopolitan Justice, Responsibility, and Global Climate Change' (2005) 18 *Leiden Journal of International Law* 747 at 757–62 (discussing the limitations of inter-generational concepts of justice).

[276] Note also that, by 1990, states were without question aware of the climate consequences of their emissions.

is not contradictory to, the objective of the climate regime. After all, demanding that developing countries undertake commitments that they would find impossible to meet would not only run afoul of another legality requirement, but would not ultimately further the convention objective. The idea of differentiated responsibility might also contradict the principles of the law of state responsibility. However, CBDR affects the primary obligations of states, rather than the secondary obligations that flow from violations of international law. As for the notion of historical responsibility, it would indeed be out of synch with the law of state responsibility, which presupposes a breach of international law as it stood at the time at which an action or omission took place, and by the actor whose responsibility is being invoked.[277]

As the CBDR principle has evolved, the criterion of non-contradiction also illuminates the prospects for success of the argument that differentiation should apply also among developed and developing countries, respectively. There is no doubt that the broad distinction between developed and developing countries remains central to the principle. However, the considerations that animate it, be it different economic and technical capabilities or contributions to the problem, argue in favour of further differentiation. Whether the criterion for differentiation is capacity, share of emissions, or historical responsibility, it is difficult to see why these criteria should not apply equally among all states. The 'philosophy' of the CBDR principle actually supports, and arguably even requires, such further differentiation.

The constancy and predictability requirements are generally met by CBDR. Some concerns might be raised to the extent that the principle may shift the goalposts for states' commitments as their emissions, or their capacity to combat climate change, evolve. However, the principle is inherently contextual. It may lead to different commitments in different situations, and it may entail shifting responsibilities. If differentiated responsibilities were carved in stone, the result would inevitably contradict the principle as circumstances evolve. Thus, to some extent, non-contradiction and predictability are unavoidably in tension in the climate regime. However, even when states' relative capacities and responsibilities change, the result is ultimately predictable. Consistently applied, the CBDR principle puts parties on notice that their responsibilities will

[277] Draft Articles on Responsibility of States for Internationally Wrongful Acts, in ILC, *Report of the International Law Commission on the Work of Its Fifty-third Session*, UN GAOR, 56th Sess., Supp. No. 10, p. 43, U.N. Doc. A/56/10 (2001).

change in certain circumstances, and maintains 'relative equality', or 'principled difference', among them.

Finally, while the post-2012 commitment regime has yet to be fully developed, the practice under the climate regime to date is congruent with CBDR. Our discussion of the shared understandings emerging around CBDR illustrates the influential role that it has played in the evolution of the regime. The principle has been consistently invoked by parties, including in the Berlin Mandate, the Kyoto Protocol, the Bali Action Plan, and individual parties' and other participants' submissions under the auspices of the latter. It has also shaped the regime itself in significant ways. The differentiation between developed and developing country parties is discernible in the UNFCCC, which establishes the distinction between Annex I and non-Annex I states, and imposes more demanding requirements upon the former. Whether developed country parties, in terms of the emissions-related requirements of the convention, have lived up to their leadership role is highly debatable. The subsequent negotiation and adoption of the Kyoto Protocol, with its strictly Annex I emission reduction commitments, certainly demonstrates parties' recognition of developed countries' particular responsibilities. Notwithstanding the resistance to the Kyoto regime by some key parties, it was arguably in conformity with CBDR, and with the notion that developed countries should take the lead in combating climate change. However, as developing country emissions rise and the shared understandings concerning differentiation evolve, the protocol itself may come to be less and less congruent with CBDR. In any case, Annex I states' actual emissions performance and hence their adherence to their leadership responsibility, has been decidedly mixed.

This all said, the debate surrounding the US rejection of the Kyoto Protocol, the fact that it nonetheless entered into operation, and the fact that discussions are now underway on an extension of Kyoto commitments, all show that CBDR has shaped the practice of states within the climate regime. Even the United States has revised its position to accord with CBDR, acknowledging the greater responsibility and leadership role that its position as a major developed country emitter entails. Current debates about developing country commitments and differentiation amongst developing countries signify not a deviation from CBDR, but a refinement and, possibly, realignment of its meaning. These subtle but significant shifts were reflected in the language of the Bali Action Plan, which abandoned the rigid Annex I and non-Annex I groupings and adopted the more fluid categories of developing and developed countries. As we have seen, it also signalled the possibility that some emissions-related 'action' will be taken by developing countries in a post-2012 commitment regime. Interestingly, recent polls suggest that sizeable majorities of people in both industrialized and developing countries support limits on developing country emissions 'in the context of a deal that requires the wealthy countries to provide aid and technology'.[278] Going forward, then, congruence with CBDR will depend on whether states agree on a new commitment regime, and on the extent to which this regime is consonant with their evolving understanding of CBDR. We will shortly turn to an assessment of the Copenhagen Accord against this backdrop.

In sum, the climate regime's core principle of CBDR measures up to the requirements of legality, including clarity. As the underlying normative understandings are developing, the lack of clarity of the regime's textual references to the principle is being addressed through the parties' practice.

5. Practice of legality

Earlier parts of this chapter already touched upon aspects of the practice of legality that has unfolded with the climate change regime. In our discussion of shared understandings we illustrated the manner in which a community of practice is upholding, and further developing, a global legal regime.

As our assessment of the criteria of legality confirms, for the time being the regime's practice is predominantly procedural in nature. We did not discuss the procedural dimensions of the Kyoto Protocol in any detail, but the same applies here as in the case of the UNFCCC. Indeed, we have here an illustration of one of the strengths of the framework-protocol approach. Since the Kyoto Protocol developed within a broader regime, it could draw on the regime participants' procedural understandings, especially concerning law-making processes. This foundation of understandings allowed protocol parties to focus on fleshing out the procedural rules needed to operationalize the emission reductions regime, such as those concerning emissions inventories, and emissions trading. Furthermore, contentious debates about emission reductions could take place on a foundation of well-developed procedural understandings and practices. We have also shown how the rules and principles of the convention have

[278] See *BBC Global Poll*, above note 113 (noting that '[t]he only country with a substantial minority opposing such a deal is Nigeria (46%)').

shaped the evolution of the climate regime, as well as the negotiations for a new commitment regime. Seen through the lens of the practice of legality, the parties' rhetorical activities and their evolving practice can be understood as efforts to ensure that ambiguities in the climate treaties are clarified and that new elements are consistent with the existing legal framework.

In this section, rather than revisit these previously discussed points, we turn our attention to the compliance mechanism of the Kyoto Protocol, another important procedural element that, through its practice, can reinforce the protocol's substantive requirements. The protocol's compliance procedure, then, provides us with an opportunity to examine an important aspect of the regime's practice of legality more closely, and allows us to connect our discussion of compliance issues in Chapter 3 to a concrete example. To this end, we begin by reiterating the central themes of that chapter. We then sketch out the main features of the compliance procedure, relate these features to the requirements of legality and, finally, illustrate how the compliance procedure is contributing to the regime's practice of legality.

As we explained in Chapter 3, a distinguishing feature of the compliance theory that follows from our interactional framework is that it draws on both norm properties (grounding in shared understandings and conformity with criteria of legality) and legal process factors (practice of legality) to explain how obligation is generated and shapes conduct (fidelity or commitment). Law-making and compliance, we argued, are not radically distinct, but part of a continuum of legal interaction. Building upon these premises, we suggested that compliance is promoted by law-making that meets the requirements of interactional law. Shared understandings and a sustained practice of legality are more likely to be cultivated when spaces and opportunities for regular interaction are provided. International institutions and meetings can provide these interactional settings, as can appropriate non-compliance processes. The latter are important both because they can help ensure the congruence of states' practice with the requirements of a regime and because they provide opportunities for developing and reinforcing the regime's practice of legality.

Our discussion so far has shown that the climate regime meets these requirements to a remarkable extent. We have described how law-making efforts are proceeding gradually to generate shared understandings and build up legality. We have also illustrated that the various plenary and subsidiary bodies of the regime, as well as its Secretariat, promote continuing interaction through regular meetings and other exchanges between regime participants. What remains to be examined more closely are the 'Procedures and Mechanisms Relating to Compliance under the Kyoto Protocol', upon which we touched briefly earlier in this chapter.[279]

As we noted in our earlier discussion, the declared goal of the Kyoto Protocol's compliance procedure is to 'facilitate, promote and enforce compliance' with the protocol. [280] The regime's institutional core is the Compliance Committee, comprised of the previously mentioned 'facilitative' and 'enforcement' branches. The committee has twenty members, with each branch comprising ten members.[281] Elected by the parties to the protocol, committee members serve in their personal capacities and, according to the committee's Rules of Procedure, must 'act in an independent and impartial manner and avoid real or apparent conflicts of interest'.[282] Each branch must include one member from each of the five UN regional groups and one member from the small island developing states. Each branch must also include two Annex I party members, and two non-Annex I party members.[283] Decisions are to be made by consensus and, as a last resort, by a three-quarters majority. In the latter case, decisions by the Enforcement Branch require simple majorities of both developing and developed countries.[284]

These features are directly relevant to the requirements of interactional law, for at least two reasons. First, they enhance the inclusiveness and representativeness of the compliance body. Both are particularly important given the compliance body's task of addressing issues that are of common concern to all parties, whether they are directly affected by an instance of non-compliance or not. In other words, since all parties have a legal interest in compliance with Kyoto commitments, as well as a practical interest in promoting the widest possible implementation of

[279] See above notes 253–4 and accompanying text. We leave aside other potential avenues for compliance assessment, such as the multilateral consultative process under Art. 13 of the UNFCCC and the regime's dispute settlement clauses (Art. 14 UNFCCC and Art. 19 Kyoto Protocol). None of these avenues has been used to date.

[280] Procedures and Mechanisms, above note 253, section I.

[281] *Ibid.*, section II.3.

[282] *Ibid.*, section II.3 and 6. And see *Rules of procedure of the Compliance Committee of the Kyoto Protocol* (as amended by the Committee in December 2008 – see *Fourth meeting of the Conference of Parties to the Kyoto Protocol*, Decision 4/CMP.4, U.N. Doc FCCC/KP/CMP/2008/11/Add.1), Rule 4, at http://unfccc.int/files/kyoto_protocol/compliance/background/application/pdf/rules_of_procedure_of_the_compliance_committee_of_the_kp.pdf.

[283] Procedures and Mechanisms, above note 253, sections IV.1 and V.1.

[284] *Ibid.*, section II.8–9.

the protocol, compliance issues are typically polycentric in nature.[285] Adjudication or other conventional dispute settlement processes are ill-suited to such polycentric issues,[286] which may be one reason why they have remained largely unused in the environmental context.[287] A non-compliance procedure, with a compliance body such as the one established under the Kyoto Protocol, is better suited to ensuring that all treaty parties are represented in decisions that affect their shared interest. Second, the composition and voting rules of the compliance body emphasize the generality of the Kyoto commitments to which we adverted in our discussion of the criteria of legality.[288] Although only Annex I parties have emissions targets, all parties are represented in the Enforcement Branch, which reviews compliance with these targets. Indeed, all decisions of the Enforcement Branch to date have been reached by consensus.

The Facilitative Branch is responsible mainly for questions concerning the implementation of protocol commitments other than those related to Annex I parties' emission reductions.[289] Emission reduction commitments under Article 3.1, and the related inventory and reporting commitments under Articles 5 and 7, are within the purview of the Facilitative Branch only when referred to it by the Enforcement Branch, or during a given commitment period.[290] The mandate of the Facilitative Branch is to address compliance problems through advice and facilitation of assistance to individual parties, facilitation of financial and technical assistance, and recommendations to the party concerned.[291] The work of the Facilitative Branch, then, is intended to minimize the circumstances in which parties will find compliance with the protocol to be impossible.

[285] See Jutta Brunnée, 'The Kyoto Protocol: A Testing Ground for Compliance Theories?' (2003) 63 *Zeitschrift für ausländisches öffentliches Recht und Völkerrecht (Heidelberg Journal of International Law)* 255 at 263.

[286] See also Lon L. Fuller, 'Adjudication and the Rule of Law' (1960) 54 *American Society of International Law Proceedings* 1 (arguing more broadly that adjudication is ill-suited to resolving international, and so typically polycentric, questions because it does not enable all parties affected by a decision to participate meaningfully in the process).

[287] See Edith Brown Weiss, 'Understanding Compliance with International Environmental Agreements: The Baker's Dozen Myths' (1999) 32 *University of Richmond Law Review* 1555 at 1582.

[288] See above notes 253–4 and accompanying text.

[289] Procedures and Mechanisms, above note 253, section IV.5

[290] *Ibid.*, sections IV.6; IX.12. Compliance with the emission reduction commitment under Art. 3.1 can be assessed only at the end of the five-year commitment period. However, there is room for 'promoting compliance and providing for early warning of potential non-compliance' during the commitment period (section IV.6).

[291] *Ibid.*, section XIV(a)–(d).

However, by limiting facilitation to specific types of commitments and situations, the compliance procedure also tries to maintain the generality and predictability of the target-related commitments.

Hence it is the Enforcement Branch that is tasked with the resolution of all compliance questions relating to the emission reduction, inventory and reporting commitments, as well as relating to eligibility for the Kyoto mechanisms.[292] The enforcement process is triggered by 'questions of implementation' raised by expert reviews under Article 8 of the protocol, or raised by a protocol party, either with respect to itself or with respect to another party.[293] The expert review trigger ensures that *all* questions of implementation concerning emission reductions will come before the compliance committee. This feature further enhances the generality of the reduction commitments and promotes the predictability of the regime. But there is another, perhaps even more important, dimension to the expert review trigger. We explained in Chapter 3 that compliance procedures or enforcement measures do not necessarily promote compliance. Failure to address non-compliance, or selective enforcement, may actually undercut legality.[294] In turn, consistent compliance review and predictable responses to non-compliance help build legality. The automatic review feature of the Kyoto compliance procedure, then, helps promote congruence between norms and practice.

This effect is further enhanced by the fact that the Enforcement Branch not only determines whether a party is in compliance with its commitments, but also applies 'consequences' to non-compliance.[295] The consequences in question differ depending on the underlying commitment. In cases of non-compliance with inventory or reporting commitments, consequences will consist in a declaration of non-compliance and in the requirement that the party concerned prepare a 'compliance action plan'.[296] That plan must include an analysis of the causes of non-compliance, a description of the measures that the party intends to take to remedy the non-compliance, and a timetable for their implementation. Progress in the implementation of the plan must be reported to the Enforcement Branch.[297] When it has determined that a party has not met

[292] *Ibid.*, section V.4. [293] Procedures and Mechanisms, above note 253, section VI.1.

[294] See Chapter 3, text accompanying notes 85–92.

[295] Procedures and Mechanisms, above note 253, I, sections V.6 and XV. These consequences are cast not as punitive, but as providing for 'the restoration of compliance to ensure environmental integrity', and 'for an incentive to comply'.

[296] *Ibid.*, section XV.1. [297] *Ibid.*, section XV.2 and 3.

one or more of the eligibility requirements for the Kyoto mechanisms, the consequence will be suspension of the party from participation in the mechanisms.[298] Finally, when compliance with the emissions reduction commitments is assessed at the end of the commitment period, there will be a grace period after the completion of the expert review, during which parties can acquire emission rights or credits to bring themselves within their assigned amounts.[299] Where a party nonetheless exceeds its emissions entitlement, it will suffer suspension from eligibility to transfer emission units under Article 17, and it will be required to develop a compliance action plan.[300] In addition, the excess emissions will be deducted, at a penalty rate of 1.3, from that party's assigned amount for the next commitment period.[301] This deduction is cast in the compliance procedure as aimed at 'restoration of compliance to ensure environmental integrity' and as providing an 'incentive to comply', rather than as a penalty.[302]

The non-compliance consequences envisaged by the Procedures and Mechanisms invite some further observations. First, the parties enshrined a set range of pre-determined consequences in the decision establishing the compliance procedure. As a result, the Compliance Committee does not actually decide on whether or not to impose consequences, or which consequence to impose. It merely assesses whether a party is in non-compliance and, if so, 'applies' the pre-determined consequences. Along with the automatic review dimension, this feature significantly enhances the predictability of the process and the congruence between norms and practice. Second, one of the main consequences to non-compliance, the compliance action plan, is explicitly interactional. It establishes an exchange between the compliance body and the non-compliant party, requiring the latter actively to engage with the Enforcement Branch until the compliance problem is resolved.

A number of other aspects of the compliance procedure are worth mentioning in the present context. First, the enforcement process is essentially interactional in nature. The party concerned is notified of

298 *Ibid.*, section XV.4. 299 *Ibid.*, sections XIII, XV.5.

300 *Ibid.*, sections XV.5(a) and (b), 6 and 7.

301 *Ibid.*, section XV.5(c). The penalty rate is intended to discourage parties from simply postponing their emission reductions to the subsequent commitment period. See Jutta Brunnée, 'A Fine Balance: Facilitation and Enforcement in the Design of a Compliance Regime for the Kyoto Protocol' (2000) 13 *Tulane Environmental Law Journal* 223 at 248–9.

302 Procedures and Mechanisms, above note 253, section V.6.

the proceeding, and given the opportunity to make a written submission as well as participate in a hearing. Based on these exchanges, the Enforcement Branch may end the process, or make a preliminary finding of non-compliance. After a further opportunity for submissions by the concerned party, the Enforcement Branch makes a final decision. As we have already seen, one of the possible consequences to a finding of non-compliance, the compliance action plan, further extends the interactional process. The Procedures and Mechanisms provide for strict timelines for all the steps of the enforcement process,[303] another feature designed to enhance the predictability of the process for the parties directly involved as well as for all regime participants.

Second, the Procedures and Mechanisms go to some length to provide access to non-state actors. While the compliance procedure can only be triggered by questions raised by expert reviews or by protocol parties, competent intergovernmental or NGOs can submit 'relevant factual and technical information' to either branch of the compliance committee.[304] Unless the relevant branch decides otherwise, and subject to rules of confidentiality, all information considered by the branch is made public.[305] In addition, unless the Enforcement Branch decides otherwise, any hearings that it holds will be public.[306] In all cases, final decisions will be available to the public.[307] These arrangements enhance the transparency of the compliance process and expose proceedings and outcome to public scrutiny. They also enable at least some measure of active engagement with the compliance process by the non-state members of the climate regime's community of practice.

Third, the compliance procedure allows for an appeal of Enforcement Branch decisions relating to a party's compliance with Article 3.1. Since these decisions expose parties to the most significant consequences, the Procedures and Mechanisms permit an appeal to the Meeting of the

[303] Procedures and Mechanisms, *ibid.*, sections VII.3 and 4 (initial screening of implementation questions and allocation to branches); and IX (procedures of the enforcement branch). An expedited procedure is provided for proceedings to suspend eligibility to participate in the protocol's emissions trading mechanisms and proceedings to have eligibility reinstated: *ibid.*, section X.1–4.

[304] *Ibid.*, section VIII.4. Each branch may also seek expert advice: *ibid.*, section VIII.5.

[305] Subject to rules of confidentiality, all information must be made public once a final decision is reached. *Ibid.*, section VIII.6.

[306] *Ibid.*, section IX.2; *Rules of procedure*, above note 282, rule 9. In the practice of the Committee, any member of the public, whether registered as a UNFCCC observer or not, may register as an observer of the proceedings.

[307] Procedures and Mechanisms, above note 253, section VIII.7.

Parties if the affected party 'believes it has been denied due process'.[308] The plenary, therefore, cannot revisit the substance of the decision, but can focus only on procedural considerations. The Meeting of the Parties must agree by a three-quarters majority vote to override the decision of the Enforcement Branch and send the matter back for review.[309] Importantly, appeals do not stay the decision of the Enforcement Branch.[310] This aspect maintains the predictability of the penalty system, while underscoring the importance of the procedural practices of the climate regime.

Finally, we return to our earlier observations about the legal form in which the protocol's compliance procedure was adopted,[311] a non-binding decision by the plenary body.[312] This route was chosen despite the stipulation in Article 18 of the Kyoto Protocol that any compliance procedures and mechanisms entailing binding consequences must be adopted by amendment. The adoption by simple decision was designed to avoid the difficulties inherent in the amendment route. An amendment would have entered into force only after the required number of ratifications had been obtained, and would have applied only to those states that had ratified it. As the interactional framework serves to highlight, the effect would have been to undercut the generality and predictability of the compliance procedure, and to severely weaken its potential to promote congruence between norms and practice. The amendment dilemma illustrates a point that we have made repeatedly in this book: formally binding law-making does not necessarily enhance legality. In the present circumstances, at least, the decision route was more conducive to legality, ensuring both immediate operation and its applicability to all parties. We would argue, in any case, that the adherence of the procedure to the requirements of interactional law is more important than its formal legal status.

In the non-compliance cases involving Greece and Canada the non-binding nature of the compliance procedure has not been an issue in its operation to date. Neither Greece nor Canada questioned the process as such, and both accepted its conclusions, including, in Greece's case, the 'consequences' that it entailed. The Enforcement Branch found Greece to be in non-compliance with the requirements concerning national emissions inventories. It determined that Greece had to prepare an

[308] *Ibid.*, section XI.1. [309] *Ibid.*, section XI.3. [310] *Ibid.*, section XI.4.

[311] See above notes 258–9 and accompanying text.

[312] See Procedures and Mechanisms, above note 253, preamble (noting that it remains the prerogative of the parties 'to decide on the legal form of the procedures and mechanisms relating to compliance in terms of Art. 18').

action plan detailing how it would remedy the compliance problems and suspended Greece from eligibility to participate in emissions trading.[313] Within several months of that decision, Greece had met the attendant requirements and its eligibility for emissions trading was reinstated.[314]

Canada's case involved a question of implementation relating to its national registry for emissions credits. In its preliminary finding, the Enforcement Branch concluded that Canada's registry was not in accordance with guidelines for the preparation of information required under Article 7 of the Kyoto Protocol.[315] Canada addressed all issues of concern in response to that finding. After a written submission explaining the steps it had taken and a hearing on 15 June 2008, the enforcement branch decided not to proceed further with the implementation question with respect to Canada.[316] Specifically, the Enforcement Branch concluded that, while 'the status of Canada's national registry resulted in non-compliance with the guidelines on the publication date of the review report',[317] there was now a 'sufficient factual basis' to avert a finding of non-compliance against Canada.[318] This conclusion prompted Canada to make a further written submission, suggesting that the branch's reference to past non-compliance was outside its mandate, and should therefore be struck from the record.[319] Canada argued that the provision that

[313] See Enforcement Branch of the Compliance Committee, 'Final Decision', CC-2007–1-8/Greece/EB, 17 April 2008, at http://unfccc.int/files/kyoto_protocol/compliance/enforcement_branch/application/pdf/cc-2007–1-8_greece_eb_final_decision.pdf.

[314] Enforcement Branch of the Compliance Committee, 'Decision under paragraph 2 of section X', CC-2007–1-13/Greece/EB, 13 November 2008, at http://unfccc.int/files/kyoto_protocol/compliance/enforcement_branch/application/pdf/cc-2007–1-13_greece_eb.pdf.

[315] Enforcement Branch of the Compliance Committee, 'Decision on Preliminary Examination', CC-2008–1-2/Canada/EB, 2 May 2008, at http://unfccc.int/files/kyoto_protocol/compliance/enforcement_branch/application/pdf/cc-2008–1-2_canada_eb__decision_on_preliminary_examination.pdf.

[316] Enforcement Branch of the Compliance Committee, 'Decision Not to Proceed Further', CC-2008–1-6/Canada/EB, 15 June 2008, at http://unfccc.int/files/kyoto_protocol/compliance/enforcement_branch/application/pdf/cc-2008–1-6_canada_eb_decision_not_to_proceed_further.pdf.

[317] *Ibid.*, para. 17(a). [318] *Ibid.*, para. 17(b).

[319] See Enforcement Branch of the Compliance Committee, 'Further Written Submission of Canada', CC-2008–1-7/Canada/EB, 14 July 2008, paras. 5 and 8, at http://unfccc.int/files/kyoto_protocol/compliance/enforcement_branch/application/pdf/cc-2008–1-7-canada_eb_document_Entitled_further_written_submission_of_canada.pdf.

sets out the mandate of the Enforcement Branch uses the present tense, tasking the branch with determining whether an Annex I Party "*is*" or "*is* not" in compliance with Kyoto guidelines.[320] Since a final decision of the Enforcement Branch cannot be appealed except on the grounds of due process violations, there was no room under the Procedures and Mechanisms for a further decision by either the Enforcement Branch or the COP. To address the concern expressed by Canada, the Enforcement Branch resorted to issuing an 'Information Note', inviting Canada to request that its further submission be appended to the annual report of the Compliance Committee to the protocol's plenary body.[321]

Canada's meticulous responses stand in some contrast to its blunt statements that it would not meet its emission reduction commitments. In the context of the current non-compliance proceeding, Canada has shown itself quick to adjust its performance to meet the procedural requirements of the protocol, keen to ensure careful interpretation of the relevant procedural rules, and intent on avoiding even a statement on past non-compliance with a procedural commitment. Arguably, the contrast between its emissions-related posture and its responses in the non-compliance proceeding reflects a tension between statements that result from political decisions by the government of the day and the day-to-day practice of the diplomats and bureaucrats engaged in the regime. However, it may also reflect the phenomenon that our interactional law analysis of the climate regime has revealed: the presence of strong shared understandings and the strong adherence to legality in the case of the regime's procedural aspects, and fragility of its substantive aspects.

It remains to be seen, of course, how Canada and other parties will handle the assessment of their emissions reduction performance at the end of the commitment period, assuming the Kyoto Protocol remains in effect. A rationalist account of compliance might predict that the higher stakes that a finding of non-compliance with the emissions target entails will lead states to challenge the non-binding compliance process and resist

[320] *Ibid.*, para. 8 (referring to Decision 27/CMP.1, section V(4)) (emphasis in the submission).

[321] See Enforcement Branch of the Compliance Committee, 'Information Note', CC-2008-1/Canada/EB, 1 August 2008, at http://unfccc.int/files/kyoto_protocol/compliance/enforcement_branch/application/pdf/information_note.pdf. Canada followed this advice – see 'Annual report of the Compliance Committee to the Conference of the Parties serving as the meeting of the Parties to the Kyoto Protocol', CC/5/2008/3, 30 September 2008, pp. 39–42, at http://unfccc.int/files/kyoto_protocol/compliance/plenary/application/pdf/cc-5-2008-3_annual_report_of_the_committee_to_the_cmp.pdf.

its more costly consequences. We suggest that a compliance assessment and even an 'enforcement' process can operate effectively without being formally binding, provided that it meets the requirements of interactional law and that a strong practice of legality evolves. A compliance process that operates on this basis will be widely seen as legitimate, will enhance parties' sense of obligation and enmesh them in a compelling justificatory discourse,[322] and will give decisions of the Enforcement Branch a quality of genuinely collective enforcement, consisting in powerful collective disapprobation rather than penalty.[323] As we have shown, the Kyoto compliance procedure fares well when measured against the criteria of legality. And while the two cases we have described cannot provide conclusive evidence, they do suggest that the particular features of the compliance procedure, and its interactional nature, also help extend the climate regime's practice of legality. However, our account also shows that the success of such a compliance process depends on the sustained efforts of all regime participants to do just that: practice legality at all points in the continuum that runs from law-making to implementation to compliance assessment and enforcement, and back to law-making. As we are about to suggest, the outcome of the negotiations in Copenhagen has put in question whether the type of compliance assessment that has evolved under the Kyoto Protocol will continue to be part of the climate regime.

6. The Copenhagen Accord

In December 2009, the eyes of the world were on the Danish capital, Copenhagen. The Copenhagen meetings of the parties to the UNFCCC and Kyoto Protocol were to yield a global regime that would commit all major economies to a long-term curbing of their greenhouse gas emissions. As noted earlier in the chapter, expectations for the outcome of the meeting were scaled back further and further as it approached. The draft texts that had been produced by the convention and protocol working groups were so unwieldy, and the positions of key parties so far apart, that a fully fledged agreement on post-2012 commitments became increasingly unlikely. Instead, hopes were pinned on a political agreement, or decisions of the parties, that would sketch at least the contours of a long-term regime.[324]

[322] See above Chapter 3, notes 47–52 and accompanying text.

[323] See above Chapter 3, notes 87–8 and accompanying text.

[324] See Lavanya Rajamani, 'The Copenhagen Agreed Outcome: Form, Shape & Influence', *Centre for Policy Research (CPR) Climate Brief*, November 2009, at www.cprindia.org/policyupload/1259569856-CPR%20Polic%20Brief2.pdf.

But Copenhagen did not go as planned. It produced only a slim document dubbed the 'Copenhagen Accord', negotiated at the eleventh hour by only five countries (Brazil, China, India, South Africa and the United States) and later taken 'note' of by the 194 parties to the Climate Convention just before their meeting was gavelled to a close.[325] Many parties, most notably many developing countries, expressed dismay at the process through which the Accord was produced, including the fact that US President Barack Obama, who had brokered the deal, announced it to the media before it had been released to, let alone sanctioned by, the parties to the climate agreements.[326] An acrimonious session of the COP was suspended when it proved impossible to gain consensus on the adoption of the Accord. The parties' decision to take note of the arrangement was a compromise facilitated by the UN Secretary-General, Ban Ki-Moon, to overcome the deadlock.[327]

The immediate reactions to the Copenhagen Accord were decidedly mixed. President Obama called it a 'meaningful and unprecedented breakthrough'.[328] But for many others the outcome spelled failure, both in the world's fight against climate change and for the UN climate change regime.[329] Leaving aside process concerns, many observers were bitterly disappointed by the substance of the Accord, and its uncertain legal footing. Before we turn to an assessment of the Accord through the lens of our interactional framework, we offer a brief sketch of its main features.

6.1 Key features

The submissions by parties under the Bali Action Plan that we discussed earlier in the chapter foreshadowed some of the dynamics that played out in Copenhagen. In the months leading up to the Copenhagen meetings,

325 See Copenhagen Accord, above note 19.

326 See Drexhage, above note 203 at 2.

327 See IISD, 'Summary of the Copenhagen Climate Change Conference: 7–19 December 2009', *Earth Negotiations Bulletin*, Vol.12, No. 459 (22 December 2009), pp. 7–9, at www.iisd.ca/download/pdf/enb12459e.pdf.

328 The White House, 'A Meaningful and Unprecedented Breakthrough Here in Copenhagen,' at www.whitehouse.gov/blog/2009/12/18/a-meaningful-and-unprecedented-breakthrough-here-copenhagen.

329 See e.g. James Kanter, 'E.U. Blames Others for "Great Failure" on Climate', *The New York Times*, 22 December 2009; at www.nytimes.com/2009/12/23/world/europe/23iht-climate.html; and Donna Bryson, 'South Africa Blasts Copenhagen Failure', *The Associated Press*, 22 December 2009; at www.google.com/hostednews/ap/article/ALeqM5hshRkwauciAwG_LbxRGBwzE7STrQD9CO9JPO0.

it became apparent that many developing countries saw a continuation of the Kyoto Protocol as essential to the further development of the climate regime. For some developing states, notably small island states, this position reflected their desire to maintain the only instrument that contained legally binding emission reduction commitments by industrialized countries.[330] For others, led by China and India, Kyoto appeared to enshrine the only acceptable model of differentiation – the distinction between industrialized states that had binding emission reduction commitments and developing countries that did not.[331] By contrast, most industrialized countries wished to see Kyoto replaced by a single, comprehensive instrument with appropriately differentiated commitments for all countries, including emissions-related commitments for the major developing economies.[332]

In other words, the fate of the Kyoto Protocol became one of the battle grounds for the underlying questions of principle. The stark distinction drawn in the UNFCCC and the Kyoto Protocol between Annex I and non-Annex I parties, was seen by some developing countries as a bulwark against efforts to single out some developing countries on account of their growing greenhouse gas emissions. As we saw earlier in the chapter, the Bali Action Plan had begun to weaken the bulwark, replacing the Annex I–non-Annex I dichotomy with a more open-ended distinction between developed and developing countries.[333] Still, for many developing countries, it maintained at least a 'fire-wall' against emission reduction commitments for developing countries.[334]

[330] See e.g. *Proposal by the Alliance of Small Island States (AOSIS) for the Survival of the Kyoto Protocol and a Copenhagen protocol to Enhance the Implementation of the United Nations Framework Convention on Climate Change*, in UNFCCC, *Ideas and proposals on the elements contained in paragraph 1 of the Bali Action Plan*, AWGLCA, 8th Sess., UNFCCC Doc., FCCC/AWGLCA/2009/MISC.8 (18 December 2009), p. 15, at http://unfccc.int/resource/docs/2009/awglca8/eng/misc08.pdf. And see, generally, Rajamani, above note 78 at 2.

[331] See e.g. '"Kyoto Principles" crucial in climate talks: China', *Reuters*, 14 November 2009, at www.reuters.com/article/idUSTRE5AD0NV20091114; and 'Big developing countries form climate change front', *Reuters*, 29 November 2009, at www.reuters.com/article/idUSPEK20047.

[332] Lavanya Rajamani, 'The "Cloud" Over the Climate Negotiations: From Bangkok to Copenhagen and Beyond', *Centre for Policy Research (CPR) Climate Brief*, October 2009, at 2–3, at www.cprindia.org/policyupload/1256103508-CPR%20Polic%20Brief.pdf.

[333] See Bali Action Plan, above note 20, paras. 1 (b)(i) and (ii) and Spence *et al.*, above note 66 at 150 (commenting on the subtle, but significant shift in the language of the Action Plan).

[334] See Rajamani, above note 332 at 2.

At the time of writing, the ultimate fate of the Kyoto Protocol is uncertain. A Danish proposal that would have set the post-2012 climate regime on a single instrument track was leaked to the press shortly after the beginning of the Copenhagen talks.[335] Developing countries, led by a small but determined group of states that were widely seen to operate with at least the backing of China and India, resisted the formal introduction of the text into the negotiating process.[336] The fact that the proposal had apparently been developed in consultation with only the United States and the United Kingdom did not help matters, nor did the fact that many developing countries saw its content as skewed towards industrialized country preferences.[337] Whereas the Danish proposal appeared designed to lead to a replacement of the Kyoto Protocol, the last-minute 'Copenhagen Accord' leaves the issue unmentioned. Apparently, an earlier draft of the document had been unacceptable to developing countries because of a preambular statement affirming parties' 'firm resolve to adopt one or more legal instruments', thereby acknowledging the possible demise of the Kyoto Protocol.[338]

Nonetheless, the Accord suggests some softening in the resistance by China and India to emissions-related measures. Indeed, the document contains at least three genuine breakthroughs. First, in addition to 'quantified economy-wide emissions targets for 2020' by industrialized countries, it envisages for the first time an international commitment to 'mitigation actions' by developing countries.[339] The former are to be 'measured, reported and verified ... in accordance with ... guidelines adopted by the Conference of the Parties' to the UNFCCC.[340] The latter are to be reported through national communications under the convention and, if supported through international financing, will be 'subject to international measurement, reporting and verification', also

[335] See John Vidal, 'Copenhagen climate summit in disarray after "Danish text" leak', *The Guardian*, 8 December 2009, at www.guardian.co.uk/environment/2009/dec/08/copenhagen-climate-summit-disarray-danish-text. The text is posted at the newspaper's website, at: www.guardian.co.uk/environment/2009/dec/08/copenhagen-climate-change.

[336] See Dan Bodansky, 'The Illegitimacy of "Legitimacy"', *Opinio Juris*, 17 December 2009, at http://opiniojuris.org/2009/12/17/the-illegitimacy-of-%e2%80%9clegitimacy.

[337] See Vidal, above note 335.

[338] See Jonathan Watts, 'What was agreed at Copenhagen – and what was left out', *The Guardian*, 19 December 2009, at www.guardian.co.uk/environment/2009/dec/18/how-copenhagen-text-was-changed.

[339] Copenhagen Accord, above note 19, paras. 4 and 5. This approach does, however, follow the course charted in the Bali Action Plan. See above note 71 and accompanying text.

[340] *Ibid.*, para. 4.

in accordance with guidelines adopted by the COP.[341] These provisions reflect the desire of industrialized countries to anchor their commitments in the same instrument as commitments by major developing country emitters, and to have at least some international oversight – a notion that had been strongly resisted by China.[342] At the same time, the Accord caters to the developing country demand for clear differentiation between the two groups. Aside from the distinction between 'targets' and 'actions', the Accord reverts to the rigid categorization of states as 'Annex I' and 'non-Annex I'.[343] Furthermore, it calls upon Annex I parties to opt into the arrangement by registering their target pledges in one appendix, and on non-Annex I parties to register their emissions intensity pledges in another.[344]

Second, the Accord commits industrialized countries to providing 'new and additional resources … approaching USD 30 billion for the period 2010–2012', and to mobilizing 'USD 100 billion a year by 2020 to address the needs of developing countries'.[345] It appears as if these financing commitments are to be 'measured, reported and verified' along with Annex I parties' emission reductions.[346]

Third, without doing so explicitly, the Accord suggests that the idea of differentiation among developing countries is taking hold and is gaining the acceptance of China and India, notwithstanding their public statements to the contrary. Within the group of 'non-Annex I parties', the Accord singles out least developed countries and developing nations that are especially vulnerable to climate change. Notably, whereas non-Annex I states 'will implement' mitigation actions, least developed and small island developing countries 'may undertake actions voluntarily and on the basis of support'.[347] The Accord also identifies 'the most vulnerable developing countries, such as the least developed countries, small island developing States and Africa' as priority recipients of adaptation funding.[348] In these respects, then, the Accord reflects the differentiations that had gained increasing support in the course of the Bali process.[349]

The 2° C benchmark for temperature increases was also confirmed in the Copenhagen Accord.[350] African and small island states especially

[341] *Ibid.*, para. 5. [342] See Drexhage, above note 203 at 3.

[343] See above notes 71 and 333–4 and accompanying text on the language in the Bali Action Plan.

[344] Copenhagen Accord, above note 19, para. 4. [345] *Ibid.*, para. 8.

[346] *Ibid.*, para. 4. [347] *Ibid.*, para. 5. [348] *Ibid.*

[349] See above notes 147–54 and accompanying text.

[350] See Copenhagen Accord, above note 19, para. 1.

had been pushing for recognition of a more ambitious temperature limit of 1.5° C,[351] but in this respect the Accord only calls for an assessment of its implementation by 2015, including 'in light of the Convention's ultimate objective' and 'consideration of strengthening the long-term goal'.[352]

Notwithstanding its origins in a five-party negotiation, the Copenhagen Accord is intended to operate in the context of the UNFCCC. It declares itself to be guided by the convention principles, including CBDR.[353] It also envisages drawing on the convention to implement a number of its key provisions. For example, in the context of the funding commitments by developed countries, the Accord contemplates a 'Copenhagen Green Climate Fund', to be 'established as an operating entity of the financial mechanism of the Convention'.[354] Yet, while connecting itself to UNFCCC processes, the Accord at the same time loosens the ties between implementing actions and the convention. The 'bottom-up' approach inherent in the pledge system reflects this fact,[355] as does the supervision system. Thus, the COP is to adopt guidelines for the measuring, reporting and verification of Annex I emission reductions and financing, as well as for national communications by non-Annex I countries on their actions.[356] But the language in the Accord suggests that the measuring, reporting and verification as such can be domestic action.[357]

The ultimate relationship between the Accord and the climate regime is difficult to predict, and the document does not provide guidance on the matter. It merely endorses two parallel decisions under the convention and Kyoto Protocol, respectively, to extend by one year the formal negotiations towards an agreed outcome on post-2012 climate action.[358] Many parties are still looking to bring the Accord more resolutely into the climate regime than was accomplished when the plenary decided only to

351 David Doniger, 'The Copenhagen Accord: A Big Step Forward', *Climate Progress*, 28 December 2009, at http://climateprogress.org/2009/12/28/the-copenhagen-accord-a-big-step-forward/.

352 Copenhagen Accord, above note 19, para. 12.

353 See *ibid.*, preamble and para. 1.

354 *Ibid.*, paras. 8 and 10.

355 The 'bottom up' approach had been advocated by the United States and Australia. See Rajamani, above note 332 at 2.

356 Copenhagen Accord, above note 19, paras. 4 and 5.

357 See above notes 340–1 and accompanying text.

358 See UNFCCC, *Draft Decision -/CP.15, Outcome of the Ad Hoc Working Group on Long-term Cooperative Action under the Convention*, para. 1; at http://unfccc.int/files/meetings/cop_15/application/pdf/cop15_lca_auv.pdf; and UNFCCC, *Draft Decision -/CMP.5, Outcome of the Ad Hoc Working Group on Further Commitments for Annex I Parties under the Kyoto Protocol*, para. 2; at http://unfccc.int/files/meetings/cop_15/application/pdf/cmp5_awg_auv.pdf.

take note of the Accord.[359] Indeed, earlier drafts of the Accord had envisaged that it be converted into a legally binding instrument within a year's time. However, the relevant text was dropped, apparently in the face of resistance by some states, including China, India and Saudi Arabia.[360]

6.2 Shared understandings

For all its flaws, the Accord is consistent with the evolution of shared understandings concerning the regime objective and the CBDR principle that we traced earlier in the chapter. However, given the manner in which the Copenhagen Accord was negotiated, the document per se cannot be seen as expressing the convention parties' shared understandings. Indeed, even representatives of one of the five states involved in the negotiations subsequently criticized both the process that led to the Accord and its substance.[361] Furthermore, many developing countries insisted on maintaining the consensus approach to decision-making that had become the default practice in the climate regime, and complained bitterly about the lack of access to and transparency of the negotiations that produced the Copenhagen Accord.[362]

In any case, negotiations among a small number of parties, by definition, cannot produce shared understandings among non-participants in the salient interactions. For it to endure, all parties must now engage with the Accord and embrace it as it stands, or agree on anchoring its approach in the climate regime in some other fashion. The final hours of the Copenhagen meeting suggest that most convention parties are willing to at least contemplate building on the Accord. According to observers of the negotiations, it was in fact a relatively small number of developing countries that blocked consensus decision-making at several crucial junctures, while many other developing countries desperately wanted progress to be made.[363] What is more, notwithstanding the

[359] See e.g. 'UK's Brown says climate change agreement possible', *The Times of India*, 4 January 2010, at http://timesofindia.indiatimes.com/home/environment/developmental-issues/UKs-Brown-says-climate-change-agreement-possible/articleshow/5409324.cms.

[360] See Bryson, above note 329; and Pew Center on Global Climate Change, 'Summary of COP 15 and CMP 5 prepared by the Pew Center on Global Climate Change', December 2009, at www.pewclimate.org/docUploads/copenhagen-cop15-summary.pdf.

[361] See Bryson, *ibid.* [362] See Drexhage, above note 203 at 2.

[363] See Drexhage, *ibid.*; Bodansky, above note 336; Dan Bodansky, 'Sleepless in Copenhagen', *Opinio Juris*, 19 December 2009, at http://opiniojuris.org/2009/12/19/sleepless-in-copenhagen-2/; Doniger, above note 351.

misgivings about the closed door negotiations among five parties, the emerging Accord seems to have had the support of the leaders of key industrialized and developing states from around the world.[364] Similarly, during the plenary debate on the Accord, a large majority of developed and developing states threw their support behind it.[365] As we have seen, the Accord rests on the premise that parties to the UNFCCC will associate themselves with it, and register any emissions pledges in the Accord's appendices. The number of such endorsements and registrations will provide an early indication of whether or not the Accord contains the seeds of a 'shared vision'.

6.3. *The criteria of legality*

Earlier in this chapter we noted that the universal participation in the UNFCCC bolsters the generality of the convention and so its legality and legitimacy.[366] Measured against this criterion, the Copenhagen Accord has yet to prove itself. As we have seen, the intention is for the Accord to be tied into decision-making under the auspices of the UNFCCC. Therefore, it would seem that the Accord, even on its own terms, will only be viable if it can attract the support of the parties to the convention. If it does, the demands for universality will be met, even in the face of differentiated commitments by only some of the parties.[367] However, whether the Accord will fully meet the generality requirement is a more complicated question, given that states' commitments are defined by their unilateral pledges and so are entirely beyond the control of other states that endorse the Accord.

The Copenhagen Accord does address the promulgation requirement, which as we have seen is not co-extensive with the adoption of an instrument in legally binding form.[368] However, it is weakened on this score by the fact that, at least for the moment, the UNFCCC parties have merely taken note of the Accord, leaving its future and precise relationship to the convention uncertain.

[364] Bodansky, above note 336; Doniger, above note 351 (citing support by leaders of 28 developed and developing countries).

[365] See IISD, above note 327 at 28–9 (noting that 'all developed countries, most developing countries, as well as spokespersons for AOSIS, LDCs and the African Group, recognized that the negotiating process had been legitimate and urged COP 15 to adopt the Copenhagen Accord').

[366] See above notes 234–9 and accompanying text.

[367] See text following above note 234.

[368] See above notes 258–9 and accompanying text.

As for the clarity requirement, the fact that various aspects of the Accord require fleshing out through subsequent action under the auspices of the convention (e.g. measuring, reporting and verification requirements) is not fatal. The relevant gaps in the Accord can be filled through decisions of the UNFCCC parties, an incremental approach to rule-making that is in keeping with the practice under the convention.[369] In other respects, however, the Accord deviates substantially from past practice under the convention. As already noted, the lack of adoption through a plenary decision of the parties leaves its relationship to the convention undefined. Further, the Accord's approach is fundamentally different from the 'targets and timetables' approach of the Kyoto Protocol. It provides no parameters for individual states' commitments beyond the broad requirements that Annex I states pledge 2020 'quantified economy-wide' emission reduction targets and non-Annex I states 'nationally appropriate mitigation actions'.[370] Annex I states must index their targets against a base year, but the Accord leaves the choice of that reference year to them.[371] In combination with the unilateral pledge mechanism envisaged by the Accord, its emissions-related elements therefore lack in clarity. It could be said that parties ultimately opt into all international agreements and that, for example, the emission reduction requirements of the Kyoto Protocol were equally determined by national preferences. The Kyoto model is nonetheless different, as parties' emissions pledges were negotiated and then fixed upon adoption of the protocol. The Copenhagen model of unilateral pledges only approximates this effect to the extent that, given the announcements made by major emitters prior to the conference, parties can predict 'with a reasonable degree of certainty' what others will inscribe.[372] Unlike the Kyoto Protocol, the Accord also leaves open whether and how parties can withdraw or adjust their pledge over time. Aside from the call for a 2015 review of its implementation, the Accord is silent on this question.

While the Accord's clarity concerning at least the initial emissions-related measures will be enhanced as states begin to opt into its appendices, problems may well persist in relation to the requirement of non-contradiction. Broadly speaking, the emissions regime it contemplates is consonant with the CBDR principle. If, procedurally, the Copenhagen Accord was squeezed out from between a rock and hard

[369] See e.g. above note 241 and accompanying text.

[370] See Copenhagen Accord, above note 19, paras. 4 and 5, and Appendices I and II.

[371] *Ibid.* [372] See Doniger, above note 351.

place, its substance is generally in line with the idea of common responsibility. As we have seen, the Accord brings the commitments of industrialized and developing countries into one instrument, and in turn aims to tie that instrument into the UNFCCC. The Accord is also consonant with the convention parties' emerging understanding of differentiation, providing for differentiation between both industrialized and developing countries and between developing countries. However, within these parameters there is considerable room for parties' pledges to follow national priorities rather than the principles underpinning the instrument, or the climate regime as a whole.[373]

Indeed, the Copenhagen Accord will almost certainly be at odds with the objective of preventing dangerous climate change. To be sure, it declares itself to be in pursuit of the objective, and endorses the 2° temperature goal.[374] However, collectively, the reduction pledges made by Annex I countries in the lead-up to the Copenhagen meetings have been calculated to promise a reduction between only 13 per cent and 19 per cent below 1990 emissions.[375] Although significant, these pledges remain considerably below the reduction range said to be required to meet the convention objective. As a result, and assuming that parties' pledges will track previous announcements, the Accord will not live up to the UNFCCC objective. In fact, when the most ambitious emissions pledges for 2020 by developed countries are combined with those made by China and India, recent estimates suggest that these efforts would put the world on track for a minimum temperature increase of 3.2° C by 2100.[376] It is not clear at this point in which direction this internal tension between the temperature goal and the current emissions pledges will pull the Accord. The fact that over 115 heads of state and government attended the summit attests to the importance that governments and people around the

[373] In fact, this type of flexibility is the very point of the 'bottom up' approach enshrined in the Accord. See e.g. Robert N. Stavins, 'A Portfolio of Domestic Commitments: Implementing Common but Differentiated Responsibilities', *Viewpoints – Harvard Project on International Climate Agreements*, 19 October 2009, at http://belfercenter.ksg.harvard.edu/files/DomesticCommitments_final.pdf.

[374] Copenhagen Accord, above note 19, preamble and paras. 1 and 2.

[375] See Kelly Levin and Rob Bradley, 'Comparability of Annex I Emission Reduction Pledges,' *World Resources Institute Working Paper*, December 2009, at 2, at http://pdf.wri.org/working_papers/comparability_of_annex1_emission_reduction_pledges_2009-12-04.pdf.

[376] See Niklas Höhne *et al.*, *Copenhagen Climate Deal – How to Close the Gap*, Briefing Paper, Ecofys & Climate Analytics, 15 December 2009, at 6, at www.climateactiontracker.org/briefing_paper.pdf.

world now attach to climate change.[377] It is perhaps for this reason that US President Obama described the Copenhagen Accord as a 'first step',[378] as have others.[379]

If the likely pledges under the Accord run up against the requirement of non-contradiction, especially as it relates to the objective of the climate regime, they also ensure its compatibility with the demand that law not ask the impossible. One of the arguments in favour of the 'bottom up' approach is that it would guard against unrealistically ambitious emissions requirements that parties would ultimately find themselves unable to meet.[380] Indeed, in view of the mid- and long-term horizon of the post-2012 regime and fluctuations in economic development over time, fixed targets can make emissions trajectories and ultimate costs of emissions actions hard to predict. While these factors may not make implementation impossible, as some Kyoto parties have claimed,[381] the Accord's pledge system, along with its planned review in 2015, will certainly make the costs of implementation more predictable. Unfortunately, the flip-side is that the emission reductions that the Accord will deliver are less predictable, especially since it is unclear whether and how parties can withdraw or reduce their commitments in light of domestic circumstances.

It is not possible at this time to comment on the congruence between parties' practice and the Accord. To the extent, however, that the Accord is in turn understood as practice under the climate regime, it does appear to raise some congruence questions. More specifically, a number of questions arise when the Accord and the Copenhagen negotiations are considered through the lens of the practice of legality, to which we now turn.

6.4 *Practice of legality*

The Copenhagen process and the resultant climate accord pose a number of challenges to the practice of legality that had evolved within the climate change regime. As we have shown in earlier parts of the chapter, that practice is primarily procedural in nature and has played an important

[377] See IISD, above note 327 at 27. [378] See The White House, above note 328.

[379] See e.g. BBC News, 'UN says Copenhagen deal "a start"', 19 December 2009, at http://news.bbc.co.uk/2/hi/science/nature/8422133.stm.

[380] See e.g. Shinya Murase, 'The Post-Kyoto International Framework – a WTO/GATT-Model', at 2 (commenting on the rigid nature of Kyoto targets), at www.meti.go.jp/english/press/data/pdf/20_Murase(English).pdf.

[381] See above note 268 and accompanying text.

role in sustaining the climate regime. We single out two issues that raise particular concerns in light of that fact: the practices relating to consensus-based decision-making, and the fate of the Kyoto Protocol's compliance procedure.

Our earlier discussion suggested that the climate regime's consensus decision-making practice has some benefits in terms of promoting the emergence of shared understandings as well as reinforcing the generality of the regime, especially in the face of the need to engage not only emitters but all states affected by climate change. At the same time, consensus decision-making enables a small number of states to exert disproportionate pressure on or even to prevent decision-making. Hence, although consensus decision-making appears at first glance to be conducive to interactional law-making, it can also hinder decision-making in situations where a large or even predominant majority of states have arrived at shared understandings. When the consensus practice prevents parties from acting on those understandings, it comes to undercut interactional law-making, rather than enhance it.

The climate regime has long wrestled with the frustrations generated by perceived abuses of the consensus decision-making approach. Indeed, repeated efforts have been made to supplement the consensus practice with a fall-back option of majority decision-making, as is common within most multilateral environmental agreements.[382] Since 1995, a proposal by Papua New Guinea to allow adoption of decisions by three-quarters majority if consensus cannot be reached has been placed before the annual meetings of the convention parties. Consultations among parties during the Copenhagen meetings made clear that, as in previous years, the proposal would falter on the very consensus principle that it was designed to supplant.[383] By all accounts, an odd coalition of states, including Bolivia, Venezuela, Ecuador, and Sudan, played the spoiler on this and other key issues that required consensus to be resolved, including the endorsement of the Copenhagen Accord.[384]

The Copenhagen process made clear that a consensus rule without a majority-vote fall-back has become untenable. It threatens both to undermine the all-important procedural legality of the regime, and to push parties who wish to make progress on climate action into smaller negotiating and decision-making groups. For now, the Copenhagen Accord,

[382] See Széll, above note 244.

[383] See Drexhage, above note 203 at 2; and IISD, above note 327 at 4.

[384] See Drexhage, above note 203; Bodansky, above note 336.

which was at least in part the result of the blockage in the Copenhagen process, is intended to be tied back into the UNFCCC. However, unless the decision-making rules of the convention are modified, the parties endorsing the Accord may well look for ways to bypass the treaty's choke points. This development, in turn, would undercut the equally important universality of the climate regime, a domino effect that could ultimately unravel it.

A second challenge to the procedural practice of legality that has evolved in the climate regime rests in the bottom-up approach of the Copenhagen Accord, and the attendant move to domestic compliance assessment that is merely guided by UNFCCC-based standards. The combination of these elements would spell the end of the compliance assessment practice that has been developing under the Kyoto Protocol and which, as we have shown, has become an important part of the regime's practice of legality. If the Kyoto Protocol, and its approach to commitments and review, wither away, the central challenge for the climate regime will be to find alternative settings in which to nurture the regime's practice of legality. Prima facie, the more promising venue for the evolution of a sustained practice of legality would seem to be the regular and increasingly dense and patterned interactions that evolve within an international review process.[385] But the approach hinted at in the Copenhagen Accord could lead to the emergence of credible domestic review practices. Such practices, in turn, could actually play an important role in fostering communities of practice that transcend the boundaries between the international and domestic spheres.[386] If such a development is to be promoted, it is crucial that the international guidelines to be adopted for domestic compliance assessment are indeed 'rigorous, robust and transparent' and,[387] we would add, help ensure that domestic practices can evolve into practices of legality.

7. Conclusion

Climate change presents one of the most complex regulatory challenges imaginable, due to the multi-faceted issues that must be addressed by actors with widely divergent perspectives and priorities. This chapter has illustrated that building a global legal regime is about much more than

[385] See Chapter 3, sections 4.2 and 4.3.

[386] See Chapters 2 (on communities of practice) and 3 (section 4.4 on the challenges posed by the interface between international and domestic law).

[387] Copenhagen Accord, above note 19, para. 4.

adopting a treaty or negotiating a deal on actions to curb climate change. We have shown that a long-term agreement on emission reductions is unlikely to be attainable, and unlikely to have lasting obligatory force, unless it rests on a strong foundation of shared understandings, respects the requirements of legality, and is embedded in a vibrant practice of legality.

As the evolution of the global climate regime attests, building up these conditions can be a long and difficult process. The regime certainly confirms our observation in earlier chapters that formal law will often be the starting point for interactional law-making, rather than the end point. Our assessment is that the climate regime has been successful in cultivating a sound basis of shared procedural understandings and fostering procedural legality, both in terms of attention to the criteria of legality, and in terms of the procedural practices within the regime. These procedural elements illustrate that interactional law can emerge without strong substantive agreement among parties. At the outset, the treaty parties agreed that climate change was of concern and that it should be addressed on the basis of a global legal regime, but in just about every other respect they were deeply divided. In particular, power imbalances between developing and industrialized countries, and a legacy of distrust, were – and continue to be – among the challenges that climate law-making must overcome. The instantiation of procedural legality is an indispensable part of this process, since parties must first develop a setting in which contentious substantive issues can be legitimately addressed, and in which all parties can participate in the development of shared understandings. We would argue, then, that the climate regime has given rise to procedural interactional law, which has helped generate a sense of commitment of the participants to the regime and accounts at least in part for its resilience. However, as the Copenhagen Accord and the events surrounding its adoption so vividly illustrate, procedural legality too rests on practices and so is potentially fragile, and dependent upon the sustained efforts of a community of practice. Maintaining, or restoring, the legitimacy of the climate regime's decision-making practice arguably is one of the urgent challenges confronting those who wish to ensure its continuing influence.

We suggest that the existence of procedural interactional law has assisted the growth of broader substantive understandings amongst participants, including those concerning CBDR and the emerging contours of a new emission reductions regime. Whether substantive interactional law has emerged is more difficult to say. An agreed meaning of CBDR that meets the requirements of legality appears to be emerging. The principle has certainly been influential in shaping the evolution of the climate regime as well as the arguments offered by states and other participants. Indeed, the experience with the climate regime to date shows that any new emissions regime will have to be consistent with the agreed meaning of CBDR in order to meet the criteria of legality (notably, non-contradiction) and to be legitimate in the eyes of all regime participants. This assessment finds confirmation in the fact that the shared understandings concerning the regime's existing emission reductions provisions seem to be fragile, as is their conformity with the criteria of legality. Specifically, the fact that only some of the major global emitters have reduction obligations under the Kyoto Protocol, the evolution of global emission patterns, and the shifts in the parties' understandings of the regime's conceptual underpinnings, including CBDR and the regime's objective, all put pressure on this reduction framework. While the Kyoto Protocol's compliance procedure has begun to develop a new practice of legality, for now it is focused primarily on procedural commitments. It is too soon to fully assess whether the parties' practice is congruent with the emission reduction commitments and, in light of the Copenhagen Accord, it is difficult to predict the ultimate fate of those commitments, or of the Protocol's approach to compliance assessment. Whether the Copenhagen Accord will lead to the emergence of a credible domestic alternative to the Protocol's international compliance assessment is also unclear at this point.

What we do know is that the Accord is broadly consistent with, and indeed even confirms, the shifts in the understanding of the CBDR principle that we have traced in this chapter. By contrast, it appears to be in tension with the objective of the climate regime, as specified through the widely shared 2° C temperature goal. The Accord as it currently stands falls short on a number of the criteria of legality that we posit. This fact leads to the conclusion that the Copenhagen Accord, quite apart from the manner and form in which it was adopted, is a political and not a legal agreement. To be sure, it can serve as a focal point for further interactions of the parties and the gradual evolution of interactional law. But to that end, the various legality issues that we have highlighted would have to be addressed by the parties as they work build on and flesh out the Accord.

As we have suggested at various points in the preceding chapters, an interactional understanding of international law implies neither the inevitably progressive development of international law, nor a success story for international law. The climate change regime is a case in point. The

1992 United Nations Framework Convention on Climate Change has been ratified by all states and the EU. The 1997 Kyoto Protocol, too, is an agreement with almost universal membership. The climate regime was structured from the beginning in a manner that promotes interaction. The convention established institutions and opportunities for repeated, long-term engagement between states parties and other actors, and between these actors and the norms of the regime. The protocol grew out of these deliberations, as have the negotiations for future, long-term commitments. And yet, almost twenty years after the adoption of the framework convention, we still cannot be certain that a global emissions regime capable of averting dangerous climate change and its potentially disastrous effects on human life and the environment will be adopted. The interactional law framework requires us to closely examine existing norms – be they customary, treaty, or soft law – and the processes through which law is made and applied. Our analysis in this chapter illustrates that some of the law-making under the climate regime has been influential. But it also illuminates the regime's weaknesses. Above all, our assessment of the climate regime underscores the theme that runs throughout this book: international law is made, upheld, and developed through the continuous, hard work of the participants.

5

Torture: undermining normative ambition

> Tell me yourself directly, I challenge you – reply: imagine that you yourself are erecting the edifice of human fortune with the goal of, at the finale, making people happy, of at last giving them peace and quiet, but that in order to do it it would be necessary and unavoidable to torture to death only one tiny little creature, that same little child that beat its breast with its little fist, and on its unavenged tears to found that edifice, would you agree to be the architect of those conditions, tell me and tell me truly?
>
> Ivan to Alyosha, Dostoevski, *The Brothers Karamozov*, Tome I, Book V, Ch. 4[1]

> Freedom from torture is an inalienable human right, and we are committed to building a world where human rights are respected and protected by the rule of law. ... Many have been detained, arrested, thrown in prison and subjected to torture by regimes that fail to understand that their habits of control will not serve them well in the long term.
>
> President George W. Bush, Statement, 26 June 2005[2]

1. Introduction

In the United Nations Convention against Torture, torture is described as:

> ... any act by which severe pain or suffering, whether physical or mental, is intentionally inflicted on a person for such purposes as obtaining from him or a third person information or a confession, punishing him for an act he or a third person has committed or is suspected of having committed, or intimidating or coercing him or a third person, or for any reason based on discrimination of any kind, when such pain or suffering

[1] Fyodor Dostoyevsky, *The Brothers Karamazov: A Novel in Four Parts and an Epilogue*, David McDuff (trans.), (London: Penguin, 2003), Book V, Chapter 4, p. 321.

[2] George W. Bush, 'Bush Calls Freedom from Torture "Inalienable Human Right"', 26 June 2003, at www.america.gov/st/washfile-english/2005/June/20050626155951521elootom0.6794702.html.

> is inflicted by or at the instigation of or with the consent or acquiescence of a public official or other person acting in an official capacity ... [3]

The United Nations Committee against Torture has stated that the prohibition against torture in international law is absolute; that it is a norm of customary international law that must be met at all times.[4] Doctrinal and popular writers typically adopt the same position: torture is subject to 'one of the few worldwide legal prohibitions'[5] and is 'absolutely forbidden by the law of civilized nations'.[6] In this chapter, we test these statements by applying the framework of interactional international law.

However powerful the anti-torture norm may have been historically, there can be no doubt that it was severely challenged in the months and years following the attacks of 11 September 2001. Certainly within the United States, a relatively wide consensus seemed to emerge that torture might be justifiable, even a necessity, in circumstances where deep threats to national security – like global terrorism – were present. In political discourse and on the radio and television talk shows, 'ticking time bomb' scenarios were invoked routinely as examples of when torture might be justified, or at least excused.[7] Popular culture seemed even to glorify acts of patriotic security agents who would torture when necessary to protect their country from harm. The most prominent example of that cultural trend was the hit television thriller *24*, which premiered only 25 days after 11 September 2001.

[3] *United Nations Convention against Torture and Other Cruel, Inhuman or Degrading Treatment or Punishment*, 26 June 1984, 1465 U.N.T.S. 85, (1984) 23 I.L.M. 1027 Part I, Art. 1(1) (entered into force 26 June 1987).

[4] UN Committee against Torture, 'General Comment No. 2: Implementation of Article 2 by States', CAT/C/GC/2/CRP.1/Rev.4, 23 November 2007, para. 1.

[5] Philip B. Heymann, 'Torture Should Not Be Authorized', *The Boston Globe*, 16 February 2002.

[6] Sanford Levinson, 'Contemplating Torture: An Introduction', in Sanford Levinson (ed.), *Torture: A Collection* (New York: Oxford University Press, 2004), p. 23.

[7] See Jane Mayer, 'Whatever it Takes', 83 (1) *New Yorker*, 19 February 2007, p. 66 at 68. ('According to Darius Rejali, a professor of political science at Reed College and the author of the forthcoming book "Torture and Democracy," the conceit of the ticking time bomb first appeared in Jean Lartéguy's 1960 novel *Les Centurions*, written during the brutal French occupation of Algeria. The book's hero, after beating a female Arab dissident into submission, uncovers an imminent plot to explode bombs all over Algeria and must race against the clock to stop it. Rejali, who has examined the available records of the conflict, told me that the story has no basis in fact.') On the argument that torture might be banned in principle, but that officials, invoking the criminal law defence of necessity, might be excused in specific cases, see Jean Bethke Elshtain, 'Reflection on the Problem of "Dirty Hands"', in Levinson, above note 6, p. 77; and John T. Parry, 'Escalation and Necessity: Defining Torture at Home and Abroad', in Levinson, *ibid.*, pp. 158–60.

Although *24* was planned before the assaults of 11 September, it soon became identified with a frightening new era of global terrorist threats against the United States:

> During its first five years on television, the terror-thriller '24' built a huge fan base by creating the first true superhero of the post-Sept. 11 era: special agent Jack Bauer. Ruggedly handsome and righteously defiant, Jack was willing to do anything to defend his country.
>
> That 'anything' has always included torture. Jack has snipped off fingers, poisoned associates, shot through kneecaps and faked executions, all in the pursuit of national security. ...
>
> Jack's interrogation techniques and the numerous 'ticking time bomb scenarios' he confronts – situations where he must quickly extract critical information from a suspect to deter an imminent threat – were raised during serious discussions of terror and torture on Sunday morning talk shows, in Republican and Democratic presidential debates, on newspaper editorial pages and in the halls of Congress.[8]

The question that arises, from the standpoint of interactional international law, is whether or not *24* is indicative of changing shared understandings within and outside the United States in the aftermath of 11 September 2001 that might have undermined any previously existing international norms against torture.

To answer that question, it is first necessary briefly to trace the history of the rule prohibiting torture and to assess whether or not the rule was firmly grounded in widely shared understandings before Osama bin Laden's shocking assault on the United States of America. We will then assess the evolution of the shared understandings underpinning the anti-torture norm from 12 September 2001 to 2009. If we discover that the norm prohibiting torture is supported by widely shared understandings, the framework of interactional international law still requires the application of the criteria of legality and a further assessment of whether or not the norm continues to be buttressed by a practice of legality.[9] Only after pursuing this analysis will it be possible to determine the current legal force of the international legal norm prohibiting torture.

[8] Rebecca Dana, 'Reinventing "24"', *The Wall Street Journal*, 2 February 2008.

[9] See detailed discussion of the conceptual framework of interactional international law above in Chapters 1 to 3.

2. Shared understandings

2.1 Shared understandings and the anti-torture norm before 11 September 2001

The imposition of severe physical pain to extract information or to punish or degrade human beings has been practised throughout human history by sadistic criminals, warriors, religious officials, and the state. For much of that history, such actions have been officially sanctioned by religious and state institutions. For example, the Roman Catholic Church allowed brutal physical torment to be imposed on suspected heretics during the Inquisition from the early Middle Ages[10] until the use of such techniques was formally abolished by Papal Bull in 1816.[11] But it was the ancient Greek authorities who first came to rely on what would come to be called 'torture' to support an emerging law of evidence. They permitted the torture of slaves in order to prove the innocence of a master in a criminal case or to support the master's word in a civil case.[12] The Romans followed suit, but seem initially to have limited the torture of slaves to criminal cases only.[13] However, the combination of a growing centralization and capriciousness of power in the hands of the emperors resulted in the widespread use of torture when prosecuting accusations of treason;[14] here we have the precursor to the link between torture and state security that has defined the use of torture in the twentieth and early twenty-first centuries. The Roman law, including the use of torture, was resurrected in the twelfth century across much of Europe, confession becoming the preferred mode of resolving criminal cases, 'the queen of proofs', with torture as its handmaiden.[15]

Edward Peters argues in his history of torture that the distinguishing feature of the evolution of torture in Western societies was its essentially public character. 'Torture' is not the application of physical force by anyone; it emerged as a legal process linked closely to judicial procedure.[16] During the period of the *anciens régimes* on the European continent,

[10] In 1252 Pope Innocent IV issued the Papal Bull 'Ad extirpanda', which authorized the torture of heretics. Edward Peters, *Torture* (New York: Basil Blackwell Inc., 1985), p. 65.

[11] 'Codex Juris Canonici' issued by Pope Pius VII, 1816.

[12] Peters, above note 10, pp. 14–15. [13] *Ibid.*, pp. 18 and 28–9.

[14] *Ibid.*, pp. 22–6. [15] *Ibid.*, p. 40 *et seq.*

[16] *Ibid.*, p. 4. Although the link to judicial process has been severed, the public nature of torture is reaffirmed in contemporary international law because the very definition of torture requires the intervention or connivance of state officials. See above note 3.

judges selected specific methods of torture, including sleeplessness, leg screws or the tying of hands behind the back and the hauling of the victim into a suspended position (*strappado*). Judges also determined the duration of the torture.[17] Although Blackstone famously resisted the description of torture as 'legal' – he viewed it as an abhorrent continental tradition outside the law[18] – recent scholarship shows that torture emerged in most of the West as an adjunct to processes of public law.[19]

In his magisterial *Torture and the Law of Proof*,[20] John Langbein traced the legal history of torture in England and continental Europe, and its connection to the laws of proof over time. In a recent reflection on that history in the light of events after 11 September 2001, Langbein reminds us: 'For half a millennium the law courts of continental Europe tortured suspected people to obtain evidence. They acted openly and according to law'.[21] He explains how the criminal procedure became dependent on torture, and why the torture-centred law of proof failed, as well as the differences between England (where torture never became ordinary) and continental Europe, where it did. Langbein suggests that the refusal of English common law to adopt torture was not, *pace* Blackstone, primarily the result of moral superiority, but because the English laws of proof were so primitive that torture would not have been useful.[22] Moreover, torture was known in the fifteenth to seventeenth centuries in England through the use of royal 'torture warrants' in cases of alleged treason, and often for other offences as well; the torture was used primarily to gain information, rather than as an instrument to elicit judicially cognizable

[17] Peters, above note 10, pp. 67–8.

[18] William Blackstone, *Commentaries on the Laws of England* (1765), vol. iv, p. 321. ('The rack, or question, to extort a confession from criminals, is a practice of a different nature: this being only used to compel a man to put himself upon his trial; that being a species of trial in itself. And the trial by rack is utterly unknown to the law of England; though once when the dukes of Exeter and Suffolk, and other ministers of Henry VI, had laid a design to introduce the civil law into this kingdom as the rule of government, for a beginning thereof they erected a rack for torture; which was called in derision the duke of Exeter's daughter, and still remains in the tower of London: where it was occasionally used as an engine of state, not of law, more than once in the reign of queen Elizabeth but when, upon the assassination of Villiers duke of Buckingham by Felton, it was proposed in the privy council to put the assassin to the rack, in order to discover his accomplices; the judges, being consulted, declared unanimously, to their own honour and the honour of the English law, that no such proceeding was allowable by the laws of England.')

[19] See generally John H. Langbein, *Torture and the Law of Proof* (University of Chicago Press, 1977).

[20] See generally *ibid.*

[21] John H. Langbein, 'The Legal History of Torture', in Levinson, above note 6, p. 93.

[22] *Ibid.*, p. 99.

evidence.[23] When the Star Chamber was abolished in England in 1641, suspected traitors were sent to Scotland where torture still existed as a legal process.[24] The central point for our purposes is that for much of the evolution of western law, torture was an accepted practice (except in the common law of England);[25] it was an instrument of the state judiciary reliant upon its application to support the use of confessions as the primary mode of criminal evidence.[26]

Torture has long existed in cultures outside western Europe as well. For example, although Shari'a law does not recognize a confession gained through coercion or even a threat of coercion, Ottoman law allowed for torture in circumstances where an accused had a criminal record. In practice torture was much more widespread, and seems to have been used before trial by prosecutors looking to introduce confessions.[27] Torture was also permitted in the laws of Japan and Russia.[28]

As early as the Renaissance, however, resistance to the use of torture was building, on grounds of legal logic and moral opprobrium.[29] European states formally abolished the legal use of torture over the course of two centuries during the Enlightenment.[30] Given the domination of Enlightenment discourse over nineteenth-century legal and social historiography, the story of the formal abolition of torture in the late eighteenth and early nineteenth centuries across Europe has often been read together with the end of slavery as a triumph of 'progressive' sensibility, as part of a narrative of moral perfectibility. Both Langbein and Peters debunk this notion, emphasizing that the 'end' of torture was never

[23] Peters, above note 10, pp. 79–80. Note Professor Alan Dershowitz's resurrection of the concept of 'torture warrants' in Alan M. Dershowitz, *Why Terrorism Works: Understanding the Threat, Responding to the Challenge* (New Haven: Yale University Press, 2002), pp. 141 and 156–63 (arguing that in an era of unprecedented global security threats, torture might be necessary in certain circumstances, especially in situations of a 'ticking time bomb', but that the use of torture should be controlled through judicial authorization, thereby protecting society from abuse and precluding criminal prosecution against the perpetrators who would, after all, be doing society's unpleasant task).

[24] *A(FC) and others* v. *Secretary of State for the Home Department* [2005] UKHL 71; 3 All ER 169, at para. 107 ('When the jurisdiction of the Star Chamber was abolished in England prisoners were transferred to Scotland so that they could be forced by the Scots Privy Council which still used torture to provide information to the authorities. … There is a warning here for us').

[25] See *ibid.* at para. 64 ('Torture is not acceptable. This is a bedrock moral principle in this country. For centuries the common law has set its face against torture.').

[26] Langbein, above note 19, p. 9; and Peters, above note 10, p. 72.

[27] Peters, *ibid.*, pp. 92–3. [28] *Ibid.*, pp. 93–7. [29] *Ibid.*, pp. 79–89.

[30] *Ibid.* pp. 89–91; and Langbein, above note 21, p. 97.

actually accomplished in state policy, or even in law. As soon as treason was suspected, forms of law permitted torture.[31] With the growth of state power in the later nineteenth and twentieth centuries, in many countries such legal limitations on torture as existed were increasingly ignored. A key development was the emergence of state security police who borrowed practices of aggressive interrogation from the military, and applied them off the battlefield in cases of what came to be viewed as 'political crime',[32] so the 'abolition' of torture even in Europe was but a fleeting achievement, overrun by the emergence of totalitarian regimes in the USSR, Spain, Italy, and Germany (along with its mimickers and minions in other parts of the world).[33] In the late 1950s, revelations of the routine use of torture by the French in Algeria demonstrated that even democratic regimes could succumb to the temptations of torture in the name of national security.[34]

In the twentieth century, further revelations of torture committed by colonial powers emerged in Africa and Asia.[35] In South Africa, the use of torture actually became more widespread with the consolidation of power in the apartheid government.[36] With the growth of independent human rights organizations like Amnesty International (founded in 1961), documentation of torture became more systematic, implicating scores of regimes including those in Greece,[37] Argentina,[38] Brazil,[39] Chile,[40]

[31] *Ibid.*, pp. 103–4. [32] Peters, above note 10, pp. 114–21. [33] *Ibid.*, pp. 104–6.

[34] *Ibid.*, pp. 103–9 and 121–35. See also generally Rita Maran, *Torture: The Role of Ideology in the French Algerian War* (New York: Praeger, 1989).

[35] See generally Darius Rejali, cited in Mayer, above note 7. See also Peters, above note 10, pp. 136–8; and Anupama Rao, 'Problems of Violence, States of Terror: Torture in Colonial India' (2001) 3 *Interventions* 186. But see Christopher J. Einolf, 'The Fall and Rise of Torture: A Comparative and Historical Analysis' (2007) 25 *Sociological Theory* 112.

[36] See Don Foster, *Detention and Torture in South Africa* (London: James Currey Ltd., 1987).

[37] Amnesty International, *Torture in Greece: The First Torturers' Trial* (London: Amnesty International, 1975); and Peters, above note 10, p. 158.

[38] Amnesty International, *Report of an Amnesty International Mission to Argentina* (London: Amnesty International, 1977); Donald C. Hodges, *Argentina's 'Dirty War'* (Austin: University of Texas Press, 1991), especially pp. 176–7 and 180; Richard Gillespie, *Soldiers of Peron* (Oxford: Clarendon Press, 1982); Americans Watch (A Division of Human Rights Watch), *Police Violence in Argentina: Torture and Police Killings in Buenos Aires* (New York: Human Rights Watch, 1991); and Marguerite Feitlowitz, *A Lexicon of Terror: Argentina and the Legacies of Torture* (New York: Oxford University Press, 1998).

[39] Amnesty International, *Report on Allegations of Torture in Brazil* (London: Amnesty International, 1972); Archdiocese of Sao Paulo, Jaime Wright (trans.) and Joan Dassin (ed.), *Torture in Brazil* (New York: Vintage/Random House, 1985).

[40] Amnesty International, *Chile: Amnesty International Briefing* (New York: Amnesty International, 1986); Ariel Dorfman, 'The Tyranny of Torture: Is Torture Inevitable in Our Century and Beyond', in Levinson, above note 6, pp. 3–18; Hugh O'Shaughnessy,

Guinea,[41] Iran,[42] Kenya,[43] India,[44] Israel,[45] Nicaragua,[46] Syria,[47] Turkey,[48] and even arguably the United Kingdom (in Northern Ireland).[49] Secret experiments with and the use of psychological torture in Asia and Latin America by the CIA from the 1950s to the 1970s are now well documented.[50] These only came to a halt when media and Amnesty International reports broke the secrecy and led to congressional

Pinochet: The Politics of Torture (London: Latin American Bureau Ltd., 2000); and Roger Burbach, *The Pinochet Affair* (New York: Zed Books, 2003), especially pp. 52–3, 60 and 86.

41 Amnesty International, *Torture in the Eighties* (London: Amnesty International Publications, 1984), pp. 114–15; and Clifford D. May, 'In Post-Coup Guinea, A Jail Is Thrown Open', *The New York Times*, 12 April 1984.

42 Darius Rejali, *Torture and Modernity: Self, Society, and State in Modern Iran* (Boulder, Colo. and Oxford: Westview Press, 1993).

43 Amnesty International, *Kenya: Torture, Political Detention and Unfair Trials* (New York: Amnesty International, 1987).

44 Human Rights Watch, *Punjab in Crisis: Human Rights Crisis in India* (Human Rights Watch: New York, 1991).

45 H.C. 428/86, *Barzilai* v. *Government of Israel*, 40(3) P.D. 505 (1986); Neve Gordon and Ruchama Marton (eds.), *Torture: Human Rights, Medical Ethics and the Case of Israel* (New York: Zed Books, 1995).

46 Amnesty International, *The Republic of Nicaragua* (London: Amnesty International Publications, 1977), especially p. 32.

47 Amnesty International, *Syria: Torture by Security Forces* (New York: Amnesty International, 1987).

48 *Askoy* v. *Turkey* (1996), 23 Eur. H.R 553; Jane Cousins, *Turkey: Torture and Political Persecution* (London: Pluto Press, 1973); Helsinki Watch (A Division of Human Rights Watch), *The Kurds of Turkey: Killings, Disappearances and Torture* (New York: Human Rights Watch, 1993).

49 *Ireland* v. *United Kingdom*, 1976 Y.B. Eur. Conv. on H.R. 512, at paras. 167–8 (the European Court of Human Rights found that various interrogation techniques employed by the British security forces in combating Irish terrorism constituted 'cruel and unusual' treatment, falling short of torture, but resulting nonetheless in a breach of the European Convention on Human Rights. Given the high political stakes, it is possible that the Court took a safer route in finding cruel and unusual treatment rather than torture). See Fionnula Ní Aoiláin, 'The European Convention on Human Rights and Its Prohibition on Torture', in Levinson, above note 6, p. 216 (arguing that the *Ireland* case 'must be read in the context of its time as a highly sensitive political case'). The House of Lords has also suggested that the distinction between what is 'cruel, inhuman and degrading' treatment and what is 'torture' might alter over time. See *A(FC)*, above note 24, at paras. 53 and 126.

50 See e.g. Alfred W. McCoy, *A Question of Torture: CIA interrogation, from the Cold War to the War on Terror* (New York: Metropolitan Books Henry Holt and Company, 2006); Harvey M. Weinstein, *Psychiatry and the CIA: Victims of Mind Control* (Washington, DC and London: American Psychiatric Press, 1990); and The National Security Archive, 'Prisoner Abuse: Patterns from the Past', at www.gwu.edu/~nsarchiv/NSAEBB/NSAEBB122/index.htm.

investigations in the 1970s.[51] Similarly, US army training manuals disseminating these techniques to regimes in Latin America were only declassified when freedom of information legislation was invoked and lawsuits threatened.[52]

However, in parallel to these chastening practices was the increasingly forceful rhetorical condemnation of the use of torture in all circumstances by the United Nations system and by regional intergovernmental organizations. In the immediate aftermath of World War II, and into the 1980s, more and more universally applicable legal instruments were created that sought to outlaw the use of torture in all situations.[53] Similar initiatives were undertaken at the regional level in Latin America,[54] Europe[55] and Africa.[56] With the entry into force of the Rome Statute of the International Criminal Court in 2002, torture was categorized as an international crime.[57]

Throughout western societies, national legal systems, often relying on the formal international legal condemnations of torture, have issued ringing statements upholding the absolute prohibition on the use of torture. In a powerful decision, the Israeli Supreme Court declared that some interrogation techniques employed by Israeli security forces upon terrorism suspects amounted to torture, and were therefore illegal. In an oft-cited passage, the Court held:

> This decision opened with a description of the difficult reality in which Israel finds herself [in confronting terrorism]. We conclude this

[51] McCoy, above note 50, pp. 53 and 60.

[52] Christy Pardew, 'Counterintelligence Training Manuals Timeline', May 2004, School of the Americas Watch, at www.soaw.org/new/docs/timeline%20final.pdf.

[53] See e.g. *Geneva Convention relative to the Treatment of Prisoners of War*, 12 August 1949, 75 U.N.T.S. 135, 6 U.S.T. 3316 (entered into force 21 October 1950); *Geneva Convention relative to the Protection of Civilian Persons*, 12 August 1949, 75 U.N.T.S. 287 (entered into force 21 October 1950), Art. 147 (in relation to the laws of war and the treatment of prisoners and civilian populations, esp. Common Article 3); see more generally in all circumstances *International Covenant on Civil and Political Rights*, 19 December 1966, 999 U.N.T.S. 171, (1967) 6 I.L.M. 368 (entered into force 23 March 1976), Art. 7; and *Convention against Torture*, above note 3.

[54] *American Convention on Human Rights*, 22 November 1969, (1969) 9 I.L.M. 99 (entered into force 18 July 1978).

[55] *Convention for the Protection of Human Rights and Fundamental Freedoms*, 4 November 1950, 213 U.N.T.S. 221 at 223, Eur. T.S. 5 (entered into force 3 September 1953).

[56] *African Charter on Human and People's Rights*, 27 June 1981, 1520 U.N.T.S. 217 (entered into force 21 October 1986).

[57] *Rome Statute of the International Criminal Court*, 17 July 1998, 2187 U.N.T.S. 90, (1988) 37 I.L.M. 999 (entered into force 1 July 2002), Art. 7 (1)(f) and (2)(b).

> judgement by revisiting that harsh reality. We are aware that this decision does not make it easier to deal with that reality. This is the destiny of a democracy – it does not see all means as acceptable, and the ways of its enemies are not always open before it. A democracy must sometimes fight with one hand tied behind its back. Even so, a democracy has the upper hand. The rule of law and the liberty of the individual constitute important components in its understanding of security. At the end of the day, they strengthen its spirit and this strength allows it to overcome its difficulties.
>
> Deciding these petitions weighed heavily on this Court. True, from a legal perspective, the road before us is smooth. We are, however, part of Israeli society. Its problems are known to us and we live its history. We are not isolated in an ivory tower. We live the life of this country. We are aware of the harsh reality of terrorism in which we are, at times, immersed. The possibility that this decision will hamper the ability to properly deal with terrorists and terrorism disturbs us. We are, however, judges. We must decided according to the law. This is the standard that we set for ourselves. When we sit to judge, we ourselves are judged.[58]

This decision carries heavy weight morally, politically and legally because Israel has struggled with terrorism throughout its existence. The decision to reinforce the subjugation of national security forces to the rule of law suggests a powerful stream of contemporary practice seeking to eliminate torture.

In 1999, the UK House of Lords went a step further, concluding that the prohibition on torture constitutes *jus cogens*, a peremptory norm of international law stronger than any treaty or customary rule, and therefore only subject to displacement by another peremptory norm.[59] The same position was adopted by the Supreme Court of Canada in *Suresh*,[60] the

[58] *Public Committee against Torture* v. *Israel* (1999) HCJ 5100/94 at 37; (1999) 7 BHRC 31 at 39.

[59] *R.* v. *Bow Street Metropolitan Stipendiary Magistrate, ex parte Pinochet Ugarte (Amnesty International and others intervening) (No. 3)* [1999] 2 All ER 897 (HL). The House of Lords accepted this characterization of the anti-torture norm more recently in *A(FC)*, above note 24, especially at paras. 33–4 (Lord Bingham noted that the *jus cogens* nature of the absolute prohibition against torture was 'common ground' in the proceedings and affirmed *Pinochet*).

[60] *Suresh* v. *Canada (Citizenship and Immigration)*, 2002 SCC 1; [2002] 1 SCR 3 at paras. 62–4 (the Supreme Court of Canada listed three reasons to assume the prohibition on torture was *jus cogens*: (1) the 'great number of multilateral instruments that explicitly prohibit torture'; (2) domestic administrative practices – 'no state has ever legalized or admitted to its deliberate practice and that governments accused of practising torture regularly deny their involvement'; and (3) 'international authorities state that the prohibition on torture is an established peremptory norm.'

UN Torture Committee,[61] and by the International Criminal Tribunal for the former Yugoslavia in *Furundzija*.[62]

Parallel sentiments have been expressed by thoughtful western legal and political commentators. The burden of the argument is that the taboo on torture goes to the heart of what it means to be a liberal democracy. In the words of Jean Bethke Elshtain: 'Torture invariably appears on the "never" list of the "forbiddens" of human politics. Genocide tops that list but torture follows closely behind.'[63] Jeremy Waldron posits that the prohibition against torture is a 'legal archetype', a reference point that expresses and epitomizes an entire set of legal principles. Waldron argues that the prohibition of torture represents the broader principle of the rule of law: a commitment against brutality and the breaking of people's wills.[64] David Luban suggests that torture is especially abhorrent to liberalism because it is essentially absolute tyranny writ small (in number of people), but writ at its highest intensity possible (in its totality of terror, humiliation, and de-reasoning of the world of the victim).[65]

Similarly, Michael Ignatieff argues that the political identity of democracy, which attempts to limit government power over human beings, must 'include an absolute ban on subjecting individuals to forms of pain that strip them of their dignity, identity and even sanity'. He concludes that, even if we accept that torture sometimes works and there are costs to an absolute ban, we 'cannot torture because of who we are'.[66] Given the comprehensive international legal ban on torture, and the fact that the Torture Convention is one of the most widely ratified treaties in history, the 'we' of Ignatieff's statement should probably be read to include states

[61] UN Committee against Torture, *General Comment No. 2: Implementation of Article 2 by States*, 23 November 2007, CAT/C/GC/2/CRP.1/Rev.4, paras. 1 and 5.

[62] *Prosecutor* v. *Furundzija*, IT-95–17/1-T, Trial Judgment (10 December 1998) at para. 154 (International Criminal Tribunal for the Former Yugoslavia, Trial Chamber) ('Clearly, the *jus cogens* nature of the prohibition against torture articulates the notion that the prohibition has now become one of the most fundamental standards of the international community').

[63] Elshtain, above note 7, p. 77. However, Elshtain goes on to argue that while there is an absolute prohibition on torture, there are circumstances where individuals may believe that it is necessary, but then they should be subjected to punishment (*ibid.* pp. 82–4). See also Henry Shue, 'Torture', in Levinson, above note 6, p. 47 (… '[n]o other practice but slavery is so universally and unanimously condemned in law and human convention').

[64] Jeremy Waldron, 'Torture and Positive Law: Jurisprudence for the White House' (2005) 105 *Columbia Law Review* 1681.

[65] David Luban, 'Liberalism, Torture, and the Ticking Bomb' (2005) 91 *Virginia Law Review* 1425 at 7.

[66] Michael Ignatieff, 'If Torture Works …', *Prospect Magazine*, April 2006, Issue 121.

that are not liberal democracies, but that still view themselves as 'civilized nations', to adopt the terminology of the Statute of the International Court of Justice.[67]

We are left with a disturbing conundrum, well expressed by the Chilean poet and essayist, Ariel Dorfman: 'we live in a world where torture is practiced on a regular basis in more countries than ever – 132 at latest count ... and where torture is being contemplated as inevitable and even beneficial in nations that call themselves democratic'. Yet, we also live in a world where 'there have been some startling advances in the last twenty-five years in the struggle to abolish torture'.[68] Dorfman goes on to argue that the creation of formal legal instruments outlawing torture, along with the outstanding work of NGOs, has been monumentally important. But there is a conceptually worrying caveat: 'There can be no exaggerating the momentousness of these treaties and agreements, even if they were, for the most part, ignored by the signatories in the name of national sovereignty.'[69]

The description of what is meant by 'torture' in the United Nations Convention against Torture focuses, as we have seen, on the intentional infliction of pain or suffering (whether mental or physical) that is designed to extract information or a confession, or that seeks to intimidate or coerce, or results from discrimination of any kind. To be 'torture' for the purposes of the convention, state officials must be implicated directly or through acquiescence.[70] Given its widespread ratification, we will use the convention definition as the touchstone for the rule against torture that we evaluate in this chapter.

Torture so defined is banned absolutely in all circumstances by international treaty and customary law, and this ban is said by many learned jurists to be *jus cogens*. Yet in practice, torture has been widely employed across the globe by states with all forms of government, including by liberal democracies. Darius Rejali, who has researched modern torture for the last twenty years, suggests that torture practices are 'shockingly common in many democracies – we just don't notice because under the spotlight of human rights monitors, torturers have refined their techniques so victims have no visible scars'.[71] Although it is difficult to assimilate all

[67] *Statute of the International Court of Justice*, Art. 38(1)(c), as annexed to the *Charter of the United Nations*, 1 U.N.T.S. 3 (signed at San Francisco, 26 June 1945; entered into force 24 October 1945).

[68] Dorfman, above note 40, p. 5. [69] *Ibid.*, p. 6.

[70] *United Nations Convention against Torture*, above note 3.

[71] Editorial, 'Modern barbarity; The idea that torture can be "clean" needs refuting', *New Scientist, UK*, 23 February 2008, Vol. 197, Issue 2644, at 3.

this contradictory information, we must assess in a dispassionate way whether or not there existed, prior to the events of 11 September 2001, a widely shared understanding that torture is a completely unacceptable practice in all circumstances.

We are forced to a troubling conclusion that by the end of the twentieth century, the norm against torture was strong as an aspiration but was only weakly supported by a shared understanding around the globe. Although in art and the public imagination, torture had been a broadly shared taboo since the Enlightenment,[72] its rhetorical condemnation was matched by use around the globe. We have already argued that legal rules do not need to be uniformly supported to retain their force as interactional law. Legal obligation can exist even in the face of contrary practice. However, a widespread failure to uphold the law as formally enunciated leads to a sense of hypocrisy which undermines fidelity to law, and may ultimately destroy the posited rule.

Although before 11 September 2001 the vast majority of states had ratified the principal treaties outlawing torture, many seem to have done so for the presumed reputational benefit, or because opposition to torture was viewed by state leadership as being theoretically part of 'who we are'.[73] When confronted by significant threats to national security, however, and when comforted by the legal concept of 'necessity', and given the opportunity to keep torture from public scrutiny,[74] state leaders often looked the other way or tacitly sanctioned the use of torture by agents of the state. This connivance was present in regimes of many hues, including in some liberal democracies. When Al Qaeda succeeded in its attacks on

[72] Beethoven's opera *Fidelio* (1805), is a castigation of arbitrary power where the hero, Florestan, is held captive in isolation and starved. Goya's painting *The Third of May 1808* captures the terrible treatment of rebels as they are lined up for execution. Picasso depicts torture in his magnificent *Guernica*, where at the top of the centre-left of the canvas, the bull's eye is commonly interpreted to represent the interrogator's light bulb in a torture cell. In *1984*, George Orwell describes Room 101 as 'the worst thing in the world', because it is where the Party tortures individuals to break their will. A war character in Ernest Hemmingway's *For Whom the Bell Tolls* contemplates suicide to preclude capture by the enemy and the horrible torture that might ensue. Alexander Solzhenitsyn's descriptions of the oppressive treatment of political prisoners (including sleep deprivation, isolation and forced standing for hours on end) in *One Day in the Life of Ivan Denisovich* and *The Gulag Archipelago* galvanized anti-Soviet activists inside and outside Russia in the 1970s.

[73] See e.g. Oona A. Hathaway, 'The Promise and Limits of the International Law of Torture', in Levinson, above note 6, pp. 199–212.

[74] Henry Porter, 'Now the talk is about bringing back torture', *The Observer*, 11 November 2001.

the United States, the shared understanding supporting the prohibition on torture was fragile. One might go so far as to say that the real shared understanding was that torture was wrong, but sometimes necessary, and would be tacitly supported by state authorities, especially if the torture could be kept secret.

2.2 Shared understandings and the anti-torture norm after 11 September 2001

Not surprisingly, in the months immediately following the 2001 terrorist attacks on the United States, debates arose as to what means states, especially liberal democracies, should be willing to employ in their own defence. In the context of heightened fear and deep frustration, when the president of the world's most powerful state declared that he wanted Osama bin Laden 'dead or alive',[75] the question of the use of torture came to the forefront. It was in this period that the television programme, *24*, with its routine subjugation of terrorist suspects to torture, burst onto the scene. At its height, the show drew roughly 17 million viewers a week in the United States, and sold millions of DVD copies.[76] Reports suggest that it was especially popular with the average US soldier:

> The office desk of Joel Surnow – the co-creator and executive producer of '24', the popular counterterrorism drama on Fox – faces a wall dominated by an American flag in a glass case. … Surnow received it as a gift from an Army regiment stationed in Iraq; the soldiers had shared a collection of '24' DVDs, he told me, until it was destroyed by an enemy bomb. 'The military loves our show', he said recently.[77]

Opinion leaders in the United States also embraced the show during the years of the Bush administration. In a panel discussion on *24*, sponsored by a conservative think tank, Homeland Security Secretary Michael Chertoff described the show glowingly as 'trying to make the best choice with a series of bad options'. He added: 'Frankly, it reflects real life.'[78]

In a moment of high drama during an otherwise staid discussion between Canadian and American judges, US Supreme Court Justice Scalia chastised a Canadian Federal Court judge who had offered the

[75] Tony Harnden, 'Bin Laden is wanted: dead or alive, says Bush', *The Telegraph* (UK), 18 September 2001.

[76] Dana, above note 8. [77] Mayer, above note 7, p. 66.

[78] *Ibid.*, p. 82. See also Paul Fahri, 'Calling on Hollywood's Terrorism Experts: Homeland Security Chief Compares Reality and *24*', *The Washington Post*, 24 June 2006.

comment: 'Thankfully, security agencies in all our countries do not subscribe to the mantra "What would Jack Bauer do?"' Justice Scalia pushed back: 'Jack Bauer saved Los Angeles. ... He saved hundreds of thousands of lives ... Are you going to convict Jack Bauer? Say that criminal law is against him? "You have the right to a jury trial?" Is any jury going to convict Jack Bauer? I don't think so. So the question is really whether we believe in these absolutes. And ought we believe in these absolutes?'[79] Justice Scalia implies that the 'necessity' defence would weigh strongly in the minds of American jurors on any charge of torture against Jack Bauer.

Bauer's fictional methods may even have had a more direct effect upon US interrogation practices in the years after 11 September 2001. In a remarkable admission, the junior army legal officer who wrote the original opinion justifying the use of 18 'aggressive' interrogation methods at Guantánamo Bay told an interviewer that the hero of *24* 'gave people lots of ideas' – she was referring to soldiers who conducted the Guantánamo interrogations. Apparently, many soldiers watched *24* while stationed at Guantánamo: 'it was hugely popular'.[80]

Nor was *24* a unique phenomenon:

> Since September 11th, depictions of torture have become much more common on American television. Before the attacks, fewer than four acts of torture appeared on prime-time television each year, according to Human Rights First, a nonprofit organization. Now there are more than a hundred, and, as David Danzig, a project director at Human Rights First, noted, 'the torturers have changed. It used to be almost exclusively the villains who tortured. Today, torture is often perpetrated by the heroes.'[81]

The increasingly routine infiltration of torture into the popular imagination was not limited to the United States. The television show *24* was shown widely and became popular in countries as diverse as Australia, Brazil, Bulgaria, Canada, Finland, Germany, Hungary, Israel, Mexico, the Netherlands, Poland, South Korea, and Turkey.[82] The recent James Bond

[79] Quoted in Colin Freeze, 'What would Jack Bauer do? Canadian jurist prompts international justice panel to debate TV drama 24's use of torture', *The Globe and Mail*, 16 June 2007. See also Editorial, 'Torture[:] Don't go to bat for Jack Bauer', *The Globe and Mail*, 9 July 2007.

[80] Philippe Sands, *Torture Team* (New York: Palgrave Macmillan, 2008), pp. 61–2.

[81] Mayer, above note 7, p. 68.

[82] Internet Movie Database, *"24" (2001) – Release Dates*, at www.imdb.com/title/tt0285331/releaseinfo.

thrillers *Casino Royale* and *Die Another Day*, which attracted large audiences globally, also portray grim scenes of torture that are far more explicit than anything shown earlier in the franchise, as did the most recent instalment of the Batman series, *The Dark Knight*.[83] In Mexican director Guillermo Del Toro's 2006 film, *Pan's Labyrinth*, one torture scene is extraordinarily graphic.

Aside from the evolution of popular culture, there are other indications that the shared understanding supporting an absolute prohibition on torture was weakening in the years immediately following 11 September 2001. In his 2005 report, the United Nations Special Rapporteur on the Promotion and Protection of Human Rights and Fundamental Freedoms while Countering Terrorism pointed to 'increased questioning or compromising of the absolute prohibition on torture and all forms of cruel, inhuman or degrading treatment' as a global phenomenon.[84] In human rights reports dating from the early to late 2000s, independent investigators from NGOs, as well as official sources in the US government, detailed a worrying list of states from around the globe that committed torture: Albania,[85] Burundi,[86] Cameroon,[87] China,[88] Egypt,[89]

[83] See also John Ip, 'Two Narratives of Torture' (2009) 7 *Northwestern University Journal of International Human Rights* 35 (comparing *24* and *Battlestar Gallactica*).

[84] Martin Scheinin, 'Report of the Special Rapporteur on the promotion and protection of human rights and fundamental freedoms while countering terrorism', E/CN.4/2006/98, 28 December 2005, Commission of Human Rights, 62nd session, Item 17 of provisional agenda, p. 16 at http://daccessdds.un.org/doc/UNDOC/GEN/G05/168/84/PDF/G0516884.pdf?OpenElement.

[85] Amnesty International, *Amnesty International Report 2006*, 22 May 2006, p. 53, at www.amnesty.org/en/library/asset/POL10/001/2006/en/59ad70c9-d46f-11dd-8743-d305bea2b2c7/pol100012006en.pdf; US Department of State, Bureau of Democracy, Human Rights, and Labour, *2008 Human Rights Report: Albania*, 25 February 2009, at www.state.gov/g/drl/rls/hrrpt/2008/eur/119064.htm.

[86] US Department of State, Bureau of Democracy, Human Rights, and Labour, *2006 Human Rights Report: Burundi*, 6 March 2007, at www.state.gov/g/drl/rls/hrrpt/2006/78722.htm; Human Rights Watch, *World Report 2008: Events of 2007*, 30 January 2008, pp. 84–5, at www.hrw.org/legacy/wr2k8/pdfs/wr2k8_web.pdf.

[87] Amnesty International 2006, above note 85, pp. 83–4; US Department of State, Bureau of Democracy, Human Rights, and Labour, *2008 Human Rights Report: Cameroon*, 25 February 2009, at www.state.gov/g/drl/rls/hrrpt/2008/af/118990.htm.

[88] US Department of State, Bureau of Democracy, Human Rights, and Labour, *2004 Human Rights Report: China*, 28 February 2005, at www.state.gov/g/drl/rls/hrrpt/2004/41640.htm; Amnesty International 2006, above note 85 pp. 89–91; Human Rights Watch 2008, above note 86, pp. 264–5.

[89] US Department of State, Bureau of Democracy, Human Rights, and Labour, *2004 Human Rights Report: Egypt*, 28 February 2005, at www.state.gov/g/drl/rls/hrrpt/2004/41720.htm; Human Rights Watch 2008, above note 86, pp. 465–6.

Iran,[90] Kahzakstan,[91] Myanmar,[92] North Korea,[93] Pakistan,[94] Russia,[95] Syria,[96] Turkey,[97] Uzbekistan[98] and Zimbabwe[99] are but some examples.[100] Governments of these states often invoked 'terrorism' as the scourge that they were trying to suppress, although they would, of course, deny the epithet 'torture' being applicable to their detention and interrogation practices.

Recent reports suggest that the UK government may have been complicit in torture practised in other countries, relying on the information

90 US Department of State, Bureau of Democracy, Human Rights, and Labour, *2004 Human Rights Report: Iran*, 28 February 2005, at www.state.gov/g/drl/rls/hrrpt/2004/41721.htm; Amnesty International 2006, above note 85 pp. 141–2; Human Rights Watch 2008, above note 86, p. 473.

91 US Department of State, Bureau of Democracy, Human Rights, and Labour, *2004 Human Rights Report: Kazakhstan*, 28 February 2005, at www.state.gov/g/drl/rls/hrrpt/2004/41689.htm; Amnesty International 2006, above note 85, p. 157.

92 US Department of State, Bureau of Democracy, Human Rights, and Labour, *2004 Human Rights Report: Burma*, 28 February 2005, at www.state.gov/g/drl/rls/hrrpt/2004/41637.htm; Amnesty International 2006, above note 85, pp. 253–4; US Department of State, Bureau of Democracy, Human Rights, and Labour, *2008 Human Rights Report: Burma*, 25 February 2009, at www.state.gov/g/drl/rls/hrrpt/2008/eap/119035.htm.

93 US Department of State, Bureau of Democracy, Human Rights, and Labour, *2002 Country Reports on Human Rights Practices: Korea, Democratic Peoples' Republic of*, 31 March 2003, at www.state.gov/g/drl/rls/hrrpt/2002/18249.htm; Human Rights Watch 2008, above note 86, p. 302.

94 US Department of State, Bureau of Democracy, Human Rights, and Labour, *2002 Country Reports on Human Rights Practices: Pakistan*, 31 March 2003, at www.state.gov/g/drl/rls/hrrpt/2002/18314.htm; Amnesty International 2006, above note 85, pp. 202–3.

95 US Department of State, Bureau of Democracy, Human Rights, and Labour, *2004 Human Rights Report: Russia*, 28 February 2005, at www.state.gov/g/drl/rls/hrrpt/2004/41704.htm; Human Rights Watch 2008, above note 86, pp. 413, 416–19.

96 US Department of State, Bureau of Democracy, Human Rights, and Labour, *2004 Human Rights Report: Syria*, 28 February 2005, at www.state.gov/g/drl/rls/hrrpt/2004/41732.htm; Amnesty International 2006, above note 85, pp. 248–51

97 Amnesty International 2006, *ibid.*, pp. 260–3; US Department of State, Bureau of Democracy, Human Rights, and Labour, *2008 Human Rights Report: Turkey*, 25 February 2009, at www.state.gov/g/drl/rls/hrrpt/2008/eur/119109.htm.

98 Human Rights Watch, *World Report 2006: Events of 2005*, 17 January 2006, pp. 423–4, at www.hrw.org/sites/default/files/reports/wr2006.pdf; US Department of State, Bureau of Democracy, Human Rights, and Labour, *2008 Human Rights Report: Uzbekistan*, 25 February 2009, at www.state.gov/g/drl/rls/hrrpt/2008/sca/119143.htm.

99 US Department of State, Bureau of Democracy, Human Rights, and Labour, *2004 Human Rights Report: Zimbabwe*, 28 February 2005, at www.state.gov/g/drl/rls/hrrpt/2004/41634.htm; Human Rights Watch 2008, above note 86, pp. 178–80.

100 The preceding listing is representative, not exhaustive. We have kept citations of NGO and official reports on torture in individual states to a reasonable sampling, but more complete citations are on file with the authors.

extracted to pursue anti-terror investigations.[101] At the level of official action in the world's remaining superpower, conscious and forceful attempts were made by the Bush administration to re-interpret the very idea of torture so as to render 'aggressive interrogations' by US and allied intelligence agencies lawful. Given its importance in global society and the special status of the United States as the state directly affected by the 11 September 2001 attacks, its response deserves careful attention.

In retrospect, one can see the beginnings of this process of justification as early as 14 September 2001 when a congressional resolution authorized President Bush to use 'all necessary and appropriate force' against the perpetrators of the terrorist attacks against the United States,[102] and on the same day Vice-President Cheney vowed to use 'any means at our disposal' to fight what was already being described as the 'War on Terror'.[103] Just two days later, Cheney declared on national television that the US government would have to work through 'the dark side'[104] to fight against potential terrorist attacks. By December 2001, the General Counsel's Office of the Department of Defense was asking for information on detainee 'exploitation' from the government agency charged with advising on counter-interrogation techniques. This was the first time that the SERE (Survival, Evasion, Resistance, and Escape) strategies taught to US soldiers and other officials threatened with capture by hostile forces were engaged; soon they would be re-engineered to shape aggressive interrogation techniques employed by agents of the US government against terrorist suspects.[105]

101 See below note 236.

102 House Joint Resolution No. 64 *Authorizing the Use of United States Armed Forces Against Those Responsible for Recent Attacks Against the United States*, 14 September 2001, s. 2(a) at www.fas.org/irp/threat/useofforce.htm. This wording is the traditional Congressional formulation giving US presidents authorization to use force in times of 'war'. The Bush administration's designation of the response to the events of 11 September 2001 as a 'War on Terror' has been highly controversial. See Jack Goldsmith, *Terror Presidency[:] Law and Judgment Inside the Bush Administration* (New York: W.W. Norton & Co., 2007), pp. 102–7.

103 The following paragraphs describe the history of Bush administration attempts to alter the legal understanding of 'torture'; they are derived primarily from Annie Lowrey, 'The Torture Timeline', *Foreign Policy Online* at www.foreignpolicy.com/story/cms.php?story_id=4891&print=1; and Scott Shane, David Johnston and James Risen, 'Justice Dept. Said to Back Harshest Tactics After Declaring Torture "Abhorrent"', *The New York Times*, 4 October 2007.

104 Mayer, above note 7, p. 68 (The Vice-President went on to say that 'it's going to be vital for us to use any means at our disposal, basically, to achieve our objective').

105 Scott Shane and Mark Mazzetti, 'Report Blames Rumsfeld for Detainee Abuses', *The New York Times*, 11 December 2008; Mark Mazzetti, 'Bush Aides Linked to Talks

In February 2002, arguing that the United States needed 'new thinking in the law of war',[106] President Bush issued an Executive Order denying Taliban and Al Qaeda prisoners the protections of the Geneva Conventions.[107] Although it can be fairly argued that the decision of the Bush administration to deny prisoner of war status to 'terrorists and other enemy fighters who did not wear uniforms or carry their arms openly' was aligned with past US interpretations of the Geneva Conventions, it did not meet with evolving interpretations in wider international society, nor with the specific context of a 'war on terror' that was not viewed as entirely legitimate even by traditional US allies.[108] By April a document on the SERE techniques was circulating through the Department of Defense, and by September the techniques were being taught to CIA operatives.[109] Meanwhile, in July 2002, National Security Advisor Rice and CIA Director Tenet agreed that the CIA should go ahead with interrogations of top Al Qaeda suspect Abu Zubayda, once the Department of Justice signed off.[110] Later that month Attorney-General Ashcroft determined that 'waterboarding' (pouring water over a constrained prisoner's cloth-covered face to induce fear of suffocation) is legal, permitting its use during interrogations of Zubayda.[111]

On 1 August 2002, the head of the Office of the Legal Counsel (OLC) in the Department of Justice, Jay Bybee, sent a memo to the Counsel to the CIA, saying that ten techniques, escalating in force up to waterboarding, did not constitute torture.[112] On the same day, a second memo from the

on Torture', *The New York Times*, 25 September 2008. See also Sands, above note 80, pp. 47–8.

[106] The White House, 'Memorandum Re: Humane Treatment of al Qaeda and Taliban Detainees', 7 February 2002, p. 1, at www.gwu.edu/~nsarchiv/NSAEBB/NSAEBB127/02.02.07.pdf.

[107] *Ibid.*, p. 2 at para. 2(c) and (d). For a description of the internal administration process that resulted in this decision by the president, see Sands, above note 80, pp. 30–6.

[108] See Goldsmith, above note 102, pp. 113–20.

[109] See e.g. Executive Summary, *Senate Armed Services Committee Inquiry into the Treatment of Detainees in U.S. Custody*, 12 December 2008 at xiv, at http://armed-services.senate.gov/Publications/EXEC%20SUMMARY-CONCLUSIONS_For%20Release_12%20December%202008.pdf.

[110] Senator John D. Rockefeller, 'Release of Declassified Narrative Describing the Department of Justice Office of Legal Counsel's Opinions on the CIA's Detention and Interrogation Program', 22 April 2009, pp. 2–4, at http://intelligence.senate.gov/pdfs/olcopinion.pdf.

[111] *Ibid.*, p. 4.

[112] Assistant Attorney-General Jay S. Bybee, US Department of Justice, Office of Legal Counsel, 'Memorandum for John Rizzo, Acting General Counsel of the Central Intelligence Agency Re: Interrogation of al Qaeda Operative', 1 August 2002, p. 18, at

OLC, also signed by Bybee, but written primarily by John Yoo, was sent to the White House Counsel, Alberto Gonzales.[113] In implementing the Convention against Torture,[114] the US Congress had already defined torture narrowly, limiting 'torture' which might give rise to criminal prosecution within the United States to acts 'specifically intended' to cause 'severe physical ... pain'[115] or 'prolonged mental harm'.[116] Yoo sought to limit the concept of torture even further, interpreting the US statute so that only pain 'associated with a sufficiently serious physical condition or injury such as death, organ failure, or serious impairment of bodily functions' constitutes physical torture.[117] What is more, the 1 August memo also argued that the powers of the president as Commander-in-Chief could override even the modest limitations on torture contained in the statute because the limitations prevented the president 'from gaining the intelligence he believes necessary to prevent attacks upon the United States'.[118]

Apparently, Yoo was referred to as 'Dr Yes' by Attorney-General Ashcroft, for Yoo's inclination to give the White House whatever it needed as legal cover for its anti-terrorism policies.[119] Even a high-ranking administration official who continued to defend the overall arc of the Bush anti-terrorism strategy after leaving office concluded that this OLC memo improperly suggested that 'the President could disregard legal prohibitions on torture'.[120] During the month of August, Zubayda was subjected to waterboarding more than 80 times.[121] Other authorized harsh

http://luxmedia.vo.llnwd.net/o10/clients/aclu/olc_08012002_bybee.pdf (Bybee Memo); see also Scott Shane, David Johnston and James Risen 'Secret U.S. Endorsement of Severe Interrogations', *The New York Times*, 4 October 2007.

113 Assistant Attorney-General Jay S. Bybee, US Department of Justice, Office of Legal Counsel, 'Memorandum for Alberto R. Gonzales, Counsel to the President Re: Standards of Conduct for Interrogation under 18 U.S.C. §2340–2340A', 1 August 2002, at www.washingtonpost.com/wp-srv/politics/documents/cheney/torture_memo_aug2002.pdf (Yoo Memo). On the real authorship of the memo, see Goldsmith, above note 102, p. 142.

114 United Nations Convention against Torture, above note 3, Art. 1(1).

115 18 U.S.C. § 2340 (1) (1994). 116 *Ibid.*

117 Yoo Memo, above note 113, p. 46. Strangely, and inappropriately, this definition was borrowed from another US statute authorizing health benefits. See Goldsmith, above note 102, p. 145.

118 See Goldsmith, *ibid.*, p. 144 (Goldsmith argues that it was an over-reaching as to the prerogative powers of the president that was one of the greatest weaknesses in the legal analysis of the Yoo Memo. When serving as the head of the OLC, Goldsmith withdrew this and other memos authored by Yoo). *Ibid.*, pp. 144–51 and 159–60.

119 Shane, Johnston and Risen, above note 112. 120 Goldsmith, above note 102, p. 135.

121 Principal Deputy Assistant Attorney-General Steven G. Bradbury, US Department of Justice, Office of Legal Counsel, 'Memorandum for John A. Rizzo, Senior Deputy General

interrogation techniques 'included slaps to the head; hours held naked in a frigid cell; days and nights without sleep while battered by thundering rock music; [and] long periods manacled in stress positions ...'.[122]

From 25 to 26 September, senior administration legal officials David Addington, Alberto Gonzales, Jim Haynes, and John Rizzo visited Guantánamo Bay. A few weeks later the Guantánamo commander requested the authorization of new interrogation techniques, supported by a legal memorandum authored by an inexperienced Staff Judge Advocate, Diane Beaver, who had tried futilely to have her legal opinion checked and corrected by superiors.[123] In November 2002, a CIA detainee in a secret prison in Kabul died of hypothermia after he was stripped and chained outside for many hours.[124] The next month, Secretary of Defense Donald Rumsfeld authorized aggressive interrogation techniques for prisoners at Guantánamo Bay, relying on the legal opinion authored by Diane Beaver. The opinion was simply attached to the authorization signed by Rumsfeld, who in turn relied on the covering memo authored by his General Counsel, William J. Haynes II.[125] In March 2003 US and Pakistani forces captured the main planner of the 11 September attacks, Kalid Sheikh Mohammed, who was then waterboarded 183 times during the month.[126]

That same March, John Yoo sent another memo, this time to the Counsel to the Department of Defense, detailing the international and domestic law applicable to the treatment of detainees. He argued that 'national defense' and executive power are paramount considerations, trumping all legal constraints.[127]

Counsel, Central Intelligence Agency Re: Application of United States Obligations Under Article 16 of the Convention Against Torture to Certain Techniques that May Be Used in the Interrogation of High Value al Qaeda Detainees', 30 May 2005, p. 37, at http://luxmedia.vo.llnwd.net/o10/clients/aclu/olc_05302005_bradbury.pdf (Bradbury Memo, 30 May); see also Scott Shane, 'Waterboarding used 266 Times on 2 Suspects', *The New York Times*, 19 April 2009.

122 Shane, Johnston and Risen, above note 112.

123 Sands, above note 80, pp. 63–4.

124 Dana Priest, 'CIA Holds Terror Suspects in Secret Prisons', *The Washington Post*, 2 November 2005.

125 William J. Haynes II, General Counsel for the Department of Defence, 'Memo to the Secretary of Defence Re: Counter Resistance Techniques', 27 November 2002, p. 1, at www.gwu.edu/~nsarchiv/NSAEBB/NSAEBB127/02.12.02.pdf (Haynes Memo). For a full description of the process of authorization, see Sands, above note 80, Chapters 1 to 8.

126 Bradbury Memo (30 May), above note 121, p. 37; see also Shane, above note 121.

127 Deputy Assistant Attorney-General John C. Yoo, US Department of Justice, Office of Legal Counsel, 'Memorandum for William J. Haynes II, General Counsel of the

The overall thrust of the advice being offered to US interrogators was that aggressive techniques were necessary in the war on terror, and that 'torture' could be read so narrowly as to allow techniques that might otherwise be contrary to international and US law. In other words, by fiat of re-definition in the name of national security, no 'torture' was being committed. A mantle of legitimacy was being crafted to place on the shoulders of all US interrogators; the subsequent actions of these interrogators cannot, therefore, be classified as 'rogue'.

In 2003 and 2004, information began to emerge about the treatment of Al Qaeda and Taliban detainees by the US government. The Red Cross issued a rare public statement in October 2003 detailing the deterioration in the psychological health of a large number of detainees at Guantánamo Bay.[128] That same month, photographic evidence was circulated widely over the internet suggesting serious abuse of prisoners at the Abu Ghraib prison in Iraq. In March 2004, three British ex-detainees at Guantánamo Bay were repatriated to the UK and released without charge. They alleged severe beatings at the hands of US guards while in detention.[129] The existence of the 'torture memos' was revealed in June by the *Washington Post*,[130] and the new head of the OLC, Jack Goldsmith, withdrew the August 2002 memo and subsequently resigned.[131] In December 2004, the acting head of the OLC, Daniel Levin, publicly issued a new memo stating that torture is illegal and 'abhorrent', and widening its definition to provide constraints on CIA and other US interrogators.[132]

However, in February 2005, Alberto Gonzales became the eightieth Attorney-General of the United States, and in May, Steven G. Bradbury of the OLC sent a new and more comprehensive memo to the CIA Counsel,

Department of Defence Re: Military Interrogation of Alien Unlawful Combatants Held Outside the United States', 14 March 2003, pp. 80–1, at http://media.washingtonpost.com/wp-srv/nation/pdfs/OLCMemo60-81.pdf (Second Yoo Memo).

128 Neil A. Lewis, 'Red Cross Criticizes Indefinite Detention In Guantánamo Bay', *The New York Times*, 10 October 2003.

129 Shafiq Rasul, Asif Iqbal and Rhuhel Ahmed, 'Composite statement: Detention in Afghanistan and Guantanamo Bay', 26 July 2004, at http://ccrjustice.org/files/report_tiptonThree.pdf.

130 Dana Priest and R. Jeffrey Smith, 'Memo Offered Justification for Use of Torture', *The Washington Post*, 8 June 2004.

131 Jeffrey Rosen, 'Conscience of a Conservative', *The New York Times*, 9 September 2007. See also Goldsmith, above note 102, pp. 161–2.

132 Daniel Levin, Acting Assistant Attorney-General, Office of Legal Counsel, United States Department of Justice, 'Memorandum Opinion for the Deputy Attorney General Re: Legal Standards Applicable Under 18 U.S.C. §§ 2340–2340A', 30 December 2004, at www.usdoj.gov/olc/18usc23402340a2.htm (Levin Memo).

supplanting the Levin memo and arguing once again that the techniques of coercive interrogation used by the CIA, including waterboarding, were lawful.[133] This secret memo provided explicit authority to subject detainees to 'a combination of painful physical and psychological tactics, including head-slapping, simulated drowning and frigid temperatures'.[134] The memo was issued over the strong objections of the Deputy Attorney-General, James Comey, who was in the process of leaving the Department of Justice because of clashes with the White House. Mr. Comey warned that the OLC would be 'ashamed' when the existence of the secret memo came to light.[135]

The 2005 Justice Department OLC opinion remained effective throughout the last years of the Bush administration. Indeed, the legal conclusions were reaffirmed in later memos, revealing the extent to which the administration succeeded in preserving a narrow interpretation of the concept of torture, allowing for the use of harsh and coercive interrogation techniques.

In November 2005 the *Washington Post* revealed the existence of CIA-controlled secret detention sites outside the United States,[136] and the CIA destroyed videotapes of the interrogation of 'high-value' detainees.[137] In October 2006, Vice-President Cheney defended the use of waterboarding as a necessary tool to defend the nation, describing it as 'a no-brainer'.[138] President Bush stopped congressional attempts to limit CIA interrogation techniques in July 2007 by issuing a secret Executive Order authorizing 'enhanced' interrogation techniques.[139] In November 2008 the Senate

[133] Principal Deputy Assistant Attorney-General Steven G. Bradbury, US Department of Justice, Office of Legal Counsel, 'Memorandum for John A. Rizzo, Senior Deputy General Counsel, Central Intelligence Agency Re: Application of 18 U.S.C. §§ 2340–2340A to Certain Techniques that May Be Used in the Interrogation of a High Value al Qaeda Detainees', 10 May 2005, p. 47, at http://luxmedia.vo.llnwd.net/o10/clients/aclu/olc_05102005_bradbury46pg.pdf (Bradbury Memo, 10 May).

[134] Shane, Johnston and Risen, above note 112.

[135] *Ibid.* See also Goldsmith, above note 102, pp. 159–60.

[136] Priest, above note 124.

[137] Mark Mazzetti and Scott Shane, 'C.I.A. Destroyed Tapes as Judge Sought Interrogation Data', *The New York Times*, 7 February 2008.

[138] MSNBC News, *Cheney endorses simulated drowning, says use of water boarding to get terrorist intelligence is 'no brainer'*, 26 October 2006, at www.msnbc.msn.com/id/15433467/.

[139] The White House, 'Executive Order 13440 of 20 July 2007 Re: Interpretation of the Geneva Conventions Common Article 3 as Applied to a Program of Detention and Interrogation Operated by the Central Intelligence Agency', 20 July 2007, p. 1, at http://edocket.access.gpo.gov/2007/pdf/07-3656.pdf.

Armed Services Committee received a report suggesting that harsh interrogation techniques were used before the issuance of the OLC memos declaring the techniques to be lawful. The report also clarified that harsh techniques were used by US agents on detainees at Guantánamo, Bagram Air Force Base in Afghanistan and Abu Ghraib Prison in Iraq. [140]

For much of the period from 2001 to 2005, the US public was either unaware or unconcerned about the evolution of US policy on interrogations of terrorist suspects. In a major poll conducted in 2005, 58 per cent of US respondents supported the use of torture if it prevented a major terrorist attack.[141] By June 2006, the mood in the United States had begun to shift, after revelations of secret CIA detention sites and growing suggestions that aggressive interrogation, perhaps amounting to torture, had been undertaken not just by low-level 'rogue' soldiers,[142] but by US agents acting under full authorization. In a World Public Opinion Poll, 75 per cent of US respondents approved of the rule against torture, 60 per cent supported the rule against even threatening physical torture and 61 per cent approved the rule against humiliating or degrading treatment of detainees.[143] However, still only 47 per cent believed that the US was currently allowing interrogators to use torture.[144] By September 2006, 57 per cent of respondents answered that US army interrogators, if faced with a terrorist suspect whom they believe have information about possible terror plots against the United States, should not be permitted to use more forceful interrogation techniques than permitted by the Geneva Convention standard, while 38 per cent thought they should.[145]

These polling results show that the Bush administration, for a time, had considerable success first in shielding 'harsh' interrogation techniques from public view, and second in convincing many members of the US

140 Armed Services Committee Executive Summary, above note 109.

141 Newsweek Poll conducted by Princeton Survey Research Associates International, 10–11 November 2005. N=1,002 adults nationwide. MoE ± 3 (for all adults).

142 On 7 May 2004, the International Committee of the Red Cross Operations Director stated that the ICRC's inspection visits to Coalition detention centers in Iraq did 'not allow us to conclude that what we were dealing with … were isolated acts of individual members of coalition forces. What we have described is a pattern and a broad system.' He went on to say that some of the incidents they had observed were 'tantamount to torture'. BBC News Service, *Red Cross saw 'widespread abuse'*, 8 May 2004, at http://news.bbc.co.uk/1/hi/world/americas/3694521.stm.

143 The WorldPublicOpinion.Org, *American and International Opinion on the Rights of Terrorism Suspects* (Poll), 17 July 2006, p. 7, at www.worldpublicopinion.org/pipa/pdf/jul06/TerrSuspect_Jul06_rpt.pdf.

144 *Ibid*, p. 9.

145 USA Today/Gallup Poll, 15–17 September 2006. N=1,003 adults nationwide. MoE ± 3.

public that the ill-defined 'harsh' techniques being authorized in the War on Terror were consonant with existing international and domestic law. And the widespread invocation of 'ticking time bomb' scenarios, both by administration officials and in the popular media, also helped to convince many people that there were circumstances in which torture was simply necessary to prevent greater evil.[146] As *The Economist* magazine pointed out in 2007, '[t]he 11 September attacks have not driven any rich democracy to reverse itself and make torture legal. But they have encouraged the bending of definitions and the turning of blind eyes.'[147]

The popular willingness to turn a blind eye to torture was less apparent in other liberal democracies as more time elapsed after 11 September 2001. An October 2006 BBC Global Poll of public opinion in 25 countries is interesting both in how it poses the question of torture, and in the responses. Respondents were asked to choose between two positions: (1) 'Terrorists pose such an extreme threat that governments should now be allowed to use some degree of torture if it may gain information that saves innocent lives'; or (2) 'Clear rules against torture should be maintained because any use of torture is immoral and will weaken international human rights standards against torture.' Highest support for the first position, accepting the use of torture, was found in Israel (43%), Iraq (42%), Indonesia and the Philippines (40%), Nigeria (39%), Kenya (38%), China (37%) and the United States (36%). Only 22 per cent of Canadian, and 24 per cent of UK respondents answered that their position was closer to position (1) – some degree of torture could be justified. Strongest support for the second position, favouring clear rules against torture, was found in Italy (81%), Australia and France (75%), Canada (74%) and the UK (72%). Interestingly, 58 per cent of Americans and 48 per cent of Israelis also agreed with the second statement.[148]

Declining support for the use of torture against suspected terrorists was also manifested in responses to popular media as the decade progressed.

[146] It must be said, however, that even in 2005, some polls began to show that a significant majority of Americans believed that torture was most often, if not always, wrong. In a 2005 ABC News–*Washington Post* poll, 63% of respondents regarded the use of torture by the United States in the campaign against terrorism as unacceptable. In the same poll, 56% believed torture was being used, while 39% believed it was not being used. ABC News–*Washington Post* Poll, 15–18 December 2005. N=1,003 adults nationwide. MoE ± 3 (for all adults). Fieldwork by TNS.

[147] 'Is Torture Ever Justified?', *The Economist*, 22 September 2007.

[148] See BBC News Service, *Global Poll: 25 Nation Poll on Torture*, October 2006, at http://news.bbc.co.uk/2/hi/in_depth/6063386.stm#table.

Whereas *24* had ridden a wave of support for harsh anti-terrorist actions over its first five years on-air, the mood shifted markedly in 2006–2007:

> Ratings dropped by a third over the course of last year's sixth season. Producers would later experience trouble casting roles, once some of the most desirable in television, because the actors disapproved of the show's depiction of torture. 'The fear and wish-fulfillment the show represented after 9/11 ended up boomeranging against us,' says the show's head writer, Howard Gordon. 'We were suddenly facing a blowback from current events.'[149]

In a remarkable twist, high-ranking US military officers also began to express deep concern about the effects of *24* on rank-and-file soldiers. In November 2006, the dean of the United States Military Academy at West Point, Brigadier General Patrick Finnegan, participated in a meeting with the writers of *24*. He brought with him three experienced military and FBI interrogators. According to Jane Mayer of the *New Yorker* magazine, the Brigadier General wanted to challenge the very premise of the show, 'that the letter of American law must be sacrificed for the country's security.' He apparently argued that this idea was promoting 'unethical and illegal behavior and had adversely affected the training and performance of real American soldiers.' He suggested that the writers should create a show where torture has a negative effect on the torturers' goals, and produces bad information.[150]

Meanwhile, in a number of western democracies, including the United States, courts were issuing judgments by 2004 that had begun to limit the powers asserted by officials in the prosecution of the war on terror. The United States Supreme Court reaffirmed the fundamental nature of a citizen's right to be free from involuntary confinement by his own government without due process of law in a case concerning a US citizen held as an enemy combatant.[151] The right of *habeas corpus* was then extended by the Court to foreign nationals held at Guantánamo Bay.[152] When the US government tried to limit the right through legislation, the Supreme Court said that the constitutional right of a Guantánamo detainee to *habeas corpus* trumped the US legislation.[153] Indirectly, these decisions

149 Rebecca Dana, 'Reinventing "24"', *Wall Street Journal*, 2 February 2008.

150 Mayer, above note 7, p. 72.

151 *Hamdi* v. *Rumsfeld*, 542 US 507 (2004).

152 *Rasul* v. *Bush*, 542 US 466 (2004).

153 *Boumediene et al* v. *Bush*, 553 US 723 (2008) at 14; 128 S. Ct. 2229 at 2247 (cited to S. Ct.). (For the plurality, Kennedy J. argued, at 2247, that the writ of *habeas corpus* is a 'time-tested device' that allows the Judiciary to 'maintain the "delicate balance of governance" that is itself "the surest safeguard of liberty"').

have been important in bringing to light the treatment of detainees, giving rise to further investigation into the use of 'aggressive' interrogation. What is more, the cases served as the basis for conclusions of courts in other countries that the processes of detention and possible trial by military commissions at Guantánamo Bay breached international law.[154]

Although the United States Supreme Court has not yet had the opportunity to consider directly the legality of torture within the context of anti-terrorist policies, the UK House of Lords has done so in robust fashion.[155] In a case concerning the admissibility of evidence obtained through suspected torture outside the UK, Lord Bingham emphasized that even though members of the UN and the Council of Europe have been 'strongly urged since 11 September 2001 to cooperate and share information in order to counter the cruel and destructive evil of terrorism ... these calls have been coupled with reminders stressing that human rights, and international and humanitarian law, must not be infringed or compromised.'[156] He went on to conclude:

> The principles of the common law, standing alone, in my opinion compel the exclusion of third party torture evidence as unreliable, unfair, offensive to ordinary standards of humanity and decency and incompatible with the principles which should animate a tribunal seeking to administer justice. But the principles of the common law do not stand alone. Effect must be given to the European Convention, which itself takes account of the all but universal consensus embodied in the Torture Convention. The answer to the central question posed at the outset of this opinion is to be found not in a governmental policy, which may change, but in law.[157]

Lord Hoffman's speech was even more forceful; he concluded that the 'word honour ... is what underlies the legal technicalities of this appeal. The use of torture is dishonourable. It corrupts and degrades the state which uses it and the legal system which accepts it.'[158] Lord Hope opined that '[t]he use of such evidence is excluded not on the grounds of its unreliability ... but on grounds of its barbarism, its illegality, and its inhumanity. The law will not lend its support to the use of torture for any purpose whatever. It has no place in the defence of freedom and democracy, whose

[154] See e.g. *Canada (Justice)* v. *Khadr*, 2008 SCC 28, at para. 24, [2008] S.C.R. 125. ('The violations of human rights identified by the United States Supreme Court are sufficient to permit us to conclude that the regime providing for the detention and trial of Mr. Khadr at the time of the CSIS [Canadian Security and Intelligence Service] interviews constituted a clear violation of fundamental human rights protected by international law.')

[155] *A(FC)*, above note 24. [156] *Ibid.*, para. 41. [157] *Ibid.*, para. 52.

[158] *Ibid.*, para. 82.

very existence depends on the denial of the use of such methods to the executive.'[159]

It seems that as more time passed after 11 September 2001, Americans became increasingly shaken by the 'aggressive' interrogation amounting to torture undertaken in their name. The editor of the magazine *Vanity Fair* argued that '[a] nation that used to be better than its enemies has, under the Bush administration, become its own worst enemy.'[160] In the words of a former chief prosecutor of the Military Commissions at Guantánamo Bay, who refused to use evidence obtained through waterboarding: 'We must restore our reputation as the good guys who refuse to stoop to the level of our adversaries. We are Americans, and we should be able to state with conviction, "We don't do stuff like that."'[161] The moral debate within the United States over torture has 'seeped deeply' into popular culture and the media.[162] The titles of a random selection of articles in the mainstream press are revealing: 'We are all Torturers Now';[163] 'We are All Guilty';[164] 'When We're the Evildoers in Iraq …';[165] 'We, The People Behind the Abuse';[166] and 'A Prison of Shame, And It's Ours'.[167]

By 2007, after the revelations of the secret torture memos and of abuse in Guantánamo, Abu Ghraib and in secret detention centres operated by the CIA with US allies,[168] the sense of moral crisis found expression in groups not normally associated with strong stances against US government policy. In July 2007, a group of 17 prominent evangelical Christian leaders and scholars released 'An Evangelical Declaration Against Torture: Protecting Human Rights in the Age of Terror'. While the Declaration drew fire

[159] *Ibid.*, para. 112.

[160] Graydon Carter, 'We Are All Guilty[:] Editor's Letter', *Vanity Fair*, December 2007, p. 88.

[161] Morris Davis, 'Unforgivable Behavior, Inadmissible Evidence', *The New York Times*, Op-Ed, 17 February 2008.

[162] Scott Shane, 'On Torture, 2 Messages And a High Political Cost', *The New York Times*, 30 October 2007.

[163] Mark Danner, 'We are all Torturers Now', *The New York Times*, 6 January 2005.

[164] Carter, above note 160.

[165] Robert Scheer, 'When We're the Evildoers in Iraq [:] With Immoral U.S. Leadership, is it so Shocking to find Torturers in the Ranks?', *The Los Angeles Times*, 4 May 2004.

[166] Manohla Dargis, 'We, The People Behind the Abuse', *The New York Times*, 25 April 2008.

[167] Nicholas Kristof, 'A Prison of Shame, And It's Ours', *The New York Times*, 4 May 2008.

[168] See Leila Sadat, 'Extraordinary Rendition, Torture, and Other Nightmares from the War on Terror' (2007) 75 *George Washington Law Review* 1200; Editorial, 'Rule of Lawlessness', *The Washington Post*, 2 May 2004; and UN Committee against Torture, General Comment No. 2: Implementation of Article 2 by States, CAT/C/GC/2/CRP.1/Rev.4, 23 November 2007.

from some religious conservatives, it was unanimously endorsed by the National Association of Evangelicals.[169]

The tone of criticism was becoming even more pointed, and the sense that all relevant actors had to 'resist' the attenuation of the norm prohibiting torture was palpable. Referring to a 2008 speech by President Bush, the *New York Times*' editorial team was scathing: 'President Bush used his radio address on Saturday to try to scare Americans into believing they have to sacrifice their rights and their values to combat terrorism .... This is not the first time Mr. Bush had misled Americans on intelligence-gathering and antiterrorism operations, and it may not be the last. It will be up to the next president to restore the rule of law.'[170] The same tone was adopted in the United Kingdom by the *Economist* editors. They suggested that although governments, particularly the British and American, had attempted to significantly erode rights generally, the 'story is not over yet. It could turn into a tale not of liberties being frayed, but of democracy's underlying strength. For, in both America and Britain, the doctrine of the balance of powers has passed a test. The executive branch made a grab for more authority; but courts and legislators have tried hard to push back.'[171]

It should not come as any surprise, then, that one of the very first acts of President Obama, only two days after his inauguration, was to issue a series of Executive orders distancing the US government from the practices adopted by the Bush administration in the war on terror. As concerns 'aggressive' interrogations amounting to torture, the new president ordered:

> From this day forward, unless the Attorney General with appropriate consultation provides further guidance, officers, employees, and other agents of the United States Government may, in conducting interrogations, act in reliance upon Army Field Manual 2 22.3, but may not, in conducting interrogations, rely upon any interpretation of the law governing interrogation – including interpretations of Federal criminal laws, the Convention Against Torture, Common Article 3, Army Field Manual 2 22.3, and its predecessor document, Army Field Manual 34 52 issued by the Department of Justice between September 11, 2001, and January 20, 2009.[172]

169 Peter Steinfels, 'An Evangelical Call on Torture and the U.S.', *The New York Times*, 21 July 2007.

170 Editorial, 'Radio Fear America', *The New York Times*, 11 March 2008.

171 'The stuff of nightmares; Civil liberties: detention without a trial', *The Economist*, 6 October 2007.

172 'Executive Order – Ensuring Lawful Interrogations', 22 January 2009, at www.whitehouse.gov/the_press_office/EnsuringLawfulInterrogations/.

The order specifically repudiates the Yoo–Bybee torture memos, and although some commentators argue that President Obama has left loopholes in his anti-torture declarations,[173] it seems that the new administration is largely in tune with the evolving US rejection of torture as an evil necessity in the battle against global terrorism.[174]

We have taken care to trace a rather long and complicated story blending together popular culture and official responses to global terrorism in the post-11 September era because the assessment of the 'shared understanding' concerning the prohibition on torture in international law needs be complex. For the first few years after 11 September 2001, there appears to have been a further eroding of the already weak shared understanding precluding torture. The striking fear present in international society, and especially in the United States, gave rise to seemingly convincing arguments that 'necessity' drove widening exceptions to the prohibition on torture. These exceptions were often framed in terms of 'ticking time bomb' scenarios, even though those scenarios bore little or no resemblance to the actual use of 'aggressive interrogations' amounting to torture in concrete cases. In addition, fear prompted attempts to significantly limit the definition of torture, attempts that for some time succeeded in changing the practice of US interrogators. Meanwhile, the rhetoric of the 'war on terror' was invoked by scores of other states to justify repressive policies and extremely harsh methods of interrogation.

There is, however, one important difference between what was happening in the United States and in other states. Whereas the Bush administration sought to keep its interrogation practices within a framework of 'law' through the vehicle of wholesale definitional reinterpretation, in other states the claim was more typically that an individual interrogation did not amount to torture, or the practice of aggressive interrogations was simply denied altogether. The point to remember is that the US government for a time became an active 'norm entrepreneur' in seeking to alter two distinct aspects of the international prohibition on torture: first, that torture was outlawed in all circumstances (leading figures in the administration argued that the president retained absolute discretion to use all means necessary to protect US citizens from terrorism);

[173] See e.g. Andy Worthington, 'Obama's mixed messages on torture', *Huffington Post*, at www.huffingtonpost.com/andy-worthington/obamas-first-100-days-mix_b_198696.html.

[174] See e.g. 'Undoing the Damage', *The New York Times*, 12 July 2009 (applauding the White House's support for a draft bill from Senator Levin of Michigan which includes provisions barring the use of evidence obtained through torture).

and second, that torture could be defined to allow waterboarding and other techniques that did not produce pain equivalent to the spasms of death or 'organ failure'. We have argued that this norm entrepreneurship failed to generate shared understandings to support normative change. We will soon see that part of the reason for this failure is that the new norms posited in the Yoo–Bybee 'torture memos' failed to meet important criteria of legality.

By 2006 the tide had begun to turn. Popular opinion worldwide, and especially in the United States, has subsequently moved away from relatively broad support for the necessity of torture in combating global terrorism. Indeed, it seems that the Bush administration, in arguing for an untrammelled right of the president to do 'whatever it takes' to fight terrorists, including the de facto authorization of torture, had over-reached and created strong pushback across the world, and within America itself. Perhaps ironically, instead of further undermining the weak shared understanding supporting the prohibition on torture that existed in 2001, events over the years from 2005 to 2009 have ultimately reinforced that shared understanding, potentially making the anti-torture rule stronger. It is therefore worthwhile asking whether or not the absolute prohibition on torture meets the eight criteria of legality we discussed in detail in Chapter 1.[175]

3. The prohibition on torture and the criteria of legality

The rule against torture as exemplified by the United Nations Convention against Torture clearly meets the requirement that legal norms be general, in this case prohibiting particular conduct. The anti-torture norm is said to be universal in application, and it specifically precludes the infliction of 'severe pain or suffering, whether physical or mental'. Interestingly, the same cannot be said for the attempt in the Yoo–Bybee 'torture memos', and subsequent secret orders, to narrow the definition of torture. The new rule they posited was not intended to be general, for it was limited to the 'necessity' of the United States to act forcefully in its war on terror. Any narrowing of the definition of torture would certainly have been resisted by the United States if applied by its enemies against US security forces or other citizens.

The absolute prohibition on torture as set out in the convention is also promulgated, and is completely accessible to the public. It permits

[175] See Chapter 1, text accompanying notes 24–40.

everyone to know what the law requires. On the other hand, one of the many reasons that the Yoo–Bybee and consequent orders to interrogators ultimately failed to change the definition of torture is that they were clandestine. They were only promulgated when political pressure and legal process forced their release. Whereas the anti-torture norm clearly met the criterion of promulgation, the challenge to the norm did not.

Nothing in the Torture Convention makes the anti-torture norm retroactive. Indeed, as we have noted above, the rule precluding torture pre-dates the convention and is widely accepted as a fundamental rule of customary international law, with many arguing that it has become *jus cogens*.[176] Whether or not that claim can be made out satisfactorily, the rule against torture is certainly not retrospective, so all citizens can take the law into account in their decision-making.

Clarity of the rule against torture is a more complicated issue. At first blush, the rule is exquisitely clear because it is said to be a blanket prohibition without exception under any circumstances, and specifically not in the case of security claims after 11 September 2001.[177] If that were true, all relevant actors would be able to understand what is permitted, prohibited or required by the law. The difficulty is that there is no commonly accepted definition of what constitutes 'severe pain or suffering, whether physical or mental'. The Torture Convention does not further define these terms; it merely draws a distinction between torture and other 'cruel, inhuman or degrading treatment or punishment'. Implicit in this distinction, however, is the assumption that there are forms of abusive treatment that do not amount to torture. No guidance is provided as to how to draw the distinction. The Geneva Conventions ban torture and other forms of mistreatment, but contain no definition of the term.[178] Nor is there an authoritative detailed definition of torture, beyond the statement of an absolute prohibition, in customary international law[179] or in the practice of the UN Torture Committee. One might say with justification that there is a common-sense understanding of what torture is. It might be similar

[176] See the courts and committees cited above, notes 58–62.

[177] UN Committee against Torture, *General Comment No. 2: Implementation of Article 2 by States*, CAT/C/GC/2/CRP.1/Rev.4, 23 November 2007, paras. 5–6.

[178] Above note 53.

[179] Although torture has been discussed in a series of national and international cases, these cases do not focus on the definition of torture. See above notes 58–60 and 62. They do establish that some 'combinations of conduct' can amount to torture, and some try to explain the difference between torture and 'cruel and inhuman treatment'. See Parry, above note 7, p. 147.

to pornography, notoriously hard to define with precision but sometimes subject to a legal 'I know it when I see it' test.[180]

But that common-sense approach is problematic because there are serious disagreements amongst fair-minded people about what constitutes torture, both physical and mental. For example, when Botswana ratified the Torture Convention in 1994, it entered the following declaration: 'The Government of the Republic of Botswana considers itself bound by Article 1 of the Convention to the extent that "torture" means the torture and inhuman or degrading punishment or other treatment prohibited by Section 7 of the Constitution of the Republic of Botswana.' It thereby appropriated to itself the definition of torture by which it would be bound. Qatar declared that it would interpret the entire treaty, including the definition of torture, in the light of Islamic law. When the United States ratified the treaty, it lodged a series of reservations and 'Understandings'. Included in the latter category was the following:

> That with reference to article 1, the United States understands that, in order to constitute torture, an act must be specifically intended to inflict severe physical or mental pain or suffering and that mental pain or suffering refers to prolonged mental harm caused by or resulting from (1) the intentional infliction or threatened infliction of severe physical pain or suffering; (2) the administration or application, or threatened administration or application, of mind altering substances or other procedures calculated to disrupt profoundly the senses or the personality; (3) the threat of imminent death; or (4) the threat that another person will imminently be subjected to death, severe physical pain or suffering, or the administration or application of mind altering substances or other procedures calculated to disrupt profoundly the senses or personality.[181]

The US 'Understanding' remains one of the most comprehensive definitions of torture available in the international law literature. However, it was the subject of criticism, prompting two states to deliver 'Objections' to the United Nations Treaty Depositary. The Netherlands declared that the US definition of torture was unacceptably narrow and should have 'no impact' on the obligations of the United States under the treaty. Sweden

[180] See e.g. *Jacobellis* v. *Ohio*, 378 U.S. 184 (1964) at 197 ('I shall not today attempt further to define the kinds of material I understand to be embraced within that shorthand description [hard-core pornography]; and perhaps I could never succeed in intelligibly doing so. But I know it when I see it, and the motion picture involved in this case is not that').

[181] All of these declarations are from *Declarations and Reservations [to the UN Torture Convention] as of 5 February 2001*, available at www.unhchr.ch/html/menu3/b/treaty12_asp.htm.

took the same view. The declarations of Botswana and Qatar received even more strenuous and widespread Objections.[182]

Doctrinal writers, NGOs and UN special rapporteurs have offered a wide variety of approaches to the definition of torture. Expansive definitions have been promoted by the UN Special Rapporteur on Torture and at least implicitly by the UN Special Rapporteur on the Promotion and Protection of Human Rights and Fundamental Freedoms while Countering Terrorism.[183] Relatively wide definitions are also put forward by human rights NGOs. Amnesty International issued a definition in 1973 that is often treated as 'classic' in the literature: 'Torture is the systematic and deliberate infliction of acute pain by one person on another, or on a third person, in order to accomplish the purpose of the former against the will of the latter.'[184] The definition is so laconic that its scope can be expanded with ease. Being potentially over-broad, this definition is also unclear. That is why some commentators have taken a different approach entirely. In considering the concept of torture post-11 September, Sanford Levinson emphasizes that distinctions must be drawn between methods of interrogation that are 'merely unattractive' and those that amount to torture and are forbidden.[185] The distinguished philosopher Jean Bethke Elshtain agrees, arguing that torture must be a circumscribed construct: if 'everything from a shout to the severing of a body part is "torture", the category is so indiscriminate as to not permit those distinctions on which the law and moral philosophy rest.'[186]

In attempting to systematically frame the permissible techniques of interrogation in 2002, and to narrow the definition of torture, a group of US administration lawyers met with the military leadership at Guantánamo Bay. Very quickly, they deferred to the expertise of the CIA. In minutes of the meeting released to a US Senate hearing, a CIA lawyer is quoted as suggesting that the definition of torture is 'written vaguely' and that it 'is basically subject to perception'. He added: 'If the detainee dies, you're doing it wrong.'[187] In this context of competing and uncertain definitions,

[182] *Ibid.*

[183] See a succession of reports by Manfred Nowak (Torture) and Martin Scheinin (Human Rights and Terrorism). These reports are available on the website of the Office of the United Nations High Commissioner for Human Rights, at www.ochr.org.

[184] Amnesty International, *Report on Torture* (London: Duckworth International and Amnesty International Publishers, 1973) p. 31.

[185] Levinson, above note 6, p. 27. [186] Elshtain, above note 7, p. 79.

[187] Quoted in Mark Mazzetti and Scott Shane, 'Notes Show Confusion on Interrogation Methods', *The New York Times*, 18 June 2008.

the Yoo–Bybee torture memos found at least temporary traction. Yoo later suggested that he never doubted that there was a ban on torture, only that the term needed more precise definition. 'But,' he asks, 'would limiting a captured terrorist to six hours' sleep, isolating him, interrogating him for several hours, or requiring him to exercise' amount to torture?[188] Phrased in this rather anodyne manner, the answer might be 'no'.[189] But what if one were closer to the actual practices used on some 'high value' detainees at Guantánamo Bay and elsewhere? What if the isolation went on for months; if the deprivation of sleep were repeated for days on end? What if the interrogations included threats of rape, slaps, the use of pornography, and subjection to extremely loud music for hours at a time? What if, interspersed amongst the questions, was repeated waterboarding?

These questions reveal the difficulties in arguing about what constitutes torture, and suggest the reason that the international law prohibition is said to be absolute: allowing the use of 'aggressive' techniques of interrogation opens up vistas of abuse that may be hard to resist, as the interrogator becomes frustrated with a perceived lack of 'cooperation' or with his own failure to generate actionable information; the temptation to go just that one step further to produce results is enormous. In other words, torture may come to seem both necessary and, by steps, normal. Speaking of the history of torture, Michael Ignatieff argues:

> This is the way with torture: it is originally justified as a lesser evil, as a regrettable necessity in the struggle to extract timely information to prevent greater harms, and slowly but surely it becomes a standard technique, explicitly used to humiliate, terrify, degrade, and subdue entire populations.[190]

Aside from the potential to 'normalize' abuse, attempting to severely limit what constitutes torture, as was done in the Yoo–Bybee memos and in subsequent secret orders, also exposes government agents to terrible moral hazard.[191] Torture damages the perpetrator as well as the victim;

[188] John Yoo, *War by Other Means* (New York: Atlantic Monthly Press, 2006), pp. 171–2.

[189] But see Jessica Wolfendale, 'The Myth of "Torture Lite"' (2009) 23 *Ethics and International Affairs* 47 at 47, 50 and 52–4 ('[D]espite the frequency with which the term is used, the distinction between torture and torture lite [e.g. loud music, sleep deprivation] is not one that is recognized in any of the international conventions dealing with torture', but it's embraced by democratic regimes as a partial mitigation of the use of "torture" broadly').

[190] Michael Ignatieff, *The Lesser Evil: Political Ethics in the Age of Terror* (Toronto: Penguin Group, 2004), p. 136.

[191] *Ibid.*, pp. 142–3.

asking security forces to cross lines that have long been taboo puts them in impossible situations. That may be why the FBI refused to allow its agents to participate in some of the interrogation sessions at Guantánamo Bay.[192] Even worse is the situation of junior agents who are given confusing instructions that force them to choose whether or not to commit torture.[193] The CIA seems to have realized the dreadful positions into which its agents were thrust. In 2007 at least two tapes of interrogation sessions at Guantánamo Bay were destroyed by the CIA, likely because the brutality of the sessions had led to fears of prosecution and political repercussions.[194] Interestingly, it appears that some US allies were also concerned that the Bush administration's attempts to redefine torture could lead to moral and legal culpability. A senior aide to Secretary of State Rice revealed that 'at the height of the War on Terror' some European allies refused to share intelligence with the United States for fear that they would be complicit in torture.[195]

Assessing the criterion of clarity in the face of this conflicting data is difficult. We cannot argue that any particular approach is logically compelled. Unlike the rule concerning the use of force that we will discuss in the next chapter, where there is an absolute prohibition, matched with specific legal exceptions, the anti-torture rule has long been phrased to admit of no exceptions whatsoever. Attempts made by the Bush administration

[192] See CNN News Service, *Inquiry clears FBI in harsh interrogations*, 20 May 2008, at www.cnn.com/2008/POLITICS/05/20/fbi.interrogations/index.html (reporting on a Justice Department investigation that concluded that FBI agents had 'separated themselves from other agencies' interrogators who were using techniques that the FBI didn't approve of'.). See also Drew Brown, 'FBI Blasts Guantánamo Interrogators; Memo Indicates Detainees were Clad in Israeli Flags and Shown Porn under Strobe Lights', *The Houston Chronicle*, 24 February 2006. From 2002 to 2004, FBI agents had sent 54 e-mail complaints to their superiors, claiming that interrogations at Guantánamo were unduly harsh. See Dan Eggen and R. Jeffrey Smith, 'FBI Agents Allege Abuse of Detainees at Guantanamo Bay', *The Washington Post*, 21 December 2004. Lawyers with the FBI also raised serious concerns over the interrogation practices at Guantánamo Bay. See Jane Mayer, 'The Memo: How an internal effort to ban the abuse and torture of detainees was thwarted', *New Yorker*, 27 February 2006; and Sands, above note 80, pp. 112–21.

[193] This was the effect of the reliance of senior Bush administration officials on the weak legal memo provided by junior lawyer Diane Beaver. See Sands, *ibid.*, p. 135 (describing how Alberto Mora, General Counsel to the US Navy, evaluated the Beaver Memo which authorized 18 coercive interrogation techniques: 'I was looking for the language of limitations, and it just wasn't there'; the advice given was 'wholly inadequate'.)

[194] See e.g. Mark Mazzetti, 'CIA Destroyed 2 Tapes Showing Interrogations', *The New York Times*, 7 December 2007.

[195] See Tony Allen-Mills, 'Allies split with US over torture', *The Times Online*, 26 April 2009 at www.timesonline.co.uk/tol/news/world/us_and_americas/article6169041.ece.

to create exceptions of necessity and overwhelming national security interests have failed because they have not generated sustained shared understandings. In that sense, the absolute prohibition has been reaffirmed and made clearer. Necessity might be a defence to a criminal prosecution for torture; more likely it would only be a mitigating element in sentencing. It is not an *ex ante* justification for torture. 'National security' has never been and is not now a free card that allows the jettisoning of all international legal constraint. We will see this point reaffirmed in Chapter 6 on the use of force.

The precise content of the anti-torture norm is more difficult to assess because of the lack of any widely accepted definition of what constitutes 'severe pain or suffering, whether physical or mental'. However, we can conclude that since 11 September 2001, the conscious efforts made to narrow the definition of torture have been rejected. As soon as the full scope of these efforts became known, they generated intense resistance within the United States and elsewhere. What has emerged is a reaffirmation that it is impossible to create acceptable gradations of aggressive interrogation that can be sustained in practice over time. Trying to do so leads to moral hazard for interrogators, and to dangerous slippery slopes towards methods that fundamentally challenge accepted perceptions of 'who we are'. We conclude, therefore, that the existing prohibition on torture, although not without grey definitional edges, is clear enough to satisfy the criteria of clarity. We would add that virtually all legal norms contain such 'grey areas'; that is why we emphasize the importance of interpretation through continuing practice in our interactional framework.

Law should also avoid contradiction, not requiring or permitting and prohibiting at the same time. This criterion is met by the absolute prohibition on torture. There is no rule in international law that would ever require torture. Given our assessment of the relative clarity of the rule against torture, it also meets the requirement that a rule not demand the impossible. In fact, it could be argued that any move away from an absolute prohibition of torture, making its application less certain, pushes potential perpetrators (usually lower-level security force agents) into situations of impossibility where they cannot know how to act, and where they might later be exposed to criminal liability, either in domestic law, or under the Statute of the International Criminal Court.

Senior government officials might suggest that an absolute prohibition on torture does potentially create a situation of political and moral impossibility for them by removing an instrument that should be deployed to protect the population. This argument links 'ticking time bomb' scenarios with the idea that the duty to provide security is fundamental to high political office. Implicitly, John Yoo's suggestion that the US president has whatever powers it takes to attack terrorism fits within this specific 'impossibility' framework.

The argument might have some merit if it could be proved definitively that torture produces reliable and actionable intelligence. Demanding that the instrument be given up might then place high officials in situations of political and moral impossibility: but there is no clear proof that torture saves lives. In fact, much psychological evidence points in the opposite direction. Before the Arar Commission in Canada, one of the world's leading experts on confessions, Professor Richard Ofshe, stressed that torture is a 'powerful motivator' to confession. That is no surprise. What may be more surprising is that:

> [i]f the individual has already been convinced that the interrogator is unmovable, then it makes no sense to resist the torture. The only thing in front of them is to minimize the amount of torture. That is the only choice they've got. And they can do that by complying.[196]

For this reason alone, torture tends to produce information that is entirely unreliable and that wastes scarce intelligence resources tracking down false leads. Professor Ofshe also testified that one might be more likely to force a false confession through torture when the person being tortured actually has no knowledge of what is being investigated. Such a person has nothing much to lose by offering a false statement; the torture will continue if he offers nothing of 'value'. But the true believer in a cause (the real terrorist) has a profound sense of commitment and a web of personal loyalties that may enable him to resist the application of physical and psychological abuse more effectively than the innocent person.[197] In 'ticking time bomb' situations, the resulting delay in extracting information makes the torture utterly inefficacious.

Practitioners of interrogation also call into question the utility of torture. In fact, in response to the Bush administration's attempts to narrow the definition of torture and to extend its use on the grounds of necessity, many senior military officers spoke out to condemn these trends in US policy. Aside from complaints about the morality of torture, a common

[196] Commission of Inquiry into the Actions of Canadian Officials in Relation to Maher Arar, *Report of the Events Relating to Maher Arar*, 2006, at www.sirc-csars.gc.ca/pdfs/cm_arar_rec-eng.pdf (Toope, co-author of this book, served as fact-finder for the Arar Commission), p. 193.

[197] Ofshe testimony before the Arar Commission (8 June 2005; on file with the authors).

refrain was that torture simply does not produce results. In the words of former Judge Advocate General for the Navy, John Hutson:

> Another objection is that torture doesn't work. All the literature and experts say that if we really want usable information, we should go exactly the opposite way and try to gain the trust and confidence of the prisoners. Torture will get you information, but it's not reliable. Eventually, if you don't accidentally kill them first, torture victims will tell you something just to make you stop. It may or may not be true. If you torture 100 people, you'll get 100 different stories. If you gain the confidence of 100 people, you may get one valuable story.[198]

Even the conservative *Armed Forces Journal* issued an editorial calling waterboarding a form of torture that should be precluded in part because 'it is … an inherently flawed method for gaining reliable information. In short, it doesn't work.'[199]

The absolute prohibition against torture has also remained relatively constant in international law, certainly since the promulgation of comprehensive international human rights treaties in the aftermath of World War II, and so the seventh criterion of legality is met.

We conclude that the absolute prohibition on torture meets seven of Fuller's criteria of legality, admitting that the analysis around clarity is complicated. The final requirement, that there be congruence between legal norms and the actions of officials operating under the law, also presents significant problems. However, before we engage in that assessment, it might be helpful to step back for a moment to place that analysis in the wider conceptual context of interactional law.

Torture presents an unusual case for our interactional framework because its solidity as a norm has always been weaker that its absolutist formulation would suggest. As we have already noted, the absolute nature of the prohibition actually distinguishes the anti-torture norm from the seemingly comparable prohibition on the use of force. Although the latter norm is also said to be absolute, it has long been matched with explicit exceptions that we will discuss in detail in Chapter 6. Because the anti-torture norm has no lawful exceptions, it has been harder to uphold; it demands real discipline and commitment, often lacking in practice. We

[198] Amnesty International USA, *Military, Intelligence and Law Enforcement Officers Opposing Torture*, at www.amnestyusa.org/war-on-terror/reports-statements-and-issue-briefs/military-intelligence-and-law-enforcement-officers-opposing-torture/page.do?id=1031036.

[199] Armed Forces Journal, 'To Rudy Giulliani and Attorney General Nominee Michael Mukasey', at www.armedforcesjournal.com/2007/12/3230108.

have already seen that the shared understandings supporting the norm were weak before 11 September 2001. We will now see that even though the shared understandings seem subsequently to have solidified, the practice of security officials in many countries is certainly not congruent with the norm. Even though the norm may once have solidified, it has remained unstable. Furthermore, the 'practice of legality' that must continue to support a norm after it has been brought into existence looks to be weak in the case of the anti-torture norm. In other words, at every stage of analysis for interactional international law, it is the concrete practice of torture that calls into question the reality of the prohibition. So as to avoid repetition, we will blend our consideration of congruence, as a criterion of legality, into our investigation of the last step in determining the legal force of the prohibition on torture, deciding whether or not the practice of legality continues to uphold the norm. If there is no such practice, we will also be able to conclude that the final criterion of legality is not met.

4. Prohibiting torture and the practice of legality

We know that torture has been committed round the world since time immemorial. What concerns us now is the extent to which torture has been committed by security forces, or with their acquiescence, after 11 September 2001. In examining this question, we are completing the analysis of 'practice' that is required under our interactional framework. We previously cited evidence of widespread torture before 11 September 2001, as part of our assessment of shared understandings concerning the anti-torture norm.[200] We extended that assessment into the post-11 September era, concluding that although the attempts of the Bush administration to narrow the definition of torture did not generate support, many states around the world continued to practise torture, usually in secret, and routinely denying the practice.[201] This reality supports our argument in Chapter 3 that norms not rooted in robust shared understandings are less likely to generate fidelity, and are more likely to be breached.[202]

It could be argued, on the other hand, that the secrecy with which most states undertake torture demonstrates that these states understand that what they are doing is illegal, and therefore may actually go to support a shared understanding that torture is prohibited. But this sanguine approach does not exhaust the required analysis. Indeed, the further

[200] See above section 2.1. [201] See above section 2.2.
[202] See above Chapter 3, notes 30–3.

requirement that a norm meet the legality criterion that official action must match the norm is a particularly tough-minded aspect of the interactional analysis, as is the need to study the subsequent practice of legality surrounding the norm. In standard accounts of international law, it has been too easy to argue that a rule exists despite widespread failure to uphold it simply because states try to justify their breaches or keep them secret. These actions are said to show that the rule has real power despite its failure to shape behaviour. In our view, this type of argument has always been an unsatisfying attempt to gloss over weaknesses in the law. It has led to charges that international lawyers are naīve idealists.

To underscore our point that one must look carefully at the actions of officials to meet the last criterion of legality, and to assess whether or not there exists a continuing practice of legality supporting a posited norm, we briefly offer further evidence that the anti-torture rule is broken on a daily basis around the world. Sadly, this evidence could be expounded for pages on end. For present purposes suffice it to note that the report of the Arar Commission in Canada, demonstrates that torture is routinely practised in Syrian detention centres, especially in Far Falestine.[203] The Agiza case from Sweden reveals similar patterns of torture in Egypt.[204] Russian security forces have been implicated in torture, especially in the context of suppressing Chechen rebels.[205] Credible reports from global human rights NGOs suggest that the Chinese government has authorized or tolerated the torture of Muslim Uighurs in Xinjiang province.[206] Pakistan, a favoured ally in the war on terror, is reported by major human rights organizations to practise torture in many locations across the country.[207] Iranian authorities use

[203] Arar Commission Report, above note 196.

[204] *Agiza* v. *Sweden*, 24 May 2005, Communication No. 233/2003, UN Doc. CAT/C/34/D/233/2003. See also Amnesty International, *Sweden: The case of Mohammed El Zari and Ahmed Agiza: violations of fundamental human rights by Sweden confirmed*, 27 November 2006, EUR 42/001/2006, at www.unhcr.org/refworld/docid/45bc855a2.html.

[205] See e.g. Krystyna Kurczab-Redlich, 'Torture and rape stalk the streets of Chechnya', *The Observer*, 27 October 2002; and C.J. Chivers, 'Slain Reporter's Last Story Bares Chechen Torture', *The New York Times*, 13 October 2006.

[206] See e.g. Human Rights Watch, *Devastating Blows: Religious Repression of Uighurs in Xinjiang*, at www.hrw.org/reports/2005/china0405/12.htm.

[207] See e.g. Asian Human Rights Commission, 'PAKISTAN: 52 illegal torture and detention centres identified', 5 June 2008, at www.ahrchk.net/statements/mainfile.php/2008statements/1574/; and Human Rights Watch, *Pakistan: Military Torturing Farmers in Punjab*, 20 July 2004, at www.hrw.org/en/news/2004/07/20/pakistan-military-torturing-farmers-punjab.

torture to stifle dissent.[208] For Uzbek security forces, torture is a routine means of extracting confessions to be used in criminal trials.[209] In Myanmar, torture is used to further repression of all dissent.[210] Torture also seems to be a routine practice in North Korea, again as an instrument of control.[211] Torture also exists in sub-Saharan Africa, with reliable reports of torture practised by security forces or their agents in Zimbabwe,[212] Equatorial Guinea,[213] Cameroon,[214] and The Gambia.[215] Even in Latin America, where enormous political and legal efforts have been made to move away from the abuses of authoritarian regimes in the 1970s and 1980s, torture continues to be employed by some security forces, with credible reports emerging from Mexico,[216] Venezuela,[217] and Paraguay.[218]

Equally disturbing are the growing reports, containing more and more detail, of the complicity of western security forces in torture committed

[208] Human Rights Watch. *Like the Dead in Their Coffins: Torture, Detention, and the Crushing of Dissent in Iran*, 6 June 2004, at www.hrw.org/en/reports/2004/06/06/dead-their-coffins-0.

[209] International Federation for Human Rights (FIDH), *The Death Penalty in Uzbekistan: Torture and Secrecy*, 10 October 2005, at www.fidh.org/The-Death-Penalty-in-Uzbekistan.

[210] See e.g. Amnesty International, *Myanmar: Torture of Ethnic Minority Women*, 17 July 2001, at www.unhcr.org/refworld/docid/3b83b6f815.html; and Amnesty International, *Myanmar: Torture and ill-treatment*, 12 May 2005, at www.amnesty.org/en/library/info/ASA16/018/2005/en.

[211] See e.g. Antony Barnett, 'Revealed: the gas chamber horror of North Korea's gulag', *The Observer*, 1 February 2004.

[212] See Hilary Andersson (BBC News Service), *Zimbabwe's torture training camps*, 27 February 2004, at http://news.bbc.co.uk/2/hi/africa/3493958.stm.

[213] UN News Centre, *Torture is rife in Equatorial Guinea's prisons*, says UN expert, 19 November 2008, at www.un.org/apps/news/story.asp?NewsID=28998&Cr=torture&Cr1=rapporteur (detailing a report by UN Special Rapporteur on Torture, Professor Manfred Novak).

[214] FIDH, 'Torture in Cameroon: an 'ordinary' reality, a systematic impunity', 29 October 2003, at www.fidh.org/Torture-in-Cameroon-an-ordinary.

[215] Amnesty International, *Gambia: Government must stop repression*, 11 November 2008, at www.unhcr.org/refworld/docid/491d3d51c.html.

[216] Steve Fainaru and William Booth, 'Mexico Accused of Torture in Drug War', *The Washington Post*, 9 July 2009.

[217] BBC News Service, *Venezuela troops 'used torture'*, 26 March 2004, at http://news.bbc.co.uk/2/hi/americas/3571383.stm (reporting on an investigation by the government-appointed Human Rights Defender).

[218] UN News Centre, *'Widely practiced' police torture in Paraguay must be fully criminalized: UN expert*, 30 November 2006, at www.un.org/apps/news/story.asp?NewsID=20802&Cr=torture&Cr1=&Kw1=Paraguay&Kw2=&Kw3 (detailing a report by UN Special Rapporteur on Torture, Professor Manfred Novak).

in secret detention sites in various locations around the globe. Here we can see clearly the point we emphasized in Chapter 2, that communities of practice are not intrinsically positive; practices that emerge can undermine legality, just as they can support it.[219] In a report to the Human Rights Commission in February 2004, the UN Working Group on Enforced or Involuntary Disappearances identified a disturbing trend in the war on terror. The Working Group had begun to receive credible information revealing the existence of secret detention centres in several countries.[220] These centres were said to exist in the developing world, but it appeared that they were created at the behest of other governments, especially that of the United States.

Since these secret detentions were first drawn to the attention of the Working Group, evidence of secret detention sites, or 'ghost prisons', has multiplied. Early reports suggested that a secret detention facility had been created at Guantánamo Bay for unacknowledged prisoners, and that other secret facilities existed in Afghanistan, Egypt, Jordan, Pakistan, Thailand, and at the US base on Diego Garcia in the Indian Ocean. Human Rights Watch detailed the cases of 11 men who had disappeared in US custody.[221] Then Amnesty International revealed the cases of three Yemeni men who had disappeared at the hands of US agents for over a year and a half.[222] In November 2005, the *Washington Post* published a powerful piece of investigative journalism connecting many of the dots, and revealing that ghost prisons may have existed in eight countries, including some EU member states in Eastern Europe and candidate countries for EU membership.[223]

More recently, even harder evidence surfaced that ghost prisons existed in Eastern Europe. An Egyptian government fax intercepted by

[219] See Chapter 2, note 42.

[220] United Nations Human Rights Council, *Report of the Working Group on Enforced or Involuntary Disappearances*, 23 December 2004, E/CN.4/2005/65, para. 368, at http://daccessdds.un.org/doc/UNDOC/GEN/G04/169/65/PDF/G0416965.pdf?OpenElement. (Toope, co-author of this book, was Chair of the Working Group at the time that this report was issued.)

[221] Human Rights Watch, *The United States' 'Disappeared': The CIA's Long-Term 'Ghost Detainees'*, 12 October 2004, at www.hrw.org/en/reports/2004/10/12/united-states-disappeared-cias-long-term-ghost-detainees.

[222] See e.g. Amnesty International, *Case Sheet (USA/Yemen)*, at www.amnesty.org/en/library/info/AMR51/176/2005.

[223] Priest, above note 124. See also Stephen Grey, *Ghost Plane: The True Story of the CIA Torture Program* (New York: St. Martin's Press, 2006) (containing a detailed account of CIA use of civilian jets to transport prisoners both to its own detention sites and those run by foreign states).

Swiss intelligence discussed 23 detainees from Iraq and Afghanistan apparently interrogated by CIA operatives at a Romanian air base on the Black Sea coast.[224] The fax was reported to have suggested that similar facilities existed in Ukraine, Kosovo, Macedonia, and Bulgaria. The existence of such facilities was confirmed by an official inquiry of the Council of Europe.[225] Outside Europe, the *Sunday Times* of London reported in February 2006 that the United States was building a new secret prison for Al Qaeda suspects near Rabat, Morocco.[226]

President Bush formally acknowledged the existence of secret detention sites run by the CIA in 2006.[227] In a televised speech, he revealed that in these secret prisons 'an alternative set of procedures' was used to obtain information from terrorist suspects. The president went on to argue that he could not 'describe the specific methods used – I think you understand why – if I did, it would help the terrorists learn how to resist questioning, and to keep information from us that we need to prevent new attacks on our country. But I can say the procedures were tough, and they were safe, and lawful, and necessary.'[228] As it turns out, their lawfulness both in international and domestic law is increasingly under scrutiny. Indeed, the US Attorney-General appointed a prosecutor in August 2009 to investigate the interrogations of some terrorist suspects by the CIA after the release of a report detailing seeming abuse, perhaps amounting to torture.[229]

The *Washington Post* stressed that the policy of secret detentions was conceived in the immediate aftermath of 11 September, and approved by 'a small circle of White House and Justice Department lawyers and officials'.[230] Jane Mayer revealed in *The New Yorker* that this policy was constructed over the forceful objections of some senior legal counsel in the Pentagon. Some of these advisers were actively misled into believing that their objections were being considered seriously when in fact these

[224] D. Rennie, 'Leaked fax "shows Romania helped CIA interrogators"', *The Telegraph* (UK), 10 January 2006.

[225] Stephen Grey, 'CIA ran secret prisons for detainees in Europe, says inquiry', *The Guardian*, 8 June 2007.

[226] T. Walker and S. Baxter, 'Revealed: the terror prison US is helping to build in Morocco', *The Sunday Times*, 12 February 2006.

[227] White House, Office of the Press Secretary, *President Discusses Creation of Military Commissions to Try Suspected Terrorists*, 6 September 2006, at http://georgewbush-whitehouse.archives.gov/news/releases/2006/09/20060906–3.html.

[228] *Ibid.*

[229] See, e.g., Mark Mazzetti and Scott Shane, 'C.I.A. Abuse Cases Detailed in Report on Detainees', *The New York Times*, 24 August 2009.

[230] Priest, above note 124.

conscientious objectors were being systematically sidelined at the behest of Secretary Rumsfeld and Vice-President Cheney.[231]

Secret detention is ripe for abuse; hiding people makes them especially vulnerable. A decade ago the UN Special Rapporteur on Torture recommended:

> Interrogation should take place only at official centres and the maintenance of secret places of detention should be abolished under law. It should be a punishable offence for an official to hold a person in a secret and/or unofficial place of detention.[232]

Although the events in Abu Ghraib showed that torture is not precluded by 'official' forms of detention,[233] abuse is easier to commit in the darkness of secret detention. And such abuse has been committed. Indeed, there is now ample evidence in the public domain that abusive interrogation, amounting to torture, has taken place in these ghost prisons.[234] In August 2009, the CIA released a 2004 report by its Inspector General that was highly critical of techniques used in some interrogations. These techniques included mock executions, used to terrify other terrorist suspects, a threat to kill the children of at least one detainee, suggestions about sexually assaulting members of a detainee's family, employment of the 'hard takedown', where a detainee was seized and thrown to the floor

[231] Jane Mayer, 'The Memo: How an internal effort to ban the abuse and torture of detainees was thwarted', *New Yorker* (27 February 2006), p. 32.

[232] United Nations Human Rights Commission, *Right to restitution, compensation and rehabilitation for victims of grave violations of human rights and fundamental freedoms*, UN Doc. E/CN.4/1995/34, at paras. 923, 926(b) and (d).

[233] See e.g. Robert F. Worth, 'U.S. Military Plans to Move detainees Out of Abu Ghraib', *The New York Times*, 9 March 2006; and Josh White, 'Military Lawyers Say Tactics Broke Rules', *The Washington Post*, 16 March 2006.

[234] See e.g. Human Rights First, *Ending Secret Detentions*, June 2004, at www.humanrightsfirst.org/us_law/PDF/EndingSecretDetentions_web.pdf (providing a comprehensive overview of known and suspected secret detention sites around the world, created at the behest of, or in collaboration with, US security forces, and highlighting specific examples of prisoner abuse); Mark Danner, 'US Torture: Voices from the Black Sites', *New York Review of Books*, 9 April 2009, at www.nybooks.com/articles/22530 (providing specific examples of torture at secret detention sites); Eric Schmitt and Carolyn Marshall, 'In Secret Unit's "Black Room," a Grim Portrait of U.S. Abuse', *The New York Times*, 19 March 2006 (detailing abusive interrogations in a secret detention facility in Iraq); Amnesty International Australia, *USA/Jordan/Yemen: Torture and Secret Detention Centres*, 26 August 2005, at www.amnesty.org.au/news/comments/480/ (discussing abuse at secret detention sites in Yemen and Jordan); and Human Rights Watch, 'The Case of Marwan Jabour', in *Report 2007*, at www.hrw.org/reports/2007/us0207/2.htm (revealing abuse in a specific case at a secret detention site in Pakistan).

before being moved to a sleep-deprivation cell, and at least one instance of a threat with a gun and a power drill.[235]

Meanwhile, in the UK a highly credible parliamentary report was issued alleging that UK security forces colluded in torture committed by the intelligence services of Egypt, Pakistan, the United States, and Uzbekistan.[236] Although these reports have been strenuously denied by the head of MI6 (Britain's secret intelligence service),[237] two senior cabinet ministers have admitted rather blandly:

> When detainees are held by our police or armed forces we can be sure how they are treated, and whether our standards are met. By definition, we cannot have that same level of assurance when they are held by foreign governments, whose obligations and practices may differ from our own.[238]

Thanks to powerful investigative journalism, the existence of access to information legislation in western democracies, and the change of administration in the United States, it is possible to conclude that torture was committed in secret detention facilities operated by or in cooperation with US security forces. Other western intelligence agencies seem to have colluded in torture as well.

In considering whether a practice of legality existed after 11 September 2001 to support the absolute prohibition on torture, it would seem that the answer is that the practice tends to run in the opposite direction, allowing for torture despite formal statements of law to the contrary. Torture is practised in all regions of the globe, and it is sanctioned even by western democracies. Were this conclusion to stand unvarnished, a further implication would be that the last criteria of legality, that official action must mesh with a purported rule of law, would not be met. On two grounds, then, breaching a criterion of legality and failing to find a continuing

[235] Office of the Inspector General, Central Intelligence Agency, *Special Review: Counterterrorism Detention and Interrogation Activities (September 2001–October 2003)*, 7 May 2004 (released 24 August 2009), at http://image.guardian.co.uk/sys-files/Guardian/documents/2009/08/24/cia04report.pdf.

[236] See UK House of Lords and House of Commons, *Human Rights Joint Committee – Twenty-Third Report[:] Allegations of UK Complicity in Torture*, 21 July 2009, at www.publications.parliament.uk/pa/jt200809/jtselect/jtrights/152/15202.htm. See also Richard Norton Taylor, 'Pressure mounts over allegations of British complicity in torture', *The Guardian*, 4 August 2009.

[237] John F. Burns, 'Head of MI6 Denies Role of Agency in Torture', *The New York Times*, 10 August 2009.

[238] See Patrick Hennessy, 'We cannot eliminate all risk of torture, ministers admit', *The Telegraph* (UK), 8 August 2009.

practice of legality, the absolute prohibition on torture would not qualify as interactional international law. Although attempts to explicitly narrow the norm failed, the prohibition itself is undermined by widespread contrary practice.

However, our final conclusion must be more nuanced because the practices of torture since 11 September 2001 are increasingly under scrutiny, at least as they implicate western intelligence services, and strong evidence is emerging that a reassertion of the absolute prohibition may be underway. Even in the darkest days after the September 11 attacks, rays of light were penetrating the cells of secret detention. A number of former FBI and ex-CIA agents, retired military leaders, and some members of the US government and military legal services, spoke out strongly against secret detention and torture.[239] A recently retired general counsel of the United States Navy, Alberto J. Mora, was particularly forthright:

> If cruelty is no longer declared unlawful, but instead is applied as a matter of policy, it alters the fundamental relationship of man to government. It destroys the whole notion of individual rights.[240]

As early as 2007, senior members of the US Congress had also begun publicly to question the use of secret detention and the attendant likelihood of abuse.[241] Meanwhile, some US allies were putting policies in place to prevent the handing over of terrorist suspects for fear that they would be subject to torture. The Canadian and Dutch Governments were apparently so worried about US treatment of Afghan detainees that they concluded special deals to avoid passing suspects that they captured in Afghanistan to US forces; instead they were turned over to the Afghan government.[242]

[239] See e.g. Mayer, above note 192; Philip Zelikow, 'The OLC 'torture memos': thoughts from a dissenter', *Foreign Policy[:] Shadow Government*, 21 April 2009, at http://shadow.foreignpolicy.com/posts/2009/04/21/the_olc_torture_memos_thoughts_from_a_dissenter (Zelikow was Executive Director of the US government's 9/11 Commission); National Public Radio, 'Ex-CIA Officer Speaks Out Against Waterboarding', 12 December 2007, at www.npr.org/templates/story/story.php?storyId=17181403; Reuters, *Ex-generals to urge Obama action on torture issue*, 3 December 2008, at www.reuters.com/article/politicsNews/idUSTRE4B18UY20081203; Josh White, 'Waterboarding Is Torture, Says Ex-Navy Instructor', *The Washington Post*, 9 November 2007; and Danner, above note 163.

[240] Mayer, above note 231 at 5.

[241] See e.g. Shane, above note 162; and 'The Stuff of Nightmares', above note 171.

[242] See James Travers, 'Smart move to sidestep Afghanistan prison controversy', *The Hamilton Spectator*, 4 March 2006.

As we write, further important legal and political developments, some of which we have already noted, are taking place within the United States and in other western countries. In one of his very first acts, President Obama announced that he would overturn the Bush-era Executive Order authorizing 'harsh' interrogation techniques.[243] The president also ordered the review of secret detention facilities, looking for lawful options for detention.[244] He later ordered the release of the Office of Legal Counsel memos that authorized forms of 'harsh' interrogation.[245] The CIA has also been forced to release an internal report that reveals details of 'harsh' interrogations[246] and the US Attorney-General has appointed a special prosecutor to look into the actions of US officials who may have committed torture.[247] Meanwhile, a parliamentary inquiry into complicity with torture has been launched in the UK, and in Canada compensation has been given to a victim of torture after a public inquiry into the role of Canadian officials.[248]

The practice of legality on the prohibition of torture has been in a state of movement since 11 September 2001. For most of the time since the terrorist attacks on the United States, the official practice seemed to be inconsistent with an absolute ban. Indeed, one could argue that the tendency was in the opposite direction, toward the complete undermining of the prohibition. Torture was taking place around the globe, and was even being used or connived in by liberal democracies, most notably by the most important global actor, the United States. Yet the tide may be shifting. Disgust over the use of torture seems to be reasserting itself both amongst western governments and in the public. Concrete steps are being taken to reverse the trends towards the direct use and political toleration of torture. In the United States especially, since the coming into office of the Obama administration, reassertions of the traditional ban on torture are being made regularly. However, it cannot be said that the undermining of the prohibition has been completely reversed. It is not yet the case that secret detention has been precluded by Executive Order in the United States, nor that all forms of 'torture lite' are excluded from the arsenal

[243] 'Executive Order – Ensuring Lawful Interrogations', 22 January 2009, www.whitehouse.gov/the_press_office/EnsuringLawfulInterrogations/.

[244] 'Executive Order – Review of Detention Policy Options', 22 January 2009, www.whitehouse.gov/the_press_office/ReviewofDetentionPolicyOptions/.

[245] BBC News Service, *Obama publishes 'torture' memos*, 16 April 2009, at http://news.bbc.co.uk/2/hi/americas/8003023.stm.

[246] See above note 235. [247] See Mazzetti and Shane, above note 229.

[248] See above notes 196 and 236.

of US interrogators. It is also unclear whether or not the policies of the Bush administration on secret detention and torture will ever be subject to legal evaluation within US domestic law. It must also be admitted that torture is continuing in many states around the globe, and does not seem to be a particular priority for global action.

Given the conflicting data, can one clearly state that there is a practice of legality upholding the absolute anti-torture norm contained in the UN Torture Convention? Unfortunately, we do not think so.[249] However, as we will suggest in the concluding section of this chapter, this evaluation may not be quite as grim as it seems. We are left, though, with the unhappy assessment that the last criterion of legality, congruence between a norm and official action, is not met in the case of the absolute prohibition on torture because there has been no solid practice of legality upholding the norm since 11 September 2001.

5. Conclusion

The case of torture points to both the robustness of our interactional analysis of international law and to the hard-headed approach that the analysis demands. Quite frankly, we are not at all comfortable with the conclusion to which our analysis draws us in relation to the prohibition on torture, but we are firmly convinced that the analysis is nonetheless correct.

In evaluating the underlying global shared understandings supporting the absolute prohibition on torture contained in the UN Torture Convention we conclude that the understandings were weak before 11 September 2001. In an intriguing twist, the shared understandings were initially further undermined in the few years immediately following Osama bin Laden's attacks; however, by 2006, the revulsion that attended disclosures of US government complicity in torture began to reinforce a shared understanding precluding the use of torture in all circumstances.

It is already clear that the attempts made in the Yoo–Bybee memos and subsequent actions of high-ranking US officials explicitly to narrow the definition of torture to include only severe pain amounting to that experienced with the approach of death or organ failure have not succeeded. They did not generate widely shared understandings; indeed they were actively resisted by senior US military and security officials, US allies,

[249] See also Ryder McKeown, 'Norm Regress: US Revisionism and the Slow Death of the Torture Norm' (2009) 23(1) *International Relations* 5.

the media, NGOs, and the general public. We have also suggested that these attempts failed to meet important criteria of legality. They were not promulgated until disclosure was forced by law and by political change. It is unlikely that the rule they posited was intended to be general; it was limited to the self-evaluated needs of the United States, and would have been resisted by it if applied by non-allies. The memos and their follow-up orders may also have created situations of impossibility where interrogators were forced, or at least authorized, to act in contravention of law. What is more, by failing to provide strong distinctions between what was allowed and what was prohibited, the attempt to narrow the definition of torture would likely have breached the criterion of clarity. It is not enough to tell an interrogator that he has gone too far when a detainee has died.

It remains sadly true that when one considers the eighth criterion of legality, congruence of official action with a posited norm, there is strong evidence that torture is routinely practised all around the globe in the name of national security, and sometimes simply to extract confessions in criminal proceedings. The complicity, or direct action, of western security agencies in 'harsh' interrogations amounting to torture also undermined this criterion of legality in the period after 11 September 2001. The same data, credibly reported by NGO and official sources, further leads us to the conclusion that there is not a robust practice of legality continuing to support the absolute prohibition on torture. Our provisional conclusion is that the absolute prohibition on torture does not meet the standards of interactional international law. The rule is rhetorically strong but practically weak; it does not truly shape the behaviour of scores, perhaps the majority, of states.

We call this a 'provisional' conclusion because the situation is fluid, and there is good evidence to suggest that we are living through a period of normative transition as concerns the anti-torture rule. The reassertion of a robust shared understanding that the prohibition on torture is necessary, and that it should be absolute, is building. The practice of the United States is undergoing a profound re-evaluation, and this may prove globally relevant, especially amongst liberal democracies. What remains uncertain is whether there is a strong normative impulse to confront and challenge the practices of torture that seem endemic in so many states around the globe. If torture continues to be widely employed without any significant international legal and political consequences in scores of states, it will be difficult to assert that the eighth criterion of legality is met or that a practice of legality supports the anti-torture norm.

The rule prohibiting torture is a fascinating example of why we argue so strenuously that the work of international law is not done with the positing of a rule in a 'binding' convention. Rules are constructed, buttressed or destroyed through the continuing practice of states and other international actors. In the case of human rights norms, like the anti-torture rule, the work of non-state actors, particularly NGOs and the media, is particularly necessary and powerful. As we set out in Chapter 1, our interactional framework is especially sensitive to the relevance of that work, to the diversity of actors who shape the practices of legality. So the real conclusion to draw from an interactional analysis of the prohibition of torture is that the struggle to maintain the norm is never over. The rule was close-to-moribund, despite its supposed status as *jus cogens*, even before 11 September 2001. It was further undermined intentionally by a powerful global actor, the US government. But attempts to restrict the rule almost out of existence were not successful once they became publicly known because of strong domestic and international responses, in the media, and by non-governmental and inter-governmental forces. When domestic political forces were recalibrated after the 2008 US presidential election, international actors found a new domestic ally – that constellation of forces is still playing itself out. But the work is not over, for now it is necessary to redouble efforts to challenge the practice of torture in scores of states around the world. If that work is not undertaken successfully, the formal existence of an absolute prohibition on torture could still become a dead letter.

6

The use of force: normative ebb and flow

1. Introduction

In 2005, in an 'Outcome Document' encapsulating the results of a sweeping debate on UN reform, the General Assembly of the United Nations (UNGA) purported to restate the UN Charter framework on the non-use of force in international relations. The UNGA reaffirmed 'that the relevant provisions of the Charter are sufficient to address the full range of threats to international peace and security. We further reaffirm the authority of the Security Council to mandate coercive action to maintain and restore international peace and security.'[1] This sanguine conclusion was surprising given that only two years earlier, at the height of debates over the prosecution of the second Iraq war, the UN Secretary-General, Kofi Annan, had opined that the organization and its members were confronting a 'fork in the road' as concerns the prohibition on the use of force, and its exceptions.[2]

Debates surrounding the second Iraq war prompted a range of commentators to diagnose the death of the law on the use of force, to call for its adaptation to the globalization of threats and the problem of so-called failed states, and to assert the need to either overturn or defend the UN Charter framework. Our aim in this chapter is not to evaluate in detail the legality of the Iraq war. Others have done so thoroughly.[3] Rather, we are interested in using this intense period of debate as an entry point

[1] See UN General Assembly, *2005 World Summit Outcome*, UN Doc. A/RES/60/1 (24 October 2005), para. 79, at www.un.org/summit2005/documents.html.

[2] K. Annan, *Secretary General's Address to the General Assembly*, 23 Sept. 2003, at www.un.org/apps/sg/sgstats.asp?nid=517.

[3] See e.g. Sean Murphy, 'Assessing the Legality of Invading Iraq' (2004) 92 *Georgetown Law Journal* 173; Vaughn Lowe, 'The Iraq Crisis: What Now?' (2003) 52 *International and Comparative Law Quarterly* 859; and various contributions to 'Agora: Future Implications of the Iraq Conflict' (2003) 97 *American Journal of International Law* 553–642. See also Jutta Brunnée and Stephen J. Toope, 'The Use of Force: International Law After Iraq' (2004) 53 *International and Comparative Law Quarterly* 785.

into the examination of how legal norms are created, upheld, solidified, challenged, and destroyed. In so doing, we will employ the interactional law framework to demonstrate how legal norms operate when confronting problems close to the heart of state interest and state sovereignty. Some shifts in the rules governing the use of force have occurred, but eight years after the events of 11 September 2001 it is evident that they are far less dramatic than anticipated by many commentators. Our framework helps to explain why.

Against the backdrop of a sweeping prohibition on the use of force in Article 2(4) of the UN Charter, complementary rules limit the right of states to resort to war to instances of collective security intervention and self-defence. The rules in the charter ask leaders to pause and inquire whether war is truly necessary. The debate over Iraq did lay bare some persisting tensions in these rules, especially in relation to the scope of exceptions. Some politicians and commentators attempted to undermine or loosen the charter's restraints on military force by combining, shifting and reinterpreting a variety of reasons for war, arguing for expanded exceptions to the fundamental rule prohibiting the use of force. The argument ran that human rights abuses in other states are themselves dangerous to 'our' society, that global terrorism is bred in failing states, and that even a *potential* weapon of mass destruction programme, or the mere existence of a 'rogue' regime, required pre-emption.[4] In some of the justifications for the Iraq War, all of these issues were lumped together as a global super-threat, justifying war and placing it beyond challenge.[5]

In the era of the UN Charter, international law has required specific, testable claims: is a given war justified as self-defence? Is a state asserting a right to humanitarian intervention? Does it claim a threat to international peace and security that would normally require Security Council

[4] Arguments to this effect are advanced from a range of different political and theoretical vantage points. See e.g. Ruth Wedgwood, 'The I.C.J. Advisory Opinion on the Israeli Security Fence and the Limits of Self-Defense' (2005) 99 *American Journal of International Law* 52; Anne-Marie Slaughter, 'Präzisionswaffe Völkerrecht: Die Demokratien müssen sich verbünden – zu einer neuen Kraft innerhalb der UN' 28 *DIE ZEIT*, 3 July 2003; and Allen Buchanan and Robert O. Keohane, 'The Preventive Use of Force: A Cosmopolitan Institutional Perspective' (2004) 18 *Ethics and International Affairs* 1. See also The National Security Strategy of the United States of America (September 2002) at 14, at http://georgewbush-whitehouse.archives.gov/nsc/nss/2002/index.html.

[5] See e.g. Address by President George W. Bush, 7 October 2002, at http://georgewbush-whitehouse.archives.gov/news/releases/2002/10/20021007-8.html. And see Jim Garamone, 'Bush Says Trusting Saddam "Not a Strategy," "Not an Option"', *American Forces Press Service*, 29 January 2003, at www.defense.gov/news/newsarticle.aspx?id=29519.

action?[6] Given the constitutive function of the charter, and its undoubted influence in shaping the regime of post-World War II international law, the rules of the charter are owed deference; there is at least a prima facie case that they represent legitimately created obligations in international society. But merely asserting that rules are binding because they are in the charter is not sufficient to address the true state of obligation.

In this chapter we will consider the prohibition on the use of force, enshrined in Article 2(4) of the UN Charter, the exceptions to that prohibition – self-defence (Article 51) and collective action under Chapter VII of the Charter – and the emerging concept of the 'responsibility to protect'. We will examine each in the light of the interactional framework, assessing the presence of shared understandings, the fulfilment of the criteria of legality, and the existence of a continuing practice of legality buttressing the norm. If these requirements are met, the interrelated rules concerning the use of force would be 'interactional international law' and would have created binding legal obligations.

2. The prohibition on the use of force

The prohibition on the use of force contained in Article 2(4) of the UN Charter is said to be fundamental to the structure of contemporary international relations. Yet it is also the subject of continuing controversy, in large measure because the exceptions to the prohibition, which are in principle conceptually distinct, generate arguments that can actually undermine the primary rule. In simplistic terms, the wider and more uncertain the exceptions, the less robust the rule.

2.1 Shared understandings on the prohibition of force

In order to assess the debates and practices surrounding the use of force since the military intervention in Iraq, and their effect on the creation, upholding, solidification, challenge, and destruction of legal norms, it is necessary to engage in a brief historical discursion on the evolution of the rule on the non-use of force and its exceptions.

The UN Charter prohibition on the use of force is sweeping: '2(4) All members shall refrain in their international relations from the threat or use of force against the territorial integrity or political independence of any state, or in any other manner inconsistent with the Purposes of the

[6] See Lowe, above note 3 at 860–2.

United Nations.' Of course, earlier in the twentieth century, the League of Nations had been based upon similar principles of sovereignty and non-intervention. Both the League and the UN prohibitions were built on a centuries-old preoccupation with establishing limits to war. We will explore this 'just war' tradition below, in the context of exceptions to the prohibition on the use of force.

In the League, a first attempt was made to legally codify the moral limits on war, treating war as exceptional and subject to a heavy burden of justification. In further response to the suffering and atrocities of World War I, the 'civilized world' also produced the Kellogg-Briand Pact, renouncing war as an instrument of policy, and pretending to limit the use of force to self-defence. Soon after, the pact was declared moribund and treated as the prime example of naïve international idealism.

Yet the pact actually reflected sentiment that extended far beyond the corridors of formal diplomatic power. One only has to consider the explosion of artistic sources excoriating the political elites that had allowed World War I to break out and to drag on for five hideous and blood-soaked years: the poetry of Wilfred Owen and Siegfried Sassoon; the novels of Erich Maria Remarque and John Dos Passos; the paintings of Max Beckman, Otto Dix, and Wyndham Lewis. All of these creative artists drew on the widespread revulsion at the senseless death and injury experienced in modern trench warfare, and helped to create a continuing public dialogue around the 'pity of war'.[7]

Once again, after the horrors of World War II, popular sentiment was captured in artistic sources that criticized the destruction of thousands of innocent lives through genocidal hate and mechanized brutality. Consider the music of Dimitri Shostakovich, Benjamin Britten and Krysztof Penderecki; the novels of Norman Mailer, Pierre Boulle and Sven Hassel; and the paintings of Picasso, Stanley Spencer and Charles Comfort. The public revulsion provoked an even broader effort to limit recourse to war than had been made after World War I, with the drafters of the Charter of the United Nations declaring that the very purpose of the UN was to 'save succeeding generations from the scourge of war'.

The provisions on the use of force in the UN Charter were fully in conformity with one aspect of the long-standing just war tradition, that is the aspect which sought to restrict justifications for war to relatively narrow, legal criteria, rather than unilaterally assessed and open-ended

[7] See e.g. Wilfred Owen, 'Preface', in John Stallworthy (ed.), *The Poems of Wilfred Owen* (London: Hogarth Press, 1985), p. 192.

moral criteria.[8] One crucial difference, however, is that instead of presuming that a sovereign was acting justly in pursuing war, the presumption was now that war is exceptional, and that proponents must justify its necessity on a balance of probabilities. As Walzer emphasizes, it is only response to aggression that justifies war, not a seeking of advantage or a desire to preclude merely potential threats. In practical terms, the primary response to aggression was likely to be the invocation of a right to self-defence.[9]

Intermittently, in the latter years of the twentieth century, the public discomfort with policies of war re-emerged in opposition to the Vietnam War, in attempts to limit the recourse to force in the Middle East, and in widespread revulsion over continuing bloody wars in Africa, especially in Sierra Leone, Rwanda and Burundi, and Uganda. The most powerful recent illustration of deep and pervasive public sentiment in opposition to war took place in the lead-up to the second Iraq War, beginning in 2002–2003. In the Introduction to this book, we detailed the range of public demonstrations around the world, the criticism of many world leaders and the extent to which ordinary people invoked issues of legality to frame their opposition to the proposed invasion.[10] This unusual moment revealed that the shared understanding that war is to be avoided had become not just a moral question, but an international legal question as well, certainly in western societies and, as we shall see shortly, in the developing world too.

A 2006 study of the deployment in the British and Canadian print media of arguments grounded in concepts of international law with reference to the Iraq War revealed the surprising extent to which public debate came to be shaped in terms of legality and illegality.[11] While there were many more references to international law in UK papers than in the Canadian dailies, this is not surprising, given that the British public was actively struggling with the decision to participate in the invasion, whereas the Canadian public was spared that hard political choice.[12]

[8] See below.

[9] See Michael Walzer, *Just and Unjust Wars*, 3rd edn (New York: Basic Books, 2000), pp. 62–3.

[10] See Introduction.

[11] Stephen J. Toope, 'Public Commitment To International Law: Canadian and British Media Perspectives on the Use of Force', in Christopher P.M. Waters (ed.), *British and Canadian Perspectives on International Law* (Dordrecht: Martinus Nijhoff, 2006), p. 13.

[12] When the words 'international law' are linked to 'Iraq' and 'war', the largest number of references occurred in *The Guardian* at 401, followed by *The Independent* at 284, *The Times* at 193, with *The Telegraph* trailing at 109 references.

In the Canadian newspapers in which international law was invoked most often, *The Globe and Mail*, *Le Devoir* and *La Presse*, the references were typically brief, and they often arose in quoted sources. For example, in an article published just after the fall of the Saddam Hussein regime, the Swedish Prime Minister was simply quoted without further comment: 'We don't need to regret the fall of Saddam Hussein, though we can regret that it occurred in such a way that it violates international law.'[13] Or, in early 2009, *The Globe and Mail* reported in a 64-word item that, following the leaking of a 2003 government memo that suggested that the Iraq invasion might have been illegal, the Dutch Prime Minister had ordered an independent inquiry into the matter.[14]

The UK newspapers were less superficial in their treatment of international law and the use of force in Iraq. In all of the 'quality dailies', leading UK international lawyers were quoted, sometimes at length, on their understanding of the relevant issues. The letter of sixteen eminent international lawyers, including the holders of the Whewell Chair at Cambridge and the Chichele Chair at Oxford, which challenged the legality of the invasion, was published in *The Guardian* and reported upon in other dailies.[15] A similar letter in Canada was never published in full, although it was reported.[16] In a detailed piece published in March 2004, a *Guardian* journalist interviewed and reported upon the views of seven UK international lawyers and international relations scholars concerning the legality of the Iraq War.[17]

In the UK we also saw a tactical use of the letters to the editor columns and opinion pages by various international lawyers who wanted to articulate their understandings of the legality of the Iraq War. Professors Phillip Allott, Chris Greenwood and Vaughn Lowe each wrote separately in *The Times*.[18] In addition, various members of the wider legal

[13] R. Mickleburgh, 'War's critics happy to see fall of Hussein', *The Globe and Mail*, 10 April 2003 (quoting then Swedish Prime Minister Goran Persson).

[14] 'Dutch to probe decision to support Iraq invasion', *The Globe and Mail*, 3 February 2009. See also Joost Oranje, '"Iraq memo" opens door to possible government inquiry', *NRC Handelsblad*, 21 January 2009.

[15] U. Bernitz, N. Espejo-Yaksic, A Hurwitz *et al.*, 'War would be illegal', *The Guardian*, 7 March 2003, Letters to the Editor; and M. White and P. Wintour, 'No case for Iraq attack say lawyers', *The Guardian*, 7 March 2003.

[16] J. Sallott, 'Legal experts say attack on Iraq is illegal', *The Globe and Mail*, 20 March 2003; and E. Oziewicz, 'Is Iraq war justified by international agreements?', *The Globe and Mail*, 25 March 2003.

[17] O. Bowcott, 'Iraq: the legal challenge', *The Guardian*, 2 March 2004.

[18] P. Allott and A. Dashwood, 'Conflict over legality of launching an attack against Iraq', *The Times*, 19 March 2003, Letters to the Editor; C. Greenwood, 'Britain's war on Saddam

community wrote op. ed. pieces arguing pro and con, the most prolific being David Pannick Q.C. and Rabinder Singh Q.C. in *The Times*.[19] Often these columns coincided with litigation where the legality of the war was being challenged – unsuccessfully – by the Campaign for Nuclear Disarmament, or where relatives of Iraqi civilians killed during the war were seeking to invoke the European Human Rights Convention and the UK Human Rights Act to require full investigation of the circumstances of death.

The media study shows that, at least in the UK, one of the belligerents in the second Iraq War, and to a lesser extent in Canada, a non-belligerent, the moral and political arguments about war were often related in public debate to the question of legality.

Our conclusion in looking at the broad sweep of twentieth-century artistic, political, public and legal responses to war is that the prohibition on the use of force in international relations was reaffirmed as a shared expectation in many parts of the globe. That expectation was expressed powerfully in the public opposition to the proposed invasion of Iraq in 2003, and was explicitly linked to the *legal* prohibition on the use of force articulated in Article 2(4) of the UN Charter.

Although our brief tracing of the historical evolution of the prohibition on the use of force suggests that the concept is 'western' in origin, the public revulsion against war is shared in the developing world. In other words, the shared understanding grounding the prohibition on the use of force is global, reaching beyond inter-state discourse. We have already noted the anti-Iraq war demonstrations that took place in major cities throughout the world.[20] It is worth detailing that those protests extended throughout Asia, Africa and Latin America, though with smaller numbers of participants than in the developed world. Significant demonstrations were held in cities such as Accra (no estimate given), Beirut (10,000), Buenos Aires (50,000), Calcutta (10,000), Cape Town (5,000), Damascus (200,000), Dhaka (1,000), Islamabad (3,000), Jakarta (7,000), Manila (10,000), Mexico City (10,000), Montevideo (50,000)

had the law on its side', *The Times*, 22 October 2003; and V. Lowe, 'Legal queries over actions on Iraq', *The Times*, 23 September 2002, Letters to the Editor.

[19] See e.g. D. Pannick, 'Why the judges should have their say on Iraq', *The Times*, 11 March 2003; D. Pannick, 'Why we must fight with one hand tied behind our backs', *The Times*, 8 April 2003; D. Pannick, 'Goldsmith's advice on legality of war must be published', *The Times*, 4 November 2003; and R. Singh, 'Why war is illegal', *The Times*, 14 March 2003.

[20] Patrick E. Tyler, 'Threats and responses: news analysis; A new power in the streets', *The New York Times*, 17 February 2003; and 'Anti-war protesters hold global rallies', *USA Today*, 15 February 2003.

and Seoul (2,000).[21] These widespread protests prompted *New York Times* reporter Patrick Tyler to speculate that, in 2003 at least, there were 'two superpowers on the planet: the United States and world public opinion'.[22]

World opinion had already been heard in the councils of the United Nations. Developing world states joined in the Security Council's refusal to authorize a second Iraq War, resisting strong pressure from the United States and the United Kingdom.[23] When the US-led 'coalition of the willing' nonetheless invaded Iraq, a wide variety of developing world states participated directly in condemning the invasion during an unusual 'open' session held by the Security Council.[24]

In our interactional theory of international law, shared understandings are the starting point for any candidate legal norm: it is their grounding in shared understandings that gives social norms a degree of resilience. But that is not enough to show that a legal norm prohibiting the use of force exists. As we explained in Chapter 1, a legal norm only exists when it meets tests of legality and when it is continually supported by a practice of legality. What is more, even the existence of the norm in formal sources, in customary international law and in the UN Charter (a treaty), would not necessarily mean that the norm is what we call interactional law. Formal sources could, however, serve a useful purpose, indicating recognition of the norm by many relevant actors in international society. So the formal sources of law are relevant, but not determinative of legal norms

[21] See BBC News Service, *Millions join global anti-war protests*, 17 February 2003, at http://news.bbc.co.uk/2/hi/europe/2765215.stm; Gary Leupp, 'The Weekend the World Said No to War: Notes on the Numbers', *CounterPunch*, 25 February 2003, at www.counterpunch.org/leupp02252003.html; 'Anti-war protesters hold global rallies', *USA Today*, 15 February 2003, at www.usatoday.com/news/world/iraq/2003–02–15-protests_x.htm; and Haruna Mohammed, 'Anti War Protest Rocks Accra', *Accra Mail*, 3 April 2003, at http://archives.econ.utah.edu/archives/a-list/2003w13/msg00136.htm. (As is usually the case, estimates of participation numbers in public rallies vary considerably. Our only point is that all around the world, people protested.)

[22] Tyler, above note 20. (He added: 'For the moment, an exceptional phenomenon has appeared on the streets of world cities. It may not be as profound as the people's revolutions across Eastern Europe in 1989 or in Europe's class struggles of 1848, but politicians and leaders are unlikely to ignore it.')

[23] See e.g. Ian Johnstone, 'The Plea of Necessity in International Legal Discourse: Humanitarian Intervention and Counter-Terrorism' (2005) 43 *Columbia Journal of International Law* 337 at 384.

[24] United Nations Security Council Press Release SC 7705, 'Security Council Holds First Debate on Iraq since Start of Military Action; Speakers Call for Halt to Aggression, Immediate Withdrawal', 26 March 2003, at www.un.org/News/Press/docs/2003/sc7705.doc.htm.

that have obligatory force. We must still assess whether or not the shared understanding on the prohibition of the use of force in international relations meets the criteria of legality identified by Fuller. If it does not, then the norm cannot generate a sense of legal obligation.

2.2 *Criteria of legality and the prohibition on the use of force*

The prohibition on the use of force, as articulated in Article 2(4) of the UN Charter certainly meets the test of generality. It is directed at all states and applies in all cases except where a specific exception is set out in the charter, or found in customary international law.[25] Some commentators who dispute the existence of the rule have argued in recent years that the rise of violent non-state actors such as global terrorists has undermined the generality of the prohibition. It is suggested that the rule against the use of force, therefore, does not actually apply to all the salient international actors, making the rule irrelevant.[26] We suggest that it is still the case that terrorists, although destructive, remain peripheral to the broad sweep of international relations. They are not yet strong enough to displace the primary focus on states as potential purveyors of violence. It is instructive to note that the use of force by states in response to terrorists is still typically directed at other states – Iraq and Afghanistan, for example. In addition, the justification for action is often that force is needed to address 'state-sponsored' terrorism. What is more, the strong majority of states and commentators reaffirm the view that the correct legal framework to deal with terrorist violence is international and national criminal law, not the inter-state use of force.[27]

The second criterion of legality, promulgation, is met because the norm prohibiting the use of force is expressed openly in customary international law and in the UN Charter.[28] The formal sources play a crucial role by telling the world that the norm is seen by the actors in the system as a legal norm. They are a communicative device that signals the

[25] The UN Charter, including its rules on the use of force, binds all states as members of the UN. To the extent that exceptions to the prohibition exist at customary international law, they apply equally to all states.

[26] For a general discussion see Jane E. Stromseth, 'Law and Force After Iraq: A Transitional Moment' (2003) 97 *American Journal of International Law* 628 at 634–5. And see Michael Glennon, 'How War Left the Law Behind', *The New York Times*, 22 November 2002.

[27] See e.g. Mary Ellen O'Connell, 'Enhancing the Status of Non-State Actors Through a Global War on Terror?' (2005) 43 *Columbia Journal of Transnational Law* 435 at 456–7.

[28] See e.g. Christine Gray, *International Law and the Use of Force*, 3rd edn (Oxford University Press, 2008), pp. 30–1.

potential existence of an obligation and that also allows people to know prima facie what they are required to do or to refrain from doing. This signalling function is entirely distinct from the argument that the articulation of the purported norm is a 'validity' test.[29]

The third criterion, of non-retroactivity, is not engaged in any way by the prohibition on the use of force. As we have seen, the prohibition is rooted in a shared understanding that has existed for many generations, and the customary law on the non-use of force long pre-dates the charter. The norm also meets the fourth criterion of legality because it is clear. The starting proposition, in Article 2(4) of the charter, is an absolute and sweeping prohibition on the use of force in inter-state relations. Over the years – on the margins – there have been disagreements amongst international lawyers over the proper content of the idea of 'force'. For example, should economic coercion be understood as a use of force?[30] In addition, arguments have been pursued over the level of intensity of action required to rise to the level of 'force'. Is sending a few spies on an armed incursion into a neighbouring state a use of force?[31] Debates have also arisen over efforts to identify uses of military force that are said not to be directed against the territorial integrity or political independence of a state and not to transgress the purposes of the UN. For example, attempts to rescue the nationals of one state held hostage in another using precise military action, matched with immediate withdrawal, have been argued not to amount to 'force'.[32]

Despite these arguments, the prohibition on the use of force has remained whole and vital. Indeed, aside from debates over the intensity of force required to fit within the rule, all attempts to question the fundamental prohibition have been unsuccessful. Conceptually, the choice has been made to keep the sweeping prohibition intact, and to address the scope of the rule by way of specific exceptions: collective security, self-defence and, perhaps, humanitarian intervention and the responsibility to protect. It is important to say, however, that it is in these exceptions that a lack of clarity can be asserted. It is the interplay between the rule and its exceptions that the argument arises that the rule itself has been 'killed'.[33] We will address these complicated issues shortly.

[29] On validity, see above Chapter 1, text accompanying notes 105–6.

[30] See Gray, above note 28, pp. 6–7 and 30.

[31] See discussion below, text accompanying notes 78–83.

[32] See Thomas M. Franck, *Recourse to Force: State Action Against Threats and Armed Attacks* (Cambridge University Press, 2002), p. 12.

[33] See Thomas M. Franck, 'Who Killed Article 2(4)? or: Changing Norms Governing the Use of Force by States' (1970) 64 *American Journal of International Law* 809 and

In current international law, there is no situation where abiding by the prohibition on the use of force would conflict with a requirement to use force, so the fifth criterion of avoiding contradiction is satisfied. If, over time, a more expansive interpretation of human rights provisions of the charter took hold, one could imagine a situation where the 'purposes' of the UN, including the promotion and protection of human rights, could be contradicted by the non-use of force. This could theoretically arise if a robust 'responsibility to protect' doctrine emerged that contained a duty to intervene to protect a vulnerable population.[34] Such a duty is not yet in sight. In any event, it is arguable that a robust duty to protect would merely be a specific exception to the rule, not a contradiction. It would be necessary, however, that any such rule be circumscribed by predictable limits, so that it would not come to overwhelm the primary rule.

The sixth criterion of legality requires that a norm not demand the impossible. This criterion is not problematic in relation to the prohibition on the use of force itself, for the rule requires refraining from action, which is always within the power of a state. However, we will soon explore problems with some interpretations of the exceptions to the rule, especially the right to self-defence, that do give rise to claims that the right is cast in such a way that it could require the politically and morally impossible of state governments. For example, should a state have to wait until an armed attack is launched before it is allowed to pre-empt the risk? Should serious internal instability in a neighbouring state be irrelevant in considering pre-emption even if there is an imminent threat for the instability to cross over the border of a neighbouring state?[35]

Constancy and predictability of a rule make up the seventh criterion of legality, and they are met by the prohibition on the use of force. However, predictability can be damaged fatally if the exceptions come to displace

'What Happens Now? The United Nations After Iraq' (2003) 97 *American Journal of International Law* 607 at 618–20.

[34] Stephen J. Toope, 'Does International Law Impose a Duty upon the United Nations to Prevent Genocide?' (2000) 46 *McGill Law Journal* 187. Of course, there is already a specific obligation to prevent genocide, enshrined in the widely ratified Genocide Convention. Arguably, however, this duty has not been extended yet outside that particular regime. See Louise Arbour, 'The Responsibility to Protect as a Duty of Care in International Law and Practice' (2008) 34 *Review of International Studies* 445 at 449–50. And see *Case Concerning the Application of the Convention on the Prevention and Punishment of the Crime of Genocide (Bosnia and Herzegovina* v. *Serbia and Montenegro)*, Judgment, I.C.J. Reports 2007, paras. 425–38, at www.icj-cij.org/docket/files/91/13685.pdf (on the treaty-based duty to prevent genocide).

[35] See the general discussion of 'imminence' of the threat below, text accompanying notes 117–34.

the rule. In our later discussion of the exceptions to the prohibition on the use of force, we will show that attempts have been made, especially in the context of the second Iraq War, to promote interpretations of the existing exceptions and to create new exceptions in response to supposedly novel threats that would have resulted in almost total unpredictability of the basic prohibition. This would have resulted in a failure to meet a fundamental criterion of legality, and the entire prohibition on the use of force would have become illegitimate. This analysis, derived from interactional international law, explains why resistance to changing the scope of the exceptions to the prohibition or of creating new exceptions was so strong during debates over the 2003 Iraq War.[36]

The eighth and last criterion of legality is congruence of subsequent practice (or in Fuller's terms, of the actions of officials) with the purported rule. This is the criterion that is most difficult to satisfy in the case of the prohibition on the use of force. Over the period after the norm prohibiting the use of force had solidified, there have been many breaches of the rule. In the latter part of the twentieth century, a partial catalogue would include the Argentinean invasion of the Falklands, the Vietnamese invasion of Cambodia, the Soviet invasion of Afghanistan, the US invasion of Grenada, the Ethiopian and Eritrean border war, the US- and UK-led invasion of Iraq, and the Russian invasion of Georgia. One could add to the list with ease.[37] Although the International Court of Justice (ICJ) ruled in the *Nicaragua* case that violations do not undo the rule,[38] this is hardly a satisfying response for sceptics who have long claimed that Article 2(4) of the charter is dead.[39] The central question is whether the breaches of the rule have been so widespread and consistent that the rule has fallen into desuetude,[40] or whether, rather, it is the exceptions to the rule that have been attacked and undermined.

One of the challenges of dispassionate assessment is that it is hard to show support for an existing rule precluding the use of force because the

[36] See discussion below, text accompanying notes 135–7.

[37] For a discussion of state practice from the end of World War II to 1991, see A. Mark Weisburd, *Use of Force: The Practice of States since World War II* (The Pennsylvania State University Press, 1997). And see Gray, above note 28.

[38] *Military and Paramilitary Activities in and against Nicaragua (Nicaragua* v. *United States of America)*, Judgment, I.C.J. Reports 1986, para. 186, at www.icj-cij.org/docket/files/70/6503.pdf.

[39] See discussion in Franck, 'What Happens Now?', above note 33 at 607.

[40] See Michael Glennon, 'How International Rules Die' (2005) 93 *Georgetown Law Journal* 939 ('one has to know how often a rule has been breached to know whether the rule is law').

rule entails doing nothing, rather than acting. How can we know how many times calm heads in defence departments and foreign offices have argued successfully that the use of force is both unwise and illegal in a given situation?[41] Throughout the latter part of the twentieth century scores of inter-state disputes were addressed without recourse to force. We also saw an increased use of arbitration and adjudication to settle border disputes, which previously might have generated armed action.[42] What may be most telling is that even when states do have recourse to the use of force, they typically offer justifications that relate to the accepted exceptions to the use of force contained in the charter and related customary law. For that reason in particular, we conclude that even though there have been numerous breaches of the prohibition on the use of force, the prohibition itself has withstood the breaches; there is general congruence of international practice with the norm. However, that conclusion should not be read as sanguine, for we must still assess whether or not the justifications used to invoke the exceptions to the rule have themselves been so strained as to undermine the legality of the exceptions. If this is so, then the entire framework on the use of force could be rendered meaningless because it would be practically void of obligatory force.

2.3 *Practice of legality*

The practice of legality is closely connected to one specific criterion of legality: the congruence of practice with the underlying rule, what Fuller examined in the domestic law context as congruence of 'official action' with a norm. However, this congruence alone is not enough to generate robust law. In addition, the practice of legality requires a sustained and continuous effort to realize all the criteria of legality. This is not to say that

[41] See also Gray, above note 28, pp. 25–6. As Gray points out, Abram Chayes's detailed account of the role of US State Department lawyers in the 1962 Cuban missile crisis remains unusual. See Abram Chayes, *The Cuban Missile Crisis: International Crises and the Role of Law*, 2nd rev. edn (Lanham, Md: Rowman & Littlefield Publishers, 1988).

[42] See *Report of the International Court of Justice*, 1 August 2004–31 July 2005, General Assembly Official Records, Sixtieth Session Supplement No. 4 (A/60/4), para. 9, at www.icj-cij.org/court/en/reports/report_2004–2005.pdf ('Over the past year, the number of cases pending before the Court has remained high. Whereas in the 1970s the Court had only one or two cases on its docket at any one time, between 1990 and 1997 this number varied between nine and 13. Since then it has stood at 20 or more. As a consequence of the fact that the Court, during the period under review, has disposed of ten cases, the number now stands at 11'); see also Human Security Centre, University of British Columbia, *Human Security Report 2005* (Oxford University Press, 2005), 'Less Interstate Conflict', at www.humansecurityreport.info/figures/Figure1.1.pdf.

practice must be absolutely consistent with the criteria of legality for legal rules to be created and upheld: but, recurring failures to meet the various criteria will ultimately erode, and even destroy, law.

'Practice' is made up of two distinct, but often interrelated elements: deeds and rhetoric, both in justifying action and in responding to that action. Although intuitively the act or failure to act, i.e. to refrain from or to use force, is the primary consideration in assessing relevant practice, it is always important to evaluate the conduct with reference to explicit justification and reaction. Because the primary rule on the use of force is matched with complex exceptions, *why* force is said and understood to be used or not used is relevant to assessing legality. Therefore, to assess the practice of legality concerning the use of force, we must first treat the exceptions. As will become apparent in that discussion, actions or rhetoric that over-extend or otherwise abuse the exceptions will also tend to eviscerate the prohibition on the use of force itself.

3. Exceptions to the prohibition on the use of force

As we have already seen, long-standing moral and legal tradition treats war as exceptional, legitimately justified only by a 'just cause'. Therefore, given the reality of inter-state conflicts of interest and purpose, much of the debate over the last few centuries has revolved around exceptions to the general prohibition. Of these exceptions, self-defence is the most clearly established. The use of force for humanitarian reasons has some historical grounding, although the practice has been scant and inconsistent. The use of force to uphold 'collective security' is essentially a twentieth-century innovation that focuses on the prevention of unilateral action. We now turn to the shared understandings that give rise to potential norms justifying exceptions to the prohibition on the use of force, first in general, and then in relation to specific exceptions. We then examine each of these exceptions in relation to both the criteria and the practice of legality.

3.1 Shared understandings concerning exceptions to the prohibition on the use of force

Since its modern emergence in the seventeenth century, international law on the use of force has been conceived to sit comfortably within the 'just war' tradition of western philosophy and theology. The tradition is rooted in an ancient Roman practice that required priests (*feliales*) to declare whether or not a wrong had been committed against Rome before the state could respond with military force. If a wrong was discerned, the perpetrator was given roughly a month to offer satisfaction to Rome's claim. If no satisfaction was forthcoming, the *feliales* would visit the Senate and certify the existence of a 'just cause' for war.[43] It is worth noting that these causes related to relatively objective assessments of fact, such as: (a) violation of Rome's borders; (b) attacks upon or insults to Roman ambassadors; (c) breaches of treaties made with Rome; and (d) a Roman ally supporting an enemy of Rome.[44]

The Roman tradition was altered significantly during the early Christian era when Augustine refined the concept of just war by focusing upon moral obligations.[45] Thomas Aquinas further developed the tradition through his formulation of three conditions to establish a 'just' war: war had to be waged under the authority of a sovereign, be undertaken for a just cause, and waged with right intention.[46] This last point is important, for it suggests that *why* one wages war matters to the justness of the cause. We will return to this issue, but suffice it to say for present purposes that assessing the true motivations of a state is notoriously difficult.[47]

It was Aquinas who pushed the doctrine of just war firmly into a moral framework, separated from *realpolitik*. Aside from his focus upon intention, Aquinas argued further that it was not injury alone that gave rise to a right to war; it was injury suffered through the fault of the perpetrator. War became a form of punishment for subjective guilt. Here we see the move from war as an instrument of inter-state relations, a policy tool designed to protect interests and restore order (or Augustine's 'peace'), to war as a means to punish aggressors.[48] Yet even with this move, it still appears that Aquinas was not concerned primarily with justice or the theoretical value of law. He continued to be interested primarily in

[43] G.I.A.D. Draper, 'Grotius' Place in the Development of Legal Ideas About War', in Hedley Bull, Benedict Kingsbury and Adam Roberts (eds.), *Hugo Grotius and International Relations* (Oxford University Press, 1992), p. 178.

[44] *Ibid.*, p. 179 (quoting Cicero).

[45] For an overview of the historical development of the just war tradition, and of its moral foundations, see James Turner Johnson, *Just War Tradition and the Restraint of War: A Moral and Historical Inquiry* (Princeton University Press, 1981).

[46] Thomas L. Pangle and Peter J. Ahrensdorf, *Justice Among Nations* (University Press of Kansas, 1999), p. 87.

[47] See below, text accompanying notes 138–40.

[48] St. Thomas Aquinas, *Summa Theologica*, Fathers of the English Dominican Province (trans.) (Westminster, Md: Christian Classics, 1982), Part II, Question 40. See also Sydney D. Bailey, *Prohibitions and Restraints in War* (Oxford University Press, 1972), p. 10. In an ironic twist, the version of just war as punishment was later adopted by the realist-positivist scholar Hans Kelsen. See Pangle and Ahrensdorf, above note 46, p. 108.

order: aggression breaches social order, giving rise to guilt, which must be punished through just war.

Grotius moved the framework into a form that continues to shape debates today.[49] He analogized the just cause in war to the lawful cause necessary to launch a civil lawsuit, thereby establishing clearly that a belligerent state had to meet a burden of proof on the balance of probability that its cause was just. This standard was meant to be demanding; Grotius said that the just cause had to be 'perfectly evident'.[50] Factors to be evaluated included whether the belligerent was acting in defence against an injury, actual or immediately threatened, not merely anticipated, or whether the war was for recovery of what was legally due. For Grotius, the punishment of a wrong was a just cause for war, so he reintegrated the interest-based and moral accounts of the earlier just war tradition.[51] Thus it would not be correct to see the Grotian version of just war as a presumption against war per se, but rather as 'a presumption against *injustice* focused on the need for responsible use of force in response to wrongdoing'.[52] Grotius further articulated what today might be called a precautionary principle: if the justness of a cause was in any way in doubt, war should not be pursued. Moreover, following Aquinas, Grotius argued that if success could not reasonably be anticipated, war could not be just, as the harms would outweigh the benefits.

Drawing upon Grotius's refinements to the ancient and medieval just war framework, but rooting the framework solidly in Augustine and Aquinas, Johnson suggests that one can identify seven criteria for a just war: (1) a just cause; (2) lawful authority within the state; (3) right intention; (4) a reasonable probability of success; (5) proportionality in the use of force; (6) war is the last resort; and (7) the goal of war must be peace.[53] Johnson argues that the first three criteria are original, derived from Aquinas, and should be given pre-eminence, with the final four criteria applying only when the first three are met.

[49] Brian Orend, *Michael Walzer on War and Justice* (Montreal and Kingston: McGill-Queen's University Press, 2000), p. 87 ('Hugo Grotius probably deserves credit for being the most comprehensive and formidable member of the [just war] tradition').

[50] Pangle and Ahrensdorf, above note 46, p. 173.

[51] Hugo Grotius, *The Rights of War and Peace (De Jure Belli ac Pacis)*, Richard Tuck (trans.) (Indianapolis, Ind: Liberty Fund, 2005), Book II, Chapter 20 (On Punishments).

[52] James Turner Johnson, *Morality and Contemporary Warfare* (New Haven: Yale University Press, 1999), p. 35 (commenting on the entire just war tradition, but in our view speaking most accurately about Grotius). But see Barrie Paskins and Michael Dockrill, *The Ethics of War* (Minneapolis: University of Minnesota Press, 1979), p. 194 (treating the entire just war tradition as a set of moral principles operating as prohibitions on war).

[53] Johnson, above note 52 at 27.

In his important work, *Just and Unjust Wars*, Michael Walzer connects the just war tradition to what he calls a 'legalist paradigm', most clearly set forth in the Charter of the United Nations. It is assumed that there exists an international society composed of nation states. This society is governed by a set of laws establishing the rights of its members, especially the rights of territorial integrity and political sovereignty. Any use of force by one state against the territorial integrity and political sovereignty of another is prima facie aggression, a criminal act.[54] Only specific exceptions to the prohibition on the use of force are allowed.

In the post-charter era, then, we see a continuity of moral and legal tradition supporting the idea that although there is a prima facie prohibition on the use of force, there are some circumstances where exceptions are justified. No state argues today that force is precluded in all events; nor would the proverbial person on the street. However, it is equally clear that the tradition and current law frame exceptions in specific and relatively narrow terms.

It is noticeable that scholars and publics in the developing world have played a relatively minor role in detailed debates over the use of force in international relations. As we have seen, they have participated in the broad shared understanding concerning the prohibition on the use of force, but have been relatively inactive in debates over exceptions to the rule. Does this mean that the exceptions are purely 'western'; that they are unsupported by a broad participation that lends legitimacy to international rules? We do not think so, for two distinct reasons.

First, and not surprisingly, the attention of many writers and activists from the developing world was long focused on a very precise exception to the non-use of force in international relations: the struggle against colonialism. This exception was highly contentious and complex. Was there a right to resist colonial power with force? If so, was that right vested only in domestic populations, a so-called right to revolution? In that case, inter-state conflict would not arise directly. Or could the right of populations to resist colonial power be aided by newly liberated states and their supporters? Could self-determination movements count on the military assistance of sympathetic state governments?[55] As it turns out, the 'terrorists' of the 1950s and 1960s (and 1970s and 1980s in South Africa) became 'freedom fighters' once they had succeeded, and the entire

[54] Walzer, above note 9, pp. 62–3.

[55] For a detailed discussion of state practice and academic debate see Heather A. Wilson, *International Law and the Use of Force by National Liberation Movements* (Oxford University Press, 1990), pp. 95–117.

controversy over state-aided self-determination movements largely dissipated in the 1980s and 1990s.[56] We can conclude, however, that developing world populations and scholars of law and politics did support the principle that exceptions exist to the primary rule of the non-use of force in international relations.

Second, we have seen that states from Africa, Asia and Latin America participated actively in the condemnation of the US- and UK-led 2003 invasion of Iraq, as did people on the street through large demonstrations. During the relevant debates in the United Nations a wide range of states from the developing world supported one of the two key exceptions to the prohibition on the use of force: collective security under Chapter VII of the UN Charter.[57] International law scholars from the developing world have also accepted the existence of both a charter and 'inherent' customary right to self-defence.[58] Many states in the developing world have also asserted a right to self-defence, and participated actively in the debates on the charter framework on the use of force in the lead-up to the 2005 World Summit.[59] We conclude

[56] See Gray, above note 28 at 63–4.

[57] In the post-invasion open debate in the Security Council, the Egyptian Ambassador argued that the 'international community must consider collective action to bring fighting in Iraq to an end and initiate political action to achieve a peaceful settlement to the crisis'. The Yemeni Ambassador lamented that the 'Council had been marginalized and paralysed in its role as the organ responsible for the maintenance of international peace and security'. In a particularly strong statement, the Indonesian Ambassador argued that 'the [US-led] aggression must be immediately stopped … The Member States' shared commitment to save succeeding generations from the scourge of war demanded that the United Nations not stand idle'. The Brazilian Ambassador said that 'his country profoundly deplored the initiation of military action in Iraq, especially since it had occurred without the express authorization of the Council'. UN Security Council, above note 24.

[58] See e.g. S.K. Verma, *An Introduction to Public International Law* (Delhi: Prentice Hall of India Private Ltd., 1998), p. 371 *et seq.*; Niaz A. Shah, 'Self-defence, Anticipatory Self-defence and Pre-emption: International Law Response to Terrorism' (2007) 12 *Journal of Conflict and Security Law* 95; and Muge Kinacioglu, 'A Response to Amos Guiora: Reassessing the Parameters of Use of Force in the Age of Terrorism: Pre-emptive Action and International Law' (2008) 13 *Journal of Conflict and Security Law* 1.

[59] See below, text accompanying notes 61–7. And see the views expressed by developing countries in *Review of the Secretary-General's Report 'In larger freedom: towards development, security and human rights for all'*, 6–8 April 2005, Verbatim Records A/59/PV.85, A/59/PV.86, A/59/PV.87, A/59/PV.88, A/59/PV.89, and A/59/PV.90, at www.un.org/ga/59/hl60_plenarymeeting.html#debates (on the need for a restrictive interpretation of Article 51 and the existence of a right to anticipatory or pre-emptive action); and see *Comments of the Non-Aligned Movement on the Observations and Recommendations Contained in the Report of the High-level Panel on Threats, Challenges and Change*, 28 February 2005, paras. 23–4, at www.un.int/malaysia/NAM/Positionpaper280205.doc.

that participation in the evolution of the lawful exceptions to the prohibition on the use of force has been widespread, engaging a wide range of actors from around the globe. Limited exceptions to the prohibition on the use of force are supported by shared understandings in international society. We now move on to consider the precise exceptions to the prohibition on the use of force in turn, looking first at underlying shared understandings, and then focusing upon the criteria of legality and practice of legality that either buttress or undermine the exceptions.

3.2 Self-defence

3.2.1 Shared understandings

For hundreds of years, it has been widely accepted that a political entity can use force to repulse an armed attack. For example, for all practical purposes the Grotian view of legitimate recourse to force, even if expressed in a variety of 'just causes', was that war could only be lawfully waged in self-defence.[60] The shared understanding supporting the concept of self-defence in international law may have developed in western doctrine, but it has been widely accepted around the globe. Self-defence has been invoked time and again by developing states around the world. In 1979, China justified its invasion of Vietnam on the grounds of self-defence, arguing that the Vietnamese had engaged in cross-border raids and were pursuing a policy of 'hegemony' in South-east Asia.[61] Kuwait claimed self-defence in 1990, after the invasion by Iraq, a claim later extended to 'collective self-defence' by the UN Security Council.[62] In 1997, Tanzania asserted that its shelling of the territory of neighbouring Burundi had been provoked by the Burundian military, and that Tanzania was simply asserting its inherent right to self-defence.[63] Ethiopia's President invoked a right of self-defence against the 'warmongering' regime in Eritrea in 2000.[64] Colombia

60 Grotius, above note 51, Chapter 1, Book II, xvi.

61 See e.g. Xiaoming Zhang, 'China's 1979 War with Vietnam: A Reassessment' (2005) 184 *The China Quarterly* 851.

62 Kuwait's individual right to self-defence was transformed into a 'collective right' of Kuwait and its allies, operating through the United Nations by Resolution 661 (affirming 'the inherent right of individual or collective self-defence, in response to the armed attack by Iraq against Kuwait'). See United Nations Security Council Resolution 661, 6 August 1990, UN Doc. S/RES/0661, at www.un.org/Docs/scres/1990/scres90.htm.

63 'Tanzania Refutes Cross-Border Shelling', *Tanzania News Online*, 22 November 1997.

64 See BBC News Service, *Ethiopian President Hails Victories*, 28 May 2000, at http://news.bbc.co.uk/1/hi/world/monitoring/media_reports/767936.stm. An international claims

sent an armed force into the territory of Ecuador in March 2008 to attack guerrillas of the FARC movement, claiming that Ecuadorean harbouring of the guerrillas gave Colombia the right to exercise self-defence.[65] Later in 2008, Cambodia and Thailand each vowed to engage in 'self-defence' if the other side resorted to force in a border dispute involving an ancient temple,[66] already the subject of an ICJ ruling in 1962.[67]

However, when one examines the scope of the right to defend against a use of force, the precise parameters of the shared understandings are far more difficult to trace. Indeed, it is highly unlikely that in any field of legal regulation a precise shared understanding exists in relation to specific rule formulations. Instead, the shared understanding is likely to be a general sense of what is reasonable and permissible, given particular circumstances. Self-defence is no exception. Some international lawyers argue, for example, that the express terms of Article 51 of the UN Charter strictly limit self-defence to responses to 'armed attacks'.[68] It is true that whenever there is an actual armed attack, there is no question of the underlying shared understanding giving rise to a right to take necessary and proportional measures of defence.

Complexity arises when one begins to consider whether or not the right to repel can be extended to a right to prevent the armed attack.[69] In other words, is there a shared understanding allowing for a norm of 'anticipatory' self-defence? We suggest that there is indeed such a shared understanding, but it is not nearly as powerful as the understanding in relation to the right to respond to an existing armed attack. Indeed, this

commission later supported the view that Eritrea had waged a war of aggression and that Ethiopia could exercise its inherent right to self-defence. See BBC News Service, *Eritrea Broke Law in Border War*, 21 December 2005, at http://news.bbc.co.uk/1/hi/world/africa/4548754.stm.

65 'Colombia and its neighbours: on the warpath', *The Economist*, 8 March 2008 at 53.

66 See e.g. 'Thailand will act in self-defence: Cambodia told', *The Nation* (Thailand), 5 November 2008.

67 *Case Concerning The Temple of Preah Vihear (Cambodia* v. *Thailand)*, Judgment, I.C.J. Reports 1962, p. 6, at www.icj-cij.org/docket/files/45/4871.pdf.

68 See e.g. Ian Brownlie, *International Law and the Use of Force by States* (Oxford: Clarendon Press, 1963), p. 265; *Principles of Public International Law*, 6th edn, (Oxford University Press, 2003), p. 702; and Michael Byers, 'Preemptive Self-Defense: Hegemony, Equality and Strategies of Legal Change' (2003) 11 *Journal of Political Philosophy* 171 at 180.

69 See *Report of the High-level Panel on Threats, Challenges and Change, A More Secure World: Our Shared Responsibility*, 2 December 2004, UN. Doc. A/59/565, paras. 188–92, at www.un.org/secureworld/report.pdf (concluding that, alongside Article 51, there existed a right to anticipatory self-defence against imminent attacks, but no right to use force to prevent emerging threats). And see *Comments of the Non-Aligned Movement*, above note 59.

is an area where there may indeed be a division of opinion, in particular as between western and developing world states. For almost 200 years, customary law, rooted in the well-known *Caroline* incident, has arguably permitted anticipatory action necessary to forestall an imminent attack, as long as it is proportional to the threat.[70] The challenge is to agree upon the scope of 'imminence', or on when it is that an 'armed attack' can be said to be underway, for those who prefer to accommodate anticipatory action within Article 51.[71] Some instances will be relatively uncontroversial, for example, when missiles have already been launched, but have not yet struck.[72] Other cases might involve the placement of missiles that might be used for an attack, in a context of high political tension; the Cuban missile crisis comes to mind immediately.[73] In yet other circumstances, the development of uranium enrichment facilities and missile delivery capacity might be viewed as evidence of an intention to attack imminently.[74] Finally, knowledge of a possible attack may come from the clandestine work of security services, but this work may be shoddy. The weapons of mass destruction (WMD) programme asserted by the US government to have existed in Iraq in 2003 is an example of this form of supposedly imminent threat.[75]

[70] J.B. Moore, '*The Caroline* (1837)' (1906) 2 *A Digest of International Law* 409; and see Derek W. Bowett, *Self Defense in International Law* (Manchester University Press, 1957), pp. 188–9. See also *Report of the High-level Panel*, above note 69 at para. 188; and Shah, above note 58 at 101. But see e.g. Gray, above note 28, pp. 160–5 (arguing that, before 9/11, states usually attempted to bring their actions within Article 51 by claiming the existence of an armed attack, rather than rely explicitly on a customary right to anticipatory self-defence).

[71] See Mary Ellen O'Connell, 'The Myth of Preemptive Self-Defence', *American Society of International Law Task Force Papers* (August 2002), p. 9, at www.asil.org/taskforce/oconnell.pdf (arguing that the *Caroline* 'formula represents common sense and fits the letter and the spirit of the Charter when used to determine when an armed attack has begun'). See also *In Larger Freedom: Towards development, security and human rights for all*, Report by the Secretary-General, UN Doc. A/59.2005, 21 March 2005, para. 124, at www.un.org/largerfreedom/contents.htm.

[72] For example, the British decision to send a task force to the Falklands on the day of the Argentine invasion. See Judith Gardam, *Necessity, Proportionality and Use of Force by States* (Cambridge University Press, 2004), p. 151.

[73] See Mary Ellen O'Connell and Maria Alevras-Chen, 'The Ban on the Bomb – and Bombing: Iran, the U.S., and the International Law of Self-Defence' (2007) 57 *Syracuse Law Review* 497 at 504–5 (commenting on the Cuban Missile Crisis).

[74] For a detailed discussion of the Iranian nuclear programme and the arguments surrounding the legality of the preventive use of force against Iran, see O'Connell and Alevras-Chen, *ibid.*

[75] United Nations News Centre, *Powell presents US case to Security Council of Iraq's failure to disarm*, 5 February 2003, at www.un.org/apps/news/storyAr.asp?NewsID=6079&Cr=iraq&Cr1=inspect (quoting Powell as asserting: 'My colleagues, every statement I

Obviously, the further one moves from an actual attack to a threat that has not yet materialized, or even solidified,[76] the less likely it is that a widespread consensus exists around the norm.[77] That is why many developing states challenge the notion of anticipatory self-defence. They fear that the concept will be hard to limit, and that they will be the likely objects of anticipatory action. In addition, as we will see shortly, an attenuated conception of 'imminence' also challenges legality. We believe that these understandable objections, and potential failures of legality, can be addressed through the criteria that limit the invocation of anticipatory self-defence.

Two other issues arise in assessing any shared understanding around the scope of self-defence. First, there is some debate over the 'intensity' of an attack required to justify lawful response. Does a small border incursion, now completed, constitute an attack that would give rise to the use of force in self-defence, or would this be an unlawful 'reprisal'?

While some observers maintain that any armed action constitutes an 'armed attack' in the sense of Article 51,[78] the dominant opinion seems to be that some intensity is required. ICJ stressed the need to 'distinguish

make today is backed up by sources, solid sources. These are not assertions. What we're giving you are facts and conclusions based on solid intelligence'). A year later, Powell acknowledged that the evidence he presented to the Council may have been wrong – see BBC News Service, *Powell admits Iraq evidence mistake*, 3 April 2004, at http://news.bbc.co.uk/2/hi/middle_East/3596033.stm. See also U.S. Senate Select Committee on Intelligence, *Report on the U.S. Intelligence Community's Prewar Intelligence*, July 2004, at www.globalsecurity.org/intell/library/congress/2004_rpt/iraq-wmd-intell_toc.htm (finding that the Bush administration's threat assessment was either overstated or unsupported by intelligence). In turn, deliberate 'spinning' of intelligence appears to have resulted in the British government's 'claims that Saddam Hussein could mount a missile strike on his neighbours within 45 minutes of ordering an attack'. See e.g. Nigel Morris 'Secret emails show Iraq dossier *was* "sexed up": Intelligence chiefs criticised "iffy drafting" of key document', *The Independent*, 13 March 2009.

[76] Introducing the 2002 National Security Strategy of the United States, President Bush asserted boldly – and controversially: 'As a matter of common sense and self-defense, America will act against such emerging threats before they are fully formed.' See Security Strategy, above note 4, Introduction.

[77] See *Review*, above note 59.

[78] See Gardam, above note 72, p. 144; Elizabeth Wilmshurst, 'The Chatham House Principles of International Law on the Use of Force in Self-Defence' (2006) 55 *International and Comparative Law Quarterly* 963 at 966 (an 'armed attack means any use of armed force, and does not need to cross some threshold of intensity'); and Dominic Raab, '"Armed Attack" After the *Oil Platforms* Case' (2004) 17 *Leiden Journal of International Law* 719 at 725 (pointing to 'substantial academic support for the view that "gravity" is irrelevant to the question of whether there has been an armed attack by regular military forces').

the most grave forms of the use of force (those constituting an armed attack) from other less grave forms' in the 1986 *Nicaragua* case,[79] a position it has since reiterated in the 2003 *Oil Platforms* case.[80] In a similar vein, the Ethiopia–Eritrea Claims Commission concluded in 2005 that '[l]ocalized border encounters between small infantry units, even those involving loss of life, do not constitute an armed attack for the purposes of the Charter'.[81] One legal implication of this approach is that the victim of an illegal use of force that does not rise to the level of an armed attack is limited to responding by non-forcible countermeasures. This limitation, which follows from the general understanding that armed reprisals are no longer permitted by international law,[82] has attracted the criticism that the gravity requirement condemns states to having to tolerate low-level violence.[83]

Although, in practice, it is often hard to construe reactions to completed, smaller scale attacks as anything but retaliatory,[84] states have preferred to justify military responses as self-defence. Frequently, the argument is that several smaller attacks or cross-border incursions, even if none amounts to an armed attack individually, can accumulate to such an extent that, taken together, they do constitute an armed attack that justifies forcible self-defence measures. This line of argument has been used on numerous occasions by the United States and Israel, notably to justify 'surgical strikes' or other limited armed responses to state-sponsored terrorist attacks.[85]

This reasoning presupposes the lawfulness of some forms of anticipatory self-defense, a question to which we return below. Since the attacks to

[79] *Nicaragua*, above note 38, para. 191. For a detailed discussion of the reactions to the Court's approach, see Gray, above note 28 at 145–51.

[80] See *Oil Platforms (Islamic Republic of Iran* v. *United States of America)*, Judgment, I.C.J. Reports 2003, para. 51, at www.icj-cij.org/docket/files/90/9715.pdf.

[81] Eritrea Ethiopia Claims Commission, Partial Award – Jus Ad Bellum, Ethiopia's Claims 1–8, 19 December 2005, para. 11, repr. (May 2006) 45 I.L.M. 430.

[82] See also the approach of the International Law Commission (ILC), *Report of the International Law Commission on the work of its fifty-third session* (Draft Articles on Responsibility of States for Internationally Wrongful Acts), UN General Assembly Official Records, 56th Session, Supplement no. 10, UN Doc. A/56/10, p. 128, at www.untreaty.un.org/ilc/reports/2001/2001report.htm (explaining that '[t]he term "countermeasures" covers that part of the subject of reprisals not associated with armed conflict').

[83] See Tarcisio Gazzini, *The Changing Rules on the Use of Force in International Law* (Manchester University Press, 2005), p. 138.

[84] See Gray, above note 28, pp. 196–7.

[85] *Ibid.*; and see Derek Bowett, 'Reprisals Involving Recourse to Armed Force' (1972) 66 *American Journal of International Law* 1 at 6.

which the measures are responding are by definition complete, the justification for a military response turns on the prevention of further attacks. The claim is that several smaller attacks are in fact an ongoing attack, and that self-defence is available to prevent a continuation through further attacks. This argument is meant to distinguish the response action from unlawful armed reprisals. In any event, when self-defence is invoked, the response must be both necessary and proportional, so we do not believe that fundamental conceptual questions are engaged by the issues surrounding the 'intensity' of an attack, notwithstanding the lingering debate.[86]

The second issue, whether an attack by non-state actors such as insurgent groups or terrorists can constitute an 'armed attack' giving rise to lawful self-defence, is far more troubling. It is fair to suggest that the charter regime is predicated upon the assumption of direct action by states.[87] However, the language of the charter does not refer to state action specifically: 'nothing in the present Charter shall impair the inherent right of individual or collective self-defence if an armed attack occurs against a member of the United Nations …'.[88] It is instructive to note that if the right is inherent, it pre-dates the charter, and customary law becomes relevant. In the *Caroline* case, the initial 'armed attack' was perpetrated by non-state actors, Fenian raiders who used British territory (in Upper Canada) to attack a US vessel, burning it and sending it over Niagara Falls.[89] It is therefore plausible to argue that the charter, when read with pre-existing custom, allows for the initial attack, justifying self-defence, to be carried out by non-state actors.[90]

While this proposition was controversial before the terrorist attacks of September 2001, a new shared understanding concerning non-state actor attacks appears to have developed since. It is important to bear in mind,

[86] See also Gazzini, above note 83, p. 138 (observing that '[t]he limits of immediacy, proportionality and necessity would provide adequate safeguards against abuses').

[87] See e.g. Gazzini, *ibid.*, p. 139; and Gray, above note 28, p. 199.

[88] Charter of the United Nations, San Francisco, 26 June 1945, in force 24 October 1945, 1 UNTS 16, Art. 51. And see e.g. Wedgwood, above note 4 at 58 (arguing that 'the Charter's language does not link the right to self-defense to the particular legal personality of the attacker').

[89] See Moore, above note 70. See also e.g. Sean Murphy, 'Terrorism and the Concept of "Armed Attack" in Article 51 of the U.N. Charter' (2002) 43 *Harvard International Law Journal* 41 at 50; and Christopher Greenwood, 'War, Terrorism, and International Law' (2003) 56 *Current Legal Problems* 505 at 517.

[90] See e.g. Nico Schrijver, 'Responding to International Terrorism: Moving the Frontiers of International Law for "Enduring Freedom"?' (2001) 48 *Netherlands International Law Review* 271 at 284–5.

however, that in most cases the response in asserted self-defence actually takes place in the territory of another state, so the question of imputability arises no matter the scope of the notion of 'armed attack' in Article 51.

Under what circumstances can one consider the actions of non-state groups to be undertaken on behalf of a state? This was how the ICJ in the *Nicaragua* case posed the question, concluding that a strict direction and control test had to be applied in relation to the specific armed operation at issue.[91] In its more recent judgments, the Court has avoided explicit pronouncements on the issue, but it appears to maintain that Article 51 presupposes inter-state use of force and so requires direct involvement of a state in an attack carried out by non-state actors.[92] In the 2004 Advisory Opinion in the *Wall* case, the Court notes that Article 51 recognizes 'an inherent right of self-defense in case of armed attack by one state against another state', and finds Article 51 to be of 'no relevance' in the case.[93] However, it appears that the Court reached this conclusion not because the attacks in question emanated from a non-state entity, but because they emanated from territory under Israel's control (rather than outside its borders).[94] In turn, in its 2005 decision in *Congo* v. *Uganda*, the ICJ did not consider it necessary to decide whether international law had evolved to encompass a right of self-defence against attacks by non-state actors.[95] The ruling nonetheless suggests that the Court holds fast to the requirement of direct state involvement.[96] The Court observes that 'the legal and

[91] *Nicaragua*, above note 38, para. 195.

[92] For a discussion, see Christine Gray, 'The Bush Doctrine Revisited: The 2006 National Security Strategy of the USA' (2006) 5 *Chinese Journal of International Law* 555 at 570–2.

[93] *Legal Consequences of the Construction of a Wall in the Occupied Palestinian Territory*, Advisory Opinion, I.C.J. Reports 2004, para. 139, at www.icj-cij.org/docket/files/131/1671.pdf. But see the Declaration of Judge Buergenthal, para. 6, at www.icj-cij.org/docket/files/131/1687.pdf. See also the Separate Opinion of Judge Higgins, para. 33, at www.icj-cij.org/docket/files/131/1681.pdf; and the Separate Opinion of Judge Kooijmans, para. 35, at www.icj-cij.org/docket/files/131/1683.pdf.

[94] *Legal Consequences*, *ibid.*, para. 139 (observing that 'the threat ... originates within, not outside, the territory [of Israel]').

[95] *Case Concerning Armed Activities on the Territory of the Congo* (*Democratic Republic of Congo* v. *Uganda*), Judgment, I.C.J. Reports 2005, para. 147, at www.icj-cij.org/docket/files/116/10455.pdf ('the legal and factual circumstances for the exercise of a right of self-defense by Uganda against the DRC were not present'). However, as in the *Wall* case, some of the judges disagreed with the Court's holding on this issue. See Separate Opinion by Judge Kooijmans, paras. 26 and 28, at www.icj-cij.org/docket/files/116/10463.pdf; and Separate Opinion of Judge Simma, para.12, at www.icj-cij.org/docket/files/116/10467.pdf.

[96] Note also that in *Bosnia* v. *Serbia*, above note 34, paras. 396–407, the ICJ confirmed that the 'effective control test' remained the test for questions of state responsibility. It thereby rejected, for these purposes, the broader 'overall control' test that had been

factual circumstances for the exercise of a right of self-defence by Uganda against the DRC were not present', but a closer look reveals that the relevant circumstances pertained to the absence of a link between the irregular forces and Congo.[97]

Meanwhile, international practice seems to have evolved both to allow self-defence against armed attacks by non-state forces, and to loosen the required link between such forces and a state in which armed defence measures are undertaken.[98] The view appears to be gaining ground that lesser forms of involvement may put a state in the cross-hairs of a military response, so long as it can be justified as a necessary and proportional exercise of the right to self-defence.[99] It has been suggested that a crucial factor in such circumstances will be whether the defending state is acting against the target state, or merely within its territory.[100]

For now, in relation to evolving shared understandings, suffice it to note that, immediately after the attack of 11 September 2001, the Security Council unanimously adopted Resolutions 1368 and 1373, both of which point to an acceptance of a right to use force in self-defence against the terrorists.[101] At the time of the invasion of Afghanistan in 2001, there was no evidence of direction and control of the September 11 terrorists by the Taliban government of Afghanistan, yet there was almost no international outcry against the invasion.[102] On 12 September, the North

articulated by the ICTY in *Prosecutor* v. *Dusko Tadic (Appeal Judgement)*, IT-94-1-A, International Criminal Tribunal for the former Yugoslavia, 15 July 1999, para. 114, at www.unhcr.org/refworld/docid/40277f504.html.

97 See Yaël Ronen, 'Israel, Hizbollah, and the Second Lebanon War', Research Paper No. 10–08 (September 2008), Hebrew University of Jerusalem Faculty of Law, at note 91.

98 See Steven R. Ratner '*Jus ad Bellum* and *Jus in Bello* After September 11' (2002) 96 *American Journal of International Law* 905 at 908–10; Stephanie A. Barbour and Joe A. Salzman, '"The Tangled Web": The Right of Self-Defense Against Non-State Actors in the *Armed Activities* Case' (2008) 40 *Journal of International Law and Politics* 53 at 65; and G. Travalio and J. Altenburg, 'State Responsibility for Sponsorship of Terrorist and Insurgent Groups: Terrorism, State Responsibility and the Use of Military Force' (2003) 4 *Chicago Journal of International Law* 97 at 102–11.

99 See e.g. André Nollkaemper, 'Attribution of Forcible Acts to States: Connections Between the Law on the Use of Force and the Law of State Responsibility', in N. Blokker and N. Schrijver (eds.), *The Security Council and the Use of Force: Theory and Reality – A Need for Change?* (Leiden: Martinus Nijhoff Publishers, 2005), p. 136; and Wilmshurst, above note 78 at 970.

100 See Kimberley N. Trapp, 'Back to Basics: Necessity, Proportionality, and the Right to Self-Defence Against Non-State Terrorist Actors' (2007) 56 *International and Comparative Law Quarterly* 141. And see Gray, above note 28, p. 136.

101 For a discussion, see Gray, *ibid.*, pp. 198–9.

102 See Gazzini, above note 83, p. 77 (discussing the overwhelmingly positive international reaction). For a detailed evaluation of state reactions and academic commentary, see Tal

Atlantic Council determined that the September 11 attacks 'were directed from abroad against the United States', giving rise to the first application of the mutual assistance provision, Article 5, of the Washington Treaty.[103] The NATO Secretary-General, Lord Robertson, asserted that Al Qaeda was 'protected' by the Taliban.[104] In their respective letters to the Security Council, the United States and the United Kingdom justified the pending invasion of Afghanistan by invoking the right of self-defence against the ongoing threat emanating from Afghan territory.[105] In the US letter, the Taliban was accused of allowing 'the parts of Afghanistan that it controls to be used by ... Al Qaeda ... as a base of operations'.[106]

The circumstances surrounding the intervention in Afghanistan may be contrasted with those that led to Turkish strikes against Kurdish rebels based in Northern Iraq. Kurdish rebels have launched attacks against Turkish forces on numerous occasions, and Turkey has in the past responded with cross-border military action.[107] While the Taliban regime did have some links to Al Qaeda, there were no links between the Iraqi government and the Kurdish rebels. It appears, rather, that the Iraqi government was unable or unwilling to control the activities of the rebels in the northern part of its territory. Arguably, it is in part for this reason that the Turkish government has never explicitly justified its cross-border strikes as self-defence.[108] Turkey maintained this stance even after the developments prompted by the September 11 attacks, suggesting that it did not consider that its right to self-defence extended to incursions into Iraqi territory.[109] At the time of Turkey's 2007–2008 offensive against the

Becker, *Terrorism and the State: Rethinking the Rules of State Responsibility* (Oxford: Hart Publishing, 2006), pp. 211–38 (suggesting a broader approach has gained acceptance). But see also Nollkaemper, above note 99, pp. 168–71 (questioning that conclusion).

103 Statement by the North Atlantic Council, 12 September 2001, at www.nato.int/docu/pr/2001/p01-124e.htm.

104 Statement by NATO Secretary-General, Lord Robertson, 2 October 2001, at www.nato.int/docu/speech/2001/s011002a.htm.

105 U.S. Letter to the President of the U.N. Security Council (7 October 2001), UN Doc. S/2001/946; and UK Letter to the President of the U.N. Security Council (7 October 2001), UN Doc. S/2001/947.

106 U.S. Letter, above note 15.

107 See Molly Moore, 'Turkey Authorizes Iraq Incursion', *The Washington Post*, 18 October 2007.

108 See Gazzini, above note 83, pp. 206–10 (suggesting that Turkey instead relied upon arguments of necessity).

109 Curiously, however, US officials did suggest that Turkey was acting in self-defence. See Stephen Farrell, 'Turkey Says its Raids in Iraq Killed 150 Rebels', *The New York Times*, 26 December 2007.

rebels, an added difficulty stemmed from the fact that there was no prior incursion by Kurdish rebels; indeed it has been reported that the mission was explicitly 'pre-emptive'. What is more, the use of force was much more significant than that of the rebels, who have far less firepower.[110]

Yet another example is furnished by the Israeli claims that its invasion of Lebanon in 2006 and its incursion into Gaza in 2009 were justified as self-defence, as means of protecting Israeli citizens primarily against rocket attacks, but also against terrorists.[111] These claims were supported by some states,[112] notwithstanding the fact that most states did not consider Lebanon to be responsible for the attacks. However, in each case, many of the same states ultimately condemned the Israeli actions as disproportionate.[113]

[110] See BBC News Service, *Turkish troops enter north Iraq*, 22 February 2008, at http://news.bbc.co.uk/2/hi/europe/7258323.stm ('Turkish broadcaster NTV reported that 10,000 soldiers had crossed the border on Thursday, a Turkish military source also confirmed for Reuters news agency that two brigades had been deployed'); 'After 8 Days, Turkey Pulls Its Troops Out of Iraq', *The New York Times*, 1 March 2008; and CNN News Service, *Turkey Launches Major Iraq Incursion*, 23 February 2008, at www.cnn.com/2008/WORLD/meast/02/22/turkey.iraq.

[111] On the 2006 Lebanon campaign, see Ronen, above note 97 at 23. On the 2009 Gaza incursion, see Letter of the Government of Israel to the UN Security Council (6 January 2009), UN Doc. S/2009/6, at www.securitycouncilreport.org/atf/cf/%7B65BFCF9B-6-D27–4E9C-8CD3-CF6E4FF96FF9%7D/Gaza%20S20096.pdf.

[112] On the 2006 Lebanon campaign, see discussion of international responses in Ronen, above note 97 at 23–5 and 29; and see ABC News Online, *Israel acting in self-defence, says Howard*, 16 July 2006, at www.abc.net.au/news/newsitems/200607/s1687707.htm ('Prime Minister John Howard has blamed Hezbollah for starting the current crisis between Lebanon and Israel, saying the group provoked the Jewish state into "self-defence" by going across the border and seizing soldiers'). On the Gaza campaign, see Spiegel Online, *Merkel Blasts Hamas for Middle East Violence*, 29 December 2008, at www.spiegel.de/international/world/0,1518,598724,00.html; and 'Australia Labour Party, Libs back Israel self-defence right', *Sydney Morning Herald*, 5 January 2009.

[113] See e.g. on Lebanon, the critique of President Chirac that the Israeli use of force was 'completely disproportionate', 'Diplomatic timeline: Lebanon and Israel, July 2006', *The Guardian*, 2 August 2006; and see Ronen, above note 97, at note 169 (detailing the critical responses of numerous states). On Gaza, see 'Israel's bombardment of Gaza is not self-defence – it's a war crime', *The Times*, 11 January 2009, Letters to the Editor – international law experts from around the world; Statement of Panama, January 16 at the Tenth Emergency Special Session of the General Assembly, UN Doc. GA/10809/Rev. 1, at www.un.org/News/Press/docs/2009/ga10809.doc.htm ('Panama had also condemned the attacks of Hamas and supported Israel's right to defend itself. But, that right must be applied with proportionality'); Polish Ministry of Foreign Affairs, Statement of 29 December 2008, at www.msz.gov.pl/Statement,by,the,Ministry,of,Foreign,Affairs,regarding,the,situation,in,the,Middle,East,24160.html ('We condemn rocket attacks against Israel by Hamas. We also find no justification for the scale of military operation taken in response by the Israeli side'); CBC News Service, *International community calls for end*

It would seem, therefore, that the shared understandings of when actions by a non-state actor can justify the invocation of self-defence are shifting. The new understanding has not yet fully emerged. But recent practice suggests that something more than mere presence of the attackers in another state's territory is required to justify defence measures in or even against that state. We return to this issue in our discussion of the criteria of legality.

Concerning the right to self-defence more broadly speaking, we can conclude that the attacks of 11 September initially generated a great deal of sympathy for the United States, and gave rise to arguments that new threats required new legal approaches. We suggest below that this normative opening was exploited in dangerous ways by the United States and some allies, and that this may have resulted in a reassertion of older shared understandings that are more restrictive in allowing for self-defence.[114]

3.2.2 Criteria of legality and the practice of legality

In this section, we will focus our analysis upon the criteria of legality that must be met to support the creation of international law as to exceptions on the prohibition of the use of force. In looking at specific exceptions we will also assess the practice of international actors in relation to the rules on self-defence to evaluate whether or not purported rules are being buttressed or destroyed.

If one considers the narrowest understanding of lawful self-defence, that it can only be invoked within the charter in response to a pre-existing armed attack, no significant issues arise with the criteria of legality. However, for a long time commentators have questioned the reasonableness of the narrow view. In 1957, in his formative treatise on self-defence, Sir Derek Bowett argued: 'No state can be expected to await an initial attack, which in the present state of armaments, may well destroy the state's capacity for further resistance and so jeopardize its very existence.'[115] Within

to violence in Middle East, 27 December 2008, at www.cbc.ca/world/story/2008/12/27/mideast-international.html (Israel acting within its 'clear right to defend itself' – Canadian Foreign Affairs Minister, Lawrence Cannon); 'Brown condemns Israeli attack as "indefensible"', *The Independent*, 15 January 2009, at www.independent.co.uk/news/world/middle-east/brown-condemns-israeli-attack-as-indefensible-1379873.html; and Reuters, *Bush puts onus on Hamas for any Gaza truce*, 5 January 2009, at www.uk.reuters.com/article/latestCrisis/idUKN05508075.

114 See below, text accompanying notes 121–37 (discussing the reactions to US attempts to assert a right to preventive self-defence).

115 Bowett, above note 70, pp. 191–2. See also Kinacioglu, above note 58 at 6 (commenting on the situation after 11 September 2001).

theories of the state and in domestic constitutional law it is generally accepted that one of the primary responsibilities of a government is to provide security for the population. It seems counter-intuitive at the very least to insist that a state sit idly by, waiting for the attack that might kill thousands, or even annihilate a population.[116]

As soon as one extends the concept of self-defence beyond the strict charter framework into anticipatory self-defence, however, significant problems can arise with regard to the criteria of legality. While the narrow charter view has the virtue of clarity and predictability, it can sometimes demand of states the politically and ethically impossible. An expanded view including anticipatory self-defence may in some cases be more reasonable, but can lead to a sacrifice of clarity and predictability if the extension is carried too far. Generality may be affected as well.

The customary law of self-defence recognized the risk. Although it arguably extended the margin of appreciation surrounding the right to self-defence, it never allowed for entirely self-serving claims that destroy clarity and predictability. Anticipatory self-defence is constrained by an imminence requirement and must be assessed against the criteria of necessity and proportionality.

These requirements are contextual and can therefore accommodate 'new threats'. Thus, in an era of global terrorist networks and proliferation of weapons of mass destruction, it is as apposite to ask whether a state has 'no choice of means and no moment for deliberation' in the face of an imminent attack as it was when the phrase was coined in the context of the *Caroline* case in 1837.[117] The same is true for the concepts of necessity and proportionality. In combination, these requirements impose external measures of evaluation, and enhance clarity and predictability.[118]

This approach to conditioning the right to self-defence accords with the synthesis of the classical just war tradition offered by Grotius, who argued

[116] See e.g. Richard B. Miller, 'Justifications of the Iraq War Examined' (2008) 22 *Ethics and International Affairs* 43 at 49 (discussing moral justifications for preventive use of force).

[117] Moore, above note 70. For a thoughtful discussion of the risks of over-extending the doctrine of anticipatory self-defence and the attendant concept of imminence, see U.K. House of Commons – Foreign Affairs Committee, *Foreign Policy Aspects of the War Against Terrorism*, Seventh Report of Session 2003–04, Volume I, at 137–41. See also Philippe Sands, 'International Law and the Use of Force', in U.K. House of Commons – Foreign Affairs Committee, *Foreign Policy Aspects of the War Against Terrorism*, Seventh Report of Session 2003–04, Volume II (Oral and Written Evidence), Ev. 91, at 92–3.

[118] But see below, text accompanying notes 163–70 (discussing difficulties that can nonetheless arise in debates over the parameters of necessity and proportionality).

that the theory of just war could not be invoked to 'guarantee' security. The human condition is such that threat is a reality of existence,[119] and:

> [f]ear with respect to a neighbouring power is not sufficient cause. For in order that a self-defence may be lawful it must be necessary; and it is not necessary unless we are certain, not only regarding the power of our neighbour, but also regarding his intention; the degree of certainty required is that which is accepted in morals.[120]

These observations also connect to the criterion of generality, requiring that a rule not address only one case, but apply in principle to all. The criterion is fully met by the charter version of self-defence, and the limited customary law extension to anticipatory self-defence. The rules can be invoked by all states, and the conditions of imminence, necessity and proportionality are generally applicable. By contrast, the purported extension of the concept of self-defence to broadly conceived 'pre-emption' that the United States advanced in its 2002 National Security Strategy statement,[121] fails the test of generality because the entire structure of the strategy is predicated upon the very thing against which Grotius cautioned: unilateral assessments as to when pre-emption is justified to protect national security interests. Indeed, the strategy document asserts that '[t]he United States has long maintained the option of preemptive actions to counter a sufficient threat to our national security'.[122]

A 'rule' that has no parameters, and that is subject to entirely unilateral assessment of what amounts to a 'sufficient threat' is simply a self-constructed permission to act. It is intriguing, therefore, that President Bush asserted that 'America will never seek a permission slip to defend

[119] See Grotius, above note 51.

[120] *Ibid.*, Chapter 22, Book II, v. These observations still resonate in today's world. Consider the strikingly similar statements in the 2004 *Report of the High-level Panel on Threats, Challenges and Change*, above note 69, paras. 188 and 191:

> 188. (…) The problem arises where the threat in question is not imminent but still claimed to be real: for example the acquisition, with allegedly hostile intent, of nuclear weapons-making capability.
>
> 191 (…) in a world full of perceived potential threats, the risk to the global order … is simply too great for the legality of unilateral preventive action … Allowing one to act is to allow all.

[121] See Security Strategy, above note 4 at 15. See also The National Security Strategy of the United States of America (March 2006), at 18 (reasserting the 'inherent right' to 'pre-empt emerging threats' in self-defence) and 23 (stating that the 'place of pre-emption in our national security strategy remains the same'), at http://georgewbush-whitehouse.archives.gov/nsc/nss/2006/.

[122] Security Strategy, above note 4 at 15.

the security of our country.'[123] It does not need one, on this view, because America gives itself *carte blanche* permission in advance. But there can be no doubt that the same permission was not accorded to other states by the US administration: to do so would be to recognize the end of all constraint of law.[124] So the proposed rule on pre-emption cannot be general without undermining all law on the use of force; this the United States has no desire to do.[125]

As Michael Walzer suggests, the characterization of another state as a 'threat' is essentially a moral claim.[126] If the argument of the US *National Security Strategy* were to be accepted by international society, each state would be able to attack another whenever a vaguely plausible claim could be made that the defending state constituted a danger.[127] The morally and legally restrictive concept of anticipatory self-defence against imminent attacks risks becoming prevention of vaguely emerging threats. The inevitable evolution of this idea is illustrated by North Korea's claim that its 2006 tests of long-range ballistic missiles were designed to enhance its self-defence capabilities, and in Japan's statements about possible pre-emptive action against North Korean missile bases.[128] The potential pattern is also reflected in the Russian *National Security Concept*, which was refined and adapted in 2000 and reflects the tension in the relations between Russia and western states surrounding NATO's use of force against Yugoslavia. The document states that one of the major sources of

[123] President George W. Bush, *State of the Union Address 2004*, at http://georgewbush-whitehouse.archives.gov/news/releases/2004/01/20040120-7.html.

[124] See also Miller, above note 116 at 52–3 (noting that '[p]reventive war doctrine is not generalizable to situations of parity between states').

[125] Security Strategy, above note 4 at 15–16 hints at this when it concludes the discussion of preventive action by stating:

> The United States will not use force in all cases to preempt emerging threats, nor should nations use preemption as a pretext for aggression. Yet in an age where the enemies of civilization openly and actively seek the world's most destructive technologies, the United States cannot remain idle while dangers gather.
>
> We will always proceed deliberately, weighing the consequences of our actions. (...) The purpose of our actions will always be to eliminate a specific threat to the United States or our allies and friends. The reasons for our actions will be clear, the force measured, and the cause just.

[126] Walzer, above note 9, p. 79.

[127] See also David Luban, 'Preventive War' (2004) 32 *Philosophy and Public Affairs* 207 at 227 (suggesting that the 'doctrine actually *makes* rival states into potential threats to each other by permitting preventive invasion of potential adversaries'); and Miller, above note 116 at 52 (observing the preventive war doctrine 'makes the world more dangerous').

[128] See Gray, above note 28, pp. 223–4.

external threats to Russian national security is 'attempts of certain states and inter-state alliances to diminish the role of existing mechanisms of international security'.[129] While the Russian *National Security Concept* does not contain explicit references to a resultant need for a pre-emptive strike posture, it does allow for the 'realization of operational and long-term measures aimed at prevention and neutralization of internal and external threats'.[130]

In distinction to the circumscribed doctrine of anticipatory self-defence, then, 'threat pre-emption' as set forth in the 'Bush Doctrine' was the launching of a concept that could not provide normative guidance. Its reliance on unilateral evaluations of distant threats not only undercut its generality but also entailed a lack of clarity and predictability.[131] The result was to posit what may superficially have looked like a legal norm, but was actually no norm at all.[132] Professor Abraham Chayes emphasized this point in his remarkable analysis of the role of law during the Cuban Missile Crisis of 1962:

> In retrospect ... the central difficulty with the Article 51 argument is that it seemed to trivialize the whole effort at legal justification. No doubt the phrase 'armed attack' must be construed broadly enough to permit some anticipatory response. But it is a very different matter to expand it to include threatening deployments or demonstrations that do not have imminent attack as their purpose or probable outcome. To accept that reading is to make the occasion for forceful response essentially a question for unilateral national decision that would not only be formally unreviewable, but not subject to intelligent criticism either. There is simply no standard against which this decision could be judged.[133]

[129] Cited in A. I. Nikitin, 'Preemptive military action and the legitimate use of force: A Russian View', Presentation to CEPS/IISS European Security Forum (Brussels, 13 January 2003) at 1, at www.eusec.org/nikitin.htm. See also BBC News Service, *Russia Targets Top Chechen Rebels*, 8 September 2004, at http://news.bbc.co.uk/2/hi/europe/3636818.stm (following the Beslan school siege in 2004, Russia declared that it would launch pre-emptive strikes against terrorist bases 'in any region of the world').

[130] Nitkin, above note 129. See also Yevgeny Bendersky, 'Russia's Foray into Preemptive Warfare a New Challenge to its Security Establishment', *Asian Tribune*, 21 September 2004.

[131] See also Lowe, above note 3, at 865.

[132] For an even more pointed assessment, see Franck, 'What Happens Now?', above note 33 at 620 (referring to the pre-emptive strike doctrine of the US National Security Strategy as 'not system transformation but system abrogation').

[133] A. Chayes, *The Cuban Missile Crisis* (New York: Oxford University Press, 1974), p. 65.

Chayes served as the Legal Advisor to the US Department of State during the crisis, so his insider's view is particularly pertinent.[134]

Debates over the legal status of the 2003 Iraq War again illustrated why relatively well-defined exceptions to the prohibition on the use of force are necessary, and how those exceptions have functioned. Legal rules cannot, by their mere existence, prevent the use of force; nor can they prevent violations that states perceive to be necessary, or in their fundamental interests. Rather, as Chayes rightly stressed, international law provides a framework against which states' actions should be assessed, and imposes a heavy burden of justification.[135] The law of self-defence demands that, whenever possible, this assessment and justification take place in advance of action. That is why, for example, Article 51 of the UN Charter requires that states immediately notify the Security Council of any action in self-defence.[136] This focus on prior assessment and justification is rooted in a rational assessment of human nature. If justifications are going to have any power to constrain states' resort to the use of force, one had best require that they be offered in advance, whenever this is possible: otherwise they are almost certain to be both unclear and unpredictable. After the event, the temptation to offer explanations for action that are entirely self-serving is great, and they will usually be moulded into shapes that conform to what has actually occurred.[137]

To be clear: legal justification is not the same as political justification, even though legal norms need to be grounded in shared understandings (that may have a strong political flavour). The requirement of adherence to the criteria of legality ensures that social norms, which are often politically motivated, must be assessed against other non-political criteria. In political decision-making, 'justification' will in any event often be distinct from true motivation. It is possible that this was the case in the US

[134] In his analysis of the role of law during the Cuban Missile Crisis, Professor Louis Henkin reveals: 'Report has it that reference to Article 51 was several times proposed for insertion in statements by the President and others, and every time alert and insistent lawyers succeeded in eliminating it.' L. Henkin, *How Nations Behave: Law and Foreign Policy*, 2nd edn (New York: Columbia University Press, 1979), p. 294.

[135] See Jutta Brunnée and Stephen J. Toope, 'International Law and Constructivism: Elements of an Interactional Theory of International Law' (2000) 39 *Columbia Journal of Transnational Law* 19; and Jutta Brunnée and Stephen J. Toope, 'Persuasion and Enforcement: Explaining Compliance with International Law' (2002) 13 *Finnish Yearbook of International Law* 273.

[136] See *Nicaragua*, above note 79, para. 200; and see discussion in Gray, above note 28, p. 121 (observing that, since the *Nicaragua* case, 'it is noticeable that states on the whole do comply with the ... requirement').

[137] See discussion in Miller, above note 116 at 62–4.

administration's calculations leading up to the invasion of Iraq. For the purposes of assessing the fit of an action within a normative framework, however, one must focus upon justifications actually offered rather than suspected motivations.[138] It is difficult to tease out the 'true' motivations of political actors, hence the various conspiracy theories that Iraq was 'really about' access to oil, or paying back Saddam for the attempt on the life of George Bush Sr. Less conspiratorially, one might argue that Iraq was 'about' a long-term threat that the acquisition of WMD might pose to Israel or the United States. But it is equally plausible that the invasion of Iraq was 'about' a belief that installing a democratic regime in Iraq would lead to wider political changes in the Middle East. In short, assessing motivation is a mug's game, at least when it comes to states. It is analytically important, therefore, to distinguish legal justification, and political motives or political rhetoric.[139] This point underscores our observation in Chapter 1 that the interactional law framework helps to explain the traditional concept of *opinio juris* in a relatively objective fashion. Instead of trying to understand the motivation or belief of a state, one can ground law in the concrete evidence of a practice of legality.[140]

It would appear that the Bush administration too drew a distinction between political rhetoric and legal justifications and that, ultimately, it recognized that threat pre-emption, or prevention, is a dangerously unlimited concept.[141] In providing a legal justification for its intervention in Iraq, the US government chose not to rely on the doctrine of preventive self-defence, as articulated in the *National Security Strategy*. Instead, in its 20 March 2003 letter to the Security Council, the United States claimed

[138] See D. Kritsiotis, 'Arguments of Mass Confusion' (2004) 15 *European Journal of International Law* 233.

[139] See *Nicaragua*, above note 38, paras. 70–1 (where the Court carefully distinguishes the legal justification offered by the United States from other motives it may have had for its activities). For a detailed discussion, see Kritsiotis, *ibid*.

[140] We are indebted to Professor Beth Simmons for observations that helped us to clarify this point.

[141] However, note also that commentators with personal involvement in the development of the Security Strategy have suggested that the open-endedness of the document reflects deliberate strategic choices for US foreign policy. Notably, it is said to reflect the Bush administration's preference for an inductive method of decision-making that 'draws ideas from many sources and adapts them to specific conditions'. This approach is said to contrast with deductive strategies, which 'develop abstract principles and develop them into generic, universal solutions'. See P. Zelikow, 'The Transformation of National Security: Five Redefinitions' (2003) 17 *The National Interest* 17 at 25. If accurate, these observations would further support our earlier argument that the concept of preventive self-defence is antithetical to the legality requirements of clarity, predictability and generality.

that its military measures were authorized under a series of Council resolutions, empowering individual states to respond to Iraq's repeated 'material breaches' of these resolutions.[142] So the self-defence argument was put aside in favour of an argument based upon collective security, to which we will return shortly. This decision of the US government was legally important because it reaffirms the practice of legality supporting a carefully circumscribed set of exceptions to the prohibition on the use of force. Despite rhetorical claims made in the *National Security Strategy* and in media statements, when pushed for legal justification for the invasion of Iraq, the United States did not choose to advance an extended version of anticipatory self-defence. Given its own practice, then, and the reaction to the US-led invasion from the vast majority of other states, which explicitly and unequivocally rejected the invasion as unlawful on any grounds,[143] practice does not support any extension of the right to anticipatory self-defence beyond that which is necessary and proportional to a pre-existing, and clearly established, threat.

Fuller's most problematic criterion of legality in relation to anticipatory self-defence is congruence. Congruence is a particularly important idea within our theory of interactional international law because it relates both to a fundamental criterion of legality, and connects legality to the community of practice that we believe supports shared understandings underlying all attempts at norm creation and maintenance.[144] On the

[142] On the US position, see Permanent Representative of the United States of America to the United Nations (J.D. Negroponte), 'Letter to the President of the United Nations Security Council', 20 March 2003, UN Doc. S/2003/351. The letter relies primarily on Security Council authorization and makes only passing reference to self-defence, suggesting vaguely that the actions of coalition forces were 'necessary steps to defend the United States and the international community from the threat posed by Iraq and to restore international peace and security in the area'. However, in the US domestic context, self-defence and pre-emption were offered as part of the legal justification for war. See the *Report in Connection with Presidential Determination Under Public Law 107–243*, repr. in 149 *Congressional Records*, H1958, H1959 (daily edn 19 March 2003), which notes that 'Iraq harbors terrorists and because Iraq could share weapons of mass destruction with terrorists who seek them for use against the United States' and that 'based on existing facts, including the nature and type of the threat posed by Iraq, the United States may always proceed in the exercise of its inherent right to self-defense, recognized in Article 51 of the UN Charter'. *Ibid.*, at H1960.

[143] See Anne-Marie Slaughter, 'Is the U.S. at Risk of Violating International Law?' *Council of Foreign Relations*, 3 March 2003 (stating, in response to the question whether an invasion without specific Security Council authorization would violate international law, that 'it is certainly true that eight out of 10 international lawyers would say that would be a violation … That view would also be supported by the legal advisers of most other countries in the United Nations').

[144] See above Chapter 3, text accompanying notes 23 to 32.

narrow reading of self-defence, that it exists only in response to a prior armed attack, there is little problem with the criterion of congruence. The core notion of self-defence seems to be strongly rooted in basic human interaction and in most legal systems: if one is struck, it is lawful to strike back in defence. The practice of states is consistent on this point, as we have seen.[145]

As we have already suggested, the more unpredictable and uncertain a supposed rule becomes, the more difficult it will be to meet the congruence requirement. If we do not know what the rule is, or we find that the rule is actually without constraining content (because it is entirely self-assessed, as was the case with the 'Bush doctrine'), then congruence becomes a meaningless concept; there is nothing to be congruent with. This is not the same issue as debates over legal categories. Some commentators argue that anticipatory action is actually folded into justifications rooted in a continuing armed attack. For example, an armed attack is said to 'occur' already when missiles are launched or a military operation is being planned and set in motion.[146] Or, as we noted earlier, a series of smaller attacks is not treated individually but cumulatively to justify anticipatory action against further attacks.[147] Alternatively, subsequent to an attack, states may argue that defensive action is necessary to avert a continuing threat of further attacks.[148] All of these justificatory approaches would bring anticipation within the confines of Article 51 of the charter. Alternatively, one can argue for a separate customary right to anticipatory self-defence, as we have done above.[149] In either case, however, the constraining requirements of imminence, necessity and proportionality must be met, so that congruence of practice with the norm (whatever its category) can be assessed, and is in fact assessed in the practice of states. Such assessment is impossible when the rule is so attenuated and so dependent upon unilateral evaluation that no common thread of practice could possibly be discerned.

Turning to the criteria of legality in relation to non-state actor involvement in the use of force, the traditional narrow view articulated by the

[145] See above, text accompanying notes 60 to 68.

[146] See Gazzini, above note 83 at 152–3; and Franck, above note 33 at 107.

[147] Gazzini, above note 83, at 143–4. And see Gray, above note 28, pp. 196–7; and text accompanying note 84.

[148] This appeared to be the justification that the United States and the UK offered to the Security Council for their pending intervention in Afghanistan. See US Letter and UK Letter, above note 105. For a discussion, see O'Connell, above note 71 at 9–11.

[149] See above, text accompanying notes 69–71.

ICJ met the criteria of legality, with the possible exception of impossibility. As we saw earlier in this chapter, in the *Nicaragua* case, the Court asserted that the violent activities of non-state actors could not be considered an 'armed attack' for the purposes of justifying self-defence in or against another state unless that state had actual control over the attack. Even significant financial or logistical support was not enough.[150] The Court's view, to which it appears to adhere still today,[151] was that a distinction had to be drawn between illegal uses of force under Article 2(4) and the concept of 'armed attack' under Article 51.[152] In other words, 'armed attack' is a sub-class of 'use of force', and self-defence is available not against all illegal uses of force but only against armed attacks.[153] In adopting this approach, the Court was promoting both de-escalation of tension and probably the use of non-forcible countermeasures and criminal law processes, rather than employment of the inter-state framework on the use of force.

Even in 1986 when the *Nicaragua* case was decided, some commentators argued that the approach taken by the Court was unrealistic because it allowed states to conduct proxy wars while depriving the victim of effective response options.[154] The debate raised similar issues as the debate over whether or not self-defence could be extended to incorporate a right to anticipatory self-defence. Is it politically and ethically impossible to demand of states that they sit by as 'terrorists' or other armed bands attack their population? Why was there no right to self-defence? At the time of the Court's decision, the risk of terrorism, though serious, had not penetrated the public consciousness as it has in the era after 11 September 2001. With changes in both technology and strategy – and potential access to weapons of mass destruction – the threat of non-state actors and the dangers of global terrorism have grown. For these reasons, a rule that may not have been unreasonable in 1986 may have become so in 2008.

What, then, should be the required link between the target state of a self-defence action and perpetrators of attacks, including terrorists? We suggested in our discussion of evolving shared understandings that something more than mere presence of the attackers in another state's territory

[150] See *Nicaragua*, above note 38, e.g. para. 195.

[151] See above, text accompanying notes 92–7.

[152] *Nicaragua*, above note 38, para. 228. [153] *Ibid*., para. 249.

[154] See Dissenting Opinion of Judge Schwebel, para 167, reprinted at www.icj-cij.org/docket/files/70/6523.pdf; also see Dissenting Opinion of Judge Sir Robert Jennings, pp. 543–4, repr. at www.icj-cij.org/docket/files/70/6525.pdf.

is required to justify defence measures in or even against that state.[155] The criteria of legality provide some guidance in answering the difficult questions about attribution and help explain the evolution of international practice. For example, at the opposite end of the spectrum from the ICJ's narrow control test would be a rule according to which the mere presence on a state's territory of terrorists who had perpetrated an attack on another country sufficed to expose the state to military action. Such a rule would run afoul of the predictability requirement. States would at all times be exposed to self-defence measures by third states, even if unaware of the presence of the terrorists within their territory.[156] Such a rule would also touch upon the 'impossibility' criterion. If the unknown presence of terrorist attackers on a state's territory were enough to place it in the crosshairs, it would have no option to behave so as to avoid exposure to defence action. For this reason, the rule would also contradict the basic principles upon which the legal framework governing the inter-state use of force has rested. Consider that, according to the ICJ, self-defence measures can be taken only against a state that has perpetrated an armed attack. It is one thing to loosen the rules of attribution for an attack from the ICJ's agency requirement to a lesser standard such as complicity, assistance or even tacit approval. When there is no link whatsoever between the state's conduct and the terrorists' actions, it is difficult to see how the state could be said to have been involved in an armed attack. This fact, in turn, raises the question why such a state should lose the protection of the prohibition on the use of force and the rule against non-intervention, and suffer a violation of its sovereignty. Lastly, a rule predicated upon mere presence of an attacker also contradicts basic tenets of the law of state responsibility, such as the rules of attribution of private conduct to a state and the rule against forcible countermeasures.[157]

155 Indeed, even the Bush administration seemed to endorse this approach. Immediately after the 9/11 attacks, President Bush stated that the United States would 'make no distinction between the terrorists who committed these acts and those who harbour them'. See President George W. Bush, Statement by the President in His Address to the Nation, 12 September 2001, at http://georgewbush-whitehouse.archives.gov/news/releases/2001/09/20010911–16.html. (The threshold was later tightened. For example, the Security Strategy, above note 4 at 5 states: 'We make no distinction between terrorists and those who knowingly harbor or provide aid to them').

156 See Derek Jinks, 'State Responsibility for the Acts of Private Armed Groups' (2003) 4 *Chicago Journal of International Law* 83 at 92 (arguing that the 'harbor or support' rule articulated by the Bush administration after 9/11 would attribute Al Qaeda's activities to too many states, 'including Yemen. Saudi Arabia, Pakistan, Sudan and the Philippines').

157 ILC, above note 82, pp. 47 (Art. 8) and 131 (Art. 50).

Some states and commentators have suggested that necessity and proportionality can adequately circumscribe the right of self-defence against attacks by non-state actors.[158] Unless the threat is grave and imminent, force cannot be used unless the harbouring state has been given the opportunity to remove the threat from its territory.[159] In addition, with reference to proportionality, the level of support provided to terrorist organizations by a harbouring state determines the permissible military response. If a state merely allowed its territory to be used but provided no active support, defensive use of force would be limited to targeting the terrorist threat itself, rather than attacking the harbouring state or its infrastructure. By contrast, if the harbouring state provided significant material or logistical support, the facilities and personnel directly engaged in providing that support could be subject to defensive action.[160] However, such an approach would not address all of the above-mentioned legality concerns. For example, in situations where the defending state deems that there is no time to ask the target state for assistance, immediate self-defence measures may be necessary and proportional. Exposure to this type of self-defence action would be entirely unpredictable and impossible to avoid.

A somewhat more narrowly cast rule, requiring proof of direct support or at least tacit approval,[161] goes a long way toward satisfying the legality requirements. These requirements may not in all cases address the impossibility concern, such as in situations where a state is incapable of controlling its territory.[162] However, they will meet the demand for predictability and they mitigate the tension between the expanded self-defence rule and the use of force and state responsibility frameworks, respectively. On the

[158] See e.g. Statement of Attorney General, Lord Goldsmith, to the House of Lords, Hansard, 21 April 2004; and the response of Sir Michael Wood, then Legal Adviser at the UK Foreign and Commonwealth Office, in 'Principles of International Law on the Use of Force by States in Self-Defence – Responses to the Questionnaire', Chatham House – International Law Programme, ILP WP 05/01 (October 2005) at 29. In the literature, see e.g. Trapp, above note 100 at 146.

[159] See Travalio and Altenburg, above note 98 at 112–14.

[160] *Ibid.*, at 112.

[161] Tacit approval could be shown by a refusal to hand over terrorist suspects that have been identified within the borders of a state.

[162] See Travalio and Altenburg, above note 98 at 111–13. States without any effective government may be an exception. In such cases of 'state failure', the simple presence of terrorists may be enough to justify a carefully targeted armed response, addressed at the terrorists alone. This approach would, of course, amount to an extension of self-defence to resist the armed attacks or imminent attacks of non-state actors, but only in the rare situations where no state authority exists.

former, while the concept of 'armed attack' may be stretched, it would seem to be wide enough to accommodate lesser forms of involvement than agency. Support or approval of an attack also provides better justification for exposing a state to military measures. Finally, the links of support or approval are also compatible with the rules of state responsibility, both on attribution and on exceptions to the rule against non-forcible countermeasures.

In our earlier discussion of anticipatory self-defence, we adverted to the importance of the congruence criterion. Given that shared understandings concerning attacks by non-state actors are only emerging,[163] it is too soon to assess congruence of international practice with one or the other version of the linkage requirement. Nonetheless, before concluding our discussion of the right to self-defence, we return to the criterion of congruence to make a broader point concerning necessity and proportionality, two conditions on which states' arguments will frequently turn.

For example, as we already suggested, in responding to Israel's 2006 Lebanon and 2009 Gaza incursions, many of the same states who had accepted the self-defence argument in principle, also condemned Israel's actions as disproportionate.[164] Proportionality was also a major concern in the context of the Russian invasion of South Ossetia in 2008. Russia offered a range of justifications for its armed intervention in Georgian territory, including that it was providing assistance to South Ossetia in defending against Georgian 'aggression', and that it was defending Russian citizens against 'genocide',[165] thereby implying that it was acting in pursuit of states' emerging responsibility to protect. Although, in light of the facts, these justifications were tenuous at best,[166] the international

[163] See above, text accompanying notes 87–113.

[164] See above, text accompanying notes 111–13.

[165] See Peter Roudik, 'Russian Federation: Legal Aspects of War in Georgia', *Law Library of Congress*, September 2008 (Document Number 2008–01474) at 8–10, at www.loc.gov/law/help/russian-georgia-war.pdf.

[166] Notwithstanding secessionist ambitions, South Ossetia was a Georgian province at the time of the intervention so that self-defence is not a viable argument for that reason alone. Similarly, a dubious policy of granting Russian citizenship to South Ossetians undermines arguments about defence of nationals abroad. For a detailed assessment, see Roudik, *ibid.*, at 10–11. As for the implicit responsibility to protect argument, whether 'genocide' was under way is one issue. But even leaving this point aside, the emerging concept does not entitle a state to defend its own nationals in another state, nor does it justify an intervention without Security Council authorization. See Gareth Evans, 'Russia in Georgia: Not a Case of the "Responsibility to Protect"' (2008) 25 *New Perspectives Quarterly* 53. For a discussion of the emerging doctrine of the responsibility to protect, see below, section 2.4.

response to the initially limited intervention was muted.[167] However, when Russian military forces expanded their operation,[168] many states, including the United States, declared this disproportionate to any threat posed from Georgia.[169]

Both of our examples involved situations in which the applicability or scope of the self-defence norm were at issue, but they also illustrate how congruence could be problematic even at the core of the right to self-defence (i.e. response to an armed attack), precisely when states argue over the conditions of necessity and proportionality.[170] The conceptual problem is not with some conduct that fails to conform to rules; rules of international law can withstand breaches, as is true in any legal system. The conceptual issue is whether or not the practice has become so disconnected from an asserted rule, the breaches are so widespread and unchallenged, that the rule is entirely undermined. At customary law, this dynamic is familiar to international lawyers. We explained in chapters 1 to 3 that this issue is relevant to all norms, because all norms must be maintained by a community of practice.

[167] Contrast the official position of the United States Ambassador to the United Nations, Zalmay Khalizad, at the 5952nd Security Council meeting on the afternoon of 8 August 2008, with his statements at the 5953rd meeting on the morning of 10 August 2008 (respectively at www.securitycouncilreport.org/atf/cf/%7B65BFCF9B-6D27-4E9C-8CD3-CF6E4FF96FF9%7D/Georgia%20SPV%205952.pdf and www.securitycouncilreport.org/atf/cf/%7B65BFCF9B-6D27-4E9C-8CD3-CF6E4FF96FF9%7D/Georgia%20SPV%205953.pdf. At the 5952nd meeting, Indonesia regretted 'that the Council missed an opportunity to pronounce itself clearly and with a single voice on this unfolding grave situation'; also note the change in Costa Rica's statements between the two meetings (from calling 'on all parties to halt military action', to deploring 'the fact that [hostilities] have spread beyond the conflict zone').

[168] See Anna Barnard, 'Georgia and Russia Nearing All-Out War', *The New York Times*, 10 August 2008 at A1.

[169] See e.g. Joint Statement on Georgia by the Foreign Ministers of Canada, France, Germany, Italy, Japan, the United States and the United Kingdom, 28 August 2008, at www.mofa.go.jp/announce/announce/2008/8/1182961_1040.html (*inter alia* deploring 'Russia's excessive use of military force in Georgia'); see also Council of the European Union, 'Georgia-Russia Conflict: Extraordinary European Council Presidency Conclusions', 1 September 2008, at www.eu-un.europa.eu/articles/en/article_8116_En.htm (declaring itself to be 'gravely concerned by the open conflict which has broken out in Georgia, by the resulting violence and by the disproportionate reaction of Russia'). And see Jules Cavendish, 'Russia-Georgia Reaction: World Leaders Condemn Moscow', *Times Online*, 10 August 2008, at www.timesonline.co.uk/tol/news/world/europe/article4497344.ece.

[170] See Gardam, above note 72, pp. 152 (discussing the issue of necessity in the *Nicaragua* case) and 157 (asserting that in both the Falklands and 1990–1 Persian Gulf campaigns, 'despite the fact that compliance with legal norms was regarded by the defending States and their allies as an integral part of their campaigns, questions were raised as to the proportionality of the actions taken to dislodge the invading force').

In other words, the criterion of congruence and the continuing action and response of communities of practice are both required to uphold legal rules; indeed, the action and response of communities of practice is, practically speaking, the measure of congruence. Although violations of and disputes over a norm will not necessarily render the norm meaningless, there may come a time where the divergence between the purported norm and actual practice is so great that congruence is destroyed and legality is impaired. As the examples illustrate, international responses to violations are as important in this process as the violations themselves.

In summary, the charter rules on self-defence, when read with the older customary law, are rooted in widely shared understandings, and they meet the criteria of legality. Over time, and especially since 11 September 2001, attempts have been made to stretch the self-defence exception in ways that seem not to have been built upon new shared understandings. We suggest that this is in large measure because they failed to meet the criteria of legality. Interestingly, although the practice of states shows some extension of the established framework (e.g. to the lawful justification of attacks on states 'harbouring' and actively supporting terrorists), by and large the rules have not changed in appreciable ways. The continuing practice of legality in relation to self-defence buttresses the charter regime and the established custom on anticipatory self-defence and the role of non-state actors.

3.3 Collective security

Strongly shared understandings exist concerning the collective security system set out in the UN Charter. In the aftermath of the World War II, not only was the revulsion against war strong, it gave rise to a widespread acceptance of the need for an international organization, the United Nations, specifically charged with the duty to prevent war, in part through the creation of mechanisms of collective security. The Security Council was established to provide the central global forum for the mutual engagement of states, a forum in which processes of deliberation and justification could take place and a practice of legality could be built up. The Council's primary task being the promotion of international peace and security, it was specifically designed to operate at the intersection of law and politics.[171] Notwithstanding widespread dissatisfaction with its

[171] See United Nations Charter, Arts 2(1) and 27; D.W. Bowett, *The Law of International Institutions*, 4th edn (London: Stevens & Sons, 1982), pp. 24, 26 and 33–42; and

performance over the years, the Security Council does seem possessed of a unique and enduring ability to lend legitimacy to international action, including the use of force.[172]

The interplay between collective process and substantive considerations in decisions on the use of force is complex. While Security Council endorsement does seem to be an important indicator of legitimacy,[173] it is arguably not sufficient in and of itself. The considerations that animate an individual decision whether or not to employ force must also resonate with widely shared understandings of international society, and must be attentive to legal norms and to the criteria of legality.

It is striking that states and NGOs alike call for extraordinary sessions of the UN to deal with emerging crises and fundamental security challenges. In recent years, such calls have been made in relation to events in India–Pakistan (1998), Iraq (2003), Sudan (2007), Sri Lanka (2009), and to deal with the problem of women in armed conflict (2000).[174] The most powerful recent example is found in the weeks leading up to the US- and UK-led invasion of Iraq. The general public and the media debated the need for Security Council authorization of any intervention, and even more precisely the need for a 'second resolution' of the Council that would specifically authorize a war.[175] Similarly, even the governments

F.L. Kirgis Jr., 'The United Nations at Fifty: The Security Council's First Fifty Years' (1995) 89 *American Journal of International Law* 506 at 506–9.

172 See Adam Roberts and Benedict Kingsbury, 'The UN's Roles in International Society', in Adam Roberts and Benedict Kingsbury (eds.), *United Nations, Divided World* (New York: Oxford University Press, 1993), p. 57. See also *Review*, above note 59. While many states called for a more representative, effective and transparent Security Council, the overwhelming majority endorsed the idea of the collective security system and the role of the Council.

173 See e.g. I. Hurd, 'Legitimacy, Power, and the Symbolic Life of the UN Security Council' (2002) 8 *Global Governance* 35.

174 See CNN News Service, *U.N. calls on Pakistan to halt nuclear tests*, 30 May 1998, at www.cnn.com/WORLD/asiapcf/9805/30/pakistan.update ('U.N. action taken in a rare Saturday emergency session called by Japan'); CBC News Service, *Canada calls for Security Council to issue deadline for Iraqi compliance*, 20 February 2003, at www.cbc.ca/world/story/2003/02/19/canadairaq030219.html; Fédération internationale des ligues des Droits de l'Homme, 'Security Council Should End Sudan's Obstruction Act to Enhance Protection for Civilians in Darfur', 20 December 2007, at www.fidh.org/Security-Council-Should-End-Sudan; Amnesty International, 'Sri Lankan government and LTTE must heed demands from UN Security Council', 14 May 2009, atwww.amnesty.org/en/news-and-updates/news/sri-lankan-government-and-ltte-must-heed-demands-un-security-council-20090514; and UN Wire, *UN Wraps Up Extraordinary Session*, 26 October 2000, at www.unwire.org/unwire/20001026/11445_story.asp (UN Security Council first-ever discussion on women and armed conflict).

175 See e.g. Stephen Castle, 'Cautious EU backs second resolution before war in Iraq', *The Independent*, 11 January 2003; Richard W. Stevenson with Julia Preston 'Threats and

preparing for intervention, for all their criticism of the UN's inaction, sought Security Council authorization and, when it could not be secured, developed an argument, strained though it was,[176] according to which a previous resolution of the Security Council provided the necessary legal authority for the invasion.[177] What these events reveal is that the core norm of collective security, requiring that inter-state recourse to armed force, save for self-defence measures, must be authorized by the Security Council, is a resilient and widely shared understanding in international society.

The Security Council's ability to lend legitimacy derives from the manner in which collective process and substantive assessment blend together in the work of the Council.[178] As a matter of process, rather than permitting unilateral assessments of the existence of a threat to international peace and security, a discipline was imposed demanding that a range of states be convinced of the reality of the threat and the utility of forceful intervention.[179] In other words, as a matter of process, multilateral checks are imposed on purely self-serving arguments.[180] As a matter of substance, proposed action must measure up to a blend of legal, prudential and political assessments.[181] As we will demonstrate, even in the politically charged

Responses: Washington; Bush Meets Blair Amid Signs Of Split On U.N. War Role', *The New York Times*, 1 February 2003; and B. Muralidhar Reddy, 'Pak. to abstain from second resolution on Iraq', *The Hindu*, 12 March 2003.

176 See Slaughter, above note 143.

177 See Letter dated 20 March 2003 from the Permanent Representative of the United Kingdom of Great Britain and Northern Ireland to the United Nations addressed to the President of the Security Council, UN Doc. S/2003/350; Letter dated 20 March 2003 from the Permanent Representative of the United States of America to the United Nations addressed to the President of the Security Council, UN Doc. S/2003/351; and Letter dated 20 March 2003 from the Permanent Representative of Australia to the United Nations addressed to the President of the Security Council, UN Doc. S/2003/352. See also detailed discussion in Gray, above note 28, pp. 354–66.

178 See Michael Barnett, 'Bringing in the new world order: liberalism, legitimacy, and the United Nations' (1997) 49 *World Politics* 526 at 539–43 (reviewing different conceptions of the interplay between procedural and substantive legitimacy of UN action). And see generally Brunnée and Toope, 'Interactional Theory', above note 135 at 56–7 (on the pervasive interaction between procedural and substantive legitimacy).

179 See Andreas L. Paulus, 'Antimonies of Power and Law: A Comment on Robert Kagan' (2003) 9 *German Law Journal* 871 at 877–9. See also, Andreas L. Paulus, 'The War against Iraq and the Future of International Law: Hegemony or Pluralism?' (2004) 25 *Michigan Journal of International Law* 691.

180 See Ian Johnstone, 'Security Council Deliberations: The Power of the Better Argument' (2003) 12 *European Journal of International Law* 437 at 454.

181 See *ibid.*, at 452–3 (on the interplay between political and legal factors in Security Council decision-making).

context of the Security Council, the criteria of legality do a significant amount of work in guiding and constraining the international practice of legality.[182]

The decision to entrust matters of international peace and security to a collective deliberative process was fundamentally sound. It is a separate issue whether the range of states to be convinced and the precise processes of decision-making within the Council remain appropriate. Many observers have criticized the system, and especially the UN Security Council, as impotent in the face of power politics,[183] or at least dysfunctional because it often is so difficult for the Council to act. In a speech before the UN General Assembly in 2002, former US President George W. Bush famously challenged the Security Council to stand up to Iraq's alleged WMD programme and asked: 'Are Security Council resolutions to be honored and enforced, or cast aside without consequence? Will the United Nations serve the purpose of its founding, or will it be irrelevant?'[184] Even though the complaint turned out not to be well founded, it is important to note that Bush's concern related to the *practice* of the Security Council. Even he, in a moment of intense political drama, did not explicitly question the norms that underpin the collective security system.

From altogether different political perspectives, critiques are launched against the Council because of its unrepresentative quality.[185] The central concern is with the permanent membership, the composition of which may have been politically logical in 1945, but which makes increasingly less sense today. For example, the role of the EU is undervalued, and European political power dynamics are confused by the presence of France and the UK, but not of Germany. There is no African, Arab or

[182] See also Ian Johnstone, 'Legislation and Adjudication in the UN Security Council: Bringing Down the Deliberative Deficit' (2008) 102 *American Journal of International Law* 275 at 276 (suggesting that, while 'deliberations in the UN Security Council are highly politicized, they are also surprisingly structured … Legal discourse looms large in that setting').

[183] See e.g. Michael J. Glennon, 'Why the Security Council Failed' (2003) 82 *Foreign Affairs* 16.

[184] Statement by President Bush to the United Nations General Assembly, UN Headquarters, New York, 12 September 2002, at www.un.org/webcast/ga/57/statements/020912usaE.htm.

[185] See *Review*, above note 59. While some states expressly challenged the Council's current configuration (e.g. Algeria and Cuba), most endorsed the idea of a reforms to make the Council more representative and transparent (e.g. the statements of the Eastern European Group, the African Union, Chile, China, Egypt, India, Pakistan, Turkey, and Vietnam).

Latin American state amongst the permanent members. Emerging economic powerhouses such as India and Brazil are left out. Reform will be highly problematic and may prove elusive. Already, in the 2003 report of the High-level Panel on Threats, Challenges and Change, proposals for changes to Security Council membership were offered up, but no action was taken. To achieve meaningful reform, significant political capital would need to be expended by a range of states, most notably by the permanent members. Options for reform include the identification of new permanent members or an enlarged rotating membership. In any event, voting rules would have to be changed. At least in certain circumstances, the exercise of a determinative veto by individual permanent members does not make sense. Instead, super-majorities or the exercise of joint vetoes might be required. Even if one imagines that these ideas could be broadly acceptable to the majority of permanent members, and that is highly doubtful, they would likely be entirely unacceptable to the United States, largely in view of its domestic political dynamics.[186]

As difficult as institutional reform may prove to be, there is no plausible alternative to the collective legitimation of the use of force through the Security Council, either inside or outside the UN.[187] The General Assembly lacks an appropriate sense of responsibility in actions relating to the use of force because its decision-making authority is too diffuse. Ad hoc 'coalitions of the willing' typically lack neutrality and therefore have no legitimacy.[188] Suggestions that a more permanent 'coalition of liberal democratic states' might serve as a supplementary decision-making authority to authorize the use of force when the Security Council is paralysed are deeply flawed.[189] Developing states have been fighting for years to

[186] See David M. Malone, 'The Security Council in the Post-Cold War Era: A Study in the Creative Interpretation of the UN Charter' 35 (2003) *New York University Journal of International Law* 487 at 514 and 516.

[187] See Barnett, above note 178 at 540–1.

[188] It might be objected that NATO's intervention in Kosovo is an example where a self-appointed coalition achieved a degree of legitimacy. However, the Kosovo intervention can be distinguished from the invasion of Iraq on a number of counts. First, in Kosovo there was credible evidence of actions amounting to a continuing, even escalating, genocide. Second, the inability of the Security Council to act resulted from the threatened veto of a single state, and not from a broader resistance to the proposed use of force. The reasons for that threatened veto are complex, and cannot be considered here. Third, the NATO intervention took place after an extended and intense multilateral effort to broker a peaceful settlement. See also Tom Farer, 'The Prospect for International Law and Order in the Wake of Iraq' (2003) 97 *American Journal of International Law* 607 at 625–6.

[189] See Slaughter, above note 4; Anne-Marie Slaughter, 'Notes from the President: A Fork in the Road' (September/October 2003) *American Society of International Law Newsletter*,

destroy the outmoded notion that there is a core group of 'civilized states' that provides the sole model to emulate if a state seeks international credibility.[190] Were the idea to be implemented through the banding together of a coalition of democratic states, it would only serve to further poison international relations.

We signal the importance of potential Security Council reform, especially in membership, because the interactional framework we describe is predicated upon inclusive participation in the development of law. In fact, a failure to allow for broader participation undermines the core idea of shared understandings in which all norms are rooted. It also calls into question the potential of the Council to encourage and facilitate a widespread practice of legality.

To return to the collective security norm per se, Chapter VII of the UN Charter requires that the Security Council 'determine the existence of any threat to the peace, breach of the peace, or act of aggression'.[191] Only on the basis of such a determination can the Council 'decide what measures' should be taken 'to maintain or restore international peace and security'.[192] In other words, within the UN Charter framework, military force can be employed only on the basis of a decision of the Council, which in current practice means that coalitions of UN member states are authorized to use force. The contemporary norm reflects an evolution of shared understandings on the legality of collective action that moves away from the text of the charter, which had envisaged that the Council alone could take military action, working through standing forces supplied by member states.[193]

For practical purposes, then, the elements of the collective security norm are: (i) determination by the Security Council of a threat to the peace, breach of the peace, or act of aggression (combining legal and

p. 4 (suggesting a 'caucus of democracies' or other 'alternative fora of discussion in the UN, and perhaps ultimately of legitimation for action taken by some subset of UN actors'); and James M. Lindsay, 'The Case for a Concert of Democracies' (2009) 23 *Ethics and International Affairs* 5. But see also Stephen Schlesinger, 'Why a League of Democracies Will Not Work' (2009) 23 *Ethics and International Affairs* 13; and Kishore Mahbubani, 'The Dangers of Democratic Delusions' (2009) 23 *Ethics and International Affairs* 19. See also below, text accompanying notes 288–90.

190 See e.g. Mohammed Ayoob, 'Humanitarian Intervention and State Sovereignty' (2002) 6 *International Journal of Human Rights* 81 at 84–5.

191 United Nations Charter, Art. 39.

192 *Ibid.*

193 See *ibid.*, Arts. 42 and 43–7. And see discussion in Franck, above note 32, pp. 21–31; and Gazzini, above note 83 at 43–63.

political considerations); and (ii) authorization by the Council of recourse to armed force to restore international peace and security. This authorization is itself normatively constrained, as we will argue below. The norm itself is unproblematic from the perspective of the criteria of legality. It meets the requirements of generality, promulgation, non-retroactivity, non-contradiction, and constancy over time. The only issue concerning constancy is the practice that emerged in light of the failure of states to provide a standing army under direct UN control. However, this detail does not fundamentally affect the operation of the rules concerning collective security. What the collective security norm demands of UN member states is certainly within the realm of the possible.

The criterion of clarity poses some problems. The authorization requirement itself is clear. However, the notions of peace, breach of the peace, and aggression are notoriously ill-defined, notwithstanding the requirement of Security Council determination. The notion of aggression has remained so contentious that a 1974 General Assembly resolution that purported to define – and so clarify – aggression with a view to assisting Security Council decision-making still remains controversial.[194] Similarly, in the context of the Rome Statute of the International Criminal Court, it has not been possible to agree on a definition of aggression for the purposes of determining the Court's jurisdiction.[195] At least in part as a result of this ambiguity, the Security Council has preferred to rely upon

194 See UN General Assembly Resolution 3314 (XXIX), Definition of Aggression, UN Doc. A/RES/29/3314 (14 December 1974).

195 Pursuant to Art. 5(1) of the Rome Statute, the Crime of Aggression is one of the crimes under the jurisdiction of the Court. However, the exercise of that jurisdiction depends on Art. 5(2), according to which the Court's jurisdiction is contingent upon the adoption of an amendment 'defining the crime and setting out the conditions under which the Court shall exercise jurisdiction' with respect to it. A Special Working Group on the Crime of Aggression was established in 2002 by the Assembly of States Parties to continue discussions on the definition, elements and jurisdictional conditions of the Crime of Aggression. A press release regarding a February 2009 meeting of the working group illustrates the ongoing problems with the definition:

> The draft provisions on the crime of aggression under consideration include a definition of the act of aggression, which is based on United Nations General Assembly resolution 3314 (XXIX), with a threshold, an open-ended lists of acts that would qualify as an act of aggression and wording on the requisite leadership element to establish individual criminal responsibility for the act. There are divergent views regarding a possible role for the United Nations Security Council prior to the initiation of an investigation by the Prosecutor.

See Assembly of States Parties to the International Criminal Court, 'Assembly of States Parties concludes the second resumption of its seventh session', Press Release ICC-ASP-20090213-PR390, 16 February 2009.

a determination of the existence of threats to or breaches of international peace and security to trigger the toolkit of Chapter VII.[196] In any event, all of these concepts are dominated by political considerations though, as we will argue, legal considerations are not entirely absent. But because consistent practice is not available to flesh-out the concepts, they do not furnish an entirely clear legal standard.

A closer look reveals that the considerable problems with the collective security norm arise not from the norm itself, but from a lack of congruence of international practice with the norm. What is more, inconsistencies in the practice have undermined any coherent 'practice of legality' that might reinforce the underlying norm. For example, on many occasions, the Security Council has refrained from determining the existence of threats to or breaches of international security, let alone aggression, even when the circumstances would have warranted such a determination. Often, this failure is due to the exercise, or anticipated exercise, of a veto by one of the permanent members. A recent example is the failure of the Council to deal assertively with the invasion of Georgian territory by one of the Council's permanent members, Russia.[197] Older examples include India's 1961 invasion of Portugese Goa,[198] the 1962 Cuban Missile Crisis,[199] the 1962 Chinese invasion of India,[200] the 1965 US intervention in the Dominican Republic,[201] the 1971 war between India and Pakistan over East Pakistan,[202] the 1971 Russian invasion of Afghanistan,[203] and Israel's 1982 invasion of Lebanon.[204] Similarly, on some occasions, the Council has failed to authorize the use of force to restore international peace and security even after a threat or breach had been determined.[205]

Such failures implicate several of the legality criteria. For example, variable practice of the Council undermines the general and non-contradictory nature of the collective security norm, further erodes its clarity,

[196] See Gray, above note 28, p. 256.

[197] See BBC News Service, *UN Security Council Fails to Agree on Georgia*, 20 August 2008, at www.news.bbc.co.uk/2/hi/europe/7571506.stm. See also above, text accompanying notes 165–9 (discussing the Russian incursion).

[198] See Weisburd, above note 37, p. 36.

[199] *Ibid.*, pp. 217–18. [200] *Ibid.*, pp. 261–4.

[201] *Ibid.*, pp. 223–4. [202] *Ibid.*, pp. 149–50.

[203] *Ibid.*, pp. 44–6. [204] *Ibid.*, pp. 161–6.

[205] See United Nations Security Council Resolution 598, 20 July 1987, UN Doc. S/RES/598, at www.un.org/Docs/scres/1987/scres87.htm ('determining that there exists a breach of the peace as regards the conflict between Iran and Iraq', yet not authorizing the use of force).

and can destroy constancy over time. The criterion of impossibility can also be engaged. For example, when a state is faced with a serious but not imminent threat to its security, so that no right of self-defence arises, a failure of the Security Council to authorize appropriate response measures may put the state in a situation that makes compliance with the collective security norm difficult, if not impossible. This problem may help to explain the confused international response to the Israeli attack on the Osirak Nuclear reactor in 1981. The same issue has confronted states with the possibility of nuclear weapons development in Iran and North Korea over the last decade.

Alternatively, a failure of the Council to authorize intervention in a humanitarian crisis can put UN member states in an impossible political and ethical situation (not dissimilar to the issues raised by anticipatory self-defence). The Council's inaction on Kosovo and the Rwandan genocide, while formally its prerogative, is widely seen as having damaged its credibility.[206] To be sure, even if the Security Council identifies a 'threat to international peace and security', but then refuses to authorize collective military intervention, this is not in all cases a failure of legality. It may mean that members of the Council are simply not convinced that the use of force is an effective response to the threat.[207] After all, recourse to force, even if authorized by the Security Council, must be necessary to address a threat to or breach of peace and security, and must be proportional to it.

Thus, in the case of the 2003 Iraq invasion,[208] the Council's refusal to adopt an authorizing resolution actually showed the Council members' adherence to the criteria of legality, even in the face of extreme pressure from some of its most powerful members.[209] The Council had already determined that there had been a breach of peace and security by Iraq,[210] and the Council was therefore within its power to take action. However,

[206] For a detailed discussion, see Michael Barnett, *Eyewitness to a Genocide: The United Nations and Rwanda* (Ithaca: Cornell University Press, 2002).

[207] See Franck, 'What Happens Now?', above note 33 at 616; and Lowe, above note 131 at 867.

[208] For a detailed discussion of the events and deliberations in the Security Council, see Gray, above note 28, pp. 354–66.

[209] See Johnstone, above note 23 at 384 (noting that Angola, Cameroon, Chile, Guinea, Mexico and Pakistan, which were non-permanent members of the Council at the time, did not commit to voting for a second resolution, notwithstanding their exposure to both pressure and incentives).

[210] See e.g. United Nations Security Council Resolution 1441, 8 November 2002, UN Doc. A/RES/1441.

within the framework of Chapter VII of the charter, the use of force is to be applied only when other enforcement options have been exhausted or have proved to be inadequate (Articles 41 and 42). Another way of phrasing this requirement is that the Council is subject to the rule of necessity, just as are states in their invocation of a right to self-defence.[211] The Council had already authorized continuing inspections of Iraqi facilities by the International Atomic Energy Agency, and the majority of Council members were not convinced that this option to control Iraq had been exhausted. Moreover, in authorizing any use of force, the Council is also bound by the rule of proportionality.[212] Council members remained unconvinced that an all-out invasion of Iraqi territory was proportional to any threat. This requirement blends with the political reality that the evidence gathered by the United States and the UK was widely debated and doubted in public as the Security Council was making its decisions. Although politics was of course relevant to the deliberations of the Council, the legal requirements of necessity and proportionality were also powerful. Therefore, the decision not to authorize a use of force was entirely congruent with the underlying norm, and was itself an expression of a practice of legality.

It is open to debate whether, on identical facts, the mere formality of a 'second resolution' would have imbued the intervention in Iraq with greater legitimacy. As many observers have noted, in the case of Iraq the Council actually functioned as intended when, on the available evidence, it declined to authorize a full-scale war.[213] This example illustrates the crucial difference between legalism and legality, and shows that the Council, although it operates at the interface between politics and law, is enmeshed in the requirements of legality.

Two further points are worth raising with respect to the requirement of Security Council authorization and the constraints imposed on practice by the criteria of legality. One concerns the criterion of non-retroactivity. While the collective security norm as such meets this criterion, the practice of the Security Council is uneven. The criterion helps explain the discomfort of many states and observers with the notion of a 'retroactive' authorization of military action, as was argued the Council provided in the case of the Kosovo intervention.[214] At the very least, this practice

[211] See Gardam, above note 72, p. 189. [212] *Ibid.*

[213] See Franck, 'What Happens Now?', above note 33 at 616; Lowe, above note 3 at 867; and Johnstone, above note 180 at 478.

[214] See Jules Lobel and Michael Ratner, 'Bypassing the Security Council: Ambiguous Authorizations to Use Force, Cease-Fires and the Iraqi Inspection Regime' (1999) 93 *American Journal of International Law* 124 at 130–4.

undercuts the clarity and predictability of the collective security norm. Similarly problematic is the notion of an 'implied authorization', that is sometimes invoked by states and academic commentators to justify a use of force – for example, US, French and UK no-fly zones in Iraq, based on implied authorization in Resolution 688 of the Security Council.[215]

In summary, the shared understanding buttressing the collective security regime of the UN Charter remains strong.[216] The norms themselves generally meet the legality criteria, although problems arise with respect to clarity because of the uncertain nature of concepts such as peace and security. In addition, the practice of the Security Council in applying the norm gives rise to serious concerns relating to congruence. In other words, it is doubtful that one could claim a robust 'practice of legality' flowing from Security Council decisions. These conclusions should come as no surprise, given the strong political dimensions of Security Council decision-making. Nonetheless, it seems that legality criteria do function to constrain the actions of the Council. This was certainly the case in the deliberations concerning the second Iraq War. Although powerful states worked hard to alter the collective security framework, it was ultimately reaffirmed.

Although the Security Council is the only international body with any legitimacy in the collective authorization of the use of force, that legitimacy is fragile because of the problems we have identified with the 'clarity' criterion of legality, and even more with the failure to build a robust practice of legality in the decisions of the Council. These weaknesses help to explain the widespread discomfort with the Council, especially when linked to the outmoded membership and unjustifiable veto structure that undermine the possibility of widely shared understandings properly informing the evolution of Security Council legal rulings.

3.4 *Responsibility to protect*

So far in this discussion of the use of force, we have explored norms that are well established. The right to self-defence has a long lineage in customary

[215] Gray, above note 28, pp. 348–51

[216] See also *Comments of the Non-Aligned Movement*, above note 59, para. 16 (stating that 'The Non-Aligned Movement reiterates the importance of the promotion and strengthening of the multilateral process, and addressing international challenges and problems by strictly abiding by the UN Charter and the principles of international law and further stresses its commitment to multilateralism. In this regard, NAM also stresses the central role of the UN in the maintenance of international peace and security …').

law, dating from the emergence of the inter-state system. The collective security norm is much more recent, but was established relatively solidly in the immediate aftermath of World War II. Now we shift to new terrain, explaining how in the interactional law framework new norms can emerge and become relatively stable. We will trace out the development of the concept called 'the responsibility to protect' (R2P), relating it to its precursor, 'humanitarian intervention'. What interests us is the fact that humanitarian intervention never achieved the solidity that its promoters sought, and it remains unclear whether the responsibility to protect will fare any better. Because the responsibility to protect is at best a candidate norm, the structure of our analysis will be different from our approach to self-defence and collective security. We will examine in tandem whether or not the norm is rooted in a robust shared understanding on the duty to protect vulnerable populations facing humanitarian crises, and whether or not the proposed norm meets the criteria of legality. We argue that the mere articulation of a norm through norm entrepreneurship is not enough to create law, because part of the success of candidate norms is determined by the extent to which actors in a legal system view a social norm as having the capacity to meet the criteria of legality. The process leading to the articulation of the responsibility to protect is fascinating because it is one of the clearest cases of intentional norm entrepreneurship, but there remains considerable doubt as to whether the norm can and will solidify into customary law. Our interactional framework helps to explain why.

3.4.1 Shared understandings and the criteria of legality

The responsibility to protect began as a set of ideas promoted by various norm entrepreneurs, academic and diplomatic.[217] The idea was designed to help the world escape from the quagmire of 'humanitarian intervention' that had trapped theorists and state leaders for at least a generation. Debates had swirled around whether or not such a right existed in any configuration. If it did, a question then arose whether the right was purely collective, or could be exercised unilaterally. If it was collective, which collectivity was empowered to act? Only the Security Council? Regional political organizations such as the African

[217] On the concept of 'norm entrepreneurship', see Martha Finnemore and Kathryn Sikkink, 'International Norm Dynamics and Political Change' (1998) 52 *International Organization* 887; and Emanuel Adler, 'Imagined (Security) Communities: Cognitive Regions in International Relations' (1997) 26 *Millenium, Journal of International Studies* 249 at 267 and 277.

Union? Regional military alliances such as NATO? If individual states or ad hoc alliances could act, what were the legal preconditions for such action?[218]

The questions surrounding who could intervene to stop or prevent a humanitarian crisis took on great urgency in 1999 with the NATO intervention in Kosovo.[219] What Kosovo brought to the fore was a dual dilemma. First was the fundamental issue whether or not a norm of humanitarian intervention existed. Second was the question, who could invoke the norm, only the Security Council or individual states? The latter issue was pointed out clearly when a threatened Russian veto precluded any Security Council authorization to use force. In a failed attempt to avoid the dilemma, most of the NATO states refused to posit any general norm of humanitarian intervention, the exception being Belgium.[220] Instead, the NATO partners argued a 'moral duty' to act, or a 'necessity' to act.[221]

Humanitarian intervention had never been rooted in a robust shared understanding of the right to act in the face of humanitarian crises, except, perhaps, in cases of impending genocide.[222] It was not referred to explicitly in any provision of the UN Charter, although it has been implicit in

[218] See e.g. J. L. Holzgrefe and Robert O. Keohane (eds.), *Humanitarian Intervention: Ethical, Legal and Political Dilemmas* (Cambridge University Press, 2003); Simon Chesterman, *Just War or Just Peace? Humanitarian Intervention and International Law* (Oxford University Press, 2001); and Antonio Cassese, 'Ex iniuria ius oritur: Are We Moving Towards International Legitimation of Forcible Humanitarian Countermeasures in the World Community?' (1999) 10 *European Journal of International Law* 23.

[219] See Independent International Commission on Kosovo, *The Kosovo Report: Conflict, International Response, Lessons Learned* (Oxford University Press, 2000).

[220] *Legality of use of Force Case* (*Yugoslavia* v. *Belgium*), Provisional Measures, I.C.J. 1999, pleadings of Belgium, 10 May 1999, CR 99/14 (uncorrected translation), at www.icj-cij.org/docket/files/105/4515.pdf ('this is an armed humanitarian intervention, compatible with Article 2, paragraph 4, of the Charter, which covers only intervention against the territorial integrity or political independence of a State').

[221] See e.g. Press Statement, Javier Solana, Secretary-General of NATO, NATO Press Release (1999) 040, 23 March 1999, at www.nato.int/docu/pr/1999/p99–040e.htm, repr. Jeffrey L. Dunoff, with Steven R. Ratner and David Wippman (eds.), *International Law, Norms, Actors, Process* (New York: Aspen Law and Business, 2002). Or see the argument of the United Kingdom, expressed in the *Declaration by the Parliamentary Under Secretary of State*, repr. in (1998) 69 *British Yearbook of International Law* 593 (claiming that 'in the exceptional circumstances of Kosovo it was considered that the use of force would be justified on the ground of overwhelming humanitarian necessity, without Security Council authorization').

[222] See Toope, above note 34. We introduce the doubt because even though the Genocide Convention, which contains a duty to prevent, is widely ratified, there is simply no consistent practice of legality supporting the right of humanitarian intervention.

certain findings of and responses to 'threats to international peace and security' under Chapter VII.[223] Somalia was the high point of this modest trend, but it quickly turned into the low point, which helps in part to explain, if not excuse, the failure of international society to act in the face of the Rwandan genocide.[224]

Nonetheless, the moral urgency underlying a perceived duty of humanitarian intervention was never satisfied. The impulse to act in the face of humanitarian catastrophe is strong, so strong that Canada and a group of major foundations sponsored an International Commission on Intervention and State Sovereignty (ICISS). In its effort to reframe the debate from a question of right to one of duty, the commission posited a 'responsibility to protect' particularly threatened populations.[225] The ICISS report rests on the premise that:

> [w]here a population is suffering serious harm, as a result of internal war, insurgency, repression or state failure, and the state in question is unwilling or unable to halt or avert it, the principle of non-intervention yields to the international responsibility to protect.[226]

This idea signals a fundamental shift in international law. Force would be authorized not only to defend a state's integrity and political independence, not only to defuse threats to international peace and security through collective action, but also to bolster a moral claim that people are more important than state sovereignty.

In its report, the commission confronted some of the difficult issues that must be addressed if the responsibility to protect is to find a place in international law: in what precise circumstances, and by whom, can force be used to avert or halt humanitarian disasters? The report argued forcefully that the primary approach to discharging the international responsibility to protect must be to prevent extreme crisis through measures ranging from various forms of assistance to non-military forms of coercion.[227] While stressing the need for decisive and speedy action in some

[223] See W. Michael Reisman, 'Hollow Victory: Humanitarian Intervention and Protection of Minorities' (1997) 91 *American Society of International Law Proceedings* 431.

[224] See Barnett, above note 178 at 34–9.

[225] International Commission on Intervention and State Sovereignty (ICISS), *The Responsibility to Protect*, December 2001, at www.iciss.ca/pdf/Commission-Report.pdf. See also G. Evans, 'The Responsibility to Protect' (2002) 81 *Foreign Affairs* 99.

[226] ICISS, above note 225, at XI

[227] *Ibid.*, at 19–31. See also J. Tanguy, 'Redefining Sovereignty and Intervention' (2003) 17 *Ethics and International Affairs* 141 at 144 (describing the ICISS approach as a 'responsibility continuum' that encompasses responsibilities to prevent, to react and to rebuild).

circumstances, the commission cast military intervention for human protection as a last resort for 'extreme and exceptional cases'.[228] The goal was to create some shared ground by expressly limiting the application of the new concept, and by making it clear what is encompassed within the responsibility to protect. This attempt also relates to the criteria of legality, especially clarity.

In the same vein, the ICISS went on to outline a 'just cause threshold', a set of 'precautionary principles', and criteria for 'right authority'.[229] The just cause criteria were tied to objective indicators that identify the extreme and exceptional cases to which military intervention should be restricted. Specifically, military intervention is warranted only when serious and irreparable harm to human beings, such as massive loss of life or large-scale ethnic cleansing, is occurring or immediately likely to occur.[230] The commission's precautionary principles demanded that the primary purpose of the intervention is to halt human suffering (right intention), that the intervention is a measure of last resort, that it employs proportional means, and that it holds reasonable prospects of success.[231] Finally, in terms of right authority, the commission identified the Security Council as the most appropriate body for decisions on military intervention for human protection purposes.[232] To enable Council action, the report suggested that permanent members agree to a 'code of conduct' for the use of the veto concerning actions needed to stop or avert a significant humanitarian crisis. Essentially, in matters that do not involve its vital national interests, a permanent member would 'not use its veto to obstruct … what would otherwise be a majority decision'.[233] The idea of demanding express decision-making parameters is also grounded in criteria of legality such as generality, clarity and constancy over time.

The responsibility to protect concept was then adopted in modified form by another panel of eminent persons, this time appointed by the Secretary-General with the broad mandate to consider options for UN

[228] ICISS, above note 225, at 31. [229] *Ibid.*, at XII.

[230] *Ibid.*, at XII and 32. [231] *Ibid.*, at XII and 35–7.

[232] *Ibid.*, at XII and 47–55. However, the ICISS report also reminds the Security Council that 'if it fails to discharge its responsibility to protect in conscience-shocking situations crying out for action, concerned states may not rule out other means to meet the gravity and urgency of that situation'. *Ibid.*, at XIII.

[233] *Ibid.*, at XIII and 51. As Tanguy, above note 227 at 145, points out, while this proposal was guided by the need for political buy-in, it does not suggest how the international responsibility to protect might be exercised *vis-à-vis* the Chechens or Tibetans, to take but two contemporary examples.

reform.[234] However, the issue had by then been caught up in a much wider debate over the future of the UN and the role of the Security Council in authorizing the use of force. The complicating factor was the divisive debate over the unilateral military action taken against Iraq in the wake of the attacks of 11 September 2001. By November 2003, the worry over the 'lack of agreement amongst Member States on the proper role of the United Nations in providing collective security'[235] prompted the UN Secretary-General to create the High-level Panel on Threats, Challenges and Change. The panel was mandated to: (i) examine contemporary global threats and future challenges to international peace and security, including the connections between them; (ii) identify the contribution that collective action could make in addressing these challenges; and (iii) recommend the changes necessary to ensure effective collective action, including a review of the principal UN organs.[236] The desire to complete a comprehensive review on all the rules concerning the use of force reflects the need for generality and non-contradiction, two criteria of legality. In other words, the elements of self-defence, collective security and the responsibility to protect should each partake of certain core values and processes of decision. For example, that is why the requirements of necessity and proportionality apply in all lawful uses of force.

The High-level Panel's report was published in December 2004.[237] With respect to the use of force for the protection of people, the report drew extensively on ICISS's recommendations. The panel specifically endorsed 'the emerging norm that there is a collective international responsibility to protect, exercisable by the Security Council authorizing military intervention as a last resort'.[238] Building on the ICISS criteria, the panel outlined 'five basic criteria of legitimacy' for the Council to consider in making decisions on the use of military force, be it to deal with external threats to states' security or to address grave humanitarian crises within states. These criteria, which the panel suggested should be 'embodied in declaratory resolutions of the Security Council and the General Assembly', were:

[234] It is important to note the presence, and leadership role, of Gareth Evans, the former Foreign Minister of Australia, on both the ICISS and the High-level Panel. His contributions highlight the opportunities that exist for individual norm entrepreneurship in international society.

[235] *In Larger Freedom*, above note 71, para. 76

[236] See UN Press Release SG/A/857, 'Secretary General Names High-Level Panel to Study Global Security Threats, and Recommend Necessary Changes', 4 November 2003, at www.un.org/News/Press/docs/2003/sga857.doc.htm.

[237] See *Report of the High-level Panel on Threats, Challenges and Change*, above note 69.

[238] *Ibid.*, para. 203.

seriousness of threat, proper purpose, last resort, proportional means and balance of consequences.[239]

In suggesting this approach, which would apply to all three elements of the use of force regime, the panel was trying to address criteria of generality, clarity and non-contradiction and the problem of the lack of congruence between the norms on the use of force and the practice of the Security Council. The High-level Panel emphasized that criteria or guidelines on the use of force could 'maximize the possibility of achieving Security Council consensus' and 'minimize the possibility of individual Member States bypassing the Security Council'.[240] As we argued in Chapter 1, adherence to the criteria of legality gives rise to a distinctive form of legal legitimacy, and this is a helpful way to understand the recommendations of the panel.

The panel also took up the ICISS suggestions regarding self-discipline of the permanent members in exercising the veto, which goes as well to generality and congruence of practice with norm.[241] The effect would be to constrain what might be a purely political set of decisions by encouraging a practice of legality. Inversely, the work of the panel reveals that one cannot build a practice of legality upon norms that do not meet the criteria of legality. If the criteria are not met, the subsequent practice will likely be unpredictable, issue-specific and unclear. However, it may be possible to start with a social norm, well-supported by shared understandings, that fails to meet the criteria of legality. Through continuing negotiation and practice, the criteria of legality may be built into the norm, enabling the norm to become law. This legal norm is then supported and reinforced by a subsequent practice of legality. We have suggested above that this is what happened with the concept of anticipatory self-defence. It has not yet happened with the responsibility to protect.

So far, we have focused upon the High-level Panel's recommendations concerning the criteria that should apply to all decisions of the Security Council when authorizing the use of force. Before applying those criteria, however, one must identify clearly the circumstances that could possibly

[239] *Ibid.*, paras. 207–8. For a discussion of the idea of overarching criteria for decisions on the use of military force, see Gareth Evans, 'When is it Right to Fight?' (2004) 46 *Survival* 59. Of course, these criteria are derived from traditional just war theory. See Jutta Brunnée and Stephen J. Toope, 'Slouching Towards New "Just Wars": International Law and the Use of Force After September 11th' (2004) 51 *Netherlands International Law Review* 363.

[240] *Report of the High-level Panel on Threats, Challenges and Change*, above note 69, para. 206.

[241] *Ibid.*, para. 256.

trigger any use of force. It is worth re-emphasizing that the jurisdictional approach that states merely that the Security Council can act when there is a threat to or breach of 'peace and security' is a deliberately fluid and broadly political idea. Hence the difficulty faced by the Council in creating clarity or constancy in decision-making on the use of force. Therefore in the context of the responsibility to protect, the panel attempted to provide a more precise trigger for action. It invoked in modified form the criteria for military action proposed by the ICISS: 'genocide and other large scale killing, ethnic cleansing or serious violation of international humanitarian law'.[242]

In his response to the report of the High-level Panel, the Secretary-General highlighted the question whether states have the right, or even obligation, to use force protectively to rescue citizens from genocide or comparable crimes against humanity.[243] Note the important shift in emphasis, from a list of grave human rights violations, to the concept of international crime as the trigger for action. Another shift is equally important. Whereas both ICISS and the High-level Panel had left open the possibility for unilateral action in a case where the Security Council could not act, the Secretary-General's response emphasized that '[t]he task is not to find alternatives to the Security Council as a source of authority but to make it work better'.[244]

The Secretary-General then endorsed ICISS's and the High-level Panel's call for criteria. He suggested that the 'Council should come to a common view on how to weigh the seriousness of the threat; the proper purpose of the proposed military action; whether means short of the use of force might plausibly succeed in stopping the threat; whether the military option is proportional to the threat at hand; and whether there is a reasonable chance of success.'[245] He stressed that the effort to articulate and apply criteria for authorizing the use of force for protective purposes was essential to achieve legitimacy amongst states and global public opinion for any Council action.[246] That legitimacy would be achieved, we suggest, to the extent that certain criteria of legality are met, notably generality, constancy and clarity.

The concept of the responsibility to protect survived the difficult negotiations leading to the adoption of the 2005 United Nations Summit

[242] *Ibid.*, para. 203. Arguably the reference to 'serious violations of international humanitarian law' widened the scope of triggering events for intervention that ICISS had envisaged.

[243] *In Larger Freedom*, above note 71, paras. 122 and 125.

[244] *Ibid.*, para 126. [245] *Ibid.* [246] *Ibid.*

Outcome Document, but not-so-subtle shifts in emphasis occurred. The responsibility to protect was now described as primarily a responsibility of individual states to protect their own populations. In addition, the link to international crime was solidified. States are only called upon to protect their populations from 'genocide, war crimes, ethnic cleansing and crimes against humanity'.[247] A role was posited for international society, but this role is first to 'encourage and help States' to exercise their responsibility to protect their own people, and secondly to 'use appropriate diplomatic, humanitarian and other peaceful means … to help protect populations'.[248] The Security Council was authorized to take collective protection action under Chapter VII on a 'case-by-case basis' and 'should peaceful means be inadequate and national authorities manifestly fail to protect their populations' from the listed international crimes.[249]

What these alterations reveal is that the shared understandings around any duty to address humanitarian crises are so thin that member states wanted to track as closely as possible the existing normative framework on the use of force. This framework is shaped by the continuing power of the norms of sovereignty and non-intervention. For example, the requirement that domestic action should have manifestly failed means that the Council cannot take preventative action, but can only authorize intervention in response to a continuing crisis. Nonetheless, the Security Council is reaffirmed as the appropriate decision-making body on the use of force. In addition, it is arguable that the Council can authorize intervention in situations of grave humanitarian crises, not amounting to a threat or breach of international peace and security, as long as those crises contain elements that can be described as international crimes.

This last nuance is important, for it may mean that there has actually been a narrowing of the potential for action when compared, say, with the situation in Somalia in 1992. When the Security Council authorized military force to restore order in Somalia, an authorization first taken up by the United States, the situation could best be described as one of chaos. Indeed, Somalia became the prototype for arguments over how to address so-called 'failed states'. But because of the lack of a functioning government, and the widespread distribution of responsibility for violence, it is very hard to discern how any 'international crime' could have been identified. In 1992 the Security Council demonstrated the malleability of the concept of 'international peace and security' extending it to a situation

[247] See UN General Assembly, above note 1, para. 138.

[248] *Ibid.*, paras. 138 and 139.

[249] *Ibid.*, para 139.

of internal chaos.[250] Today, if the framework of the Outcome Document proved determinative, the Security Council might decide that it can no longer employ the trigger of threat or breach of international peace and security in the case of humanitarian crisis. Relying on the new trigger of international crime, it might refuse to authorize intervention.

Furthermore, by asserting that decisions on the use of force must be made on a 'case-by-case' basis without generally applicable criteria, the states who agreed to the Outcome Document effectively reaffirmed their desire for political space in use of force decisions. The overall balance of the Outcome Document is that the triggering criteria for any use of force to protect vulnerable populations are made legal (through the vehicle of international crime) but that the considerations that affect concrete decisions are left in the political realm. The member states did not take up the consistent recommendations of ICISS, the High-level Panel and the Secretary-General, to develop criteria for intervention. The only charge was to the General Assembly to 'continue consideration of the responsibility to protect … and its implications, bearing in mind the principles of the Charter and international law'.[251]

In January 2009, Ban-Ki Moon, Kofi Annan's successor as UN Secretary-General, released a major report on 'Implementing the responsibility to protect'. The report stresses the strict focus of the concept on genocide, war crimes, ethnic cleansing, and crimes against humanity, which firmly anchors the responsibility to protect in existing international law.[252] It also emphasizes that the responsibility to protect, as endorsed by the General Assembly in 2005, 'is an ally of sovereignty, not an adversary' and 'seeks to strengthen sovereignty, not weaken it'.[253] As well, we see a conceptualization of 'sovereignty as responsibility' and a further effort to distance the responsibility to protect from the controversial notion of a 'right' to humanitarian intervention.[254]

Yet, the Secretary General's report is also clear that 'sovereignty does not bestow impunity' and that there is an international responsibility to 'respond collectively in a timely and decisive manner' when a state is manifestly failing in its protective responsibility.[255] However, as the

[250] Gray, above note 28, pp. 287–8.

[251] UN General Assembly, above note 1, para. 139.

[252] *Implementing the Responsibility to Protect*, Report by the Secretary-General, UN Doc. A/63/677, 12 January 2009; http://daccessdds.un.org/doc/UNDOC/GEN/N09/206/10/PDF/N0920610.pdf?OpenElement, paras. 2 and 3, and 10(b).

[253] *Ibid.*, para. 10(a).

[254] *Ibid.*, paras. 7 and 10(a).

[255] *Ibid.*, paras. 11(c), 54.

report underscores, 'the responsibility to protect does not alter, indeed it reinforces, the legal obligations of Member States to refrain from the use of force except in conformity with the Charter.'[256] Coercive military action is reserved for 'extreme cases' and must be authorized by the Security Council 'or by regional or subregional arrangements under Article 53 [of the charter], with the prior authorization of the Security Council'.[257]

The report offers two further observations in relation to possible military action, both of which pick up on recommendations in earlier reports. First, the Secretary-General's report urges the five permanent members of the Security Council to 'reach a mutual understanding' to refrain from employing or threatening the use of their veto power 'in situations of manifest failure to meet obligations relating to the responsibility to protect, as defined in paragraph 139 of the Summit Outcome'.[258] Second, the report asks UN members to 'consider the principles, rules and doctrine that should guide the application of coercive force', pointing out that 'the credibility, authority and hence effectiveness of the United Nations in advancing the principles relating to the responsibility to protect depend, in large part, on the consistency with which they are applied.'[259]

The Secretary-General's report was presented to the UN General Assembly in July 2009. A formal plenary debate ensued, during which speakers representing all parts of the world took the floor to offer the views of member states and various groupings of states. Taken together, these interventions suggest gathering support for the responsibility to protect, especially when compared to the debates leading up to the 2005 Summit. Almost sixty member states echoed the Secretary-General's view that the responsibility to protect was anchored in existing international law.[260]

Many states, including the members of the European Union, Benin, Costa Rica, Lesotho, Qatar, and Timor-Leste, also agreed that mass atrocities within states could constitute threats to international peace and security, such as to enable the Security Council to take collective action.[261] The United States noted, in very general terms, that collective action would

256 *Ibid.*, para. 3. 257 *Ibid.*, para.56.
258 *Ibid.*, para. 61. 259 *Ibid.*, para. 62.
260 See Global Centre for the Responsibility to Protect, *Implementing the Responsibility to Protect – The 2009 General Assembly Debate: An Assessment*, August 2009, p. 1; at www.responsibilitytoprotect.org/index.php/component/content/article/35-r2pcs-topics/2522-report-by-the-global-centre-for-r2p-the-2009-general-assembly-debate-an-assessment-, p. 5.
261 *Ibid.*

'[o]nly rarely, and in extremis, ... include the use of force'.[262] In any case, as with all operational aspects of the responsibility to protect, including action through the Security Council, responsibility could arise only in relation to the international crimes identified in the *Summit Outcome*.[263] Not surprisingly, the role of the Security Council and questions concerning recourse to military measures continued to be among the most controversial topics of debate.[264]

On 14 September 2009, the General Assembly adopted a short and carefully balanced resolution on the responsibility to protect.[265] In it, it reaffirms its respect for the principles and purposes of the UN Charter, recalls paras. 138 and 139 of the *Summit Outcome*, takes note of the Secretary-General's report on implementation and the 'timely and constructive' debate on the report, and decides 'to continue its consideration of the responsibility to protect'. Revealing the reservations that some states continue to have, it was only the removal of the words 'with appreciation' from the operative paragraph taking note of the Secretary-General's report that enabled adoption of the resolution by consensus.[266]

A full review of the interventions in the debate is beyond the scope of this chapter, but it is safe to conclude that the understanding of the responsibility to protect that is outlined in paras. 138 and 139 of the *Summit Outcome* is shared by a growing number of states from all parts of the world.[267] While concerns about potential abuses of the concept linger, the group of states that are categorically opposed to its collective action aspects, including use of force through the Security Council as a last resort, appears to be shrinking.[268] It is also noteworthy that the NAM

[262] Remarks by Ambassador Rosemary A. DiCarlo, at a General Assembly Debate on the Responsibility to Protect, in the General Assembly Hall, 23 July 23 2009, at http://responsibilitytoprotect.org/USA_ENG-1.pdf.

[263] Global Centre for the Responsibility to Protect, *Implementing the Responsibility to Protect*, above note 260, p. 6.

[264] *Ibid.*, p. 7.

[265] UN General Assembly Resolution 63/308, UN Doc. A/RES/63/308, 7 October 2009, at http://daccessdds.un.org/doc/UNDOC/GEN/N09/513/38/PDF/N0951338.pdf?OpenElement.

[266] See Global Centre for the Responsibility to Protect, *Summary of Statements on Adoption of resolution RES A/63/L80 Rev. 1 – September 2009*; at http://globalr2p.org/media/pdf/GCR2P_Summary_of_Statements_on_Adoption_of_Resolution_on_R2P.pdf.

[267] Global Centre for the Responsibility to Protect, *ibid.*, pp. 10–11 (detailing the patterns of support in Africa, Asia and Pacific, Latin America and the Caribbean, the Middle East, and Eastern and Western Europe).

[268] Cuba, Nicaragua, Pakistan, Sudan, the People's Republic of Korea, and Venezuela are the most vocal of these states. See International Coalition for the Responsibility to Protect,

statement offered on the occasion of the debate was considerably softer than the earlier statements of the movement. The statement merely notes 'mixed feelings' about the implementation of the responsibility to protect, and 'concerns' about its possible abuse beyond the four crimes listed in the *Summit Outcome*, 'to legitimize unilateral coercive measures or intervention in the internal affairs of States'.[269] Furthermore, it has been noted that many of the 118 NAM member states 'appeared to break with tradition by not explicitly aligning themselves with the NAM statement'.[270]

The emphasis of much of the continuing debate appears not to be on challenging the concept of the responsibility to protect as such, but on refining it, especially as it relates to the use of force. Indeed, seen through the lens of our conceptual framework, the proposals in the Secretary-General's report, as well as many of the interventions in the General Assembly debate, seem at least in part designed to strengthen the legality of the norm. For example, the calls for a more representative Security Council speak to the concern about generality. The question who would decide whether a crisis situation involved a triggering crime speaks to the clarity requirement, as well as to the delineation between legal and political space. The same is true for requests for clarification on the circumstances in which the Security Council could resort to collective action. In turn, the strong emphasis, in the Secretary-General's Report and in several states' plenary statements, on the need for guidelines on the use of force underscores the importance of generality, clarity and constancy. Guidelines, such as those proposed by ICISS or the High-Level Panel, would significantly enhance the legality of the norm by subjecting case-by-case decisions to overarching criteria that identify the extreme and exceptional cases to which military intervention should be restricted. They would also highlight cases in which force should in fact be used, and demand a reasoned justification of inaction. Finally, the call for non-use of the Security Council veto in cases involving one of the listed crimes is also related to legality considerations. The veto power for the five permanent members undercuts the generality of

Report on the General Assembly Debate on the Responsibility to Protect., 15 September 2009, pp. 7–8, at http://responsibilitytoprotect.org/ICRtoPGAdebate.pdf.

269 See Statement by Egypt on behalf of the Non-Aligned Movement, Agenda Item 44 and 107: 'Integrated and coordinated implementation of and follow-up to the outcomes of the major United Nations conferences and summits in the economic, social and related fields; Follow-up to the outcome of the Millennium Summit: report of the Secretary-General', p. 1, at www.responsibilitytoprotect.org/NAM_Egypt_ENG.pdf.

270 See Global Centre for the Responsibility to Protect, *Implementing the Responsibility to Protect*, above note 260, p. 4.

protective force option, and weakens the potential for consistent decision-making by the Council.

The norm of responsibility to protect has now been articulated, formally endorsed and invoked positively with increasing frequency in General Assembly debates. It could potentially present a fundamental challenge to structural imperatives that have long shaped international law and politics.[271] This is precisely why it will be so difficult for shared understandings to arise that displace or significantly alter foundational principles and that support the new norm. It goes without saying that the principal institution of international relations since the Westphalian compact has been anarchic sovereignty. Anarchy may not have been inevitable, and may even have been intentionally constructed, but it has been determinative nonetheless.[272] This reality was codified in the United Nations Charter's recognition of the 'sovereign equality' of states in Article 2(1) and in the principle of 'non-intervention in the internal affairs of states' in Article 2(7). However, the charter also contained provisions that allowed for challenges to sovereignty, so the new approach contained in the responsibility to protect is not without some support in related areas of established law. The ambition of the drafters was to subject sovereignty both to human rights norms and to the constraints of collective security. In large measure, for at least forty years, this ambition remained unfulfilled. The continuing influence of state-centrism and the imperatives of power politics, especially as constructed in the Cold War, made any incursion on the principles of sovereignty and non-intervention extraordinarily difficult. Modest advances were made, however.

The 'responsibility to protect' could entail a fundamental conceptual shift, rooted in prior developments, but going much further and calling upon states to reconsider the essentials of their role and powers. Anne-Marie Slaughter has described the rise of the responsibility to protect as a 'tectonic shift' in the very definition of sovereignty.[273] For example, if the responsibility to protect were fully implemented, a state would owe

[271] See discussion in Heather Jacques Wood, Taylor Nuttall and Kendall W. Stiles, 'Humanitarian Intervention', in Wayne Sandholtz and Kendall W. Stiles (eds.), *International Norms and Cycles of Change* (Oxford University Press, 2009), p. 263.

[272] Hedley Bull, *The Anarchical Society* (New York: Columbia University Press, 1977); Alexander Wendt, 'Anarchy is What States Make of It: The Social Construction of Power Politics' (1992) 46 *International Organization* 391; and Alexander Wendt, 'Collective Identity Formation and the International State' (1994) 88 *American Political Science Review* 384.

[273] Anne-Marie Slaughter, 'Security, Solidarity, and Sovereignty: The Grand Themes of UN Reform' (2005) 99 *American Journal of International Law* 619 at 627.

obligations of protection to its own people. But the responsibility to protect also implies that the state is accountable to other states if it fails to protect its people. The accountability is not simply at the level of state responsibility; it can actually trigger the duty of third parties to intervene, including ultimately military intervention. This also implies an *erga omnes* obligation on the part of other states to act – whether collectively or unilaterally remains uncertain – in the face of a limited category of massive human rights abuses, amounting to international crimes.[274]

We do not believe that this tectonic shift has yet occurred, though pressure seems to be building.[275] Given the potential for transformative change in the deep structures of sovereignty, and hence of international law and politics, it is not surprising that although they agreed to its inclusion in the Outcome Document of the 2005 Summit, many states have sought to limit the impact of the responsibility to protect. The key limitation negotiated in the Outcome Document is that all responsibilities are triggered only in relation to international crimes.[276] This limitation was taken up in Secretary-General Moon's 2009 implementation report, and reaffirmed by many states in the subsequent General Assembly debate.

Leaving aside the issue of limitations on the scope of the responsibility to protect, the very creation of any set category of offences that might justify collective military action can have both positive and negative effects. On the positive side of the ledger, reliance on a fixed category of relatively well-established international crimes could prevent sterile definitional debates, thereby advancing generality, clarity, non-contradiction, and constancy over time. The focus on widely accepted categories of offence might also have broader normative implications. Read in conjunction with the accountability regime envisaged in the Statute of the International

[274] See Arbour, above note 34 at 450–1. But see also José E. Alvarez, 'The Schizophrenias of R2P', Panel Presentation, *Hague Joint Conference on Contemporary Issues of International Law: Criminal Jurisdiction 100 Years After the 1907 Hague Peace Conference*, The Hague, 30 June 2007, at www.asil.org/pdfs/r2pPanel.pdf (calling the idea that, for example, the UN could be legally responsible for a failure to act 'absurdly premature and not likely to be affirmed by state practice').

[275] See also Gareth Evans, 'The Responsibility to Protect: An Idea Whose Time has Come … and Gone?' (2008) 22 *International Relations* 283.

[276] In the Outcome Document responsibility is linked to 'genocide, war crimes, ethnic cleansing and crimes against humanity'. Although 'ethnic cleansing' is not established as a distinct international crime, it is arguably included in the concepts of 'genocide', 'extermination', 'deportation or forcible transfer of population' and 'enforced disappearance' as set out *inter alia* in Arts. 6 and 7 of the Rome Statute of the International Criminal Court, UN Doc. A/CONF.183/9 (17 July 1998). Depending upon factual circumstances, it might also be a 'war crime'.

Criminal Court, the linkage between a responsibility to protect and specific triggering offences could lead to a clarification and consolidation of the concept and content of international crimes, and import substance into the heretofore rather vague construct of *erga omnes* obligations.[277]

On the negative side of the ledger, the mere existence of accepted categories justifying collective action may not pre-empt definitional debates. The question whether a particular set of circumstances amounts to 'genocide' or to 'war crimes' can still arise, but this becomes a legal, rather than purely political, question. We are not suggesting that this takes away all the controversy, but only that in requiring a legal assessment, a normative change has occurred. In the case of genocide, one of the triggering crimes, we already know that disagreements over the question whether the facts fit the definition has stymied action on a number of occasions.[278] And as is well known, recognition that a crime exists will not necessarily lead to action, as the Rwanda case so sadly demonstrated. That is because, as we argued above, the triggering question is only one point in the decisional process.

Once it is determined that we confront a situation in which force could be authorized, it still remains to be decided whether or not it should be. Indeed, even in grave situations such as the crisis in Darfur, it is less than clear that a UN-authorized military intervention would achieve the ends that proponents might envisage.[279] In other words, it would arguably fail on at least one of the threshold criteria envisaged in the ICISS, High-level Panel, and Secretary-General's reports – reasonable chance of success. It may even worsen the situation by exacerbating the humanitarian situation and increasing instability in the region. Either way, when there are

[277] See Jutta Brunnée, 'International Law and Collective Concerns: Reflections on the Responsibility to Protect', in Tafsir Malick Ndiaye and Rüdiger Wolfrum (eds.), *Law of the Sea, Environmental Law and Settlement of Disputes* (Leiden: Martinus Nijhoff, 2007), pp. 48–51.

[278] See e.g. Mahmood Mamdani, 'The Politics of Naming: Genocide, Civil War, Insurgency', *London Review of Books*, 8 March 2007 (discussing US media reports and the determination of the US House of Representatives that Darfur was the site of an ongoing genocide, while a UN Commission on Darfur found that there was no policy of genocide but that actions in Darfur might constitute crimes against humanity).

[279] See Alex de Waal, 'No Such Thing as Humanitarian Intervention: Why We Need to Rethink How to Realize the "Responsibility to Protect" in Wartime', in *Harvard International Review* 2007, at www.harvardir.org/index.php?page=article&id=1482&p=1 (arguing that an international intervention in Sudan, for example, is unlikely to protect civilians, and that debates about intervention have diverted efforts from achieving a peace agreement); and Evans, above note 256 at 292 (noting that it is 'accepted by most governments and relief organizations on the ground … that a non-consensual military intervention … would almost certainly be disastrously counterproductive').

no established guidelines to shape judgement on the 'should' question, political calculations generally prevail, which is exactly what many states want. Guidelines would not eliminate political considerations or provide easy answers, but they would demand more transparent and accountable decision-making.

On balance, and given the potentially fundamental importance of the challenge to sovereignty contained in the responsibility to protect, it is difficult to dismiss the Outcome Document as mere 'cheap talk'.[280] The stakes were too high, and the implications fundamental. Some states worked hard to modify and limit the concept through its various iterations.[281] These efforts suggest that at least some states believe that the responsibility to protect actually means something – or at least that it could mean something if they are not careful to constrain the concept now. These states may believe that the limitations negotiated preclude the further evolution of a robust responsibility to protect. For other states, the central goal will be to strike the appropriate balance between sovereignty and intervention. These states would not want to disable the responsibility to protect completely, but they might want to further qualify and limit its application.[282] We saw these approaches clearly articulated in the 2009 General Assembly debate on the Secretary-General's implementation report.

Our evaluation of the status of the responsibility to protect is that it remains only a candidate norm in international relations.[283] Much work remains to be done before it can plausibly be considered a binding norm of international law.[284] The need for a continuing commitment to norm

[280] See Thomas Risse, '"Let's Argue!" Communicative Action in World Politics' (2000) 54 *International Organization* 1 at 8.

[281] See Evans, above note 275 at 292 (referring to US efforts to avoid constraints on decisions on the use of force, and Southern countries concerned about enabling interventionism).

[282] A review of the comments made by states during the debates on the 2005 World Summit suggests a spectrum of views. Some states reject R2P as an unacceptable intrusion into state sovereignty (e.g. Arab states, Cuba, Iran, Pakistan, Venezuela and Vietnam). Others were more open to the idea, but concerned that collective security might become defined in terms of R2P and serve as a pretext for intervention (e.g. Malawi, on behalf of the Group of African States). Yet others are non-committal, calling for more discussion (e.g. Colombia, Indonesia, Mexico), or insisting on the role of the Security Council (e.g. Bulgaria, Chile, Russia, Tanzania). Strong support for the concept comes largely from northern countries, such as the members of the EU, Australia, Canada, Iceland, Japan, New Zealand and Norway. See *Review*, above note 59.

[283] See also Carsten Stahn, 'Responsibility to Protect: Political Rhetoric or Emerging Legal Norm?' (2007) 101 *American Journal of International Law* 99.

[284] See also Evans, above note 275 at 289.

entrepreneurship is implicit in the process that led up to the unanimous adoption of the responsibility to protect in the Outcome Document of the 2005 summit. So far, the norm has been articulated in expert reports, in the response of the UN Secretary-General and in the final statement of an international gathering of heads of state and government. The concept was widely supported by states in the debate over Secretary-General Moon's implementation report. However, it has never been included in a treaty. Meanwhile, Canada, originally a forceful proponent of the responsibility to protect, seems to be taking a more cautious line under a new government, of a different political stripe.[285]

Other states have thrown their support behind the new norm, including Australia, Bangladesh, Korea, the Netherlands, and the United Kingdom.[286] Various NGOs are also actively promoting the norm,[287] as is the UN Secretary-General, Ban Ki-Moon.[288]

In any event, the interactional international law framework reveals that norm entrepreneurship is not in itself enough to create law. Articulating candidate norms, and generating increasing support can help to create the shared understandings that allow norms to emerge. In the case of the responsibility to protect even this process is not complete. Granted, following the world summit, the Security Council adopted a resolution that endorsed the concept of R2P,[289] and one that invoked it with respect to the

285 It is interesting to note that the leader of the official opposition in Canada, as of 2009, is Michael Ignatieff, who served as a member of the ICISS panel. See Anthony Fenton, 'Haiti and the Danger of the Responsibility to Protect (R2P)', *Upside Down World*, 23 December 2008, at www.upsidedownworld.org/main/content/view/1638/1 ('And waiting in the wings to take political power is the new leader of Canada's Liberal Party, Michael Ignatieff, cheerleader for the Iraq and Afghanistan wars, advocate of "Empire Lite", and member of the R2P's ICISS').

286 See Meeting Summary, 'Uniting to Support the Responsibility to Protect: Preserving the Spirit of the 2005 Agreement', Global Centre for the Responsibility to Protect, 25 September 2008, at www.globalr2p.org/pdf/related/Sept08mtg.pdf.

287 See e.g. the recently launched (28 January 2009) *Responsibility to Protect – Engaging Civil Society*, at www.responsibilitytoprotect.org; *Global Centre for the Responsibility to Protect*, at www.globalcentrer2p.org; *R2P Coalition*, at www.r2pcoalition.org; and the *Asia-Pacific Centre for the Responsibility to Protect*, at www.r2pasiapacific.org.

288 See United Nations Secretary-General Ban Ki-Moon, *Address to the Summit of the African Union*, Addis Abbaba, 31 January 2008, at www.un.org/apps/news/infocus/sgspeeches/search_full.asp?statID=180 (stating that he was 'fully committed to keep the momentum ... made at the 2005 World Summit and will spare no effort to operationalize the responsibility to protect').

289 See United Nations Security Council Resolution 1674, 28 April 2006, UN Doc. S/RES/1674, para. 4 (reaffirming paras. 138 and 139 of the 2005 Outcome Document, which relate to R2P), at www.un.org/Docs/sc/unsc_resolutions06.htm.

situation in Darfur.[290] Still, there is no widely shared understanding that the Security Council should authorize states to fulfil a duty to protect vulnerable populations in times of humanitarian crisis.[291] Notwithstanding the many positive signs, in some parts of the developing world scepticism, or even hostility to the doctrine, remains.[292] Indeed, representatives of some Latin American, Arab and African states have since claimed that the relevant paragraphs in the 2005 Outcome Document were intended to deal with the protection of civilians from specific crimes, and not to endorse the concept of R2P.[293]

In any event, even when a shared understanding arises, any norm must still be built within the parameters of the criteria of legality. In the case of the responsibility to protect, we have shown that some substantive elements of the emerging norm meet the criteria of legality. For example, anchoring the responsibility in the framework of 'international crime' provides for greater clarity, enhances constancy over time, and minimizes the possibility of norm contradiction. A triggering approach resting in the political assessment of threat or breach of international peace and security does not meet these criteria. Other elements of the responsibility to protect candidate norm are problematic, and may make it difficult for the norm ever to achieve the status of customary international law. This includes the refusal of the 2005 summit to agree to guidelines that would constrain and shape decisions on the authorization of military action to protect vulnerable populations.

In summary, the responsibility to protect does not benefit from a widespread shared understanding that would allow the Security Council to authorize the use of force in cases of humanitarian emergency. The specific normative content of the proposed responsibility is also problematic in some details from the perspective of the criteria of legality. Given the

290 United Nations Security Council Resolution 1706, 31 August 2006, UN Doc. S/RES/1706, preamble (recalling Resolution 1674, as well as paras. 138 and 139 of the 2005 Outcome Document), at www.un.org/Docs/sc/unsc_resolutions06.htm.

291 See *Comments of the Non-Aligned Movement*, above note 59, paras. 14–15 (stating that 'NAM reiterates its rejection of the so-called "right" of humanitarian intervention, which has no basis either in the UN Charter or in international law', ... 'observes the similarities between the new expression "responsibility to protect" and "humanitarian intervention", and wishes to carefully study and consider further the expression "responsibility to protect" and its implications on the basis of the principles of non-interference and non-intervention as well as the respect for territorial integrity and national sovereignty of States').

292 See Evans, above note 275 at 288–9 (referring to the 'Arab-Islamic and Latin American worlds", sub-Saharan Africa, and Asia).

293 *Ibid.*, at 288; and see Stahn, above note 283 at 108.

inchoate status of the concept, there is no practice of legality surrounding the responsibility to protect. It follows that there is certainly no emerging unilateral duty, let alone 'right', to engage in protective military action.

3.4.2 Failed norm entrepreneurship

Before we conclude this chapter, it is worth delving into efforts to link the emerging norms on the responsibility to protect to those governing self-defence. After the attacks of 11 September 2001, it became intellectually fashionable in some circles, especially within the United States, to attack the framework on the use of force, and to argue that it was outdated or ineffective in addressing the threats of global terrorism.[294] This tendency was exacerbated during the worldwide debates concerning the most prudent approach in dealing with the alleged existence of WMD in Iraq. Given the contemporaneous promotion of the concept of the responsibility to protect, it is perhaps not surprising that some commentators attempted to link together the notions of threat said to justify intervention to protect vulnerable populations and the threat posed by terrorists and by the existence of weapons of mass destruction in the hands of 'rogue' regimes. This was, after all, the era in which an American president could single out threatening states as members of an 'axis of evil'.[295] Human rights concerns were not actually invoked as an independent legal justification for action in Iraq,[296] but they were used *ex post facto* to reinforce other rhetorical claims, notably to extend the concept of 'threat prevention'.[297]

[294] See Charles Krauthammer, 'Unilateralism, Yes indeed', *The Washington Post*, 14 December 2001; Marc A. Thiessen, 'World Pax, Not World Pacts' (Debate) (March/April 2001) *Foreign Policy*; Michael Reisman, 'In Defense of World Public Order' (2004) 95 *The American Journal of International Law* 833 at 834; Glennon, above note 26; and Michael Glennon, 'The Fog of Law: Self-Defense, Inherence, and Incoherence in Article 51 of the United Nations Charter' (2001–2002) 25 *Harvard Journal of Law and Public Policy* 539 at 540 (stating that 'the Charter's use-of-force regime has all but collapsed').

[295] President George W. Bush, *State of the Union 2002*, at http://georgewbush-whitehouse.archives.gov/news/releases/2002/01/20020129-11.html. See also David Frum and Richard Perle, *An End to Evil: How to Win the War on Terror* (New York: Random House, 2003).

[296] See Jutta Brunnée, 'On the Legality of the Use of Force against Iraq' (2003) 59 *Behind the Headlines* 1 at 3.

[297] See President George W. Bush, Radio Address, 5 Apr 2003, at http://georgewbush-whitehouse.archives.gov/news/releases/2003/04/20030405.html ('Village by village, city by city, liberation is coming. The people of Iraq have my pledge: Our fighting forces will press on until their oppressors are gone and their whole country is free'). See also Jack Straw, 'We are in Iraq to Bring about Democracy', speech by Foreign Secretary Jack Straw, Labour Party Conference, Brighton, 28 September 2005, at www.jackstrawmp.org.uk/speeches_detail.asp?id_content=120.

For example, the distinguished American scholars Alan Buchanan and Robert Keohane argued for a recasting of the security concern over threats such as those posed by WMD into a broader cosmopolitan concern for the protection of human rights. Their premise was that massive human suffering and human rights violations had to be averted 'regardless of whether the rights endangered are those of our fellow citizens or foreigners'.[298] In view of the nature of the WMD threat, Buchanan and Keohane argued that the limits on military action imposed by existing international law were too narrow. To arrive at appropriate parameters for preventive force, they suggested that we eliminate the distinction that international law had drawn between defensive actions and humanitarian intervention in another state. According to Buchanan and Keohane:

> reducing the grounds for preventive use of force to self-defense ... conceives of the potential aims of preventive action too narrowly. It fails even to consider the possibility that there are circumstances in which the preventive use of force would be justified to protect the rights of persons other than one's fellow citizens.[299]

Traditional just war theory, for Buchanan and Keohane, furnished sufficient substantive standards for preventive force, such as proportionality, non-combatant immunity and avoidance of excessive force.[300] What was missing was an institutional framework. The solution to the normative dilemma surrounding preventive war was to embed just war principles in 'mechanisms that help to ensure that they are applied correctly and that there are effective sanctions to increase compliance with them'.[301]

As will be obvious from our previous discussion, we agree that an effective forum for collective deliberation and decision-making is crucial to legitimate uses of force designed to prevent threats to peace and security or to avert massive human rights violations. We also agree that it is important to combine strong institutional disciplines on forcible intervention with justificatory disciplines that are as focused and transparent as possible. However, we do not agree that a 'cosmopolitan' choice of human rights protection as the overarching theme improves on the justificatory requirements already imposed on the collective use of preventive force. At the institutional level, it is not clear that either type of threat is

[298] See Buchanan and Keohane, above note 4 at 5.

[299] *Ibid.* [300] *Ibid.*

[301] *Ibid.*, at 12. For Buchanan and Keohane, institutional accountability has an *ex ante* and an *ex post* dimension. Prior to taking preventive action, states must make an evidence-based case for force to the relevant institution. After the resort to force, they must submit themselves to an evaluation of their earlier justification. *Ibid.*, at 1–2 and 13–16.

better addressed by limiting participation in decisions on the preventive use of force to 'those states that have decent records regarding the protection of basic human rights', which Buchanan and Keohane preferred amongst the various institutional models they proposed.[302]

Similarly, resting a system of cosmopolitan accountability on a 'coalition of reasonably democratic states' where the Security Council fails to authorize preventive use of force is problematic.[303] Practically speaking, any such proposal is likely to meet with the fierce and effective resistance of developing states.[304] At a conceptual level, although cosmopolitan in name, the idea risks undermining the pluralist aspirations of international law, and the diversity of its sources, which are the markers of a truly cosmopolitan spirit. Buchanan and Keohane were well aware of these concerns, but suggested that they could be addressed through broadly construed criteria that would admit a 'fairly wide range of political institutions and cultures' and would exclude from the coalition only 'states that are unambiguous violators of human rights'.[305] In addition, they suggested that the continued operation of the Security Council would reduce the likelihood of 'creating a schism between the democracies and the other members of the UN'.[306] We do not share their optimism in this regard because, as we have discussed briefly already, the Security Council is itself subject to increasing critique in relation to its representative quality.

Anne-Marie Slaughter, too, has advocated the idea of a coalition of liberal democratic states within the UN that might authorize the use of force when the Security Council cannot act.[307] In a contribution with

[302] *Ibid.*, at 10. [303] *Ibid.*, at 18.

[304] See also *Comments of the Non-Aligned Movement*, above note 59, para. 17 (stating that 'The Non-Aligned Movement strongly condemns the labelling of countries as good or evil and repressive based on unilateral and unjustified criteria, and reiterates its firm condemnation of all unilateral military actions without proper authorization from the Security Council, as well as of threats of military action against the sovereignty, territorial integrity and independence of NAM Member Countries, which constitute acts of aggression and blatant violations of the principle of non-intervention and non-interference').

[305] Buchanan and Keohane, above note 4 at 18. Note that Buchanan and Keohane also canvass a range of options for reforming the Security Council to enable it to provide for 'cosmopolitan accountability'. *Ibid.*, at 16–17.

[306] *Ibid.*, at 20.

[307] See Anne-Marie Slaughter, 'The Liberal Agenda for Peace: International Relations Theory and the Future of the United Nations' (1994) 4 *Transnational Law and Contemporary Problems* 377 at 406–7 and 416–17; Slaughter, above note 4; and Slaughter, above note 189 (suggesting a 'caucus of democracies' or other 'alternative fora of discussion in the UN, and perhaps ultimately of legitimation for action taken by some sub-set of UN actors').

Lee Feinstein, Slaughter echoed Buchanan and Keohane's cosmopolitan premise, arguing: 'Whether individuals are targeted for execution over time or vaporized in a single instant [by WMD], the result is the same: a massive and senseless loss of life.'[308] However, for Feinstein and Slaughter this point served mainly as support for the argument that the ICISS's proposal of a 'responsibility to protect' should be emulated in the WMD context through a 'duty to prevent'.[309] Feinstein and Slaughter were not advocating military intervention as the primary tool to forestall threats posed by states seeking WMD or sponsoring terrorism. Rather, as the ICISS did in the context of the responsibility to protect, they envisaged a range of other early action strategies, with force being a measure of last resort.[310]

However, whereas the ICISS tied military intervention to actual or imminent large-scale human rights violations, and the UN Summit Outcome document further narrowed the triggering mechanism to require the engagement of international criminal law, no limiting conditions were offered by Feinstein and Slaughter.[311] Indeed, the very point of the duty to prevent was to overcome the fact that the existing criterion of imminent threat (an element of the necessity test that applies to all use of force decisions) is difficult to meet in the context of early action on terrorist and WMD threats.[312] Instead, the proposed 'duty to prevent' was specifically related to the profile of states. It focused on states without internal checks that might possess WMD, or that were suspected of sponsoring terrorism and might be seeking to obtain WMD. The duty to prevent would apply in cases where existing agreements had not prevented such

[308] Lee Feinstein and Anne-Marie Slaughter, 'A Duty to Prevent' (2004) 83 *Foreign Affairs* 136 at 142.

[309] *Ibid.*, at 137. Whereas Buchanan and Keohane suggest that, given the overarching concern for the protection of human life, there is no meaningful distinction between defensive and protective action.

[310] *Ibid.*, at 145–6.

[311] Feinstein and Slaughter do outline a series of precautionary principles, but they largely address the extent of allowable force, rather than providing limits on the initial triggering: 'Force must be exerted on the smallest scale, for the shortest time, and at the lowest intensity necessary to achieve its objective; the objective itself must be reasonably attainable when measured against the likelihood of making matters worse. Finally, force should be governed by fundamental principles of the laws of war ...' *Ibid.*, at 149.

[312] *Ibid.* Feinstein and Slaughter observe: 'Consider, for instance, how recognizing a duty to prevent could have changed the debate over the war in Iraq ... Under existing law ... the United States could not argue that Saddam posed a threat warranting intervention simply because of his absolute power, his past behavior, and his expressed intentions.' *Ibid.*, at 138–9.

states from pursuing WMD.[313] These criteria, along with a state's record of threatening past behaviour,[314] bear considerable resemblance to elements of the 2002 US *National Security Strategy*'s concept of 'rogue state'.[315]

The dangers of proposals such as those made by Buchanan and Keohane, and Feinstein and Slaughter are illustrated by the fact that less internationally minded commentators who 'doubt whether Charter use-of-force rules remain legally binding', continue to offer very similar arguments.[316] The criteria of legality illustrate why blending a variety of reasons for war inherent in the claim that 'the justifications for a preventive war … have a deep resemblance to the justifications now commonly given, and accepted, for preventive "humanitarian" interventions',[317] undermines the legal restraints on military force. Such blending promotes the collapse of legally distinct categories such as self-defence, protection of human rights, and threats to international peace and security into one super-category of 'threat prevention', using the other categories simply as examples of dangers that can be invoked to justify action as either defensive or protective.

This effect, of course, is at least in part intended by those who argue that the normative concern should be protection of human life against grave danger, regardless of whether those at risk are 'fellow citizens or foreigners'.[318] Yet, however much one may agree with the latter proposition in principle, it does not address the thorny question of what threshold of threat must be crossed for military force to be the appropriate response. No one would deny that there are linkages amongst humanitarian crises, repressive regimes, collapsing states, terrorism, and international security threats. But neither intelligent policy response nor international law is aided by simply lumping all of these issues together. Linkages should be carefully considered, but interventions must be justified on grounds that relate to the actual problems that one is seeking to alleviate.[319] That is why so much effort has been expended over so many years to articulate, explain and uphold the distinct normative frameworks governing

313 *Ibid.*, at 142. 314 *Ibid.*, at 139.

315 *Security Strategy*, above note 4 at 13–14. See also J. Gross Stein, 'Pandora's box of pre-emption', *The National Post*, 25 October 2002 (suggesting that the *Security Strategy* uses judgments about character, based on past behaviour, as criteria for pre-emptive military attack).

316 See Robert J. Delahunty and John Yoo, 'The "Bush Doctrine": Can Preventive War Be Justified?' (2009) 32 *Harvard Journal of Law and Public Policy* 1 at 4.

317 *Ibid.*, at 23.

318 Buchanan and Keohane, above note 4 and accompanying text.

319 See Lowe, above note 3 at 861.

self-defence and collective security. The parallel but separate practices of legality that have grown up around these frameworks, and that continue to buttress them, has made it very hard for norm entrepreneurs to blend either self-adjudged humanitarian concerns or auto-determined 'threats' into the other frameworks so as to create a supposed 'duty to prevent' or a 'right' to engage in 'preventive war'.

In any event, collapsing all the use of force justifications into one goal of 'threat prevention' undermines the generality of law. If only some actors can invoke the supposed legal principles to justify military action (the United States unilaterally; liberal democratic states; states that meet ill-defined tests of human rights accountability), then the law is not available to all. Clarity is also fundamentally challenged: given the absence of any constraining trigger for the duty to prevent, it is simply not possible to know when any given coalition of the willing would choose to act. The same problem ensures that constancy over time will be impossible to achieve; the decision to act would remain essentially a political judgment, unshaped by legal conditions.

It is also very likely that the criteria of non-contradiction would be breached, for without any guiding framework to shape decisions on the use of military force for prevention, states could be told that they have a 'duty' to intervene at the same time that they are told that 'non-intervention' remains a powerful norm of international law. Both principles would be equally powerful (and contradictory), which is entirely different, for example, from the possibility that the responsibility to protect is a limited exception to the non-intervention rule, constrained by the need to link the rule to the framework of international criminal law.

Finally, it is certain that given the lack of any clear triggering mechanism or shaping guidelines that would require transparency and accountability in the decision to employ preventive force, this supposed duty would not allow for congruence between the norm and subsequent practice. Decisions to act would be entirely ad hoc and unpredictable. It is hard to see how any continuing practice of legality would be possible. Instead, the norm would be beholden to raw politics. It could be argued that this is exactly as it should be, that decisions on preventing massive threats to people are political. We are doubtful that leaving such important and consequential decisions entirely outside the framework of law would be wise. The risks of generating enormous political tensions, and further resort to violence are great. In any event, our principal point is more limited: the notion of preventive war as articulated by some influential American scholars or as mooted in the 2002 US *National Security Strategy* purports to address a legal framework and seeks modification of that framework, but the proposals are actually outside law because they cannot meet the criteria of legality.

The criteria of legality underscore that, to discharge their important justificatory function, legal categories must retain relative normative clarity and coherence. This point is especially important in the case of exceptions to fundamental, and broadly stated, rules. Legal norms are typically applied by analogy to a broader framework of norms and to past practices that circumscribe plausible interpretation.[320] Legal norms are not self-applying, but neither are they infinitely malleable.[321] It is not enough that 'an argument' can be made; the argument must have the power to persuade and thereby to generate adherence.[322] In other words, the criteria of legality not only determine the strength of legal norms, but also serve to discipline legal arguments. Relative clarity and coherence also help to avoid the problem of mixed motives on the part of international actors. If discipline is required in justifying resort to the use of force, it becomes harder for states simply to pick and choose amongst an available menu of justificatory options.

The failed attempt to instantiate the concept of preventive war illustrates the point. The concept purported to extend the self-defence norm beyond the point at which it could no longer provide meaningful guidance, and so would effectively have destroyed the law of self-defence by dislodging the norm from the terrain of legality. Similarly, in extending the idea of prevention to a duty to prevent all massive human rights violations, but without any clear triggering standard or guidelines to shape the decision to act, the realm of law was actually abandoned. Precisely because the proposed concept failed on several of the legality criteria, it is also arguable that it lacked the capacity to convince the majority of international actors that the concept was legitimate or even plausible as a legal norm. There is no evidence that the doctrine of preventive war has achieved the status of a shared understanding. Here we have an attempt at norm entrepreneurship that simply failed.

[320] Gerald J. Postema, 'Implicit Law' (1994) 13 *Law and Philosophy* 361; and Lowe, above note 3 at 861–4 (speaking of 'coherence' of a given claim with existing law). See also *Comments of the Non-Aligned Movement*, above note 59, para.18 (stating that 'The Non-Aligned Movement has called for evolving common perceptions and agreed approaches to address both the new and existing threats to international peace and security … Such common perceptions and approaches to collective security would only be legitimate if they are developed in accordance with the principles and purposes of the UN Charter and by all Member States acting together').

[321] Johnstone, above note 180 at 448–50, 475–6; and above note 182 at 280.

[322] Johnstone, above note 180 at 448–50, 475–6; and above note 182 at 280.

4. Conclusion

Notwithstanding assertions that the prohibition on the use of force had fallen into desuetude or had died, eight years after 11 September 2001, we conclude that the rule encapsulated in Article 2(4) remains healthy as a binding legal obligation. As we have illustrated, the prohibition is one of the most widely shared understandings in international society and it substantially meets the criteria of legality. Recourse to armed force continues to require justification on exceptional grounds, notably the right to self-defence or Security Council authorization. It is on these exceptions that most of the debate surrounding the rules on the use of force has focused.

The most significant changes have occurred in the law of self-defence. Still, no radical overhaul along the lines of the Bush administration's 'preventive war' argument has ensued. Instead of accepting a definition of self-defence that risked making the exception a matter of unilateral assessment, states appear to have settled on two more narrowly circumscribed expansions of the concept of self-defence. First, it now seems to be settled that defensive action can be taken not just when an armed attack has occurred or is in progress: states can also take defensive measures in anticipation of an imminent attack, as long as the measures are necessary and proportionate to the threat. Second, it appears that attacks by non-state actors can now trigger a right to self-defence, although it remains to be confirmed what links are required to the state against which, or within which, response action is taken.

While the concept of responsibility to protect has gained considerable currency, it remains only a candidate norm in international law. No new exception to Article 2(4) has emerged. It has, however, become legally clear that the Security Council may intervene in grave humanitarian crises, even when the situation does not occasion a threat to international peace and security.

The interactional framework helps us to understand why some normative changes were possible, and others failed, despite concerted efforts by powerful and committed norm entrepreneurs.

Conclusion

In this book, our primary goal has been to trace out a theory of international obligation that makes sense of the contemporary practice of international law, and distinguishes between legal and other social norms. In this conclusion, we will re-state the core conceptual arguments, drawing upon the three case studies, of climate change, torture and the use of force, to illustrate how the elements of our interactional framework play out in practice. We close with a summary of the main implications that the interactional theory holds for international law-makers.

1. Shared understandings

Social norms can only emerge when they are rooted in an underlying set of shared understandings supporting first the need for normativity, and then particular norms intended to shape behaviour. In the climate context, for example, the growing consensus about the human origins of climate change has anchored the realization that a global legal regime is required. Specific norms also evolve over time, as shared understandings are built up or shifted. Consider the continuing efforts to flesh out the meaning of 'common but differentiated responsibilities'. It is not enough to look only at the surface of the norm as stated in a formal source, but we must examine with care the underlying shared ground, as well as contested meanings. A detailed example was provided in the discussion of common but differentiated obligations, but the same process can be observed in the definitional arguments over what constitutes torture, and what is meant by self defence.

Particular ideas may be promoted by epistemic communities, as is the case with the Intergovernmental Panel on Climate Change and the definition of 'dangerous' climate change. Norms may also be promoted directly by 'norm entrepreneurs' as with the Responsibility to Protect in the use-of-force context. However, constructivists show that these norms can only become social norms through sustained mutual engagement in communities of practice, as illustrated in the engagement of a broad range of actors in the climate regime, or in the distinctive interactions within the Security Council on matters of the use of force. In all cases, we saw that norms are not unidirectional projections; they are created and sustained in social interaction.

For international lawyers, this concept of the growth of normativity reveals that meaningful norms cannot simply be posited. Stating a norm, even through formal means like treaties or custom, may be a step in creating law: but without the mutual engagement of social actors in a community of practice, the formal norm will not exert social influence. The prohibition on torture, for example, is contained in one of the most widely ratified treaties in the human rights domain. But the norm is constantly challenged through contrary practice and attempts at redefinition. The need for basic congruence between norms and social understandings helps to explain why ambitious international regimes often founder: they have no social grounding.

2. Adherence to the criteria of legality

However, shared understandings alone do not make law. Many social norms exist that never reach a threshold of legal normativity. While there may be a global social consensus that significant emission reductions are required to avert dangerous climate change, we do not yet know whether or not this shared understanding will be translated into legal commitments. Even the existing foundation of procedural legality could be undermined if continuing climate negotiations fail to produce substantive norms that are clear, general and that produce congruent practice.

To reiterate, what distinguishes legal norms from other types of social norms is not form or pedigree, but adherence to specific criteria of legality. Fuller set out eight such criteria: legal norms must be general: prohibiting, requiring or permitting certain conduct. They must be promulgated, enabling citizens to know what the law requires. Law should be prospective, not retroactive, allowing citizens to take rules into account in their decision-making. The law must be clear; citizens must also be able to understand what is permitted, prohibited or required. Law should avoid contradiction, not requiring or permitting and prohibiting at the same time. Law should not demand the impossible, but should be realistic. Its requirements of citizens must remain relatively constant. Finally, there should be alignment between legal norms and the actions of officials operating under the law.

In applying these criteria, we found that the procedural elements of the climate change regime generally meet the requirements of legality and have generated a robust continuing practice of legality. By contrast, the legality of the regime's substantive rules is very much a work in progress. The prohibition on torture presents significant problems with the criterion of clarity, because of the failure to generate a commonly accepted definition, and fails on the criterion of congruent practice. The exceptions to the prohibition on the use of force meet the legality requirements, and although the prohibition itself was threatened by a lack of congruent practice, more recently the norm has been reinforced.

In international law, it is important to appreciate that the last criterion of legality – congruence of norm and practice – encapsulates a larger idea, that there is a need for 'reciprocity' amongst actors in the international legal system. Any kind of official action, for example by the International Court of Justice or by the UN Security Council, must adhere to known and promulgated rules. But in addition, a majority of states and other international actors must support the rules if they are to retain influence. In other words, the concept of reciprocity translates the idea of a community of practice into the legal realm. That is why the criteria of legality are not just a checklist for the existence of formal law. Adhering to the criteria means engaging in a practice of legality – day in, day out. The ebb and flow of state practice around the anti-torture norm and the prohibition on the use of force demonstrates how important reciprocity is in the maintenance of a legal rule.

3. Continuous practice: the hard work of international law

For law to exist and to endure, a community of practice needs to maintain or expand underlying shared understandings (which, as we saw in the case of climate change, can be purely procedural or substantive), and to embed those understandings in a legal practice that assures day-to-day application in concrete settings of the criteria of legality. We call this a 'practice of legality'. In other words, law does not exist merely because legal norms are declared; they must be continuously maintained or they can be destroyed. The threats to the fundamental prohibition on the use of force and the anti-torture norm after the attacks of 11 September 2001 are sobering examples.

Formal law can be made into interactional law by building up a practice of legality. This process is underway in the compliance regime of the Kyoto Protocol. But without constant attention, interactional law can fall into desuetude or can be undermined by inconsistent practice, as we saw clearly in the case of torture. The need for a community of practice underscores the dynamic and continuous nature of law-making in international society. Citizens in domestic systems are not mere consumers, but can be builders of law. Similarly, states and all other international actors must be active participants in the process of creating and maintaining law.

Although we emphasize 'communities of practice' in explaining the evolution of interactional law, this concept of 'community' is utterly different from the notion of community underlying older universalist claims of international law. A community of practice is constituted by mutual engagement, not by shared values or goals. Within the climate change regime, various actors including states, NGOs and international organizations, pursue diverse values and interests. In terms of states' commitments, a diversity of outlook and interest is acknowledged in the core principle of common but differentiated obligations. As this example suggests, membership in a community of practice neither presupposes nor necessarily leads to homogeneity. The creation and maintenance of international law requires a commitment to communication, a willingness to listen, and openness to reciprocal modification of outlook. At first glance, the existence of any international law may seem very unlikely in our world. Yet, the interactional understanding of law also demonstrates that despite diversity, thin initial commitments to legality are possible and shared legal understandings may deepen through mutual engagement in communities of practice, as is illustrated by the evolution of the climate change regime.

The reciprocity requirement of interactional law implies that legal norms can be constructed and maintained even in situations where there is an imbalance in material power. The successful resistance in the Security Council, and more broadly in international society, to the self-defence claims of the Bush administration reveals how even strong states cannot re-interpret international law at will. Obviously, no normative system can eliminate power imbalance. Stronger actors will have more resources at their disposal to influence the evolution of law. Nonetheless, the interactional framework shows that all participants in the community of practice can exert some normative influence. Recall the unexpected survival of the Kyoto Protocol after its blunt rejection by the United States. What is more, interactional law undercuts the ability of powerful actors to put forward self-serving or perverse normative claims because the claims will have to be measured against the eight criteria of legality, and will have to fit within shared understandings generated through inclusive participation of all social actors. Efforts to re-define torture are an obvious example, but the same observation applies in the use-of-force context where some states and academic commentators sought to merge self-defence claims and humanitarian intervention. The attempt failed because it would have resulted in a supposed norm that violated several of the criteria of legality including clarity and generality.

4. Interactional international law: what we do not claim

Given the overwhelming force of state-centric, hierarchical conceptions of law since the nineteenth century, matched with the dominance of rationalism in international relations theory, any approach to international law that rejects the exclusive explanatory power of positivism and rationalism bears a heavy burden of justification. Indeed, over the last few years, as we have presented parts of this analysis, we have confronted challenges suggesting that interactional international law is overly optimistic, representing a new strain of naïve liberal internationalism. Yet our case studies have illustrated that the interactional approach is in many ways more hard-headed than sources-based positivist accounts of international law. We demonstrated, for example, that the torture norm, which we would obviously wish to uphold, and is often claimed to be *jus cogens*, is actually fragile. Nonetheless, in this Conclusion, we want to be explicit about what interactionalism does not claim.

First, suggesting that all norms, including legal norms, are rooted in shared understandings does not mean that law must defer to existing practice, that law inevitably reinforces the status quo. The point is quite the opposite: as we have shown throughout this book, law can help to shape interactions in international society, and is in turn modified by those interactions. To ensure that interactional law is built and maintained, it is necessary to understand the existing shared expectations. But as mutual engagements deepen in a community of legal practice, it may be possible to enrich shared expectations to allow for more demanding substantive rules to be constructed. Participants in an inclusive process of law-making can learn through law, but this is a difficult and complicated process. Merely declaring a rule does not ensure any learning.

Second, interactional international law is not founded on any presumption of universally shared values. In fact, one of our central points is that it is possible to build procedural law that shapes the parameters of social relations, even with only weak shared values. All that is required to begin the process of law-building in international society is a shared understanding that law is needed in a given context. On that base can be built over time, with inclusive processes of participation in communities of legal practice, agreement on the parameters of coordinated social action that generate more substantive legal norms that meet the criteria of legality. Around certain concrete issues it may even be possible over time, and with deepening mutual engagement, to cultivate stronger and more demanding legal regimes.

Third, we do not suggest that the reality of unequal power is entirely displaced by interactional processes. However, power and its concomitant, material interests, do not operate in isolation within international society. Power and interests strongly influence social interactions but they are not the only relevant considerations. The interests generated by power differentials are actually shaped in part by identity concerns of states and other actors. So power itself is not purely material, but is affected by ideas rooted in self-perceived and relational identity construction. Moreover, power can be constrained by the need to justify actions within the criteria of legality as applied in a community of practice.

Fourth and finally, interactional international law is not premised on a claim that enforcement of rules is irrelevant to effective law. Instead, the argument is that enforcement is not the *sine qua non* for the existence of law. Law's existence is grounded in shared understandings, buttressed by adherence to the criteria of legality in day-to-day practice. Enforcement, or its lack, is especially relevant to one of the criteria of legality: the congruence of rules and international practice. When posited rules are consistently evaded or undermined without legal consequence, the rules themselves are compromised because the community of practice recognizes that the declared rule is hypocritical, or that power is being abused without response. In such cases, law itself is undermined. Enforcement matters not because force is necessary for the existence of law, but because adherence is necessary, and enforcement can support or diminish adherence.

5. Implications for international law-makers

Law is not simply declared through formal processes. It is built in everyday interactions. It can also be destroyed in the same way. Formal law, be it in treaty, custom or even soft law, plays an important role in providing fixed points for social engagement. If the hard work of law-building has been done, those fixed points will have emerged through inclusive processes of participation and may reflect shared understandings. They will be interactional law. But even if this has not happened, it is possible that posited law will serve as a basis for future interaction that can turn mere declarations of norms into interactional law.

Even when they arise from shared understandings, norms will not become law unless they are constructed with due regard to the criteria of legality. As we have illustrated at various points, when concluding a treaty, state representatives must ensure that the language is clear enough to ensure that it is understood in commensurable ways by participants in the regime. The treaty must not ask the impossible or contradict other rules of international law. Eventually, the treaty must actually come to shape the actions and decisions of parties. If there is no widespread adherence to the treaty norms, an individual state party can fairly conclude that there is no congruence between the rules of the treaty and their concrete application. The treaty will become a dead letter, for it will have inspired no fidelity. In building and maintaining a customary rule, it is equally important to ensure that the rule is clear, and that it does not require the impossible. Inherent in the very idea of custom is the congruence of practice with the norm. However, the eighth criterion of legality, which requires reciprocity among a significant majority of participants in the legal system, demands that we analyse with care exactly whose practice is being assessed in declaring the continuing existence of a customary rule. We have also shown that legality can be built on the basis of what international lawyers refer to as 'soft law'. Such norms can in fact reflect strongly shared understandings and can meet the criteria of legality, and be embedded in a rich practice of legality.

For those who seek to build and uphold international law, the message of this book is that it is crucial for them to open up spaces where sustained mutual engagement and robust interaction can take place. These spaces include international intergovernmental organizations, treaty regimes embedded in institutions such as conferences of the parties, treaty implementation mechanisms including compliance procedures, conferences that include state and other international actors, intergovernmental and non-governmental networks, expert and advocacy groups that promote norms and monitor implementation, and transnational media. Dense communities of practice are more likely to arise in situations where there is relatively institutionalized and sustained legal interaction.

Law begins in shared understandings coupled with a sustained effort to link those understandings to criteria of legality. To engender fidelity, legal norms must continue to meet the criteria of legality. Ultimately, then, law is created, maintained or destroyed through day-to-day interactions in communities of legal practice. Legal obligation cannot be reduced to the existence of formal rules; it is made real in the continuing practice of communities that reason with and communicate through norms. Over time, as mutual engagement increases, the normative community may become tighter, and the norms may become richer and more demanding. International law today is largely a set of interlocking communities of practice that uphold relatively weak norms, but there are some sites of richer normativity. To expand those sites, to include more people within deeper normative communities, and to create spaces for sustained legal interaction, is the challenge for all those people who want to build up international law.

BIBLIOGRAPHY

Books and Articles

Aaken, Anke van, 'To Do Away with International Law? Some Limits to "The Limits of International Law"' (2006) **17** *European Journal of International Law* 289.

Abbott, Kenneth W., Robert Keohane, Andrew Moravcsik, Anne-Marie Slaughter and Duncan Snidal, 'The Concept of Legalization' (2000) **54** *International Organization* 401.

Abbott, Kenneth W., and Duncan Snidal, 'Hard and Soft Law in International Governance' (2000) **54** *International Organization* 421.

Acharya, Amitav, 'How Ideas Spread: Whose Norms Matter? Norm Localization and Institutional Change in Asian Regionalism' (2004) **58** *International Organization* 239.

Adler, Emanuel, *Communitarian International Relations: The Epistemic Foundations of International Relations* (London and New York: Routledge, 2005).

'Barry Buzan's Use of Constructivism to Reconstruct the English School: "Not All the Way Down"' (2005) **34** *Millennium: Journal of International Studies* 171.

'Constructivism in International Relations', in Walter Carlsnaes, Thomas Risse and Beth Simmons (eds.), *Handbook of International Relations* (London: Sage, 2002), p. 95.

'Seizing the Middle Ground: Constructivism in World Politics' (1997) **3** *European Journal of International Relations* 319.

'Imagined (Security) Communities: Cognitive Regions in International Relations' (1997) **26** *Millennium: Journal of International Studies* 249.

Adler, Emanuel, and Steven Bernstein, 'Knowledge in Power: The Epistemic Construction of Global Governance', in Michael Barnett and Raymond Duvall (eds.), *Power in Global Governance* (Cambridge University Press, 2005), p. 294.

Ago, Roberto, 'Positivism', in Rudolph Bernhardt (ed.), *Encyclopedia of Public International Law*, vol. VII (Amsterdam: North-Holland, 1984), p. 385.

Alkoby, Asher, 'Theories of Compliance with International Law and the Challenge of Cultural Difference' (2008) **4** *Journal of International Law and International Relations* 151.

Alley Richard B. *et al.*, 'IPCC 2007: Summary for Policymakers', in Susan Solomon *et al.* (eds.), *Climate Change 2007: The Physical Science Basis. Contribution of Working Group I to the Fourth Assessment Report of the Intergovernmental Panel on Climate Change* (Cambridge and New York: Cambridge University Press, 2007).

Allott, Philip, *Eunomia: New Order for a New World* (Oxford University Press, 1990).

Alvarez, José E., 'The Schizophrenias of R2P', 30 June 2007, Panel Presentation, *Hague Joint Conference on Contemporary Issues of International Law: Criminal Jurisdiction 100 Years After the 1907 Hague Peace Conference.*

'Do States Socialize?' (2004) **54** *Duke Law Journal* 961.

Anderson, Terry L. and J. Bishop Grewell, 'It Isn't Easy Being Green: Environmental Policy Implications for Foreign Policy, International Law and Sovereignty' (2001) **2** *Chicago Journal of International Law* 427.

Angelova, Anastasia A., 'Compelling Compliance with International Regimes: China and the Missile Technology Control Regime' (1999) **38** *Columbia Journal of Transnational Law* 419.

Anghie, Antony, *Imperialism, Sovereignty and the Making of International Law* (Cambridge University Press, 2005).

'Universality and the Concept of Governance in International Law', in Edward Kofi Quashigah and Obiora Chinedu Okafor (eds.), *Legitimate Governance in Africa: International and Domestic Legal Perspectives* (The Hague: Kluwer Law International, 1999), p. 21.

'"The Heart of My Home": Colonialism, Environmental Damage, and the Nauru Case' (1993) **34** *Harvard International Law Journal* 445.

Aquinas, St. Thomas, *Summa Theologica*, trans. Fathers of the English Dominican Province (Westminster, Md: Christian Classics, 1982).

Arbour, Louise, 'The Responsibility to Protect as a Duty of Care in International Law and Practice' (2008) **34** *Review of International Studies* 445.

Archdiocese of Sao Paulo, Jaime Wright (trans.) and Joan Dassin (ed.), *Torture in Brazil* (New York: Vintage/Random House, 1985).

Aristotle, *The Nicomachean Ethics*, J.A.K. Thomson (trans.) (Harmondsworth: Penguin 1976).

Rhetoric, E.S. Forster (trans.) (Cambridge, Mass.: Harvard University Press, 1966).

Aust, Anthony, *Modern Treaty Law and Practice*, 2nd edn (Cambridge University Press, 2007).

Austin, John, *Lectures on Jurisprudence*, 5th edn (London: John Murray, 1885).

Axelrod, Regina, Norman J. Vig and Miranda Schreurs, 'European Union as an Environmental Governance System', in Regina Axelrod, David Leonard Downie and Norman J. Vig, *The Global Environment: Institutions, Law and Policy*, 2nd edn (Washington, DC: CQ Press, 2005), p. 200.

Axelrod, Robert, *The Evolution of Cooperation*, rev. edn (New York: Basic Books, 2006).

The Evolution of Cooperation (New York: Basic Books, 1984).

Ayoob, Mohammed, 'Humanitarian Intervention and State Sovereignty' (2002) **6** *International Journal of Human Rights* 81.

Bailey, Sydney D., *Prohibitions and Restraints in War* (Oxford University Press, 1972).

Barbour, Stephanie A. and Joe A. Salzman, '"The Tangled Web": The Right of Self-Defense Against Non-State Actors in the Armed Activities Case' (2008) **40** *Journal of International Law and Politics* 53.

Barker, Terry *et al.*, 'Technical Summary', in B. Metz *et al.* (eds.), *Climate Change 2007: Mitigation. Contribution of Working Group III to the Fourth Assessment Report of the Intergovernmental Panel on Climate Change* (Cambridge and New York: Cambridge University Press, 2007).

Barkun, Michael, *Law without Sanctions: Order in Primitive Societies and the World Community* (New Haven: Yale University Press, 1968).

Barnes, Jonathan, 'Introduction', in Aristotle, *The Nicomachean Ethics*, J.A.K. Thomson (trans.) (Harmondsworth: Penguin, 1976), p. 9.

Barnett, Michael, *Eyewitness to a Genocide: The United Nations and Rwanda* (Ithaca: Cornell University Press, 2002).

'Bringing in the new world order: liberalism, legitimacy, and the United Nations' (1997) **49** *World Politics* 526.

Barnett, Michael and Raymond Duvall, 'Power in International Politics' (2005) **59** *International Organization* 39.

Barnett, Michael and Martha Finnemore, *Rules for the World: International Organizations and Global Politics* (Ithaca, NY and London: Cornell University Press, 2004).

Barrett, Scott, *Environment and Statecraft: The Strategy of Environmental Treaty-Making* (Oxford University Press, 2003).

Barsoom, Peter N., Kyle W. Danish and George W. Downs, 'The Transformational Model of International Regime Design: Triumph of Hope or Experience?' (2000) **38** *Columbia Journal of Transnational Law* 465.

Baumert, Kevin and Jonathan Pershing, *Climate Data: Insights and Observations* (Washington, DC: Pew Center on Global Climate Change, 2004), at www.pewclimate.org/global-warming-in-depth/all_reports/.

Becker, Tal, *Terrorism and the State: Rethinking the Rules of State Responsibility* (Oxford: Hart Publishing, 2006).

Bederman, David, 'Constructivism, Positivism, and Empiricism in International Law' (2001) **89** *Georgetown Law Journal* 469.

Bedjaoui, Mohammed, *Towards a New International Economic Order* (New York: Holmes & Meier Publishers, 1979).

Benevenisti, Eyal, 'Domestic Politics and International Resources: What Role for International Law?', in Michael Byers (ed.), *The Role of Law in International Politics* (Cambridge University Press, 2000), p. 109.

Benford, Robert D. and David A. Snow, 'Framing Processes and Social Movements: An Overview and Assessment' (2000) **26** *Annual Review of Sociology* 611.

Bergman, Marcelo, *Tax Evasion and the Rule of Law in Latin America: The Political Culture of Cheating and Compliance in Argentina and Chile* (Philadelphia: Penn State University Press, 2009).

Beyerlin, Ulrich, P. T. Stoll and R. Wolfrum (eds.), *Ensuring Compliance with Multilateral Environmental Agreements: A Dialogue between Practitioners and Academia* (Leiden: Brill Academic Publishers, 2006).

Bhaskar, Roy, *The Possibility of Naturalism: A Philosophical Critique of the Contemporary Human Sciences* (Brighton: Harvester Press, 1979).

Biermann, Frank, 'The Case for a World Environment Organization' (2004) **42** *Environment* 22.

Biniaz, Susan, 'Common But Differentiated Responsibility – Remarks' (2002) **96** *American Society of International Law Proceedings* 358.

Birnie, Patricia, Alan Boyle and Catherine Redgwell, *International Law and the Environment*, 3rd edn (New York: Oxford University Press, 2009).

Blackstone, William, *Commentaries on the Laws of England* (1765).

Blanning, Tim, *The Pursuit of Glory: Europe 1648–1815* (London: Allen Lane, 2007).

Blomquist, Robert F., 'Ratification Resisted: Understanding America's Response to the Convention on Biological Diversity, 1989–2002' (2002) **32** *Golden Gate University Law Review* 493.

Bodansky, Daniel, 'International Law in Black and White' (2006) **34** *Georgia Journal of International and Comparative Law* 285.

'Bonn Voyage: Kyoto's Uncertain Revival' (2001) *The National Interest* 45.

'The United Nations Framework Convention on Climate Change: A Commentary' (1993) **18** *Yale Journal of International Law* 451.

Bodansky, Daniel, Jutta Brunnée and Ellen Hey, 'International Environmental Law: Mapping the Field', in Daniel Bodansky, Jutta Brunnée and Ellen Hey (eds.), *Oxford Handbook of International Environmental Law* (Oxford University Press, 2007), p.1.

Bolton, John, 'Address before the Federalist Society at the 2003 National Lawyers Convention', 13 November 2003, at www.fed-soc.org/doclib/20070324_bolton.pdf.

'Is There Really "Law" in International Affairs?' (2000) **10** *Transnational Law and Contemporary Problems* 1.

Book, Leslie, 'The Collection Due Process Rights: A Misstep or Step in the Right Direction?' (2004) **41** *Houston Law Review* 1145.

Bowett, Derek W., *The Law of International Institutions*, 4th edn (London: Stevens & Sons, 1982).

'Reprisals Involving Recourse to Armed Force' (1972) **66** *American Journal of International Law* 1.

Self Defense in International Law (Manchester University Press, 1957).

Boyd, Emily *et al.*, 'The Clean Development Mechanism: An assessment of current practice and future approaches for policy', Tyndall Centre Working Paper 114, October 2007, at www.tyndall.ac.uk/publications/working_papers/twp114_summary.shtml.

Boyle, A. E., 'Some Reflections on the Relationship of Treaties and Soft Law' (1999) **48** *International and Comparative Law Quarterly* 901.

Bradford, William, 'International Legal Compliance: Surveying the Field' (2005) **36** *Georgetown Journal of International Law* 495.

Brierly, J.L., *The Law of Nations: An Introduction to the International Law of Peace*, 6th edn, Humphrey Waldock (ed.) (Oxford: Clarendon Press, 1968).

Brown Weiss, Edith, 'Understanding Compliance with International Environmental Agreements: The Baker's Dozen Myths' (1999) **32** *University of Richmond Law Review* 1555.

Brownlie, Ian, *Principles of Public International Law*, 6th edn (Oxford and New York: Oxford University Press, 2003).

International Law and the Use of Force by States (Oxford: Clarendon Press, 1963), p. 265.

Brunnée, Jutta, 'Climate Change, Global Environmental Justice and International Environmental Law', in Jonas Ebbesson and Phoebe Okowa (eds.), *Environmental Law and Justice in Context* (Cambridge University Press, 2009), p. 316.

'Europe, the United States, and the Global Climate Regime: All Together Now?' (2008) **24** *Journal of Land Use and Environmental Law* 1.

'International Law and Collective Concerns: Reflections on the Responsibility to Protect', in Tafsir Malick Ndiaye and Rüdiger Wolfrum (eds.), *Law of the Sea, Environmental Law and Settlement of Disputes* (Leiden: Martinus Nijhoff, 2007), p. 35.

'Shifting the Global Climate Debate: When Bad News is Good News' (Summer 2007) *Nexus* 30.

'Enforcement Mechanisms in International Law and International Environmental Law', in Ulrich Beyerlin *et al.* (eds.), *Ensuring Compliance with Multilateral Environmental Agreements: A Dialogue between Practitioners and Academia* (Leiden: Brill Academic Publishers, 2006), p. 1.

'Review: Legalization and World Politics. Edited by Judith L. Goldstein, Miles Kahler, Robert O. Keohane, and Anne-Marie Slaughter (2001)' (2003) **1** *Perspectives in Politics* 231.

'On the Legality of the Use of Force against Iraq' (2003) **59** *Behind the Headlines* 1.

'The Kyoto Protocol: A Testing Ground for Compliance Theories?' (2003) **63** *Zeitschrift für ausländisches öffentliches Recht und Völkerrecht (Heidelberg Journal of International Law)* 255.

'COPing with Consent: Lawmaking under Multilateral Environmental Agreements' (2002) **15** *Leiden Journal of International Law* 16.

'A Fine Balance: Facilitation and Enforcement in the Design of a Compliance Regime for the Kyoto Protocol' (2000) **13** *Tulane Environmental Law Journal* 223.

Brunnée, Jutta and Stephen J. Toope, 'Norms, Institutions and UN Reform: The Responsibility to Protect' (2006) **2** *Journal of International Law and International Relations* 121.

'Slouching Towards New "Just Wars": International Law and the Use of Force after September 11th' (2004) **51** *Netherlands International Law Review* 363.

'The Use of Force: International Law After Iraq' (2004) **53** *International and Comparative Law Quarterly* 785.

'Persuasion and Enforcement: Explaining Compliance with International Law' (2002) **13** *Finnish Yearbook of International Law* 273.

'International Law and Constructivism: Elements of an Interactional Theory of International Law' (2000) **39** *Columbia Journal of International Law* 19.

'Environmental Security and Freshwater Resources: Ecosystem Regime Building' (1997) **91** *American Journal of International Law* 26.

Buchanan, Allen and Robert O. Keohane, 'The Legitimacy of Global Governance Institutions' (2006) **20** *Ethics and International Affairs* 405.

'The Preventive Use of Force: A Cosmopolitan Institutional Perspective' (2004) **18** *Ethics and International Affairs* 1.

Bull, Hedley, *The Anarchical Society* (New York: Columbia University Press, 1977).

Burbach, Roger, *The Pinochet Affair* (New York: Zed Books, 2003).

Burley, Anne-Marie, 'Law Among Liberal States: Liberal Internationalism and the Act of State Doctrine' (1992) **92** *Columbia Law Review* 1907.

Byers, Michael, 'Preemptive Self-Defense: Hegemony, Equality and Strategies of Legal Change' (2003) **11** *Journal of Political Philosophy* 171.

Custom, Power and the Power of Rules (Cambridge University Press, 1999).

Caney, Simon, 'Cosmopolitan Justice, Responsibility, and Global Climate Change' (2005) **18** *Leiden Journal of International Law* 747.

Caron, David D., 'Between Empire and Community – The United States and Multilateralism 2001–2003: A Mid-Term Assessment' (2003) **21** *Berkeley Journal of International Law* 395.

Cassese, Antonio, 'Ex iniuria ius oritur: Are We Moving Towards International Legitimation of Forcible Humanitarian Countermeasures in the World Community?' (1999) **10** *European Journal of International Law* 23.

C.D. Howe Institute, *Burning Our Money to Warm the Planet – Canada's Ineffective Efforts to Reduce Greenhouse Gas Emissions*, No. 234, May 2006, at www.cdhowe.org/pdf/commentary_234.pdf.

Center for Human Rights and Global Justice, *Beyond Guantanámo: Transfers to Torture One Year After* Rasul v. Bush (New York University School of Law, 2005).

United Kingdom All Party Parliamentary Group on Extraordinary Rendition *Briefing: Torture by Proxy: International Law Applicable to 'Extraordinary Renditions'* (New York University School of Law, 2005).

Charnovitz, Steve, 'WTO Dispute Settlement as a Model for International Governance', in Alexandre Kiss, Dinah Shelton and Kanami Ishibashi (eds.), *Economic Globalization and Compliance with International Environmental Law* (The Hague: Kluwer Law International, 2003).

'Rethinking WTO Trade Sanctions' (2001) **95** *American Journal of International Law* 792.

Chayes, Abram, *The Cuban Missile Crisis: International Crises and the Role of Law*, 2nd rev. edn (Lanham, Md: Rowman & Littlefield, 1988).

The Cuban Missile Crisis (New York: Oxford University Press, 1974), p. 65.

'On Compliance' (1993) **47** *International Organization* 175.

Chayes, Abram and Antonia Handler Chayes, *The New Sovereignty: Compliance with International Regulatory Agreements* (Cambridge, Mass.: Harvard University Press, 1995).

Checkel, Jeffrey T., 'Why Comply? Social Learning and European Identity Change' (2001) **55** *International Organization* 553.

'The Constructivist Turn in International Relations Theory' (1998) **50** *World Politics* 324.

Chee, Yoke Ling, *How Big Powers Dominate the Third World: The Use and Abuse of International Law* (Penang: Third World Network, 1987).

Chesterman, Simon, *Just War or Just Peace? Humanitarian Intervention and International Law* (Oxford University Press, 2001).

Chimni, Bhupinder S., 'Third World Approaches to International Law: A Manifesto', in Antony Anghie, B.S. Chimni, Karin Mickelson and Obiora Chinedu Okafor (eds.), *The Third World and International Order: Law, Politics and Globalization* (Leiden: Brill Academic Publishers, Martinus Nijhoff, 2003), p. 47.

Chinkin, Christine, 'The Challenge of Soft Law: Development and Change in International Law' (1989) **38** *International and Comparative Law Quarterly* 850.

Churchill, Robin and Geir Ulfstein, 'Autonomous Institutional Arrangements in Multilateral Environmental Agreements: A Little-Noticed Phenomenon in International Law' (2000) **94** *American Journal of International Law* 623.

Climate Group, The, *China's Clean Revolution* (July 2008), at www.theclimate-group.org/assets/resources/Chinas_Clean_Revolution.pdf.

Corbett, P. 'The Consent of States and the Sources of International Law' (1925) **6** *British Yearbook of International Law* 20.

Cortell, Andrew P. and James W. Davis, 'When Norms Clash: International Norms, Domestic Practices, and Japan's Internalisation of the GATT/WTO' (2005) **31** *Review of International Studies* 3.

Cousins, Jane, *Turkey: Torture and Political Persecution* (London: Pluto Press, 1973).

Cullet, Philippe, *Differential Treatment in International Environmental Law* (Brookfield, Vt: Ashgate Publishing Co., 2003).

Danish, Kyle, 'Management v. Enforcement: The New Debate on Promoting Treaty Compliance' (1997) **37** *Virginia Journal of International Law* 789.

Darian-Smith, Eve, and Peter Fitzpatrick (eds.), *Laws of the Postcolonial (Law, Meaning, Violence)* (Ann Arbor: University of Michigan Press, 1999).

Delahunty, Robert J. and John Yoo, 'The "Bush Doctrine": Can Preventive War Be Justified?' (2009) *32 Harvard Journal of Law and Public Policy* 1.

Dernbach, John, 'U.S. Adherence to Its Agenda 21 Commitments: A Five Year Review' (1997) **27** *Environmental Law Reporter* 10504.

Dershowitz, Alan M., *Why Terrorism Works: Understanding the Threat, Responding to the Challenge* (New Haven: Yale University Press, 2002).

Doniger, David, 'The Copenhagen Accord: A Big Step Forward', *Climate Progress*, 28 December 2009, at http://climateprogress.org/2009/12/28/the-copenhagen-accord-a-big-step-forward/.

Dorfman, Ariel, 'The Tyranny of Torture: Is Torture Inevitable in Our Century and Beyond?', in Sanford Levinson (ed.), *Torture: A Collection* (New York: Oxford University Press, 2004), p. 3.

Dostoyevsky, Fyodor, *The Brothers Karamazov*, Constance Garnett (trans.), large print edn, 2 vols. (San Diego, Calif.: Huge Print Press).

Downs, George W., Kyle W. Danish and Peter N. Barsoom, 'The Transformational Model of International Regime Design: Triumph of Hope or Experience?' (2000) **38** *Columbia Journal of Transnational Law* 465.

Downs, George W., David M. Rocke and Peter N. Barsoom, 'Is the Good News About Compliance Good News About Cooperation?' (1996) **50** *International Organization* 379.

Draper, G.I.A.D., 'Grotius' Place in the Development of Legal Ideas About War', in Hedley Bull, Benedict Kingsbury and Adam Roberts (eds.), *Hugo Grotius and International Relations* (Oxford University Press 1992), p. 177.

Drexhage, John, 'Copenhagen: A memorable time for all the wrong reasons?' International Institute for Sustainable Developments, December 2009, at www.iisd.org/pdf/2009/cop_memorable_time_wrong_reasons.pdf.

Dunoff, Jeffrey L., 'Constitutional Conceits: The WTO's "Constitution" and the Discipline of International Law' (2006) **17** *European Journal of International Law* 647.

(with Steven Ratner and David Wippman) *International Law: Norms, Actors, Process* (New York: Aspen Law and Business, 2002), p. 892.

Dupuy, Pierre-Marie, 'The Place and Role of Unilateralism in Contemporary International Law' (2000) **11** *European Journal of International Law* 19.

'Soft Law and the International Law of the Environment' (1991) **12** *Michigan Journal of International Law* 420.

Dworkin, Ronald, 'Philosophy, Morality, and Law – Observations Prompted by Professor Fuller's Novel Claim' (1965) **113** *University of Pennsylvania Law Review* 668.

Dyzenhaus, David, *The Constitution of Law: Legality in a Time of Emergency* (Cambridge University Press, 2006).

'Fuller's Novelty', in Willem J. Witteveen and Wilbren van der Burg (eds.), *Rediscovering Fuller: Essays on Implicit Law and Institutional Design* (Amsterdam University Press, 1999), p. 78.

Einolf, Christopher J., 'The Fall and Rise of Torture: A Comparative and Historical Analysis' (2007) **25** *Sociological Theory* 112.

Elshtain, Jean Bethke, 'Reflection on the Problem of "Dirty Hands"', in Sanford Levinson (ed.), *Torture: A Collection* (New York: Oxford University Press, 2004), p. 77.

Esty, Daniel C. and Maria H. Ivanova, 'Revitalizing Global Environmental Governance: A Function-Driver Approach' in Daniel C. Esty and Maria H. Ivanova (eds.), *Global Environmental Governance: Options and Opportunities* (New Haven: Yale School of Forestry and Environmental Studies, 2002).

Evans, Gareth, 'The Responsibility to Protect: An Idea Whose Time has Come … and Gone?' (2008) **22** *International Relations* 283.

'Russia in Georgia: Not a Case of the "Responsibility to Protect"' (2008) **25** *New Perspectives Quarterly* 53.

'When is it Right to Fight?' (2004) **46** *Survival* 59.

'The Responsibility to Protect' (2002) **81** *Foreign Affairs* 99.

Farer, Tom, 'The Prospect for International Law and Order in the Wake of Iraq' (2003) **97** *American Journal of International Law* 607.

Fearon, James and Alexander Wendt, 'Rationalism v. Constructivism: A Skeptical View', in Walter Carlsnaes, Thomas Risse and Beth Simmons (eds.), *Handbook of International Relations* (London: Sage, 2002), p. 52.

Feinstein, Lee and Anne-Marie Slaughter, 'A Duty to Prevent' (2004) **83** *Foreign Affairs* 136.

Feitlowitz, Marguerite, *A Lexicon of Terror: Argentina and the Legacies of Torture* (New York: Oxford University Press, 1998).

Fierke, Karin M., 'Constructivism', in Timothy Dunne, Milja Kurki and Stephen Smith (eds.), *International Relations Theory: Discipline and Diversity* (Oxford University Press, 2007), p. 166.

Finnemore, Martha, 'Are Legal Norms Distinctive?' (2000) **32** *New York University Journal of International Law and Politics* 699.

National Interests in International Society (Ithaca, NY: Cornell University Press, 1996).

'International Norm Dynamics and Political Change' (1998) **52** *International Organization* 887.

Finnemore, Martha and Kathryn Sikkink, 'Taking Stock: The Constructivist Research Program in International Relations and Comparative Politics' (2001) **4** *American Review of Political Science* 391.

Finnemore, Martha and Stephen J. Toope, 'Alternatives to "Legalization": Richer Views of Law and Politics' (2001) **55** *International Organization* 743.

Fitzmaurice, Sir Gerald, 'The Foundations of the Authority of International Law and the Problem of Enforcement' (1956) **19** *Modern Law Review* 1.

Flockhart, Trine, '"Complex Socialization": A Framework for the Study of State Socialization' (2006) **12** *European Journal of International Relations* 89.

Foster, Don, *Detention and Torture in South Africa* (London: James Currey Ltd., 1987).

Fox, Gregory H. and Brad R. Roth (eds.), *Democratic Governance and International Law* (Cambridge University Press, 2000).

Franck, Thomas M., 'What Happens Now? The United Nations After Iraq' (2003) **97** *American Journal of International Law* 607.

Recourse to Force: State Action Against Threats and Armed Attacks (Cambridge University Press, 2002).

'Legitimacy in the International System' (1998) **82** *American Journal of International Law* 705.

Fairness in International Law and Institutions (Oxford: Clarendon Press, 1995).

'The Emerging Right to Democratic Governance' (1992) **86** *American Journal of International Law* 46.

The Power of Legitimacy Among Nations (Oxford and New York: Oxford University Press, 1990).

'Who Killed Article 2(4)? Or: Changing Norms Governing the Use of Force by States' (1970) **64** *American Journal of International Law* 809.

Friedmann, Wolfgang, *The Changing Structure of International Law* (New York: Columbia University Press, 1964).

Frost, Mervyn, *Ethics in International Relations: A Constitutive Theory* (Cambridge University Press, 1996).

Frum, David and Richard Perle, *An End to Evil: How to Win the War on Terror* (New York: Random House, 2003).

Fuller, Lon L., 'The Forms and Limits of Adjudication' (1978) 92 *Harvard Law Review* 353; repr. in Kenneth I. Winston (ed.), *The Principles of Social Order: Selected Essays of Lon L. Fuller*, rev. edn (Oxford: Hart Publishing, 2001), p. 86.

'Human Interaction and the Law'(1969) 14 *American Journal of Jurisprudence* 1; repr. in Kenneth I. Winston (ed.), *The Principles of Social Order: Selected Essays of Lon L. Fuller*, rev. edn (Oxford: Hart Publishing, 2001), p. 211.

The Morality of Law, rev. edn (New Haven: Yale University Press, 1969).

'The Law's Precarious Hold on Life' (1969) **3** *Georgia Law Review* 530.

'Freedom as a Problem of Allocating Choice' (1968) **112** *Proceedings of the American Philosophical Society* 101.

'A Reply to Professors Cohen and Dworkin' (1965) **10** *Villanova Law Review* 655.

'Adjudication and the Rule of Law' (1960) **54** *American Society of International Law Proceedings* 1.

'Positivism and Fidelity to Law – A Reply to Professor Hart' (1958) **71** *Harvard Law Review* 630.

'American Legal Philosophy at Mid-Century' (1954) **6** *Journal of Legal Education* 457.

The Law in Quest of Itself (Chicago: The Foundation Press, 1940).

Gardam, Judith, *Necessity, Proportionality and Use of Force by States* (Cambridge University Press, 2004).

Gardiner, Stephen M., 'Ethics and Global Climate Change' (2004) **114** *Ethics* 555.

Gazzini, Tarcisio, *The Changing Rules on the Use of Force in International Law* (Manchester University Press, 2005).

Giddens, Anthony, *The Constitution of Society: Outline of the Theory of Structuration* (Cambridge: Polity Press, 1984).

'Agency, Structure', in Anthony Giddens (ed.), *Central Problems in Social Theory* (Berkeley, Calif.: University of California Press, 1979), p. 49.

Gillespie, Richard, *Soldiers of Peron* (Oxford: Clarendon Press, 1982).

Glennon, Michael J., 'The Emerging Use-of-Force Paradigm' (2006) **11** *Journal of Conflict and Security Law* 309.

'How International Rules Die' (2005) **93** *Georgetown Law Journal* 939.

'The UN Security Council in a Unipolar World' (2004) **44** *Virginia Journal of International Law* 91.

'Why the Security Council Failed' (2003) **82** *Foreign Affairs* 16.

'The Fog of Law: Self-Defense, Inherence, and Incoherence in Article 51 of the United Nations Charter' (2002) **25** *Harvard Journal of Law and Public Policy* 539.

Global Centre for the Responsibility to Protect, *Implementing the Responsibility to Protect – The 2009 General Assembly Debate: An Assessment*, August 2009, at www.responsibilitytoprotect.org/index.php/component/content/article/35-r2pcs-topics/2522-report-by-the-global-centre-for-r2p-the-2009-general-assembly-debate-an-assessment.

Goldsmith, Jack, *Terror Presidency[:] Law and Judgment Inside the Bush Administration* (New York: W.W. Norton & Co., 2007).

Goldsmith, Jack L. and Eric A. Posner, *The Limits of International Law* (Oxford University Press, 2005).

Goldstein, Judith L. *et al.* (eds.), *Legalization and World Politics* (Cambridge, Mass.: MIT Press, 2001).

Goodman, Ryan and Derek Jinks, 'International Law and State Socialization: Conceptual, Empirical, and Normative Challenges' (2005) **54** *Duke Law Journal* 983.

'How to Influence States: Socialization and International Human Rights Law' (2004) **54** *Duke Law Journal* 621.

'Toward an Institutional Theory of Sovereignty' (2003) **55** *Stanford Law Review* 1749.

Gordon, Neve and Ruchama Marton (eds.), *Torture: Human Rights, Medical Ethics and the Case of Israel* (New York: Zed Books, 1995).

Gray, Christine, *International Law and the Use of Force*, 3rd edn (Oxford University Press, 2008).

'The Bush Doctrine Revisited: The 2006 National Security Strategy of the USA' (2006) **5** *Chinese Journal of International Law* 555.

Greenwood, Christopher, 'War, Terrorism, and International Law' (2003) **56** *Current Legal Problems* 505.

Gregg, Benjamin, *Coping in Politics with Indeterminate Norms: A Theory of Enlightened Localism* (Albany: State University of New York Press, 2003).

Grotius, Hugo, *De Jure Belli ac Pacis*, Richard Tuck (trans.) (Indianapolis, Ind.: Liberty Fund, 2005), Book II.

Grovogui, Siba N., 'Postcolonialism', in Timothy Dunne, Milja Kurki and Stephen Smith (eds.), *International Relations Theory: Discipline and Diversity* (Oxford University Press, 2007), p. 229.

Sovereignty, Quasi-Sovereigns and Africans: Race and Self-Determination in International Law (Minneapolis: University of Minnesota Press, 1996).

Grubb, Michael and Joyeeta Gupta, 'Implementing European Leadership', in Joyeeta Gupta and Michael Grubb (eds.), *Climate Change and European Leadership: A Sustainable Role for Europe* (Berlin: Springer, 2000), p. 287.

Grubb, Michael and Farhana Yamin, 'Climatic collapse at The Hague: what happened, why, and where do we go from here?' (2001) **77** *International Affairs* 261.

Guzman, Andrew T., *How International Law Works: A Rational Choice Theory* (Oxford University Press, 2008).

'The Promise of International Law' (2006) **92** *Virginia Law Review* 533.

Haas, Ernst, *When Knowledge is Power* (Berkeley: University of California Press, 1990).

Haas, Peter, 'Epistemic Communities', in Daniel Bodansky, Jutta Brunnée and Ellen Hey (eds.), *Oxford Handbook of International Environmental Law* (Oxford University Press, 2007), p. 791.

'Introduction: Epistemic Communities and International Policy Coordination', in Peter Haas (ed.), 'Special Issues: Knowledge, Power, and International Policy Coordination' (1992) **46** *International Organization* 1.

Habermas, Jürgen, *Between Facts and Norms: Contributions to a Discourse Theory of Law and Democracy* (Cambridge, Mass.: MIT Press, 1996).

Harrison, Kathryn and Lisa McIntosh Sundstrom, 'The Comparative Politics of Climate Change' (2007) **7** *Global Environmental Politics* 1.

Hart, Henry Jr. and Albert Sacks, *The Legal Process: Basic Problems in the Making and Application of Law* (Westbury, New York: Foundation Press, 1994).

Hart, H.L.A., *The Concept of Law*, 2nd edn (Oxford University Press, 1994).

Essays in Jurisprudence and Philosophy (Oxford: Clarendon Press, 1983).

The Concept of Law (Oxford: Clarendon Press, 1961).

'Positivism and the Separation of Law and Morals' (1958) **71** *Harvard Law Review* 593.

Hathaway, Oona, 'Why Do Countries Commit to Human Rights Treaties?' (2007) **51** *Journal of Conflict Resolution* 588.

'Between Power and Principle: A Political Theory of International Law' (2005) **71** *University of Chicago Law Review* 469.

'The Promise and Limits of the International Law of Torture' in Sanford Levinson (ed.), *Torture: A Collection* (New York: Oxford University Press, 2004), p. 199.

'Do Human Rights Treaties Make a Difference?' (2002) **111** *Yale Law Journal* 1935.

Hathaway, Oona A., and Ariel N. Lavinbuk, 'Rationalism and Revisionism in International Law' (2006) **119** *Harvard Law Review* 1404.

Henkin, Louis, *How Nations Behave: Law and Foreign Policy*, 2nd edn (New York: Columbia University Press, 1979).

Higgins, Rosalyn, *Problems and Process: International Law and How We Use It* (Oxford: Clarendon Press, 1994).

Hodges, Donald C., *Argentina's 'Dirty War'* (Austin: University of Texas Press, 1991).

Höhne, Niklas *et al.*, *Copenhagen Climate Deal – How to Close the Gap*, Briefing Paper, Ecofys & Climate Analytics, 15 December 2009, at www.climateactiontracker.org/briefing_paper.pdf.

Holmes, Oliver Wendell, Jr., 'The Path of the Law' (1897) **10** *Harvard Law Review* 457.

Holzgrefe, J. L. and Robert O. Keohane (eds.), *Humanitarian Intervention: Ethical, Legal and Political Dilemmas* (Cambridge University Press, 2003).

Holzscheiter, Anna, 'Discourse as Capability: Non-State Actors' Capital in Global Governance' (2005) **33** *Millennium: Journal of International Studies* 723.

Honkonen, Tuula, 'The Principle of Common But Differentiated Responsibility in Post-2012 Climate Negotiations' (2009) 18 *Review of European Community and International Environmental Law* 257.

Hourcade, Jean-Charles and Thierry Le Pesant, 'Negotiating Targets, Negotiating Flex-Mex: The Economic Background to the US-EU Controversy', in Carlo Carraro (ed.), *Efficiency and Equity of Climate Change Policy* (Dordrecht: Kluwer Academic Publishers, 2000), p. 63.

Hovi, Jon, Steinar Andresen and Tora Skodvin, 'The Persistence of the Kyoto Protocol: Why Other Annex I Countries Move on Without the United States' (2003) **3** *Global Environmental Politics* 1.

Hunter, David, 'The Future of U.S. Climate Change Policy', in Steven Bernstein, Jutta Brunnée, David Duff and Andrew Green (eds.), *A Globally Integrated Climate Policy for Canada* (University of Toronto Press, 2007), p 79.

Huntington, Samuel P., *The Clash of Civilisations and the Remaking of World Order* (New York: Simon & Schuster 1996).

Hurd, Ian, 'Legitimacy, Power, and the Symbolic Life of the UN Security Council' (2002) **8** *Global Governance* 35.

Hurrell, Andrew, 'Power, Institutions, and the Production of Inequality', in Michael Barnett and Robert Duvall (eds.), *Power in Global Governance* (Cambridge University Press, 2005), p. 33.

'Global Inequality and International Institutions', in Thomas W. Pogge (ed.), *Global Justice* (Oxford: Blackwell, 2001), p. 32.

'International Law and the Changing Constitution of International Society', in Michael Byers (ed.), *The Role of Law in International Politics* (Cambridge University Press, 2000), p. 327.

Ignatieff, Michael, 'If Torture Works ...', *Prospect Magazine*, April 2006, Issue 121.

The Lesser Evil: Political Ethics in the Age of Terror (Toronto: Penguin Group, 2004).

Ikeme, Jekwu, 'Equity, environmental justice and sustainability: incomplete approaches in climate change policies' (2003) **13** *Global Environmental Politics* 195.

Intergovernmental Panel on Climate Change, *Climate Change 2007: Working Group I Report: The Physical Science Basis* (February 2007).

Climate Change 2007: Working Group II Report: Impacts, Adaptation and Vulnerability (April 2007).

Climate Change 2007: Working Group II Report: Mitigation (May 2007).

Ip, John, 'Two Narratives of Torture' (2009) **7** *Northwestern University Journal of International Human Rights* 35.

Jackson, Robert and Georg Sørensen, *Introduction to International Relations* (Oxford University Press, 1999).

Jacobson, Harold K., 'Climate Change: Unilateralism, Realism, and Two-Level Games', in Stewart Patrick and Shep Forman (eds.), *Multilateralism and U.S. Foreign Policy: Ambivalent Engagement* (Boulder, Colo.: Lynne Rienner Publishers, 2001), p. 415.

Jenks, Wilfred C., *The Common Law of Mankind* (London: Stevens, 1958).

Jinks, Derek, 'State Responsibility for the Acts of Private Armed Groups' (2003) **4** *Chicago Journal of International Law* 83.

Johnson, James Turner, *Morality and Contemporary Warfare* (New Haven: Yale University Press, 1999).

Just War Tradition and the Restraint of War: A Moral and Historical Inquiry (Princeton University Press, 1981).

Johnston, Alastair Ian, 'Treating International Institutions as Social Environments' (2001) **45** *International Studies Quarterly* 487.

Johnstone, Ian, 'Legislation and Adjudication in the UN Security Council: Bringing Down the Deliberative Deficit' (2008) **102** *American Journal of International Law* 275.

'The Plea of Necessity in International Legal Discourse: Humanitarian Intervention and Counter-Terrorism' (2005) **43** *Columbia Journal of International Law* 337.

'The Power of Interpretive Communities', in Michael Barnett and Raymond Duvall (eds.), *Power in Global Governance* (Cambridge University Press, 2005), p. 185.

'Security Council Deliberations: The Power of the Better Argument' (2003) **12** *European Journal of International Law* 437.

Joyner, Christopher C. *et al.*, 'Common But Differentiated Responsibility' (2002) **96** *American Society of International Law Proceedings* 358.

Kahan, Dan M., 'The Logic of Reciprocity: Trust, Collective Action, and Law' (2003) **102** *Michigan Law Review* 71.

Kahn, Paul W., 'Speaking Law to Power: Popular Sovereignty, Human Rights and the New International Order' (2000) **1** *Chicago Journal of International Law* 1.

Katzenstein, Peter J., Robert O. Keohane and Stephen D. Krasner, 'International Organization and the Study of World Politics' (1998) **52** *International Organization* 645.

Keene, Edward, *Beyond the Anarchical Society: Grotius, Colonialism and Order in World Politics* (Cambridge University Press, 2002).

Kelsen, Hans, *General Theory of Law and State*, Anders Wedberg (trans.) (New York: Russell & Russell, 1961).

Principles of International Law (New York: Rinehart & Company, 1952).

Kennan, George F., *American Diplomacy 1900–1950* (University of Chicago Press, 1984).

Keohane, Robert O., 'Reciprocity in International Relations' (1986) **40** *International Organization* 1.

Keohane, Robert O. and Joseph S. Nye, 'Power and Interdependence Revisited' (1987) **41** *International Organization* 725.

Kinacioglu, Muge, 'A Response to Amos Guiora: Reassessing the Parameters of Use of Force in the Age of Terrorism: Pre-emptive Action and International Law' (2008) **13** *Journal of Conflict and Security Law* 1.

King, David A., 'Climate Change Science: Adapt, Mitigate or Ignore?' (2004) **303** *Science* 176.

Kingsbury, Benedict, 'International Law as Inter-Public Law', in Henry R. Richardson and Melissa S. Williams (eds.), *NOMOS XLIX: Moral Universalism and Pluralism* (New York University Press, 2009), p. 167.

'Sovereignty and Inequality' (1998) **9** *European Journal of International Law* 599.

'The Concept of Compliance as a Function of Competing Conceptions of International Law' (1998) **19** *Michigan Journal of International Law* 345.

'Legal Positivism as Normative Politics: International Society, Balance of Power and Lassa Oppenheim's Positive International Law' (2002) **13** *European Journal of International Law* 401.

Kingsbury, Benedict and Adam Roberts 'The UN's Roles in International Society', in Adam Roberts and Benedict Kingsbury (eds.), *United Nations, Divided World* (New York: Oxford University Press, 1993), p. 1.

Kirgis, F.L. Jr., 'The United Nations at Fifty: The Security Council's First Fifty Years' (1995) **89** *American Journal of International Law* 506.

Klabbers, Jan, 'Constitutionalism and the Making of International Law: Fuller's Procedural Natural Law' (2008) **5** *No Foundations: Journal of Extreme Legal Positivism* 84.

'Compliance Procedures', in Daniel Bodansky, Jutta Brunnée and Ellen Hey (eds.), *Oxford Handbook of International Environmental Law* (Oxford University Press, 2007), p. 995.

'The Relative Autonomy of International Law or the Forgotten Politics of Interdisciplinarity' (2005) **1** *Journal of International Law and International Relations* 35.

'The Redundancy of Soft Law' (1996) **65** *Nordic Journal of International Law* 167.

Knop, Karen, 'The Hart–Fuller Debate's Silence on Human Rights', in Peter Cane (ed.), *The Hart–Fuller Debate: 50 Years On* (Oxford: Hart Publishing, 2010), p. 61.

Knopf, Jeffrey W., 'The Importance of International Learning' (2003) **29** *Review of International Studies* 185.

Koh, Harold H., 'Internalization through Socialization' (2005) **54** *Duke Law Journal* 975.

'The 1998 Frankel Lecture: Bringing International Law Home' (1998) **35** *Houston International Law Journal* 623.

'Why Do Nations Obey International Law?', Book Review of *The New Sovereignty: Compliance with International Regulatory Agreements* by A. Chayes and A. Handler Chayes (1997) **106** *Yale Law Journal* 2599.

'Transnational Legal Process – The 1994 Roscoe Pound Lecture' (1996) **75** *Nebraska Law Review* 181.

Koskenniemi, Martti, 'What is International Law for?', in Malcolm D. Evans (ed.), *International Law*, 2nd edn (Oxford University Press, 2006), p. 57.

From Apology to Utopia: The Structure of International Legal Argument, reissue with a new Epilogue (Cambridge University Press, 2005).

The Gentle Civilizer of Nations: The Rise and Fall of International Law 1870–1960 (Cambridge University Press, 2001).

'Carl Schmitt, Hans Morgenthau, and the Image of Law in International Relations', in Michael Byers (ed.), *The Role of Law in International Politics* (Cambridge University Press, 2000), p. 17.

'Breach of Treaty or Non-Compliance? Reflections on the Enforcement of the Montreal Protocol' (1992) **3** *Yearbook of International Environmental Law* 123.

Krämer, Ludwig, 'The Roots of Divergence: A European Perspective', in Norman J. Vig and Michael Faure (eds.), *Green Giants? Environmental Policy of the United States and the European Union* (Cambridge, Mass.: MIT Press, 2007) p. 53.

'Regional Economic Integration Organizations: The European Union as an Example', in Daniel Bodansky, Jutta Brunnée and Ellen Hey (eds.), *Oxford Handbook of International Environmental Law* (Oxford University Press, 2007), p. 853.

Kratochwil, Friedrich V., 'How Do Norms Matter?', in Michael Byers (ed.), *The Role of Law in International Politics: Essays in International Relations and International Law* (Oxford University Press, 2000), p. 35.

Krisch, Nico, 'More equal than the rest? Hierarchy, Equality and US Predominance in International Law', in Michael Byers and Georg Nolte (eds.), *United States Hegemony and the Foundations of International Law* (Cambridge University Press, 2003), p. 135.

Kritsiosis, Dino, 'Arguments of Mass Confusion' (2004) **15** *European Journal of International Law* 233.

'Imagining the International Community' (2002) **13** *European Journal of International Law* 268.

Kumm, Matthias, 'The Legitimacy of International Law: A Constitutionalist Framework of Analysis' (2004) **15** *European Journal of International Law* 907.

Kurki, Milja and Adriana Sinclair, 'Hidden in Plain Sight: Reflections on the Limitations of the Constructivist Treatment of Social Context' (manuscript on file with authors, 2007).

Kwakwa, Edward, 'The International Community, International Law, and the United States: Three in One, Two Against One, or One and the Same?', in Michael Byers and Georg Nolte (eds.), *United States Hegemony and the Foundations of International Law* (Cambridge University Press, 2003), p. 25.

Langbein, John H., 'The Legal History of Torture' in Sanford Levinson (ed.), *Torture: A Collection* (New York: Oxford University Press, 2004), p. 93.

Torture and the Law of Proof (University of Chicago Press, 1977).

Lave, Jean, and Etienne Wenger, *Situated Learning: Legitimate Peripheral Participation* (Cambridge University Press, 1991).

LeBel, L., and G. Chao, 'The Rise of International Law in Canadian Constitutional Litigation: Fugue or Fusion? Recent Developments and Challenges in Internalizing International Law' (2002) **16** *Supreme Court Law Review* 23.

Legro, Jeffrey W., 'Which Norms Matter? Revisiting the "Failure" of Internationalism' (1997) *51 International Organization* 31.

Lessig, Lawrence, 'Social Meaning and Social Norms' (1996) **144** *University of Pennsylvania Law Review* 2181.

Levin, Kelly and Rob Bradley, 'Compatibility of Annex I Emission Reduction Pledges', *World Resources Working Paper*, December 2009, at http://pdf.wri.org/working_papers/comparability_of_annex1_emission_reduction_pledges_2009-12-04.pdf.

Levinson, Sanford, 'Contemplating Torture: An Introduction' in Sanford Levinson (ed.), *Torture: A Collection* (New York: Oxford University Press, 2004), p. 23.

Lindsay, James M., 'The Case for a Concert of Democracies' (2009) **23** *Ethics and International Affairs* 5.

Lobel, Jules and Michael Ratner, 'Bypassing the Security Council: Ambiguous Authorizations to Use Force, Cease-Fires and the Iraqi Inspection Regime' (1999) 93 *American Journal of International Law* 124.

Lowe, Vaughan, 'The Iraq Crisis: What Now?' (2003) **52** *International and Comparative Law Quarterly* 859.

'The Politics of Law-Making: Are the Method and Character of Norm Creation Changing?', in Michael Byers (ed.), *The Role of Law in International Politics* (Cambridge University Press, 2000), p. 207.

Luban, David, 'Liberalism, Torture, and the Ticking Bomb' (2005) **91** *Virginia Law Review* 1425.

'Preventive War' (2004) **32** *Philosophy and Public Affairs* 207.

'Rediscovering Fuller's Legal Ethics', in Willem J. Witteveen and Wilbren van der Burg (eds.), *Rediscovering Fuller: Essays on Implicit Law and Institutional Design* (Amsterdam University Press, 1999), p. 193.

Lutz, Ellen L. and Kathryn Sikkink, 'International Human Rights Law and Practice in Latin America', in Judith L. Goldstein, Miles Kahler, Robert O. Keohane and Anne-Marie Slaughter (eds.), *Legalization and World Politics* (Cambridge, Mass.: MIT Press, 2001), p. 249.

Macdonald, Roderick A., 'Legislation and Governance', in Willem J. Witteveen and Wilbren van der Burg (eds.), *Rediscovering Fuller: Essays on Implicit Law and Institutional Design* (Amsterdam University Press, 1999), p. 279.

Mahbubani, Kishore, 'The Dangers of Democratic Delusions' (2003) **23** *Ethics and International Affairs* 19.

Malone, David M., 'The Security Council in the Post-Cold War Era: A Study in the Creative Interpretation of the UN Charter' (2003) **35** *New York University Journal of International Law* 487.

Mamdani, Mahmood, 'The Politics of Naming: Genocide, Civil War, Insurgency', *London Review of Books*, 8 March 2007.

Maran, Rita, *Torture: The Role of Ideology in the French Algerian War* (New York: Praeger, 1989).

March, James G. and Johan P. Olsen, 'The Institutional Dynamics of International Political Orders' (1998) **52** *International Organization* 943.

Democratic Governance (New York: Free Press, 1995).

Rediscovering Institutions (New York: Free Press, 1989).

Matsui, Yoshiro, 'Some Aspects of the Principle of "Common but Differentiated Responsibilities"' (2002) **2** *International Environmental Agreements* 151.

Mayer, Jane, 'Outsourcing Torture', *The New Yorker*, 14 February 2005.

McCoy, Alfred W., *A Question of Torture: CIA interrogation, from the Cold War to the War on Terror* (New York: Metropolitan Books Henry Holt and Company, 2006).

McKeown, Ryder, 'Norm Regress: US Revisionism and the Slow Death of the Torture Norm' **23**(1) *International Relations* 5.

McKibbin, Warwick J. and Peter J. Wilcoxen, 'Estimates of the costs of Kyoto: Marrakesh versus the McKibbin-Wilcoxen blueprint' (2004) **32** *Energy Policy* 467.

McKinstry, Robert B. Jr., 'Laboratories for Local Solutions for Global Problems: State, Local and Private Leadership in Developing Strategies to Mitigate the Causes and Effects of Climate Change' (2004) **12** *Penn State Environmental Law Review* 15.

Meinshausen, Malte *et al.*, 'Greenhouse-gas emission targets for limiting global warming to 2 C' (2009) **458** *Nature* 1158.

Mickelson, Karin, 'South, North, International Environmental Law, and International Environmental Lawyers' (2000) **11** *Yearbook of International Environmental Law* 52.

Miller, Richard B., 'Justifications of the Iraq War Examined' (2008) **22** *Ethics and International Affairs* 43.

Mitchell, Ronald B., 'Compliance Theory', in Daniel Bodansky, Jutta Brunnée and Ellen Hey (eds.), *The Oxford Handbook of International Environmental Law* (Oxford University Press, 2007), p. 893.

Moore, J.B., '*The Caroline* (1837)' (1906) **2** *A Digest of International Law* 409.

Mootz, Francis J. III, 'Natural Law and the Cultivation of Legal Rhetoric', in Willem J. Witteveen and Wilbren van der Burg (eds.), *Rediscovering Fuller: Essays on Implicit Law and Institutional Design* (Amsterdam University Press, 1999), p. 425.

Moravcsik, Andrew, 'Taking Preferences Seriously: A Liberal Theory of International Politics' (1997) **51** *International Organization* 513.

Morgenthau, Hans J., *Politics Among Nations: The Struggle for Power and Peace*, 2nd edn (New York: Knopf, 1954).

Politics Among Nations: The Struggle for Power and Peace, 1st edn (New York: Alfred A. Knopf, 1948).

Scientific Man vs. Power Politics (University of Chicago Press, 1946).

'Théorie des sanctions internationales' (1935) **16** *Revue de Droit International et de Legislation Comparée* 474.

Müller, Harald, 'Arguing, Bargaining and All That: Communicative Action, Rationalist Theory and the Logic of Appropriateness in International Relations' (2004) **10** *European Journal of International Relations* 395.

Murphy, Colleen, 'Lon Fuller and the Moral Value of the Rule of Law' (2005) **24** *Law and Philosophy* 239.

Murphy, Sean, 'Assessing the Legality of Invading Iraq' (2004) **92** *Georgetown Law Journal* 173.

'Terrorism and the Concept of "Armed Attack" in Article 51 of the U.N. Charter' (2002) **43** *Harvard International Law Journal* 41.

Mutua, Makau W., 'What Is TWAIL?' (2000) **94** *American Society of International Law Proceedings* 31.

'Why Redraw the Map of Africa: A Moral and Legal Inquiry' (1995) **16** *Michigan Journal of International Law* 1113.

Nardin, Terry, 'Legal Positivism as a Theory of International Society', in David R. Mapel and Terry Nardin (eds.), *International Society: Diverse Ethical Perspectives* (Princeton University Press, 1998), p. 17.

Nedelsky, Jennifer, 'Judgment, Diversity, and Relational Autonomy', in Ronald Beiner and Jennifer Nedelsky (eds.), *Judgment, Imagination, and Politics: Themes from Kant and Arendt* (Lanham, Md: Rowman & Littlefield, 2001), p. 103.

'Communities of Judgment and Human Rights' (2000) **1** *Theoretical Inquiries in Law* 245.

Neuwirth, Jessica, 'Inequality Before the Law: Holding States Accountable for Sex Discriminatory Laws under the Convention on the Elimination of all Forms of Discrimination Against Women and Through the Beijing Platform for Action' (2005) **18** *Harvard Human Rights Journal* 19.

Ní Aoiláin, Fionnula, 'The European Convention on Human Rights and Its Prohibition on Torture' in Sanford Levinson (ed.), *Torture: A Collection* (New York: Oxford University Press, 2004), p. 213.

Nisbet, Matthew C. and Teresa Myers, 'The Polls – Trends: Twenty Years of Public Opinion about Global Warming' (2007) **71** *Public Opinion Quarterly* 1.

Nollkaemper, André, 'Attribution of Forcible Acts to States: Connections Between the Law on the Use of Force and the Law of State Responsibility', in N. Blokker and N. Schrijver (eds.), *The Security Council and the Use of Force: Theory and Reality – A Need for Change?* (Leiden: Martinus Nijhoff Publishers, 2005), p. 133.

Norman, George and Joel P. Trachtman, 'The Customary International Law Game' (2005) **99** *American Journal of International Law* 541.

Nye, Joseph S. Jr., *Soft Power: The Means to Success in World Politics* (New York: Public Affairs, 2004).

'Nuclear Learning and U.S.–Soviet Security Regimes' (1987) **41** *International Organization* 371.

O'Connell, Mary Ellen, 'Enhancing the Status of Non-State Actors Through a Global War on Terror?' (2005) **43** *Columbia Journal of Transnational Law* 435.

'The Myth of Preemptive Self-Defence', *American Society of International Law Task Force Papers* (August 2002), p. 9.

O'Connell, Mary Ellen and Maria Alevras-Chen, 'The Ban on the Bomb – and Bombing: Iran, the U.S., and the International Law of Self-Defence' (2007) **57** *Syracuse Law Review* 497.

Onuma, Yasuaki, 'A Transcivilizational Perspective on Global Legal Order in the Twenty-first Century', in Ronald St. J. Macdonald and Douglas M. Johnston, *Towards World Constitutionalism: Issues in the Legal Ordering of the World Community* (Leiden: Martinus Nijhoff, 2005), p. 151.

Orend, Brian, *Michael Walzer on War and Justice* (Montreal and Kingston: McGill-Queen's University Press, 2000).

O'Shaughnessy, Hugh, *Pinochet: The Politics of Torture* (London: Latin American Bureau Ltd., 2000).

Ott, Herrmann, 'Climate Policy post 2012 – A Roadmap: The Global Governance of Climate Change,' Discussion Paper for the 2007 Tällberg Forum (Stockholm: Tällberg Foundation, 2007), at www.wupperinst.org/uploads/tx_wibeitrag/Ott_Taellberg_Post-2012.pdf.

'The Bonn Agreement to the Kyoto Protocol – Paving the Way for Ratification' (2001) **1** *International Environmental Agreements: Politics, Law and Economics* 469.

'The Kyoto Protocol: Unfinished Business' (1998) **40** *Environment* 3.

Otto, Dianne, 'Subalternity and International Law: The Problem of Global Community and the Incommensurability of Difference' (1996) **5** *Social and Legal Studies* 337.

Owen, Wilfred, 'Preface', in John Stallworthy (ed.), *The Poems of Wilfred Owen*, original definitive paperback edn (London: Hogarth Press, 1985), p. 192.

Özsu, Umut, 'Towards a Critical Constructivist Theory of Legal "Norm-Internalization": Two Cases from Early Republican Turkey' unpublished LL.M. thesis, University of Toronto, Faculty of Law (2007), Chapter 1.

Pachauri, R.K and A. Reisinger (eds.), *Climate Change 2007: Synthesis Report. Contribution of Working Groups I, II and III to the Fourth Assessment Report of the Intergovernmental Panel on Climate Change* (Geneva: IPCC, 2008), at www.ipcc.ch/pdf/assessment-report/ar4/syr/ar4_syr.pdf.

Pallemaerts, Marc, 'International Law and Sustainable Development: Any Progress in Johannesburg?' (2003) **12** *Review of European Community and International Environmental Law* 1.

Pangle, Thomas L. and Peter J. Ahrensdorf, *Justice Among Nations* (University Press of Kansas, 1999).

Paradell-Trius, Lluís, 'Principles of International Environmental Law: an Overview' (2000) **9** *Review of European Community and International Environmental Law* 93.

Pardew, Christy, 'Counterintelligence Training Manuals Timeline', May 2004, School of the Americas Watch.

Parry, John T., 'Escalation and Necessity: Defining Torture at Home and Abroad' in Sanford Levinson (ed.), *Torture: A Collection* (New York: Oxford University Press, 2004), p. 145.

Paskins, Barrie and Michael Dockrill, *The Ethics of War* (Minneapolis: University of Minnesota Press, 1979).

Paulus, Andreas L., 'The War against Iraq and the Future of International Law: Hegemony or Pluralism?' (2004) **25** *Michigan Journal of International Law* 691.

'Antimonies of Power and Law: A Comment on Robert Kagan' (2003) **9** *German Law Journal* 871.

Die Internationale Gemeinschaft im Völkerrecht (Munich: Verlag C.H. Beck, 2001).

Payne, Roger A., 'Persuasion, Frames and Norm Construction' (2001) **7** *European Journal of International Relations* 37.

Perelman, Chaim, *The New Rhetoric and the Humanities: Essays on Rhetoric and Its Applications*, W. Kluback (trans.) (Dordrecht: D. Reidel Publishing Company, 1979).

Logique Juridique (Paris: Dalloz, 1976).

Pew Centre on Global Climate Change, 'California Global Warming Solutions Act of 2006'.

Pope Pius VII, 'Codex Juris Canonici' (1917).

Postema, Gerald J., 'Custom in International Law: A Normative Practice Account', in Amanda Perreau-Saussine and James Bernard Murphy (eds.), *The Nature of Customary Law: Legal, Historical and Philosophical Perspectives* (Cambridge University Press, 2007), p. 279.

'Implicit Law' (1994) 13 *Law and Philosophy* 361; repr. in Willem J. Witteveen and Wilbren van der Burg (eds.), *Rediscovering Fuller: Essays on Implicit Law and Institutional Design* (Amsterdam University Press, 1999), p. 255.

Price, Richard, 'Nuclear Weapons Don't Kill People, Rogues Do' (2007) **44** *International Politics* 232.

'Emerging Customary Norms and Anti-Personnel Landmines', in Christian Reus-Smit (ed.), *The Politics of International Law* (Cambridge University Press, 2004), p. 106.

Provost, René, *International Human Rights and Humanitarian Law* (Oxford University Press, 2002).

Raab, Dominic, '"Armed Attack" After the *Oil Platforms* Case' (2004) **17** *Leiden Journal of International Law* 719.

Rabkin, Jeremy, *Law Without Nations? Why Constitutional Government Requires Sovereign States* (Princeton University Press, 2005).

Rajagopal, Balakrishnan, 'International Law and Third World Resistance: A Theoretical Inquiry', in Antony Anghie, Bhupinder Chimni, Karin Mickelson and Obiora Chinedu Okafor (eds.), *The Third World and International Order: Law, Politics and Globalization* (New York: Kluwer Law International, 2003), p. 145.

'Locating the Third World in Cultural Geography' (1998–9) *Third World Legal Studies* 1.

Rajamani, Lavanya, 'Addressing the "Post-Kyoto" Stress Disorder: Reflections on the Emerging Legal Architecture of the Climate Regime' (2009) 58 *International and Comparative Law Quarterly 803.*

'The Copenhagen Agreed Outcome: Form, Shape & Influence', *Centre for Policy Research (CPR) Climate Brief*, November 2009, at www.cprindia.org/policyupload/1259569856-CPR%20Polic%20Brief2.pdf.

'The "Cloud" Over the Climate Negotiations: From Bangkok to Copenhagen and Beyond', *Centre for Policy Research (CPR) Climate Brief*, October 2009, at www.cprindia.org/policyupload/1256103508-CPR%20Polic%20Brief.pdf.

'The Copenhagen Agreed Outcome: Form, Shape & Influence', *Centre for Policy Research (CPR) Climate Brief*, October 2009, at www.cprindia.org/policyupload/1259569856-CPR%20Polic%20Brief2.pdf.

'From Berlin to Bali and Beyond: Killing Kyoto Softly' (2008) 57 *International and Comparative Law Quarterly* 909.

'China and India on Climate Change and Development: A Stance that is Legitimate but not Sagacious?', in Steven Bernstein, Jutta Brunnée, David Duff and Andrew Green (eds.), *A Globally Integrated Climate Policy for Canada* (University of Toronto Press, 2007), p. 104.

'From Stockholm to Johannesburg: The Anatomy of Dissonance in the International Environmental Regime' (2003) **12** *Review of European Community and International Environmental Law* 23.

'The Principle of Common but Differentiated Responsibility and the Balance of Commitments under the Climate Regime' (2000) **9** *Review of European Community and International Environmental Law* 120.

Rao, Anupama, 'Problems of Violence, States of Terror: Torture in Colonial India' (2001) **3** *Interventions* 186.

Ratner, Steven, '*Jus ad Bellum* and *Jus in Bello* After September 11' (2002) **96** *American Journal of International Law* 905.

Raustiala, Kal, 'Form and Substance in International Agreements' (2005) **99** *American Journal of International Law* 581.

'The Architecture of International Cooperation: Transgovernmental Networks and the Future of International Law' (2002) **43** *Virginia Journal of International Law* 1.

'Non-State Actors in the Global Climate Regime', in Urs Lauterbacher and Detlev F. Sprinz, *International Relations and Global Climate Change* (Cambridge, Mass.: MIT Press, 2001), p. 95.

'Compliance and Effectiveness in International Regulatory Cooperation' (2000) **32** *Case Western Reserve International Law Journal* 387.

Raustiala, Kal and Anne-Marie Slaughter, 'International Law, International Relations and Compliance', in Walter Carlsnaes, Thomas Risse and Beth

Simmons (eds.), *Handbook of International Relations* (London: Sage, 2002), p. 538.

Rawls, John, *The Law of Peoples; with 'The Idea of Public Reason Revisited'* (Cambridge, Mass: Harvard University Press, 1999).

Raz, Joseph, *The Authority of Law, Essays on Law and Morality* (Oxford: Clarendon Press, 1979).

Reisman, Michael, 'In Defense of World Public Order' (2004) **95** *The American Journal of International Law* 833.

'Hollow Victory: Humanitarian Intervention and Protection of Minorities' (1997) **91** *American Society of International Law Proceedings* 431.

Rejali, Darius, *Torture and Modernity: Self, Society, and State in Modern Iran* (Boulder, Colo., and Oxford: Westview Press, 1993).

Reus-Smit, Christian, 'Constructivism', in Scott Burchill *et al.*, *Theories of International Relations*, 3rd edn (Houndmills, Basingstoke: Palgrave Macmillan, 2005), p. 188.

'Society, Power and Ethics', in Christian Reus-Smit (ed.), *The Politics of International Law* (Cambridge University Press, 2004), p. 272.

Risse, Thomas, 'Transnational Actors and World Politics', in Walter Carlsnaes, Thomas Risse and Beth Simmons (eds.), *Handbook of International Relations* (London: Sage, 2002), p. 255.

'"Let's Argue!": Communicative Action in World Politics' (2000) **54** *International Organization* 1.

Cooperation Among Democracies: The European Influence on US Foreign Policy (Princeton University Press, 1995).

Roberts, J. Timmons, and Parks, Bradley C. *A Climate of Injustice: Global Inequality, North–South Politics, and Climate Policy* (Cambridge, Mass.: MIT Press, 2007).

Ronen, Yaël, 'Israel, Hizbollah, and the Second Lebanon War', Research Paper No. 10–08 (September 2008), Hebrew University of Jerusalem Faculty of Law.

Rorty, Richard, *Contingency, Irony, and Solidarity* (Cambridge University Press, 1989).

Roudik, Peter, 'Russian Federation: Legal Aspects of War in Georgia', *Law Library of Congress*, September 2008 (Document Number 2008–01474).

Rubenfeld, Jed, 'Unilateralism and Constitutionalism' (2004) **79** *New York University Law Review* 1971.

Ruggie, John G., 'What Makes the World Hang Together? Neo-utilitarianism and the Social Constructivist Challenge' (1998) **52** *International Organization* 855.

Rundle, Kristen, 'The Impossibility of an Exterminatory Legality: Law and the Holocaust' (2009) **59** *University of Toronto Law Journal* 65.

Russett, Bruce, *Grasping the Democratic Peace: Principles for a Post-Cold War World* (Princeton University Press, 1993).

Sands, Philippe, *Torture Team* (New York: Palgrave Macmillan, 2008).
Principles of International Environmental Law, 2nd edn (New York: Cambridge University Press, 2003).

Scelle, Georges, 'Le Phénomène Juridique de Dédoublement Fonctionnel', in Walter Schätzel and Hans-Jürgen Schlochauer (eds.), *Rechtsfragen der internationalen Organisation: Festschrift für Hans Wehberg zu seinem 70. Geburtstag* (Frankfurt: Klostermann, 1956), p. 324.

Schachter, Oscar, 'New Custom: Power, *Opinio Juris* and Contrary Practice', in Jerzy Makarczyk (ed.), *Theory of International Law at the Threshold of the 21st Century* (The Hague: Kluwer Law International, 1996), p. 531.

Schauer, Frederick, 'Fuller on the Ontological Status of Law', in Willem J. Witteveen and Wilbren van der Burg (eds.), *Rediscovering Fuller: Essays on Implicit Law and Institutional Design* (Amsterdam University Press, 1999), p. 124.
'Fuller's Internal Point of View' (1994) **13** *Law and Philosophy* 285.

Schiff Berman, Paul, 'From International Law to Law and Globalization' (2005) **43** *Columbia Journal of Transnational Law* 485.

Schlesinger, Stephen, 'Why a League of Democracies Will Not Work' (2009) **23** *Ethics and International Affairs* 13.

Schreurs, Miranda and Yves Tiberghien, 'Multi-Level Reinforcement: Explaining European Union Leadership in Climate Change Mitigation' (2007) **7** *Global Environmental Politics* 19.

Schrijver, Nico, 'Responding to International Terrorism: Moving the Frontiers of International Law for "Enduring Freedom"?' (2001) **48** *Netherlands International Law Review* 271.

Searle, John, 'An Iterative Perspective on Treaties: A Synthesis of International Relations Theory and International Law' (1996) **37** *Harvard International Law Journal* 139.
The Construction of Social Reality (London: Penguin, 1995).

Shah, Niaz A., 'Self-defence, Anticipatory Self-defence and Pre-emption: International Law Response to Terrorism' (2007) **12** *Journal of Conflict and Security Law* 95.

Shannon, Vaughn, 'Norms Are What States Make of Them: The Political Psychology of Norm Violation' (2000) **44** *International Studies Quarterly* 293.

Shaw, Malcolm N., *International Law*, 5th edn (Cambridge University Press, 2003).

Shklar, Judith, *Legalism: Law, Morals, and Political Trials* (Cambridge, Mass.: Harvard University Press, 1986).

Shue, Henry, 'Torture', in Sanford Levinson (ed.), *Torture: A Collection* (New York: Oxford University Press, 2004), p. 47.

Sikh Coalition, The, 'United States Judicial Opinions Regarding Sikh Religious Identity' (2009).

Simmons, Beth, 'The Legalization of International Monetary Affairs' (2000) **54** *International Organization* 573.

Simmons, Beth and Daniel Hopkins, 'The Constraining Power of International Treaties' (2005) **99** *American Political Science Review* 623.

Simpson, Gerry, *Great Powers and Outlaw States: Unequal Sovereigns in the International Legal Order* (Cambridge University Press, 2004).

Slater, David, 'Contesting Occidental Visions of the Global: The Geopolitics of Theory and North–South Relations' (1994) **4** *Beyond Law* 97.

Slaughter, Anne-Marie, 'Security, Solidarity, and Sovereignty: The Grand Themes of UN Reform' (2005) **99** *American Journal of International Law* 619.

'Notes from the President: A Fork in the Road' (September/October 2003) *American Society of International Law Newsletter*, p. 4.

'Is the U.S. at Risk of Violating International Law?', *Council of Foreign Relations*, 3 March 2003.

'A Liberal Theory of International Law' (2000) *Proceedings of the 94th Annual Meeting of the American Society of International Law* 240.

'Building Global Democracy' (2000) **1** *Chicago Journal of International Law* 223.

'International Law in a World of Liberal States' (1995) **6** *European Journal of International Law* 503.

'The Liberal Agenda for Peace: International Relations Theory and the Future of the United Nations' (1994) **4** *Transnational Law and Contemporary Problems* 377.

Sołtan, Karol, 'A Social Science That Does Not Exist', in Willem J. Witteveen and Wilbren van der Burg (eds.), *Rediscovering Fuller: Essays on Implicit Law and Institutional Design* (Amsterdam University Press, 1999), p. 387.

Spence, Chris *et al.*, 'Great Expectations: Understanding Bali and the Climate Change Negotiation Process' (2008) **17** *Review of European Community and International Law* 142.

Stahn, Carsten, 'Responsibility to Protect: Political Rhetoric or Emerging Legal Norm?' (2007) **101** *American Journal of International Law* 99.

Stavins, Robert N., 'A Portfolio of Domestic Commitments: Implementing Common but Differential Responsibilities', *Viewpoints – Harvard Project on International Climate Agreements*, 19 October 2009, at http://belfercenter.ksg.harvard.edu/files/DomesticCommitments_final.pdf.

Stern, Todd and William Antholis, 'A Changing Climate: The Road Ahead for the United States' (2007) **31** *The Washington Quarterly* 175.

Stromseth, Jane E., 'Law and Force After Iraq: A Transitional Moment' (2003) **97** *American Journal of International Law* 628.

Sunstein, Cass, 'Of Montreal and Kyoto: A Tale of Two Protocols' (2007) **31** *Harvard Environmental Law Review* 1.

Széll, Patrick, 'Decision Making under Multilateral Environmental Agreements' (1991) **26** *Environmental Policy and Law* 210.

Tamanaha, Brian Z., *On the Rule of Law* (Cambridge University Press, 2004).

Tanguy, Joelle, 'Redefining Sovereignty and Intervention' (2003) **17** *Ethics and International Affairs* 141.

Teachout, Peter R., '"Uncreated Conscience": The Civilizing Force of Fuller's Jurisprudence', in Willem J. Witteveen and Wilbren van der Burg (eds.), *Rediscovering Fuller: Essays on Implicit Law and Institutional Design* (Amsterdam University Press, 1999), p. 229.

Teske, Sven *et al.*, *Energy [R]evolution: A Sustainable Canada Energy Outlook*, (Greenpeace and the European Renewable Energy Council, 2009).

Thuo Gathii, James, 'Alternative and Critical: The Contribution of Research and Scholarship on Developing Countries to International Legal Theory' (2000) **41** *Harvard International Law Journal* 263.

'The Limits of the *New* International Rule of Law on Good Governance', in Edward Kofi Quashigah and Obiora Chinedu Okafor (eds.), *Legitimate Governance in Africa: International and Domestic Legal Perspectives* (The Hague: Kluwer Law International, 1999), p. 207.

'International Law and Eurocentricity' (1998) **9** *European Journal of International Law* 184.

Toope, Stephen J., 'Formality and Informality', in Daniel Bodansky, Jutta Brunnée and Ellen Hey (eds.), *Oxford Handbook of International Environmental Law* (Oxford University Press, 2007), p. 107.

'Public Commitment To International Law: Canadian and British Media Perspectives on the Use of Force', in Christopher P.M. Waters (ed.), *British and Canadian Perspectives on International Law* (Dordrecht: Martinus Nijhoff, 2006), p. 13.

'Powerful but Unpersuasive? The Role of the United States in the Evolution of Customary International Law', in Michael Byers and Georg Nolte (eds.), *United States Hegemony and the Foundations of International Law* (Cambridge University Press, 2003), p. 287.

'Does International Law Impose a Duty upon the United Nations to Prevent Genocide?' (2000) **46** *McGill Law Journal* 187.

Trapp, Kimberley N, 'Back to Basics: Necessity, Proportionality, and the Right to Self-Defence Against Non-State Terrorist Actors' (2007) **56** *International and Comparative Law Quarterly* 141.

Travalio, Greg and John Altenburg, 'State Responsibility for Sponsorship of Terrorist and Insurgent Groups: Terrorism, State Responsibility and the Use of Military Force' (2003) **4** *Chicago Journal of International Law* 97.

Ulfstein, Geir, Thilo Marauhn and Andreas Zimmermann (eds.), *Making Treaties Work: Dispute Settlement, Compliance Control and Enforcement in Human Rights, Environmental and Arms Control Agreements* (Cambridge University Press, 2006).

Vandenbergh, Michael P., 'Climate Change: The China Problem' (2008) **81** *Southern California Law Review* 905.

VanDeveer, Stacy D., 'Green Fatigue' (2003) **27** *Wilson Quarterly* 55.

Verma, SK, *An Introduction to Public International Law* (Delhi: Prentice Hall of India Private Ltd., 1998).

Victor, David G., *The Collapse of the Kyoto Protocol and the Struggle to Slow Global Warming* (Princeton University Press, 2001).

Vining, Joseph, 'Fuller and Language', in Willem J. Witteveen and Wilbren van der Burg (eds.), *Rediscovering Fuller: Essays on Implicit Law and Institutional Design* (Amsterdam University Press, 1999), p. 453.

Visscher, P. de, 'Cours général de droit international public' (1972) **136** (II) *Recueil des Cours de l'Academie de Droit International* 1.

Waal, Alex de, 'No Such Thing as Humanitarian Intervention: Why We Need to Rethink How to Realize the "Responsibility to Protect" in Wartime' *Harvard International Review* (21 March 2007).

Waldron, Jeremy, 'Torture and Positive Law: Jurisprudence for the White House' (2005) **105** *Columbia Law Review* 1681.

'Why Law – Efficacy, Freedom, or Fidelity?' (1994) **13** *Law and Philosophy* 259.

Walzer, Michael, *Just and Unjust Wars*, 3rd edn (New York: Basic Books, 2000).

Spheres of Justice: A Defense of Pluralism and Equality (New York: Basic Books, 1983).

Wedgwood, Ruth, 'The ICJ Advisory Opinion on the Israeli Security Fence and the Limits of Self-Defense' (2005) **99** *American Journal of International Law* 52.

Weil, Prosper, 'Le droit international en quête de son identité' (1992) **237** *Recueil des Cours de l'Academie de Droit International* 13.

'Towards Relative Normativity in International Law?' (1983) **77** *American Journal of International Law* 413.

Weinstein, Harvey M., *Psychiatry and the CIA: Victims of Mind Control* (Washington, DC and London: American Psychiatric Press, 1990).

Weisburd, A. Mark, *Use of Force: The Practice of States since World War II* (The Pennsylvania State University Press, 1997).

Wendt, Alexander, *Social Theory of International Politics* (Cambridge University Press, 1999).

'Collective Identity Formation and the International State' (1994) **88** *American Political Science Review* 384.

'Anarchy is What States Make of It: The Social Construction of Power Politics' (1992) **46** *International Organization* 391.

'The Agent-Structure Problem in International Relations' (1987) **41** *International Organization* 335.

Wenger, Etienne, *Communities of Practice: Learning, Meaning, and Identity* (Cambridge University Press, 1998).

Werksman, Jacob 'The Clean Development Mechanism: Unwrapping the Kyoto Surprise' (1998) 7 *Review of European Community and International Law* 147.

Westerman, Pauline, 'Means and Ends', in Willem J. Witteveen and Wilbren van der Burg (eds.), *Rediscovering Fuller: Essays on Implicit Law and Institutional Design* (Amsterdam University Press, 1999), p. 145.

Wet, Erika de, 'The International Constitutional Order' (2006) **55** *International Comparative Law Quarterly* 51.

Whelan, Frederick G., 'Legal Positivism and International Society', in David R. Mapel and Terry Nardin (eds.), *International Society: Diverse Ethical Perspectives* (Princeton University Press, 1998), p. 36.

Wiener, Antje, 'Enacting Meaning-In-Use: Qualitative Research on Norms and International Relations' (2009) **35** *Review of International Studies* 175.

Invisible Constitution of Politics: Contested Norms and International Encounters (Cambridge University Press, 2008).

'The Dual Quality of Norms and Governance Beyond the State: Sociological and Normative Approaches to "Interaction"' (2007) **10** *Critical Review of International Social and Political Philosophy* 47.

'Contested Compliance: Interventions on the Normative Structure in World Politics' (2004) **10** *European Journal of International Relations* 189.

'Constructivism: The Limits of Bridging the Gaps' (2003) **6** *Journal of International Relations and Development* 252.

Wiener, Jonathan B., 'On the Political Economy of Global Environmental Regulation' (1999) **87** *Georgetown Law Journal* 749.

Wilmshurst, Elizabeth, 'The Chatham House Principles of International Law on the Use of Force in Self-Defence' (2006) **55** *International and Comparative Law Quarterly* 963.

Wilson, Heather A., *International Law and the Use of Force by National Liberation Movements* (Oxford University Press, 1990).

Winston, Kenneth I., 'Three Models for the Study of Law', in Willem J. Witteveen and Wibren van der Burg (eds.), *Rediscovering Fuller: Essays on Implicit Law and Institutional Design* (Amsterdam University Press, 1999), p. 51.

Wirth, David A., 'The Sixth Session (Part Two) and Seventh Session of the Conference of the Parties to the Framework Convention on Climate Change' (2002) **96** *American Journal of International Law* 648.

Witteveen, Willem J., 'Rediscovering Fuller: An Introduction', in Willem J. Witteveen and Wilbren van der Burg (eds.), *Rediscovering Fuller: Essays on Implicit Law and Institutional Design* (Amsterdam University Press, 1999), p. 21.

Wolfe, Robert, 'Decision-Making and Transparency in the "Medieval" WTO: Does the Sutherland Report Have the Right Prescription?' (2005) **8** *Journal of International Economic Law* 631.

Wolfendale, Jessica, 'The Myth of "Torture Lite"' (2009) **23** *Ethics and International Affairs* 47.

Wood, Heather Jacques, Taylor Nuttall and Kendall W. Stiles, 'Humanitarian Intervention', in Wayne Sandholz and Kendall W. Stiles (eds.), *International Norms and Cycles of Change* (Oxford: Oxford University Press, 2009), p. 263.

Yamin, Farhana and Joanna Depledge, *The International Climate Change Regime: A Guide to Rules, Institutions and Procedures* (New York: Cambridge University Press, 2004).

Yeats, William Butler, 'The Second Coming', in *Michael Robartes and the Dancer* (Churchtown, Dundrum: Cuala Press, 1920), p. 19.

Yoo, John, *War by Other Means* (New York: Atlantic Monthly Press, 2006).

Zelikow, Philip, 'The Transformation of National Security: Five Redefinitions' (2003) **71** *The National Interest* 17.

Zhang, Xiaoming, 'China's 1979 War with Vietnam: A Reassessment' (2005) **184** *The China Quarterly* 851.

INDEX

CAMBRIDGE STUDIES IN INTERNATIONAL AND COMPARATIVE LAW

Books in the series

Legitimacy and Legality in International Law: An Interactional Account
Jutta Brunnée and Stephen J. Toope

The Public International Law Theory of Hans Kelsen: Believing in Universal Law
Jochen von Bernstorff

The Concept of Non-International Armed Conflict in International Humanitarian Law
Anthony Cullen

The Challenge of Child Labour in International Law
Franziska Humbert

Shipping Interdiction and the Law of the Sea
Douglas Guilfoyle

International Courts and Environmental Protection
Tim Stephens

Legal Principles in WTO Dispute
Andrew D. Mitchell

War Crimes in Internal Armed Conflicts
Eve La Haye

Humanitarian Occupation
Gregory H. Fox

The International Law of Environmental Impact Assessment: Process, Substance and Integration
Neil Craik

The Law and Practice of International Territorial Administration: Versailles, Iraq and Beyond
Carsten Stahn

Cultural Products and the World Trade Organization
Tania Voon

United Nations Sanctions and the Rule of Law
Jeremy Farrall

National Law in WTO Law Effectiveness and Good Governance in the World Trading System
Sharif Bhuiyan

The Threat of Force in International Law
Nikolas Stürchler

Indigenous Rights and United Nations Standards
Alexandra Xanthaki

International Refugee Law and Socio-Economic Rights
Michelle Foster

The Protection of Cultural Property in Armed Conflict
Roger O'Keefe

Interpretation and Revision of International Boundary Decisions
Kaiyan Homi Kaikobad

Multinationals and Corporate Social Responsibility: Limitations and Opportunities in International Law
Jennifer A. Zerk

Judiciaries within Europe: A Comparative Review
John Bell

Law in Times of Crisis: Emergency Powers in Theory and Practice
Oren Gross and Fionnuala Ní Aoláin

Vessel-Source Marine Pollution: The Law and Politics of International Regulation
Alan Tan

Enforcing Obligations Erga Omnes *in International Law*
Christian J. Tams

Non-Governmental Organisations in International Law
Anna-Karin Lindblom

Democracy, Minorities and International Law
Steven Wheatley

Prosecuting International Crimes: Selectivity and the International Law Regime
Robert Cryer

Compensation for Personal Injury in English, German and Italian Law: A Comparative Outline
Basil Markesinis, Michael Coester, Guido Alpa and Augustus Ullstein

Dispute Settlement in the UN Convention on the Law of the Sea
Natalie Klein

The International Protection of Internally Displaced Persons
Catherine Phuong

Imperialism, Sovereignty and the Making of International Law
Antony Anghie

Necessity, Proportionality and the Use of Force by States
Judith Gardam

International Legal Argument in the Permanent Court of International Justice: The Rise of the International Judiciary
Ole Spiermann

Great Powers and Outlaw States: Unequal Sovereigns in the International Legal Order
Gerry Simpson

Local Remedies in International Law
C. F. Amerasinghe

Reading Humanitarian Intervention: Human Rights and the Use of Force in International Law
Anne Orford

Conflict of Norms in Public International Law: How WTO Law Relates to Other Rules of Law
Joost Pauwelyn

Transboundary Damage in International Law
Hanqin Xue

European Criminal Procedures
Edited by Mireille Delmas-Marty and John Spencer

The Accountability of Armed Opposition Groups in International Law
Liesbeth Zegveld

Sharing Transboundary Resources: International Law and Optimal Resource Use
Eyal Benvenisti

International Human Rights and Humanitarian Law
René Provost

Remedies Against International Organisations
Karel Wellens

Diversity and Self-Determination in International Law
Karen Knop

The Law of Internal Armed Conflict
Lindsay Moir

International Commercial Arbitration and African States: Practice, Participation and Institutional Development
Amazu A. Asouzu

The Enforceability of Promises in European Contract Law
James Gordley

International Law in Antiquity
David J. Bederman

Money Laundering: A New International Law Enforcement Model
Guy Stessens

Good Faith in European Contract Law
Reinhard Zimmermann and Simon Whittaker

On Civil Procedure
J. A. Jolowicz

Trusts: A Comparative Study
Maurizio Lupoi

The Right to Property in Commonwealth Constitutions
Tom Allen

International Organizations Before National Courts
August Reinisch

The Changing International Law of High Seas Fisheries
Francisco Orrego Vicuña

Trade and the Environment: A Comparative Study of EC and US Law
Damien Geradin

Unjust Enrichment: A Study of Private Law and Public Values
Hanoch Dagan

Religious Liberty and International Law in Europe
Malcolm D. Evans

Ethics and Authority in International Law
Alfred P. Rubin

Sovereignty Over Natural Resources: Balancing Rights and Duties
Nico Schrijver

The Polar Regions and the Development of International Law
Donald R. Rothwell

Fragmentation and the International Relations of Micro-States: Self-determination and Statehood
Jorri Duursma

Principles of the Institutional Law of International Organizations
C. F. Amerasinghe

For EU product safety concerns, contact us at Calle de José Abascal, 56–1°,
28003 Madrid, Spain or eugpsr@cambridge.org.

www.ingramcontent.com/pod-product-compliance
Ingram Content Group UK Ltd.
Pitfield, Milton Keynes, MK11 3LW, UK
UKHW042351271225
466426UK00011B/743